Walter Kolneder

THE AMADEUS
BOOK ^{OF}_{THE} VIOLIN

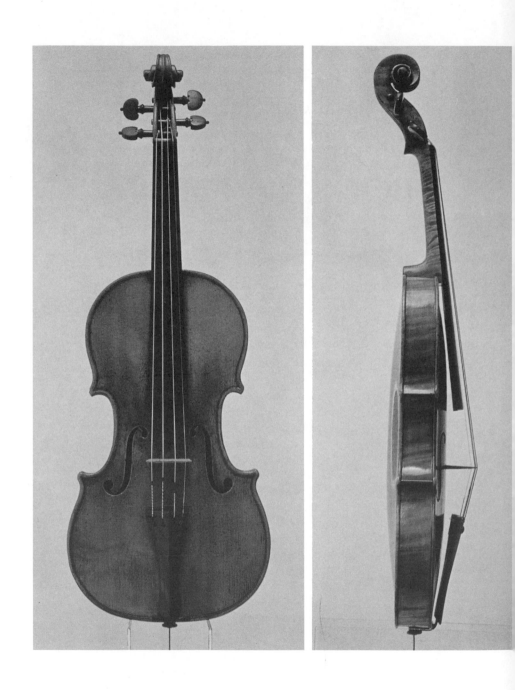

Walter Kolneder

THE AMADEUS
BOOK ^{OF}_{THE} VIOLIN

CONSTRUCTION, HISTORY, AND MUSIC

Translated and Edited
by
Reinhard G. Pauly

Amadeus Press
Portland, Oregon

This English-language edition supported by Inter Nationes, Bonn.

Frontispiece: "Il Cremonese" by Antonius Stradivarius, 1715.
Cremona, Palazzo Communale.

Jacket front: Violin by Andreas Guarnerius, 1668.
Courtesy of Schuback Violin Shop, Inc., Portland, Oregon.

ISBN 1-57467-038-7

Printed in Hong Kong

AMADEUS PRESS
The Haseltine Building
133 S.W. Second Avenue, Suite 450
Portland, Oregon 97204, U.S.A.

Library of Congress Cataloging-in-Publication Data

Kolneder, Walter.
[Buch der Violine. English]
The Amadeus book of the violin : construction, history, and music /
Walter Kolneder; translated and edited by Reinhard G. Pauly.
p.   cm.
Includes bibliographical references and index.
ISBN 1-57467-038-7
1. Violin. 2. Violin music—History and criticism. I. Pauly, Reinhard G. II. Title.
ML800.K6413   1998
787.2—dc21   97-46198
CIP
MN

CONTENTS

PREFACE TO THE
REVISED ENGLISH-LANGUAGE EDITION

Is the violin an endangered instrument? Yes and no, I would answer. It is true that pianos, trumpets, guitars, and many electronic instruments now appeal to more prospective players than do the members of the violin family. It is also true that the first few months of practicing the violin may not provide the same kind of gratification, for player or listener. Nevertheless, the violin has attracted generations of listeners, and the large body of string music written during the last three centuries has inspired many to take up the instrument. As players, their accomplishments may have been modest or magnificent, but most became more sensitive and enthusiastic listeners. Some, together with a few kindred spirits, discovered the joys of playing chamber music. Others joined school and community orchestras, or pursued their studies professionally and became members of symphony and opera orchestras. A select few succeeded on the concert stage.

For all these—players and listeners—a vast, wonderful repertory of music including the violin exists. This book was written for them.

Its author, Walter Kolneder (1910–1994), a distinguished Austrian string player, conductor, musicologist, and pedagogue, was the author of an impressive number of publications before the present volume first appeared as *Das Buch der Violine* (Zurich 1972). It has been highly successful; the fifth German edition, translated here, appeared in 1993. An early reviewer pointed out that this was the first book to deal, in one volume, with virtually all aspects of the violin: with its construction, history, and literature; with violin playing and teaching; and with violin virtuosos through the ages. "One author accomplished what normally would require five specialists." A glance at the table of contents will give an idea of the wealth of information Kolneder presents.

This first English-language edition is more than a translation. It includes many revisions, most of them dealing with recent developments. In the book's last section in particular I tried to include information, not available to the author, that may be of interest to American readers. I have also omitted some material chiefly useful for readers in German-speaking countries. This applies to much of the book, including the lists of important compositions for the violin. The so-called standard repertory has never been static. For instance, Kolneder's exclusion, in 1970, of Chausson's *Poème* from that repertory might well be questioned a generation later. The lists of twentieth-century virtuosos have also been revised.

An encyclopedic book of this kind—broad in scope, with thousands of names, dates, and other facts—will continue to need periodic updating; I therefore would welcome comments from readers that will lead to improvements in future printings.

Many fellow musicians and others (*Friends and Fiddlers*, to quote the title of a delightful earlier book) have assisted me with this revision of Kolneder's book. His daughter, Frau Marianne Lohaus, made available some of his handwritten notes, prepared after publication of the first edition. Roland Feller and David Kerr, violin makers in San Francisco and Portland, were a great help with the translation of the more technical terminology of violin making. Charles Farmer, Dr. Camille Smith, and Dr. Ulrich Wüster were kind and generous to supply information about community music schools, public school music programs, and German music schools, respectively. Dr. Abram Loft, formerly of the Fine Arts Quartet and the Eastman School of Music, patiently answered many questions. I am thankful to all of these, as I am to Frances Bertolino Farrell, my alert, conscientious copyeditor.

REINHARD G. PAULY

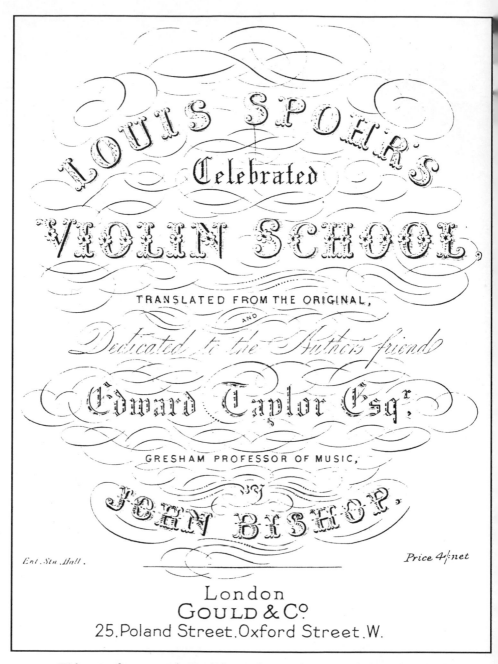

Title page from an early English translation of Louis Spohr's *Violin School* (London 1833)

PART ONE

THE INSTRUMENT

The violin emerged ca. 1500 and continued to develop up to the mid-sixteenth century, acquiring its modern shape in the seventeenth and early eighteenth centuries during the epoch of the great violin makers—Nicolò Amati, Jacob Stainer, Antonio Stradivari, and Joseph (Giuseppe Giovanni Battista) Guarneri. There have been few modifications since.

According to Hart, the violin consists of fifty-eight parts; other writers count more than seventy, Grillet, eighty-three. Different ways of counting yield various results; the back, for instance, can be made of one or two pieces. The violin's chief components are the resonating body, the neck with fingerboard, and the four strings lying across the bridge.

The body's normal length is 355 mm and consists of the back, the top (or belly), and the ribs. In the bowing area, two C-shaped indentations (the waist) accommodate the bow's motion across the strings. Both top and back are arched. Each may be made of one piece, but the top especially is usually made of two. (Throughout this book, all indications of position or direction are given as seen by the viewer, holding the violin in front of himself, resting on his lap. Thus "upper to lower" can refer to the direction "scroll to tailpiece," or "top to back." For the bow it would mean "tip to frog.")

The neck plate, at the place of the neck's attachment, is carved out of one piece with the back. The top and bottom blocks are glued to both back and top, as are the corner blocks and the ribs. The ribs are reinforced by lining

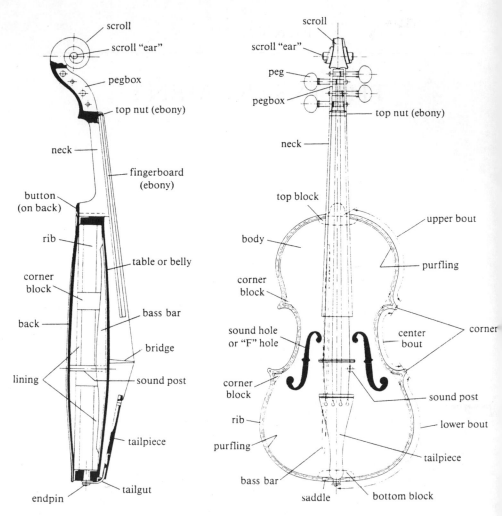

Violin: cross section and front view. Reprinted by permission of the publisher from *The New Harvard Dictionary of Music*, edited by Don Michael Randel, Cambridge, Mass.: The Belknap Press of Harvard University Press, copyright 1986 by the President and Fellows of Harvard College.

strips where they are attached to back and top. Except for the neck plate, the top has the same contour as the back. It contains the carved-out *f* holes. The bass bar is glued to the left inside of the top.

Thin strips of wood, called the purfling, are inlaid on both top and back at a distance of ca. 2.5–4 mm from the rim. The soundpost, a small piece wedged between top and back, is positioned under the bridge's right foot.

The neck, with pegbox and scroll, is inserted at the top block. It supports the fingerboard, which gradually widens in the direction of the bridge. The strings are attached to the tailpiece, strung across the bridge and nut to the

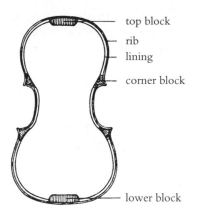

top block
rib
lining
corner block

lower block

Back with rib structure

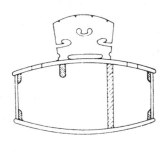

Cross section of the body,
right behind the bridge

pegbox. The tailpiece is fastened to the end button (or endpin) by a wire or gut loop.

The end button is inserted in an opening in the rib and bottom block. A fine-tuner for the E string usually is fastened to the tailpiece. Some violinists use such tuners for all four strings. The Thomastik tailpiece (named for its inventor, Dr. Franz Thomastik of Vienna) has four built-in tuners. A chin rest is normally placed near the tailpiece's left side.

The bow stick, ca. 730–750 mm long, has a slightly concave curvature and is somewhat thinner at the top than at the bottom end at the frog. Diameters are ca. 8.6 mm at the lower end and ca. 5.3 mm at the top. At the lower end, the stick is normally octagonal but becomes round after ca. 11 mm. Some bows are entirely octagonal, or round.

The playing surface, or band, of the bow hair is 640–650 mm long, gathered at both ends. At the bow's tip it is anchored in a small mortise inside the

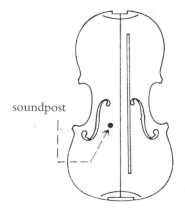

soundpost

Interior view of the top

Neck with pegbox and scroll

head with a wooden plug; at the other end it is fastened inside the frog. On the top side of the bow stick's lower end a small groove has been cut out; the frog eyelet screw lies in this groove. It is connected to the button screw, used to adjust the bow hair tension. At the frog's upper end, a round indentation supports the right thumb. The frog's sides are curved slightly inward to reduce its weight.

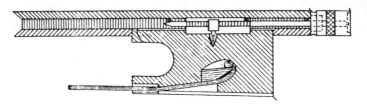

Cross section of the frog and lower end of stick

TONE PRODUCTION

The violin strings can be set into motion by pulling the bow across them, by bouncing the bow (saltato, spiccato bowings), by plucking them (pizzicato), or by striking them with the bow stick (col legno). Bowing across the string is the normal manner of tone production, but the process is actually extremely complicated and in its most minute details not yet entirely understood. Each bow hair has small, scalelike barbs, visible only under a microscope, to which the rosin adheres. If, after much playing, the hairs have lost these barbed hooks, the bow has to be rehaired. The sticky quality of the rosin and the bow's pressure exert a lateral pull, displacing the string from its resting position. The string's elasticity will then cause it to return to the resting position and to move beyond it, in the opposite direction. Pulling the bow continuously will cause the string to go on vibrating regularly. It has been claimed that the bow hair's barbs cause the string to move, but this is not true; without the use of rosin the bow will produce no tone in either direction. Nevertheless some bow makers mount half of the bow's hair in the opposite direction, wrongly assuming that this would result in the same contact with the string on up and down bows.

The string's basic pitch depends on its length, thickness, material (density, elasticity), and tension. These factors determine the frequency, that is, the number of vibrations (cycles) per second. In relation to the violin, the G string would have to be too long or too thick, but the remedy of winding it with metal was soon discovered. Most new strings have a perlon core with aluminum or silver winding.

Strictly speaking, four separate, partial motions are involved in a string's vibration. The principal motion involves the entire string, producing the fundamental pitch. At the same time, partial vibrations of the string's half, third, quarter, and other portions occur. All these vibrations are combined (see diagram), and all are transverse vibrations, that is, at a right angle to the string, for the motion that sets off the vibration (whether bow hair, plucking finger, or bow stick) is normally in that direction, displacing the string ca. 1 mm in both directions from its resting position. In addition, longitudinal vibrations coordinate with the transverse vibrations, which produce a periodic shortening of the string. The entire process is even more complex because the string turns axially at the same time, in a regular manner, returning periodically to its initial position. Finally, because of the bow stick's elasticity, bow pressure varies, which also affects the string's longitudinal vibrations. The bow in turn is also put into motion by the vibrating string.

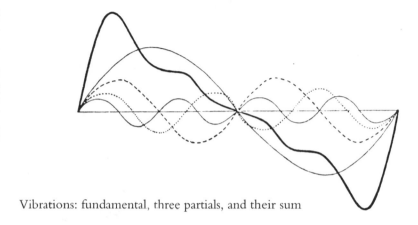

Vibrations: fundamental, three partials, and their sum

Pure longitudinal vibrations would result in squeaky sounds. Jahn points out that these sounds can be produced by rubbing a string lengthwise, with fingers to which rosin has been applied. Such longitudinal vibrations interfere with the basic transverse vibrations, resulting in nodes that cause undesirable overtones (partials) affecting tone quality.

Most important for the vibration of the violin's body is the string displacement's effect on the bridge, tailpiece, and neck. The motions of these are transmitted to the back through the upper and lower blocks. Rödig's experiments have shown that the back vibrates more strongly than the top; the top's vibration is slightly impaired by the bridge, which divides it into two vibrating fields. Contrary to popular belief, Rödig claims that the string's vibrations are not transmitted from the top to the bottom, but in the opposite direction; he stresses the important involvement of the neck in this process. Drögemeyer had stated this earlier, for which reason he attributed importance to the selection of wood for the neck and to its construction.

Roussel, on the other hand, speaks of the bridge's importance for modifying the string's vibration, the bridge transmitting it to the top in the form of impulses. Apparently both processes take place simultaneously. He also believes that the back's amplitude of vibration is smaller than the top's. The bridge's feet have different positions: the left foot stands on a freely vibrating portion of the top while the right foot is blocked by the soundpost, resulting in an extremely complicated kind of vibration. Roussel concludes, "When the foot over the bass bar exerts downward pressure on the top, it causes the back to rise, but when the foot above the soundpost presses on the top, the back is also pressed downward."

Schulze has described precisely how the vibration is started. When the bow's motion begins, the part of the string that is closest to the point of contact vibrates first. For the E, A, and D strings, this portion is ca. 8.5 mm long, producing the pitches G-sharp[7], C-sharp[7], and F-sharp[6]. Due to its thickness, the G string's tone is G[5]. As other parts of the string are set in motion, lower partials are heard. The fundamental pitch appears last.

Tone volume depends chiefly on the speed of bowing and bow pressure, which affect the amplitude of the vibration. Timbre is determined by many factors, but chiefly by the bow's point of contact with the string. A normal violin tone results from bowing at a distance of ca. 20 mm from the bridge; according to Apian-Bennewitz this is at exactly ten-elevenths of the vibrating string length. Closer to the bridge, the string is harder, offering more resistance to the bow, calling for slower bowing—the secret of the "endless" bow of many great violinists. Near the bridge the tone grows louder but also harsher because certain higher overtones are more prominent. If, while bowing at the normal contact point, one gradually moves toward the bridge, one reaches, after a few millimeters, the optimal place for a large tone. If one moves closer than that, some higher partials become prominent, causing the sound to become unpleasantly harsh and scratchy. Composers of program music especially occasionally want this effect, indicating it in the music by the words "sul ponticello" (at the bridge). Placing the bow closer to the fingerboard, closer to the largest amplitude of the string, the bow meets with less resistance; the tone is more gentle but also weaker. Composers who desire this effect indicate it with the words "sulla tastiera" (over the fingerboard). Choosing the bow's point of contact with the string is essential for regulating dynamics and timbre. When playing in the very high positions, the vibrating string is very short, which means that the place of contact must be adjusted accordingly. Gut strings especially are sensitive to pressure, so that one must play fairly close to the bridge—otherwise the tone might break because the bow "squashes" it.

The optimal ability of a string to vibrate is determined by its tension in relation to the resistance offered to this tension by the instrument. Opinions vary concerning this optimal tension; it seems to be related to the violin's tuning (higher or lower pitch), the type of string, height of the bridge, and some other factors. Möckel gives the following figures:

G string: 6.255 kg
D string: 6.327 kg
A string: 6.875 kg
E string: 8.965 kg
Total tension: 28.422 kg

If the bridge is higher than normal, the angle at which the strings rest on it is different and pressure on the bridge is greater.

Leipp (*La sonorité*) recommends a simple way to determine the appropriate calibre and density of a string for a particular instrument: tune the string up to pitch, let it adapt itself to that pitch for a few hours, then play on it. If the sound isn't right, tune the string slightly higher or lower. If it sounds better at the lower pitch, the violin requires a thinner string; if it speaks well at the higher pitch, it shows the need for a heavier string. In Frankfurt, Paganini bought strings from Pirazzi of Offenbach. To test one he stretched it with both hands at eye level and plucked it with one finger, closely observing the vibration curve. He was satisfied only if the curve looked completely even. Otherwise he would throw the string on the ground and step on it, saying, "If I can't use it, certainly no one else could." Boerner, a concertmaster in Karlsruhe, devised an ingenious method to test a string for uniform thickness. With a ruler he determined the exact middle of the vibrating string and marked the place with a pencil. He then used a pointed object to depress the string at that place, and plucked both parts. Only if they gave off exactly the same pitch was the string serviceable. Often the lower half produces a higher pitch, for it may have become thinner with heavy use.

It is important that the string's pressure and pull are in balance. Since pressure is chiefly affected by the angle the string forms with the bridge, changing the bridge's height can equalize the two opposing forces.

The string's vibration is first transferred to the surrounding air, which produces a very faint tone. This can be heard when a string is stretched in the air. Vibrations are also transmitted to the bridge, which passes them on, transformed, as impulses. This can be accomplished best if the bridge is made from wood of optimal quality and strength. But it must also stand up under the string's pressure, so that its shape represents a compromise. The bridge's modern shape goes back to Stradivari but is more closely related to that of Josephus Guarnerius del Gesù (see illustration).

The carved-out portions, the bridge's "heart" and "ear," are primarily ornamental, but they increase elasticity by reducing the amount of wood in the bridge without reducing its stability. Close examination will show that the amount of wood is nearly the same at any point in a vertical section. For a violin of average size and wood quality, the ideal dimensions of a bridge are

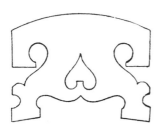 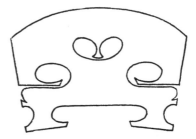

Bridges by Stradivari and del Gesù

as follows: 35 mm high; 40 mm wide; width of foot, 9–11 mm; width of bridge at the foot, 4 mm; and at the rounded top, 1.5 mm, the tapering from foot to top being gradual. Minor deviations from these norms, including the shape, will affect the violin's timbre but may be necessary for several reasons. A highly arched violin requires a lower bridge, and a violin with a weak top will be helped by a stronger bridge. If the bridge is excessively tapered toward the top a piercing tone results while a relatively thick top portion yields a more gentle tone. A bridge that is too elastic affects high tones adversely; if it is too rigid, low tones are affected. The exact position of the heart-shaped, middle excision also influences the tone. Last but not least, the type of wood used for the top must be considered: hard wood requires a soft-wood bridge and vice versa, according to Riechers. The bridge's feet must conform exactly and snugly to the top's curvature and must be very thin, for only in that way will vibrations be best transmitted.

Placing a mute on the bridge reduces tone volume, resulting in a nasal timbre. Eighteenth-century mutes were made from lead; Vivaldi uses the indication "con piombo" in some scores. Later they were made of wood; now plastic or rubber may be used. Mutes have three double prongs, a few have two, four, or five. These are placed between the strings and must fit tightly. Since a mute, being small, can easily be misplaced or forgotten at home, and since it takes time to put it on, mutes have been designed to be kept behind the bridge, so that they can be moved forward quickly against the bridge, or put on the bridge. Some users believe that one pays for the convenience of these mutes by sacrificing tone quality. The degree of muting depends not only on the material but also on the mute's weight. The top part of a very heavy mute, sometimes called "tone wolf," used for practicing, is filled with lead.

Experiments with a freely vibrating top have shown that vibration nodes exist in certain places. Depending on the pitch, some places will vibrate more strongly than others, which means that a succession of notes played would not be uniform in volume and timbre. The bass bar equalizes these various vibration centers. To offset the low notes on the G string it is fastened on the top's left inside. Its function is aided by positioning it not exactly parallel to the wood's grain but facing slightly to the upper right. This ensures the top's uniform vibrations.

These vibrations are transmitted to the back through the ribs and blocks, the air inside the violin, and probably also through the soundpost. Rödig, however, does not share this opinion, because in a violin without a soundpost the back vibrates surprisingly strongly, often more than the top. To carry out its dual function—supporting the top subjected to string pressure, and transmitting vibrations—the soundpost must be both strong and elastic. The best ones are made of light firwood and have a diameter of 5.5–6 mm, including ten to twelve annual rings. The soundpost, too, must be fitted exactly to the curvature of top and back. Its approximate location is slightly below the bridge's right foot, at the distance of the top's thickness. The ideal placement varies with each violin, depending on the wood and on the bridge.

The precise placement of the soundpost strongly affects volume and especially timbre, and since a fraction of a millimeter can make a difference, finding the right spot requires the skill and patience of an experienced luthier. Some violinists carry out their own experiments; Ole Bull, forever dissatisfied with the tone of his Strad, is said to have developed a morbid compulsion to do so.

As it is so close to the bridge's right foot, the soundpost strongly impedes the bridge's vibrations. This is easily demonstrated. If, while the violin is being played, the right foot is immobilized with a pair of pliers, the tone is barely affected; if the same is done to the left foot, volume and timbre are altered a great deal. Thus it is primarily the bridge's left foot that causes the top to vibrate, which is why the bass bar must lie under the left foot.

The violin's body, vibrating in its entirety, transmits its vibrations to the air, both inside and outside of the instrument. The outside transmissions are most important by far for volume and timbre, but the air vibrating inside the violin, emerging through the *f* holes, increases volume. The placement of the *f* holes is of great importance. The shape of the *f* holes affects the combination of inside and outside air only slightly but has a far greater effect on the top's vibration and hence on tone quality; if they are very elongated, the top's middle portion becomes overly elastic in relation to the upper and lower portions, which disturbs the uniformity of sound. Placing the holes too closely together will have the same effect. The top's center will vibrate well if the top eyes of the *f* holes are up to 43 mm apart, assuming the wood is strong enough to absorb the string pressure. Placing the holes at a slant compensates ideally for the reduction of wood. The notches are roughly in the middle between the end points of the holes. The bridge should stand on the line connecting the two inside notches and is thus symmetrically placed.

How the player holds the instrument will also affect its sound. In early times, players merely rested it against the chest or clavicle, which allowed the top to vibrate freely. Later, playing in the higher positions, and especially the need to shift down, caused violinists to hold the instrument firmly under the chin. This reduced vibration, especially because players used chin rests or small cushions to facilitate holding the instrument, thus partially blocking the back's free vibration.

Varnish has little positive influence on the violin's sound. It serves primarily to preserve the wood, protecting it from perspiration, dust, dirt, and humidity. Testing violins before and after they have been varnished has shown that varnish has a slightly dampening effect on the sound. The instrument responds more quickly and easily as a result, but it also loses some of the high overtones that add brilliance, which results in a more gentle, milder tone. None of these differences, however, are pronounced.

If the varnish is too hard, the effect will be negative, for the wood will also harden and lose some of its ability to vibrate. In that sense, varnish does affect the sound materially, but it is impossible to improve the poor sound of an unfinished violin by applying good varnish. The "white," unvarnished instrument already has the best tone quality its maker could impart to it.

Varnish has another characteristic: it will slightly raise the violin's basic (fundamental) pitches—something that needs to be considered in the early stages of construction. If the body at that point is designed with overly high fundamental pitches, varnishing may cause it to have an inferior sound. Problems of this kind caused Franz Ludwig Schubert to call varnish a necessary evil, while Drögemeyer concluded that varnish undoubtedly had "an adverse effect on tone quality."

Does a new violin have to be "broken in"—does it have to be played for a certain length of time before it produces its best sound? In 1816, Spohr tried out four Strads from the collection of Count Cozio di Salabue, instruments that looked as though they had just been finished. He described their tone thus: "It is full and strong, but raw and wooden; they must be played for ten years before they reach perfection." Another opinion was expressed in the essay *Verbessert das Alter und vieles Spielen wirklich den Ton und die Ansprache der Geige? Eine ketzerische Studie von Dr. Max Grossmann* (Does age and intensive playing really improve the tone and response of a violin? A heretical study by Dr. Max Grossmann, Berlin 1904). The author, in eighty-two pages, attempts to prove the opposite point of view. Actually, the problem is far more complicated than is generally assumed, for in all questions relating to timbre, observations tend to be highly subjective, and scientific processes are difficult to control.

In his book on the Guarneri family, Alfred Ebsworth Hill dealt in depth with the "breaking in" question and gave the following recommendations:

> Stainer: 10–15 years
> Amati (medium model): 20–25 years
> Amati (large model): 30–35 years
> Strad (Amati type): 30–35 years
> Strad (long model, unlike Amati): 40–50 years
> Strad (from 1726 to 1736): 40 years
> Strad (standard model): 50–60 years
> Strad (from 1737 to 1743, large model): 60–80 years
> Carlo Bergonzi (medium model): 40–60 years
> Carlo Bergonzi (large model): 60–80 years

Hill considers these the required periods not so much for breaking in a violin but for "the tone of these instruments, made by the most famous luthiers, to mature." He further states that age alone is not the decisive factor—to sound its best a violin must be played, which eventually brings about a oneness of player and instrument.

Apian-Bennewitz observed three stages of breaking in a violin: at first its sound improves, then it becomes rougher, and after about three months it again improves. According to Sibire, a violin should sound brittle at first; if it sounds good immediately, the tone is likely to deteriorate later.

It is to be expected that after a major repair, a violin needs to be broken in again. Joachim's Strad was consigned to Bausch's shop in Leipzig for repairs. When he got it back he apologized to Brahms (letter of 15 May 1860) for not having the time to visit Hamburg: "My violin and my fingers are very much in need of being thoroughly broken in for the music festival." Kreisler even believed that a string instrument that had not been played for a long time would lose its tone. He concedes that a violin, like an athlete, now and then needs a period of rest, but that for a violin that period should not exceed a year, lest the beauty of its timbre be lost.

VIOLIN MAKING

THE WOOD

As suitable wood is the most important requirement for a violin to vibrate well, obtaining wood that will sound good is always the luthier's greatest concern. From examining their instruments we know that many Italian masters in their youth used inexpensive, local wood; only after having established themselves comfortably could they afford to buy wood of better quality from abroad. Legend has it that Nicolò Amati and Jacob Stainer would walk through the woods during thunderstorms, on the lookout for trees hit by lightning. As a tree crashed to the ground, the sound it made told them whether it was suitable for violin making. Others, Vuillaume among them, traveled far and wide to find good wood. Indeed, very little wood is suitable, and logging is threatening to diminish the small remaining supply. With this in mind, Walter Scheidt published a memorandum in 1947 about protecting Alpine lumber suitable for instrument making.

It is often thought that the wood's age is partly responsible for the quality of old master instruments. Luthiers everywhere looked for wood that was as old and dry as possible, buying furniture, paneling, and other objects, and showing up wherever an old building was being torn down. Some instruments by the luthier Alois Palfner were made from wood that came from the Graz town gates. James Andersen of Scotland declared that his "Paisley Abbey" violin was made from seven-hundred-year-old wood from Paisley Abbey, and that it was equal to the best Cremona violins. James William Briggs of Glasgow used three-hundred-year-old wood from a church in Warsaw that was scheduled to be razed. At times luthiers in the New World pointed with pride to instruments made from local wood. One violin in the Stearns collection at the University of Michigan was "made by N. W. House in Ann Arbor, out of wood that came from a table that had been built by the first settlers in that city." How to use this kind of wood became the subject of detailed studies, including a publication by Raffaele Cormio, *L'impiego di legni tratti dalle demolizioni di vecchi edifici nella costruzione dei violini* (Use of wood salvaged from razed old buildings in the construction of violins). Forgers in particular are eager to use old wood, for one of the chief giveaways of fake "old master" violins is wood that is too new.

Others believe that the importance of the wood's age as a factor determining sound quality can be overestimated, Riechers among them. Calling five years of drying entirely adequate, he weighed various pieces of violin wood after five years and again after ever-longer intervals; he noted that even after twenty years there had been no weight loss, meaning that no further moisture had been lost. Maugin also considered an interval of five to six years (after cutting) to be adequate; Apian-Bennewitz mentioned four to five years for spruce and up to ten years for maple. Other luthiers favor a drying period of up to fifty years.

Open-air drying of the wood, while protecting it from sun and rain, is generally considered better than any artificial drying process. Climate has some influence; Bagatella judged three years an adequate drying time in Italy. Artificial drying, for instance by steam, shortens the time considerably but brings with it the danger that the useful life of the wood (that is, its capacity to vibrate) will be shortened. To test whether the wood of an instrument has been treated with a drying preparation, Alton recommends touching it with the tip of the tongue. A slightly sour taste indicates that chemicals were used. Vuillaume's method of "baking" wood to age it will occupy us later. Infrared rays have been used experimentally for drying wood, along with ozone boxes that "age" the wood to a beautiful color but make it brittle, with disastrous results.

A good procedure, especially in regions with high humidity, is to store the wood in temperature- and humidity-controlled sheds with good air circulation. Apian-Bennewitz considers 12–18 degrees centigrade to be the best storage temperature. Since freshly cut firwood contains as much as 45 percent moisture, the drying process is extremely important. Trees intended for violin making therefore are best logged during the winter months, preferably in January, because the sap content then is lowest. Insufficiently dried wood vibrates poorly, chiefly because it contains too much resin. In England, wood for string instruments is treated similarly to wood intended for top quality construction work: the logs are stored under water for up to two years before the air-drying process begins. This is said to extend the wood's life span.

Experience over hundreds of years has led to red fir, hazel fir, silver fir, and white fir being preferred for the top, soundpost, and bass bar. (In the United States, the most commonly used woods are Engelmann spruce and Sitka spruce.) Various kinds of maple are preferred for the back, neck, ribs, and bridge. For the fingerboard, tailpiece, and several small parts, other woods, such as ebony, are used. Balfoort lists fifty to sixty different degrees of quality for spruce, maple, and ebony; Sibire lists twenty-two for spruce alone. This is credible considering that there are a hundred thousand species of trees, whose wood may be divided into more than thirteen hundred kinds.

For the violin top, spruce is used more often than fir. According to Apian-Bennewitz, this is due to the scarcity of good fir, though luthiers prefer fir because of its full, large tone. Heavy wood brings out the fundamentals and low partials; light wood, the upper partials. As early as the fourteenth century, fir was not considered suitable for the back of string instruments.

Cell structure of conifers

Konrad von Megenberg recommended it for the top, saying that it produced a sweet tone. Wood from nut trees is seldom used for the back, but there are good violins with backs made from oak or beechwood. Experimentation continued during the sixteenth century to determine the most suitable types of wood. At that time backs were also made from poplar, linden, and pear wood, as Gasparo da Salò continued to use at times. Several reasons led to the preference for maple: it ideally combines hardness, elasticity, and light weight, to say nothing of its beauty.

To use the same type of wood for top and back normally results in poor sound. Apparently the entire instrument's ability to vibrate is greatly affected by the different basic pitches of different kinds of wood. Violins in which spruce was used for top and back turned out to have a sound that is robust but not beautiful, while using maple for both resulted in weak sound. The importance of choosing the right wood is also proved by the velocity of sound produced: the sound of heavy woods such as beech and oak travels at only 3400–4400 m per second, while that of fir travels more than 5000 m. Savart's experiments showed that firwood has approximately the same elasticity as steel and glass. According to Riechers, the wood of American balsam spruce is hardly suitable for instruments because of its high resin content. Attempts to tap the resin before felling the tree were not successful.

The nature and condition of the wood's fiber also affect its ability to vibrate. Distances between the annual rings should be nearly equal, preferably not more nor less than 1 mm. Climate evidently has an influence, as a dry climate will cause slow growth resulting in dense rings and fibers. Temperature is another determining factor, as is the soil's content of minerals and chemicals. The initially good sound of instruments with wide grain may not last, since very porous wood is likely to change. Doubts have been raised about the fibers' influence on tone quality, for some fine old Italian violins are made from wood with irregular growth patterns. One Strad has a very powerful tone even though its top has a knothole. The Milan museum's collection includes a violin by Giovanni Godoni, the top of which has *three* knotholes! Some luthiers prefer wood from a tree's sun side, believing its structure to be better for instruments.

The best sprucewood has always come from the North and South Tyrol, Bavaria, Switzerland, the Bohemian forests, and the Carpathian mountains, while the best maple hails from Hungary, Romania, Dalmatia, Bavaria, and also the Tyrol. Best conditions exist at an altitude of 1000–1500 m in valleys that are protected from wind. Old trees are preferred as their wood is most stable. Early Italian luthiers obtained maple from Venice, a city-state with much shipbuilding that had established good sources of supply from Dalmatia, Croatia, and Turkey.

Within each type of wood, pieces that are of medium hardness and also quite light are preferred. One can determine the special qualities by tapping on the wood, obtaining light or muffled sound. Trees for cutting are selected with this in mind. Furnishing wood for instruments has become a special branch of the lumber industry, relieving the luthier of selecting raw material unless he or she has special requirements. Amazing quantities of wood were formerly needed. Thus from 1 January to 8 April 1896, eighty-one carloads of 10,000 kg each were delivered to Schönbach for instrument making, which amounts to ca. three hundred carloads per year. To supply wood on such an industrial scale does have a disadvantage. Only small quantities of the same wood are available at any one time, so that the violin maker cannot experiment with a specific model, always using the same wood. Many master luthiers of the past laid in large supplies of wood, so that they could work with the same material for the longest possible time. Johannes Cuypers's supply was not exhausted until thirty-two years after his death!

PREPARING THE TOP AND BACK

The rough-cutting of the wood is done by the supplier. As in a pie, wedge-shaped segments, or quarter cuts, are cut out, usually ca. 50 mm longer than required for the finished product and at least 40 mm thick at the edge.
These are cut once more (along the dotted line), almost but not quite to the center. In that way, pieces with the same flaming or grain are held together until they arrive in the violin maker's shop.

He now separates the pieces completely and gives them a first smoothing or polishing. Wood used for the top, taken from straight-grained spruce must be "book-match" cut, so the grain of the two halves will be mirror images. The joining of the two pieces then follows—a difficult but important operation. Both contact surfaces must be completely smooth, without the

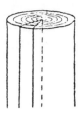

Quarter cut

slightest humps or gaps. Only then may they be glued together with color-less [neutral] glue of the best quality.

In preparing the glue, all ingredients must be dissolved completely by boiling. Considered best for violins are Cologne, Breslau, and Russian glues, which names refer to the glue's types rather than provenance, for they are now made everywhere. "Hide glue" is most commonly used in America. Glues are first softened in cold water, then heated and dissolved in a double boiler. In winter, the pieces to be glued are slightly warmed to prevent the glue's drying too quickly. Any glue that oozes out must be removed at once lest it penetrate the wood. Failure to do so might damage the varnish later, when repairs are made. In its dry state, glue is very sensitive to the air's humidity; luthiers in countries with a wet climate use a special glue. Most glues require three to ten hours for drying, depending on the time of year.

Aside from the quartersawn, there is another way to cut wood intended for the back, namely tangent-sawn or slab-cut. For this the board that includes the core cannot be used, but one gains uniform flaming across the entire back, whether it is made of one or two pieces. Andrea Amati and the Brescia masters preferred this cut, while Nicolò Amati used the quarter cut. It is a matter of aesthetics. Quarter-cut pieces give symmetry, for the axis provides the eye with a point of repose in the wood's flaming, while a back flamed in its entirety creates a restless impression. According to Möckel, a slab cut reduces the back's firmness, causing it to have insufficient resistance for its many tasks. Other writers maintain the opposite.

For the top it is preferable to have the closer grain at the center and the wider grain on the outside. The top's two pieces are not cut parallel to the grain but in such a way that toward the top they form a slightly acute angle. This provides increased tension for the top and better friction for the glue. If a top is carved from one piece, the wider rings should be on the left and the closer ones on the right, due to the location and pressure of the lower and higher strings. Dealers often praise violins with one-piece tops, and espe-cially backs, hoping to obtain higher prices, but experience has shown that over time such a back stands up less well under pressure.

It stands to reason that all this working with wood requires not only a great deal of experience but also the greatest care in preparing, treating, and handling it. All these operations are still basically carried out as they were in Amati's time; only the tools have been improved. In violin making as in other fields, people continually seek better ways of carrying out the same tasks. Those who have read the chapters on tools by Möckel and by the Millants are aware of the amazing wealth of ideas and minor inventions that facilitate the modern luthier's work.

THE MODEL

All violin makers follow a specific model, at times more than one. They occasionally may treat them freely, or change them as time goes on, but they usually adhere to one model for some time. The Strad model is currently the one most often adopted, unless a customer has other wishes. In that case a specially prepared drawing with all needed measurements is transferred to the wood with the help of fairly complicated protractors—a cumbersome, time-consuming procedure. Yet considerations of price demand that a minimum of time be devoted to this. To make a white (unvarnished) violin takes 150–180 hours, and this only if the same model is used for some time, so that templates or molds can be made for all parts. This too at first is time-consuming but in the long run significantly reduces the overall time needed. Möckel (1930) includes drawings for no fewer than twenty-seven templates, from the outline of the entire body to the bridge's curvature; they make the luthier's work easier and prevent slipups. For the templates Schulze prefers thin zinc or brass since wood is too sensitive to changes in temperature and humidity.

Though the use of a mold is important, its significance should not be exaggerated. Even though expertly and flawlessly followed, it only assures the violin's beautiful appearance, not its sound, which largely depends on the wood's characteristics. To understand these and to modify the model accordingly as work progresses—this is the mark of an artist-luthier. Pieces of wood may belong to the same kind of tree but may vary greatly according to the location of the individual tree, the soil in which it grew, and the climatic factors that affected it. Even the same tree has wood of different qualities at its root, middle, and top. To adhere rigidly even to the best model would be disregarding all these factors as they affect sound.

MAKING THE TOP AND BACK

When the parts that have been securely clamped together have dried for ca. twenty-four hours, work on top and back can be resumed. With the help of a template, the body's outline is transferred to the wood, which then is cut out, using a carpenter's saw with a very thin blade. The resulting piece should be ca. 1 mm larger than the template, and the excess will then be taken off with a fine file. For this procedure, too, much experience is needed. Cutting out the middle bouts in particular requires much practice. The following are average dimensions for violins from the golden age:

Length: 355 mm
Inside length: 343 mm
Width (lower bout): 208 mm
Width (upper bout): 168 mm
Width at waist: 112 mm
Distance between corners on the same side: ca. 76 mm

In the following pages, mention will often be made of large, medium, or small models; this should not be confused with so-called full-size, three-quarter-size, half-size, or quarter-size violins. Actually, the three-quarter-size violin amounts to seventeen-eighteenths, and the half-size violin to eight-ninths of a full-size violin. The body length of a quarter-size violin is 297 mm; half-size, 320 mm; and three-quarter-size, 335 mm.

Once the outer dimensions have been established, the extra wood is removed, as required by the arching, partly by using a gouge, partly by using special finger planes. An arching of 15 mm each, for top and back, measured at its highest point, is generally considered best. Only slight deviations from this are acceptable without an adverse effect on the instrument's sound. As the top near the soundpost is very fragile, and as so-called soundpost cracks in the top are almost impossible to repair, the top for 5 mm around the soundpost is often left somewhat thicker than the rest. The scooping out of the arching can be done freehand (i.e., "by eye") or with the help of templates as described by Roger and Max Millant.

To simplify this task and to prepare for it, Möckel recommended drilling several hundred small holes into the wood that is to be removed. The depths of the holes must correspond exactly to the curvature of the arching. By using templates, the exact number of the holes and the relief lines are first traced on the wood. Rödig describes a simple way of indicating the top's varying thicknesses: beginning at the soundpost, lines are drawn in all directions and are divided as often as desirable; by connecting all points representing the same division, lines are obtained that indicate asymmetrical layers that have the soundpost at their center.

When both top and back have been planed down to the bottom of the bore holes, the edge can be cut to a thickness of 4 mm with knives and files of various sizes. Once the thicknesses of top and back have been definitively established, the groove for the purfling is cut and scooped out with the purfling tool, 4 mm from the edge and 1.5 mm wide. The purfling is then inserted. It usually consists of three strips of wood, each .5 mm wide. The one in the middle is made of light-colored wood, most often maple; the outer ones of black wood (ebony; sometimes whalebone or stained pearwood). Purfling may be furnished to the luthier by outside suppliers, but before it can be inserted it must be bent to the appropriate shape. Once it has been installed, top and back are essentially complete. For increased tension, a slight indentation known as the channel is scooped out with a scraper, ca. 2–2.5 mm from the edge. It leads gradually into both the edge and the arching. The channel's depth and exact shape vary from model to model.

Luthier scooping out the channel (photo: Klaus Grandpierre)

Sandpapers of increasingly fine quality are employed for the finishing work, which has a substantial effect on the violin's tone. With this work the luthier aims to achieve optimal wood thickness for all parts of the instrument. Excessive thickness will result in distortions and impurities of sound; if the wood is too thin, the timbre (especially of the lower strings) is adversely affected by the insufficient mass of the vibrating body. For the back, Riechers recommends 4 mm as the best thickness, reducing it slightly near the upper and lower blocks, and 3 mm near the middle ribs. The Millants prefer a thickness of 5 mm for the back. Rödig tried to calculate exact dimensions; his results come close to the measurements of old Italian violins. For Strad models he believes that the top should have a consistent thickness of 2.5 mm; the Millants claim that Stradivari used 3 mm, with a slight reduction (2.5 mm) near the ribs. For both top and back, the area where the two halves are joined is usually somewhat stronger. A reduction of up to 1.5 mm near the edges has been recommended. If other authors indicate different measurements, this is due to the different models used by the masters, and to differences in wood. Violins with little or no arching require thicker wood to withstand string pressure. Wood quality also must be taken into consideration: hard wood will tolerate more thinning.

Needless to say, finishing work calls for great skill and craftsmanship. This work is checked with a micrometer that registers tolerances of one-hundredth of a millimeter. But aside from great skill the violin maker must have a sure instinct for arriving at the desired tone quality. Slight irregularities that no longer can be corrected may greatly affect an instrument's tone. In their desire to achieve the best possible sound, luthiers are tempted to remove as much wood as possible. When too much has been removed, the result may be a "wolf tone," the extraneous, unpleasant sound that occurs if a tone's node of vibration is near a place on the top that is too thin. The cause can be demonstrated easily enough: a finger placed on the top shows that inadequate thickness (meaning insufficient weight) is to blame. Wolf tones occur even in beautifully finished instruments made by master builders; they are rarely heard in factory-made instruments. They are more noticeable in dry weather. On the violin, the wolf tone occurs chiefly near C-sharp on the G string. Players try to cope with it by wedging a small cork between top and fingerboard, and cellists may avoid it by extra knee pressure on the ribs. This has little effect on timbre or tone volume but may suppress the wolf. Luthiers have tried various modifications of the instrument to eliminate the problem.

During the finishing work the basic vibration tone or tap tone of both top and back must be continually checked, as the tones of both must stand in a good interval relationship to each other. Different ways of checking them have been developed. The oldest and simplest consists of tapping (with one's knuckle) the individual pieces, suspended so that they can vibrate freely. More complex methods have been used by Savart, Möckel, and others, but all are problematic because the loose, individual pieces vibrate quite differently from a complete instrument. Only very experienced luthiers know how to take this into account.

By measuring master violins and by various experiments it has been established that the interval of a major second (such as E to F-sharp) is best, meaning that the back must have a higher tap tone than the top. If both are tuned to the same pitch, a rather dull, muffled tone quality results. Schulze considers G to be the most desirable tone for the top. He recommends an interval of a minor or major third with the back but has had good results with intervals up to a major sixth. Balfoort recommends a fifth for the upper bouts and an octave for the edges. Möckel lists the dimensions of ten master violins along with their tap tones. A luthier may have made instruments of different measurements in different years, suggesting that he experimented with his model, but differences may also have been due to the properties of the wood. A top with a thickness of more than 4.5 mm will lack elasticity and therefore will produce a harsh, piercing tone, even if very soft sprucewood is used. Tops that are too thin, on the other hand, may lose some arching, even if very hard wood is used, and an uneven tone quality will result. Möckel provides these tabulations, with thicknesses measured at the following places:

Top	Back
1) At the bridge	1) As for the top, under the bridge
2) Betw. bridge and lower block	2) Betw. soundpost and lower block
3) Betw. bridge and top block	3) Betw. soundpost and top block
4) In the upper bouts	4) In the upper bouts
5) In the lower bouts	5) In the lower bouts
6) Very near the edges	6) Near the edges
7) Close to the *f* holes	7) Near the middle bouts (waist)

Gasparo da Salò

	Top	Back
1)	2.8–3.0	4.3
2)	2.8	4.1
3)	3.0	3.4
4)	2.1	
5)	2.2	2.6–2.7
6)	2.6–2.8	2.5
7)	3.1–3.4	3.0
	F	F-sharp ¼

Nicolò Amati

	Top	Back
1)	2.6	4.8–5.1
2)	2.3	3.7
3)	2.5	4.1
4)	2.2	1.5
5)	2.2–2.4	1.6–1.8
6)	1.8–2.2	1.8–2.4
7)	2.7–2.9	3.2
	D-sharp	F

Nicolò Amati (another violin)

	Top	Back
1)	3.8	5.8–6.1
2)	3.0	3.9
3)	2.7–2.8	4.3
4)	2.3–2.9	2.3–2.4
5)	2.5–2.6	2.3–3.0
6)	2.2–2.3	1.9–2.4
7)	2.8	2.8
	F-sharp	E

Antonius Stradivarius (long model)

	Top	Back
1)	1.8	4.2
2)	2.1	3.0
3)	2.0	4.0
4)	1.8–1.9	2.7
5)	1.8–2.2	2.5
6)	2.5–3.2	2.6–3.0
7)	2.6–3.2	3.3
	F	[not given]

For the top, the given tap tone assumes the inclusion of the bass bar.

As to the measurements of old violins, Apian-Bennewitz has pointed out that over the course of 150 to 200 years wood is likely to shrink or diminish. When making copies of old violins it is therefore wise to add .5 mm to the thickness of both top and back. Fuhr has rightly stated that one cannot indicate any one precise tap tone for top or back, for different tones will be heard at different places. Balfoort too has pointed this out. He chose four places, at the most important points of vibration, saying that those tones should be considered in finishing an instrument. The highest tone, between D-sharp and F, is produced between the C bouts.

In discussions of measurements and proportions, notable discrepancies between old and modern writers exist. This is due in part to our steadily rising concert pitch, which has affected the way violins were made during various periods. [For further technical information, see Stowell 1992, "The Physics of the Violin" by Bernard Richardson. *Ed.*]

THE *f* HOLES AND BASS BAR

Once top and back, through constant checking and improving, have acquired the ideal thickness, the points of contact on the back are reinforced with small cleats made of maple, each having the dimensions $10 \times 10 \times 2$ mm. Usually there are seven of these, placed at equal distances from each other. For better adhesion they are glued in place so that their fibers run at a right angle to those of the back. Two important procedures involving the top then follow: cutting the *f* holes and inserting the bass bar. Beautifully cut *f* holes testify to the luthier's skill; they will please professional musicians and knowledgeable amateurs and collectors. Special care is therefore devoted to this operation. Finding the right place for the holes is facilitated by an *f* hole template, which also fixes their distance from the center seam or joint. Schulze gives a detailed description of Stradivari's method of making the *f* holes; he considers Guarneri's method "somewhat bizarre" because that maker supposedly cut the holes freehand.

Tracing the holes on the violin's top is difficult due to the arching. Assuming the vibrating part of the string is 325 mm, the inner notches of the holes must be located at a distance of 195 mm from the edge of the body's

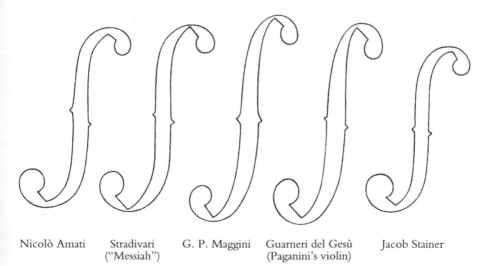

| Nicolò Amati | Stradivari ("Messiah") | G. P. Maggini | Guarneri del Gesù (Paganini's violin) | Jacob Stainer |

f holes of old masters (from Niederheitmann 1877)

upper part. This applies to the Strad model, and Riechers considers these the standard measurements. A nasal tone results if the holes are too close to each other or too small.

After the tracing, the circular ends, or eyes, are cut out first, with a fret saw or special tool; then the connecting parts are cut. Finishing is accomplished with a special kind of knife that is also used for shaping the bridge. Finally, the *f* holes are smoothed with small files. Apian-Bennewitz pointed out that the size of the holes must correspond exactly to the violin's dimensions, otherwise the *eigentone* (the tone produced by the air vibrating inside the violin) will be too high or too low.

The bass bar has several functions. It counteracts the pressure of the D and G strings and is therefore attached to the top's left side in such a way that the bridge's left foot is later positioned exactly above the bass bar—i.e., at a distance of 19–20 mm from the top's center joint. The bass bar also slows the top's vibration, or, as Apian-Bennewitz put it, it compensates for the loss of wood caused by carving out the *f* holes. If it is too thick, however, it will impede vibration. One of its chief functions is to distribute the vibrations evenly along the various areas of the top. For that reason it is mounted not quite parallel to the grain of the top's wood, but with a deviation of 3–6 mm, at a slight angle from bottom left to top right. This also protects the top against cracks. Together with the soundpost the bass bar imparts to the top's left half a different vibration pattern from the right half.

There is no one correct length or thickness; the bass bar must complement the top's thickness, which in turn depends on the wood. If the top is very thin, a somewhat heavier bass bar will increase the top's elasticity and will supply the needed mass of wood. Leonhardt observed that the bass bar's length is also related to the top's width, and to the wood's firmness and arching. Very flexible wood requires a longer bass bar. Hill (1902) gave the following measurements for bass bars:

	Length	Height	Width
1621 Antonio and Girolamo Amati	269.88	6.35	4.76
1650 Nicolò Amati	219.08	6.35	4.76
1716 Antonio Stradivari	254	7.94	4.76
1789 Gagliano	273.05	17.46	4.29
An Andrea Amati, measured by Simoutre	220	8.00	4.00

These figures can be updated as follows:

	Length	Height	Width
Since 1859	266.7	11.11	6.35
1997	270–280	20–29	5–6

These changes in the bass bar's dimensions are largely due to the steadily rising pitch, which puts more and more strain on string instruments. The ends of the bass bar are now ca. 42 mm away from the upper and lower edges of the top. The upper end has a distance of ca. 18 mm from the joint of the top's two parts, the lower end ca. 21 mm. That way, the bass bar is positioned exactly under the bridge's left foot. In determining the top's tap tone or vibration frequency, the bass bar's weight (added to the top's weight) must be taken into consideration. The tap tone of the entire top, established after the bass bar has been glued in, is called the bass-bar tone by Fuhr.

Very light but hard sprucewood is most suitable for the bass bar (its rough-cut shape is shown here). Its final attachment to the finished top is a delicate operation that requires constant probing, observing the top's arching and the thickness of its wood.

Bass bar model

THE RIB STRUCTURE

Preparation of the ribs and inner parts of the violin and their subsequent combination into the rib assembly take place independently of the luthier's work described so far. Usually, the six rib strips are made of maple and are prepared in rough form by an outside shop or firm. The luthier then planes them down to a width of 30–32 mm and a thickness of 1.2–1.5 mm. The individual pieces are moistened slightly; they are then bent over a heated bending iron under gradually increasing pressure. This process requires much patience. It is fairly easily accomplished for the upper and lower ribs but is quite difficult for the middle ribs (at the waist) because of their great curvature. Some violin makers oppose this method of bending the wood; it tends to harden it and thereby affects its vibration adversely. They prefer fitting the thoroughly moistened pieces to the mold while applying pressure.

The ribs' height has not remained uniform. Since the time of Stradivari it has gradually and slightly decreased, from the lower block (30–31.75 mm) toward the upper block (28.5–30 mm). This increases the top's tension.

Other preparations are needed before the rib structure can be completed. Upper and lower blocks must be shaped, as well as the four corner blocks and the twelve rib linings. The corner blocks prevent lateral changes of top and back. Upper and lower blocks counteract string pressure, while the linings provide better adhesion of top and back to the ribs. The fitting of the lining must be done with great precision; it will protect the completed violin from excessive pressure and from blows. Spruce, willow, linden, poplar wood, or occasionally whalebone is used for the lining. All these are hard enough for the purpose, but also light enough so that not too much weight is added to the violin's body. For these reinforcing or lining pieces a height of 8 mm and width of 2.5 mm are optimum, though during the eighteenth century they were considerably thinner.

Gluing is facilitated by the use of molds, including small auxiliary molds for the middle ribs or C bouts. Both interior and exterior molds are used. There is disagreement about which is preferable. Modern Italian luthiers

Cross section of a rib with lining

object to the exterior mold because it fixes the shape definitively, whereas an interior mold allows for some later modifications. Molds are not normally employed when only a single violin of a particular type is to be made; it would not be worth the time and effort.

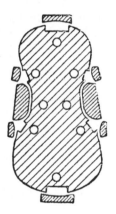 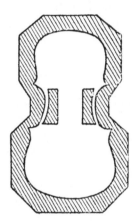

Interior and exterior molds (with counterparts)

Counterparts are needed for the gluing. Small blocks of soft wood (at times padded with cork) are inserted between clamp and violin to protect the violin from damage. The rib structure, by the way, is somewhat smaller than the top's circumference. The top should have an overhang of ca. 2 mm to protect the ribs from damage.

While work on the ribs progresses, the upper and lower blocks must be glued to the back. Once the glue has dried, the rib structure can be attached to the back. Excess glue must be removed quickly; if it penetrated the adjacent wood, it would adversely affect the wood's capacity to absorb varnish.

When the rib structure has been glued to the back, finishing work on the insides of blocks and linings takes place. Only then can the top be glued on, again protecting it from the clamps with small wooden blocks. To make it easier, later, to remove the top for repairs, a thinner glue is used than for the back. Small adjustments to the ribs are still possible after the glue has dried; then those parts made of maple (back and ribs) are finished with a special kind of sandpaper. The softer top, however, made of spruce, remains in its present condition in order not to hinder the absorption of the varnish undercoat.

In addition to the body, and independently of it, the neck, scroll, and fingerboard must be finished. The neck block—a piece of maple roughly precut in the shape of the neck—has the dimensions 260 × 55 × 42 mm. Neck and scroll are then cut out (with a saw and using several templates) and planed down. The neck's thickness can be adjusted to accommodate a violinist's hand; its normal width is 16–18 mm near the pegbox and 24 mm near the violin's body. Leonhardt gives detailed instructions for positioning the neck and fingerboard. According to Schulze and Riechers, the distance from the top nut (on the fingerboard) to the top's upper edge should be 130 mm. With the vibrating portion of the string being 325 mm long, and a distance of 195 mm between the body's upper edge and the bridge, this represents a proportion of two-fifths to three-fifths, which both believe are ideal proportions for a violin. The proportion of body to neck should be 7:5.

The scroll model is also transferred to the wood with the help of special templates, unless the luthier wishes to demonstrate his skill by carving it freehand, giving the scroll a distinctive, personal touch. According to Apian-Bennewitz, some artisans specialize in making scrolls, following the models of certain old masters.

When the scroll is complete, the pegbox is cut out and the peg holes are drilled. To stand up under the pressure of the pegs, the pegbox walls should be at least 4–7 mm thick at the bottom and 3 mm thick at the top.

Fingerboards can also be obtained from suppliers in rough-cut form. Smooth ebony with a dense grain is best suited. Normal dimensions are as follows:

> Length: 267–270 mm
> Width at the nut: 24–25 mm
> Width near the bridge: 45 mm
> Thickness: 4–5 mm

The fingerboard's lower end will lie exactly over the imaginary line connecting the *f* hole notches. To reduce its weight, the underside of the part that extends beyond the neck is slightly carved out. The luthier does the precision cutting and planing, using templates, but the final preparation of the fingerboard surface is after the fingerboard has been glued to the neck. In this process, and in shaping and mounting the nut, one must consider that the thicker G string requires more room to vibrate than the other strings. The nut therefore must be somewhat higher on the G string side. Spohr noted that the fingerboard of Romberg's cello had a scoop almost 1.5 mm deep under the G string in order to avoid the string's touching the fingerboard under heavy bow pressure. Since then this has sometimes been done under the violin's G string, with a much shallower scoop under the E string.

On the nut, notches for the strings are now made with a file. If the instrument is made for a particular person, it is possible to take the thickness of the player's fingers into consideration, to facilitate the playing of true fifths. The distance between the outer notches usually is 16–18 mm. They should not be very deep, for the strings must merely lie on the notches without being pinched. Nut and notches should allow the upper three strings to lie .5 mm, and the G string 1 mm above the fingerboard.

The angle the fingerboard forms with the violin's body must be correct in relation to the height of the bridge. This is important, both for ease of playing and for the violin's tone. The angle is correct if a vertical line over the line connecting the *f* hole notches meets the extension of the fingerboard line 27 mm away from the top. At the lower end of the fingerboard, this means for the E string a distance of 2.5–3 mm from the fingerboard; for the G string ca. 4 mm. It is possible to correct the fingerboard angle by mounting a wedge under it. An angle of 155 degrees was considered ideal by Greilsamer; Delezenne and Roussel advocate 156 degrees, Fuhr 155–157 degrees (see illustration). The more acute the angle, the greater the string pressure will be. If the angle is too acute the violin will not speak readily and extraneous noises will interfere.

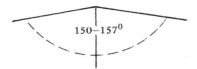

Angle formed by string, both sides of the bridge

Once the fingerboard is in place, the neck is carefully smoothed with files, scrapers, and very fine sandpaper wherever it will come in contact with the player's left hand, which would be disturbed by even the slightest unevenness. To facilitate moving the left thumb, the neck's left side is somewhat reduced. All these fine points or niceties are more likely to be considered if the luthier also plays the violin. Some of these small adjustments will not be made until the neck has been glued to the body. The neck's foot is mounted on the button, a semicircular continuation of the back that supports the neck. In Stradivari's day, one to four nails were used to attach the neck to the top block. More recently the nails have been removed from all old instruments; the nail holes may still be visible.

With the neck attached to the body, the unvarnished (white) violin is complete. According to Leonhardt it weighs 380–390 g without the chin rest. Alton recommends letting the violin dry out thoroughly for a few months. He exposes it to sunlight, which imparts to it a natural, warm color, and he recommends that it be played often during this period. Other luthiers disagree, worried about the adverse effect of hand perspiration to the unvarnished wood.

VARNISHING

Before the actual varnishing takes place, an undercoat is applied. It stains the wood, but most importantly it makes it harder and keeps the varnish itself from penetrating the wood directly, which would reduce its ability to vibrate. Luthiers used to treat the wood with substances such as potassium bichromate, solutions of ammonium chloride, potash, or similar caustic, corroding chemicals. They did this in order to give the new wood an aged appearance. The practice was gradually discontinued because it affected the wood's lifespan adversely. Violins that were so treated may have looked like old Italian instruments when new, but in time their resonance would deteriorate. Only those substances that enhance the normal process of darkening brought on by age without penetrating the wood's cell structure seem to work well. Such substances include, above all, various oils, especially linseed oil, to which coloring agents such as dragon's blood or saffron are added. Grounding substances of this kind are called filler. Rödig has discussed various problems associated with them.

After the wood is sealed or sized, the instrument must dry for a long time, to prevent later mixing of the varnish with the ground. During this period the instrument should be protected from light, which might have an undesirable effect on the color. There are, however, sizings that bring out the full beauty of the wood after it has been exposed to sunlight for a long time. In the Mittenwald violin makers school, instruments are exposed to direct sunlight for a year, a practice that may go back to the Klotz tradition. According to Leonhardt, after the violin has been grounded with linseed oil, a long period of drying and exposure to sunlight will result in a beautiful, golden brown color.

Resins of varying degrees of hardness are essential ingredients of varnish. Very hard resin will impede the wood's ability to vibrate, while varnish containing excessively soft resin will fail to protect the wood against perspiration; moisture from the player's breath; dust from rosin and other sources; dirt; and weather or climatic influences. Medium–hard resins therefore are preferred. One obtains them by scratching the tree trunk and collecting the resin that exudes and hardens. Mastic from the island of Chios and African copal are often used. Fuhr is against the use of copal, shellac, or amber as they are too hard. Oil or alcohol are used as solvents, both for resin and color additives; we therefore speak of oil or spirit varnishes. Each has advantages and disadvantages; a luthier's decision about which to use depends in part on his manner of working. Oil varnishes are slow–drying, which facilitates corrections; some take as long as a year to dry. Since spirit varnishes dry almost as soon as they are applied, one must work with a fast and sure hand, for it is virtually impossible to make corrections. Varnishes rich in fat, recommended especially by Mailand, require a drying time of about a week after the application of each layer of varnish.

Once the resin has been dissolved, only small amounts of coloring agents are added, so that the true color of the wood is not completely obscured. Dragon's blood is one of the coloring agents most often used; it is obtained from palm trees growing in the Moluccas (Spice Islands). According to some luthiers, the solvents do not affect the quality or lifespan of the varnish because both oil and alcohol evaporate during the drying, so that only resin remains. It has been claimed that spirit varnish tends to crack easily, and that it does not bind resin and pigment as well as oil varnish does. When oil is used as a solvent an oxidation process takes place that goes on for several years.

The actual varnishing involves several stages or steps. Varnish is applied with a soft brush. The number of coats required depends on its composition, on the intended hue, and on the wood. After each coat is applied the violin must air dry in a dust-free place. Since varnishing is facilitated by rapid drying, summer is the preferred time for it. The first layers will penetrate the wood to some extent; only when a layer remains on the surface is the varnishing process complete.

Once a coat of varnish has dried completely, the varnished parts must be rubbed down with pumice, fine sandpaper, linseed oil, or a special rubbing oil. The next coat is then applied, and this process is repeated until the desired color has been attained. Riechers gives the weight of a violin (both his own and those by Stradivari) as 260–275 g without the fingerboard. Fry gives 285–317 g for an unvarnished violin, to which the varnish adds 13–26 g. For an unvarnished violin Angeloni gave the following weights:

Back: 100–110 g
Top: 80–91 g
Rib structure with blocks: 50–55 g
Neck: 70–75 g
Fingerboard: 45–60 g
Finished accessories: 40–45 g

Except for the fingerboard, the exact weight depends less on the model than on the kind of wood.

The neck also is given a colorless spirit varnish that must be very hard, because the neck is subjected to the constant friction of the hand and to its perspiration.

With varnishing, the acoustical properties of the violin will change. The tap tones of the various pieces will rise, that of the (softer) top more than that of the (harder) back. As he assembles the violin, the luthier must take these changes into consideration.

ADJUSTING THE VIOLIN

The term "adjusting" refers to providing the violin's completed body with pegs, tailpiece, strings, bridge, and soundpost, usually added in that order. Many musicians, even professional ones, have no clear notion of their importance, including their effect on the violin's tone quality.

Pegs are made from very hard wood, such as rosewood, yellow boxwood, ebony, or mountain mahogany. They usually are mass-produced and supplied to the luthier who selects and fits them, cutting off the ends that protrude too far. Chalk or soap can be used to improve their fit if they are too easy or too hard to turn; it must be possible to turn them without undue effort. Peg holes also frequently need adjusting. Once the pegs fit well, holes through which to thread the strings are drilled. For easy tuning and quick replacement of a broken string, several factors must be considered: the pegbox dimensions, the best placement of peg holes and holes for the strings, and the quality of the pegs.

Tailpieces are also supplied ready-made to the luthier. Its curvature at the top must correspond exactly to the bridge's curvature, and its width must equal the width of the fingerboard, which is 45 mm. The tailpiece's length must be such that the string's length, from the bridge to its point of contact with the tailpiece, is exactly 55 mm. The holes through which the strings are fastened should be positioned to allow the G and E strings to be 30 mm apart. Riechers has demonstrated convincingly the importance of measurements behind the bridge. A string's tension extends from its peg to the tailpiece, even though the vibrating part is shorter; conditions of the string behind the bridge affect the conditions of the vibrating portion. Rödig has shown that the hole for fastening a string should lie in the straight line formed by the string's resting point on the bridge and the saddle. He points to the oblique upper part found in the tailpieces of old gambas and viols, which made it possible to place the holes exactly in the direction of string pull without having to put them too close to each other.

A tailpiece's quality is chiefly determined by the choice of wood. Ebony, very hard and very light, offers great resistance to string tension. In earlier days a piece of gut string ca. 2 mm in diameter was used to attach the tailpiece to the end button, which in turn is inserted into the rib and lower block. Wire was later used for the same purpose—unfortunately, for it is less elastic. Currently, nylon is preferred to wire. To protect the violin's top, a small ebony saddle is placed under the wire or nylon.

One or several fine-tuners attached to the tailpiece are needed for steel strings whose thinness and density make it nearly impossible to tune them precisely with a peg. A fine-tuner with a regulating screw has been necessary since the introduction of steel E strings. The strings' proper thickness depends on the violin's wood and construction, and also on the bridge. One has to know an instrument well to determine what strings are best suited. The Millants give the following ranges in diameters:

> Steel E: .26 mm
> Gut A: .75–.77 mm
> Aluminum D: .85–.87 mm
> Silver G: .8 mm

Wunderlich gives similar dimensions for old Italian violins. Möckel provides detailed charts for violin, viola, cello, bass, and guitar. String making is constantly changing, however, partly because of the use of synthetic materials, so that these figures no longer are entirely valid. The strings' material and quality will also affect the bridge.

After the luthier has attached the strings loosely to pegs and tailpiece, the bridge will be cut and adjusted. Bridges of various sizes and types are provided in rough-cut form by manufacturers. Maplewood without flaming, or symmetrically cut with slight flaming, will furnish a bridge that is both strong and elastic. Hardwood will result in light, softwood in dark tone color. Bridges made of very hard wood prevent the violin from speaking easily, but soft wood reduces tone volume. In its finished shape the bridge should be 40 mm wide and 32–35 mm high, though these measurements also depend on the arching and thickness of the top and on the characteristics of the bridge wood. The rule of thumb is high arching, low bridge; thin top, sturdy bridge.

A bridge should have feet that are ca. 4 mm thick and 9–11 mm wide; they should conform exactly to the top's arching. Giving the bridge the appropriate curve is the next step. This can be done with a template, though care must be taken to have the curve conform to the fingerboard as well as the requirements of the future owner-player. Often the bridge is cut somewhat higher toward the G string, observing the general rule that at the end of the fingerboard the E string should lie 3 mm, the G string 5 mm above it.

Once the desired curvature has been made, the bridge will be cut to the correct thickness since this strongly influences tone color. Its upper part should be thinner than the lower part. Here again one must establish the right balance between strength and elasticity. As to strength, it is worth noting that even with the strings and tuning common in the nineteenth century, the bridge's right foot had to support a weight of 4.2–5.2 kg, the left foot 3.4–4.4 kg. Minimum thickness at the bridge's top is 1 mm. In a thick bridge, the mass of wood has the effect of a mute. Roussel has established wood thicknesses for what he considers the ideal bridge:

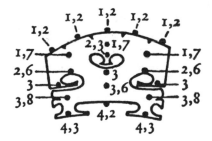

From Roussel *Traité de lutherie*

Grooves for the strings must be very shallow as the strong pressure of each string will deepen it somewhat. They must not be too deep, otherwise the strings might at times touch the fingerboard. Distances between the strings may have to be adjusted to a player's preference. All this shows that adjusting the bridge is an important process, requiring a well-versed professional.

When all these tasks have been accomplished, the bridge is given its final smoothing and polishing with files and sandpaper. This is important for the violin's sound but chiefly for its appearance. Now the bridge can be positioned along the imaginary line drawn between the notches of the *f* holes. Some luthiers have the habit (disapproved of by others) of removing the varnish from the places on which the feet stand, intending to bring about the closest possible contact between bridge and top. When mounting the bridge, string tension should not yet be high, for a part of the instrument is still missing—one that is hardly visible but of fundamental importance for the violin's sound and stability. This is the soundpost, called the soul ("l'anima") of the violin by the Italians.

Light sprucewood has proven most satisfactory for the soundpost. It is marketed in the shape of small, square rods. A violin maker may drop it on a wooden surface to determine its sound quality: the higher its pitch, the greater its elasticity and capacity to vibrate. Its grain should have annual rings .5 mm distant from each other. The little rods are planed down to be round, with a diameter of 6–7 mm. These dowels are carefully smoothed and cut into pieces 80–100 mm long. The exact length will depend on the violin's arching and is determined with the help of a small metal rod, which is inserted through the upper part of the *f* hole and placed on the back. The necessary height is then marked by a notch. To be of the right length, the soundpost, when inserted, must raise the top by .5 mm. If it is too long, the tone will be piercing and thin. To shape the points of contact with top and back requires much experience, for the arching of both must be accommodated precisely. Proper fit is ascertained with a small mirror similar to the one used by a physician to examine the larynx. When finished, the soundpost's diameter is 5.5–6 mm. It is positioned with a simple yet ingenious metal tool (see illustration) that is inserted through the right *f* hole. The soundpost should be placed so that its annual rings are at a right angle to those of the violin's top.

Angeloni has developed a way of using the metal tool together with a string, to keep the soundpost from falling down while it is being positioned. Generally speaking, it should stand below the bridge's right foot, about 2–3 mm away from it toward the player. In violins that are highly arched and made of thin wood it stands near the bridge; in flat violins and those made of thicker wood it stands farther away. To find the best location for a particular instrument can be a laborious task, requiring constant testing of the resulting sound. It also calls for keen, critical hearing. Möckel said that this work must be interrupted frequently since the ear tires easily and soon loses its ability to make comparisons. The Millants even recommended a few days' pause after each attempt to find the optimal position. According to Schulze, the thickness and position of bass bar and soundpost are related to each other somehow. Mordret describes experiments with a bass bar placed at a slight angle, with its upper end slightly to the right and outside of the bridge's foot. This supposedly reduces the harsh sound of the E string and generally improves the instrument's ready response.

In the first few months of a new violin's life the complex tensions within it change significantly, causing a noticeable deterioration of tonal strength and beauty. The new situation may mean that the soundpost is too short. This can be determined easily by loosening all the strings. If the soundpost falls down, it must be replaced by a larger one. Carl Flesch has pointed out how an instrument's adjustment is affected by climate, especially by excessive humidity or dryness, which affects not only the soundpost but also the bow hair, bridge, and other parts of the violin.

Strictly speaking, mounting the chin rest is not part of a violin's adjustment, since the violin's purchaser chooses a chin rest according to his own preferences and normally will mount it himself. Chin rests were not yet used in the early nineteenth century, and old instruments may still show the place where perspiration from the chin damaged the varnish. This place may be to the right or left of the tailpiece, or on both sides if several players used the violin. As violin technique more and more involved playing in the high positions it became imperative to hold the instrument securely under the chin, especially when shifting down again, so that the left hand no longer had to hold the violin. Spohr concerned himself with this problem; he may have been the first to design a chin rest, ca. 1820. In his *Violin School* he said,

> On the lower part of the representation of the instrument, above the tailpiece, is seen a contrivance of my own invention, called the *fiddle-holder*, which, after having been used for upwards of ten years by myself, my numerous pupils, and many other violinists, has fully proved its utility; and concerning which, therefore, I may perhaps be permitted to say a few words in this place.

Spohr then explains the need for a chin rest, the advantages it offers, and describes it in detail. In his violin method of 1858, Bériot describes the chin rest as a German innovation. Countless models have been introduced since Spohr's time; some did not last long. While Spohr's chin rest was mounted above the tailpiece, later models were attached to its left. It is difficult to make general recommendations about the chin rest, especially about its height, for every violinist must find the one best suited to his or her physique and way of holding the violin. No chin rest, however, must touch the tailpiece, and contact with the violin's top and back should be minimal, so as not to inhibit vibration.

Spohr's chin rest (from his *Violin School*)

BOW MAKING

Beginning with the French bow maker François Tourte (1747–1835), high-quality bows have been made from Pernambuco wood, a special variety of Brazil wood, named after that country's Pernambuco state. Ordinary Brazil wood, which is abundant there, is used for bows of lesser quality. Beechwood, especially red beech, is used for inexpensive student bows. Vuillaume experimented with metal tubes, and Bériot tried them out with a view to artistic performance. For some time, bows have been made of aluminum. They do not meet artists' requirements, but they are unbreakable. Fiber glass bows have been made in Japan recently, that material having already proven itself in pole vaulting.

Pernambuco wood is usually cut into boards by the supplier and transported in pieces ca. 1.2 m long, 10–15 mm in diameter. Most bow makers are not violin makers but specialists, who cut the bow's straight, basic form according to a pattern; a small block indicates the tip's location. The wood must be cut in the direction of the annual rings to ensure firmness and elasticity. In this rough-cut form the wood must dry, preferably for several years. The stick is then given its initial planing. Though better bow sticks are usually octagonal, a round stick, made from comparable wood, provides the same elasticity. In this initial work, the weight distribution, so important for playing, is already considered.

At this point the bow stick is still straight. Before it is bent (manually, over the knee) it must be thoroughly warmed, usually over an alcohol flame. At first the wood tends to return to its original shape, so the bending process must continue until the desired curvature has been reached. The difficulty is that the curve must not be even; its lowest point must be ca. 40 cm from the stick's lower end.

There follows the most delicate operation, the shaping of the tip, which is ca. 23 mm long. Models are used to facilitate this work. Because of the bow hair's tension the tip might easily break off, for which reason it is reinforced.

Two face plates—the inner one made of ebony, the outer one of ivory—can be glued on to protect the tip.

The crucial task now is to achieve optimal weight distribution within the stick. It weighs ca. 35 g and is 73–75 cm long. Wunderlich has prepared charts indicating that the stick should have a constant thickness (8 mm diameter) for about 25 cm, approximately its first third. From there on it should taper gradually, so that a few centimeters from the tip its diameter is ca. 5 mm. Its center of gravity should be at about 25 cm from the frog; Balfoort, Roda, and others mention 19 cm. Tourte bows have a diameter of ca. 8.6 mm for the first 11 cm and then taper to 5.3 mm.

The frog of good bows is almost always made from very hard ebony, rarely from ivory or tortoise shell; pressed wood has been used for inexpensive student bows. Madagascar and Mauritius furnish the best ebony for frogs. According to Wunderlich, normal dimensions are a length of 45 mm, height 20 mm, and width 13 mm. Since the frog is attached to a stick that is slightly curved, not all its parts form right angles. Metal parts (usually silver or a silver compound) give greater stability to the frog and make it heavier, providing a good counterweight against the stick's center of gravity. If a customer wants the metal parts (slide, heel, and ring) to be made of gold, this does not necessarily represent snobbism, for because of its specific weight, gold provides the needed balance very well.

Once the wooden upper part of the frog has been completed in its rough form, the slide and heel are fitted and the button is cut to accommodate the ring. The track for the underslide is carved out, and the slide is glued on and fastened with screws. Just below its middle it supports the screw-eye, usually made of brass. The underslide's shape is determined by the shape of the bow stick, octagonal or round. Finally, the mortise in which the hair is attached must be carved out and the "little foot" must be rounded, so that it will support the thumb's shape evenly.

This completes the frog. Now the groove in which the screw (made of iron or stainless steel) moves will be bored at the bow's end. The frog can now be inserted in this opening, where its screw-eye will connect with the screw.

The end of the bow hair is fastened in another mortise cut out at the bow's tip. Bow hair consists of selected horsehair, weighs ca. 4 g, and may be naturally white or bleached. Only about 5 percent of all horsehair is suitable for bows; the best quality horsehair comes from Hong Kong or from wild horses in Asia (including Siberia), Argentina, and Poland. In our motorized age, horsehair has become rare, but experiments with metal, nylon, or gut substitutes have so far been unsuccessful. Some claim that synthetic materials have produced better results. Earlier bow makers used 100 to 150 hairs, partly depending on thickness; 200 to 250 hairs are sometimes used lately, for a larger tone. They must be distributed evenly across the band's entire width to produce even tension. To equalize weight, the thicker part of the hair, at its root, must be attached at the frog, the thinner end at the tip. Distributors bundle the hair that way. Hair length, of course, must be exactly right for each individual bow. If it is too short, it will not be possible to loosen it. Before the bow hair is attached, the hair ends are singed slightly over a flame, resulting in little knots that make for better adhesion in the mortise, where they are glued with warm rosin and tied with thin thread.

The ribbon of hair is 10–12 mm wide at the frog, 8–10 mm wide at the tip. It is tucked in at both ends with small wedges or plugs. Rosin is then applied, and the final adjustments of the bow's balance are made. The stick is then stained, oiled, and varnished, unless its natural color is preferred. Schulze advises against varnishing because most kinds of bow wood, including Pernambuco, are hardened by the air, thereby becoming more elastic while maintaining the same weight. He does recommend repeated applications of linseed oil.

A finished bow ideally weighs 58–60 g; according to Wunderlich the outside limits are 53–63 g, according to Roda 42.5–63.7 g. The player chooses between these extremes according to individual preference. Flesch (*The Art of Violin Playing*, vol. 1) considers 58 g the ideal weight and rejects bows weighing less than 54 g because they require too much energy to obtain the necessary pressure at the tip. The Millants note the tendency to prefer heavier bows since ca. 1900, possibly because of the ever-rising concert pitch. Currently, 61 g is the norm. Bows by François Nicolas Voirin, made between 1860 and 1885 and weighing 50–55 g, are of good quality and, though out of favor for some time, are again in demand.

Rosin ("Kolophonium" in German, "colophane" in French, "colofonia" in Italian) is named after the Colophon region in the part of Asia Minor settled by the Greeks. Its quality is important, for the string's vibration depends on it rather than on the bow hair's small barbs. The various materials of which strings are made, along with their thickness, require different kinds of rosin for violin, viola, cello, and bass. Climate is also a factor. Basic ingredients are spruce resin, paraffin oil, beeswax, and mineral oils. Manufacturers of rosin closely guard information on how and at what temperatures these are treated and mixed. Jacob Augustus Otto (1817) gave a detailed account of how rosin was prepared in a small shop.

MANUAL WORK AND MACHINES

A violin and all its parts rarely were made by one luthier, for violin shops almost always employed apprentices and journeymen. Those parts that had little or no bearing on the sound, and those easily made, were always crafted, at least in their rough form, by apprentices. A certain division of labor was the norm, as it had been in the ateliers of the great painters of the sixteenth and seventeenth centuries. In 1568, Girolamo Virchi employed and housed a "maestro de intalij" (carving master) for the preparation of gamba heads and lute roses, and perhaps violin scrolls and *f* holes. Similar division of labor soon gave rise to auxiliary shops. Especially in places such as Markneukirchen, Mirecourt, and Mittenwald, highly specialized shops were established. As early as 1820 a separate shop for making pegs existed in Schönbach, followed soon by independent establishments for making violin tops, backs, necks, fingerboards, bridges, tailpieces, and other parts. Polishing was entrusted to women, but the master himself did the varnishing. To bring about greater economy in making all these parts, machines were introduced in the late eighteenth century. The nineteenth-century Industrial Revolution favored this development, and as early as ca. 1850 all violin parts could be produced by machine. Only gluing continued to be done by hand and was entrusted to quickly trained helpers. In 1862 Michael Schuster, Jr., of Markneukirchen introduced water power to run machinery used in violin making; electricity was employed soon thereafter.

The middle class's rise, furthered by the French Revolution, led to an incredible flourishing of musical activity, especially of music making in the home, and is reflected in the founding of many conservatories and other music schools, many catering to the amateur. Without machines this growing demand, for inexpensive student violins in particular, could not have been met. The Parr string instrument factory in Idaho successfully used specialized machinery to produce instruments of above-average quality.

One of the chief disadvantages of machine production is that the distinctive properties of various kinds and pieces of wood are largely ignored. Great quantities of wood of varying provenance are subjected to the same production processes. If factory-made violins nevertheless sound good this is fortuitous, for the wood usually is too thick and of inferior quality, resulting in a tone that is not noble and does not carry well. To improve quality, factory-preformed parts are manually refined. All hand work requires additional wages, so the quality of such violins is determined by the price for which they are meant to sell. Cheap, assembly-line "boxes" therefore will continue to be made, along with instruments made partly by machine, partly by hand. With very high costs and a limited pool of potential buyers, the number of violins created in all their essential parts by master luthiers will continue to be small.

What has been said here about violin making also applies to bow making, although that craft has relied more heavily on manual work, through the nineteenth century and even to our own time. For the production of superior bows machines can be enlisted only in the preliminary stages, except for routine processes such as screw making.

STRING MAKING

If it is true that the first string instruments were inspired by the hunting bow, string making may be considered to be one of the world's oldest crafts.

Silk strings, introduced from Asia, were used in the middle ages; they continued to be preferred in China and Japan, but elsewhere strings were made from twisted animal gut, also introduced from the Orient and already known to the Greeks. Bachmann cites a fourteenth-century source that describes the making of gut strings. Sheep intestines were soaked in water or lye for at least half a day, to remove meat remnants. For two more days they were submerged in a strong alkaline solution or in red wine. While still wet, two, three, or four strands were twisted to form a string that was then stretched for drying. Metal strings were rare, though preferred in Arabia and India. Strings were also made of horsehair, hemp, and linen fibers; in 1677 hemp strings were still used in Europe. In primitive civilizations lianas and root fibers served as strings.

At the time of the violin's origin, string making had already reached a high degree of perfection, especially of gut lute strings, which were durable and vibrated well. Siena, Florence, Venice, and other Italian cities soon became centers of string making, supplying high-quality goods to much of Europe. Gasparo da Salò obtained his strings from Rome, where a monk attended to his business affairs. In a 1588 tax statement Salò wrote, "I also owe 42 lire to the Reverend Father Marco Antonio of the Order of S. Piero Oliviero, for strings he sent me from Rome, so that I can supply violins." In 1708, on a diplomatic mission to Rome, Johann Philipp Franz von Schönborn, a music enthusiast from a well-known family in the Rhine-Main region, purchased good strings for his uncle's violin, cello, and theorbo. To be sure of obtaining the right string dimensions he requested samples; he then entrusted his treasures to a custodian from the Mainz cathedral, for the northbound journey.

String making improved continually. In the early eighteenth century, three pieces of gut were required for an E string, seven for a G string, and 120 for the heaviest contrabass string. Domenic-Antonio Angelucci introduced improvements that for a long time put Italian string making ahead of other countries, and even abroad, Italians were often in charge of string making. A well-known Offenbach firm was founded in 1798 by Pirazzi, a Roman, who received advice from Paganini. The famous Savaresse string factory in Lyon was founded by Savarezze, an Italian who is said to have come to France in the late seventeenth century. His many descendants more or less dominated string making in France for years. *Mémoire sur la fabrication des cordes d'instruments de musique* (Paris 1822) lists a Savaresse as the author. To be sure, not all "Italian" strings were made in that country, or even in factories directed by Italians. Morris claims there is as much fraud in selling strings as there is in the violin trade.

Scientific contributions to string making go back to early days. Through experimentation, Mersenne (d. 1648), who wrote on acoustics, discovered laws governing the vibration of strings; these were scientifically explained by Taylor (d. 1731), an English mathematician. In 1796 Chladni of Erfurt published his study about the longitudinal vibrations of strings and rods. A dissertation by Ernst G. Fischer ("Experiments with the Vibrations of Strings, with a View to Establishing a Reliable Standard for Their Tuning") was published in 1822–1823 by the Berlin Academy of Sciences. Substantial improvements were made in Markneukirchen, where a process of cutting intestines lengthwise into strips was developed, so that one string consisted of a large number of thin parts.

Again and again the use of silk was considered, though silk strings had disappeared several centuries previously. In 1774 Peter Nonaille obtained a patent for "a method to make silk strings for all kinds of musical instruments." The *Allgemeine Musikalische Zeitung* of 15 May 1799 reported, "Citizen Baud of Versailles, a man of great knowledge especially in the field of music, some time ago invented a process for spinning strings from silk. He used these at first for the harp, but now substitutes them for gut strings on all instruments." In 1803 Baud published his "observations about both gut and silk strings for musical instruments." Silk strings then were used throughout the nineteenth century, though not as successfully as had been hoped. They would stretch up to 20 percent and therefore were hard to keep in tune, but they were not affected by heat or humidity. A silk string normally consisted of 140 strands, each having twenty fibers, or 2800 fibers in all.

A standard process for making gut strings evolved about a hundred years ago, though individual manufacturers may have kept some secrets. Sheep gut is used exclusively; experiments with gut from other animals did not bring satisfactory results since it is too coarse. In the case of sheep gut, quality depends largely on race. The fibrous structure of gut from domestic animals makes it unsuitable for strings. Mountain and prairie sheep are the preferred sacrifice to the cause of music—and tennis. They are slaughtered when six to eight months old, at which age the intestines already are strong but still soft. Because they are raised for their wool, sheep in nordic countries are slaughtered at a much later age. The climate of England produces sheep gut particularly suitable for strings, perhaps because English sheep are fed fodder grown in maritime air. The good quality of Italian strings has been attributed to the relatively dry pastures there, which produce lean animals.

Once the animals have been slaughtered, skilled workers remove the entrails. In times past, the intestines had to be prepared at once; deep-freezing now makes it possible to store them until needed. It is also possible to purchase them in dried form. The first step in preparing strings is to immerse the intestines in a chemical solution that arrests decomposition and helps separate the adhesive substance. Later it causes the strips to hold together, making the string durable. The useless layers must then be detached and removed. An intestine has three layers, the intestine proper and an inner and outer layer of skin. Only the first of these is suitable for string making. The separation used to be done by hand; intestines were stretched on a wooden board and scraped with smooth small wooden disks until nothing but the muscular middle layer remained. Machines are now widely used for this. In between all these operations the intestine is cleaned repeatedly in water that must be carefully inspected for any ingredients that might harm the intestine. The last cleaning again is in a chemical bath, or is done by a machine that again scrapes the intestine and squeezes it, passing it between rubber rollers. The intestine is next cut into strips of uniform thickness, an operation that requires great precision. Another bath bleaches the strips, after which they are sorted according to quality and other characteristics. The most important step follows: twisting the strands. Wet gut strips of equal length are gathered and attached at both ends to a turning machine. While they are twisted, the gluelike substance is squeezed out, making one string out of many strands. When it is still wet, the string is put into an airtight chamber where it is exposed to sulfur fumes for bleaching.

Every string is then carefully inspected. Further twisting will usually be needed to obtain the required firmness. Up to this point the strings are still wet. After an initial drying they are polished and rounded until they have a uniform thickness and are completely smooth. Here too great care must be taken, for if the string's substance is damaged it will become fragile and will not last. Around 1900, Richard Baehr (d. 1945) invented an ingenious polishing machine. Only after it has been polished is the string placed in a warm-air chamber for the final drying. It is then oiled lightly to increase its resistance to humidity and perspiration from the player's hand. In a modern string factory the entire manufacture is continually controlled by chemists and other technicians who use sophisticated precision instruments.

Storing gut strings for long periods has always been a problem. Apian-Bennewitz recommended treating them with almond oil and storing them in a calf's or pig's bladder.

If strings are tuned to a low pitch they do not sound good because they are not thick enough in relation to their tension, a problem known to Praetorius. This is why composers up to Corelli seldom wrote notes to be played on the G string. In the seventeenth century, the French physicist Saint-Colombe came up with the idea of winding low strings, thus obtaining the required mass with less volume. In 1765 he succeeded in making a copper-wound string. Later, the winding process was greatly refined by the use of special machines. The material used for winding also is important. A silver alloy has been used for some time to wrap high-quality strings; for less expensive G, D, and A strings copper, bronze, and aluminum have been employed, occasionally in alloys. Silver-wound D strings have met with resistance; in 1900 Jokisch claimed they did not have "the characteristic full, beautiful sound of a good gut D string," but that on the other hand they lacked, in the lower middle range, "the typical hoarseness and uncertain response" of the gut string.

Paganini reputedly was the first soloist to use wound strings. In Dresden ca. 1860 Weichold developed a special process for making strings with true fifths; later he improved the quality of wound D and A strings.

The E string was beset by special problems. Gut strings were problematic because of a conflict between mass and tension. They cannot be stretched more than 15 percent, which means that E strings had little tolerance and tended to break easily. Silk strings were not the answer because the ever-rising pitch to which instruments were tuned brought about increasing string tension. Now we can hardly imagine what problems gut E strings presented. A soloist could count on breaking an E string during a concert. For practicing before a recital, Dittersdorf recommended using only the three lower strings, in order to avoid embarrassment during the recital. In 1806, in a letter from Frankfurt, Boucher wrote,

As you know, I play the Adagio of my Quartet in C entirely on the E string. Here it happened that the string broke. I quickly managed with my mouth to get the dangling piece out of the way, for it would have kept me from playing on the other strings. But I played on as though no string was missing, just as I had done in Rotterdam and often elsewhere. You should have seen the musicians: they sat with their mouths wide open, full of admiration, as did the listeners. Many came closer, to hear me better and to notice whether I left out anything. As you know, I am not likely to lose my head in a tight spot.

When in 1888 Kreisler, not yet thirteen years old, played for the first time in the United States, he broke *two* E strings during the Mendelssohn Concerto. In the slow movement he continued on the A string; in the Finale he quickly seized the concertmaster's violin. Situations like these make us appreciate the two courses for the playing string (*chanterelle*) of old instruments; perhaps one of their purposes was to have an extra string in case of an accident!

Violinists gradually switched to steel strings, especially because since 1833 there had been experiments on other instruments with platinum strings. After 1835, steel strings replaced brass strings for the mandolin. Marie Tayau was the first to use steel A and E strings, for the 1876 premiere of Godard's *Concerto romantique*, on a violin made by Collin-Mezin. Witek and Burmester may have been the first, ca. 1906, to perform regularly in public on steel strings. The specific weight of steel is 5.5 times that of silk or gut. After much experimentation, Swedish steel produced with charcoal turned out to be best, and production methods were constantly improved. At first the steel E string's sound seemed harsh and unrefined; it is improved by placing a small piece of leather on the bridge underneath the string. Still, as late as 1938 Siegfried Eberhardt published a book in Copenhagen entitled *Wiederaufstieg oder Untergang der Kunst des Geigens: Die kunstfeindliche Stahlsaite* (Resurrection or decline of the art of violin playing: Steel strings, the enemy of art). On the other hand, Flesch wrote as early as 1923 that steel E strings undoubtedly resulted in better performances in the concert hall, gut strings always having been unreliable (*The Art of Violin Playing*, vol. 1).

Many musicians welcomed the new E string, especially those who played in dance bands and other popular-music groups. They often had to play in smoke-filled, overheated rooms, bathed in perspiration, or had to contend with outdoor conditions. Steel strings were less affected by weather and lasted almost indefinitely. They also made it possible to produce high notes that projected well and could compete with trumpet, saxophone, and percussion. These musicians clamored for all four strings to be made of steel. For artistic purposes this has been only partly satisfactory, but it led to the use of steel or another metal as the core for wound strings. Since gut strings were largely unavailable in the United States during World War I, having been imported from Germany, steel strings became common. In Germany, however, contracts signed by players in professional orchestras as late as 1920 stipulated that steel strings were not to be used. It is true that steel strings do not sound good on all instruments, especially on highly arched violins.

Objections to steel strings continue. In 1949 Mingotti reopened the battle, with some justification. Flesch, in the first chapter of his book on violin fingering, devotes much space to one particular problem: the open E string often fails to speak immediately at a fast tempo. He recommends using the fourth finger in ascending passages, the open string when descending. But it is generally agreed that only steel strings should be used in teaching beginners. The pupil who plays on gut strings will be more or less out of tune most of the time.

A special type of metal string, wound using a special process, was invented and produced by Vienna's Franz Thomastik, for whom it is named. They offer great advantages: they last almost indefinitely, are not sensitive to heat, humidity, or hand perspiration (which makes them ideal for tropical climates), and they stay in tune for days or weeks on end. Unfortunately, there are also serious disadvantages. Their tension is greater than usual, which could affect an instrument adversely, and because of their hardness, especially at first, they require drastically different bowing and produce a poor pizzicato sound.

Improvements have been made upon Thomastik's first experiments, dating to 1914. Otto Infeld, his co-worker and successor, introduced the flat-wound, solid steel string, followed in 1951 by the Super-Flexible string (*Künstler-Seil-Saite*), and ten years later by the Spiro-core string, which has many of the gut string's advantages. During the same period the Stockholm string maker Frøjel, further developing Thomastik's idea, came up with the Prim precision string. It comes close to settling the conflict between suppleness and elasticity on one hand and durability on the other.

Increasingly, synthetic materials are used in a range of products, including strings. Though at first problematic, nylon A strings are now much improved. String makers continue to do research; the days when a string breaking during a performance caused pain to soloists and orchestra players are largely gone.

VIOLIN MAINTENANCE

REPAIRS

Good repairers are like gold, often scarce, always wanted, and much abused . . . because they cannot perform miracles and transform wretched old fiddles with broken voices into seraphic Cremonas.

W. MEREDITH MORRIS, *BRITISH VIOLIN MAKERS*, 1904

String instruments, unless destroyed by acts of war, fire, or other disasters, will have a virtually unlimited life span if they are well cared for. Maintaining old instruments therefore has become increasingly important. Talented luthiers might deplore this, but to earn a livelihood they have to live with this state of things and make the best of it, hoping to acquire the reputation of being an outstanding repairer.

It goes without saying that serious violinists will give the best possible care to their instruments. This begins with keeping the violin in a well-padded case, wrapped in a silk or flannel cloth (preferably both) to protect it from humidity, great fluctuations of temperature, and blows. Cleaning it often is not only a matter of hygiene—it preserves its tone. Accumulations of rosin dust on the top in time will form a crust that will reduce the wood's ability to vibrate, and hence affect its sound. Rosin should also be removed from the strings frequently. Some violinists wash the bow regularly, in which case care must be taken to keep moisture out of the mortise at the tip and away from the frog; they might be damaged by the wood plug's swelling. One should also remove dust and dirt from the violin's interior. Uncooked rice or other grains are used for this purpose and inserted through the f holes, after which the violin is shaken. We need not, however, carry our care as far as did the violinist (whom Maugin described) who every morning upon rising would put his instrument in his warm bed, believing that this improved its sound.

When selecting a cleaning preparation it is wise to consult a professional, to avoid any with corrosive ingredients that might harm the varnish. Generally speaking, a violinist should not putter and experiment with his instrument; better to find a reliable person who specializes in maintaining and repairing violins. In time he or she will become familiar not only with the instrument but also with the player's requirements and preferences. On the other hand, a player should be familiar with certain basic procedures, for at times help may be needed immediately. Woodwind players in orchestras usually carry a small repair kit with them, so that even in the middle of an opera performance they will be able to make minor repairs or adjustments to the keys.

For significant repairs one will look for the best available professional, and that choice should not be guided by monetary considerations. Proper adjusting and repairing will ensure the violin's best performance. Even seemingly insignificant small parts may have a decisive effect on this.

Let us assume that a violinist buys a good instrument that has not been played in a long time and has been neglected. In that case all parts must be carefully examined, not only separately but also in their adjustment to each other. Some likely deficiencies follow:

1) Worm damage
2) Cracks in the top or back
3) Damage to the edges of the top or back, or to the ribs
4) Thin places in top or back
5) Excessive thickness
6) A weak bass bar, or one that has lost its tension
7) Damage to the varnish

8) Proportions in need of correction
9) Neck too short
10) Earlier repairs that were badly done
11) Fingerboard at incorrect angle
12) Fingerboard in need of resurfacing
13) Cracks in pegbox

For some repairs it is necessary to open the violin. To do this, a knife with a very thin blade, kept moist with alcohol, is inserted between the top and ribs. Beginning near the neck, one looks for places where the glue has already been weakened by perspiration; this often occurs near the chin rest and the place touched by the left thumb while playing in the higher positions. Places near the corner blocks are most difficult to separate, and a hammer stroke may be needed. Möckel (1930) makes this observation:

> The opening of a valuable string instrument usually affects the owner like torture, for the accompanying noise is greatly augmented by the resonating body, causing fears for the precious instrument. It is therefore best not to open it in the presence of onlookers.

Vidal recounts the story of Paganini's "Cannon," which Vuillaume had to open for repairs. It took a good deal of persuasion before the great virtuoso consented to this, and then only with the condition that it be done in his own quarters. Vuillaume complied and arrived with his tools. When he began the operation Paganini, trembling, withdrew to a corner of the room. At every sound he winced in agony, as though the knife were cutting into his own flesh.

WORM DAMAGE

Worms are apt to attack instruments that have not been played in a long time and have been stored in poorly ventilated, humid rooms. Once the instrument is played again, the worm will soon be done for as it cannot stand the vibrations. If damage is so extensive that the violin has become unplayable, it will have to be gassed in a hermetically sealed container, preferably using tetrachloride. Simoutre recommended rinsing the violin's interior with 50 g of picric acid dissolved in 1 liter of alcohol.

Various stages of worm damage may occur; they need to be clearly recognized before the instrument is repaired. These are some of the stages:

1) A small number of worm holes is found all through the instrument, so that the wood's resilience is not much affected. In that case the holes are filled in. Möckel recommends a mixture of Lycopodium and glue, to be applied warm. When dry, this mixture closely resembles wood. After staining or varnishing, repairs can hardly be noticed.

2) If an instrument is very valuable, and if the holes are close to each
   other, small plates may be inserted. They should look exactly like the
   surrounding surfaces and therefore must be selected carefully. Other
   damage to the body is repaired in the same manner.
3) If worm damage is so extensive that parts of the instrument are
   beyond repair, they must be replaced in order to restore the violin to
   playing condition. Many fine old violins have suffered this fate;
   indeed few still have all their original parts.

CRACKS IN THE TOP AND BACK

Cracks must be thoroughly cleaned first. Thin glue is rubbed into the crack;
pressure is exerted until some glue emerges on the other side. Clamps are
then fastened quickly; they must have been previously adjusted to any arching, so that the repaired portion will dry in the original position. Möckel
gives detailed instructions for preparing such clamps. Clamping can be very
difficult if the crack is complicated or occurs in an awkward place, in which
case small cleats also have to be used. These also help to distribute the clamps'
pressure. None of these devices must damage the varnish. After the crack
has dried and any traces of glue have been wiped off, a kind of beauty plaster is applied by filling in the (usually slightly depressed) crack with varnish.
Only after this a general layer of varnish is applied. It must be so similar to the
surrounding varnish that the crack is no longer visible.

It is an old and persistent misconception that cracks reduce the wood's
strength and resilience and therefore reduce an instrument's value. On 17–18
October 1777 Mozart wrote to his father about his acquaintance with the
Augsburg piano maker Stein and his work:

> His pianos are really built to last. He guarantees that the soundboard will
> not break or crack. Once he has made a soundboard he exposes it to the
> fresh air, rain, snow, the heat of the sun, and God knows what else, so
> that it will crack. Then he glues in wedges, making it as strong and firm
> as possible. He is glad if it does crack, for that way he is assured that noth-
> ing further will happen to it. Often he cuts into the soundboard himself,
> then glues it again, making it all the stronger.

Cracks at or near the violin's soundpost are particularly dangerous. The
back is very vulnerable in this regard since the strings' counter pressure is
lacking. There is the possibility that a glued crack might open again, gradually or suddenly. In that case the repairer will have to use a cleat or a so-called
soundpost patch. A cleat consists of a small lining patch made of spruce (occasionally parchment is used) glued over the crack, with its fibers running across
those of the top and back. This is done to ensure greater adhesion, not for reasons of tone production. If a larger area has to be reinforced, lining becomes
necessary. Fitting such pieces of wood is difficult because they must adhere
perfectly, even in arched places. If the instrument in question is made of wood

of ideal thickness, these linings should be used only if absolutely necessary, since they add to the thickness and are likely to affect sound adversely.

DAMAGE TO THE EDGES OF THE TOP AND BACK, AND TO THE RIBS

Damage to the edges is usually easily repaired, for the purfling will keep it from extending far into the wood. If a replacement piece of wood must be underlaid or added, it must be chosen with great care and the varnish skillfully applied for the repair to be invisible. Violinists with careless bowing often cause damage to the top of the waist. When playing popular music they are especially prone to hit this place with the frog.

Tears in the ribs usually require painstaking work before gluing, for in the affected places the ribs (due to the great pressure on them) tend to be deformed. To restore them to the original form, small patches are added. They too must fit very exactly. After gluing, the rib parts that have been repaired must be clasped firmly for as long as possible, so that they will again be able to withstand great pressure.

On an instrument that sees heavy use, the spot on the rib that is touched by the thumb when playing in the high positions, and when changing positions, will gradually lose its varnish. Once it is gone, the wood itself will suffer. In extreme cases it may be necessary to add rib lining.

If a rib is damaged beyond repair the affected piece must be replaced. Again, skillful repairers carefully select wood and varnish, priding themselves on making the replacement indistinguishable from the original rib.

VARIOUS CHANGES IN THE WOOD

The wood in old violins often is too thin. This may be due to the maker's eagerness to have the instrument sound good; it may also be the result of later "scraping," or of using material that was not completely dry, leading to a loss of wood. Such an instrument requires lining, of a small area or even of the entire top or back. According to Möckel there are different types of lining for the soundpost, bass bar, under the chin, and between the *f* holes. Fine old violins often require such lining, since the wood in those places is apt to be weak, yet in those days was not subjected to such strong string pressure. To find the correct place and thickness for this kind of lining is an important part of the repair.

There are two techniques for applying lining: to attach the lining after first having removed the equivalent amount of the original wood; or to apply the lining on top of the existing wood. Luthiers have learned from experience that the first way is risky, and that it is better to preserve as much of the original wood as possible.

It is generally preferable not to apply lining to large areas, for the glue impedes vibration with a resulting loss in tone quality. In his memoirs, Flesch (1957) remembered how a fine instrument was ruined by lining:

I was still playing the Guadagnini violin I had acquired eight years before in Bucharest, an instrument that sounded well but was at times unreliable because the wood was not sufficiently thick. I had been persuaded to hand it over to a Düsseldorf violin maker who had an unfortunate mania for "lining" instruments, that is, strengthening the wood by insertions. By this process, many a valuable instrument was spoiled, including my Guadagnini, which returned from his workshop unmanageably rough in tone.

Also on the subject of lining, Flesch (*The Art of Violin Playing*, vol. 1) observed,

Although a small lining where the soundpost fits at either the top or back hardly affects [the violin] adversely (the tone of an instrument being otherwise good, and may in course of time become absolutely necessary in order to strengthen the belly, because of the unrelieved pressure of the bridge), a lining inside of the belly (top), or other lining even more extended, especially when the weather is damp, unquestionably makes the instrument sadly unreliable.

Glue tends to attract water. Therefore under conditions of great humidity a repaired instrument will be affected adversely, to the extent that many a fine violin will be virtually useless in certain countries or regions.

LOSS OF WOOD IN THE TOP AND BACK

Sometimes a basically good violin, made of good wood, may have a disappointingly small tone. This may be because excessively thick wood was used, in general or in certain places. It takes much experience to establish this and to locate the places in question; a good luthier also has a sixth sense for detecting them. With thickness calipers, an ingeniously constructed tool, one can obtain precise measurements, but there is no one ideal thickness. The type of wood, its density, and the amount of arching largely determine optimal thickness, to mention only the most important factors. By systematically tapping the instrument, a person with a sensitive ear can locate places that are too thick. If they are in the top, it is possible to compensate for them by installing a lighter bass bar. Even though taking away wood is a technique with which every violin maker is familiar, a conscientious repairer will consider all possible other remedies before deciding to reduce the wood's thickness, for it is well known that this can easily be carried too far.

REPLACING THE BASS BAR

The bass bar is subjected to a great amount of tension by virtue of its attachment to the violin's top. That, along with its constant participation in vibration, causes a bass bar to lose its usefulness rather soon. If, after some years, an

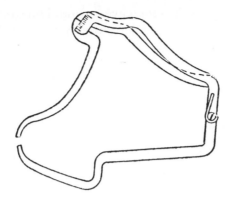

Thickness calipers

instrument's tone volume and quality deteriorates noticeably, a tired bass bar is usually to blame. If steel strings are used, the bass bar may have to be replaced after five years; gut strings will extend its useful life to twenty years. For the last two hundred years the ever-rising pitch to which we tune our instruments has had an adverse effect on them, necessitating among other measures a change in the bass bar's dimensions.

To install a new bass bar differs in no way from inserting one in a new violin. When the necessary proportions have been determined, the most important part of the work has been done. Removing the old bass bar, however, requires special care. The violin's top is easily damaged, which can result in adverse changes in the proportions of the body as a whole.

DAMAGE TO THE VARNISH

Several operations may be needed:

1) Varnishing replacement pieces
2) Touching up varnish that has peeled off or has been otherwise damaged
3) Repairing places where varnish has worn off, due to friction or perspiration
4) Rejuvenating varnish that has lost its sheen
5) Removing a second layer of varnish that was improperly applied
6) Removing the original varnish

It is always difficult, if not impossible, to predict how the varnish will be affected, in time, by the drying process. For that reason replacement pieces should not be made from white wood; rather, one should use spare parts from older instruments that no longer are playable or have been destroyed. They offer a better chance of bringing about a perfect match. If replacement pieces are made of untreated, white wood, an undercoating must be applied to them to adapt them to the hue of the surrounding area. Varnish is then applied layer by layer, until its color harmonizes completely with the surrounding area.

Retouching is desirable only for places where small chips of varnish have come off. Before attempting it, the luthier must prepare new varnish that is similar to the original one: oil varnish for instruments originally treated with oil varnish, spirit varnish for others. It takes a long time for oil varnish to dry. The damaged place must be cleaned carefully, and the actual varnishing, with very soft brushes, must take place in a warm room. The newly varnished place must then be polished. Möckel recommends lightly polishing the surrounding area as well, to achieve a good blend.

If larger areas have lost their varnish, by contact with perspiration from the left hand or the chin, the repair procedure is similar, except that the wood must first be treated with extremely fine sandpaper. When the wood is completely smooth, an undercoat sealer is applied.

There is disagreement on whether polishing can restore varnish that has lost its gloss. Varnish on very old violins typically has a somewhat "tired" appearance that should not be tampered with unless there is a special reason to do so. If it is to be refreshed, restraint should be exercised; an old violin should not have the looks of a new one. For polishing such instruments Möckel recommends well-filtered gum benzoin dissolved in alcohol, though there is the danger that alcohol will harm the original varnish. Some makers apply a layer of colorless varnish to an instrument that has been generally restored or whose varnish has been retouched in places. It is a questionable way to rejuvenate the appearance of an old violin.

To remove a layer of varnish that has been applied over the original varnish is a most difficult task, requiring a solvent that is strong enough to work on the upper layer, yet mild enough not to harm the original varnish. Möckel advises dabbing the violin carefully with a piece of cotton soaked in the solvent, continually monitoring the cotton's color to determine whether it is working on a layer of dirt, or the second varnish, or whether the original varnish already is being affected.

Many violins from the eighteenth and nineteenth centuries are made of superior wood and display fine workmanship, but an entirely unsatisfactory varnish was applied to them, the usual reason being that luthiers, fond of experimenting, wanted to delight their fellows by a better-than-ever varnish of their own invention. In such cases replacing the varnish is justified. To remove it, chemical rather than mechanical means must be employed lest the wood be damaged. Even these chemicals must not be overly strong, else they might have a corroding effect on the wood and affect its life span adversely.

CORRECTION OF MEASUREMENTS

Violins with the measurements or proportions customary up to the end of the eighteenth century are known as "short-neck" violins; their necks are 5–8 mm shorter. Playing on such instruments today requires quite an adjustment, for ca. 1800, old violins were remodeled and new violins built according to new measurements. This involves the proportion between the vibrating length of the string and the body and neck. The calculation assumes that the *f* holes (or more precisely the notches in the *f* holes) will be accurately placed. In violins with *f* holes in a different position, the calculation will be slightly off. If the bridge stands exactly on a line drawn between the two notches, the string length should be 327 mm, which approximately corresponds to a 5:7 or 2:3 ratio. This establishes the correct length of the neck as 135 mm, and the distance from the line between the notches to the body's upper end as 189 mm:

$$135/5 \times 7 = 189 \quad 135 + 189 = 324 \text{ (plus a correction of } + 3 \text{ mm} = 327)$$

For easy checking of these proportions, luthiers use a compass with legs set at the 5:7 ratio. Möckel has described the ingeniously constructed proportional divider, which automatically measures and divides according to this proportion.

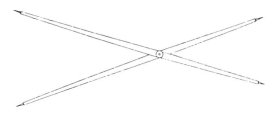

Proportional divider

If the measurements of a violin do not reflect these proportions, some adjustments will be necessary. Small deviations are fairly easily corrected, for instance, by moving the bridge and soundpost, or by slight changes in the body. But if the deviations are substantial, the neck will have to be lengthened, so that the original short-neck violin will have modern proportions. For this the old neck must be cut from the scroll in such a way that the new neck will have the largest possible surface to which to adhere.

The repairer will want to save the old pegbox and the original scroll of a valuable violin. For this, a similar cut is made at the place where the neck leads into the pegbox. The replacement piece should be selected from good and beautiful wood; it is attached in its unfinished state. Again, the fit must be perfect for successful and long-lasting gluing. When the glue is completely dry, the finishing work takes place.

FINGERBOARD REPAIRS

If an old instrument is to be played again after a long interval, the fingerboard must be closely inspected. The strong downward pressure of fingers gradually wears at the fingerboard, even if made of the hardest ebony, resulting in depressions, even grooves, that cause rattling when certain notes are played in certain positions. Actually, very tiny grooves are needed for the strings' proper vibration, especially for the wound G string, but wear enlarges these.

To examine the fingerboard, the strings and also the top nut must be removed. The surface is then closely scrutinized with the aid of an iron ruler. If there are flaws, the fingerboard is planed, followed by touch-up work with files, scrapers, and sandpaper of different grades. The final smoothing is done with a rag saturated in a mixture of alcohol, linseed oil, and finely powdered pumice.

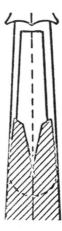

Fitting the neck into the scroll

If the fingerboard required extensive planing, the surface may now lie too low in relation to string length and bridge. This may also happen if the fingerboard has come down, due to weather conditions such as an extremely humid climate or great fluctuations in temperature. To remedy this, a wedge can be placed under the fingerboard. It is very thin near the top nut, its thickness gradually increasing as needed. To glue on the wedge the fingerboard, of course, has to be removed.

It is also possible to bring about the desired angle of the fingerboard by changing the neck's angle, thereby lowering the scroll. For this the top must be removed and a small wedge added to the top at the place where the neck is attached. But the neck will be more firmly positioned if a new top block is installed. It should be shaped in such a way that the newly attached neck gives the proper incline to the fingerboard.

PEGBOX REPAIRS

Constant use of an instrument may cause the peg holes to become worn or enlarged, so that the pegs no longer hold. Larger pegs may take care of the problem, but in the long run it is better to fill in the old holes and to bore new ones. This is imperative if the holes are in the wrong places—if, for instance, opposite holes are so near each other that the strings wound around the pegs touch each other. In that case the old holes are closed by inserting plugs that fit exactly and then are glued. After they have dried completely, any protruding ends are cut off, and the places for the new holes can be marked with the help of a stencil. For boring the new holes Möckel recommends beginning with a very fine drill and gradually increasing the size, in order to avoid any tearing around the edges.

If the wood of the pegbox is weak, tearing may occur. It may be caused by a peg that does not fit both holes equally, so that one hole has to bear most of the peg's pressure. Tears of this kind are glued, if necessary attaching a thin liner strip to the pegbox's interior wall in order to reinforce it. In difficult cases a wooden plug can be inserted across the tear, strengthening the connection of the two parts.

These are only the principal repairs a luthier may have to undertake. They require much experience, patience, and a good set of tools and materials. Among these are a veritable arsenal of clamps and counterparts, for any place that has been glued must be carefully clamped. This can be difficult in some places, such as tears in the pegbox near the scroll. A good luthier will, of course, choose appropriate wood and varnish, so that the repair will be virtually invisible.

PART TWO

THE HISTORY OF THE VIOLIN

The origin of the violin family is obscure, and it is only
by conjectures, analogies, and inferences that we are able
to proceed in tracing the instrument.

KATHLEEN SCHLESINGER,
THE PRECURSORS OF THE VIOLIN FAMILY, 1910

S chlesinger's statement is as true today as it was in 1910, though there
certainly has been no dearth of research. Heron-Allen's *De fidiculis bibliographia* of 1890–1894 lists thirteen hundred studies, most of which deal
primarily or partly with the violin's history. Since then the number of studies has reached astronomic proportions, with many writers uncritically
repeating what has been said before.

To bring some kind of order into all this material it seems necessary to
divide it into three chronological sections: the violin's prehistory, its early history, and the history of the instrument as we know it. The prehistory might
be seen as beginning with the first instruments showing some characteristics
of the violin. This stage lasted roughly to the first half of the fifteenth century.
The early history begins at about that time and lasts until ca. 1500, when an
instrument appeared that we can, with some caution, call the first violin. At
that point the true history of the violin begins.

For now these time periods must be considered tentative. As our investigation proceeds we may be able to determine their accuracy.

THE PREHISTORY

If in the violin's prehistory we wanted to include all instruments that had
any of its characteristics, we would have to go back to primitive man. As he

plucked the string of his hunting bow he might have become aware of a musical sound. More realistically one might say that the prehistory begins with the invention of a bow with which a string is set in motion.

For a long time opinions about the approximate date of this event differed widely. Leopold Mozart's statement (in his 1756 treatise on violin playing) now seems simplistic: "Orpheus, Apollo's son, invented the violin. The poet Sappho gave us the bow, strung with horsehair; she was the first to play as we do today." Even in the scholarly encyclopedia *Die Musik in Geschichte und Gegenwart* (Kassel 1949, vol. 1, col. 211; henceforth *MGG*) we read, "In the Old Testament (Book of Exodus) Jubal (ca. 2000 B.C.) is mentioned as the father of fiddlers and pipers." Werner Lottermoser, the author of this article, unquestioningly accepted a misleading translation that goes back to Luther. Leopold Mozart had taken his own statement verbatim from P. Zacharias Teve's book *Il musico testore* (Venice 1704).

The view that bowed string instruments had been in use in ancient Greece and Rome dates from the Renaissance. Painters and sculptors who were not concerned with historical accuracy depicted gods of antiquity playing Renaissance instruments. One of the most famous art works of this kind is by the sculptor Bertoldo (ca. 1420–1491); his *Orpheus* (also called *Apollo* or *Amphion*) plays a kind of fiddle. Later, and especially during the late phase of humanism (when the forging of art works became a lucrative business), many such works were claimed to be original creations from antiquity. As ever, many credulous collectors were victimized. Thus the famous *Apollo fidicen*, at one time owned by the Medici Cardinal Hippolyt and now in Florence, actually dates from the seventeenth century. *Hieroglyphica commentarii Joannis Petri Valeriani* (Basel 1617) contains an especially large number of errors relating to the study of musical instruments. Vidal (1876–1878, vol. 1) showed in detail how, in a medallion of the ancient Roman family Scribonia, Valerianus replaced the lyre originally depicted there with a kind of viola da bracchio, resulting in the translation of "lyra" as "viola" and "plectrum" as "bow"— and thus rendering ancient Greeks and Romans string players par excellence! To be sure, as early as 1581 Vincenzo Galilei refuted the notion that the term "plectrum" referred to the bow for a string instrument, but his statement did not become generally known.

In the eighteenth century, research by Gemsage (*Origin and Introduction of the Violin*, London 1757) and Le Prince le Jeune (*Observations sur l'origine du violon*, Paris 1782) came closer to the truth—that the instrumental bow could not have existed before the Middle Ages, which fact Johann Tinctoris (1445–1511) seems to have been aware of three hundred years earlier. In *De inventione et usu musicae* (ca. 1487) he refers to contemporary use of a small bow, "whereas the ancients had the plectrum." Also in 1782 appeared Sonnerat's book *Voyages aux Indes et à la Chine*, in which he describes a certain string instrument: "Some special instruments are found in the temples. . . . The Pandarons, members of a large monastic order, accompany themselves with a kind of violin called ravanastron. Its name derives from the giant Ravanen, king of the island of Ceylon, who invented it almost five thousand years ago." Sonnerat's claim gave new credence to the belief that bowed string instruments were played in very ancient times, and that the bow had made its way from India by way of Asia Minor to Mediterranean civilizations. It seemed all the more likely because ancient string instruments such as the kemanghe and rebab were used by Persians and Arabs. The slogan "ex oriente lux" (or, as Fétis put it, "Nothing exists in the West that did not originate in the Orient") helped advance the theory, popular during the entire nineteenth century, that the bow had come from India.

Rühlmann (*Die Geschichte der Bogeninstrumente*), however, objected that neither the instruments' great age nor their having come from India and Persia could be proved. Instead, Rühlmann believed—and this seems plausible—that subjecting a string to continuous friction was such a basic invention that it could easily have been made in several civilizations, independently of each other.

For a while the pendulum swung in the opposite direction, and northern countries were favored as the likely origin of bowed instruments. The opening ("Esquisse de l'histoire du violon") of Fétis's 1851 book on Paganini contains this statement:

> In spite of all other claims, allegedly based on documentary evidence, bowed instruments were unknown in ancient, oriental, Greek, or Roman civilizations. No evidence exists in India and Egypt, nor in Italy or any other parts of the ancient world. As I have stated in my *Philosophical Outline of Music History*, the bow originated in the West. Nordic peoples introduced it to all Europe.

This theory was strongly supported by the crwth of Welsh bards, which very ancient instrument, according to many sources, was played with a bow. The earliest references to its existence, however, were written; neither actual instruments nor pictorial records were found.

Even if the names "ravanastron" and "crwth" occur during a relatively early period, the question remains whether these instruments were plucked or bowed. The first known use of the name "crwth" is an oft-quoted remark by St. Fortunatus (b. 530, d. after 600), bishop of Poitiers: "Romanusque lyra plaudat tibi, Barbarus harpa Graecus Achilliaca, Chrotta Britanna cantat" (Romans praise you with the lyre, Barbarians with the harp, Greeks with the cythara, and Bretons with the crwth). Yet the first illustration of a crwth occurs in an eleventh-century manuscript from Limoges (Paris, Bibliothèque Nationale, fonds latin, 1.118, p. 104). To interpret the word "cantat" as "plays with a bow" is far-fetched; its many possible meanings include "sing," "croak," "intone," "play an instrument," "praise with song," "announce," and others. Interpreters, eager to declare the sixth-century crwth a bowed instrument, translated the passage in question in such a way that "plaudat" refers to harpa and Achilliaca, but "cantat" only to chrotta.

As to the development of instruments in Europe during the early Middle Ages, beginning in the twelfth century, all bowed instruments were originally plucked. Some continued to be plucked. In Gottfried of Strasbourg's *Tristan and Isolde* (written ca. 1210), lira and rotta are mentioned as both plucked and bowed instruments. In Spain, various types of fiddles existed, called "vihuela a mano" or "vihuela a arco," depending on their use. In the case of the crwth, a written document from the seventh century was related to a pictorial document from the eleventh century in order to prove the existence of a bow in the seventh century. To do so is to disregard important stages in the development of medieval instruments. The example of the crwth shows how careful one must be in interpreting written documents.

Since the publication of Rühlmann's book, scholars have continued to investigate the origin of the bow, but several specialized studies have failed to solve the problem. Not until 1969 did Werner Bachmann (*The Origins of Bowing*) throw some light on the subject. Based on earlier research he proved that the fiddle had originally been a plucked instrument. In the early Middle Ages the term merely indicated a string instrument; it did not yet imply a specific manner of tone production. In other words, "fidula" in its earlier uses did not yet refer to a bowed instrument. It is also true that the kemanghe (Persia, Afghanistan) and the rubab or rebab (Arabia, Ethiopia) had been plucked or strummed before they became bowed instruments. During the centuries that were so important in the development of the bow, many musical terms underwent significant changes in meaning. A single reference to an instrument and to the manner in which it was played cannot safely be taken at face value, unless the context clearly indicates a manner of tone production.

Careful research has established that the three Sanskrit terms "kona," "sarika," and "parivada," probably referring to a bow, are not found before the seventh century, but that kona well into the twelfth century also meant "claves," "plectrum," and "drumstick." Visual evidence confirms these findings: the reliefs at the Borobudur temple, erected in Java by ninth-century Indian settlers, do not depict any bowed instruments. Rather, they show scenes from Hindu life before the Islam invasions; quite a few music scenes are included.

Generally speaking in the field of organology, visual documents need to be interpreted with great caution before they are introduced as proof for certain theories. This applies especially to precise dating. Archeological methods are becoming increasingly sophisticated; as a result, certain visual representations of instruments, often pointed to in the past, now make less convincing evidence. Bachmann has clearly indicated these limitations for European art works.

> My research has not led to a single representation [of a bow] during the first millennium. There is only one such representation that clearly dates from the tenth century; it is of Mozarabic origin and reveals oriental influence.

The illustration to which he refers (Bachmann 1969, ill. 1), captioned "Four musicians habentes citharas dei" (related to Apocalypse 15.1–4), is found in the Mozarabic manuscript *S. Beati de liebana explanatio in apokalipsis S. Joannis* (Madrid, Biblioteca Nacional, Hh 58, fol. 127r). The Spanish manuscript dates from ca. 920 to 930.

The famous Utrecht Psalter, probably dating from ca. 860, provides another example of the caution needed when interpreting pictorial evidence. Only a portion of it is usually reproduced, but it seems indeed to reveal the earliest European example of a bow. The musician represented carries in his left hand a harp and a long-necked lute; in his right hand he holds a stick which, at 1.6–2 m in length, could hardly be a bow. The artist illustrated Psalm 107, with particular reference to the verses "Exsultabo et partibor Sichem, et vallem Succoth dimetiar" (I shall rejoice, partition Sichem, and portion out the valley of Succoth). Thus this stick, and another depicted next to the carrier, is in all likelihood a measuring stick.

Most recent research (Bachmann) places the origin of the bow in Central Asia, southeast of Lake Aral, especially near the river Oxus (Amu-Darja), where small, rich, highly civilized states developed during the early Middle Ages. Unfortunately, foreign influences virtually destroyed the civilizations (the eighth-century Arab conquest largely eradicated their affluence), and their documents were lost. Among these peoples, known and respected for their cultivation of music, a bow strung with horsehair was already in use during the ninth century, according to reliable sources. Quite likely it evolved from the older friction stick. Its use spread rapidly because musicians from this region were much in demand. Moreover, Arabs deported musically knowledgeable slaves to Baghdad and other cultural centers of the Arabic-Islamic realm.

More sources are available from the tenth century, and documentary evidence from ca. 1000 shows that a bowed instrument of the rebab type was in use in Persia, Afghanistan, and other regions of the Orient. These sources usually indicate that the instruments had come from Central Asia; by the late tenth century they were widely used in the Arabic-Islamic and Byzantine empires. In 711 the Arabs conquered parts of Spain, a development that was to have far-reaching consequences for European cultural history.

A critical and somewhat polemic attitude toward the musical sound produced by a bow is evident in a tenth-century literary source. Al-Farabi (b. ca. 870 in Transoxania, the cradle of the bow) writes in his most important work, the *Kitab al-mūsīqī al-kabīr* (cited after Bachmann): "Because of the rebab's construction its sound is not as forceful as that of certain other instruments. It therefore occupies a lower position than most other instruments."

Nevertheless, the sound of a bowed instrument opened up new possibilities for folk music. A flat bridge resulted in the simultaneous sound of the two (normally) strings. If one fingered only the higher string, allowing the lower one to sound along, a drone effect resulted. On three-string instruments, the drone strings might be tuned at the interval of a fifth, producing an effect known to us from bagpipes. These string instruments did not have frets, which means they were able to produce the micro-intervals that so characterize the tonal systems of Asiatic people, especially of India. They could also imitate the oriental manner of singing, using glissando and an occasional slow vibrato. Previously, wind instruments were capable of doing this in a very limited way, and string instruments, therefore, were favored in making music with singers. Despite initial reservations (they were first encountered only among the lower classes), they were soon widely accepted and counted among the most important instruments in the Arab cultural realm.

A growing amount of pictorial and written material since the early eleventh century documents the bow's existence in Europe. It seems that string instruments that later were bowed at first were only plucked, with a finger or plectrum. An elongated form of the plectrum was also used as a "beating stick"; often it was applied not only to one string but, drone fashion, to two or more strings. Our first illustration of a bow, among European sources, dates from ca. 920 to 930. Outside the Mozarabic realm, the first depictions of instruments played with a bow date from the eleventh century and are found chiefly in manuscripts from Catalonia, and in numerous manuscripts from northern Italy and northern France. Documentation from the Rhineland also exists. By the twelfth century the instruments were generally found throughout southern and western Europe and England.

The bow appeared, early and simultaneously, in widely separated parts of Europe. To account for this we must remember that it came not only from North Africa and Moorish Spain (as did so many other material and intellectual goods), but also by way of Byzantium. In Europe this marked the beginning of the age of polyphonic music. String instruments could produce drone effects and even play organum at the interval of a fourth or fifth. This may have helped to quickly overcome any initial aesthetic objections to bowed string instruments.

STRING INSTRUMENTS IN THIRTEENTH-AND FOURTEENTH-CENTURY EUROPE

As the bow appeared in Europe, some instruments that previously were plucked were now bowed, while others continued to be plucked. Still others were played, as Jerome of Moravia (thirteenth century) said, "aut arcu aut tactu" (bowed or plucked). By bowing, one or more strings were set into continuous and simultaneous vibration. As this also tended to enlarge the amplitude of the vibration, some structural modifications of the instruments became necessary, and drastic changes began to take place in European instrument making. One of the first major changes affected the height of the bridge, so that the vibrating strings would not touch the instrument's body or fingerboard. An increase in string tension resulted. Because of this, the earlier way of attaching strings to a cross-stay (as is still the case for guitars and lutes) no longer sufficed; they now had to be fastened to the rib. At times this was done directly, but more often with the help of a tailpiece, which in turn was fastened to the rib with a loop made of wire, gut, or other string. (Here we have the origin of the end button.) These changes occurred very gradually, as is demonstrated by a fifteenth-century fiddle in which the strings were still attached to a cross-stay (Denis, *De Muziekinstrumenten in de Nederlanden en in Italie*, Antwerp 1944, ill. 3).

An important consequence of bowing was the creation of space for bowing on the instrument's sides, which eventually led to the division of the body into upper and lower bouts. This seems at first to be a contradiction, given the above-mentioned practice of drone (simultaneous) playing on two or more strings, made possible by the flat bridge. It has also been pointed out that even in ancient times instruments that featured such indentations at the waist existed, and that for reasons of symmetry these were not always at the place where, later on, the bow would cross the strings. Another consideration was that a rectangular instrument is very sensitive to blows and to pressure, while a more or less oval shape offers far more resistance, thus increasing the instrument's life span. To make room for the bow became necessary for broad instruments such as oval fiddles, especially since the greatest width is found near the point of contact with the bow. Since the bow was not always applied near the rather flat bridge, this change in the instrument's shape became all the more necessary, but less so in the case of the pear-shaped rebec, a rather narrow instrument. It was also easy to avoid the instrument's edge by playing closer to the other, fingering, hand. Yet even the rebab occasionally displayed indented portions on the sides (see Sachs 1940, ill. 72). The changes in the instruments' shapes, necessitated by bowing, led to the separation of plucked and bowed instruments. Still, the common ancestry is often apparent.

To understand the violin's early history, an overview of bowed instruments from the thirteenth and fourteenth centuries is necessary. In regard to European instruments it should show what features existed, at the time when the changes became necessary, that eventually gave rise to the violin family. Here we must restrict ourselves to elements essential to that development, disregarding the special types that were so abundant at a time when standardization did not yet exist. Nor can we discuss in detail the many problems of terminology. Even specialists often cannot establish with certainty the meaning of a term such as lyra (lira) in a specific context.

During the High Middle Ages the following bowed instruments were in use in Europe:

1)   The crwth (chrotta, crotta, cruit, crwt, crouth, crudh, crowd). First used by bards to accompany singing; later a folk instrument. Used in the United Kingdom, especially in Ireland and Wales, and in northern France. Shape: 50–60 cm long; back at first flat, later also arched. Flat top; ribs ca. 5 cm high. Carved-out portions for the playing (left) hand to the right and left of the course of strings. Played in the manner of a gamba. In its early stage, three strings (crwth trithand); later with fingerboard and six strings, two of which were strung next to the fingerboard and served as drones. Occasionally these two may have been plucked with the left thumb. One of the

King David playing a crwth, from a troper, St. Martial Abbey, Limoges
(Paris, Bibliothèque Nationale)

crwth's most important structural details: an almost flat bridge with one short and one long foot. The former rested on the crwth's top, the latter, through a hole in the top, rested on the inside bottom or back, thus having one of the functions of the soundpost. In its late form the crwth displayed several structural elements of the violin, so that it has been called its immediate predecessor. Actually it is more likely that the crwth was refined after the violin family had begun to evolve, so that some of its details were incorporated in the crwth. The three-string crwth used the tunings e′ a′ d″ and g′ d′ a′.

2)   The fiddle (Latin: fidula; Middle Latin: vitula; Late Latin: fitola, figella; Spanish: vigola, viguela; French: vièle, vielle, viole; Old Norse: fuðlu; Anglo Saxon: feðilo, fithele, fythele; Old High German: fidula, vidula, viula; Middle High German: videle, fiedel; English: fiddle; Norwegian: fidla, fiol).

Found throughout Europe in various forms and families. Sound box usually oval, flat, with ribs and attached neck; normally without frets. Slight lateral indentations, occasionally approaching the shape of an 8. Oval form still found in the fifteenth century. Almost always held with the instrument resting on the left shoulder, also in front of the body. Only a few illustrations show the instrument being held with the chin, probably because the fiddle was often used to accompany the player's own singing, so that the chin had to remain free. Remarkably long bow. Number of strings varied from one to six, at times including lateral drone strings.

According to Jerome of Moravia, the drone fiddle was tuned d G g d′ d′, or d G g d′ g′, or G c g d′ d′. Strings were attached to pegs; these were inserted from the top into a flat pegboard, or sagittal attachment. Later the pegboard was made into a box, probably to protect the pegs. Beginning in

Fidula player, from a miniature in the Velislav Bible (Prague, University Library)

the early fifteenth century, pictures show a violinlike pegbox with pegs inserted laterally.

3)   The rebec (Latin: rubeba; German: Rubebe, with many variants). Found throughout Europe. Shaped like half a pear, arched back, with neck and fingerboard forming one continuation, all carved of one piece. Flat top, attached with glue. No ribs, no frets, one to three strings. Tuned in fifths; in the case of three strings g d' a'.

A special form of the rebec is the lyra, a Byzantine form of the rebab. Until recently it was widely used as a folk instrument in the Balkan countries, especially in Greece. The name "lyra" is also used for the one-string rebec.

4)   The giga (French: gigue). Term not used consistently. Really a rebec with flat back and with ribs. Number and tuning of strings similar to the rebec. Virdung (1511) mentions "clein Geigen"; the illustration shows a rebec. At this time the word "Geige" does *not* mean violin. In 1545 Sebastian Hurlacher is mentioned as having played at the Munich court "Zynnckhen, Busaunen, pfeiffen, geigen," but it is doubtful that this refers to violin playing. Since the word "Geige" was not adequately defined, there was much confusion about its use, especially in the early sixteenth century. Boetticher, for instance, states that Hans Gerle (b. ca. 1500 in Nuremberg) became especially famous as a player of the lute and the large and small "Geige"; Gerle discusses these extensively in his pedagogical works (*MGG*, article "Gerle"). But the first such work appeared in 1552, and it is quite certain that Gerle did not yet play a violin at that time. (In order to avoid ambiguous terminology, I do not use the words "Geige" and "violin" as synonyms during this period of transition.)

5)   The tromba marina (German: Trumscheit, Marientrompete; French:

From an English psalter manuscript (Cambridge, St. John's College Library)

trompette marine (or, de Marie). An instrument up to 2 m long, originally having one string. Its narrow body is tapered at the top. The string crosses the bridge's right side; the bridge's left foot, however, is unattached and vibrates freely, lightly touching the instrument's body. The bow's point of contact with the string is near the upper end; the left hand produces harmonics (the natural overtone series) below the bow.

If we consider lyra, rebec, and giga as variants of *one* type, and if we disregard the rotta (a harplike instrument rarely played with a bow), we have four basic types of medieval bowed instruments. Though morphologically quite different from each other, they are based on the same structural idea (except for the tromba marina, which uses only harmonics). Evidence for this derives from our knowledge of their tunings. They have in common the flat or nearly flat bridge, indicating that several or all strings were played simultaneously. If an instrument had two strings, the upper one was bowed while the lower one was a drone that usually provided the lower fourth or fifth (see Bachmann 1969, ill. 48). Stopping two or more strings simultaneously also seems to have occurred. According to Al-Farabi, the rebab also employed two courses, that is, the one-string rebab could have two strings tuned to the same pitch, and the two-string instrument could have four, tuned in pairs. This resulted in an effect known to us from the mandolin: a slight, intentional "beat," since in practice the two strings never were completely in unison. Stopping two strings with one finger was quite customary during the High Middle Ages. It is documented by pictures, though we cannot be entirely certain about the accuracy with which these represent playing technique. The crwth player from St. Martial (see illustration on p. 72)

Tromba marina

uses *barré* fingering, thus creating organum effects on his instrument. Bach-mann has further illustrations. It must have seemed new and fascinating to twelfth-century players and listeners that a string instrument could play organum at the fourth or fifth, with just as much intensity as that produced by singers.

Three-string instruments, using the tunings described for the crwth, could produce two types of polyphony: a drone in fourths and fifths to accompany a single melodic line (this is the period when the hurdy-gurdy and bagpipe evolved), or organum at the fourth or fifth with drone. Here the two upper strings were cross-fingered while the lower, open string or strings were bowed (see Bachmann 1969, ill. 22, where this manner of playing is clearly indicated). Many medieval pictures show that the thumb was used to stop the lowest string, indicating that the pitch of the drone could be varied.

That such a use of drones was an imitation of organum is mentioned in literary sources, for instance, by Johannes de Garlandia (ca. 1215): "Giga est instrumentum musicum de quo dicitur organicos imitata modus" (It has been said that the giga is an instrument that can imitate the sound of organum).

General preference for a fuller sound inspired makers to provide suitable instruments. One might compare their efforts to those of Perotin who, in the early thirteenth century, augmented the sound of his predecessor's compositions, making them "melior quam Leoninus" (better than those of Leonin). The same rationale applies to the stringing of instruments: the number of strings grew. Tunings related by Jerome of Moravia show that the drone fifth was doubled at the lower octave. Since this caused an imbalance between accompaniment and melody, the melody string also was doubled. Cross-fingering of the two melody strings produced a "beat," thereby restoring some balance. We know of two interesting couplings of drone sound with stronger melody sound. These occurred in tunings of the crwth, and though their descriptions date from 1711 and 1801, they no doubt reflect medieval practice:

g g′ c′ c″	d′ d″	and	a a′ e′ e″	b′ b″
(drone)	(melody)		(drone)	(melody)

Such tuning of neighboring strings in octaves was rare. By using cross-fingering an octave-coupling for the melody was produced.

In conclusion we can say that bowed instruments of the thirteenth and fourteenth centuries were employed for drone and organum effects. With the increased number of strings they were entirely adequate for the musical requirements of the age. There is an indication that these instruments were highly valued: in medieval illustrations they are almost always played by angels. King David, though often thought of as a harpist, is frequently shown as a fiddle player. Fiddle, rebec, giga, and tromba marina were not only associated with music at court; they also served to praise God.

Near the end of the fourteenth, and especially in the fifteenth century, fiddle and rebec suffered a loss in social standing. Like the hurdy-gurdy, they came to be viewed as appropriate for lowly wandering minstrels, even beggars. This lower prestige can be attributed to changes in musical styles: parallel organum and drones gradually ceased to represent the expressive and formal ideals of art music. As polyphony with independent voice leading became the ideal for composers and listeners, the earlier styles increasingly were considered old-fashioned.

THE VIOLIN'S EARLY HISTORY

Undoubtedly [the violin] was not created or suddenly invented by one master; rather, its form is the result of extensive experiments by many who wished to construct an instrument having a lighter timbre and higher range than the old viols.

FRIEDRICH NIEDERHEITMANN, *CREMONA: EINE CHARAKTERISTIK DER ITALIENISCHEN GEIGENBAUER UND IHRER INSTRUMENTE*, 1877

In spite of its variety and the confusing, frequently overlapping terminology, the medieval instrumentarium presents a fairly clear picture. The fifteenth century, however, brought changes to traditional instruments and the invention of new ones, developments that led to a completely new array. One product of this revolution is the violin. To shed some light on its origins one must examine what methods researchers have employed, and how fruitful and reliable these have been.

The first approach would be that of the collector. To the naive observer, the task of solving the problems of fifteenth-century instrumental evolution seems simple: an examination of the instruments themselves would provide the answer. Unfortunately, very few instruments from the fifteenth and sixteenth centuries have been preserved, and most of these no longer are in their original condition. Later changes were so manifold and drastic that we can rarely establish the most important original features. The reasons for structural changes are clear. In an age not yet concerned with museums, with preservation, instruments that no longer were adequate for new musical purposes were considered obsolete, but their wood at least was preserved, recarved and re-fashioned to meet the new needs. When this no longer was possible, the original wood might still have been used for repairs. Instruments that no longer were usable might be highly interesting to us as evidence of various stages of experimentation, but such research objects, in conditions that permit reliable conclusions, are extremely rare. If such an instrument was preserved, it was pure chance; an early collector might have kept it as a mere curiosity. We therefore depend essentially on written and pictorial documents.

Written documents include theoretical treatises, memoirs, travel diaries, descriptions of festive events, personal documents, inventories, payrolls, and other account books. Many exist, but there are obstacles to their use. Obscure terminology in various languages and many special local developments often make it impossible to correlate one term with one specific instrument, unless that instrument is clearly identified in other ways.

The name "viola" serves as an example. It probably is derived from the word "vidula" (viula, vihuela, viuola), but we do not know whether the change in name also represents a structural change, or whether such a change caused a name change. In the fifteenth century two types of viola emerged in Italy. According to the manner of playing they were called viola da (or in) bracchio (arm viola) and viola da gamba (leg viola). In ordinary parlance one often did not bother with the full name and referred to both of them as violas. The similar short forms were used in French (viole) and English (viol), and even in modern writings it is not always clear which instrument is meant.

So far, our most informative source regarding the violin's early history has been iconography—the description and interpretation of early illustrations, yet even this source must be used with great caution. Sure attribution to a specific painter, and hence to a specific date, is not always possible, yet such a date often would be a decisive factor. Nor did all painters from ca. 1500 endeavor to give realistic representations of instruments and their playing techniques. The most famous example of this is the angel playing a gamba in the Isenheim altarpiece: he holds the wrong end of the bow. Surely no gamba was ever played in this manner. An angel painted by Memling plays the tromba marina holding it up in the air—a position requiring strength such as even an angel would hardly possess! In other paintings we may note that one instrument is drawn very accurately, another one very vaguely; perhaps the artist knew the former very well because he played it himself. The

Italian art historian Vasari tells us that many Renaissance artists sang and played the lute well; two known fifteenth-century engravers were even "pifferi de la Signoria di Firenze" (members of the Florence town band). It is quite possible, then, that in the same painting we may see imaginary, fantastic instruments next to others reproduced so precisely that the artist must have had intimate knowledge of them.

Another research problem stems from a certain manner of deduction derived from biology. In the nineteenth century it was applied to organology and its methods. A statement by Curt Sachs (1920) reflects this:

> Revolutionary changes affected instrument making around 1500. Old traditions, persistently observed before, were suddenly abandoned. Instruments that for centuries had jealously kept their distinct identities now abolished these and intermingled, resulting in bastard instruments.

Here instruments are viewed as living beings, having the urge and the ability to choose mates, producing new traits through cross-breeding. This, of course, is not exactly what Sachs meant, but his words gave rise to this kind of thinking, leading to dangerous trends in instrumental research. There is a simpler explanation for the mutual influences, the transfer of structural features from one instrument to another: right into the seventeenth century, few makers specialized in only one plucked or bowed instrument. One and the same luthier made fiddles, gambas, lutes, and liras, along with all members of the violin family, from violin to double bass. To this day, the Italian word for violin maker is "liutaio" (luthier), though he or she may never have built a lute. Only when for legal reasons a precise definition was needed did the Italians use the term "violinaro." In his second will, Andrea Guarneri referred to himself as "liutaro, violinaro e chitarraro."

If, during the fifteenth and sixteenth centuries, an all-around maker of plucked or bowed instruments came up with an innovation for one instrument, he most likely tried it out on others as well. Some such experiments were abandoned, for various reasons. They may have had an adverse effect on the instrument's tonal characteristics. Experiments may have been due to considerations of timbre; others may have been instigated by a customer's wishes, by the mere curiosity of the builder, or by events in a particular community. To see, among such diverse conditions, a line of development comparable to the laws of genetics has led to questionable conclusions and prefabricated opinions contradicted by research.

A crucial question regarding the violin's origin is this: which structural features determine the sound, and which are merely aesthetic? When it comes to making instruments, what pleases the eye does not necessarily have a positive effect on the sound, though there are those who believe it. Pictures merely reveal an instrument's appearance; they may also lead us to *imagine* its sound. Classification systems used in organology are largely morphological. Therefore there is the danger that in music iconography, as in organology in general, aspects of construction that have nothing to do with sound receive the bulk of attention. Sachs, comparing an instrument from Turkmenistan with its European equivalent, mentions almost exclusively features that are of little consequence to the sound. Morphological considerations dominate; sound is hardly mentioned. Superficial features, such as how the strings are attached, become criteria for classification. Sachs places the violin among the large group of instruments featuring the end button, and the lute among those having a frontal string holder. Again and again, as one reads organological studies one is reminded of the classification systems of botany. When organologists began developing their own system, they evidently failed to base it, primarily and consistently, on characteristics of sound. Instead it followed other branches of science in which entirely different premises and laws apply. It would be absurd to classify flowers scientifically according to their scent, but it makes sense to classify instruments according to their sound, even though no system is without problems. Only in those cases where morphological characteristics determine sound can both classification systems be applied.

The violin sounds quite different from earlier bowed instruments. It is entirely possible that the first instruments to sound approximately like violins may have displayed structural features not found in our later, standard violin. In exploring the instrument's early history it might be wise to adopt a definition that may seem sacrilegious to traditionalists: the violin is an instrument that sounds like a violin, regardless of its appearance.

Research methods employed in the past have revealed interesting details but have thrown little light on the violin's early history. As a result, dates given in reference works and special studies vary greatly. From *Everyman's Encyclopedia* (2d ed. London 1931–1932) we learn that Giovanni Kerlino, a lute maker in Brescia, built violins as early as 1449. In his book *Das Konstruktionsgeheimnis der alten italienischen Meister: Der Goldene Schnitt im Geigenbau* (Berlin 1925–1927), the Berlin violin maker Max Möckel tells us that Leonardo da Vinci undertook many mathematical measurements and that since he built lutes, viols, and liras, "It seems safe to conclude that due to his knowledge of mathematical measurements he may well have been the true creator of the violin's classic shape and of the Italian art of building violins."

Leonardo died in 1519 and spent his last years in France. Thus his influence on violin making presumably took place ca. 1500. On the other hand Sachs (1920) states, "We cannot prove the violin's existence before the 1590s." In a 1962 book on organology the author expresses amazement: "Three hundred years ago an instrument had evolved empirically that still lives up to our highest standards today." This implies a date ca. 1662! In all, opinions differ by about two hundred years—a remarkable discrepancy when we are dealing with what is, perhaps, the most important instrument of our musical environment. In short, we have very little precise information.

We might therefore try to approach the problem from a different angle. Strangely enough, hardly anyone has taken up the question: *why* did the violin come into being? Except for the products of inconsequential tinkering, the development of music does not include a single case of an instrument (or an important structural detail) that did not evolve to satisfy needs related to sound. One thinks of the hammer-action keyboard, the valves for brass instruments, and of Boehm's groundbreaking ideas affecting the construction of woodwind instruments. In his study about the trombone's origin, Heinrich Besseler provided impressive documentation of the causal connection between the development of music and instruments. He first searched for the raison d'être of the trombone and found it in the drone contratenor as developed by Dufay ca. 1430. Using this (at first hypothetical) date as a point of departure, Besseler drew on many kinds of evidence, from compositional techniques to organology, iconography, and written documents. He was able to establish that the trombone's slide had been in use at the Burgundian court from 1434 to 1468.

The original concept of the violin can only be related to the wish for an instrument that had a stronger tone, at a time when traditional bowed instruments no longer were adequate in that respect. Our first task will be to establish the point in time at which musical needs, also related to timbre, caused changes in instrument building that eventually resulted in the violin.

MUSICAL DEVELOPMENTS IN THE FIFTEENTH CENTURY

As the fourteenth century drew to a close, the Western world was increasingly aware of a new spiritual, intellectual movement, at first characterized by a gradual outgrowing of medieval concepts, followed by a conscious discarding of medieval scholastic thinking. A new type of person emerged, inspired by the ideals of Greece and Rome. In 1550, Vasari used for the first time the word "rinascità" (rebirth) to characterize the epoch. It does characterize the period well, if we apply it less to a rebirth of the ancient world than to man being "born again" out of the spirit of antiquity. This "re-naissance" inspired all fields of human endeavor; it especially gave new impetus and new forms to all the arts. In the music of Ockeghem and Dufay a new feeling for harmony led to greater sonority and to an extension of range, especially lower range. Praetorius noted the gradual rise of the Chor-Ton (choir pitch). But the most telling manifestation of a new human spirit is reflected in festivities that took place in the open air, in front of many spectators. At such events the Renaissance prince demonstrated his position of power, making use of every opportunity and of all artistic representational media. Tremendous masses of sound were employed to accomplish this. In Rimini in 1475, at the wedding of the son of Sigismondo Malatesta, fifty trumpets and a hundred transverse pipes were heard during the solemn nuptial mass, at the elevation. When in 1487 Lucrezia d'Este and Annibale Bentivoglio were married in Bologna, the procession to the San Petronio cathedral was accompanied by "100 trombita e 70 piffaria e trombuni e chorni e flauti e tamburini e zamamele." On such occasions, trumpets were the preferred instruments, symbolizing princely glory. For other occasions, such as masques, intermezzi, mythological ballets, and similar entertainments presaging opera, we may assume that soft fiddles were no longer adequate. The wish for louder bowed instruments came not only from the musicians employed for such events, but also from the courts themselves, especially from those multitalented artists whose chief function it was to direct these celebrations.

A basic error about violins has been passed on from one writer to another, leading not only to entirely false notions about the instrument's origin but leaving the reader completely in the dark as to the *why*. One such writer was Philibert Jambe-de-Fer, a musician from Lyon who perished there in the St. Bartholomew Massacre of 1572. In 1556 (*Épitome musical*) he wrote about the difference between gamba and violin, saying that the latter was smaller and had a flatter body and rougher sound. [See also Anthony 1997, ch. 19. *Ed.*]

> Viols are played by noblemen, merchants, and other persons of means to while away the time. . . . The other instruments are called violins. They generally are used for dancing, for a good reason: they are easier to tune, for the ear detects a fifth more easily than a fourth. The violin also is easier to carry, which is useful when leading wedding or maskers' processions.

Jambe-de-Fer's statements have been interpreted to mean that for a long time the violin was basically associated with taverns and was late in assuming its place in the realm of art music—a view that, with few modifications, has been generally repeated to the present day. There is, however, an important objection: do we really believe that all those early instrument makers who showed an interest in the violin created such fine specimens only to sell them cheaply to "beer fiddlers" and to those who played for dancing? We are thinking of the first great master builders such as Andrea Amati, whose first preserved violin is dated 1546, and Gasparo Bertolotti, called da Salò. If Jambe-de-Fer was right, would they not rather have made better money by building gambas for noble lords and rich merchants? Jambe-de-Fer's "mommeries" and "noces" seem to have involved only the lower classes, but this would leave totally unexplained the developments, over decades, that finally led to the violin. He surely was also referring, and perhaps primarily so, to great festive events of the Renaissance. For these, all professional and other competent players would be enlisted, not only locally but from neighboring courts and towns. To create the necessary instruments for such large events must have been what makers were challenged and commissioned to do. The need for an extended lower range resulted in the gamba; the need for a strong sound in the upper register (and to balance the newly acquired low range) led to the violin.

The mid-fifteenth century is the period under discussion. Another half century was needed to progress from the initial idea to its realization. Wilhelm Joseph von Wasielewski (*Die Violine und ihre Meister*, 1869) was one of the few authors who understood the musical reasons for the violin's emergence:

> For some time there had been the need for an instrument corresponding in range to the soprano voice. . . . Earlier, the cornetto had assumed that role because the timbre of the viols did not resemble that of the soprano. But the cornetto's sound did not blend with that of the viols, so that the need arose for a bowed instrument related to the viols but closely resembling the soprano.

Almost all violin makers who commented on the violin's origin agree. They are opposed by some authors who completely misinterpret the relation between social necessity and its consequences for the violin. Emanuel Winternitz (*Musical Instruments of the Western World*) belonged to these:

> The frequent assumption that the invention of new instruments can be attributed exclusively either to technological progress or to new musical ideas has often led to an oversimplified interpretation of musical history. Actually, generalizations are not possible and each case has to be investigated on its own merits. . . . The violin . . . existed a considerable time before its inherent dynamic and tonal resources were exploited by Vivaldi, and later, in an unforeseeable way, through the invention of a supplementary tool, the Tourte bow. Sometimes it is another factor, the visual appeal of the shape, that contributes to the invention or improvement of an instrument. Here again, one exemplary case in point is the violin. Its "invention" must, in fact, have been due to the aesthetic sensitivity of unknown master craftsmen in the early sixteenth century who, searching for a "perfect" form—that is, for an organic and unified whole—brought about the crystallization of older types and forms of the fiddle into a balanced union of undulating contours and gracefully molded planes.

Others (for instance, Hajdecki in *Die italienische Lira da Bracchio*) have voiced similar views, probably because they lacked familiarity with fifteenth-century musical developments. They imply that the violin was created regardless of any need and without considering any possible use. Only much later did Vivaldi further exploit the violin's potential in remarkable ways, but this is no reason for denying the musical causes of its origin.

VIOLA DA GAMBA AND VIOLA DA BRACCHIO

In the first half of the fifteenth century, the extension of the lower range led to a revolution in instrument making. Trombone, gamba, bass rebec, bass lute, bass bombard, curtal or dulcian, and bassoon represent milestones along this road. Ingenious inventions include the slide and bent tubing. According to Besseler, the trombone stood at the beginning of these developments; a bill issued by an instrument maker in Bruges and dated 1423 already documents the existence of a bass bombard.

Pictures tell us that the medieval fiddle was primarily an alto instrument. The rebec was the preferred instrument in the soprano range, and the cornetto in mixed scoring. The painting from the 1432 Ghent altarpiece informs us of the tendency to extend the fiddle's range downward, thus producing a family of instruments with a homogeneous sound.

At first there was no precedent for developing a bass fiddle; no doubt this took decades of experimentation. Unfortunately, instruments from this age are nonexistent, making it impossible to trace their development with any degree of accuracy.

Tuning was a special problem. The fiddle was a drone instrument on which only the upper strings were fingered. To judge by the approximate string length, the fingering of whole tones and half tones resembled that of the modern viola. Such fingering is difficult even on a tenor-range instrument, especially for small hands, unless we assume the technique later developed by cellists. The bass fiddle therefore was tuned in fourths and one third, as had proven satisfactory for the lute. The third was necessary so that triads based on the instrument's lowest note could be played. Tuning consistently based on the interval of a fourth would have produced the dissonance E–F between the outer strings. Adopting the lute tuning and forgoing the use of drones had an important result: the instrument was no longer a true member of the fiddle family. Fiddlers who wanted to play it had to adjust to an entirely different stringing and tuning; the change amounted to having to learn the technique of a completely new instrument. Omitting the playing of drones led to the curved bridge and the lateral indentations.

There were other, less important changes due to the instrument's tenor and bass range, such as the rather high ribs, and holding the instrument between the legs. Morphologically, a new instrument had evolved. Later it was named the viola da gamba.

Adopting the lute tuning proved advantageous: after a few bowing exercises, lutanists could play the viola da gamba. Since then, many musicians have played both instruments. French court musician Nicolas Hautman (d. 1663), for instance, was "luthiste et virtuose de la basse de viole." The gamba also retained the lute's frets—a fortuitous byproduct contributing to its distinctive and attractive sound, resembling that produced by open strings.

The evolution from the bass fiddle to the gamba must also have been based on more profound musical necessities affecting especially soprano and alto fiddles. Players were increasingly called upon to play the vocal lines in polyphonic music, to reinforce the vocal parts, or to fill in for missing singers. Moreover, instrumental ensemble playing largely made use of vocal compositions. Besides the aforementioned changes in tuning, playing vocal parts on fiddles required important modifications of the instrument:

1) A curved bridge, so that the bow could play on a single string.
2) More distance between the strings, which made playing on a single string easier, leading in turn to a reduction in the number of strings. Given the range of vocal music, the large number of strings was unnecessary.
3) Deeper lateral indentations to make room for the bow. Because of the curved bridge the bow arm required a much greater radius of movement.

For Tinctoris (*De inventione et usu musicae*) fiddles and rebecs were the preferred instruments for participation in church music. Around 1487 he accurately described their strings as he dealt with the difference between lute and viola (fiddle): the strings "are positioned over a bulge [the curved bridge], so that if the player wishes to touch one string the others will not sound." The precedent of tuning in fifths, set by the rebec, had been tested. In playing a diatonic scale in the first position, the third finger was followed by the next open string, providing more resonance than was possible on instruments tuned in fourths. Theoretically, and considering the player's hand, an open string following the fourth finger would have been possible, in which case strings would be tuned in sixths. But for one thing, the fourth finger was seldom used at the time. For another, a sequence of major sixths, such as G–E–C-sharp–A-sharp, would have been tonally unthinkable, while a mixture of major and minor sixths, for instance g e′ c″ a″, would have required an overly complicated fingering technique.

We cannot as yet establish precisely when the drone fiddle changed into a melody instrument suitable for polyphony; most likely this occurred during the mid-fifteenth century. Later this essentially new instrument acquired the name "viola da (in) bracchio." The term occurs for the first time ca. 1510, which means that the changes must have taken place concurrently with the evolution of the gamba or immediately thereafter. The qualifier "da bracchio" made sense only as a distinction from "da gamba," because fiddles were held against the shoulder or chest. Larger members of the family were carried with a strap around the neck and were held horizontally.

One is tempted to assume that the term "viola" came into existence as the result of changes in construction and playing technique, but it is already found in twelfth-century Provençal. It then occurs in Italian documents from Bologna dated 1261 and 1265. The term soon found its way into Latin theoretical treatises, without implying a structural change. "Viella" (used by Jerome of Moravia) and "viola" had identical meanings, just as in thirteenth- and fourteenth-century France the terms "vielle" and "viole" were used interchangeably. Only in the fifteenth century did vielle à roue come to mean hurdy-gurdy, while vielle was retained for bowed instruments. These, by the way, had no frets.

The new term viola da bracchio raises the basic question: was this arm-held instrument already a member of the violin family? In 1619 Praetorius (*Syntagma musicum*, vol. 2) declared,

[Viola da bracchio:] usually called violin, or fiddle by the common people. It is called da bracchio because it is held on the arm. Also Bass = Tenor = and Discantgeig (called violin, or violetta piccola, also Rebecchino). They have four strings; the small ones (called Pochetto in French) have three strings. All these are tuned in fifths.

Based on this terminology, the literature has largely equated "viola da bracchio" with "violin." Thus Sachs (1920):

The viola da bracchio (our violin and its sisters) has a neck almost at a right angle with the shoulders, has no frets, an arched back, low ribs, both plates extending over the rim, a scroll, and four strings.

A recent catalog (Othmar Wessely, *Die Musikinstrumentensammlung des oberösterreichischen Landesmuseums, Linz*) lists violin, viola, and cello under the subheading "viole da bracchio." Together with gamba, viola d'amore, hurdy-gurdy, and tromba marina they are listed under the larger heading of bowed lutes. This is according to Sachs and Hornbostel, who include violin, gamba, and guitar among the "boxlike instruments, with neck either attached to the sound box or carved from the same piece of wood" (*MGG*, vol. 8, col. 345).

Praetorius's terminology dates from a period long after the term "viola da bracchio" had come into use. If the violin indeed developed from that instrument, Praetorius, with some justification, equated the two terms, as had been customary almost a hundred years earlier. But the very early viola da bracchio, which existed before the name existed, certainly was not yet an alto violin, even when one disregards some structural features of the standard type of violin after ca. 1550–1560.

Soon after the emergence of the viola da gamba, which originally was only a bass instrument, a four-part choir of bowed instruments came into existence:

> Soprano: viola da bracchio
> Alto: viola da bracchio
> Tenor: viola da bracchio
> Bass: viola da gamba

(There were only minor differences between the alto and tenor viola da bracchio.) This then was a "broken" consort, not a homogeneous family. When playing with low-pitch instruments, especially trombones and shawms, the soprano viola proved to be too weak. Given the general trend of the time, soon after the fiddle gave way to the early, transitional viola da bracchio, the transformation to louder instruments in the upper range must have begun.

THE ORIGIN OF THE VIOLIN

In its early stages, the viola da bracchio was an alto fiddle with arched bridge, a body resembling the shape of an 8, a flat back, and three or four strings tuned in fifths. For the soprano instrument several names were in use, such as soprano (or sopranino) di viola, violetta, viola piccola, rebecchino, and violino. In *Die italienische Lira da Bracchio*, Hajdecki tried to prove that "violino" is not a diminutive form of "viola" but means "viola-like." His reasoning contains flaws, for he did not take into consideration northern Italian dialects. He erred particularly in dating the violin's origin from ca. 1560, by which time the development of the gamba family from bass to soprano had been completed. According to Hajdecki, the violin arose imitating the soprano gamba's function, becoming a "viol-like" instrument.

To trace the development of the viola da bracchio to the stage where it sounded like a violin, we should imagine the situation of an instrument maker during the second half of the fifteenth century. He was searching for a viola da bracchio with greater sound volume, to meet the new requirements of professional musicians. Praetorius described instruments in general as the "artful creations of noble and profound artists whose inventions are the results of busy thinking and constant endeavor." This must apply especially to those artisans who tried to respond to their customers' requests. According to Schulze, "The loudness of a tone is determined by the force producing it, by resonance that amplifies it, and by the nature of the substance that generates it."

As we've said, the early viola da bracchio featured greater distance between the three or four strings. This, along with the carved-out sides, enabled the bow to attack the strings more vigorously. At first one tried to produce a louder sound by using thicker strings. Mersenne (*Harmonie universelle*) stated, "[The violin] might be called an imitation of the gamba . . . , but it is inferior to it, for the violin's sound is rougher, especially because one is forced to use strings that are too thick." Roussel, a more recent writer, used similar language: "The thicker the strings, the greater the sound volume." Since thicker strings offer more resistance to the bow, they require more vigorous playing. This has been accomplished by greater tension and by using more rosin and bows with more hair. The strings' greater amplitude of vibration necessitated a higher bridge, so that the string would not hit the fingerboard. A higher bridge (up to a limit) led to a bright sound rich in harmonics. The bridge's added height, along with increased string tension, meant greatly increased string pressure on the bridge and through it on the top plate. To prevent it from cracking or breaking, a support became necessary. Unlike the earlier fiddle, the violin now acquired a soundpost—a small stick that originally was meant to be a support but was soon found to influence the sound decisively, so much so that the Italians called it the "anima" (soul).

However, not only the (vertical) string pressure increased but also the (horizontal) string tension. The peg plate, lying in the same plane as the fingerboard and forming one piece with it, no longer was adequate for this strong pull; it was likely to bend, if not break. Actually, the peg plate had been in the process of modification for some time, as evidenced by illustrations. A peg that stuck out, unprotected, from the plate was easily damaged. To counteract this, a kind of enclosure had come into use in the early fifteenth century. From then on we also encounter a rounded pegbox with laterally inserted pegs, as shown in a painting by Fra Angelico. The pegbox is found more often after the mid-century: Memling's tromba marina of 1480 displays it in its definitive later shape associated with the violin, as does a drawing in the treatise *De musica tractatus* (Bologna pre-1482) by the Spaniard Ramos de Pareja. To reduce the tension, one only needed to position this pegbox slightly below the level of the strings, and to add the nut. The pegbox, then, was not invented specifically for the violin.

The larger amplitude of vibration, combined with thicker strings, had a profound effect on the shape of the instrument's body, for string vibration and body resonance are closely related. Use of thicker wood only partially counteracted the amount and intensity of vibration; if carried too far it would interfere with the body's ability to resonate. An arched body, however, made it possible to increase its tension without interfering with the elasticity of the resonating box. "Tone volume depends more on the construction of the arches than on the wood's thickness" (Max Möckel, *Das Konstruktionsgeheimnis*). But experience in shaping these arches was yet to be gained. The arched body of the lute was assembled from ribs, while the rebec and its neck were carved from one block of wood, so that the two were shaped in entirely different ways. Through arching, the interior regained in volume what had been lost to the lateral indentations.

To make up for the heavier lower strings, the left part of the upper plate needed to be stronger. Gamba makers had known this for some time; they occasionally used thicker wood for the left side of the instrument's top. A more advantageous solution, namely to fasten a bass bar to the inside, had yet to be found. The bass bar also equalized vibrations across the entire top—probably a fortuitous byproduct—and prevented excessive shaking at vibration node points.

The top's arching also affected the shape of the sound holes. Illustrations and preserved instruments from the fifteenth and sixteenth centuries show that sound holes were subject to experimentation and placed rather arbitrarily. For fiddle and rebec they were given various shapes and positioned differently. Eventually the shape of a C, most easily carved, was preferred. Two arrangements of the two holes existed: Ɔ C and C Ɔ. After 1400 the holes became larger and were put in acoustically better positions. These two shapes were favored for a good reason: they provide a better distribution of the thinner wood than would result from circular, semicircular, semioval, or elongated rectangular shapes. Holes resembling the familiar *f* shape, derived from the C shape by reversing the direction of the upper segment (see illustration on p. 88), occur fairly early; a gamba by Hans Volrat (Vienna 1475) displays *f* holes in the classic Italian shape. The *f* hole proved to be essential for arched tops, having a favorable effect on wood tension.

While the size of the aperture remained the same, it was more firmly anchored in the instrument's top. It has occasionally been claimed, for formal and aesthetic reasons, that the C shape was a "gothic" and the *f* shape a "Renaissance" style characteristic, but such claims ignore the true reasons for these changes. Apian–Bennewitz (1892) stated them clearly:

> Position and shape of the *f* holes, as of the bridge, are not the results of the whim or sense of beauty of those who first created them; they are the results of a long period of development.

To arrive at the best possible sound, lower ribs were needed. Later, a height of 3 cm became the norm.

These structural changes are the results of attempts to enhance the sound of the viola da bracchio and may have occurred more or less in the sequence of steps described here. Based on pictorial evidence, Denis stated that until 1500 the fiddle was flat, with a round peg plate, and with ribs at the outside. Later it was arched, with the ribs set back, and with the neck set at a slight angle. This also is a partial description of the violin's development. To see this in its true perspective we must get rid of the notion that the *liutai* had "wanted to invent the violin." Rather, they began to experiment with modifying the viola da bracchio's sound. Vincenzo Galilei (*Fronimo*, Venice 1568) documents this:

> The Neapolitans were the first in Italy to know the viola da bracchio, before the Spaniards. Spain gave us the first music written for the viola, but the first instruments had been built in Bologna, Brescia, Padua, and Florence. Ever since its inception, the viola showed different shapes; they underwent many transformations, as did the number of strings and their tuning. These instruments were the first to have C holes and, in the late fifteenth and early sixteenth centuries, an arch—first on the middle of the top, then also on the back. [Wood was used] with or without veins [curls]; there was no protruding rim, and the profile showed no corners. The pegboxes were in the shape of a scroll or head; others featured a small board that was circular, or in the shape of a heart. The early sixteenth century saw the devlopment of protruding rims and corners; veins in the back plate came later, as did large *f* holes that replaced the C holes.

Galilei (b. ca. 1520) reported what was happening in his own time.

As one attempts to order all these developments chronologically, one should discard another widely held notion: that the term "violin" is appropriate only from the time when it received the shape with which we are familiar. For all these investigations of terminology as related to form we must distinguish among the following:

1) Characteristics defining sound
2) Characteristics that are the result of sound requirements, having to do with construction and playing technique
3) Purely formal-aesthetic characteristics not related to specific sound qualities

A purely morphological approach brings with it the danger that the formal-aesthetic characteristics are accorded equal or greater importance than the others, inviting wrong conclusions. A violin is an instrument that produces a violin tone, whether or not it conforms to a certain standard form. This is one reason why iconography is of only limited importance for the violin's early history. It is entirely conceivable that an instrument with peg plate and C holes *sounded* like a violin. Such an instrument, with peg plate, C holes, and one indentation between upper and lower bouts, is shown in a wooden mosaic by Paolo and Antonio del Sacha in Bologna (*MGG*, vol. 2, col. 97). The instrument shown in the woodcut *St. Kümmernis* by Hans Burgkmair (Augsburg, ca. 1507) may also have sounded like a violin, granted that the artist was no expert on bowed instruments: the bridge is placed on the upper bout, and the musician plays behind the bridge.

Instruments in Baldassare Peruzzi's "Orpheus" cycle (Rome, Villa Farnesina, built 1508–1511) also depict early violin shapes. Instruments of this kind probably were very fragile, perhaps one reason why so few early specimens have come down to us. Schlesinger (1910) states that the *f* holes are the violin's most distinctive feature, and that the scroll characterizes sixteenth-century instruments. Many others have expressed similar opinions, yet they give undue emphasis to nonmusical features, such as those introduced to protect an instrument that at first was played almost exclusively outdoors.

Whoever has reflected on the imagination and thought that went into the creation of the violin, this miracle of human ingenuity, will realize that it could not have been invented by one person. Sibire (*La chélonomie*) gave eloquent expression to his reverence and admiration for those who first undertook its development:

How much labor, how much research by our ancestors was needed to bring about this instrument! How many hypotheses, how much experimentation, how much time went into the solution of the riddle! The raw material was there, but the number of possible combinations was legion; how then could anyone guess at, or discover the instrument's true—the one and only suitable form?

Without exaggeration we can say that this process of development took thirty, forty, or even more years. We cannot determine whether the first instrument that sounded like a violin was built in 1470, or not until 1480 or 1490, but certainly the process was concluded by 1500. Italian scholars including Strocchi have used the term "violino del I tempo" (violin of the first stage), while Boyden distinguishes between "early" and "true" violin. The first term is chronological, the second represents a value judgment. Cozio speaks of early violins that were later "corrected" by members of the Amati family and which may have been built at the beginning of the century or even earlier.

The evolution from the viola da bracchio to the violin presents us with a problem of terminology. The many names at first given to the viola da bracchio did not refer to our violin. Therefore the words "violino" and "violinista," when used in the second third of the fifteenth century, hardly referred to our instrument and its player, but this no longer is true after ca. 1475.

In general, too late a date has been assumed for the violin's origin; therefore the occurrence of these words caused doubts and led to attempts to interpret them differently. Actually, there is no need for this. Thus A. Rossi (*Giornale di erudizione artistica*, vol. 5, 1874) quotes a source according to which a Magister Franciscus florentinus was referred to in 1462 as "quitarista seu violinista." This may have been customary language at the time but does not prove that the instrument he played had the sound properties of a violin. Likewise Albert Jacquot (*La musique en Lorraine*) reports that in 1490 René II appointed Jehan Darmurot as regional supervisor "dans l'art et mestier de joueur de violon et autres instrumens," in order to keep nonmembers of the guild from playing for pay. This report, often discredited, receives new credibility in the light of recent research.

It stands to reason that structural details of the soprano instrument would be applied to the alto instrument, so that at the end of the fifteenth century the viola da bracchio (now meaning specifically the alto range of the family) could have been a viola in the modern sense. The rather high ribs and flat bottom, however, may have lent it a rather covered, nasal timbre; it would actually have been desirable for ensemble playing with the (bass range) viola da gamba.

Interestingly enough, the term "violina," appropriate for a small viola, is occasionally found. Heron-Allen (*De fidiculis*, no. 692) refers to an eight-page account by Giulio Grotto, published ca. 1550 in Brescia and Ferrara: *La violina: Con la sua risposta et altre canzoni musicali bellissime*. A woodcut on the title page represents a musician playing an instrument resembling a viola da bracchio, which he supports with his chin, on the left side of the tailpiece.

In the decades following 1500 the differences between gamba and soprano viola da bracchio eventually resulted in two morphologically independent families, differing greatly in timbre. This was nicely expressed by Jean Rousseau, author of a 1687 gamba method. Referring to the soprano gamba, he warns the player to stay within the expressive realm of the gamba in gay movements and not treat it like a violin. The violin should sound lively, but the soprano gamba should sound ingratiating and flattering.

The same makers who experimented with the viola da bracchio also developed the gamba. As they searched for ways to increase the volume of the violetta, they understandably took over certain proven details for the gamba, chief among them the soundpost and bass bar, which features improved the gamba's sound without destroying its characteristic timbre. The same was true of a judicious arching of the top. In this way the gamba went through a process of development that began with the tonally unsatisfactory large fiddle. The process was especially important for the tenor instrument for which the cello became a competitor. A gamba by Francesco Linarolo (1540) has the scroll and f holes of a violin; another one by Antonius and Hieronymus Amati (Cremona 1611) greatly resembles a cello.

One other instrument must be mentioned as it figures importantly in the violin's early history: the lira da bracchio. Hajdecki (1892) postulated his own theory: "Structural, musical–technical, and historical reasons, along with a direct lineage, cause us to consider the lira da bracchio to be the only predecessor and mother of the violin." This view has been repeated, widely and unquestioningly. I already have referred to Hajdecki's basic error of claiming far too late a date for the violin's origin. He further stated, "The quartet of viols evolved from the lowest to the highest range; that of the bracchios in the opposite direction." This is true, but at the time of the violin's development the gamba quartet did not yet exist. Therefore many of Hajdecki's arguments only appear to be logical; actual developments took another course.

The lira da bracchio had five playing strings and two lateral drone strings. According to Lanfranco (*Scintille di musica*, Brescia 1533) the tuning was d d' g g' d' a' e''. He gives the string names as basso grave, basso acuto, bordone grave, bordone acuto, tenore, sottanella, and canto. Praetorius gives the tuning of the highest string as d'', which may have been more customary at the time. The instrument was in use for a limited time. According to Hajdecki it appeared ca. 1490 and acquired its external form ca. 1503. Being a drone instrument it already was more or less obsolete. When around the mid-fifteenth century the drone fiddle became the viola da bracchio, which had a larger sound, the fiddle's thin and nasal tone no longer sufficed. This created the demand for an instrument that combined drone strings with the timbre of the then-new violin. It is fairly certain that the violin did not have its origin in the lira da bracchio. Rather, builders used the experience gained in developing the violin from the viola da bracchio and applied it to the almost anachronistic lira da bracchio. This accounts for the similarity of certain features of both, rightly noted by Hajdecki. The development of the lira da bracchio is clearly documented by pictures and preserved instruments:

1510   Carpaccio, *Presentation in the Temple*, Venice
1511   Instrument built by Giovanni d'Andrea, Verona, now in Vienna
1540   Instrument built by Giovanni da Brescia, allegedly made in
        Venice, now in Oxford

Boyden dates the second instrument ca. 1525. It has the body of a violin except for the way the strings are attached and for a slight indentation on the bottom of the lower bout. It must have sounded like a member of the violin family.

It is understandable that Hajdecki propounded so enthusiastically his thesis that the lira da bracchio represents the missing link between viola da bracchio and violin, and that his theory was widely accepted. So little was known about the violin's early history that one gladly embraced a fairly plausible theory that explained this embarrassing lacuna. It may speak for Hajdecki that some magnificent specimens of the lira da bracchio have been preserved, dating from the early 1500s, and that there are pictorial documents. This is not true of the violin. As a drone instrument, the lira was still popular in society, for both solo playing and accompanying. The violetta da bracchio–violin, on the other hand, belonged to the professional musicians. Furthermore, the lira was by then fully developed, whereas the violin continually underwent changes. To preserve very early models seemed uninteresting.

The development of bowed instruments as outlined here for the second half of the fifteenth century must remain largely hypothetical (especially for the early stages of the violin) until clear documentary evidence can be found. Doubtless ample material will be located once we abandon the notion that the violin did not evolve until the mid-sixteenth century. To recognize iconographic evidence we must also free ourselves of preconceived notions based on instruments of the late sixteenth century, notions that would prevent us from recognizing early violins as such. Unfortunately, no instrument from the early period (pre-1500) seems to have come down to us in its original form. There is only one such possibility: the violin with a label "Joan. Kerlino, anno 1449." Laborde mentioned it in 1780; Fétis saw it at Koliker's in 1804—but as Fétis already suspected, it seems to be a forgery. André Augustin Chevrier, a violin maker working for Jean Gabriel Koliker in Paris, supposedly made it. Koliker was known as an unscrupulous dealer; the Italian-sounding "Kerlino" supposedly was a rearrangement of "Koliker." Bertolotti, however, introduced documentary evidence that a gamba maker named Kerlino worked for the Count of Mantua ca. 1495. According to Vidal and others, the famous "first violin" originally was a soprano viola da bracchio that Koliker had remodeled.

We can obtain a fair idea of what instruments looked like ca. 1500 from three instruments in the Milan collection. Instruments nos. 12, 44, and 45 in the Milan catalog may date from the sixteenth century but display some telling archaic characteristics; the names of their makers are not known. Their measurements—of length, width (upper, middle, and lower bouts), and ribs (upper and lower bouts)—differ greatly, showing that standard dimensions were established only gradually, after experiments based on considerations of sound:

No. 12: 335 / 130 / 93 / 167 / 32 / 30
No. 44: 333 / 171 / 131 / 220 / 33 / 33
No. 45: 350 / 147 / 90 / 187 / 28 / 28

The first of the three instruments, called viola da bracchio piccolo in the catalog, actually is a true violin. Its primitive appearance is touching somehow; even if it should turn out to be a later work by a simple amateur builder, the concern for sound and shape is obvious.

THE VIOLIN IN THE EARLY SIXTEENTH CENTURY

Our investigations so far point to its being highly probable that some examples of the soprano viola da bracchio (occasionally also called violin), even if made before 1500, may have sounded like a violin. Many scholars, studying the violin ca. 1500, persisted in believing that such beautifully proportioned objects could not have been created by craftsmen alone—that a major artist must have had an important role in creating its shape. One of the first to deal with this subject was an anonymous contributor to the Leipzig *Allgemeine Musikalische Zeitung* (vol. 10), who quotes from the autobiography of Benvenuto Cellini (1500–1571):

> My grandfather Andrea Cellini was a knowledgeable architect. Giovanni, my father, followed him in this occupation. Vitruvius claims that in order to do well in it, one not only needs to draw well but must also know something about music. Therefore Giovanni, having become a good draftsman, began to study music, first mastering the basic rules and then learning to play well on viol and flute. . . . My father began began to instruct me in flute playing and singing, but I did not like it and sang and played only to obey him. He then also was building wondrous organs with wooden pipes, and other keyboard instruments, the best to be found anywhere. He also made viols, lutes, and harps. . . . When he fell in love with the woman who was to be my mother, he also became inordinately fond of the flute, so that the town pipers invited him to play with them. He did this for a while, for his own pleasure, but eventually they employed him on a regular basis and inducted him into their guild.

Though principally an architect, Giovanni Cellini (d. 1528) built instruments ca. 1505–1510.

It was mentioned earlier that Max Möckel, on the basis of detailed research, suspected that Leonardo da Vinci, whose interests were manifold, was the father of the violin. Before Möckel, Hajdecki had expressed the same belief. He quoted an account in Vasari concerning Ludovico Sforza's accession to the throne (Milan 1481). "The highly esteemed Leonardo was taken to the duke who was fond of playing the lira. Leonardo had brought along the instrument he had built himself." Möckel (1935) considered the egg (oval) shape of the lute and showed how the gamba's shape might have evolved from it:

Early violins (Milan, Museo Civico)

Let us retrace our steps and compare the egg shape, leading to the shape of the gamba, with what we have learned so far about the development of the violin's shape. Here we see ugly, unproportioned lines, there perfection of form. There can hardly be a more convincing proof of the need for proportioned development. This is where I believe that Leonardo da Vinci entered the picture. This genius, an artist of incredible versatility and a scientist, also constructed musical instruments. He of course condemned the existing bowed and plucked instruments, plump and ugly as they were. It stands to reason that he was the one who improved the form of the violin, establishing its classic, ideal shape. He was as familiar with the problem of the golden section as today's children are with the multiplication table. To fully comprehend the value of these rules, they must become second nature. The eye must be so well trained that it spontaneously detects deviations. . . . Leonardo supposedly said: "You must have a compass in your eye."

Winternitz was able to prove that Leonardo had an inventor's interest in wind instruments. The literature is full of undocumented claims that Leonardo played the violin. These claims go back to Charon and Fayolle (*Dictionnaire historique des musiciens*, 1810–1811) who rather brazenly stated that Leonardo was a violin virtuoso in Sforza's service.

Hajdecki made a strong claim for Raphael, who depicted bowed instruments in several of his paintings—instruments that reflect a certain line of development. After several attempts to prove the painter's involvement, Hajdecki states,

> Is it too daring to assume that [Raphael] was the one who first gave to the violin this variety of lines, this lively appearance—who enhanced it with such graceful, curving, and well-balanced lines? Since then they have become the standard. Might not instrument builders have adopted this idea and put it into practice? . . . It took Raphael years and years of thinking and modeling until his instrument reached its classic form.

The famous mathematician Niccolò Tartaglia (b. ca. 1500 in Brescia) has also been mentioned as possibly having made a violin. Though all these accounts are interesting and may contain some truth, they cannot be proved. This also applies to the role played by great Renaissance artists in the shaping of the violin.

The violin's history in the sixteenth century must be viewed as a family history, related to the gamba's development. In the early sixteenth century, to play a four-part choral composition with bowed instruments, one would have used a violetta piccola for the upper part—a transitional type between soprano viola da bracchio and violin. The middle voices would be given to two viole da bracchio. Both would have the same tuning, though the second one would be slightly larger, to better produce the lower notes. A viola da gamba would take the bass part. Such an ensemble produced a fairly homogeneous sound, as long as violetta and viola did not yet have a distinct violin sound. When that happened, the need arose for two distinct families: one incorporating the timbre of the top voice, the violin; the other built on the timbre of its lowest member, the (bass) viola da gamba. A contrabasso di viola da gamba already existed before 1500; quite logically it was called violone, that is, large viola. This violone, however, is *not* identical with the later contra (double) bass; it does not belong to the violin family. The development of both families took place in the first third of the century. In the first edition of his book *Musica instrumentalis* (1529), Martinus Agricola speaks of "small *Geigen* with three strings tuned in fifths." He may be referring to the rebec, but perhaps also to the violin family, though there is a discrepancy between text and illustrations. The tunings are g d' a' for the discant, c g d' for the alto/tenor, and F c g for the bass.

In *Musica Teusch* (1532), Gerle mentions "kleine Geigleyn"; these may have been violins as well as rebecs. His tunings are g d' a' for the discant, e g d for alto/tenor, and C G d a for the bass. The last is our cello tuning. Similar remarks by Lanfranco, and by Agricola in his 1545 edition, also suggest that the fourth string for the other members of the violin family may go back to the cello.

Lanfranco (1533) mentions a "bowed violetta da bracchio" with three strings and no frets. The tuning may be what Cerone (*El melopeo*, 1613) reported, based on Lanfranco: discant g d′ a′, alto/tenor c g d′, bass B–flat F c g. The last is Agricola's tuning, extended downward by a fifth.

Finally Jambe-de-Fer (1556) gives the following tunings for the violin family: discant (dessus) g d′ a′ e″, alto/tenor (taille/hautecontre) c g d′ a′, bass (bas) B–flat F c g. This is Lanfranco's tuning with violin and viola range extended upward by a fifth.

The early violin, then, usually had three strings, as did the viola. The fourth string was initially added to the bass instruments to gain lower range. By 1500, when both families were fully developed, the division into two groups with distinct timbres was complete.

Given the violin's much more brilliant tone, instrument makers continued to be tempted to apply some of its features to the gambas. One might say that there are very few "true" gambas, if by that we mean the prototype. Almost all those preserved in museums display violin-violoncello features, if only in small details. This "hankering" of gamba builders after the violin shape, and of gamba players after the cello's tonal qualities, is evident in Christopher Simpson's *The Division Violist* (1659), which includes illustrations of two gambas, one of which very much resembles the cello's shape. Simpson says that that one has a better sound.

The last step toward the completion of the violin family, the creation of the contra bass, was not taken until the second half of the sixteenth century, although contra bass gambas were used in orchestras until the early eighteenth century. Their frets greatly helped intonation, especially in the low register (players often needed years of practice before they acquired secure intonation), and the slanted back of the gamba made it easier to hold. This was so advantageous that one saw no need for adopting the violin shape.

For a long time scholars failed to know that the violin and gamba families developed simultaneously and assumed rather that the violin family lagged behind, thereby giving rise to the erroneous belief that the violin developed from the soprano gamba, as claimed by Grillet (*Les ancêtres*): "The first violin was an undeveloped and simplified soprano gamba."

Few writers believed that the violin existed in the fifteenth century, but many took up this question: who, in the sixteenth century, invented the violin? The number of makers credited with the feat is legion, including, in alphabetical order, Andrea Amati, Bertolotti (called da Salò), Bononiensis, Brensio, Bussetto, dalla Corna (father and son), Dardelli, Lanure, Linarolo, Mahler, Morella, Rolini, Testatore, Tieffenbrucker, Zanetto da Montichiaro, and Zanura.

Giambattista Rolini, active in Pesaro in 1471, has been called "first maker of violins," as has Pietro Dardelli, a Franciscan monk who lived in Mantua. Some of his instruments are dated between 1490 and 1500. According to Valdrighi (*Nomocheliurgografia*) he made "viole e bassi di viola, rebecchi, liuti." "Viole," at this time and in this context, meant "viole da bracchio"; the "bassi di viola" were gambas. Thus Dardelli may have been one of the first builders of soprano viols (violins), although Valdrighi's term "viole" is not yet precise. A lute with the label "Padre Dardelli 1497" has also been preserved.

It is doubtful that a maker named Testatore il Vecchio ever existed. He supposedly lived ca. 1500 and is credited with being one of the first to work on the transformation of the viola da bracchio into the violin. His name first appears in a rather fantastic book, *Lutomonographie* by the Russian Prince Youssoupoff, published anonymously in 1856 in Frankfurt. There is no documentary proof of Testatore.

In chronological order, the next possible early builder is Zuan Maria dalla Corna, sometimes called "da Bressa" (from Brescia). His dates are not known, but he must have been born before 1460 because his son Giovanni Giacomo was born ca. 1485. The Ashmolean Museum in Oxford has an outstanding lira da bracchio built between 1525 and 1540; the label identifies the builder as "Giovanni Maria bresciano in Venetia." Its quality suggests that the master had built especially fine instruments before this.

Zuan Maria's son Giovanni Giacomo dalla Corna (ca. 1485–1550) deserves special mention because in 1533 Lanfranco included him and Giovanni Montichiaro among the best instrument makers of the time. As he put it, one could find in Brescia "beautiful string instruments such as lutes, bass gambas, liras, and others—all sounding good, built by Giovan Giacobo dalla Corna and Zanetto da Montichiaro." The second word in the original text was "violoni," which Fétis translated as "violons." As a result, the younger dalla Corna has been consistently listed as a builder of "lutes, violins, liras, etc." right up to Vannes's *Dictionnaire* of 1951. Most likely he did make violins, but Lanfranco did not specifically say so. Boyden (1965), however, refers to a passage in Galilei's *Dialogo* (1581), according to which "lira" could also mean "viola da bracchio."

Pietro Zanura, a gamba maker in Brescia from 1500 to 1520, probably made violins also, though this is not certain. A tenor viola labelled "Pietro Lanure, Brescia 1509" displays some violin characteristics. This may be the same master.

Likewise, Antonio Brensio and Antonio Bononiensis ("from Bologna") may be one and the same builder, since a person often used the name of a hometown. According to Strocchi (1937), who gives 1485 as the date of birth, Antonio was the inventor not only of the gamba but of the violin as well. There is a painting of a violin in Bologna's S. Domenico church, which for some time was seen as proof that the violin was invented in that city, but recent research attributes the painting to Antonio Cisseti, an eighteenth-century painter.

Along with dalla Corna, Lanfranco mentions Zanetto da Montichiaro (Mentechiaro) as a major luthier ca. 1533. He most likely was one of the first, if not *the* first violin maker. In 1907, Sgarabotto repaired a very coarsely made violin with the label "Peregrino Zanetto fecit Brixiae 1532." (Brixiae, by the way, is Brescia, not Brixen or Bressanone.) Cozio also refers to him as one of the first violin makers. A "registro delle custodie" (surveillance register) of 1559–1560 refers to Zanetto's son as "Peregrinus filius Johannetti magistri a violinis." In other sources this Peregrinus (Pellegrino), detto [called] Zanetto da Montichiaro, is given as Michelis Gianetto, detto Zanetto. He died after 1607. One of his letters deals with the sale of a violin in 1552. Gambas made by him since 1547 exist, also a violin dated 1600. Its ribs are 30 mm high. The enormous length of its body approximates that of a viola.

Luca Maler (Lux Maler, Maller, Mahler), a German who worked in Bologna, enjoyed an excellent reputation but seems to have built lutes and theorbos only. Francesco Linarolo (b. ca. 1516 in Bergamo) was active in Venice. He seems to have had a hand in perfecting the violin's shape. The Musikhistorisches Museum in Vienna has a beautifully made violetta piccola labelled "Franciscus Linarolus Bergomenensis Venetiis faciebat." London's South Kensington Museum owns one of his violas dated 1563.

Giovanni Maria del Bussetto's place in the violin's early history is uncertain. He is said to have built instruments in Cremona from 1535 to 1580, and to have been Andrea Amati's teacher. The construction of his instruments made after 1560 resembles the style of Gasparo da Salò, but we do not know whether or how he was connected with him or the Brescia school.

According to instrument labels, Morglato Morella worked in Mantua and Venice between 1545 and 1602, esteemed as a maker of lutes and gambas. There is no proof that he made violins, but it is likely.

A very interesting figure in the history of violin making is Gaspard Tieffenbrucker (Duiffobruggard, Duiffoprugcar, and other spellings). For a long time, all that was known about him was that he lived in Lyon and that he built instruments of all kinds, as shown in the illustration reproduced here. Instruments by Tieffenbrucker were sold in Paris after 1827; according to their shape and manner of construction they may be the earliest preserved violins. Some are elaborately carved and painted; all are dated on labels such as "Gaspard Duiffoprugar / Bononiensis [from Bologna] / à 1515." According to Henley, eight such violins exist. The oldest, dated 1510, displays the royal crown and monogram of King Francis I of France. Another from 1511 has painted ornamentation ascribed to Leonardo da Vinci. Their sound is reminiscent of early Andrea Amati violins—so good that for many years Meerts used one of them in concerts.

Thus Tieffenbrucker acquired the reputation of being the father of the violin, and soon biographical accounts appeared. According to these he was born ca. 1480 in Bavaria; he was then active in Italy, as were famous lute makers of the same name. After his victory at Marignano in 1515, Francis I met Pope Leo V in Bologna, to ratify a concordat. There the king met Tieffenbrucker and invited him to France.

So much for what we read in numerous accounts from the nineteenth century and even later. Henry Coutagne, however, a Lyon physician, produced documentary evidence (revised and augmented in 1911 by Franz Waldner) that shed light on Tieffenbrucker's true background. He was born in 1514 in Tieffenbrugg, a small village near Füssen in Bavaria. Nothing indicates that he was active in Bologna. After an entry in the baptismal register, the first record is a Lyon customs bill for imported wine, dated 1553. Five years later he acquired French citizenship. Late in life his house was demol-

Gaspard Tieffenbrucker, engraving by Pierre Woeriot, 1562

ished during the enlargement of the city's fortifications. He received no compensation for this, which caused him financial woes. He died in Lyon in 1570. The court must have regarded him highly, for Charles IX, apparently suffering from a bad conscience, authorized a pension for his family.

Coutagne's research dispelled the legends surrounding Tieffenbrucker who, according to some labels, would have made his first instrument four years before his birth! Those early violins turned out to be forgeries by Vuillaume, who must have gloated over the success of his deception. It is strange that the royal coat of arms of 1510 did not arouse suspicion; this antedates Francis's reign. Yet on the basis of Woeriot's engraving it is quite likely that Tieffenbrucker did build violins, though there is no proof. Henley considers six of his gambas and one viola to be genuine.

Others who for a long time were credited with being inventors or perfectors of the violin are Andrea Amati, the first luthier of that family, and Gasparo da Salò. Their creations can be considered to conclude the first chapter of the violin's history. Their late instruments already represent the classic style of Italian violin making. Before we deal with these we should take note of some pictorial documents that can give us important information about the early developments.

Of special interest is the Piedmontese painter Gaudenzio Ferrari (b. ca. 1470, d. 1546). His nephew Lomazzo (*Idea del tempio della pittura*, ca. 1590) described him thus: "Born in Valdugio, he was a painter, sculptor, architect, expert on optics; a poet and a philosopher of nature. He played the lira and the lute." The musicologist Karl Geiringer was the first to call attention to his masterpiece, the cupola frescoes in the cathedral of Saronno, 22 km north of Milan. Geiringer calls them "a compendium of organology for the first half of the sixteenth century." A major Ferrari exhibit (Vercelli 1956) resulted in renewed interest in the painter, whose *oeuvre* involving musical instruments had been investigated by Emanuel Winternitz. These frescoes were commissioned in 1534 and largely completed the following year. They depict eighty-seven angels, sixty-one of whom play instruments or are part of an instrumental group. In all, fifty-six instruments are shown. Among the string instruments are several belonging to the violin family, though some of them show peculiarities of shape. One violin is being played in the third position, pizzicato; another one is highly arched. There is a viola with four strings, played in a higher position. An early cello is played with the bow held overhand and the little finger placed below.

Another painting by Ferrari is of special interest because it is reliably dated 1529. This is the altarpiece *La Madonna degli Aranci* in S. Cristoforo church in Vercelli. At the Madonna's feet a cherub plays a violin, probably having four strings, and with very typical lateral indentations and pointed corners. The neck is disproportionately long; the instrument is being played in approximately the third position; the left thumb is stopping the lowest string, something frequently seen in pictures. The strikingly elegant bow is held overhand, but the thumb is fully inserted between stick and hair. This violin, painted six years before the cupola frescoes, represents a more developed stage than that of the Saronno instruments. Winternitz believed that many apprentices helped with the giant frescoes—helpers who were not familiar with the instruments' details. An undated Ferrari sketch, *Adoration of the Magi* in Turin's Palazzo Reale, shows a violin-playing angel in almost the same pose as the one in Vercelli.

Ferrari's numerous representations of violins, including the one authenticated for 1529, suggest some conclusions. Boyden (1965) claims, "The establishment of the *latest* date that can be assigned to the emergence of the early violin has important consequences." But he fails to draw these consequences when he states,

> This date now makes it possible or even plausible that such terms as *violino*, *violon* (Fr.), and *violetta*, when found about or after 1530, may actually mean "violin," whereas previously a number of documents and treatises which used such terms in the early sixteenth century have been discounted as evidence of the existence of the violin.

Boyden adheres too closely to the year 1530. He insists that this very first experimental instrument, with a violinlike appearance, must immediately have been known to a painter of Ferrari's stature, who then at once set out to depict the entire violin family, even though no one knew how long the instrument would remain in use. This might be plausible for the Saronno frescoes, but is quite unlikely for the 1529 altarpiece. If, for such an occasion, the artist painted a violin, it is safe to assume that the instrument must already have been widely known at that time, familiar to the average churchgoer. Bessaraboff estimates that fifteen to twenty years elapsed between the instrument's first appearance and its pictorial representation. When we consider the time it took to develop a bass violin (violoncello), it seems likely that Ferrari's work documents the violin's existence before 1529, which means that it can have originated no later than 1500. Boyden's opinion, that pre-1520 documents mentioning the violin are "probably spurious," can hardly be supported.

THE RISE OF THE AMATI FAMILY

CREMONA BECOMES THE CENTER OF VIOLIN MAKING

The Amati dynasty was founded by Andrea; his brother Nicolò I, whose existence has been doubted by some, also made violins, but they are not considered to be especially valuable. A Nicolò Amati violin with a label dated 1535 (or 1532) originally had three strings. It was repaired by Gaetano Sgarabotto ca. 1920.

Accounts of Andrea's life and work somewhat resemble those of Tieffenbrucker, but they proceed in the opposite direction. Andrea's birth date was unknown; it was assumed to be between 1520 and 1535. Therefore Amati violins with dates before 1550 were at once declared to be forgeries. In 1938, on the basis of archival studies, Carlo Bonetti was able to establish with some certitude that Andrea was born in Cremona between 1500 and 1505, certainly before 1511. In a January 1580 document, the two sons Andrea and Girolamo are listed as the heirs; it is therefore likely that Andrea died in 1579 or slightly earlier. Instruments dated after 1579 may have been begun by the father and finished by the sons.

The fixing of Andrea's birth date for the years immediately after 1500 had several results. It helped to determine the authenticity of instruments; it also threw new light on the relative positions of Cremona and Brescia as centers of violin making. There is no documentary proof that violins were made in Brescia at the time Andrea took up the craft, but there is some likelihood that violin making had begun to flourish there.

Andrea came from an old Cremona family of patricians. An inheritance left him comfortably off, which must have made it easier for him to buy first-rate wood for his instruments in Venice. Giovanni Lionardo de Martinengo (b. ca. 1470) is most often mentioned as his teacher, though we know nothing precise about an apprenticeship. As early as 1526 Andrea was referred to as master; his first daughter was baptized in 1535. A violin made in 1540 is said to have reached Vuillaume by way of Tarisio; another one from 1542 was repaired by Sgarabotto in 1898. The length of its body is 334 mm; it has three strings tuned d a′ e″. Yet another violin has this label: "Andreas Amati cremonensis fecit 1546." Cozio di Salabue (*Carteggio*) described it as follows:

> Dimensions of my violin, said to be by Amati. Label reads Andrea Amatus from Cremona, 1546. Unusual shape. Neck made by Mantegazza, the father of violin makers. Originally it had only three strings. Earlier owned by Padre Vomini in S. Ambrose monastery. . . . Its sound is rather bright and even, strong, but pointed (thin) like the Amati.

One of Andrea's cellos was repaired by Darche in 1547. Other violins are dated 1549, 1551, 1561, 1562, 1563, 1564, 1566, 1570, 1572, 1574—distributed fairly evenly through his years of mastery. Nothing proves that he was in Paris in connection with an order by Charles IX to furnish twenty-four violins, six violas, and eight cellos for the court chapel, but the Ashmolean Museum has an Andrea Amati violin dated 1564 that is known to have belonged to that king. An entry in the royal account books may refer to this instrument: "27 October 1572. Nicolas Dolinet, flutist and violinist in the royal chapel, was paid 50 toursche Pfund [50 pounds in Tours currency?] for the purchase of a Cremona violin to be used in the royal chapel." A 1573 account of a concert in France by a large string orchestra makes the Amati commission credible, even if it does not authenticate Amati's stay in Paris.

Though Andrea's early instruments are in some ways reminiscent of the earlier violin type, he does seem to have brought about the instrument's standardization. Before him, the bridge was placed as it was on the viola da bracchio, where, due to the length of the vibrating string, the bridge had to have a low position. Andrea experimented, giving the bridge a higher and the *f* holes a lower position, thus in time arriving at the definitive proportions.

To judge by one of his instruments from 1565, his basic model was relatively narrow: 353 / 163 / 202 / 29 / 30. (Here and elsewhere, five numbers refer to length of body, upper bout, lower bout, upper ribs, and lower ribs, in that order.) His *f* holes are quite wide; the upper "eye" is almost as large as the lower. Thickness of the back: maximum 3.98–4.37, minimum 2.77–3.18. This corresponds to the later standard measurements. Thickness of the top: maximum 3.18, minimum 1.99–2.39. This is slightly more than those found in Stradivarius models (ca. 2.5).

Some Amati violins have been criticized for the weak tone of the G string. At the time this was not a major flaw, for the G string, because of its poor quality, was little used. Structural refinements are closely tied to intended use. For instance, as playing in the high positions became more frequent, violin makers concerned themselves chiefly with good, even tone quality from G to the highest notes on the E string, at the very end of the fingerboard. A sixteenth-century violin maker needed to consider a range of two and a half octaves at most.

In Andrea Amati's instruments the arching is even, without any scoop, almost to the rim. His early varnish was very dark; later it became yellowish brown.

The Amati family had many branches, but there may have been some builders of that name who did not belong to it. Some, such as Taronimus Amati, may never have existed; their names occur only on forged labels. There is no agreement on the actual number of Amati violin makers. Vannes lists nine; Henley seventeen! Don Nicolò is included in the genealogy offered here even though his family membership is uncertain. Dates in parentheses are taken from labels in instruments, indicating that dates of birth and death are unknown.

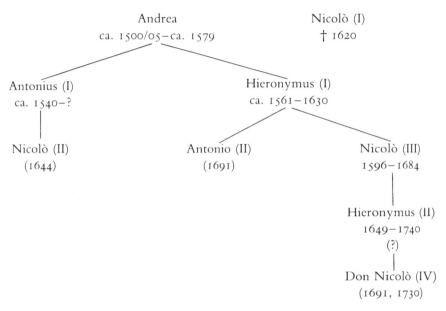

Genealogy of the Amati Family of Luthiers

Andrea's sons Antonius and Hieronymus signed some of their instruments individually, others jointly: "Antonius et Hieronymus Fr. Amati / Cremonen Andrea fil F. 15—." References to the Amati brothers always mean these two. It is extremely difficult, if not impossible, to distinguish between their violins, or to establish (if a label refers to both) who is responsible for what part of the collaboration. Quite likely, labels with both names refer to the family shop, which also included apprentices.

In their early years, both sons closely followed their father's model, especially Antonius, the older one. When the father died, Hieronymus was only eighteen or nineteen years old. The more talented son, he seems to have found it easier to free himself from his father's influence and to go his own way. Father and sons used wood of the highest quality and varnished expertly. Their model was small: Fuchs (*Taxe der Streichinstrumente*) gives 350–352 / 165 / 205–207 / 27–28 / 29–30. Antonius also used a larger model. His early violins are highly arched like his father's. Their tone is noble and sweet but no longer adequate for modern large halls.

Though the instruments of the first three Amatis show some structural differences, they sound much the same. They are rarities for collectors, but soloists no longer use them.

Both brothers built violas with substantially different dimensions:

Small model: 411 / 197 / 247 / 33 / 34
Large model: 450 / 220 / 268 / 39 / 41

This represents the old distinction between alto and tenor viola, though their tuning is identical.

Forgers were casual about dates, as evidenced by a viola d'amore in the Berlin collection. It was made in Munich in the eighteenth century and has a label that states "Antonius & Hieronymus Fr. Amati / Cremonen, Andreae fil. F. 1512." In that year their father was still a child!

GASPARO DA SALÒ AND THE EARLY BRESCIA SCHOOL

Brescia's proud citizens honored the master by erecting a monument with the inscription "GASPARO DA SALO / INVENTORE DEL VIOLINO / 1542–1609." Much ink has been spilled over that statement, with polemics supporting or disputing the claim. Rivalries between Cremona and Brescia, two cities so important in the violin's history, are to blame for much of this, as are jealousies of later generations. One positive result is that a good deal of the ensuing research brought to light new material. Certainly no one person can be considered the violin's "inventor," and the fact that Andrea Amati was thirty to forty years older than Gasparo would speak against the Brescian's priority. This is not to belittle his genius or to deny his share in developing the violin's standard form.

Gasparo Bertolotti was born 20 May 1540 in Polpenazze, a tiny hamlet belonging to the parish of Valtenes, 10 km from Salò, on Lake Como. His ancestors include many musicians and instrument makers. His birth certificate reads "Die 20 maji suprascripto [1540] Gaspar Julius et Johannes filius francisci, filius sanctini dicti violì" (On 20 May of the above year Gaspar Julius Johannes, son of Franciscus, grandson of Sanctinus, known as the violì). "Violì" is a dialect form, found in northern Italy, of "violini"; it implies that Gasparo's father, Franciscus, and grandfather, Sanctinus, were violinists or luthiers. This is all the more likely because the family lived in what was known as the "contrada violinorum" (violinists' country or region).

Gasparo received his musical training from his uncle Agostino Bertolotti, maestro di cappella at the Salò cathedral. His father probably provided first instruction in instrument making. Around 1562, Gasparo went to Brescia, to the shop of Girolamo Virchi (several spellings of the name are given by Vannes). One of Virchi's violins, labelled "1565 adi 26 agosto / Hieronimo di Vir in Brescia," is in the Milan museum. Its measurements are worth noting: 353 / 159 / 195 / 29 / 30. The distance between the two C indentations is 105 mm, making this a very slender instrument. Vannes identified four members of the Virchi family who were luthiers in Brescia. Thus the family greatly contributed to Brescia's reputation as a center of violin making.

In the 1565 baptismal certificate of his son, Gasparo is listed as "magistro," in a 1568 document as "maestro de violini." After initial financial difficulties he achieved a degree of affluence. In 1578 he opened a shop in his own house. A tax document from 1588 tells us that he purchased wood in Venice and strings in Rome. He sold many instruments to France, except for one period during the religious wars under Henry III.

Gasparo died in Brescia on 14 April 1609. His widow and his son Francesco Bertolotti, also a luthier, retired to Calvagese, an estate near Salò. She sold instruments built by Gasparo that carried dates (from 1610 to 1630), though Gasparo's own labels never included any dates. This does not mean that instruments with dates after his death are necessarily forgeries. A violin in the Berlin collection, however, with a printed label "Caspar da Salo in Brescia 1521" surely was not by him!

Gasparo's instruments are very robust. At least the early ones show little concern with symmetry or refined shapes. Many are characterized by f holes that are irregularly shaped and positioned; the right one may be thinner and placed slightly higher, while the left one points somewhat to the outside. Heron-Allen (1884) found fault with Gasparo's scrolls, saying that they reflect the generally primitive aspect of his work. This merely indicates that the master tended to neglect details that did not affect sound—details that later were important to those with a predominantly aesthetic point of view. His tops are only slightly arched; the arching begins right at the edge. For the tops he often chose wood with unusually broad grain. A very early viola, now in the Milan museum and probably built ca. 1560, is one of the first preserved violas of the modern type. Its back is made of three pieces; between two segments cut from the same wood is a broad diagonal strip of different wood. A small viola, its dimensions are 400 / 186 / 239 / 32 / 34; width at the middle, 131. It has a flat back; the C indentations are up fairly high and not deep; the f holes are irregular and clumsily cut.

Another violin in the Milan museum, probably from ca. 1570, is similar in shape to this viola, though all details are more carefully executed. The terminal curves in the f holes are large. According to Möckel and Grillet, the measurements of this violin and another one are 349 / 165 / 116 / 201 / 2.8 / 3 and 347 / 162 / 110 / 202 / 2.8 / 2.8. (Whenever six figures are given for measurements, the third one refers to the distance between the two C indentations.)

It seems that Gasparo, responding to the wishes and needs of his customers, built two types: a small instrument up to 351 mm long and a large one up to 364 mm. Arching in the earlier instruments is more pronounced than in later ones. Early f holes are narrow; later ones, wider and larger.

Though Gasparo's instruments are undated, they reveal the tremendous progress he made from his primitive beginnings to the perfection of an artist and craftsman, especially in achieving a larger tone. Even during his lifetime, his instruments were highly regarded. Many are known that carry his emblem, though a large number of these are forgeries. Vannes lists the following: twenty violins (eight or nine genuine); fifteen violas (seven genuine); four cellos (one); twelve contrabasses (five); eight gambas (four). Several of the gambas later were made into cellos or basses.

Gasparo used rather thick wood. In a violin said to date from 1580, Möckel noted the following thicknesses: middle of the back, 43; near soundpost, 41; at the upper bout, 27; lower bout, 28; corners, 25. Top, 28–30 at the bridge; 21, upper bout; 22, lower bout. A viola in the shape of a guitar, probably a very early instrument, has no bass bar, which part is found in all his other instruments. It appears that he occasionally experimented. The Ashmolean Museum has a violalike instrument with the label "Gasparo da Salò, in Brescia 1561." It lacks upper corners; the indentation for the bow flows smoothly into the upper bout. His varnish, of the best quality, is usually amber-colored, and (like Cremona varnishes) very soft: if warmed by only slight rubbing it will retain fingerprints. According to Riechers, Gasparo also applied varnish to the inside of his instruments.

With the Amatis and Gasparo da Salò we enter the age during which instruments clearly reflect the builder's personality. The medieval tradition of anonymous builders and shops now becomes a thing of the past. Increasingly instruments were regarded as unique works of art. Some were given names; they were not the mere tools of professional musicians. Amateurs and collectors displayed ever-growing interest. Some of Gasparo's instruments had their own special fates, which typifies this new state of affairs. The story of the famous "Jewel Room" violin serves as an example, even if some details may be fictional. It is said that Cardinal Aldobrandini (the later Pope Clement VIII) had commissioned it. This alone is an indication of the rapidly rising regard in which violins were held. It was beautifully decorated with an angel's head and with intaglio work reputedly by Benvenuto Cellini who, however, had died in 1571. The cardinal gave it to the Innsbruck museum, where it was kept in the treasury or jewelry room, whence its name. In 1809 it was stolen by a soldier in the French occupation army. It then found its way to Vienna, where a rich Pole named Rehatschek (Rhaczek) owned it. In his will he gave the right of first refusal to purchase to Ole Bull, the Norwegian virtuoso who had tried in vain to buy it in 1839. Bull then played it until 1842. Because of its beautiful, large tone he preferred it to his Amati and Guarneri violins. Vuillaume repaired it and adjusted it to modern measurements. In 1901, Bull's widow gave it to the museum in Bergen, on condition that it never be played again. Malicious rumors had it that the instrument in question was not the one Gasparo had made, and that at least the second part of Ole Bull's story was invented for publicity purposes. The instrument remains in the museum, a magnificent specimen that some experts attribute to Maggini. Others continue to maintain that it could very well date from 1570 to 1580. The somewhat eccentric Ole Bull absolutely worshipped it. After his concerts people often crowded into the greenroom to see it. Before he opened his violin case, however, Bull would insist that all present remove their hats!

Gasparo's choice of wood, his workmanship, his often noticeable lack of concern with aesthetic aspects, his sole interest in tone quality—all these have often been noted, as by Walter Hamma (*Meister italienischer Geigenbaukunst*):

> Most early violin makers worked on commission. Raw materials such as wood and varnish were selected according to the patron's wishes and the agreed-on fee. A generous honorarium may have inspired a maker to do his very best. In those days the raw materials were much more expensive than today; therefore cost played a more decisive role in their choice. For instance, ebony veneer was often used for the fingerboard as ebony was very expensive. Due to the high wages prevailing today, such a fingerboard would cost much more than one made of solid ebony.

Patterns or stencils were rarely used, or only for the basic shape. Free drawing and cutting was the norm, following acoustic principles as related to a particular type of wood. This led to instruments of distinctive appearance and beauty, even if the laws of symmetry were not always observed.

The violin model Gasparo developed late in life was well received by European makers. As late as 1700 Gaspar Borbon, an excellent Belgian luthier, based his work exclusively on the early Brescian model, as did Antonio Pasta (d. 1730). Soloists also thought highly of Gasparo: Ole Bull owned yet another of his instruments, and Rodolphe Kreutzer played a Gasparo. On their concert tours, Dragonetti and Bottesini, two famous contrabass virtuosos, played three-string basses by Gasparo, said to have been magnificent instruments.

Gasparo died in 1609, passing on his artistry to Maggini. The violin's sixteenth-century development had come to a close.

VIOLIN MAKING IN THE SEVENTEENTH CENTURY

THE CREMONA SCHOOL FROM NICOLÒ III AMATI TO ANTONIO STRADIVARI

When we speak of schools of violin making, such as Cremona and Brescia, we do not refer to actual schools, such as the Scuola Professionale Internazionale di Liuteria in Cremona, or the schools in Mittenwald and Brienz. Rather, we think of a group of important luthiers active at major centers of violin making—places where leading shops existed but where makers also resided who were entirely on their own or worked with only a few helpers. Such local luthiers were usually in close contact with each other, not only because there often were master–pupil relationships, but also because professional and amateur musicians tended to compare their instruments critically. In order to remain competitive, they might discuss their experiences, or at least keep an eye on each other's work. Trends of fashion may also have been a concern, as was the case with varnish colors.

All this resulted in some common characteristics among instruments made in the same town, and this justifies the term "school," if only in a loose sense. Style characteristics of a school were of course affected by the personalities of the major instrument makers and by their success as reflected in volume of sales. Further contacts were provided by membership in guildlike organizations. Establishing certified standards of proficiency for apprentices and masters also called for cooperation.

According to Vannes, twenty-four masters were active in Cremona during the seventeenth century. This does not include lesser builders who displayed good craftsmanship but worked in someone else's shop; their names are hardly known. The Amati brothers ran the leading atelier. Well set up in business by their father, they already had an excellent reputation and were swamped with commissions. Their financial solvency was of course an advantage over smaller shops when it came to buying wood, varnishes, and other supplies, as well as in preparing suitable storage and drying rooms, and in organizing their marketing. The Amati shop attracted good students and apprentices; therefore high quality was assured even with a large volume of production. Success also entailed an obligation to maintain high standards or even to raise them.

Hieronymus (d. 1630) was succeeded by his thirty-four-year-old son Nicolò (Nicola; 1596–1684), whose work represented the experience of three generations of luthiers. As his father's pupil he grew up in an ideal milieu, following his father's model until his death. A decade of experimentation and gradual improvement followed.

Only after 1640 did he affix his own labels to his instruments. A label, it would seem, did not so much signify a luthier's manual involvement; it meant that the instrument represented his own personal style. If Nicolò, between 1630 and 1640, built a violin and attached a label with his father's name, giving a date after 1630, this in no way was meant to deceive. Everyone in Cremona knew that the father had died. Rather, the label was intended to announce that the instrument was built after the father's death, but in his style.

Until 1640, Nicolò's mastery is seen chiefly in the refinement of proportions and in the steadily improving, craftsmanlike execution, all of which tended to strengthen the family tradition. Only after this period of maturation did he change his style, creating the large Amati model. It featured generally higher ribs and less arching. He also increased the top's tension by deepening the groove at the rim, the groove having been added to his father's and uncle's instruments. In this way his violins displayed a larger tone without sacrificing the timbre so typical for instruments by all members of the Amati family.

Violin by Nicolò Amati, 1660 (from Walter Hamma 1964)

With the Amati brothers (especially Nicolò), Cremona had become the leading city of violin making. In 1637 Monteverdi was asked for advice about buying a violin. He replied, "It would be easy to find violins in Brescia, but those from Cremona are far superior."

Nicolò's work is closely related to musical developments of the time. During the decades of his mastery, a massive, typically baroque style developed, especially in Rome. Its most extreme manifestation is the Salzburg Festival Mass, formerly attributed to Orazio Benevoli. It features twelve choirs and fifty-three parts. To be heard in the cavernous space of a cathedral, string instruments had to be capable of producing large volume. In the early seventeenth century numerous church orchestras were founded and existing ones enlarged. Luthiers such as Stainer responded to this specific challenge.

Nicolò Amati was even more careful than his predecessors in his selection of wood and varnishes. He also represents the tendency to build violins that not only had excellent tonal qualities but also were works of art. His instruments, especially those from 1660 to his death, represent a new standard of violin making, a standard by which violins were to be judged from then on.

Nicolò built violins in two basic sizes: medium to large, and small. The small ones were sometimes called "ladies' violins," but actually they were built mindful of the rooms in which they were to be heard. Only Nicolò's very large instruments are adequate for today's large concert halls. Their measurements, according to Fuchs, are as follows:

Medium to large model: 354–358 / 165–172 / 204–214 / 26.5–30 / 29.5–30
Small model: 352 / 162 / 202 / 28.5 / 29.5

The wording on Nicolò's labels varies. Usually it acknowledges his debt to his father and uncle:

Nicolaus Amatus Cremonen. Hieronymi Fil. ac Antonij Nepos Fecit 1679

A trend to remodeling instruments affected those of many great luthiers of the seventeenth and eighteenth centuries, including Nicolò Amati. Concerning an Amati violin, Cozio di Salabue remarked as early as 1775 that the neck was the work of another maker. Many nineteenth-century virtuosos performed on Amati violins, and often an instrument acquired the performer's name, thus we have an "Ole Bull," a "Marsick," and a "Spagnoletti." Others were given the names of collectors, such as Goding, Count de la Barre, and others. Nicolò made violas, cellos, and basses as well as violins; even one of his kits [or *pochettes*, small fiddles played by dance teachers] has been preserved. Virtuosos such as Grützmacher, Klengel, and Popper played his cellos. In 1800, Prince Carl Lichnowsky presented a complete string quartet to Beethoven consisting of one violin by Nicolò Amati, Cremona, 1690;

one violin by Giovanni Guarneri, Cremona, 1718; a viola by Vincenzo Ruggieri, Cremona, 1690; and a cello by Andrea Guarneri, Cremona, 1675. Beethoven must have heard these often in the prince's town house; they may
have influenced the sound of his op. 18 quartets, written ca. 1800.

String instruments owned by Beethoven

The Amati family tradition was carried on into the eighteenth century by
Hieronymus II (1649–1740), son of Nicolò III. The latter must have had
many apprentices. Some, among them Aegidius Barzellini and Giacomo
Gennaro (Jacobus Januarius) mentioned the master on their labels, no doubt
hoping that some of his fame might rub off on them: "Jacobus Januarius Cremonensis / Alumnus Nicolai Amati faciebat 1653." Giorgio Fraiser was one
of the pupils who had come from the Tyrol. Mathias Albani (Alban) was the
head of a large family of luthiers in Bolzano. It is an indication of Nicolò's
reputation that Mathias sent his son of the same name (1650–1715) to Cremona to perfect himself under Nicolò's tutelage. The younger Mathias later
was active in Rome and in his hometown, making excellent violins.

Two families of luthiers grew up in Cremona; their first studies were with the Amatis. These were the Ruggieris and the Bergonzis, whose instruments reveal a decidedly personal style. The founder of the former family was Francesco Ruggieri (Rugieri, Rugierius; 1655–1720), detto il Per. As Nicolò's pupil he succeeded in constructing violins with a large tone; these remain in demand by soloists. His sons Giacinto and Vincenzo also made superior violins, as did his grandson Antonio.

The Bergonzi dynasty may go back to one Francesco Bergonzi, active in Cremona during the seventeenth century. The first important luthier by this name was Carlo Bergonzi, born in Cremona in 1683. He was a pupil of Hieronymus II Amati—a "grandson pupil" of the great Nicolò. He also had studied with Josephus Guarnerius and worked with Antonius Stradivarius. Since he was active during the eighteenth century, his work will occupy us in a later chapter. Outstanding Amati pupils include Gioffredo Cappa and Paolo Grancino.

Nicolò's work as a teacher and mentor of talented young luthiers reached a high point when, ca. 1636, Andreas Guarnerius entered his shop, and when, probably more than a dozen years later, Antonius Stradivarius became his pupil.

Andreas was the oldest of a dynasty of violin makers, some of whom created true masterworks. Antonio Stradivari passed on his artistry to two of his sons; he also had other pupils. Given the many great luthiers who emerged from Nicolò Amati's shop, Cremona without a doubt became the center of violin making. Even now violinists tend to walk with awestruck reverence through the city's streets.

As the genealogy offered here indicates, five major luthiers rose out of the extended Guarneri family. Little is known about a Pietro III, and an Antonius, known from the 1722 label of a violin, probably was invented by a forger.

Like Andrea Amati, Andrea Guarneri (b. ca. 1626 in Cremona) came from a well-to-do family. His early violins are based on those of his teacher, Nicolò Amati, who at the time was still developing his own mature style. Andrea opened his own shop ca. 1655. A label from that year refers to the

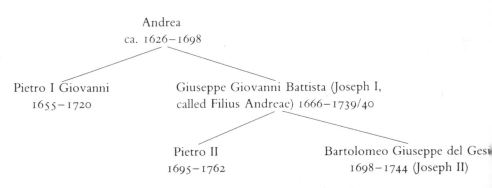

Genealogy of the Guarneri Family of Luthiers

young master as "ex alumnis Nicolai Amati." Not until the 1660s did Andrea modify his instruments, following his master's intent to gain a larger tone by reducing the arching. With this rather flat model he also inspired the next generation of builders, creating violins that could survive "battles" with the modern orchestra.

His treatment of the *f* holes reflects Andrea's concern with details that previously had been based on appearance rather than acoustical considerations. The *f* holes are very wide, but their circular ends are quite normal. The sections between these round portions and the main stem are particularly broad. Andrea evidently wished to have the largest possible opening, but to distribute it well, so that the top's ability to resonate would be minimally affected. In the process the *f* holes lost some of their elegance, but that does not seem to have bothered him. He placed the lower part of the hole very close to the lateral indentation, probably in order to widen the top's middle section (between the *f* holes) as much as possible.

From Edler 1970

According to Hill, some 250 violins, four violas, and fourteen cellos by Andrea Guarneri are extant. His labels usually read "Andreas Guarnerius fecit Cremone sub titolo Sanctae Teresiae 16—." "Sub titulo" refers to the sign hanging outside his shop; he had chosen St. Theresa as his logo. Instruments from his workshop not built by him personally have labels such as "Sub disciplina Andree Guarnerij in eius Officina sub titulo Se. Teresie, Cremone" (Made under the supervision of A. G. in his workshop under the sign of St. Theresa). This distinction, however, does not seem to apply to instruments made by his sons while they worked in his shop. Quite a few instruments with the father's labels display style features typical for the sons. Andrea's instruments differ quite a bit from each other. This could indicate that he was given to experimentation, but it may also be due to his customers' wishes. His violas and cellos remain in demand, and the Milan museum owns an outstanding contrabass made by him.

His two sons were Petrus I (b. 1655), and Josephus I (b. 1666), whose complete Italian names were Pietro Giovanni and Giuseppe Gian or Giuseppe Giovanni Battista, respectively. Both at first worked in their father's shop, but Pietro soon moved to Mantua. Their main period of violin making was in the eighteenth century.

VIOLIN MAKING IN SEVENTEENTH-CENTURY BRESCIA

Gasparo da Salò died in 1609. His reputation attracted not only pupils to his shop but also colleagues such as Giacomo (Jacope de) Lafranchini (b. ca. 1570, d. after 1630), who later assisted Maggini. For whatever reason, some co-workers did not succeed in setting up their own shops. Perhaps they did not want to risk being in business for themselves. Though they usually remained anonymous, they made important contributions to the instruments coming out of the atelier. In many cases their violins can hardly be distinguished from those made by the master.

Gasparo's favorite pupil was Giovanni Paolo Maggini (b. 1579 near Brescia, d. ca. 1630). He opened his own shop when he was twenty-nine; at the age of fifty he became a victim of the plague. His early instruments resemble those of his master. They are somewhat roughly made from wood that was not always carefully chosen. Before long he developed his own style, eventually making beautifully crafted violins with remarkable tonal qualities. His violas and cellos display the same care. He is said to have been the first to use rib lining and corner blocks, to strengthen the body. All Maggini's later violins are large and remarkably flat. Their measurements are as follows:

Larger model: 366 / 178 / 218 / 27–28 / 27–28
Smaller model: 362–363 / 168 / 208–211 / 25–28 / 25–28

According to Vannes, there are about fifty, according to Henley slightly more than seventy authentic Magginis. In the early nineteenth century his violins were little known and esteemed, but when Bériot reaped his great successes in Paris and London he played a Maggini that later was used by Léonard and Marteau, thus contributing to the artistic and commercial success of Maggini's violins.

Again one notes that a maker's concern with large sound was related to contemporary developments in music and music making. Maggini's work influenced violin making for centuries. The decade during which he achieved independence saw important musical events that affected instrument making:

1607   First performance of Monteverdi's *Orfeo*, in Mantua
1608   *Sonate a quattro, sei et otto* by Cesario Gussago (organist at S. Maria delle Grazie in Brescia), published in Venice
1610   First violin sonatas by Gian Paolo Cima (maestro di cappella in Milan), published in Venice
1617   Marini's *Affetti musicali*, op. 1, published in Venice

Might Maggini have participated in the *Orfeo* performances as an orchestra player? For such occasions, extra musicians from near and far were hired, and a violin maker was likely to play that instrument. Surely Maggini heard Gussago's music, thus learning how string instruments had to sound in large churches.

It has often been said that Maggini was influenced by the Cremona school. Quite possibly Brescia luthiers were impressed by the beautiful execution of Amati violins and imitated them. On the other hand, the excellent tonal qualities of Gasparo's and Maggini's creations left their mark on the Amatis' work. Beyond that it would be difficult to pinpoint specific details that reveal such influences.

Among the many makers in Brescia, those belonging to the older generation, including Giovita Rodiani (b. 1545), tended to follow Gasparo da Salò. Matteo Bente (Benti, Benta; b. 1580, d. ca. 1637) made outstanding violins that were still played by twentieth-century virtuosos. He may have been Gasparo's student, but he later followed Maggini's style. Tartini's favorite violin was a Bente.

Luthiers of the younger generation soon took Maggini as their model; some may have been Maggini pupils. Among these Antonio Maria Lanza, Raffaele Nella, and Giovanni Battista Bassani deserve mention; Giovanni Gaetano Pazzini was active in Florence. Some violins by Lanza (Lansa; d. 1715) reflect the Gasparo or Maggini styles. They have labels with a 1530 date. It seems that some makers considered Lanza one of the fathers of the violin. A German, Michael Eisele (Aisele; b. 1614), also worked in Brescia. Battista Vetrini (active ca. 1630) and Giovanni Maria del Bussetto (second half of the 1500s) developed styles of their own, as far as this can be determined by the small number of their instruments preserved. Bussetto first worked in Brescia, then in Cremona; he may have established a link between the two schools.

Pietro Santo, a good luthier, bought Giovanni Paolo Maggini's shop and took on the Maggini name. Because of this he was for a long time thought to be a son of the great master from Brescia.

ITALIAN SEVENTEENTH-CENTURY VIOLIN MAKERS OUTSIDE BRESCIA AND CREMONA

Boyden (*The History of Violin Playing*) supplies a geographic outline of the instrument's early history. In a region defined by Venice, Genoa, Florence, and Turin, and extended north to Switzerland, Cremona is the natural center. Most likely the violin originated in and around Milan, Brescia, and Cremona. This center of violin making expanded as word spread about the superior instruments made there. In northern Italy's leading musical centers, makers of fiddles, lutes, and viols soon turned to violin making. Quite likely some of these luthiers participated in the developmental experiments that led to the violin.

Though we no longer subscribe to the view that the violin originated in Bologna, most likely these experiments included luthiers in that city, which is only 150 km from Cremona. Music flourished at Bologna's San Petronio cathedral, and the city's famous town band, the Concerto Palatino del Senato, was imitated all over Italy.

As early as 1500, Bologna, a center of lute making, attracted instrument makers from Germany. One of them, Maler, was mentioned earlier in connection with the violin's early history. It is not certain that the gamba maker Antonio Brensio also made violins, but a viola da bracchio preserved in Bologna and made by Hieronymus Brensius may identify him as one of the city's first violin makers. Important for further developments in Bologna was Giovita Rodiani (1544–1624), who had come from Brescia. His shop had a good reputation; one document refers to him as a "fabricator a violinis." He is especially known for his violas, which represent the transition from the viola da bracchio. His style resembled Gasparo da Salò's and Maggini's, but since he was five years younger than Gasparo and thirty-six years older than Maggini he should be considered a master who established his own style, similar to Maggini's, but developed independently of him.

At the end of the seventeenth century we find lesser masters such as Giacomo Gherardi, a maker of good double basses, and Vincenzo Socchi. Giovanni Tononi, a luthier in Bologna (active 1670–1703), made violins and cellos that remain in demand. The timbre of his instruments clearly reflects concepts of the Amati family; like Rodiani's, Tononi's instruments demonstrate how Cremona and Brescia influenced violin making all over Italy. His son Carlo (1675–1730), active in Bologna and Venice, made violins that surpassed even those of his father. Carlo followed the large Amati model. Later he approached the style of Stradivari, to the extent that one of his violins from 1698 for a long time was believed to be a Strad. Instruments by members of the Tononi family are much in demand by soloists and bring high prices.

In Padua, then known chiefly as a center of lute making, many luthiers were of German origin, Wendelin Tieffenbrucker among them. Venice was famous for its flourishing musical life, at St. Mark's cathedral and in the *ospedali* (conservatories) and opera houses. There, too, outstanding lute makers resided, including five members of the Tieffenbrucker family. Bowed string instruments were also built, inspired by luthiers who had come from other cities. Dalla Corna of Brescia and Francesco Linarolo of Bergamo have already been mentioned. Francesco's son Ventura Linarolo (b. ca. 1550) and grandson Giovanni were the first major luthiers born in Venice, along with one Alessandro detto il Veneziano. A 1581 violin by Ventura Linarolo is important for the development of violin making: it does not have a bass bar, nor blocks, nor rib linings. Italian sixteenth- or seventeenth-century makers often reinforced the ribs by gluing a broad strip of cloth inside, a practice that no doubt had an adverse effect on the sound.

Whereas Venetian violin making flourished during the first half of the eighteenth century, inspired by Vivaldi, Tessarini, and other violinists, violin building in Milan developed surprisingly slowly, and the city at first relied on instruments brought in from Cremona and Brescia. The legendary Testatore supposedly lived in Milan, but the first known local luthiers were members of the Grancino family. Vannes lists nine makers of that name, but recent research has established that three alleged members (all with the first name Giovanni Battista or Giambattista) are spurious. There is only one known Giovanni Grancino (d. 1726), son of Paolo.

Giovanni was trained in Cremona. Together with his older brother Francesco he was active in Milan from ca. 1666 to ca. 1684. After that he worked alone until his death. It is known that Paolo Grancino lived in Nicolò Amati's household, but there is no proof that he made violins since no original labels exist.

The Grancino family also made good cellos. All their instruments are characterized by a large tone, though the choice of wood and details of execution reveal a certain nonchalance. Aside from the Grancinos, capable luthiers were Pietro Antonio Bellone (instruments from 1684, 1700) and a certain Santo or Santino. Eighteenth-century violin making in Milan reached its height with the instruments of the Testore, Guadagnini, and Landolfi families.

Florence was not a prominent center of violin making. Bartolomeo Cristofori (b. 1655 in Padua, d. 1731 in Florence), the famous inventor of the piano, also made string instruments including some fine cellos and basses. He was in charge of the grand duke's collection of 161 instruments, including violins by Stainer, the Amatis, and Antonio Stradivari. We do not know whether these inspired him to make violins, but he was Stradivari's friend and consulted him about the thickness of soundboards and string tensions of keyboard instruments.

Nor did violin making flourish in Rome before the eighteenth century, though Paolo Albani of Cremona had settled there. Others during the second half of the seventeenth century worked in Rome temporarily.

Violin making in Naples also developed relatively late, founded by members of the Gagliano dynasty. A romantic tale tells how the excellent violin and mandolin player Alessandro Gagliano (b. ca. 1660, d. 1725 in Naples) came to be a luthier. A member of a noble family, he had killed his opponent in a duel and had to flee. He hid in the forests, during which period he experimented with making instruments. Recognizing his gift for this, he apprenticed himself to Nicolò Amati and later to Antonio Stradivari. He returned to Naples in 1695. His violins, violas, and cellos have a beautiful tone, though craftsmanship and varnish are not always first-rate. On his labels he refers to himself as a pupil of Stradivari.

A family of luthiers named Cappa lived in Saluzzo in northern Italy. Its most distinguished member was Gioffredo Cappa (1644–1717), a pupil of Nicolò Amati in Cremona. His violins are virtually indistinguishable from those of his master, from which fact he may have derived financial advantage. More likely unscrupulous dealers sold Cappa's instruments as genuine Amatis. At any rate, he remained practically unknown until Cozio di Salabue "discovered" him. Until the late nineteenth century little was known about his life. The few violins known to be his were greatly valued by top performers such as Viotti and Pugnani. In the 1970s, a large-model Cappa might sell for 100,000 DM, while those claimed to be by Amati brought an additional 50,000 DM!

Two names should be mentioned that figure in Alberto Bachmann's study *Le violon* (Paris 1906). They are "*Acevo* (Saluzzo). 1650–1696, à Salines. Valeur de 300 à 400 fr. Élève de Cappa" and "*Sapino*. Élève de Cappa." Saluzzo, here mentioned as a person's first name, is a small town southwest of Turin. "Acevo" is the misread Italian "acero," meaning maple, found on the back of an instrument from Saluzzo. "Sapino" is the Italian word for fir. Fétis mistook these words to be the names of luthiers, an error repeated in writings by Grillet, Vidal, Bachmann, and others.

NATIONAL SCHOOLS IN EUROPE BEFORE 1700

JACOB STAINER

Before taking up the development of violin making outside of Italy we should address a question that continues to occupy lovers of the violin and to this day stirs up nationalistic sentiment: did the violin really originate in Italy? Certain references have led some to assume that the violin originated in France. In *Épitome musical*, Jambe-de-Fer describes the difference between violin and gamba, gives the tuning of the violin, and goes on to say, "The French violin, as to the manner of playing, is in no way different from the Italian violin." This could mean that two types of violins existed ca. 1556—French and Italian—a supposition supported by later references to violins "façon de Paris" and "façon italienne." In a 1523 account book at the court of the duke of Savoy, written in French, reference is made to a "vyollon," and in his *Orfeo* of 1607 Monteverdi uses the term "violini piccoli alla francese."

However, the "trompettes et vyollons" who were paid 6 scudi on 17 December 1523 came from "Verceil," that is, Vercelli, and Jambe-de-Fer's two violin types were probably just two different sizes, such as were built in Italy, especially by the Amatis. Possibly the French preferred the smaller model, easier to handle but with a smaller tone. The alto and tenor sizes of the viola da bracchio, tuned the same, may have served as models for the two sizes of violins. Vidal (1876–1878, vol. 1) thoroughly investigated the question of the French violin. "From what has been said one must conclude that Italy alone can pride itself on having transformed the viol into the violin. No other European country can seriously dispute that claim."

Leipp (*Le violon*, Paris 1965) once more took up the dispute, basing his findings on the 1562 Woeriot engraving of Tieffenbrucker. He concluded,

There is no evidence that Tieffenbrucker was the inventor of the violin, though he surely was among those who brought today's violin and its measurements into general use. The claim that the modern violin had its origin in France is given credence by the luthier from Lyon, by various implications in documents, and by Monteverdi's statement; also by remarks made by Praetorius, and by certain formal considerations.

Leipp was unaware of the results of iconographic research. His basic error consists in placing the violin's origins twenty to thirty years too late. An Italian altarpiece in which a violin is shown was painted at a time when Tieffenbrucker was still an apprentice. The decisive argument against the violin's French origin, however, is the lack of any evidence of French violin making before the mid-sixteenth century.

Instruments signed with the name Kerlino gave rise to further quarrels about the violin's national origin. Bretons claimed him because the syllable "ker" (house) is part of many Breton names. Germans declared he belonged to a Nuremberg family of luthiers named Gerle. The oldest member of that family was already well known in the fifteenth century; its most famous member was Hans Gerle, who published a treatise on instruments, *Musica Teusch* (Nuremberg 1532). The name Kerlino, then, was considered an Italian diminutive of Gerl. Others tried to explain Kerlino as "little Karl"! Eventually the belief prevailed that Kerlino, the supposed maker of the first violin, never existed, which caused the controversy to die down.

German claims even led to a book, *Der Geigenbau in Italien und sein deutscher Ursprung: Eine historische Skizze von Dr. Edmund Schebek* (Violin making in Italy and its German origin: A historical sketch by Dr. Edmund Schebek, Prague 1874). The publication attracted much attention and was translated into English in 1877. The author claimed that the decisive stage of the transition from the old viol to the violin occurred in Germany. He based his opinion on the large number of German luthiers active in Italy, on the (supposedly) German Kerlino, and on Tieffenbrucker, who was then thought to have worked in Bologna as early as 1514. There even were dubious attempts smacking of charlatanism to prove that the violin had come down from the nordic countries. In his book *Die Germanen und die Renaissance in Italien* (1905), Ludwig Woltmann derived the name Amati from Amadhilis, Guarneri from Werner, and Stradivari from Sigiwart or Tagavar!

Martinus Agricola's *Musica instrumentalis* (2d ed. Wittenberg 1545) called attention to developments in Poland. This may have led to statements by Praetorius (*Syntagma musicum*, vol. 2) about violas da bracchio being called violins or Polish fiddles because outstanding players of the violin were found there, perhaps because they had originally come from Poland.

Agricola's "Polnisch Geig" is identical with the rebec. In the early sixteenth century the word "Geige" never meant "violin." Under "viole da bracchio, Geigen," Praetorius gives the tuning g d' a' e'' for "Discant Viol. Violino." In the early seventeenth century the violin came to be called "Geige" in German-speaking regions, especially among professional musicians, but it took some time for the earlier meaning of Geige (rebec) to disappear. Around 1500 the term "Polnische Geige" meant "rebec," possibly constructed and played by Polish fiddlers in a distinctive manner.

From Italy, the violin first took hold in France, for geographic and political reasons. For one thing, the dukedom of Savoy extended to Lombardy in one direction; in the other it included the current Savoie, far beyond the Alps. It thus formed a cultural bridge between Italy and Provence. Military campaigns in northern Italy by Charles VIII, Louis XII, and Francis I had as a positive byproduct the rapid exchange of cultural achievements. The French also occupied Milan at various times and captured Brescia in 1512.

We have no information from this period about the violin in other European countries. The first references to German players of instruments belonging to the violin family come from Ulm and Worms in 1545. In 1559 one Pietro Lupo sold "cinq violons renfermés dans leur étui" to a musician sent by the town council of Utrecht. The account of this purchase includes the first known reference to a violin appraiser; the buyer had the instruments tried out by a professional violinist; his fee, including the wine consumed on this occasion, amounted to 6 pounds. There is a 1561 reference to violin playing in England. All these dates refer to documentary proof, but it is likely that violins were used several decades earlier in these and other countries.

France was the first country outside of Italy in which violin makers established themselves. Italian violinists are known to have been in the service of the French court in 1533. The important role played later by Baltazarini da Belgioioso surely inspired French luthiers to turn to the new violin. Instrument making was a well-established craft in sixteenth-century Paris. To judge by the preserved lutes and gambas, standards were high. Lesur was able to identify approximately fifty shops, all on the right bank. Luthiers, like members of other crafts and trades, customarily had their shops in the same quarter. The inventory of the estate of one of these artisans, Philippe de la Canessière (d. 1551), included "deux grans viollons" and "une violle et ung petit viollon," which might refer to two violas or cellos, a gamba, and a violin. He may have made these instruments himself or merely offered them for sale. To judge by the many accounts from the last third of the century, violin making flourished in Paris. The luthier Isaac de Bargue (d. 1599), for instance, had twenty violins in his atelier at the time of his death. The French type of instrument mentioned by Jambe-de-Fer is documented, after 1570, by at least one cello. A musician named Masnet owned, among other instruments, two cellos—one "façon de Venise," the other "façon de Paris." Seven years later a merchant ordered from the luthier Pierre Nicolas Aubry (d. 1596) four violins, "faicts à la mode de Crémone" (built in the Cremona fashion). Genuine Cremona instruments then cost three times as much as those made in Paris.

In the seventeenth century, with the support of the dukes of Lorraine, musical life flourished. Perhaps as a result, Nancy rather than Paris became the center of French violin making. The Médard family included no fewer than fifteen luthiers. It may be that the oldest Médard, a carpenter, already was a luthier, for they traditionally belonged to the woodworking trades and their guilds, as in Strasbourg. Nicolas I Médard (d. before 1628) was known as a "façonneur de violons." The family's first important luthier, said to have learned his craft in Cremona, was Henri I Médard; his 1620 marriage certificate refers to him as "faiseur de violons," and his cellos are still in demand. Henri II (b. 1629), his son, trained in Cremona and at various times was active in Turin. His brothers Antoine (1621–1678) and Nicolas II (b. 1628, d. ca. 1680) based their instruments on the Amati model. They elevated violin making in France to a level that could easily stand comparison with Italy. Labels in their instruments refer to Nancy or Paris, probably indicating that they were purveyors to the French court. An outstanding member of the family was François Médard (b. 1647 in Nancy, d. ca. 1720), probably an Amati pupil. He moved to Paris, where he was in charge of the string instruments in the orchestra of Louis XIV. Following the trend of the times and of Italian masters, he Latinized his name to Franciscus, just as Antoine's labels refer to Antonius.

Next to Nancy, the little town of Mirecourt, only 50 km away, became a center of violin making, with an emphasis on mass production. The Jacquot and Vuillaume families were the founders of this industry; they were already active in the late sixteenth and early seventeenth centuries.

String instrument making also flourished in southern Germany and the Tyrol, both qualitatively and quantitatively. The region includes the South Tyrol [now part of Italy], which at the time formed a cultural entity with the North Tyrol. Italy's vicinity was a factor, as was the availability of excellent wood suitable for instruments of the violin family. Inhabitants of this region had excelled in all kinds of carving and other woodwork for centuries.

A leading luthier north of the Alps was Jacob Stainer, born ca. 1617 in or near Absam, not far from Hall in the Tyrol. Most likely he had a thorough musical education, for he demanded that a luthier's apprentice "must first acquire some skill in violin playing, as this will be helpful and indeed necessary" in his craft (Senn 1951). Oral tradition has it that Stainer trained in Venice; other indications point to the Amati shop in Cremona, but none of this is certain. Cozio di Salabue owned one of his violins, dated 1638, that may have been made in Italy. Stainer settled in Absam ca. 1640, but he seems to have been restless and went on long journeys to Salzburg, Munich, Venice (twice), and Bolzano, frequently running afoul of the law. In his travels he may have encountered Protestant doctrine, which brought him into conflict with church authorities. During a search of his home they discovered "seditious books" and threw him into prison. The intolerance of the Counter-reformation embittered him, and he spent the last years of his life in poverty and ill health. By the time of his death in 1683 his mental health too had failed, which some considered heaven's just retribution. In his violin method Löhlein recounts, "Certain of his prejudiced countrymen held the ridiculous opinion that his excellent work was the result of a pact with the devil."

Jacob Stainer was one of the all-time greats among violin makers. His instruments resemble those of the Amati family except in some details. Henley (*Universal Dictionary*) claims that Stainer's violins were built "according to mathematical principles entirely different from those of the Amatis." They are highly arched; accordingly their tone, though noble and beautiful, is not powerful but somewhat veiled and dark—their main difference from Italian models. In Italy, since Andrea Amati, the trend had been toward increasingly large tone volume, whereas luthiers in the north preferred a gentler, gamba-like tone. This accounts for the longstanding preference, north of the Alps, for the Stainer model rather than the Guarneri/Stradivari type. Hill is probably right in relating this preference to the former gamba players, who supplied many of the younger professional violinists.

The workmanship of Stainer's instruments is outstanding. Their transparent, often amber-colored varnish equals the best in Italy. He probably knew the Italians' secret of preparing varnish and may have obtained his ingredients from Italy. A stay in Venice in 1647 lasted a year, in order, according to Senn, for Stainer to "obtain various materials needed to build the instruments he had promised for the princely court chapel (in Innsbruck)." Only the very best wood satisfied him. He allegedly collected it himself during long excursions in the mountains. For the violin's top he preferred a special variety of fir found especially in the Tyrol.

Stainer kept abreast of musical developments elsewhere, for instance through his contacts with H. I. F. v. Biber, concertmaster in Salzburg since 1670 and court kapellmeister since 1686. From 1671 to 1675 Stainer received commissions from Salzburg. The great carrying power of his instruments was well known. Correspondence from a business acquaintance who arranged the commissions makes reference to a contrabass whose "sound would fill an entire church, and could also be heard far away." Another instrument "can be heard above the sound of the full music in the Olmütz or Salzburg cathedrals."

Stainer, like all sixteenth- and seventeenth-century luthiers, made violins in several sizes. Henley mentions three, Fuchs gives the measurements for two, differing especially in the size of the lower bouts:

1658 model: 355 / 162 / 200 / 30.5 / 31
1670 model: 356 / 166 / 222 / 29 / 30

His labels are written daintily by hand:

A letter from Stainer (14 December 1678) shows how much he respected the wishes of an individual customer. The letter is addressed to the town parson in Merano, who had ordered a gamba. Since the desired dimensions had not been clearly stated, Stainer made this suggestion (quoted in

Senn 1951): "[Have] the gamba player cut out a piece of paper, showing the exact width of the fingerboard, and send it to me."

With their enchanting sound and beautiful execution, Stainer's instruments were as much in demand as the best from Italy. According to Cozio's *Carteggio*, even in the late eighteenth century Stainer violins brought prices that were higher than Nicolò Amati's and Antonio Stradivari's.

During Bach's years in Köthen, several violins, one viola, and one cello by Stainer were in use. According to his will, dated 24 September 1715, Antonio Veracini (d. 1720) owned twenty instruments, with six Stainer violins listed at the top of the inventory. During a stormy sea voyage, Francesco Maria Veracini (d. 1768) is said to have lost two Stainer violins that he had christened "St. Peter" and "St. Paul." Geminiani, since 1714 England's foremost violinist, played a Stainer instrument as did, from time to time, Tartini. In 1786 Mozart is said to have been presented a 1656 Stainer by Prince Lobkowitz. Aside from violins Stainer made excellent violas, cellos, and gambas. The Lobkowitz collection included a contrabass.

A Stainer violin inspired the Abbé Sibire (*La chélonomie*, 1806) to pen a poetic hymn of praise:

If, during a hard day's work, I need some diversion . . . I turn to my violins. . . . On a bright, sunny day I derive greatest pleasure from an excellent Cremona instrument . . . , but in the deep stillness of the night . . . I turn to the splendid Stainer. The tone bursts forth and rises up to the shining stars. I imagine that they hear me, and I am proud to have these millions of other worlds listen to me. . . . This is how much power . . . this magic, heavenly instrument has over me.

Soon after Stainer's death prices for his violins rose steeply. For a long time they exceeded those of the best Italian instruments. The *Musikalische Korrespondenz* of 1791 relates a charming story about the purchase of a Stainer. Count Wenzel von Trautmannsdorf, master of the stud farm for Emperor Charles VI, had tried unsuccessfully to purchase an Italian violin for his concertmaster.

One day an elderly man called on the count. He played so beautifully on a Stainer violin that the distinguished guests and connoisseurs soon forgot all about Cremona violins.

The count immediately resolved to buy this violin and interrupted the player. Thinking that his playing did not please his audience, the man became quite agitated. The count tried to calm him down and explained that he would like to buy the instrument, to which the player replied that losing his violin would be the end of his art and his good fortune; he would not know how to support himself without it.

Upon this the count at once paid him 50 ducats for his performance, and then made the following agreement with him: he would receive 300 florins for the violin, also a yearly supply of clothing, free

Violin by Jacob Stainer, 1682, probably his last instrument
(Innsbruck, Museum Ferdinandeum)

room and board including a jug of wine every day, two extra barrels of beer, and fuel for lighting and heating. He also would be paid 10 florins a month, and would receive every year six bushels of grain and as many rabbits as he could use in his kitchen.

Since the old man lived another sixteen years, the price of the violin came to 8733 florins and 20 farthings! In the eighteenth century, a convent in Innsbruck acquired a Stainer violin in exchange for a chalice worth 100 ducats!

Even during Stainer's lifetime, his instruments were much in demand. They were found everywhere, played by concertmasters in the orchestras of nobility and in cathedrals. As a result, his violins became the models adapted by countless other luthiers, especially in Austria, Germany, and England. The labels in many of these instruments included the name Stainer, a reference to the model only; this practice resulted in a flood of "genuine" Stainer violins, far more than the master could possibly have built in a lifetime. At that he was most industrious, completing some twenty-two instruments in a year.

Genuine Stainers, however, are now rare. Not even experts can always distinguish them from very fine copies. His instruments were subjected to the same deplorable practice that ruined so many others: attempts to improve their sound by thinning portions of both top and back. As a result, according to Drögemeyer (*Die Geige*), "Nothing but a delicate shell remained; the instrument's soul had been destroyed."

Though he had no immediate pupils, Stainer inspired violin making in the Bavarian and Austrian Alps. The name Markus Stainer, allegedly a brother, is found on the labels of good instruments, with the place names Kufstein and Lauffen. It is unlikely that he existed. The name of the only known brother was Matthias; he did not make instruments. Mathias Albani (d. 1712) of Bolzano belonged to the Tyrol school of luthiers. He worked independently of Stainer but may have been a pupil of Georg II Seelos.

The region around Füssen was of special significance for instrument making as the home of the highly talented Tieffenbrucker family, whose members then moved on to many places. In 1562 the Füssen luthiers formed a guild and agreed to require a five-year apprenticeship. The names of many of these makers are known, but only a few remained in Füssen. Georg Seelos (d. 1672) worked in Innsbruck, while the Fichtl (Viechtl) family (twenty-five members are listed by Vannes) dispersed throughout southern Germany. Many Füssen luthiers were attracted to Vienna, which at that time had few violin shops. Eight luthiers from Füssen settled there in the seventeenth century, including three Hollmayer brothers, Martin Fichtl (the founder of the family's Vienna branch), and Mathias and Johann Jakob Fux (brothers who adopted the Stainer model and reached the position of court luthiers). Nikolaus Leidolf, an excellent craftsman trained in Italy, later acquired Viennese citizenship.

Michael Fichtl may have lived off and on in Mittenwald, where he inspired local makers, but the real founder of violin making in that city was Mathias Klotz (b. 1652), who was variously claimed to be an Amati or Stainer pupil. He was apprenticed to Johann Railich from 1672 to 1678, at the Bottega di Lautaro al Santo in Padua. In 1683 he settled in his hometown of Mittenwald, where he died in 1743. His violins resemble Stainer's more than Amati's. They are beautifully crafted from the finest wood. Unfortunately Klotz used a type of glue that greatly reduced the wood's ability to vibrate. Möckel claims that once the layer of varnish has been rubbed off, the glue foundation will peel off. The Klotz family had many branches. Eight generations of luthiers with thirty-six members are known after Mathias.

The Low Countries (today's Belgium and Holland) had close musical ties to Italy, resulting in superior string instrument building: gambas at first, then also violins. It was an affluent region that supported painters and architects as well as luthiers, whose work depended on commissions from wealthy customers. Amsterdam was a center of musical activity. The earliest known local luthier was Gerrit Menslagen (d. 1670). His brother-in-law Jan Boumeester (d. 1681), considered one of Holland's best violin makers of any period, used the Amati model and varnished expertly; his fishbone inlay is a regional characteristic. Hendrick Jacobs (d. 1699) was another outstanding Amsterdam luthier whose varnish equals that of his Italian models; Möller relates that he pasted Amati labels in his violins, not with fraudulent intent but as a sign of veneration for the master. Other Amsterdam luthiers include Willem van der Sijde (Syde, Zeyden; d. 1710), who at first worked in The Hague, and Cornelis Kleynman (Kleinmann; d. 1699). Antwerp makers were Matthijs Hofmans (d. 1691) and Joannes Baptista van der Slaghmeulen (d. ca. 1700); their instruments represent the finest Italian tradition. Members of the Hendrick family worked in Ghent; the father, Willems I, died ca. 1700. Hendrick Aerninck (d. after 1701) was active in Leyden, having moved there from Westphalia.

The English fondness for the gamba can be related to the tradition of fine viol making there. During the sixteenth century and even later, good violins were imported from Italy. Thomas Lupo, an Italian, became "composer for the violins," testifying to a strong Italian influence. When a local tradition of violin making finally developed in England, the Stainer model was preferred, perhaps because its timbre resembled that of the gamba. It may also have been due to the influence of Jacob Raymann, a luthier from the Tyrol, who worked in London until 1650. The first important native London luthiers were Christopher Wise (d. ca. 1680) and Thomas Urquhart (d. 1680). Both used Stainer violins as their model. The violins of Richard Meares, who opened a London shop in 1676, are closer to the Maggini type.

ITALIAN VIOLIN MAKING
IN THE EIGHTEENTH CENTURY

ANTONIUS STRADIVARIUS AND
JOSEPHUS GUARNERIUS DEL GESÙ

The development of seventeenth-century music is characterized by an increase of instrumental music formerly inconceivable. At the century's beginning the vocal madrigal was a major type of secular music. The instrumental sonata and concerto grosso emerged as the century progressed. Composers of violin music such as Corelli, Torelli, and Vivaldi were active at the century's end, and the solo concerto achieved greatest popularity. These developments chiefly took place in Italy. Other Europeans received and developed further what Italy had offered. Whoever wanted to amount to anything in music had to study there to become acquainted with the innovations in instrumental music.

The violin, at first used for "mommeries" and "noces," and long despised by aristocrats, soon became the instrument that carried this development forward. Since ca. 1700, dozens of concerti grossi and trio sonatas were issued by publishers such as Roger in Amsterdam—able businessmen who soon recognized the demand for this music. It was heard not only in palaces and churches but also in the collegia musica of students and middle-class citizens, and in many homes.

All this activity created a need for instruments. Production had increased even during the seventeenth century, but after 1700 the demand was such that making string instruments became a flourishing enterprise. Makers could barely keep up with the demand. Superior instruments were needed for solo players in solo concerto and concerto grosso, good ones for ripieno players in the orchestras, and cheap ones for beginners. This is the age when centers of violin making developed, utilizing new methods of industrial production including division of labor.

Italy continued to excel in making high-quality instruments. Many Italian concertmasters held leading positions in the orchestras of princes and other noblemen all over Europe, and most brought along instruments from Cremona and Brescia. But these two centers were not able to keep up with the new demand, and other cities on that peninsula helped fill the gap. Venice entered the picture with the establishment of Petrus II Guarnerius (1695–1762) of Cremona ca. 1723. His instruments do not currently bring the same prices as those of his younger brother, but because of their outstanding tonal qualities they are much in demand by soloists. Santo Seraphin (d. ca. 1755) had come to Venice from Udine in 1717. He intended to study painting but turned to violin making, taking Nicolò Amati's and Stainer's violins as models. His nephew Giorgio Seraphin also worked in Venice, building fine instruments ca. 1750. The brothers Antonio, Francesco, and Matteo Gofriller probably had come from the South Tyrol. Matteo (d. 1742) was the best of the three. He tried to combine Stainer's style with Stradivari's. Francesco

Gobetti (d. 1749) probably learned his craft in Stradivari's shop. His instruments reflected Stradivari's influence before he developed an entirely personal style.

Domenico Montagnana (d. ca. 1750) was probably the outstanding Venetian luthier. As an Amati pupil he may also have had personal contact with Stradivari. His large violins and especially his cellos are still much sought after. The instruments of two able luthiers, probable brothers by the name of Deconet, are increasingly appreciated. Giovanni Battista Deconet (Deconetti; d. 1762) worked in Venice, and a Michel (Michele) Deconet was active in Venice and Padua; some writers thought them to be two different luthiers. Deconet instruments, built in the best Cremona manner, have easily been sold as works by Stradivari or Guarneri.

Bologna was the home of Don Nicolò Amati (d. ca. 1740), a priest who made violins. It is unlikely that he belonged to the famous dynasty. Members of the Guidante and Tononi families also worked in Bologna. Giovanni Guidante (Guidantus; d. 1741) was the most distinguished luthier in that family. Among the Tononis, Felice (d. 1718), his son Giovanni (d. 1740), and his grandson Carlo Antonio (d. 1730) were well known for their fine violins and cellos. [Bachmann 1925 gives Carlo Antonio's dates as 1721–1768. *Ed.*] Carlo Antonio later settled in Venice.

Four luthiers named Gabrielli and five named Carcassi made good to excellent violins in Florence. Giovanni Battista Gabrielli (d. 1787), the best-known member of his family, was given to experimentation. His best instruments are surprisingly small; one has the following dimensions: 347 / 163 / 115 / 202 / 30 / 30. Most highly regarded were the violins made by the brothers Lorenzo (d. 1776) and Tomaso Carcassi (d. ca. 1786). Sometimes their instruments are signed individually; sometimes they are signed with both names, or simply "Carcassi," probably meaning that they were built by both. We have reached the stage in violin making when it became important to some owners to have their violins repaired by a master luthier, and we therefore also find such labels as "Ristorato de me Lorenzo Carcassi / dalla Madonna de Ricci in / Firenze 17—."

Talent for violin making often seems to have been inherited, so that many dynasties of luthiers emerged. Heredity, constant involvement with the field, and experience gained while young—these were important prerequisites for excellence. The most remarkable example of such continuity is the Gagliano family in Naples. It can be traced back to Alessandro Gagliano (b. ca. 1660), whose offspring are still active participants in violin making. Their family tree includes six generations of luthiers, including the present firm of Vincenzo Gagliano e Figlio. It is not enough to own a Gagliano; now one must know the maker's first name! That, however, is often difficult if the original label no longer exists. Moreover, many instruments were built cooperatively by workers in the same shop.

Outstanding members of the family (as reflected in current prices for their violins) were Nicola I and Gennaro, but the high level of workmanship carried over to the next generation. Gradually, however, industrial methods

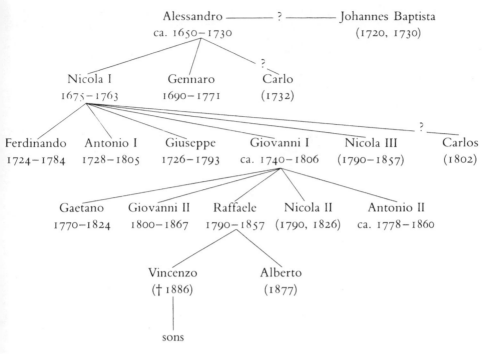

Alessandro ——— ? ——— Johannes Baptista
ca. 1650–1730   (1720, 1730)

Nicola I   Gennaro   Carlo
1675–1763   1690–1771   (1732)

Ferdinando   Antonio I   Giuseppe   Giovanni I   Nicola III   Carlos
1724–1784   1728–1805   1726–1793   ca. 1740–1806 (1790–1857)   (1802)

Gaetano   Giovanni II   Raffaele   Nicola II   Antonio II
1770–1824   1800–1867   1790–1857   (1790, 1826)   ca. 1778–1860

Vincenzo   Alberto
(† 1886)   (1877)

sons

Genealogy of the Gagliano Family of Luthiers

were introduced. Giuseppe and Antonio I often worked separately, but labels in the violins they sold read "Joseph et Antonius / Gagliani filii Nicolaj et Nepotes januarj F. Neap. 17—." Instruments produced by members of the fourth generation, while still retaining characteristics of the family, were labeled "Fabbrica di Violini, ed altri strumenti / armonici dei Fratelli Giuseppe / ed Antonio Gagliano Napoli 18— / Strada Cerriglio num. 37."

Members of the Neapolitan Vinaccia family (Henley lists eight luthiers) were mostly active in the second half of the eighteenth century. Instruments by Gennaro Vinaccia (d. 1778) are most highly regarded.

Many luthiers worked in eighteenth-century Rome, but except for David Techler (b. 1666, d. ca. 1743) of Salzburg, who was also active in Venice, few were of significance. Violin making in Milan, however, flourished due to the Grancino, Guadagnini, Landolfi, and Testore families. Their instruments are much in demand. Whoever wants to buy a Grancino should look for one by Giovanni (d. ca. 1726), Paolo's younger son, who was also active in Ferrara. His violins and cellos have a big tone that carries well. Virtuosos esteem them as much as the best of the Guarneri and Stradivari families. Giovanni Grancino's school produced Carlo Giuseppe Testore (d. 1737) and his sons Carlo Antonio (d. 1765) and Paolo Antonio (d. 1760). Noted luthiers at the end of the century were Carlo Ferdinando Landolfi (d. after 1788) and his son Pietro Antonio (d. ca. 1800).

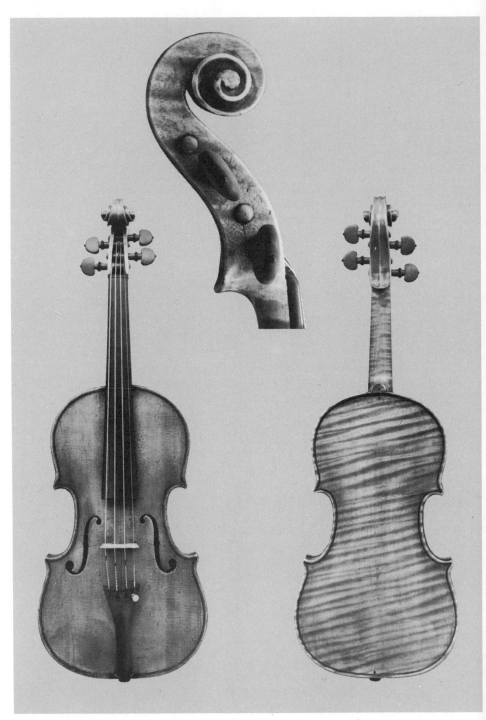

Violin by G. B. Guadagnini, Milan 1758, owned by Vieuxtemps and Suk
(photo: Archiv Hamma, Stuttgart)

Members of the Guadagnini family (Vannes lists sixteen) were active throughout northern Italy and abroad. The last descendant-luthier died as a soldier in 1942. The clan goes back to Lorenzo I (b. 1695, probably in Piacenza). A Stradivari pupil, he set up his own shop in Cremona. His son Giovanni Battista (d. 1786), also apprenticed to Stradivari, was the most renowned luthier in the family. He led a restless, vagabond existence, working in Piacenza, Milan, Cremona, and Parma before settling in Turin, where Count Cozio di Salabue became his benefactor. The count acquired all instruments that Giovanni Battista did not sell, so that at his death he owned fifty-one instruments by G. B. Guadagnini.

The wording on most of his labels is "Joannes Baptista, filius Laurentii Guadagnini," often adding "alumnus Antonii Stradivari." Like their father, his sons Giuseppe I, Gaetano, and Lorenzo II traveled widely, working in Cremona, Parma, Como, Milan, Turin, and Pavia. A nephew, Giacchino, ventured as far as Paris.

Members of the Gragnani family in Livorno built instruments of outstanding tonal quality, though at times the workmanship was very careless. Antonio Gragnani (d. 1794), the family's best luthier, made violins that are increasingly in demand by current concert artists.

In the eighteenth century Brescia did not sustain the reputation that had been established by Gasparo da Salò and Maggini. Among the lesser makers working there, only Giovanni Battista Rogeri (b. ca. 1650, d. ca. 1730) and his son Pietro Giacomo (d. ca. 1735) stood out. The father, from Bologna originally, became a Nicolò Amati pupil and settled in Brescia ca. 1670, where he lived until his death. His well-crafted instruments have such labels as "Io: Bapt. Rogerius Bon. Nicolai Amati / de Cremona alumnus Brixiae fecit, Anno Domini 16—." His son also came from the Amati workshop. His violas, cellos, and basses are now even more in demand than his violins.

The instruments of the Guarneri and Stradivari families represent the very apex of violin making, not only in Italy. Their artistry represents the sum total of two centuries of careful development and experimentation. Writers have exaggerated the contrast between the Brescia and Cremona schools, but luthiers of the two families were above any local patriotism. They accepted and adopted everything they deemed good, regardless of origin.

Petrus I Guarnerius (d. 1720), Andrea's son, went to Mantua, where he was also employed as an excellent violinist and violist in the court chapel. Andrea's grandson, Petrus II Guarnerius (d. 1762), settled in Venice. This moving on to other cities is quite typical for the younger generation of Cremona luthiers. Since that city supplied a surplus of good instruments, it seemed wise to look for opportunities in other towns with an active musical life.

Petrus I, who collaborated on instruments in his father's shop until his twenty-third year, developed a personal style quite early. But it seems that he did not get along too well with his father, which explains his moving to Mantua. He was given to experimentation; he made a viola without corners, shaped somewhat like a guitar, and some of his instruments have surprisingly broad lower bouts. They are highly arched (a Stainer influence, perhaps); on the other hand, the grooving is deeper. The tone is beautiful but small, approximating the Amati timbre. Later in his career he again strove for a larger sound. Since violin making was only his second profession, Petrus I built few instruments—fifty at most, according to Hill.

Josephus I Guarnerius, eleven years younger than his brother, took over his father's shop. He died in Cremona in 1739 or 1740, aged seventy-three. He too followed the father's model before developing a personal style. In some ways it corresponds to his brother's style; other violins, less arched, are closer to the Strad shape. At times he seems to have copied the large Strad model. Instruments by Josephus I are distinguished by very fine varnish.

Violins signed by a Caterina Guarnerius exist, the first known woman luthier. She may have been a daughter of Andrea, or perhaps she was Caterina Sussagni, wife of Petrus I or Josephus II.

Magnificent as they are, the instruments by Andrea Guarneri and his two sons are overshadowed by those of his grandson Josephus II (Bartolomeo Giuseppe; 1698–1744), called "del Gesù" (of Jesus) because he marked his labels with a cross and the letters IHS: Iesus hominum salvator (Jesus, savior of mankind). He did this to distinguish them from those made by his father, Josephus I. Some sources give a different birth date, the discrepancy arising from the fact that an uncle had four sons, all of whom died in infancy and all baptized Giuseppe. Del Gesù learned his craft from his father before beginning to work on his own in 1722. According to Hill, his first preserved violin is dated 1726. The younger Carlo Bergonzi (d. 1838) claimed that according to an oral tradition Josephus II was lazy, careless, and fond of drinking. Stories that he had committed a murder and was incarcerated for a long time may be pure fantasy.

Joſeph Guarnerius fecit ✠
Cremonæ anno 1 7   IHS

His period of mastery lasted only two decades, which suggests that in all he made only around two hundred violins. Dissatisfied with the usual models, he experimented a good deal, especially with Gasparo da Salò's type of violin. Many of his creations show less than elegant execution; Möller even speaks of a "lack of craftsmanship." Quite a few of his instruments, however, show formal perfection and indeed artistry. Eager to obtain the largest possible sound he crafted instruments that were very flat with an unusually thick (up to 5.8 mm) back. This caused them to respond rather slowly, which in turn prompted others to modify his instruments, reducing the thickness in order to achieve a better balance between volume and response. Felice Manelli specialized in this procedure; in 1805 Cozio di Salabue referred to him as "raggiustatore di strumenti" (adjuster or improver of instruments).

Abbé Antoine Sibire (1806) expressed with disarming openness the then-prevailing opinion about Josephus del Gesù violins. Asked what he would do if given a Josephus and a Petrus Guarnerius, he declared,

I would at once remove the top of both and treat each according to its own construction. At first I would remove the Josephus's bass bar, to make the instrument thinner. . . . Since the middle portions of top and back are just right I would leave them as they are, but I would ruthlessly modify the eight lateral parts, reducing their thickness to exactly that of the top's middle. This would make the violin speak more easily, and the surplus wood would be replaced by air, resulting in maximal volume in the low register. Though working on a Guarneri, I would gain a Strad. In this way, I believe, the student's work would resemble that of the master—a 100 percent improvement.

Sibire was an avid collector, but as a luthier he was a complete dilettante. He did, however, write his book *La chélonomie* in close cooperation with the famous French luthier Nicolas Lupot. Sibire's remarks about del Gesù's instruments represent those generally held by professionals.

Josephus II chose his wood according to acoustical rather than aesthetic considerations. These also account for the elegance of his famous *f* holes, said to be Gothic in style. The main stem, placed at a slight angle, becomes quite thin at both ends and terminates in relatively small round holes. This represents an ideal solution to an old problem: to have the largest opening, for the sound, with only minimal interference with the vibration of the instrument's top. In instruments by Josephus II, *f* holes are at times irregularly shaped and placed, evidence of his tendency to experiment.

To those used to the sounds of Amati and Stainer violins, the tone of a del Gesù must have seemed barbaric. Paganini played a del Gesù; he called it his "Cannon." Even those that were rebuilt were not favored by amateurs for a long time. This led to the widely held belief that Josephus II (and others) were far ahead of their time, inspired by visions of sound that were only gradually understood and appreciated. On the other hand, as Walter Hamma (*Meister italienischer Geigenbaukunst*) tells us, "From the beginning his violins were preferred by musicians. This is why among those preserved we count many that have seen heavy use, whereas Stradivari worked more for the nobility and wealthy patricians."

Del Gesù developed his "cannon" type of violin from ca. 1726 to 1736. This is the period during which the solo violin concerto of the Torelli and Vivaldi type was perfected, inspiring widespread imitation by European composers. In concerts with orchestra in the Venetian *ospedali*, a soloist had to be able to hold his own in a large hall, above a tutti of thirty to forty instruments; on major holidays the orchestra at the San Petronio cathedral in Bologna was even larger.

The drastic changes in Italian violin making in the early eighteenth century thus were related to concrete musical considerations. For music making in a smaller, family setting, instruments with a less penetrating, more flutelike tone continued to be preferred—instruments that sounded well when combined with gamba, harpsichord, and theorbo. Among well-known virtuosos of the late eighteenth century, Viotti was the first to play a del Gesù. He

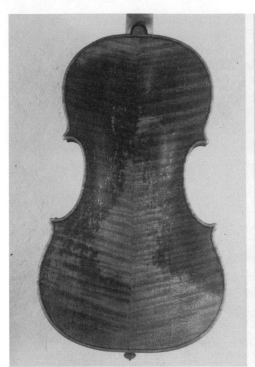

"The most beautiful del Gesù," according to both Charles Reade and
Fridolin Hamma (Germany, private collection)

gave this instrument, made in 1735, to his pupil Baillot; it changed owners
several times and is now in the United States. Luthiers of the time were reluctant to adopt Guarnerius as their model. The first known Guarneri copy outside of Italy was made by Lupot in 1806. During his triumphant concert
tours through Europe, Paganini played a del Gesù built during the master's
last years, which led to a general acceptance of his instruments and to a rapid
increase in prices. In Vuillaume's youth they rose in price, fetching from
1200 to 6000 francs. After Paganini's death in 1840, his del Gesù was kept
under lock and key, with orders that it must never be heard again. As Henley put it, it was "sentenced in 1850 to lifelong incarceration in the Genoa
museum."

Vieuxtemps called his Guarneri his "battle steed." He had bought it in
1846 from Baron Peragra in Vienna, and he preferred it to both of his Strads
and to his Maggini. The poet Nikolaus Lenau also was the proud owner of
a Guarnerius del Gesù. The times, however, when great virtuosos enchanted
their public with the sound of a del Gesù have gradually come to an end.
Among these artists were Alard, Alday, Auer, Bull, David, Heifetz, Huberman, Kreisler, Kubelik, Lipinski, Mayseder, Paganini, Pugnani, Reményi,
Rode, and Spohr. Gradually all these fine instruments are finding private

owners, who keep these precious investments in a safe. At times wealthy amateurs may scratch away on them. It does happen that a rich owner will put such an instrument at the disposal of a soloist, on a long-term basis. Thus ca. 1900, the Wittgenstein family in Vienna bought the famous "Bazzini" of 1742 in order to loan it to the virtuosa Maria Soldat. If such instruments appear on the market, they easily bring prices of 500,000 DM or more, as of 1982. Needless to say, few professional violinists can compete with collectors in purchasing power. The Hill brothers knew of 147 del Gesù violins and suspected that an additional thirty to forty may have existed. Of one hundred Guarneri labels they had seen, sixty were genuine.

Josephus Guarnerius del Gesù was somewhat of a genius, restless and unpredictable. He accomplished his most significant work within a short stretch of years. But Antonius Stradivarius (Stradivari in Italian, sometimes Stradiverti in documents) developed and matured slowly, so that he actually represented two ages of violin making. The year of his birth is unknown, as are details about his youth. He came from a fine Cremona family that traced its ancestors back to the twelfth century. Such longevity may have been due to the family having left the city at the time when the plague claimed two-thirds of Cremona's inhabitants. Some say that Antonio was born in Bergamo. For a long time his year of birth was calculated to have been 1644, for on the label of a violin from 1727 Stradivari noted "fatto di Anni 83" (made at the age of eighty-three). According to more recent research the correct year is 1648 or 1649.

Antonio was the family's first luthier. According to tradition he was a carpenter's apprentice who worked for Nicolò Amati in his spare time. His first known violins have such labels as "Antonius Stradivarius Cremonensis Alumnus / Nicolai Amati, Faciebat Anno 16—." The Hill brothers in Paris had one such violin, dated 1666; Cozio di Salabue knew one from 1665, and Henley mentions a 1664 instrument. Chanot-Chardon saw a label that read "fatto all'età di tredici anni nella bottega di Nicolò Amati" (made at the age of thirteen in Nicolò Amati's shop).

In his formative years Antonio closely followed the smaller model of his probable teacher. Several patterns or stencils that had belonged to Nicolò Amati were found in Stradivari's estate. The term "amatisé" has been applied to Stradivari's instruments from these early years up to ca. 1685. Only after that, when he was more than forty years old, did he begin to question the traditional concepts of sound and shape, apparently because he was dissatisfied with the beautiful but rather small tone of the earlier instruments. Cellos from before 1700 have surprisingly thin ribs, reinforced on the inside with glued-on strips of cloth. These instruments did not speak readily and their tone was uneven. Later the strips of cloth were replaced by rib lining. Violins from this decade of experimentation are longer and less arched; their upper and lower bouts are broader. Cozio di Salabue described a 1684 Strad as "forma grandissima, finora ignota" (very large, a previously unknown shape). For a 1691 violin Hill gave the measurements 362 / 201 / 170 / 32 / 30, which comes close to the Maggini model that Stradivari apparently examined closely at this time. While Amati used archings of up to 20 mm, Stradivari reduced these to 14–15 mm, thus achieving a considerably larger tone. Fuhr explained this very simply: "A flat back vibrates more easily than a highly arched one."

The top's dimensions also contributed to the big tone. The area near the bridge was up to 2.5 mm thick, that near the edge at least 3 mm. At the time, other makers used the opposite proportions: up to 4 mm near the upper bout, no more than 2 mm near the edge. From 1695 to 1698 he abandoned these extremes, and the typical Strad emerged in which a large and beautiful tone went hand in hand with superior craftsmanship. That Stradivari carved everything freehand is shown by slight irregularities in his instruments, as in the right *f* hole's being at times placed somewhat higher than the left. Only in instruments dating from after ca. 1725–1730 do we notice the aging master's hands gradually losing their steadiness; though the tone quality remains excellent, the workmanship is somewhat less precise. In the famous "Habeneck" Strad of 1736, for instance, the right *f* hole is placed considerably higher than the left. Four violins from the master's last years have been preserved; the one thought to be his last has been given the name "Swan Song." Stradivari died on 18 December 1737, more than ninety years old.

His grave has not been preserved. The San Domenico church in which the family vault was located was demolished in 1869. No one thought it necessary to move the master's remains to another gravesite and to mark it properly. At the time, Cremona's town council apparently was unaware that the fame of Stradivari's instruments was worldwide.

It is unclear whether Stradivari's many experiments with different sizes were based on acoustical considerations or whether he was simply fond of experimenting. Vannes said, "Stradivari, enthusiastic about violins from the Brescia school, created the longer model generally referred to as Longuet." Even if the reference to Brescia is correct, it does not explain why Stradivari developed such a large instrument, up to 362 mm long. Leipp (*Essai sur la lutherie*), one of the few who related the experimental instruments of the 1690s to musical developments of the time, said, "It is to Stradivari's credit that he adapted his instruments to the requirements of orchestral music and of modern virtuosity. No doubt he had the advice of instrumentalists and virtuosos."

What were these requirements, and who were the virtuosos? At the end of the century in northern Italy, music at St. Mark's cathedral in Venice set an example, as did San Petronio in Bologna. The distances of the two cities from Cremona are 180 km and 120 km respectively. In Bologna, leading performers included Antonii, Cazzati, Colonna, Gabrielli, Laurenti, Perti, Torelli, and Vitali. Most of them composed music for their instruments. It was the time of the solo concerto's emergence, resulting in sound requirements beyond the capabilities of instruments of the Amati and Stainer types. Might Torelli and his colleagues have journeyed to Cremona and talked with Stradivari about their needs? It is obvious that changes in music then coincided with changes in instrument making. The violinist Gasparo Visconti, born in Cremona, is said to have advised Stradivari. In 1715 Volumier, concertmaster in Saxony, spent three months in Cremona waiting to receive instruments ordered by his employer. Quite likely similar conversations between luthier and virtuoso then took place.

There is no agreement about the number of instruments Stradivari made, or about how many still exist. Riechers believes that three thousand violins issued from his atelier, which does not mean that they were all entirely made by him. That number undoubtedly is too high. Henley based his estimates on seventy productive years, with about twenty instruments per year. Subtracting time for holidays, illnesses and so on, he arrived at a figure of about a thousand. Hill's calculations came to 1116 instruments. Twelve hundred is the most commonly mentioned figure, of which six hundred are violins, twelve violas, and fifty cellos. There are no string basses, but several other instruments, including a harp and four guitars, are thought to have been preserved. Stradivari also made a *pochette* for which the composer Clapisson wrote a gavotte, used in his 1858 opera *Les trois Nicolas*.

Just how many instruments carrying the name Stradivari are authentic is another question. Doring (*How Many Strads?*) accounts for 509 registered instruments. Henley lists only four hundred violins, sixteen violas, and thirty-nine cellos. The Hill brothers knew of six hundred instruments and believed that another hundred existed.

Needless to say, Stradivari's instruments have been thoroughly studied and their exact measurements noted. Vannes's detailed tabulations do not reveal a clear line of development. Evidently the master experimented at all times with different forms. Hill refers to another problem regarding chronology: the year given on a label is not always the date the instrument was made but may indicate the year it was sold.

Vannes gives a few of the extreme dimensions:

Length: 350 (1667, 1677), 362 (1693, 1699); the average length is ca. 360 (1708, 1711, 1718, 1732, 1734).
Width (upper bout): 160 (1667), 172 (1679); a width of 170–171 is more frequently found (1704, 1707, 1708, 1710, 1711, 1714, 1718, 1732, 1734) than widths ca. 160.
Width (lower bout): 183 (1667), 213 (1679).
Height of the ribs (upper bout): 28 (1677) to 32 (twice in 1734); the average is 30.
Height of the ribs (lower bout): 30–31 at all times, except 32 (one instrument in 1699) and 33 (once in 1734).

Möckel examined eighteen violins from 1672 to 1736 and found that the top's thickness varied from 1.98 to 3.17.

Are there specific timbres that can be associated with Guarneri's and Stradivari's instruments? Möckel denies this. Each used several different kinds of wood, so that instruments by the same luthier vary greatly in tone quality. Some claim there are Guarneri violins that sound like typical Strads and vice versa. Concerning the manner in which they should be played, Flesch (1931) said, "Strads must be treated gently, considerately; a Guarneri del Gesù not only tolerates an energetic approach—it requires it."

Stradivari's instruments have always been admired, from his own day to the present, for their magnificent varnish. The secret of his varnish has fascinated researchers, luthiers, and lay tinkerers. Any number of possible and impossible theories about it have been advanced. Much of the talk has centered around amber varnish. Mailand proved that a process to dissolve amber or hard copal in oil was discovered by Delaporte in 1737. His son-in-law, the lacquer producer Simon Étienne Martin, applied for a manufacturing monopoly in 1744, but it was not until 1772 that the process became known through Watin's *Traité des vernis*. Mailand concludes that Stradivari could not have used amber since it required the same treatment as the very similar hard copal. The Hills believed Stradivari used a relatively quick-drying, pure oil varnish (varnish that was easily soluble in oil, to which pigments were added). Reade thought it likely that a small amount of alcohol was used as a solvent for the pigment. No serious researcher believed there was a secret. Stradivari obtained the ingredients from a pharmacist and prepared the varnish himself.

One romantic story continues to be told about the master's formula. As a young man, one of his descendants discovered in a family bible a varnish recipe, supposedly the one used by his famous ancestor in 1704. When the family moved, the bible was discarded, but a copy of the recipe was made. During the war years ca. 1848 this Signor Stradivari, though in financial straits, resisted repeated attractive offers to buy the recipe. It supposedly is to be preserved and guarded until another Stradivari takes up violin making.

Stradivari's fame soon spread through Italy. Strangely enough, it was based on those of his instruments that followed the Amati model. Apparently they corresponded most to the ideal of beautiful sound then held by music lovers, more so than the del Gesù sound. Orders soon came from princes and members of the high clergy, among them Frederick August II of Saxony and Poland, Grand Duke Cosimo III of Tuscany, and the dukes of Savoy and Modena. The latter ordered a cello in 1686 and, at the luthier's invitation, came to Cremona to receive it. At the age of forty-two Stradivari became court luthier to Cardinal Vincenzo Orsini of Benevento.

A quartet of string instruments that Stradivari intended to present to Philip V of Spain as a gift suffered a strange fate. In 1702, during the Spanish War of Succession, Philip was in Cremona. Stradivari was urgently advised not to make the presentation lest he be accused of being a collaborator. He heeded the advice, and the four instruments remained in the family. His son Francesco inherited them after the father's death, and after Francesco died, they went to his younger brother Paolo. He in turn sold the quartet in 1775 to a Padre Brambilla, who may have been acting as a front for the Spanish court. Through him the instruments became the property of Crown Prince Don Carlos, the later King Charles IV, who was a fine violinist. The Stradivari family tried to repurchase the quartet but did not succeed. Unscrupulous repairers continued to "improve" the instruments until they were virtually useless. This was done against the will of the king, who apparently knew more about instruments than his court luthiers.

Stradivari's instruments did not meet with much appreciation abroad before ca. 1780, nor did they exert much influence on violin making before that time. They began to bring high prices after 1782, when Viotti brought them to the attention of French violinists. Apparently many were brought to France during the Napoleonic Wars, when northern Italy was occupied by the French. Cozio di Salabue said they were the ones most in demand after the French arrived.

Fairly soon Stradivari's instruments found owners who appreciated their value, which accounts for the large number of those preserved. Their stories form an important chapter in the history of violin playing. Many famous violinists owned or at least performed on Strads, including Alard, Artôt, Auer, Baillot, Bériot, Böhm, Brodsky, Bull, Burmester, Busch, Dancla, David, de Vito, Dushkin, Elman, Ernst, Flesch, Francescatti, Grumiaux, Habeneck, Heifetz, Hubay, Huberman, Jansa, Joachim, Kreisler, Kreutzer, Kubelik, Kulenkampff, Manén, Marsick, Marteau, Massart, Menuhin, Milstein, Molique, Nachèz, Oistrakh, Paganini, Reményi, Rode, Rostal, Sarasate, Schneiderhan, Ševčík, Spohr, Stern, Suk, Szeryng, Szigeti, Thibaud, Vécsey, Vieuxtemps, Viotti, Wieniawski, Wilhelmj, Ysaÿe, and Zimbalist. Busch once made an eloquent remark about Stradivari's instruments, exclaiming after a ca. 1920 Vienna performance of Mozart's Violin Concerto K. 219, "When you hold such a violin in your hands, you might even think that you are talented!"

Members of world-famous string quartets past and present also performed on Strads. Among them are the Joachim Quartet (Joachim owned several Strads as did Halir, A. Moser, and de Ahna), the Florentine String Quartet (Jean Becker), Rosé Quartet (first violin), Brussels Quartet (Schörg), Gordon Quartet (first violin), Griller Quartet (O'Brien), New York String Quartet (Cadek), Fine Arts Quartet (Sorkin), Strub Quartet (first violin), and the Juilliard Quartet (first violin). Sprengel, a well-known benefactor from Hanover, put a Strad at the Végh Quartet's disposal.

Many patrons distinguished themselves by such gifts. Napoleon III gave a 1681 Strad to Léon Reynier. In 1876, Wilma Neruda received one from the Duke of Edinburgh and other members of the nobility. King Maximilian Joseph of Bavaria owned several that were played by members of his orchestra. One of these Strads since then has been known as the "King Maximilian." The publisher Axel Springer purchased it in the United States and gave it to Michael Schwalbé, concertmaster of the Berlin Philharmonic, as a lifetime loan. Johann Wenzel Kalliwoda, court kapellmeister in Donaueschingen, was given a Strad by Prince Karl Egon II, and in 1909 Prince Max of Baden gave one to Deman, court concertmaster in Karlsruhe. The Paris Conservatoire owns five Strads, most of them gifts; by custom, one of them was loaned to prize-winning students for their graduation recitals. A similar tradition existed in Russia. Strad owners past and present include the poet d'Annunzio and leaders in industry and banking, going back to Michele

Monzi in Venice, who in 1682 had ordered a quartet from the master and later presented it to the king of England. More recently twelve members of the first violin section of the New York Philharmonic played Strads.

Some Strads have had truly adventurous and sometimes mysterious histories, involving wars, revolutions, and law suits. The famous "Lord Nelson" Strad (1690) was on the admiral's flagship during the Battle of Trafalgar. The "Molique" was made in 1716 for George I of England. George III gave it to a Scottish officer, who carried it with him during the Napoleonic wars. He was killed in the Battle of Waterloo, and the Strad was returned to his family, who later sold it to Molique.

Fritz Meyer (1919) has this to tell about Paganini's "Cannon":

> In 1908 the Genoa city council decreed that . . . the instrument's condition should be examined annually by eight experts. It also should be played at least twice a year, since this would help to preserve it. . . . The first violinist invited by the city to perform on it was Bronislaw Huberman. The "Cannon" was taken under military escort through the streets of Genoa to the concert hall. Armed soldiers positioned themselves on the stage around the violin. The Polish violinist then performed. Nothing adverse happened to the Strad, which then was returned to its prison under similar protective measures.

[A story in the September 1997 issue of *The Strad* relates that the "Cannon," normally displayed in Genoa, will be used by violinist Shlomo Mintz at a concert in Maastricht. "It will fly in a special aircraft and will be accompanied by an entourage of four. . . . Once in Maastricht, the 'Cannon' will be at Mintz's disposal for five days, during which he will not be able to play on it for more than three consecutive hours a day." *Ed.*]

Henley relates the following tale about the "Des Rosier" Strad, made in 1733:

> During the French Revolution it caused a young corporal to be beheaded by the guillotine. When the revolutionary rabble stormed a castle, it was about to crush the Strad, seeing in it a symbol of the wealthy aristocracy. The young corporal, however, himself a violinist from Versailles, managed to grab the instrument, hide it, and run away. But five miles away he was captured and guillotined.

This Strad was bought in 1911 by Alfred Hill and in 1920 by Wurlitzer.

Merton, a Frankfurt patron of the arts, made a lifetime loan of a Strad to the noted violinist Max Strub. In 1945 Strub, an alleged high party official, had to appear before a military court martial. For this occasion he brought along the only possession he had been able to save, his double violin case containing his Strad and a Grancino. He played on the Strad to prove that he was "only" a violinist. Luck was with him, and the accusation was withdrawn. But word got around about the fine violin, and before long Russian soldiers "liberated" the violin case and its contents. Some time later, the Grancino was found on the floor of a military barracks.

The great violinist Huberman bought his first Strad in Hill's shop in 1911 for 63,000 marks. It was stolen in Vienna in 1919 and subsequently recovered, but in 1936 it was stolen again. Rumor had it that a Paris gypsy sold it for a ridiculously low price at the flea market; according to Pâris (1995) it resurfaced in Connecticut in 1987. The "General Kyd" Strad (1714) also was stolen, resulting in an insurance payment of $48,500. Only when this became known did the thief realize its value. He was afraid to sell the violin, and the insurance company was able to return it to its owner.

The number of Strads extant has decreased for several reasons. The violinists Thibaud and Neveu both died in airplane crashes, and both had Strads with them; Thibaud's Strad (1709) had been played by Baillot for Napoleon. The "Balfour" was declared a forgery even though nine French and English experts testified to its authenticity, and in Switzerland, a famous-infamous trial took place regarding the "Greffuhl" Strad. Though certified by Hill, it can no longer be declared genuine, at least in that country.

For some Strads it is possible to establish an unbroken chain of owners. According to Henley, this applies to the "Toscana," built in 1690 for Grand Duke Cosimo III of the Medici family. In 1737, after that family died out, their collection of instruments was dissolved. The "Toscana" was then purchased by the Florentine citizen G. F. Moseli. In 1794 he sold it for 24 pounds to David Kerr, an Irishman, in whose family it remained until 1876 when it was sold to M. Riccardo of Paris. It was then acquired for 240 pounds by Hill & Sons, who sold it to Sir J. J. Oldham of Brighton. In his will, Oldham directed that it should be sold at auction by Hill, for a minimum bid of 3500 pounds. If this price was not reached it was to go to the British Museum. That institution, however, declined since it wanted the instrument to remain in active musical life. It was eventually acquired by Eric H. Rose. Mussolini wanted to buy it for Gioconda de Vito, but the Italian government did not authorize a purchase for the S. Cecilia Academy in Rome until 1953. It was bought for 12,000 pounds from Hill & Sons and made available to de Vito for life. In case the academy should cease to exist, the violin is to become the property of the Italian government.

Strad admirers may see two of them in the Ashmolean Museum, along with one violin by the Amati brothers, a Nicolò Amati, and a Stainer. In 1936, Arthur and Alfred Hill began a series of gifts from their inventory, leading to a 1950 instrument exhibition.

Quite a few monographs have been written about Stradivari, among them

ca. 1889   Anonymous, *The Grenville Stradivarius of 1726*, New York
1891   James M. Fleming, *The Stradivarius Violin "The Emperor,"*
                 London
             Hill & Sons, *The Tuscan and the Salabue Stradivari (Le Messie)*,
                 London (rpt. 1976)

1892	Mougenot, *Description du superbe violon de Stradivarius, dit "Le Mercure,"* Brussels
1929	Anonymous, *Geschichte und Beschreibung von zwei Meisterwerken des Antonius Stradivarius, bekannt als die "König Maximilian" und die "Prinz Khevenhüller" (1733) im Besitze von Emil Herrmann,* Berlin
1943	H. Werro, *Die "Lady Blunt,"* Bern
1978	P. Peterlongo, *Die Geige Vecsey*, Milan

According to Fuchs, 1982 prices for Strads averaged 350,000 to 800,000 DM. A 1667 Strad brought more than 760,000 DM (34,000 pounds) at Sotheby's in London in 1995. Violins by Guarnerius del Gesù have brought upward of 500,000 DM. The difference is in part due to the many more Strads on the market. Fritz Kreisler (quoted in Lochner 1950) pointed to another factor:

> The Strad is excellent for a small concert hall. At the time when Strads were built, only small halls were available for concerts. The Guarnerius has much more power. Recently a younger violinist bought a Strad. He wondered why, although it is such a marvelous instrument, he was not doing as well with the audiences as he used to do. The answer is simple: our concert halls today for the most part are too big for a Strad.

Still, some Strads command prices up to one million DM. Some years ago Hill & Sons sold to the City of Cremona the magnificent Strad now on display in the town hall (see frontispiece). The price, 200,000 DM, was considered a charitable gesture.

The steady rise in prices can be illustrated by the Strad once owned by the violinist Rode. After his death, the duke of Albreuse bought it for 4000 francs. He in turn sold it to the firm of Gand et Bernardel in Paris for 5000 francs. The conductor Lamoureux acquired it for 6000 francs and resold it in 1890 for 30,000 francs. Given such prices, most Strads were sold to the United States; Henley noted that the "Kubelik" Strad (1687) went to that country finally, after a series of foreign owners. According to Doring (1945), 185 violins, five violas, and seventeen cellos were in the United States, 149 violins, sixteen violas, and thirty cellos in Europe.

Antonio Stradivari married twice. Of the total of eleven children, only two took up the father's craft, were trained by him, and finally were overshadowed by him. The older one, Francesco (1671–1743), kept the atelier with the help of his brother Omobono (1679–1742). Even at the age of forty-two, Omobono did not dare to sell his violins as his own creations but used the label "Homobonus Stradivarius / sub disciplina A. Stradivari 1725." Other instruments carry a notation by the father: "Revisto e Corretto da me Antonio Stradivari in Cremona 1720." Apparently the father kept a close eye on his sons' work. Such instruments, however, were not necessarily made by the sons. Both were outstanding luthiers; their violins would now bring high prices, except that they were "only" made by the sons. Still, according to Fuchs, instruments by both sons sold for 180,000 DM or more in 1982.

We know of only a few luthiers who were definitely Antonio's pupils. Unlike other authors, the Hills believe that only the two sons and Carlo Bergonzi are known pupils, but this seems too restrictive an estimate. On a 1740 label, Laurentius Guadagnini refers to himself as "alumnus Antonius Stradivarius." Assuming the label is genuine, this is apt to be correct, given the proximity in time. Whether Nicolas Duclos (d. 1780), active in Barcelona and Madrid, was an actual pupil is doubtful, even though he used labels such as "Matriti per Nicolaus Duclos / Discipulus de Stradivarius / Anno 1776." Forty years after Antonio's death, and far away from Cremona, such claims were difficult to prove or to disprove. Carlo Bomini, on the other hand, a fine but virtually unknown Cremona luthier, most likely was a pupil. One of his labels reads "Carolus Bomini, Discipulus / Antonji Stradivarji Cremonensis 1715."

Only instruments made by members of the Bergonzi family come close to those from the Stradivari and Guarneri shops. Before becoming Stradivari's apprentice, Carlo (b. 1683 in Cremona, d. 1747) learned the craft from Hieronymus Amati and Josephus Guarnerius I. He thus was able to absorb the best traditions. Highly talented, he crafted instruments that were artistically made and had superior tonal qualities. For the back and top he used rather heavy wood, probably due to the influence of Guarnerius del Gesù. His violins embody the best aspects of his models and also of his own style, resulting in instruments that are much in demand by soloists. After both Stradivari sons had died, Carlo received some of the father's raw materials and eventually took over his atelier.

The Bergonzi family had many branches. Benedetto Bergonzi (d. 1840) continued the shop in Stradivari's house. One of Carlo Bergonzi's pupils was Sebastiano Albanesi (d. 1744) of Cremona. Henley considers him one of the best of the less-known Italian luthiers.

Lorenzo Storioni (1751–1802), a very imaginative master builder, represents the last flourishing of violin making in Cremona. He understood the tonal requirements of his time and tried to meet them by building many instruments of a decidedly experimental nature. His most successful instruments represent a kind of continuation of the Guarneri style. Soloists since Vieuxtemps have prized them. According to Fuchs, a good Storioni brought 100,000 DM in 1982.

THE DECLINE OF ITALIAN VIOLIN MAKING DURING THE SECOND HALF OF THE EIGHTEENTH CENTURY

As one studies the lives of eighteenth-century Italian luthiers, one notices the surprisingly large number of major figures who died around the mid-century. This also was the time when noted families of violin makers died out, while members of other families, active until ca. 1800, no longer reached the earlier high standards of excellence. This even applies to families who continued to remain active in the field, such as the Guadagninis and Gaglianos. One of the few exceptions to this trend was Giambattista Ceruti (d. 1817), a pupil of Lorenzo Storioni in Cremona, who built instruments in the del Gesù manner. Likewise, Stradivari pupils Pietro and Tomaso Balestrieri and Treviso luthier Pietro Antonio Dalla Costa (d. 1768) built instruments in the best northern Italian tradition.

Statements noting this decline occur repeatedly in the literature, including remarks by Fuchs on Ferdinando Gagliano ("The tone quality of his instruments is quite different; [he] built with an eye to sales"), Giovanni Battista Grancino ("A decline of artistic standards; coarse craftsmanship, inferior wood; the varnish is an unsightly yellow, transparent but hard; tone quality is still good"), and Francesco Grancino ("His instruments sound good but also demonstrate an artistic decline").

Looking for possible reasons for such a decline one is tempted to make a comparison with developments in the music of the Netherlands ca. 1600, or with similar symptoms in cultural history elsewhere, and say that the talent of a people may simply have exhausted itself. But it is an oversimplification to attribute talent to a collective (in this case, a people), and not realize that special gifts are found in individuals, even if their gifts may have been nurtured by the group. Thus it seems entirely possible that, based on the examples of the Stradivari and Guarneri families, other talented luthiers might have appeared on the Italian scene ca. 1750.

More plausible is a causal relation to the development of eighteenth-century music. At the time when Italian violin making was losing its dominant position, the leading role in musical developments, held for almost two hundred years by Italians, was assumed by composers in Austria and southern Germany. Still, this did not necessarily mean that luthiers from Brescia, Cremona, and elsewhere in Italy (who had always exported many instruments) were unable to supply orchestras of the early and late classic period with high-quality instruments. The sons and grandsons of the Guadagnini, Grancino, Bergonzi, and Landolfi families (to name just a few) certainly had the talent and training to do this. Others have claimed that the best old Italian violins were made of balsam fir or spruce, which woods excessive logging had rendered unavailable. Real proof is lacking for any of these theories.

The most likely explanation may be the law of supply and demand. Ever since Andrea Amati and his predecessors, violins had been built to satisfy the demands of particular customers, be they personally known or anonymous—not to supply the world at large with immortal masterpieces. Customers determined both the quality and quantity of production. Good builders may at times have used mediocre or bad wood and cheap varnish; they did this when there were no customers who could afford the more expensive raw materials. Inevitably, a luthier's primary objective was to feed himself and his often quite large family. Soon after the mid-century the market seems to have been saturated with high-quality instruments, so that sales declined significantly. Some calculations might support this. If a luthier, during forty active years, produced approximately twenty instruments a year, he would have contributed eight hundred instruments. Vannes lists sixty luthiers before 1750 for Cremona alone, which gives us a total of ca. fifty thousand instruments. To this we should add the production of apprentices and others working in his shop; they often approached the master in skill. Nor have the names of all earlier luthiers come down to us. All this suggests that in Cremona alone, 100,000 to 200,000 instruments may have been made before the midcentury. There were few collectors in those early days, so most of this production found its way into music making in public life and in the home. Inevitably the demand for instruments of above-average quality diminished. The four violas Stainer furnished in 1669 for the Olmütz cathedral were probably all that were needed there for a long time, unless some were stolen.

Aside from these reasons for the supposed decline in Italian instrument making, we can point to the appearance of highly skilled violin makers in other European countries, and to the growing demand for inexpensive instruments, especially for beginners. Increasingly, a builder's time was needed for making repairs. Thus Pietro Giovanni Mantegazza (d. 1796 in Milan) made few new violins but was much in demand for working on those of del Gesù. Henley says that late in life Antonio (d. 1860) and Raffaele Gagliano (d. 1857), two highly talented brothers, "stooped" to making violins on a commercial basis, "for the sake of money. They neglected their talent and uncritically manufactured instruments of all degrees of quality." This censure may sound very high-minded from our vantage point, but the criticism is unjustified given the reality of the market ca. 1750.

THE "SECRET" OF THE OLD ITALIAN LUTHIERS

Having perfected his skills as a luthier, my father embarked upon the search for Stradivari's secret. In this he resembled almost all violin makers driven by a similar obsession.

FRITZ BUSCH, *AUS DEM LEBEN EINES MUSIKERS,* 1949

Violin making reached a high point in the instruments of Antonio Stradivari and Josephus Guarnerius del Gesù. Antonio and his sons died in quick succession, followed soon by del Gesù. Since no comparable talent surfaced among their successors, it seemed indeed as though those masters' secrets must have followed them to the grave. To rediscover them was seen as the most important task of luthiers and researchers—as the only way to recreate, and perhaps even surpass, the beautiful sound and appearance of the old instruments.

Antonio Bagatella (b. ca. 1715 in Padua), one of the first intent on discovering the secret, was an amateur violinist who enjoyed making violins. Though he lacked professional instruction, he soon became so proficient that Tartini engaged him to care for his instruments and those of his many

pupils. At times these repairs involved his opening the instruments and studying them closely, and thus Bagatella had no lack of opportunity to inspect
work by the masters. Antonio Amati's instruments were his favorites, for
sound and appearance; he never mentioned Nicolò Amati. He noticed in
Amati's violins that certain proportions occurred again and again, leading
him to this conclusion (quoted by Hübner): "These famous masters knew
geometry very well, or at least were instructed by an excellent mathematician." In 1748 Bagatella succeeded in detecting the structural principles
involved, which enabled him to build a model.

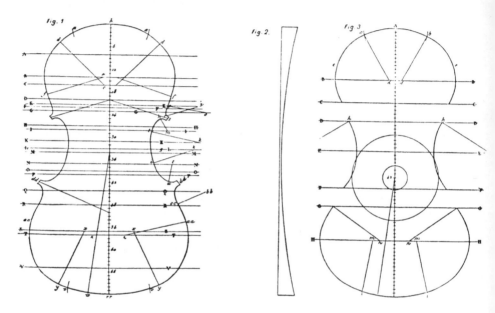

He divided the axis into seventy-two equal parts. Proceeding from the
14th, 20th, 25th, 33d, 48th, and 57th division points, and by using ruler and
compass, he constructed the body's circumference and arch. From this he
determined the thickness of the wood, especially for top and back. The number 72 (6 × 12) was derived from six Cremonese ounces, each having twelve
Cremonese points. Later experiments were based on divisions of one hundred parts.

Bagatella was convinced that his findings were significant, that they
would enable a luthier to "build good instruments, worth their price, according to firm concepts and rules—not, as has been done heretofore, haphaz-
ardly." He continues with a personal guarantee: "Everyone who follows my
instructions precisely will achieve the desired tonal qualities."

In 1782 Padua's Accademia di Scienze, Lettere ed Arti launched a contest. Bagatella participated by entering his work, *Regole per la costruzione dei
violini, viole, violoncelli e violoni*. For a year the jury undertook thorough tests
at the university's physics institute, examining instruments that Bagatella had
"proportioned" according to the measurements he had discovered. His book

was awarded the prize and was published in 1786. In the same year a German translation appeared in Göttingen. Since this study represented the first attempt to base violin making on mathematical methods of construction, it attracted much attention. It also gave rise to much speculation and experimentation in a craft that previously had been guided by purely empirical considerations.

Several objections to Bagatella's ideas can be raised. His principles of construction affect only the external form, and this form has varied even among the instruments of one luthier. Furthermore, he based his work exclusively on the Amati brothers' model. As to criticisms of Bagatella's work, Leipp (*Essai sur la lutherie*) observes, "Actually, there is no one standard recipe for the construction of a good violin. Much depends on the types of wood used since they vary greatly in quality." Mordret (1898), on the other hand, shares this belief with Bagatella: "The Amatis were well schooled in mathematics, or were advised by able mathematicians. Stainer, Stradivari, and Guarneri, who were their pupils, followed the same principles, passed on to them by their teachers."

After 1800, more and more soloists performed on great Italian instruments, providing occasions when, for repairs, instruments had to be opened. Some were in their original condition and had to be adapted to modern requirements of sound and playing technique. The German luthier August Riechers, for instance, repaired or serviced more than three hundred Strads. Many leading nineteenth-century luthiers had ample opportunities to study the construction of such violins. Vuillaume was so completely familiar with Stradivari's style that he could build copies that are still admired as works by the great master from Cremona. On one occasion he repaired Paganini's Strad, which enabled him to make a copy that Paganini himself could not distinguish from the original until he played on it.

Activities of this kind were not undertaken primarily to discover the old masters' secret. Rather, some luthiers wanted to prove, after much experimentation, that Stradivari for all time had found the ideal type of violin, and that any deviations from his model would affect the sound adversely, so that it would be best to copy his model in every detail. In Vuillaume's case, other considerations affected his beliefs.

The Berlin luthier Carl Schulze (d. 1903) had a particular talent for experimentation. Based on Helmholtz's theories, his investigations dealt chiefly with Strads from 1700 to 1725. He concluded, "Since the mid-eighteenth century no instruments have been made that are comparable to those by Stradivari and Guarneri. Those masters studied acoustics, creating violins that in every way are aesthetic works of art."

His book *Stradivaris Geheimnis: Ein ausführliches Lehrbuch des Geigenbaus* (Stradivari's secret: A detailed manual of violin making) incorporates the results of many years of intensive study and has inspired many luthiers. He found that Stradivari's instruments were constructed according to simple proportions, corresponding to musical intervals. He noted a violin with a length of 346.5 mm thus:

> Division of the body by the bridge: 6:5 = minor third
> Width (upper bout to middle): 5:4 = major third
> Width (lower bout to middle): 3:2 = perfect fifth
> Inside length (divided by soundpost): 4:3 = perfect fourth
> Inside volume (divided by soundpost): 2:1 = octave

On a purely experimental basis he made violins without ribs; for others he used elliptical shapes, parabolic and hyperbolic curves. Some of these violins sound remarkably good. Such an instrument has no sharp edges. Its longitudinal and lateral sections display carefully calculated flat ellipses.

Adolf Beck (d. 1961), a luthier from Düsseldorf, returned to Bagatella's ideas and tried to discover laws accounting for the beauty of the old Italian violins. In *Die proportionale Konstruktion der Geige: Eine Abhandlung über die Proportionsgesetze, nach welchen die klassischen Geigenmodelle konstruiert sind* (The proportional construction of the violin: A treatise about the laws of proportion according to which classical violin models have been built, Leipzig 1923) he postulated that the proportion 5:8 governed all external forms, but that all vibrating surfaces stood in a 4:5 relation. He further believed that the thickness of the wood depended entirely on the material used.

Two outstanding Berlin builders were Max and Otto Möckel (both d. 1937). After many years of research and experimentation, Max Möckel concluded that Leonardo da Vinci was involved in determining the shape of the violin, and that the classic model was constructed according to the golden section. Möckel built his first violin according to this concept in 1924; in the following year he published the results of his studies in a book, *Das Konstruktionsgeheimnis der alten italienischen Meister: Der Goldene Schnitt im Geigenbau* (The secret of the old Italian masters: The golden section in violin making, Berlin 1925–1927). The regular pentagon figures importantly in his calculations.

> We draw a circle and divide its periphery into five equal sections. We connect the five sections by straight lines, obtaining a regular pentagon. By drawing the diagonals in this pentagon we obtain a star, the pentagram. We continue to draw diagonals to construct more, smaller pentagons, as long as this is technically possible. A triangle from the first star is similarly divided. All these lines and shapes represent the proportions of the golden section. If we observe these given lines so that the larger units follow the lines of the large pentagons, and the smaller lines the smaller ones, we will have a construction based on the rules of the golden section.

He also set down procedures for constructing the curves of the arched surfaces and for details of the scroll and bridge. Some of these procedures are explained and illustrated in his book (two of Möckel's typical diagrams are included opposite).

Many critics raised their voices against Möckel's conclusion that his book offered "scientific proof for the rediscovery of something that had been con-

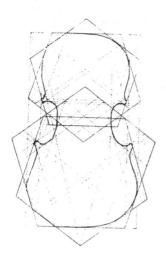
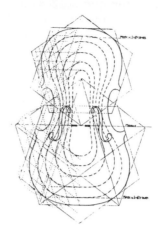

sidered lost." Fuhr (*Die akustischen Rätsel*) states categorically, "The golden section has nothing to do with acoustics." Elsewhere he claims,

> Max Möckel assumes that the Italians' chief secret lies in their determination of thickness according to the golden section. If we find this in a Strad, it would be a sure sign that it is a forgery. It would also be difficult to find an authentic violin by another superior old Italian luthier that displays the proportions of the golden section.

Concerning Möckel's procedures, Leonhardt (1969) states,

> Many constructions have been made, and models have been built, but I consider it wrong to give pride of place to geometric construction and to various calculations, and to relegate the empirical method to second place. Max Möckel defended such rationalistic speculation; as a result, neither his violins nor his writings have attracted attention.

Still, Möckel's book raised a number of important questions. Those who are a priori defenders of universal laws found themselves justified by Möckel's proof (if indeed it was proof) of the golden section applying to violin making. But in dealing with a *musical* instrument one must distinguish between sound and appearance. Such shapes might be based on the law of the golden section, but *sound* is governed by the laws of acoustics. At times, both laws may coincide, but this is pure coincidence. The properties of the specific type of wood chosen for an instrument, not preestablished proportions, are decisive.

A drawing from a fourteenth-century manuscript, in which ruler and compass are used in connection with lute construction, gives cause for further reflection. The drawing was described by Leipp (*Le violon*) who, in its proportions, noted values that approximate the golden section. That such procedures were known is also evident from a passage in Mersenne, who gives a proportion of 5:8 for neck and body of the instrument. Even if it can be proved, however, that such principles of construction existed during the golden age of Italian violin making, this does not establish that they were used by luthiers. Everyone worked with a model, for which (for the sake of efficiency) a pattern was cut out. If the builder wanted to make changes and try a different form, he would make a new mold or pattern. A master such as Stradivari, an experimenter like other Italian luthiers, probably had dozens of such patterns hanging on the walls of his shop, and some have been preserved. But changes were based on acoustical considerations, and even working with a mold, one would not follow it slavishly but with respect for the condition of the particular piece of wood.

A mold from Stradivari's shop did turn up, and a rather sensational account of the find was given by Euro Peluzzi (1941). Various lines are drawn on the mold, along with three concentric circles and more than twenty numbers (reproduced in Leipp 1969). This seemed to prove that Stradivari also used such calculations. Doubts arose about the authenticity of this mold, however, because the numbers were written in a manner not customary at the time, and with a steel pen that had not yet been invented!

In 1947 Hans Kayser, a scholar known for his work in the field of harmony, published *Die Form der Geige: Aus dem Gesetz der Töne gedeutet* (The shape of the violin: Interpreted according to the laws of acoustics), in which treatise he states, "We want to explain the violin's shape according to criteria never before employed, namely on the basis of tonal laws." His introductory historical remarks are strikingly amateurish: "It is true that gambas and viols were predecessors of the violin, but its real shape appeared around the mid-sixteenth century, suddenly and inexplicably, out of the blue. At that time, at the end of the high renaissance, it was found in the shops of da Salò and Tieffenbrucker." Aside from dwelling on the "mysterious appearance" of the violin, he reflects on its continued existence for more than two hundred years. That it did not undergo any essential changes to him is further proof of its optimal form. Kayser mentions writings by Bagatella, Beck, and Möckel, and speaks disparagingly of Carl Schulze:

> [He] and others whom we cannot discuss here use mathematical figures and geometric proportions that are rather primitive and have nothing to do with acoustical values. In view of the close links between pitch [intervals] and numbers, it should have been obvious to use these relations in analyzing the violin's body.

Schulze did note proportions such as 1:1, 1:2, 2:3, 3:4, 4:5, 5:6, 3:5, 8:15, 64:81, and 64:125 in various parts of the instrument and said specifically, "In many places we find measurements that have the proportions of musical intervals." Kayser tells us, for instance:

> The widths of the upper and lower parts of the body represent a proportion of 4:5, that is, of a major third. The measurements of the neck

and body (from the bridge to the neck's beginning) represent the ratio of 2:3 (fifth) or 5:7 (seventh). The neck's thickness (its width at the fingerboard as related to half of its diameter at a right angle to the fingerboard) represents the proportion 5:3 (minor third), increasing from the top nut toward the body. The narrowest place on the middle waist is approximately half that of the lower waist—the ratio of an octave. Even the scroll is an exact equivalent of the "tone spiral," a discovery stated here for the first time, to be proved in the final chapter.

Kayser's numerological speculations are of absolutely no significance for violin making. There may be numbers that, as Schulze put it, "express the proportions of musical intervals," but this in no way indicates a connection with music. The dimensions of a table top may express the proportion 4:5; two brothers may be sixteen and twenty years old; the upper and lower bouts of a violin may measure 165 and 206.25 mm—but none of this has anything to do with a major third.

Dr. K. Steiner of Tübingen is another researcher who tried to discover the secret of the classic violin shape by using ruler and compass; he published the results of his study in 1949 (*Die geometrische Konstruktion der Geigenform von Stradivari*). Strangely enough, and unlike Möckel's, his point of departure was a trapeze, but he also arrived at the proportions of the golden section. On this subject Leipp (1969) stated,

> It is curious that no matter how we try to analyze the violin's form, we are led to the golden section. [It] can only define its external shape, and it is untenable to attribute acoustical values to such calculations. But many authors believe that in that way they have discovered the "secret" of the old luthiers governing the sound of their instruments.

The basic error in all these calculations is that, though they may establish certain proportions, they are not likely to coincide with those required for optimal sound, which depend on the mass of the vibrating material—which in turn depends largely on the special characteristics of the wood and which will vary for different parts of the top and back. This enormously complicates proportional calculations and suggests that construction based on experiments may lead to better results. It all boils down to whether a violin is primarily a musical instrument, created according to the laws of acoustics, or whether it is an *objet d'art*, the proportions of which are intended to delight the eye. As Leonhardt said, "Intellect at first is likely to be based on preconceived notions, until experience leads us to the truth."

Nevertheless, sensational claims continued to be made and were eagerly pounced upon by the media. The well-known violinist Henry Schradieck did his share of tinkering, leading to this headline in the 19 December 1884 issue of *Tägliche Rundschau*: "How Cremona Violins Were Made. A Lost Secret Rediscovered by Henry Schradieck." Inevitably, rebuttals were quick to follow, such as Georg Gemünder's *Contradictions on the Alleged Discovery of* the *"Lost Secret" of the Cremona Violins, Claimed by Prof. Henry Schradieck of the Cincinnati College of Music.* The gist of Gemünder's argument? The secret of the Cremona violins was never lost because he, Gemünder, continues to make instruments that are every bit as good.

Otto Migge of Koblenz, a good luthier, opened an atelier "for the artistic construction of Cremona violins." In 1894 he published a book, *Das Geheimnis der berühmten italienischen Geigenbauer, ergründet und erklärt* (The secret of the famous Italian luthiers, discovered and explained), which includes such choice statements as these: "Today we can rightly say that since the deaths of the great makers, there have been no real luthiers. Only as a result of [reading] my book can instrument makers advance to the rank of true luthier." After the first wave of publicity vanished, however, and after the usual further polemics, Migge's ungrateful contemporaries decided that the secret remained to be discovered.

W. Meredith Morris (1904), a scholar with integrity, admitted, "In sooth I must confess that I know very little more about the mysteries of the Italian tone now than I did thirty-five years ago when I first took up the study of the subject." Certainly many of those seeking to discover Stradivari's secret were quite honorable, convinced of the truth of their findings. But there were others, such as the luthier mentioned by Drögemeyer, who advertised that he was "the sole proprietor of Stradivari's secrets."

THE OLD ITALIAN VARNISH

The number of those who claim to have rediscovered the recipe for Italian varnish is large and growing all the time. All claim to have inherited the formula, or to have found it in Holland, or in some monastery library, or in India. One person even claims to have successfully prepared varnish with a mixture of granular varnish, spirit, and castor oil.

HERMANN AUGUST DRÖGEMEYER, *DIE GEIGE*, 1891

About once every five years, in connection with news about the discovery of Stradivari's secret, newspaper reports announce the discovery of the secret of the old Italian varnish. The stories seem to follow a pattern: after decades of work, some elderly professor has at last succeeded in recreating the magic formula. A few weeks later the word is forgotten. No one has seen or heard the violins to which this old–new varnish was applied, but in due time the next such report is launched.

We should not assume that all these researchers and discoverers are charlatans. They did indeed spend decades on their experiments, they equipped special laboratories and invested much money. In an attempt to liquefy amber, one almost burned his house down. Some discovered partial truths, which pleased them so much that they jumped to conclusions. Others became victims of their self-deceptions.

In early times, builders soon saw the need for preserving instruments with the help of varnish, to protect the wood from hand perspiration, from dust, humidity, and very hot and cold temperatures. When a white (unvarnished) violin is played as soon as it has been completed, it reveals its optimal volume and tone quality. But if it continues to be played in this raw condition, the wood gradually loses its ability to vibrate; the violin becomes "deaf" and eventually unusable.

Various methods of varnish preparation go back as far as the craft of making wooden instruments. The oldest known source is a Turkish manual from ca. 1400 that describes how instruments were treated with a mixture of ground glass and glue. Furniture making confirmed that wood needed to be treated, and this knowledge was then applied to plucked and bowed instruments. Experiments showed how different ingredients and ways of preparing varnish affected tone quality. The same experiments may also have shown that an ideal varnish (though not yet discovered at the time) would represent a compromise between two goals: to preserve the wood and to retain its elasticity. A third factor was an aesthetic one: the brilliance of the varnish should enhance the instrument's appearance.

Varnishes on sixteenth-century instruments were dark and relatively thick, covering up rather than bringing out the wood's grain. In violins by the mature Andrea Amati and his sons, by Gasparo da Salò, and especially by Maggini, the aesthetic element was of special importance. They looked for great transparency and increasingly favored varnish that was light brown to golden yellow, slightly reddish. The high point of varnish quality was reached in Stradivari's work. Instruments from his years of greatest mastery are distinguished by varnish that furthered optimal acoustical and aesthetic qualities.

The great skill in preparing and applying varnish evident in the work of many Italian makers was gradually lost after the mid-eighteenth century. Louis Guersan (d. 1770), an excellent Paris luthier, is said to have been the first to use a new kind of varnish that, however, affected tone quality adversely. Guersan was an experimenter. His instruments vary greatly in the degree of arching, in the height of ribs, thickness of wood, shape of f holes, and details of interior finishing. Anxious to produce a varnish that was inexpensive and quick drying, he came up with a product that was beautiful and brilliant but also very hard and dry. It covered the instrument with a kind of armor that inhibited vibration and favored the upper partials, resulting in an overly piercing sound in the high register. It took some time for these disadvantages to appear; they then caused Guersan's violins, though otherwise very well made, to become practically worthless.

Apparently his process was widely adopted ca. 1750, or perhaps similar ones were developed independently of him. The Hills believed that other Italian luthiers, even before Stradivari's death, took advantage of the newly discovered method of dissolving resin in alcohol. About Francesco Stradivari, who at first followed his father's form closely, Fritz Meyer (1910) said, "Unfortunately he then deviated from his father's model and used inferior varnish."

It would be wrong, however, to reduce the varnish question to this simple pair: oil varnish (slow drying) vs. spirit varnish (quick drying). Alexis (1550) mentions a turpentine varnish that dries quickly, and Mailand (1859), in discussing Bonanni's recipes (1713) said that he wanted to correct a widespread misconception:

> Writers frequently claim that the old masters used "oil varnish," without specifying whether this was what we commonly call "oil," such as linseed oil, or whether a spirit-based oil was meant, such as turpentine oil. It has been pointed out that the old luthiers, in preparing their varnish, at first boiled oil over an open flame until it had reached the consistency required for quick drying. Once the oil had cooled somewhat, they would add pulverized rubber resin, and would then reheat the mixture to a somewhat lower temperature (100–120 degrees Celsius), for at a higher temperature the delicate resins and rubber substances would have burned. This distinguishes the way in which the early luthiers worked from the preparation customarily used today, when hard copals or amber are melted in turpentine oil at temperatures up to 300 degrees.

Mailand concludes, "The varnish of the early luthiers did not consist of fatty oils with hard resins, but of etheric oils (essence) with soft resins."

After the vogue of spirit varnish, still favored by Savart, there was a return, in the early nineteenth century, to the old masters' oil varnishes. But the mistaken belief that they had used a fatty varnish persisted for a long time.

Because of the declining quality of varnish in the second half of the eighteenth century, it was thought that the last great Italian luthiers had jealously guarded their formula for varnish preparation and had taken it with them to the grave—a romantic thought, to be sure, but not borne out by reality. An informative letter from 1526, dealing with the preparation of varnish, has been transmitted by Valdrighi. The duke of Ferrara wanted to know how the luthier Maler varnished his instruments. He sent as his intermediary a certain Jacopo Tebaldi, who wrote the duke thus: "The famous Sigismund Maler, a German, promised that he would write down the recipe for me next Monday. . . . He told me that he used two kinds of varnish that were prepared by his assistants, not by himself."

Ingredients were usually bought at the pharmacist's; the varnish was then prepared in the shop. The more ambitious luthiers tried to establish the optimal proportions, but this was not something to be kept secret from one's own colleagues or others. In a letter of 14 April 1792 to Lupot (quoted in Pierre 1893), Pique made this request:

> [I require a small supply of oil varnish], enough for a few violins. I have run out and don't have time to prepare more. Four years ago I prepared enough varnish to last me until today. This is difficult to do in Paris; one would have to have a courtyard or a garden. I urgently need to varnish two violins; I therefore would be most obliged if you could send me a small bottle, along with some Orleans yellow to add to the saffron.

Some sources even claim that an able pharmacist would prepare varnishes according to a master's specifications, all of which suggests that it was neither intended nor possible to keep varnish formulas a secret.

Whole families of luthiers, rich in tradition, continued their activities into the nineteenth century. They were familiar with the old way of making varnish but evidently used it only in special cases, because of the high costs involved. Thus there is no basis for the ongoing claim that the skill of melting amber without a loss of quality had vanished. Other writers claim that the old Italian varnish was not superior initially but rather acquired its transparency and luminescence in the course of time. It has also been claimed that by ca. 1750 one could no longer obtain the high-quality ingredients of Cremona varnish. Nevertheless, masters such as Fedele Barnia (d. 1780 in Venice) provided their very good instruments with first-rate varnish. Further explanations were related to the disappearance of the balsam fir (*Pinus balsamea*) in Italy. Because of its inferior wood, the tree itself was not considered important but was only used for its resin—so much so that the trees, not having been plentiful in the first place, became extinct.

More likely the decline in varnish quality was the result of a lessening demand for instruments, as discussed earlier. The demand for cheap, mass produced instruments called for an inexpensive varnish, one that could be applied quickly, though it was far inferior to the classic Italian varnish. Möller notes that after 1750 a luthier's time was increasingly taken up with repairing old instruments and with sales, making it necessary to use more effective, time-saving production methods, including the use of quick-drying varnishes.

Through Viotti and others, violins of the great Italian masters became known in central Europe, while Tarisio brought such instruments to Paris. Nineteenth-century luthiers therefore had ample opportunity, through repairs and sales, to become well acquainted with details of the instruments' construction, including a thorough study of the varnish. Outstanding luthiers such as Vuillaume at first tried to duplicate the quality of Italian varnish empirically, but soon a solution to the problem was sought in historical research and laboratory experiments. Both approaches were beset by great difficulties. The terminology of the old recipes was problematic, making it difficult to ascertain exactly what name was used for a certain raw material or product in a given period and a given dialect. To obtain specimens of varnish from master violins for chemical analysis was also inherently difficult, as such samples were extremely small, no longer contained ingredients that had evaporated, and had been modified by exposure to air.

The first to report on these researches in some detail was Eugène Mailand (*Découverte des anciens vernis italiens employés pour les instruments à cordes et à archet*, Paris 1859). He presented much historical material and supplied not only varnish recipes but also described processes for preparing it. Obviously, the preparation of varnish was not a secret. Mailand's main sources were Alexis 1550, Fioravanti 1564, Auda 1663, Zahn 1685, Morley 1692, Coronelli 1693, Pomet 1694, and Bonanni 1713, which cover fairly evenly the time from Andrea Amati to Antonio Stradivari. Moreover, Mailand was able to reconstruct the early procedures of varnish preparation—to enter, as it were, the old luthiers' shops. The book's importance is attested to by Vuillaume, who declared that he derived essential new insights from it. In fact, Vuillaume's instruments from this time on measure up to the best from Italy, even to the quality of the varnish. Mailand's researches were supplemented by observations made by Ole Bull, by the well-known English expert Charles Reade, by studies undertaken by George Fry and Joseph Nichelmann, and by many others up to our own time, including Lamberto Corbara.

Early descriptions of Italian master violins often refer to their dual coloring, to a certain changing of hues apparent under different light conditions. In fact these luthiers worked with two varnish applications. Tebaldi's letter to the duke of Ferrara refers to two kinds of varnish. The first, applied in three or four coats, was a base varnish whose essential ingredients were resin, linseed oil, and turpentine oil (turpentine oil evaporated rapidly, its only function being to liquefy the viscous mixture of the other two ingredients). This varnish would fill the pores and firm up the wood structure, rendering it resistant to the strong effect of the vibrations. On the other hand, since it was elastic, it did not adversely affect the wood's ability to vibrate. This base varnish was neutral in color, yet depending on the kind of resin used had a slightly golden yellow to brownish shade. From it the wood derived its beautiful, natural coloring, which remained in place even if the varnish layer on top was scraped off. Its transparency allows the eye to see the wood structure, and its smooth surface provides a good foundation for the real varnish. Thus the base varnish not only preserves the wood but also serves acoustical and aesthetic functions.

A second varnish, an oil varnish, was then applied to this foundation. It could contain alcohol components and be almost neutral in color, though rich pigments were usually added. The base and the real varnish had to be applied in the right proportion. Whether seventeenth- and eighteenth-century luthiers used oil varnish or spirit varnish has been much debated. The fact is that they used both, though the amount of alcohol in the mixture was relatively small. It is more important to note that oil containing ether, rather than fat, was used. This explains the notably short drying time. If fatty varnish had been used exclusively, the drying time would have been intolerably long. On 20 March 1678 Jacob Stainer wrote to the parson in Merano about a gamba that had been ordered. "Work on this viol is now completed. We now need a few days of sunshine for varnishing. If the weather cooperates, the instrument should be ready by Palm Sunday, God willing." On 5 April he notified the parson that the viol had been finished, blaming the delay on bad weather. We learn from this that varnishing and drying required four to five days, though Stainer did not specify whether he dried his instruments in direct sunlight, or whether he merely needed the sun's warmth. The former is more likely; a higher temperature for drying could have been obtained by heating the shop. Other sources also mention the sun's heat, for instance a 1638 letter from Cremona about delivery of a violin, and a letter by Stradivari dated 12 August 1708.

Mailand (1859) quoted Tingry and Tripier–Deveaux (two reliable writers whose works were published in 1803 and 1845 respectively) on the chief difference between using etheric (spirit) oils and alcohol in preparing varnish:

> Etheric oil has the great advantage that it permanently lends to the resinous ingredients a softening and binding quality. Alcohol, on the other hand, evaporates completely. Moreover, oil varnishes are softer and more brilliant than spirit varnishes.

> The greater solidity of oil varnish (as compared to spirit varnish) is due solely to the dried layer of the etheric oil that has not evaporated. This residue combines with the resins. It consists of fatty, concentrated etheric oil, or oxidated essence (*essence grasse*); it may thicken but will not be hardened by air except after a very long time. This is why the dried resins of an oil varnish, surrounded by a similar substance and protected by it from the air, can more effectively resist the harmful influences of the latter, while the resins in spirit varnishes are entirely exposed to it.

According to Hill, members of the Guarneri family occasionally added dry substances to the oil varnish. Apian-Bennewitz does not believe that spirit varnishes necessarily are harmful but rather that the crucial ingredients are the resins themselves, not the solvents.

The use of two varnish layers is also responsible for the tentative results of chemical analyses, since in the process the two independently prepared layers are apt to intermingle. Even if it were possible to analyze the two layers separately, this would reveal only the ingredients, not the steps involved in their application. These, however, are quite essential, since some solutions can occur only under certain conditions. One would have to prepare separately all ingredients mentioned in the recipes. That way the finished varnish, ready to be applied, would be the result of many manipulations, each requiring great skill and much experience.

When we reflect on the primitive tools and other equipment of the time, we cannot but admire those who produced the old Italian varnishes. Seemingly minor details of preparation are actually very important—for instance, the use of a double boiler for indirect heating (known since 1550). Another nicety: large pieces of resin must be added to the solvent because small pieces offer too large a surface to the detrimental influence of the air. Pulverized resin would shorten the drying time significantly but would be useless for the reason just stated.

Easily prepared spirit varnish was used almost exclusively after 1750, for commercial reasons. As a result, knowledge of the earlier techniques gradually disappeared. Twenty to thirty years sufficed for this to happen. Some blamed the decline of the guilds for this deterioration. One of the first who again advocated oil varnishes was the Paris luthier François Louis Pique. In a 1791 announcement he described violins as being "vernit à l'huile" (finished with oil varnish).

Some old recipes were rediscovered in the nineteenth century, and the components of old varnishes were analyzed, but no one knew how to put this knowledge to use at first. Actually, some investigators were not primarily interested in learning more about old Italian varnishes: they wanted to invent their own. On 8 March 1904, for instance, Fry was issued U.S. patent no. 754298 for a varnish he had invented.

Some luthiers specialized in varnish making. Hans Willi Busch, an orchestra musician and conductor in Berlin, developed several types of varnish and finished violins for other builders. A. G. Rowley, an English varnish specialist, similarly worked for violin shops in his country. John K. Empsall was an affluent member of the Bradford Symphony Orchestra. He even bought white violins in order to indulge his passion for varnishing them. Some violins from the mid-nineteenth century carry this label: "Made by F. Feilnreiter, varnished by N. Sawitzki."

Many specialized books include old and new varnish recipes. August Riechers (1893), one of the best luthiers of the last hundred years, was willing to share his "secret" and his experiences:

> Take three parts Sandarak and one part mastic. To a quantity of about half a litre of ready varnish, I add ten drops of oil of turpentine. I obtain the desired color using spirit from Kurkume and light red sandalwood, of a lighter or darker shade, as desired. In order to add a slightly brown tint to the varnish, I add a little soot color from turpentine oil, again dissolved in spirit. I have experimented much with other resins and pigments, but always have come back to these ingredients and proportions as the best ones. One should not use dragon's blood as it is not color fast.

In 1920 Morris reported that in England it was possible to buy excellent ready-made violin varnishes, some of which were prepared and offered for sale by violin researchers and chemists, others by luthiers. He mentions Whitelaw, Clark, Anderson, Harris, and Walker. Quite predictably, many modern luthiers have their own secret varnish formula, which they guard jealously. The claim always is that it goes back to the old Italians. Thus Josef Bausch, a very capable builder, uses this label in his instruments: "Tinctura vere Cremonensi / sonum reddidit meliorem / Josephus Bausch anno 19—" (J. B., by using a true Cremona varnish, restores to his instruments a superior sound).

To summarize: violin varnish and ways of applying it were essentially developed during the first half of the sixteenth century. After that they were refined, the range of varnish colors was expanded, and luminosity was enhanced. The quality of varnish declined ca. 1750, leading to efforts by countless luthiers and researchers to rediscover, through painstaking work, what had been forgotten or lost. The old Italian varnish no longer can be considered a secret; it was the product of the genius of the old masters and their helpers.

EIGHTEENTH-CENTURY VIOLIN MAKING OUTSIDE ITALY

FRANCE

For a long time, the French luthiers' concept of a violin's sound was very different from that held by their colleagues in Italy. Italian instruments were characterized by a large tone. Italian composers took advantage of this by writing sonatas, concerti grossi, and solo concertos. For the kind of dance music that continued to be favored in France, a relatively small tone sufficed, which in turn determined how French instruments were constructed and played.

François Médard (1647–1720) was the first to reach the level of Italian builders, partly because in the meantime French violin music had been exposed to strong Italian influences. For some time, French builders tended to follow the Amati model, among them Jacques Boquay (Bocquay; d. 1730 in Paris), whose small, well-made instruments had a correspondingly small sound. In his teaching at the Paris Conservatoire, Baillot used a Boquay violin. René Champion (d. 1770) was a Boquay pupil whose instruments displayed fine workmanship. Claude Pierray (d. 1729) also built fine instruments in the Amati manner. A gradual preference for the Stradivari model is shown by the violins made by François Gaviniès (1683–1772) of Bordeaux, who was active in Paris after 1741. Actually, his son acquired greater fame than his violins, which gave rise to a play on words that is difficult to translate: "François Gaviniès n'avait jamais fait qu'un bon violon, et ce violon était son fils" (François Gaviniès produced only one good violin [i.e., violinist], namely his son).

François Louis Pique (d. 1822), from the Mirecourt region, made excellent violins more representative of the Stradivari manner, as did Gérard J. Deleplanque (d. 1790) of Lille, who early on had turned to the large Strad model.

During the eighteenth century, Paris made great musical strides, which helped to attract Italian violin makers to the city, among them Louis Lagetto (Luigi Lagetoo), who used the Amati forms and who called his shop La Ville de Crémone. Others were André Castagneri (d. 1762), who followed Stradivari and Guarneri, and Vincenzo Panormo (d. 1813 in London). Franz Fendt (d. 1791) moved from the Tyrol to Paris, where he called himself François Fent. He was an important advocate of the Strad model. His success in Paris caused some family members to follow him there; others achieved importance in London.

Louis Guersan (d. 1770), the talented student of Pierray, has already been mentioned in connection with his varnish experiments. He tended to partially suffocate his instruments (otherwise well made) under a hard layer of varnish. Still, they must have sounded good at first, for his use of a quick-drying spirit varnish, which speeded up work, was widely adopted. His labels read "Ludovicus / Guersan / prope / Comoediam / Gallicam / Lutetia / Anno . . ." (L. G., near the Comédie Française, Paris, in the year . . .).

Pierre (1893) offers some interesting statistics regarding Paris luthiers in the last third of the eighteenth century. The consequences of the French Revolution on one aspect of musical activities, one that had been largely supported by the nobility and upper bourgeoisie, is obvious:

1769	1775	1777	1779	1783	1789	1791	An VII
10	40	53	45	58	43	22	19

[An (Year) VII: Revolutionary leaders had introduced a new calendar that began on 22 September 1792]

At the end of the seventeenth century, twenty-one luthiers worked in Paris; by the end of the eighteenth century this number had increased to 170.

Instruments by the Lupot family represent a high point in French violin making of this period. The founder, Jean (d. 1696), worked in Mirecourt; his son Laurent, at first a schoolteacher, was active as a luthier in Lunéville and Orléans ca. 1750. Instruments by the grandson François I (1725–1804) represent the Strad model. For a time he was employed by the duke of Wurttemberg, using the label "François Lupot, luthier de / la cour de Wirtenbergk, / à Stoutgard l'anno. . . ." His son Nicolas, the family's outstanding luthier, was born in Stuttgart but settled in Orléans and later in Paris, where he died in 1824.

In 1815, Nicolas was appointed luthier to the French court; the following year he was put in charge of instruments at the Conservatoire. During his last years he used labels that proudly referred to himself as "Luthier de la Musique du Roi / et de l'École Royale de Musique / Paris. . . ." Gaviniès established the tradition of providing all violin and cello prize winners at the Conservatoire with an instrument by Lupot. Nicolas Lupot was one of the best violin makers of all time, rightfully called "the French Strad." The sound of violins from the classic age in some instances is beginning to show signs of deterioration, while the best Italian violins continue to be taken out of circulation by wealthy collectors; more and more, concert violinists look for Lupots.

Joseph Bassot of Mirecourt was strongly influenced by Lupot. He opened an atelier in Paris, where he died in 1808. Another outstanding Paris violin maker was Jean Théodore Namy (d. 1808), reputed to be a highly skilled repairer. Sibire (1806) had words of praise for him:

A man of great merit. Talented in all aspects of his field, he made it his special task to give new life to weak centenarians. . . . From all over France, fragile instruments from centuries past find their way to his shop, which resembles an old people's home. One by one they line up for treatment. . . . Whenever I come across an instrument that has been repaired with great art and skill I recognize his workmanship, and I say without hesitation: "That is Namy's work," just as I would say: "That is a Cremona violin."

THE HISTORY OF THE VIOLIN

AUSTRIA AND GERMANY

Here, the concept of the ideal sound worked against the building of instruments comparable in quality to those of Stradivari and Guarneri. During most of the eighteenth century the Stainer type of violin, with a noble, velvety dark yet small sound, continued to be preferred in German-speaking countries, especially in Austria. A turn to the Strad model did not take place until about 1800—later, that is, than in France. Representative of this change is the career of Johann Gottlob Pfretzschner (1753–1823), who came from a well-known family of luthiers of the Vogtland region, a family that later became famous for making first-rate bows. Pfretzschner worked in Markneukirchen, initially following the Stainer model. He experimented a good deal and finally chose Stradivari as his model. His instruments are suitable for orchestral use.

Discussing the emerging fashion of preferring Italian instruments, Fuchs quotes a violin label: "Johann Gottlob Pfretzschner / prope Violino car Respontent / Romani cremona 17—." The wording makes no sense, but does include the magic word, "Cremona." Other violins carry the label "Carl Ferdinand Primerius / Musikalischer Instrumentenmacher in / Italia. . . ." None of these violins have ever been *near* Italy, having been made in Klingenthal or Neukirchen!

Eighteenth-century musical life in Germany and Italy was characterized by the many small and medium-size orchestras maintained by secular and ecclesiastical rulers. Up to Napoleon's time there were as many as 365 independent principalities, including city states. Unlike in France, power was thus decentralized, and cultural life profited from this. Given this wealth of orchestras, many luthiers not only looked after existing instruments but also built new ones, maybe not of superior quality but entirely adequate for orchestral playing.

Anton Posch (d. 1742) and his son Anton Stephan Posch (d. 1749) moved to Vienna from Bavaria. Both worked for the Austrian court. On his labels the son called himself "Königlicher Hoflautenmacher" (royal court luthier), but the title does not imply that he made lutes.

The changeover from the Stainer to the Strad model is also reflected in the work of the Stadlmann family of luthiers, five of whom worked in Vienna. The first was Daniel Achatius Stadlmann (b. 1680); the last, Michael Ignaz (d. 1813), played first violin in the court orchestra. During the eighteenth century, six members of the Partl family made violins; among them Michael Andreas Partl (d. 1788) was outstanding. Among Viennese luthiers were also five members of the Leidolf family; the first of whom probably received training in Italy. Johann Christoph Leidolf (d. 1758) and Joseph Ferdinand Leidolf (d. 1780) excelled; their violins were made following the Stainer model.

Capable luthiers belonging to the Stoss family of Füssen settled in Vienna, St. Pölten, and Innsbruck; J. Martin Stoss (d. 1838) was luthier to the imperial-royal court. Sebastian Dalinger (d. 1809) remained true to the

Stainer model as did most members of the Thir family from Bavaria, eight of whom settled in Pressburg (Bratislava) and Vienna. Johann Georg Thir (d. 1781), one of the best, unfortunately treated his instruments with nitric acid before applying the varnish, thus spoiling the beautiful wood.

The outstanding Austrian luthier during Beethoven's time was Franz Geissenhof (Gaisenhof; b. in Bavaria, d. 1821). He followed Italian models, and his best instruments approached those in quality. The violin on which the young Mozart first practiced was made in Salzburg by Andreas Ferdinand Mayr, known to have worked there until 1764. Johann Michael Alban (Albani; d. 1730), of the famous family of luthiers in Bolzano, established himself in Graz and made excellent cellos. The brothers Simon Joannes (d. 1774) and Joannes Baptista Havelka (d. 1799), probably of Bohemian origin, were active in Linz, making very fine violins in the Bohemian–Austrian style then in vogue.

Six luthiers belonging to the Leeb family worked mostly in Vienna. Andreas Carl Leeb was one of the Austrian makers who adopted the flat Strad model.

Close cultural ties joined Prague, Vienna, and southern Germany. Thomas Edlinger (d. 1729) and Joannes Udalricus Eberle (d. 1768), two Bavarians, worked in Prague. Thomas Andreas Hulinzky (d. 1788) was Eberle's student and later taught Anton Laske (d. 1805). Members of the Rauch family of Augsburg supplied luthiers for Würzburg, Komotau, and Breslau, as well as for Prague and other cities. The same is true of the Hellmer family of luthiers, active throughout southern Germany.

Füssen was the home of many talented luthiers, among them Simpert Niggell (d. 1799), Johann Anton Gedler (d. 1790), and Marcus Guggemos (d. 1791), all of whom supplied outstanding instruments according to the Stainer model. Johann Paul Alletsee (d. 1738), probably a Füssen native, moved to Munich, where he became court luthier. Because of his style and superior varnish it is likely he spent considerable time in Italy, perhaps Venice.

For several generations the Schändl family of Mittenwald continued the Klotz tradition, even into the nineteenth century; its ablest representative was Michael Schändl (d. 1750). A good luthier in Augsburg was Georg Aman (d. 1734), who followed the Amati model. The Edlinger family also came from Augsburg; some of them worked in their hometown, others settled in Prague. Three generations of the Buchstetter family established themselves in Stadtamhof near Regensburg. Christoff André Buchstetter used Gasparo da Salò as his model, while his son Gabriel David Buchstetter (d. 1780), though considering Italian models, went his own way. His instruments are so good that for a long time Spohr concertized on a Buchstetter violin. Joseph Buchstetter, a grandson (d. 1880), followed nineteenth-century practices.

In Nuremberg, Leonhard Maussiell (d. 1765) built good violins on the Stainer model and also made fine gambas. Leopold Widhalm (d. 1776) of the same city also followed Stainer. Fuchs called him one of the best German luthiers. Sebastian Schelle (d. 1747), also of Nuremberg, made violins in the Italian style as well as good lutes. Johann Georg Vogler, from the Füssen region, was active in Würzburg during the first half of the century. His instruments have increased in value, though the opposite is true of his famous son, the Abbé Vogler, who because of his "reform organ," is widely held responsible for the ca. 1800 decline in German organ building. Zacharias Fischer (d. 1812), taking advantage of the fashionable preference for old Italian instruments, used artificial methods for drying wood and chemicals to give it an antique appearance. His violins were basically good and probably found affluent buyers, but within a few decades they lost their vitality and usefulness.

In Mannheim, Jakob Rauch (d. 1763) looked after the instruments belonging to the musicians of the Johann Stamitz circle. Ellwangen, a small princely residence, attracted Benedikt Wagner (d. 1796) to the post of court luthier; his fine violins show the change from the highly arched to the flat type. Martin Diehl (d. 1786) was the founder of a family of violin makers known to have worked in Prague and later in Darmstadt and Hamburg. Johann Georg Hassert (d. 1780) lived in Eisenach, making quite good instruments based on Italian models. Anton Bachmann (d. 1800 in Berlin) took care of the instruments in the court chapel of Frederick the Great. His son Carl Ludwig Bachmann (d. 1809) at first used Stainer as his model, then Amati and Stradivari. He also played viola in the royal orchestra and together with Ernst Benda founded the Liebhaberkonzerte that flourished in Berlin from 1770 to 1797.

Similar duties—to look after the string instruments of the Leipzig musicians—were carried out by Martin Hoffmann (d. 1719) and by his son Johann Christian (d. 1750). They may also have been responsible for the upkeep of instruments in the Saxon court chapel, an important orchestra that counted Volumier, Pisendel, and at times F. M. Veracini among its members. Christian reached some fame as the builder (according to J. S. Bach's instructions) of the viola pomposa, a small cello held like a viola.

In 1703 Handel entered the orchestra of the Hamburg opera house at the Gänsemarkt as a second violinist. There, Joachim Tielke (d. 1719) was in charge of maintaining the string instruments. A famous maker of gambas and lutes, Tielke also built violins of above-average quality, following the Amati model.

HOLLAND AND BELGIUM

Established standards of violin making were maintained in these countries during the eighteenth century. Luthiers displayed an openness to French innovations. Egidius Snoeck (d. 1736), a member of an old family of organ builders, became court luthier in Brussels, a position later held by his son Marc Snoeck (d. 1762) and by his grandson Henri Augustin Snoeck, a composer who eventually became first violinist in the royal chapel. In Amsterdam, Pieter Rombouts (d. 1740), stepson and pupil of Jacobs, made violins, violas, and cellos showing fine workmanship. In The Hague, Erhard Amman (d. 1770) at first made violins in the traditional Dutch style; later he followed

Bergonzi. Jacques B. Lefèbvre (d. 1773) of Mirecourt received his training in Cremona and then settled in Amsterdam. His fine violins in the Amati style gave a new perspective to Dutch violin making. Joseph Boussu (d. 1780) of Etterbeek (a Brussels suburb) also followed Amati, as did Gosewijn Spijker (Spyker; d. 1812), while Ambroise de Comble (d. 1787) of Tournai and Johannes Theodorus Cuypers (d. 1808) and his sons in The Hague preferred the Strad model. Comble is said to have been a Stradivari pupil.

ENGLAND

Here, for a long time the preferred timbre was the gamba's, so that the Stainer and Amati models were slow in losing favor. Barak Norman (d. 1740) made more gambas than violins. The sign outside his shop showed a bass viol, and his labels read "Barak Norman / at the Bass Viol / in St. Paul's Alley / London. Fecit / 17—." He began making instruments in the Stainer manner, but later used less arching and incorporated some features of the Maggini type. Nathaniel Cross (d. 1751) at times was Norman's business partner. He apparently found it advantageous to use the name Nathanaeli Crosso on his labels. Peter Wamsley (d. 1751), an excellent London luthier, adversely affected his reputation by artificially aging his wood by treating it with chemicals. Many of his colleagues on the Continent had done the same. He tried to improve on the Strad model by using extremely thin tops, which turned out to be a mistake. Violins by Alexander Kennedy (d. 1785) and Thomas Smith (d. 1799) show that the Stainer model lasted in England for a long time. This also applies to violins by the Forster family in Brampton. Its founder, John S. Forster (d. 1781), also made spinning wheels and rifles. His grandson William Forster (d. 1808), also a luthier, founded a publishing house through which he came in contact with Haydn. What he glued to the inside of his instruments amounts to an advertising display rather than a traditional label: "William Forster / Violin, Violoncello, Tenor and Bow-maker / Also Music Seller / To their Royal Highness the / Prince of Wales and Duke of Cumberland / Opposite the Church. St. Martin's Lane, London. / N.B. / The above instruments are made in the best manner / and finished with the original varnish, / and a copy of every Capital Instrument in England / may be had."

During the last decades of the eighteenth century a change in taste took place, leading to preferences at first for violins of the Amati, then the Strad type, which shift is already evident in the instruments of Daniel Parker (d. ca. 1761 in London). For many years, Fritz Kreisler concertized on a Parker. Members of the Banks family led this new trend. Its first known luthier was Benjamin Banks (d. 1795), a pupil of Wamsley who worked in Salisbury. He tended to use Amati models unless a customer ordered a Stainer model. Good work was done by his son James Banks, who moved the firm to Liverpool jointly with his brother, who repaired pianos.

Richard Duke (d. 1780), John Barton (d. 1810), and Charles Harris (d. 1813) all worked in London. It is typical of this transitional period that John

Crowther (d. 1810), according to his customers' wishes, built instruments following Stainer, Amati, or Stradivari models.

John Edward Betts (d. 1823) was a student of Richard Duke. He opened a shop in London, was a good businessman, and was able to attract many excellent workers, mostly from abroad. He made few violins, but his shop became an important trading center for Italian instruments at a time when English collectors were just beginning to appear on the scene.

Of major importance for violin making in England was Joseph Hill, the founder of the famous shop that exists to this day. Labels from his later years read "Joseph Hill & Sons, makers / of harps and flutes / in the Haymarket / London 17—." The list of his descendants takes us to the present day.

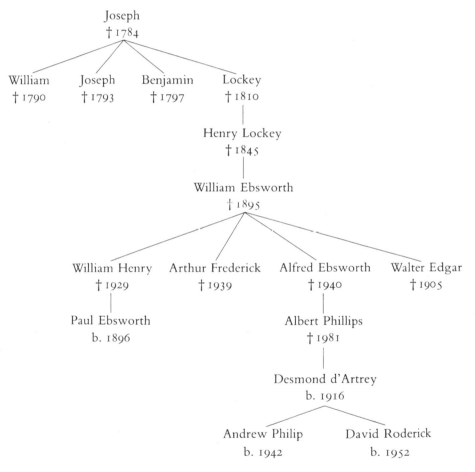

Genealogy of the Hill Family of Luthiers

THE IBERIAN PENINSULA

Instrument making in Spain and Portugal was directly influenced by Italian masters. There are quite a few fine pieces, and the names of the luthiers are righly esteemed. But quantities are limited; not enough instruments were made to satisfy even the region's needs.

ALBERT FUCHS, *TAXE DER STREICHINSTRUMENTE*, 1960

While this last observation is true, the general statement is somewhat unjust. A direct Italian influence can be explained by the close political ties between Italy and Spain. For more than two centuries Naples was part of the Spanish kingdom, and parts of northern Italy at various times were ruled by Spain until the end of the Spanish War of Succession (1714). At that time the Spanish court insisted on being supplied only by first-rate Italian luthiers. This influx of outstanding Italian instruments had a beneficial effect. Stradivari's influence was felt very early, leading in the late eighteenth century to the emergence of fine Spanish and Portuguese luthiers. Among these were José Benedict (d. 1744) of Cadiz, who was better known as a maker of guitars, and Salvadore Bofill (d. 1756) of Barcelona, who followed models by both Stradivari and del Gesù. José I Contreras (d. 1780) of Granada, called "El Granadino," worked in Madrid and also was known abroad. His instruments, based on Italian models, had labels such as "Matriti per Granadensem / Josephum Contreras / anno 17—" (Made in Madrid by Josephus Contreras of Granada). Forgers removed labels from some of his violins on the assumption that his name was little known among collectors who were always looking for old Italian instruments. His son José II (d. 1827) also made violins in the best Italian tradition. Two luthiers named Guillami (father and son) were active in Barcelona. Strad copies by Joannes I Guillami (d. 1760) currently bring good prices (Joannes II mostly made double basses). João Jozé de Souza (d. 1780) was established in Lisbon, having received his training in Mirecourt and Paris.

THE INDUSTRIALIZATION OF VIOLIN MAKING

With the advent of large violin shops, division of labor was the norm. Even before that it had been the custom to turn certain tasks over to apprentices or to poorly paid assistants, such as the making of fingerboards, pegs, bridges, and other small parts, and the rough finishing of neck and scroll. Though Stainer usually worked alone, we know that he hired an assistant to help with making a double bass, and that his wages were calculated into the instrument's cost.

The enormous popularity of violin playing, especially in the eighteenth century, greatly increased the demand for cheap student instruments. No longer could the demand be filled by the old methods. Division of labor, including specialization in certain aspects of manufacturing a product, had proved to be cost effective during the early stages of industrialization, especially in England, France, and the Netherlands, and such money-saving procedures soon came to be applied to violin making. The beginning of this trend can be seen in shops in which family members worked, including women and children. They received no real wages, which made possible more output at relatively low prices.

The little town of Mirecourt in the Vosges Mountains, south of Nancy, became one of the first centers of this kind of organized violin making. Early on two families cooperated, the Jacquot family, with twenty-three violin makers (according to Vannes), and the Vuillaume family with twenty-five. The former goes back to Claude Jacquot (b. ca. 1580), the latter to Claude Vuillaume, whose name first appears ca. 1625. For Mirecourt, Vannes found the names of no less than 830 luthiers, but during the period of its greatest flourishing, four-fifths of the entire population were involved, directly or indirectly, in making violins as well as strings, the latter forming a significant part of the operation. According to Pierre, Nicolas employed six hundred workers who produced one million string instruments, while the bow maker Pageot was responsible for some hundred thousand bows. In the late nineteenth century, the Thibouville-Lamy firm reached an average annual production of twenty-five to thirty thousand string instruments. Drögemeyer noted that ca. 1900, 360 different models of instruments were made in Mirecourt. Needless to say that a well-organized distribution system was needed to sell this mountain of instruments.

It would be wrong to assume that only cheap, mass produced instruments resulted from all this activity. In spite of industrialized methods, highly esteemed luthiers worked in these centers, insisting on quality and managing to impart their own characteristics to at least some of the local products. This is shown by the development of the Vuillaume family, up to Jean-Baptiste, who in 1818 moved to Paris. Other significant families of luthiers worked in Mirecourt. The Trévillot family flourished in the eighteenth century, and the Mougenot family, which goes back to Nicolas Mougenot, continues to include excellent luthiers to the present time. Auguste Darte (d. 1892) could fashion high-quality violins if an interested buyer asked for one, but most were labeled "Fabrique de / A. Darte / à Mirecourt."

Violin makers in Mirecourt were closely related to those in Paris, for most of the latter originally came from Mirecourt families. Many instruments from Mirecourt were given false labels, implying that they had been built in Paris, the intent being to drive up prices. Forgeries were facilitated by the fact that many Mirecourt factories were owned by Paris firms.

In German-speaking countries, the Sudeten and Vogtland regions became centers of violin making. According to Vannes, Markneukirchen counted 939 luthiers, Schönbach 378, and Graslitz 33. The tradition goes back to the Thirty Years War, when luthiers fled Bohemia for religious reasons, settling in Markneukirchen and the neighboring towns of Klingenthal, Schönbach, and Erlbach. Johann Georg Schönfelder (Schönfeld; b. 1653 in Graslitz) settled in Markneukirchen, where in 1677 he became the co-founder of a luthiers' guild. He and others organized the production and sale of reasonably priced string instruments. Large families of violin makers, some carrying on the craft for several centuries, were active in the Sudeten region around Schönbach. As given by Vannes, in Markneukirchen these included the families Dölling (with 20 members bearing the name), Ficker (26), Gläsel (26), Glier (15), Gütter (37), Heberlein (27), Kessler (24), Kretzschmann (31), Kurzendörffer (17), Nürnberger (13), Otto (14), Pfretzschner (21), Reichel (57), Schönfelder (17), Schuster (14), and Voigt (43).

Some, such as Nürnberger and Pfretzschner, became widely known as makers of excellent bows. Luthiers in Schönbach included the families Brandner (12), Buchner (15), Hoyer (19), Klier (12), Placht (28), and Sandner (21). They (and especially the Schallers) produced violins in all categories of quality and price, the best ones being eminently suitable for use in professional orchestras. In recent times women luthiers also have become masters. In Markneukirchen, Helene Johanna Voigt has made fine copies of Italian master violins.

Astounding amounts of string instruments were made as early as 1800. At that time Markneukirchen had seventy-eight shops headed by master luthiers, producing violins, violas, cellos, and string basses. Twenty-six shops specialized in bow making, thirty in string making. In Klingenthal, eighty-five masters made violins exclusively. In all, the yearly production in the Klingenthal region amounted to an average of at least thirty-six thousand instruments. By refining production methods and achieving greater efficiency, these figures were greatly increased during the nineteenth century. After 1945, when the Sudeten region became part of Czechoslovakia, many luthiers emigrated to Germany. They were welcomed there since their work brought in desirable hard currency. Major enterprises established in Bubenreuth in Bavaria exported instruments all over the world.

Luthiers in Klingenthal, located on the other side of the Sudeten mountains, across the border in Saxony, stayed in contact with their colleagues in Markneukirchen. According to Vannes's lexicon, 149 masters are established there. The local tradition can be traced back to the Dörffel family in the seventeenth century; a luthiers' guild was formed in 1716. Violins from the Vogtland were much in demand by orchestra players; they were somewhat above average in quality and reasonably priced. Comparable and better instruments were made by some members of the Hopf (14), Hoyer (15), Meinel (11; according to Henley 24), and Meisel families. Others, including the Glass family, lived elsewhere in the region. String making became increasingly important in these centers. A string makers' guild, formed in Markneukirchen in 1777, was accorded many privileges and soon acquired an international reputation. A shop specializing in making superior bows was founded by Joseph Strötz (d. 1760), who had come from Bavaria.

Mathias Klotz, a major figure, stands at the beginning of a long tradition of making fine instruments in and around Mittenwald (Bavaria). His family produced many other good luthiers, during the eighteenth century and even today. Before Klotz, Mathias Neuner made violins in Mittenwald. He too became the founder of a dynasty of luthiers who remain active, though now primarily as commercial distributors of violins. Vannes lists 276 master builders in Mittenwald, including the Hornsteiner family, with eighteen members, going back to the eighteenth century. During the nineteenth century, the two firms of Neuner & Hornsteiner and Baader were largely responsible for the production and distribution of instruments. Baader owned the Royal Bavarian String Instrument Factory, founded in 1790.

This enormous increase in the production of instruments and accessories called for extensive training—the kind of instruction that went beyond what was possible under the old master-apprentice system. Trade schools, in which music instruction formed an important part of the curriculum, were founded in Markneukirchen (1834), Klingenthal (1844), and Adorf (1860). The Mittenwald school (1858) continues to have an especially good reputation. All chiefly provide practical, "hands-on" instruction.

Some writers have looked down on this mass production of "inferior" violins. They have failed to see the connection with the enormous increase of string playing in the nineteenth and twentieth centuries, in schools and orchestras of all kinds. To buy a good violin is primarily a question of money; in fact, without affluent buyers, superior instruments would seldom be made. But almost every violinist started out on a "box," and even its purchase at a very low price may have represented a sacrifice for the parents. Those who enjoy playing on a fine old Italian instrument might well thank those who produced inexpensive violins for beginners.

VIOLIN COLLECTORS AND DEALERS

In medieval times, instruments that were not needed for ordinary daily use were stored by princes in special rooms. These "instrument rooms" were the predecessors of the instrument collections later maintained by connoisseurs and amateurs. In some cases the collections became quite comprehensive, including many kinds of instruments. Some collectors acquired objects that were beautiful, even as pieces of furniture, such as harpsichords, spinets, and small organs; they delighted the eye even if they were seldom played. Some major collections, such as those of the d'Este family in Modena, the Contarinis in Venice, and Prince Ferdinando de Medici in Florence, also contained instruments that had unusual shapes or were representative of earlier epochs. Our sense of historical consciousness developed during the renaissance; as a result, instruments that earlier would have been discarded were preserved, their wood used for repairs. Old instruments were rebuilt, adapted to modern practices since otherwise they would have become useless.

One of the most famous early collections, assembled during the sixteenth century by the Austrian archduke Ferdinand, was located in Ambros castle near Innsbruck. Most of its holdings are now in Vienna, offering unique source material for organological research.

The violin did not attract the attention of collectors until rather late. It was considered to be the instrument of professional players, and though its sound provided a welcome addition to everyday musical activities at court, violins were not yet valued by collectors. During the first century of its existence, the violin seldom was the object of lavish, artistic execution, including the varnishing; that would have increased costs and impeded sales. But with the work of Nicolò Amati, Stainer, and especially Stradivari, the artistic aspects of violin making reached a high degree of perfection. Gradually, their instruments were bought not only because of their sound but also for aesthetic reasons, or as investments. In 1716, the Venetian patrician Lorenzo Giustiniani wrote a letter to Stradivari that characterizes this new attitude.

> Everyone says that the world has no luthier who is as gifted as you are. I would be happy to have an object to remind me of such a famous man who is such an outstanding artisan. I therefore am writing to inquire whether you would make a violin for me, devoting all your talent to the task, so that this would be the very best, the most beautiful instrument you are capable of creating.

A modest collection, known to us from a Florentine testament, has as its nucleus six Stainer instruments. It is one of the earliest collections devoted to violins and was assembled by the violinist and composer Antonio Veracini, uncle of the famous virtuoso. A more significant eighteenth-century collection, held by violinist Antonio Bonazzi, contained forty-two violins, including some by Nicolò Amati, Antonio Stradivari, and del Gesù.

Count Ignazio Alessandro Cozio di Salabue of Cremona was one of the first great collectors. Born in 1755 at Casale-Monferrato castle in Piedmont, he was financially well-off. In 1720 his father bought him a Nicolò Amati violin on which Cozio played until his interests turned to the instruments themselves, rather than playing. When he was seventeen, he made the acquaintance in Turin of Giovanni Battista Guadagnini, who had recently moved there. Facing strong professional jealousy and competition, Guadagnini had not yet succeeded in establishing himself and for several years had encountered financial difficulties. Cozio was so impressed by his instruments that he bought all that were available, though he seems to have been lax about paying. Guadagnini sent him urgent requests for money; he was unable to go on working as he needed funds to purchase wood. On his death Cozio left behind fifty of the master's instruments.

Remarks by Guadagnini may have prompted Cozio to expand his interests to include Cremonese violins. Eventually he acquired (through purchase or exchange) master violins from all over northern Italy. At twenty years of age, he already owned thirteen Strads and six Nicolò Amati violins. He kept a card file to help him keep track of the location of valuable instruments that might be for sale. On one card he noted that Signor Luigi Passeri, a clergyman and musician, owned two Stainer violins, and that he lived in Pavia.

In the long run, such activities did not seem appropriate for a member of the nobility, aside from necessitating constant travel. Cozio therefore employed a middleman, the cloth merchant Giovanni Michele Anselmi Briata from Casale, who made good use of his many connections to help locate and purchase instruments. The most important contact was Paolo Stradivari, the master's youngest son. A year before his death, Antonio Stradivari had paid 20,000 lire to buy a place for his son in the cloth business of Bertio in Cremona. Antonio is said to have left about one hundred violins, some of them only half finished and later completed by his sons Francesco and Omobono. Almost all were sold, because "violins by Amati and Stradivari sell like hotcakes," as Paolo's son Antonio put it in a 1776 letter. Cozio and his agents barely managed to get in on the end of this treasure sale. Paolo still owned ten of his father's violins, and Briata bought them all for the count. The related correspondence shows, by the way, that at that time Nicolò Amati's violins brought substantially higher prices than Stradivari's.

Other valuable objects, such as models, templates, drawings, and tools used by Antonio (some originally owned by Nicolò Amati), formed part of the estate. After much bargaining, all were purchased by the count. When the French occupied Piedmont and Lombardy in 1797, he deposited his collection with Carlo Carli, a banker in Milan. Cozio's finances deteriorated during the war, and he was forced to sell some of his instruments. In a printed announcement "aux amateurs de musique" he offered his Cremona instruments for sale, "the entire collection or individual pieces," listing instruments by Antonio, Hieronymus, and Nicolò Amati; Antonio Stradivari; Ruggieri; and J. B. Guadagnini. Still, he kept five Strads, including the famous "Messiah."

The count must have been a curious mixture of idealist, researcher, dedicated collector, and clever businessman. Through his contacts with Guadagnini, who died in 1786, one of the last great Italian luthiers, he was a witness to the decline of Italian violin making. For a while he planned to establish a school for violin makers in Turin. His purchase of the tools and other materials from Stradivari's shop was not altogether due to his collector's zeal; he intended to preserve these precious documents, and the knowledge and skills to be derived from them, for later generations. It may be that Guadagnini's death, or the developments of the time, caused Cozio's plan to come to nothing. At the age of sixty-one, Cozio began to jot down his memoirs of his years of collecting instruments. These recollections are not altogether reliable, but together with his correspondence, bills of sale, and descriptions of instruments, they are valuable source material for violin research.

Cozio died in 1840, having devoted the last decades of his life to the study of Piedmont general history. His estate included seventy-four instruments, including the fifty made by Guadagnini mentioned earlier. A section of his catalogue entitled "Violini di diversi autori" includes those by Andrea Amati; Bergonzi; Andrea, Pietro, and Giuseppe Guarneri; Ruggieri; and Stainer. His heirs apparently lost no time in divesting themselves of everything. Among those interested in buying was a certain Luigi Tarisio, who succeeded in obtaining fourteen instruments right away, another twelve soon after, and two more in 1845—at ridiculous prices. The group of twelve, for instance, brought 120 lire each; the lot of fourteen on the average went for 200 francs—this at a time when in Paris one could sell a Strad for 5000 francs!

This Tarisio (b. ca. 1790) is one of the strangest figures in the history of the violin. An illiterate, he at first worked as a carpenter's apprentice. During his peregrinations, doing odd jobs and fiddling at dances, he also repaired instruments, including those of owners who had no idea of their true value. He gradually bought whatever instruments he could get a hold of, usually at absurdly low prices. As he traded violins, he gradually became an expert, quite familiar with the different schools, with specific makers, and the various stages in their careers. Meanwhile Italian violins had become very popular in France, thanks largely to Viotti. In 1824, Tarisio therefore decided to offer a small assortment of his instruments for sale in Paris. Carrying six valuable violins on his back, he set out on foot, arriving in Paris dirty and in rags. He happened to present himself to Aldric, one of the city's leading luthiers, but because of his disheveled appearance he was unable to sell his violins at a decent price. Tarisio had learned his lesson. When he returned to Paris, he arrived in an elegant carriage, presented his violins in excellent condition and perfectly adjusted. He also knew how to cash in on the rivalries between Aldric, Chanot, Thibaud, and Vuillaume, thus driving up prices and making tidy profits. In this way, Tarisio successfully sold instruments in France for almost thirty years. He used his profits for new, successful explorations in Italy, looking for new treasures chiefly in churches and monasteries. He loved his best instruments so much that he would not sell them.

Gradually, Vuillaume became a regular buyer of Tarisio's instruments, and his shop, a gathering place for violin lovers. Paris thus was the first center for the sale of Italian master violins. Upon news of Tarisio's death in Milan in 1854, Vuillaume left immediately for that city. What he found far exceeded his expectations. Though on the road much of the time, Tarisio had established a foothold in a modest Milan inn, which also served as a storehouse for his instruments. In this single room, in which Tarisio had died on a dilapidated sofa, there were stacks of instruments, 244 in all—violins, violas, cellos, basses, and other instruments. The deceased man's relatives were visibly delighted to get rid of all this "junk" at once, especially for the sum of 80,000 francs in cash. What seemed like a fairy tale to them was for Vuillaume the business deal of a lifetime. On a small farm near Novara that had also belonged to Tarisio, six more violins were found: two Strads, one del Gesù, one Carlo Bergonzi, and two J. B. Guadagninis. One of the Strads had been bought by Cozio in 1824; for years Tarisio talked to the Parisians about it. Heralded for so long and now at last appeared, it was christened "Messiah" by Vuillaume.

Quite a few of Tarisio's instruments reached English collectors by way of Paris. A kind of passion for collecting valuable violins had developed in England. As early as 1710, William Corbett, an English court musician, spent several years in Italy to look for music and musical instruments. He purchased some fine Cremona violins. Before he died in 1748 Corbett deeded his collection to Gresham College, on the condition that it be exhibited. He even established a yearly endowment for that purpose. The collection, however, was auctioned off in 1751, supposedly for lack of space.

In 1724 Corbett had offered for sale "some of the most beautiful violins made by the famous Amati, by the elder Stradivari from Cremona, by Giovanni P. Maggini and Gasparo da Salò from Brescia, and by the famous makers Albani and Stainer from the Tyrol." He apparently found no buyers at the time. Arthur Betts (d. 1847) began collecting a few decades after Corbett's death. Around 1800, the London banker Stephenson owned the largest collection of Italian instruments, while James Goding, a brewer, acquired a dozen each of Stradivari and Guarneri violins. Some collectors, such as Joseph Gillott, freely admitted that they knew nothing about instruments and regarded their purchases as mere investments, especially in view of steadily rising prices. Among knowledgeable collectors were the counts Castelbarco and Valdrighi in Italy and Wilmotte (d. 1893) in Antwerp, who owned twenty master violins. The duke of Campo Selice in Paris (d. 1887) owned twelve instruments. Other major collectors were the duke of Hamilton, Baron Knoop in London, the manufacturers Walher in Grulich (Czechoslovakia) and Hämmerle in Dornbirn (Austria), and the lawyer Geissmar in Mannheim. Most of these collections were sold at auction after the owner's death, usually because the heirs were not interested and more eager to obtain ready cash. The 1872 auction of the Gillott collection in London was a major event in collectors' circles. From another famous collection, owned by Charles Plowden, George Hart bought four Strads and four del Gesù violins.

The market for master violins grew by leaps and bounds during the nineteenth century, leading to the emergence of experts or professional appraisers. Vuillaume, for instance, had received from Tarisio instruments by the best Italian makers. Some were still in mint condition—in fact, some had hardly been played. Examining these violins made him one of the foremost experts on Italian violins. "Who is going to know anything about Italian violins after Chanot and I have died?" he once said, half in jest, yet he knew that there was some truth to the remark. True experts must have knowledge of such vast dimensions that at any one time one can count them on the fingers of one hand. The person who has tried his hand at cutting a few dozen scrolls, who has constantly experimented making the many seemingly minor small parts that go into the making of a violin—only that person will be able to size up an instrument, to recognize characteristics of a specific school, a master builder, or a certain stage in his work. Repairing instruments in particular offers opportunities to open them and to examine details of their interior construction and workmanship. Gaetano Sgarabotto, one of Italy's most knowledgeable experts, has repaired as many as 450 violins in a year, making plaster casts or sketches of noteworthy details. This offers unique opportunities for making comparisons. Over the years, an expert can thus acquire a knowledge that seems astonishing.

But such expertise also requires a phenomenal memory for shapes and colors. The Berlin luthier Schulze once recognized a violin before it had been taken out of its case—a violin he had repaired thirty years ago. He could tell the present customer who its prior owners had been. In 1851, Tarisio visited Goding in London. Goding showed him his instruments, arranged along the sides of a large room. Tarisio sat in the middle, and from a distance of several meters was able to identify not only each master builder, but in most cases the year it had been made as well. Most of these instruments at one time had been handled by Tarisio and had reached London via Paris. He had committed to his amazing photographic memory both the exact shape and varnish color of every instrument and could now identify it immediately.

Vuillaume, who came from a family of luthiers in Mirecourt, was such an expert. The ability to make authoritative judgments is highly desirable in a field such as violin making, where there probably are more forged than genuine objects.

Another problem, perhaps the most serious one, is mentioned by Iviglia in his preface to Cozio's *Carteggio*. It has to do with honesty. Usually violin experts are also dealers. We should put ourselves in the position of a dealer from whom a wealthy collector (they seldom are experts themselves) wants to buy a Strad, the authenticity of which has not been definitely established. Should the dealer tell the potential buyer about his doubts, thereby risking the loss of a lucrative sale? Albert Berr tells of a Strad copy, known as the "Balfour," for which there are no fewer than nine certificates of authenticity by outstanding English and French dealers. Some of these certificates no doubt were issued in good faith, but it is conceivable that the authors of others had reservations that they kept to themselves. On the whole, however, such certificates, if issued by top experts, can be considered reliable.

The snobs among collectors, of course, care little whether the twelve instruments in their safe are copies or genuine master violins. By the same token, professional musicians may not derive much consolation from a parcel of such certificates if the instrument does not live up to their musical expectations. Moreover, an instrument with a magnificent tone can be considered a master violin even if we do not know the name of the luthier who, due to nineteenth-century fashions, has been condemned to anonymity.

The maker of the "Balfour" most likely was Vuillaume, but even if we knew nothing about him, he must have been a highly qualified master, not much below Stradivari himself. Perhaps we should follow the example of art historians and, on the basis of such an outstanding instrument, "create" a luthier, in this case calling him "Master of the Balfour."

In the preface to Vannes's *Dictionnaire*, Iviglia makes this sober statement: "Strictly speaking, an instrument is authentic only if we watched it being built and varnished. In all other situations there are reasons for doubt." This, of course, is an exaggeration, for in that case there would not be a single authentic instrument by an old master. The very fact that such a skeptical attitude could develop tells us something about the field of selling instruments. A violin dealer's foremost purpose is (or should be) to provide the professional violinist with an instrument that sounds good. Beyond that things get murky, and the occupation deals not so much with concrete, definable questions of sound as with extramusical concepts of shape and beauty, an adoration at times reminiscent of the veneration of saints. There are obvious parallels here to the cult of relics, to the lucrative trade in "genuine" bones of the martyrs. In his violin method, Spohr (1833) did not mince words:

> It will, however, be very advantageous to him, if he can at once commence on a good, old instrument, as the acquirement of a fine tone and a perfect mechanism is thereby greatly facilitated. But the purchase of such should be made either under the inspection of the teacher, or with the advice of a competent judge, as so much deception is practiced in the fiddle trade.

Joachim, in a letter of 23 February 1862, put things even more plainly: "Luthiers who sell instruments seldom are entirely honest."

An instrument's "value" is greatly enhanced if it is reputed to have been played by one or the other great violinist. As Flesch (*The Art of Violin Playing*, vol. 2) put it, "Famous violinists, dukes, kings, and emperors, even the messiah himself will be invoked by luthiers if they want to obtain top prices." Knowing the business well, he further states, "At present there are on the international market about a dozen each of Strads said to have belonged to Viotti, Kreutzer, and Vieuxtemps."

The legal definition of forgery requires that the intent to deceive be proved, which is not always easy. It is difficult to determine whether the maker of a copy should be considered a forger, or whether it is the dealer who sells it as an old instrument. A common deception is the practice of making a new instrument look old by intentionally adding scratches and other blemishes on the varnish. Domenico Geroni, an Italian early nineteenth-century luthier, was a great master of making such copies, though his own violins do not have a significant reputation. Few luthiers were as honest as the English maker who signed his instruments thus: "Facsimile / Antonius Stradivarius / Made by Bert Smith / 'East View,' Coniston, Lancs. 19——."

Labels can play an important role in establishing authenticity, but there also are instruments about which Hill said, tongue-in-cheek, "A faithful copy, including the label." Labels have not always been considered reliable proof that a specific master made an instrument, though they sometimes are viewed that way, erroneously, in law suits. Labels indicated the shops, and normally apprentices and other workers had a part in making the instrument in question. There was no intent to deceive when John Betts used labels bearing his name in instruments made in his shop by Edward Betts, Cartier, Bernhard Fendt, Panormo, and Tobin. We should remember that the creations made in the great houses of fashion are named after the firm's owner, not after the tailor or seamstress who put them together! Only if a violin was basically the work of apprentices, the label might read "sub disciplina di. . . ." Thus there are violins with genuine, original labels, though the instruments were only partly made or finished by the master himself. Some were finished after his death, with only the date on the label indicating this.

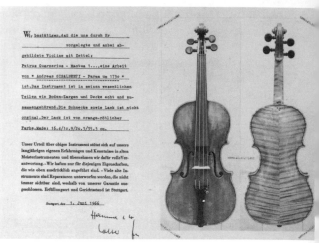

Certificate of authenticity issued by the firm of Hamma & Co., Stuttgart 1966

Count Cozio acquired white violins from the estates of various makers and then had them varnished by Mantegazza, a Milan luthier. In families of instrument makers it was customary that after the father's death, the sons for some time would continue to make instruments based on his pattern, and also use his labels. Finally, Stradivari used labels with the printed date "168," adding the last digit in ink as was customary. Being thrifty, he continued to use those labels beyond the decade, scratching out the 8 and substituting a 9. It is virtually impossible to decide whether such a correction was made by the master or by a dealer who thereby hoped to obtain a higher price.

There is nothing new about using a forged label to ascribe a violin to a maker whose instruments were much sought after. In a letter of 19 October 1685, Tomaso-Antonio Vitali asked his employer to put a stop to the practice. He had been sold a violin with a Nicolò Amati label for 12 *doppie*; it then turned out to be by Francesco Ruggieri, detto il Per, worth only 3 *doppie*. When violins by Amati and Stainer, and later by Stradivari, became sought after, it was a common trick to remove labels from master violins and glue them into copies. (A genuine master violin brought good prices, even without a label or with a forged one.) Since then, master violins with forged labels and copies of such instruments with genuine labels have circulated. Therefore great caution must be used in considering labels proof of authenticity. This is all the more advisable since forging labels has become a highly skilled activity. The instrument museum in Copenhagen owns an album of forged labels seemingly "more genuine" than the originals, as an expert once declared. There is distinguished precedent for such forgery: Vasari relates that Michelangelo made copies of his own drawings on paper that he "antiqued" with color, smoke, and dirt, keeping the original drawings for himself.

Fuhr viewed the label problem this way:

It is easy to buy a "genuine" violin, but difficult to resell it as genuine. When buying an old violin one therefore would be wise to consider only its tone, and not its label, which almost always is forged. When trying out a violin, one should not be influenced by other factors. Labels with the name of a little-known maker are more likely to be authentic, but in that case they are not of great importance.

It is no exaggeration to say that fraudulent violin dealers are as old as the violin itself. Forging has, however, assumed incredible proportions since violins began to be bought by collectors. Some fake sales were even attested to by notaries. Cozio di Salabue wrote the *proemio* (introduction) to his book in 1816, declaring that its main function was to inform and enlighten buyers of violins and to put crooked dealers out of business. He complained bitterly about the "almost general corruption," saying that he had to learn the hard way how to be knowledgeable in matters relating to the violin. One of his collection's lists of contents includes the entry "Violino tedesco col biglietto di Jacobus Stainer del 1665 / Violino di Fabrizio Zenta di Torino col biglietto di Nicolao Amati del 1666" (German violin with label by Jacobus Stainer . . .). For other violins he used the term "creduto" (believed to be by), for instance, "Violino creduto di G. B. Bergonzi con biglietto di Gerolamo Amati figlio di Nicolao del 1729 / Violino creduto di Andrea Amati," admitting that he was unable to make a reliable attribution.

Some of his descriptions are curious: "Violini di Francesco Rugier detto il Per del Gavioli con biglietto di Nicola Amati falso del 1661, tutte quattro delle cifre stampate della stampa del Mantegazza" (Violins by Francesco Rugier, called il Per [the father] of Gavioli, with a false label by Nicolò Amati dated 1661, all four digits [of the date] having been printed in Mantegazza's shop). Or: "Misure mio violino del Francesco Stradivari con biglietto suo padre del 1700" (Dimensions of my violin by Francesco Stradivari, with label by his father dated 1700).

Almost all instruments by the great luthiers, especially by the seventeenth- and eighteenth-century Italians, are now registered, described in books and professional journals, often with illustrations. The names of their owners are so well known that it has become virtually impossible to mislead people. But all kinds of fraud are still possible with violins by less renowned makers, whose instruments do not display strong personal characteristics.

Drögemeyer described the techniques of making "genuine old masters" in great detail; one is tempted to think that he must have worked in such a specialized shop for some years. His chapter "Der unlautere Wettbewerb" (On fraudulent competition) is particularly amusing and enlightening. In it he describes how an "old" or "authentic" violin is made, "so that the reader will become familiar with these procedures and can appreciate the market for these products." He then gives details about the various steps involved: what ingredients to use to obtain a varnish that looks very old; how to add small cracks, patches, and other blemishes; how to shape an equally "antique" soundpost and label; and how to give a worn appearance to those places on an instrument that normally show wear and tear. Even worm holes can be faked. Drögemeyer concludes by saying, "Such fake instruments are produced by the thousands in Bohemia, but especially in Germany, France, and Italy. . . . Occasionally such a violin, made in Germany, is sold to an Italian buyer—an 'old,' venerable Cremona violin returning home."

Given the large number of clever forgeries, a special branch of criminology has emerged to detect them. Max Frei has described this in his article "Naturwissenschaftliche Methoden zur Aufdeckung von Geigenfälschungen" (Methods from the natural sciences employed to detect fraud in violin making); appropriately enough it appeared in the *Archiv für Kriminologie* of 1955. Frei was the director of research for Zurich's Kriminalpolizei and played an important part in the Swiss "violin controversy." Some scientific methods that establish authenticity, however, are opposed by luthiers who evaluate instruments on the basis of style characteristics. Strong objections were voiced by Fridolin Hamma, honorary president of the Association of German Luthiers. He objected especially to the use of a quartz (UV) lamp. Jacques van der Meer tells me that the age of the wood cannot be determined with the UV lamp but only by radio carbon tests, which have an error factor of plus or minus twenty-five years. Modern scientific methods therefore can determine fairly accurately the age of the wood (i.e., when the tree was cut), but they cannot establish the date when the wood was made into an instrument. They therefore can expose a forger who was careless enough to use wood that was too new. Such a forger, of course, may himself use scientific methods to establish the wood's age *before* he begins work. In that case it would not be easy to detect his fraud.

VIOLIN MAKING AND THE DEVELOPMENT OF THE NATURAL SCIENCES

NEW EXPERIMENTS

The luthier who knows nothing about the acoustics of string instruments really is nothing more than a carpenter.

ANTOINE MARIUS RICHELME,
RENAISSANCE DU VIOLON ET DE SES ANALOGUES, 1883

All attempts to perfect the violin have failed.

EMILE LEIPP, *LE VIOLON*, 1965

Writers on violin making have often asked whether, or to what extent, the great masters of the seventeenth and eighteenth centuries were knowledgeable about acoustics and mathematics. Some writers have answered in the affirmative, convinced that violin making, even in its early stages, was based on scientific foundations. Most authors, however, believed that these early masters proceeded in a purely workmanlike, empirical manner. Cozio di

Salabue belonged to the former camp, saying that Antonio Stradivari, "to judge by his drawings, was no mere artisan but a learned person." Researchers, it appears, have not discovered convincing proof of this opinion. We have no information about Stradivari's specific training in mathematics or acoustics as an apprentice, nor are there statements by masters, or other written documents such as instructional materials, reports of contemporaries, letters, or memoirs, to give credence to Cozio's claims. Violin making was a skill. Apprentices were supposed to have some musical training, at least a nodding acquaintance with playing several instruments, but above all a sure hand and a gift for working with wood. An apprentice started out by doing primitive, menial jobs (including sweeping the floor); he would then advance as rapidly as his skills permitted. His progress (or lack of it) would be measured by the amount of wood he spoiled, not by his insight into acoustics.

The better luthiers had a highly developed instinct for recognizing the specific qualities of various types of wood—a sense perhaps initially sharpened by what they could detect through touching and knocking on a piece of wood. With experience came certainty and that quick recognition that to the layman often seems like a sixth sense. Wood tension in the top and back of an instrument, different arching, or the height of the ribs—these were not calculated: they were determined through experimentation. Once a musically satisfactory model had been found it was apt to be used for decades. In family shops, such a model might be used for a long time, out of respect for the elder family member who had developed it. If it was well received by the buying public, that would be an additional reason for adhering to it. When changes were made, they were not the result of calculations or laboratory tests; rather, they might be due to suggestions made by good violinists who passed on to the maker their own experiences, gained under various acoustical conditions or in connection with new musical forms or genres. It is striking how closely related in time the work of Maggini and the early stages of opera are, or Stradivari's experiments and the early history of the solo concerto. Luthiers were always eager to hear how their instruments sounded in performances in various places.

For a long time, treatises on organology did little more than describe instruments for the benefit of players. This changed drastically with the writings of the Jesuit Marin Mersenne (d. 1648 in Paris). His training included not only theology, but also logic, physics, and mathematics. He was interested in music theory and practice. Falling back to medieval concepts, he referred to music as "the enchanting part of mathematics." His findings in physics as related to music are included in several of his works, including *Harmonie universelle* (Paris 1636–1637), the most important source for organology. He may be the discoverer of a number of acoustical phenomena, or he may merely be the first to have described them. Certainly he knew some of the most important ones, such as overtones, vibration as related to pitch and timbre, and the way sound travels and is focused. The organological part of his principal work goes far beyond description; it seeks causes and proofs, which makes him the founder of the scientific study of instruments.

We cannot ascertain to what extent his findings became general knowledge during his lifetime or what direct influence they had on instrument making.

When Mersenne died, Jacob Stainer was thirty years old; it is unlikely that he knew any of Mersenne's writings. But Mersenne's approach, his basically modern attitude toward physical-acoustical phenomena, soon became widely known and profoundly influenced many scholars of the next generation, such as Athanasius Kircher (d. 1680 in Rome), whose *Musurgia universalis sive ars magna consoni et dissoni* was published in Rome in 1650. Its second and third editions appeared in 1662 and 1690; there is also a partial German translation.

It stands to reason that such a widely circulated book was known to Nicolò Amati or Antonio Stradivari. Though it may not have had a direct influence on violin making, it may have inspired speculative thinking about sound-related phenomena and their physical causes. Giuseppe Tartini is the prime example of an outstanding professional musician who was keenly interested in the secrets of sound and its production.

Once the attempt had been made to account for musical-acoustical phenomena by recourse to the natural sciences, many inquiries ensued, especially in France. Though experiments may not have affected violin making, they did involve musical instruments. Results were published in venues such as the series *Mémoires de l'Académie royale des sciences*, which in 1724 included a "Mémoire sur la forme des instruments de la musique" by J. B. Drovel de Maupertuis. It contains this sentence: "According to our observations, a vibrating string much more easily sets into motion those wood fibers that are in tune with it than other fibers . . . to proceed in such a way that the instrument's top and back contain only fibers that harmonize with each tone." The idea was impractical, for any change in the basic concert pitch would have rendered the instrument useless. Yet the underlying finding continued to be an important consideration.

The fact that Telemann translated some essays for Mizler's *Musikalische Bibliothek* (1739) shows that they were of interest to musicians. An important treatise by Urban Nathanael Beltz, *Abhandlung vom Schalle: Wie er entsteht, fortgehet, ins Ohr wirket, und wie der Empfang des Schalles kraft der innerlichen Structur des Ohres hervorgebracht wird und wie das Hören geschiehet* (A treatise on sound: How it originates, moves, reaches the ear, and how the ear's inner structure receives it, and how one hears), received a prize from the Berlin Academy of Sciences in 1764. *Abhandlung vom Instrumentalton* by Mathias Gabler was published in Ingolstadt in 1776. These are but two of many publications dealing with this subject. Others followed, such as *Untersuchungen über die Zusammensetzung der Klänge der Streichinstrumente* (Investigations into the composition of sounds produced on string instruments) by J. Ritz (Munich 1883), and further writings up to the present time.

Developments in the natural sciences and their practical applications to music were dealt with by Ernst Florens Friedrich Chladni (d. 1827 in Breslau), a physicist. In 1796 he published the essay *Über die Longitudinalschwingungen der Saiten und Stäbe* (Concerning longitudinal vibrations of strings and rods), having previously published *Theorie des Klanges* (On the theory of sound) in 1787. He lectured in many places and included practical demonstrations of his experiments, creating widespread interest in acoustical phenomena. Violin making also benefited from his intensive research, which included experiments with vibrating plates or surfaces, leading to the discovery of the "Chladni sound shapes." *Lehrbuch der Akustik* was published in 1802, including the results of these and other experiments of his. Late in life he wrote *Beyträge zur praktischen Akustik und zur Lehre vom Instrumentenbau* (Leipzig 1821), a work that reflects his tendency to put to practical use the results of his researches. Karl Christian Wilhelm Kolbe, a mining engineer from Halberstadt, provided specific ideas applicable to violin making in *Vermischte Abhandlungen besonders bergmännischen und physikalischen Inhalts* (Miscellaneous essays about mining and physics, Quedlinburg 1794). The first volume of his work is entitled *Über den Bau der Musikalischen Saiteninstrumente* (The construction of string instruments).

Chladni's work gave rise to much further experimentation. In 1800, John J. Hawkins of London was granted a patent for a violin without ribs or back; we are told that he sacrificed a Strad for his experiments. In 1801 Johann Anton Haensel, a musician in the employ of the duke of Schönburg and an amateur violin maker, made a violin with equally large upper and lower bouts. In 1810, after much experimentation, the French luthier Charles Alexis Baur built violins without bass bars. Franz Anton Ernst, concertmaster at the ducal court of Saxony-Coburg and a good luthier, warned about all such attempts at improving the instrument; in 1804, a year before his death, he published an article in the *Allgemeine Musikalische Zeitung* in which he stated that after twenty years of experimentation he had reached the conclusion that nothing about the old masters' instruments called for improvements, especially their shape.

Nevertheless, and especially because of Chladni's work, close liaison between science and practical work continued, as exemplified by the French physician Felix Savart (d. 1841). His father, a maker of precision instruments for physicists, encouraged Felix's work in acoustics; it led to several studies in the field of vibration theory. The relationship between a violin's shape and sound interested Savart early on and led him to obtain optimal results by completely turning away from traditional shapes. In 1818, the famous Paris violin shop of Gand et Bernardel built violins according to Savart's directions—instruments in trapeze form, with straight *f* holes, a bass bar exactly in the center of the top and without any arching. Such a violin was demonstrated by Lefebre, concertmaster of the Théâtre Feydeau, in the presence of scientists and artists of the Académie des Sciences and the Académie des Beaux-Arts. Among those present were Cherubini and Lesueur. Lefebre had brought along his own violin for purposes of comparison. The demonstration was entirely successful, leading Savart to publish his results in 1819. In this *Mémoire sur la construction des instruments à cordes et à archet suivi du rapport qui en a été fait aux deux Académies* (Report on the construction of bowed string instruments, followed by the report given to the two academies) he states,

The new violin displayed great purity and evenness of tone; the latter quality especially is rare but much sought after. At close range, the sound of the new violin seemed less bright than that of the other one. To help us distinguish between the two we asked M. Lefebre to go to an adjoining room and to play the identical passages alternating between the two instruments, without telling us which one he was playing at any time. It turned out that both were equally good, to the extent that the most expert listeners repeatedly mistook one for the other. The only distinguishing feature, noticed once in a while, was that the new violin's tone was slightly sweeter.

It is still possible to confirm that Savart's instruments are suitable for concert performance, though they are slightly weaker in the low register.

Savart's investigations also involved valuable Italian violins. He established that the air in violins by Stradivari and del Gesù vibrated 512 times per second, and that the basic pitch of the top lies between C-sharp and D, the basic pitch of the back, between D and D-sharp. These first discoveries were later used for well-developed procedures involving sound relationships. Vuillaume was greatly interested in Savart's experiments and furthered them by supplying precious instruments, including a Strad. Violins were completely taken apart, even cut up, and thoroughly studied in order to discover the old masters' secrets. Starcke claims that in all Vuillaume sacrificed instruments worth 150,000 francs for this purpose.

Savart's instruments attracted much attention but failed to become widely accepted, chiefly because at that time lovers of the violin had begun to cherish aesthetic aspects, as related to appearance, more than those relating to timbre or volume. To play a trapeze-shaped violin would have seemed ridiculous; even those who were impressed by its tone quality would not accept it. Yet we must acknowledge that there was more to Savart's ideas than what he could prove with his instruments. Innovations in violin making always suffer a handicap: the new instruments tend to be compared with master violins that are the result of more than two centuries of experience. Moreover, experimental violins seldom are made by first-rate luthiers, and they are not produced in quantity, in which case an innovation could be tested more widely. All this means that new ideas about violin making hardly have a chance of succeeding. Luthiers may have invested many years of intensive work and a great deal of money in their attempts to improve the violin's shape and sound, yet they were exposed to ridicule from colleagues, often out of professional jealousy. It was and is easy to declare that the old masters' instruments cannot be improved upon, yet we should acknowledge and appreciate the desire to perfect, even if (apart from some highly interesting ideas) much that was done turned out to be dilettantish and unrealistic.

Aside from his trapeze violin, Savart experimented with a kind of connecting piece, intended to strengthen the top and to give greater stability to both top and back. Nothing came of this, but Savart's ideas were considered seriously at least by some, as is shown in a manual of violin making by Domenico Angeloni (*Il liutaio*, Milan 1923) that contains a chapter seventy-six pages long entitled "Il violino trapezoidale del Dottor Felice Savart."

Savart's use of modern scientific concepts and acoustic laws inspired others, including François Chanot (b. 1787 in Mirecourt). The son of a vintner-luthier who was the founding father of an important French family of luthiers, some of whom also worked in London, Chanot studied at the École Polytechnique in Paris and became an engineer active in shipbuilding. After taking early retirement he worked in his father's shop and later in Paris. Independently of Savart he attempted to put violin making on a scientific basis. He believed that all corners of a violin inhibited vibration, and he therefore designed a guitarlike violin, modifying the sound holes and placing them close to and parallel to the sides. His purpose was to disturb the wood of the top as little as possible and to preserve intact the greatest number of long wood fibers, all in order to obtain optimal vibration. In 1817 he submitted one of his violins to the Académie des Sciences, where it was tested and compared with a Strad. The jury that included Gossec, Lesueur, and Cherubini judged it to be superior to the Strad. This seemed surprising, so a second test was scheduled for 26 July 1817. It confirmed the result of the earlier comparison. A report about these proceedings appeared in the *Moniteur Universel* of 22 August 1817, stressing how surprising it was that Chanot's violin competed successfully with the Strad, "even though it had been made from wood cut only six months ago."

In 1818, Chanot presented one of his violins to Viotti; it is kept in the museum of the Paris Conservatoire. On his labels Chanot signed himself C. I. D. (Capitaine, Ingénieur deuxième classe).

As it turned out, Chanot's violins soon lost their fine tone quality. Apparently he failed to establish the necessary balance between the various tensions. Such deterioration affected other experimental violins, which may explain why they often were at first praised but then soon forgotten. Henley (*Universal Dictionary*) relates that the instruments made by the Swiss painter Baltensperger received much praise by virtuosos who then failed to play them in public.

One very practical idea advocated by Chanot did not find acceptance either: to have the scroll face downward, in order to facilitate mounting the A string. The classic, traditional shape prevailed, and to this day violinists continue to struggle with this operation, when speed often is desirable. Actually, the specific shape of Stradivari's scroll had been intended to facilitate mounting the strings.

French attempts at innovation attracted much interest abroad, as evidenced by the 1821 publication in English of A. M. Abell's *Account of the Recent Endeavours in France to Improve the Construction of the Violin*. A German translation appeared the same year in Dingler's *Polytechnisches Journal*, while the *Wiener Conversationsblatt* (issue 66, 1821) reported on "Chanot's newly invented violins." Later violin competitions brought similar results:

1909   An instrument by Gand et Bernardel received first prize, rather than a Strad.

1910   A cello by French luthier Paul Kaul, built according to the ideas of Jules Edward Chenantais, a physician, received first prize with 465 votes; second place (288 votes) went to a Strad cello.

1912   A violin by Chenantais-Kaul, and one by Wilhelm Paul Kunze, a German maker in The Hague, were successful.

1921   Once more, two modern violins won out over a Strad, in a competition held in the auditorium of the Paris Conservatoire.

Leipp's sober comment on all this? "The tonal superiority of violins by Stradivari and others is a myth" (*Le violon*).

The guitar shape used by Chanot was not entirely new. A Gasparo da Salò viola has the same shape, as does a 1698 violin by an unknown maker. Its length is 389 mm, the bouts measure 189 and 237 mm, and its width at the waist is 157 mm. Such experiments may have been influenced by the shape of the early gamba, which also lacked lateral indentations and had the approximate shape of an 8. Chanot may also have been guided by his awareness that the inside shape of a violin resembles an 8 because of the blocks.

Another experimental shape that did not catch on was presented for discussion by the Munich court luthier Andreas Engleder (d. 1875) at the German Industrial Fair in Munich. His instruments were pear-shaped. The small upper bout, without corners, led to the indentation necessary for bowing; the intent was to facilitate playing in the high positions. The bass, at the expense of the brilliant high tones, was too weak. Eberle attributed this to the faulty proportion of upper and lower bout.

Carlo Antonio Galbusera (d. 1846), an officer from Milan, also believed that the corners inhibited vibration, a fault he tried to correct by giving the instrument a shape approximating an 8. He too received public recognition, including a silver medal at the 1832 Milan Academy of Sciences. Francesco Antolini, however, published a pamphlet opposing Galbusera's views: *Osservazioni su due violini esposti nelle sale del R. Palazzo di Brera, una di quali di forma non comune* (Observations about two violins exhibited at the Royal Palace of Brera, one of which had an unusual shape, 1832). Galbusera also made an interesting discovery about gumlike substances found in various kinds of wood. They are so strongly present in certain non-European types of wood that their ability to vibrate is extremely poor, making them unsuitable for instruments. He succeeded in extracting the gum from the wood by using chemicals. This improved the wood's elasticity for some time but reduced its lifespan. The sound of his instruments soon began to deteriorate, which his opponents blamed on faulty methods of construction.

Professor Franz Joseph Koch of Dresden conducted experiments using a different approach. As he examined old Italian instruments under the microscope he isolated a substance in the wood to which he attributed their balanced sound. In 1920 he began making his "homogenous instruments," in which this substance was evenly distributed. While his instruments for some

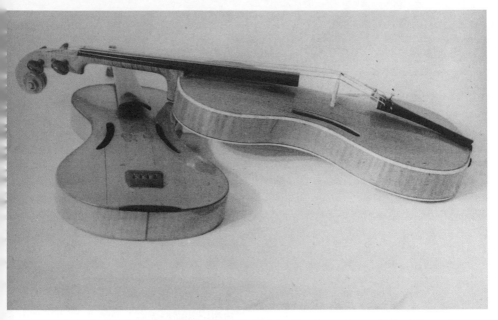

Violin and viola by Chanot (Karlsruhe, Wahl collection; photo: Erika Margraf)

time were in great demand, they were also controversial. Fuhr presented good reasons for his opposition to Koch's process.

A recent attempt to improve the violin's form was based on Galbusera's experiments. This is a violin built by Julius Zoller, an engineer from Karlsruhe. (Some of his violins have an added C string.) As the photograph on p. 186 shows, its contour features fairly straight lines, leading to the lower bout in the shape of a partial circle. There are no *f* holes, but there are striplike holes in the ribs. With two bass bars and two soundposts, this is probably the most radical attempt (next to Chanot's) to design a new shape. Möckel believed that it had potential.

Another idea, essentially going back to Savart, exists in various modifications: the attempt to increase the vibrating surface by the insertion of another plate below the top. Such violins were built by the Lyon luthier Lapostolet, based on plans by Nicolas Suleau (Sulot), a Paris violinist. These instruments can be seen in museums in Berlin, Geneva, and Brussels. In 1839 Lapostolet was granted patents for string instruments with an additional top; he called them "à double écho." He also made violins the backs of which had longitudinal ridges in wave form. Further experiments were undertaken ca. 1850 by the Englishman Henry Bell, who tried to improve the sound by installing a glass plate that contained a hole for the soundpost between top and back. Others continued to experiment with one or two inserted wooden plates that usually followed the instrument's contours but did not quite extend to the ribs. Early in the twentieth century Lewis C. Smith and Herman H. Petersen, in order to increase volume, placed freely vibrating res-

Violin by Julius Zoller (Karlsruhe, Staatliche Hochschule für Musik;
photo: Erika Margraf)

onator-posts inside the violin. In 1919 Johann Czerny, an amateur luthier from Prague, attracted attention with a combination of several ideas: he substituted a resonating device for the soundpost and used lateral openings in the middle rib instead of f holes. These devices were not glued to the top. He replaced the bass bar with a vibrating rod that was not attached with glue. Czerny won gold medals at international exhibits from 1924 to 1949, but he too did not have lasting success.

A number of inventors tried to deal with the problem caused by the strong pressure exerted on the violin's top. Realizing that older violins could hardly stand up to this pressure, due to the wood's weakness, Anton Sprenger II, a Stuttgart luthier, devised a kind of artificial support for weak violins: he inserted a slightly curved stick in the lower block and glued it to the upper block, with the curvature pointing upward. At the highest point he attached a small wood block that could be forced upward with the help of a screw, thus exerting counterpressure against the bridge.

Other drastic changes involving the violin's top and back have kept the traditional contours. In one case, both top and back were made from twelve plates that were glued together and overlapped; the wood's fibers pointed centrifugally from a place halfway between the two f holes. A bridge consisting of six parts was intended to maximize vibration. Similarly, James H. Ingram (d. 1918) constructed the top of his "twentieth-century violin" from forty-two pieces. Others, including Louis Lumière in Lyon, took up the idea of harmonic plates inside the violin.

Antoine Marius Richelme (d. 1896) of Marseille was an outstanding luthier who based his violins on Italian models. His valuable study, *Études et observations sur la lutherie ancienne et moderne*, was published in 1868. He experimented widely, including the design of a combination of chin rest and tailpiece. He also tried to improve the violin's form by designing the various archings on the basis of geometrical considerations. Building on Savart's and Chanot's ideas, he formed the upper and lower bouts in ways that led to a shape resembling the ancient viol. He published another study in 1883; it had the wordy and rather pompous title *Renaissance du violon et de ses analogues— d'après de nouvelles lois acoustiques, plaidant en faveur de la facilité, de l'exécution & des grands effets de sonorités par A. M. Richelme, luthier, inventeur du nouveau modèle de violon, d'alto, de basse et de contrebasse, à courbes circulaires pleines, d'un timbre supérieure et d'une sonorité plus puissante que celle de tout autre instrument de luthiers anciens et modernes* (Renaissance of the violin and related instruments, according to new laws of acoustics, favoring greater ease of execution and greater sound effectiveness by A. M. Richelme, luthier and inventor of new models of violin, viola, bass [cello] and contrabass, with circular inserts, having superior sound quality and greater resonance than that of any instrument made by luthiers of ancient and modern times). The presumptuous wording worked to the author's detriment, especially since his results did not live up to expectations.

Of great interest were the efforts to improve sound made by Nicolas Eugène Simoutre (d. 1908). He was born in Mirecourt, the son of the well-known Lupot pupil Nicolas Simoutre. He worked in several ateliers, including Darche's in Paris. Prior to settling in that city he had shops in Mühlhausen (Mulhouse) and Basel. He defended his ideas in various publications. For his "supports harmoniques" he was granted the German patent no. 33514. These are wooden supports for the soundpost that he made in several styles. Before Simoutre, Mordret already had tried out soundposts that were placed at an angle (see illustration). Simoutre also tried to cope with the difficulties caused by the rising pitch then coming into use. He was convinced that a thicker bass bar would destroy the functioning of vibrations inside the instrument. Similar considerations guided Claude Victor Rambaux (d. 1871), who wanted to avoid using a thicker bass bar by fastening a second bass bar to the violin's back in such a way that the soundpost rested on it.

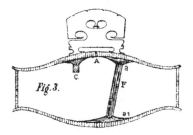

From Simoutre 1889

Though he was granted a patent in 1868, an idea developed by John Henry Schucht did not succeed. He constructed both top and back from two pieces, using both soft and hard wood for each and gluing them together. Similar experiments had already been carried out by Jacques Boquay (d. 1735). He used wide-grained wood for one half and narrow-grained wood for the other, though he used the same kind of wood for both pieces.

The fine French cellist Auguste Tolbecque (d. 1919) once again took up the idea of placing the sound holes in the ribs. In general, earlier ideas that had been discarded, or that had been adapted for other instruments, now tended to be reconsidered, such as a fingerboard with keys (as on the hurdy-gurdy); or the sympathetic strings of the viola d'amore, but mounted inside the instrument; or the double courses of strings as on the mandolin. In 1925 the American Charles C. Lock took out a patent on his "improved violin." It featured a set of strings comparable to the viola d'amore and was intended to produce a larger tone.

The ribs were seldom the object of experimentation, though there were attempts to mount them at an angle. This was accomplished by having a top that was slighly smaller than the back. J. A. Lapaix (d. 1859), a luthier in Lille, cut the ribs with all attachments from one piece of wood. By contrast, many experiments involved the soundpost. Different materials were used, such as glass. A hollow or partially hollow soundpost was to reduce weight; a second soundpost was placed below the D string. These efforts essentially go back to Savart's findings as described by Drögemeyer.

Experiments by Dr. Alfred Steltzner, a mathematician and physicist, attracted much attention during the 1890s. Following acoustical investigations on valuable master violins, he designed a model that was built by Wiedemann, a violin maker in Wiesbaden. For the traditional shape he substituted an elliptical one, giving similar shape to the upper and lower block. The rather high ribs featured parabolic curves, and he adapted the flat top to these curves before gluing. Steltzner overestimated the importance of interior vibrations, which led him to enlarge the *f* holes in order to increase sound volume. Trying to solve the problem of the tenor violin he designed a violotta (an octave lower than the violin); quite logically this led to the cellone, pitched an octave below the violotta. Steltzner's concepts, after causing quite a stir initially, did not succeed as he had hoped, which disappointment perhaps led to his suicide. He believed that instruments made according to his specifications would be superior to old Italian violins. Nevertheless, Apian-Bennewitz (1892) said of Steltzner, "It is not inconceivable that one day his ideas will be taken up again and realized in an improved manner."

Möckel described various experiments with the bass bar. The famous cellist Bernhard Romberg (1767–1841) tried to obtain a better distribution of vibrations across the entire top by gluing small wood plates across the ends of the bass bar. Ole Bull recommended placing it at an angle so that it would cross the middle joint of a back made of two pieces. Carl Grimm (d. 1855 in Berlin) drilled square apertures into the portion of the bass bar that touched the top, hoping thereby to make the top lighter and improve its ability to vibrate. Louis Löwenthal (Lowendahl) made and sold violins in Berlin and many other places. In 1900 he was granted a patent for a resonator-bass bar with many holes into which he inserted hollow soundposts. Claude-Augustin Miremont (d. 1887) was one of many who experimented with two bass bars, one of which was attached to the top's right side and was called the discant bar. Others tried out three parallel bass bars of different lengths and thicknesses, the thickest and longest one being on the left side. Some experimented with a second bass bar, placed on the back, or inserted a curved bass bar, hoping to obtain a better distribution of vibrations. Believing that the bass bar inhibited the top's vibration, the Versailles luthier Baud in 1810 constructed instruments without them, compensating for this by increasing the top's thickness. The German luthier Jacob Seelbach took out a patent for a violin without bass bar. He also eliminated the soundpost, substituting a kind of tuning fork for both that was intended to increase the tone volume.

Interestingly enough, most of these experimenters were not professional luthiers, who as a rule had little time for experimentation, being obliged to supply serviceable instruments on a competitive basis. Because of his training, the professional violin maker also had been conditioned to think along traditional lines. None of this applies to the amateur. Obtaining his income from other sources, he often devotes all his leisure time to his hobby, convinced that he will make revolutionary innovations. These the professional luthier, with many years of experience, is likely to view with skepticism.

Wealthy Paris amateur André Roussel (*Traité de lutherie*) calculated that in almost forty years of research he devoted thirty thousand hours to his avocation: about four hours daily from 1926 to 1939, two hours daily from 1939 to 1950, and about an hour every day since 1950. His work sometimes involved high–quality instruments. One day, having bought a good cello for his experiments, the seller said to him, "If you were my son I would not let you do this."

G. Tarlé (d. 1959) was a Paris physician, an imaginative, curious thinker. He went back to the bridge of the crwth that touched the instrument's body with only one foot and tried to develop this concept further. The result was the vigorine, a weight he attached to the left foot of the traditional bridge. By regulating the vibrations it was supposed to give to average violins the timbre and volume of Italian master violins. He also designed violins with up to six strings, including the range of the viola and, in some cases, the cello. Others had tried something similar, including Woldemar (d. 1816) and Urban (d. 1845), who built and played a five-string violin-viola (with C string). Ralph E. Fishburn, a British miner who claimed to have supernatural contacts with Stradivari, built violin-violas (later including the cello range), allegedly under the master's influence.

Before Tarlé, Dr. Franz Thomastik, the Viennese manufacturer of strings, occupied himself with the idea of the crwth bridge. Through a hole in the violin's top he placed the right foot of the bridge directly on the soundpost, thus increasing the back's vibration. Hermann Ritter, known for making tenor violins, also experimented with new bridges. An essay published in Würzburg in 1889 is entitled *Professor Ritters dreifüssiger Normalsteg für Geigeninstrumente (Vor Nachahmung gesetzlich geschützt). Der dreifüssige oder Normal-Geigensteg erfunden und begründet von Hermann Ritter, kgl. Professor und grossherzogl. Kammervirtuos* (Prof. Ritter's standard bridge with three feet, for instruments of the violin family. All rights reserved. Invented and explained by Hermann Ritter, royal professor and grandducal chamber virtuoso).

The "Kantusch bridge" deviates only slightly from the shape that has been traditional since Stradivari. Only the shape of the cutouts has been changed, resulting in a different distribution of material. Leonhardt reports on testing it. There were also experiments with bridges consisting of two or more parts.

The difficulty of tuning violins gave rise to countless inventions and patents. Every violinist has been exasperated at one time or other, struggling with a peg that would stop at every pitch but the right one. To tune the strings precisely some inventors transferred to the violin the screw mechanism used for string bass and guitar; others pursued similar ideas. Most of these, though good, seemed too mechanical to violinists who apparently continue to prefer playing half the time on out-of-tune strings. French luthier P. J. Masson invented a peg with a hollow end. From its middle, an opening led to the outside. The string is mounted beginning at the peg. Max Grossmann (1907) commented,

The concept of Masson's peg is ingenious and promising, if only violinists were not so terribly conservative in everything relating to their instrument! The fact that a string is mounted by beginning at the opposite end than what is customary, i.e., not at the tailpiece, is enough to arouse opposition.

Many attempts have been made to design more efficient mutes. An eighteenth-century violinist by the name of Tagnani constructed a mute that could be activated by the chin. For modern orchestra players, several types of mutes that can be placed on the bridge and taken off quickly and easily are available.

Improving the tone of violins was the concern of the Franck-Reiner firm, with shops in Schönbach and Markneukirchen. The individual pieces for a string instrument were mass produced and then subjected to a vibration treatment. The results were fairly good, though a "shoe box" violin was not transformed into a Strad by this or any other process. An American violin maker announced that through an x-ray exposure of a mere ten minutes he would transform any modern violin into one equal to an old Italian instrument; of course he was unable to substantiate his claim. Several experiments in which wood intended for violins was subjected to electrical currents also fell far short of expectations. More recently, Konrad Leonhardt (1969) investigated the influence of artificial vibration on sound. He described the tests to which two violins were subjected but concluded, "No unequivocal success was reached through artificial vibration."

An early attempt to amplify the sound of string instruments was the "funnel violin" (also known as the Tiebel violin, after its inventor), in which the string's vibration was transmitted from the bridge through a sound box to a speaker. Instead of the normal violin body it consisted of a wooden frame only. Its sound was strong but rather piercing. For some time it was popular in dance bands. Many methods of amplifying sound are now widely used, in connection with electronic music and especially in popular music. An early example of the electric violin was built by Vierling. Such instruments do not need a resonating body; sound is transmitted through a microphone attached to the bridge—a contact mike. Dynamics are regulated through volume controls. Tarlé collaborated with the Frenchman Bizos on the construction of a "super violin," also called "stereophonic violin," using similar principles; it was patented in 1931. None of these experiments provided instruments that were musically satisfactory, for an instrument without a body cannot produce a true violin sound. Moreover, electronic amplification of a vibrating string's sound results in a decidedly coarser timbre, inadequate for high musical requirements.

In the early nineteenth century, when concert tours meant long days of travel, the need arose for a "silent" violin for practicing in hotel rooms and other places with poor sound insulation. A typical practice violin consists of only a frame, fingerboard, and other parts essential for the mechanics of playing; it does not reproduce true violin sound. Excessive playing on such a "dumb" violin can have an adverse effect on the violinist's tone production.

Many attempts have been made to substitute other materials, including synthetic ones, for wood, but in spite of sensational claims no clearly adequate or superior material has been found so far. Clay and glass violins were intended as curiosities, to be seen rather than heard. Around the mid-nineteenth century, Menichetti of Faenza developed what he called a "violino ligneometallico," made of both wood and metal. His plan of having it adopted by military bands came to nothing. Late in the nineteenth century in Mirecourt, violins were made from pressed wood, known as "violons moulés." Experimentation has never ceased; in 1963 a patent was issued for a violin made from plastic. The use of such materials may never result in high-quality instruments, but it seems likely that ongoing improvements may lead to adequate, low-priced student instruments.

Many experiments did not deal so much with the instrument itself as with the manner of constructing it. In this area, Dr. Max Grossmann of Berlin seems to have made some significant discoveries, though they were widely attacked. His most important publication is *Die Theorie der harmonischen Abstimmung der Resonanzplatten bei der Geige und die hauptsächlichsten Einwände dagegen* (On the harmonic tuning of the violin's resonator plates, and the chief objections to it, Berlin 1917). Savart had already been aware of the problem. Among those voicing objections was Hans Diestel (1912), who said, "The hopes of all luthiers, who based their theories of violin making on the tuning of the plates and the enclosed air space, and on the determination of their characteristic tones, always turned out to be false." Max Möckel also was aware of the problematic aspects of plate tuning. Researchers observed that an instrument whose plates had pure vibrations and a distinct tone was superior to others. But Max Möckel (*Das Konstruktionsgeheimnis*) believed that the importance of pure vibrations was underrated by other researchers who assumed that a "harmonic relation" of the plates to each other would lead to even greater success—an assumption not verified by experiments.

In recent times, the plate tap tones have again attracted the attention of scientists. In 1960, the U.S. research team of Hutchins, Hopping, and Saunders published their lengthy investigations in *Subharmonics and Plate Tap Tones in Violin Acoustics*. Finally, Leonhardt pointed out an important factor that shed light on the nature of tap tones: "We are not primarily concerned with the pitch of the tap tone, but with its duration; it determines the resonance. The longer and louder the tap tone, the greater its resonance."

Leonhardt also contributed to improvements in violin making through his system of evaluating the degree of the wood's light transparency. He recalled that luthiers at all times had held a piece of wood up to the light of a strong lamp in order to detect potentially thin, weak places. "Today, electro-acoustical measuring techniques may provide excellent, objective tests, but they supply no sure information to the luthier about the way in which the wood should be used. Only the wood itself can do this, and whoever understands the wood's language has discovered the secret of violin making." He constructed a "light box" containing strong neon tubes. The box top had cutouts in the shapes of a violin's top and back. With some practice, the luthier can recognize many important wood characteristics, such as factors of climate as reflected in the annual rings; mineral and other deposits; differences in wood density; irregularities caused by knots; and the onset of wood rot. "The study of light transparency is not theory, but practice. It is based on the principle that a wood plate vibrates on the basis of the distribution of its mass. The wood's varying density is indicated by the different degrees of light it lets through."

For decades this question has been posed with increasing frequency: how can electro-acoustical research further our knowledge of bowed string instruments? In his new edition of Otto Möckel's *Die Kunst des Geigenbaues*, Fritz Winckel has described the current state of research. For accurate testing, the violin strings are set into motion by a mechanical device, consisting of a "continuously moving ribbon stretched across wheels, because the human hand could not draw a bow with comparable, even pressure. The tones produced in this way are transmitted through a microphone to a tape recorder. They are then electronically analyzed in regard to fundamentals and partials." In spite of this basically technological approach, Winckel frankly admits, "The secret of the ideal violin sound still has not been fully discovered." In 1922, the Berlin acoustician Alfred Seiffert constructed a device with which he was able to register vibrations at any place on a violin that was vibrating in its entirety, and to amplify these partial vibrations two hundred times. He thereby was able to detect even the slightest motions. He did this to substantiate views expressed in his publication *Eine Theorie der Geige auf mechanischer Grundlage* (A theory, based on mechanics, about the violin's function). In time, the measuring devices employed and the results they yield will become increasingly precise.

Will the increasing refinement of measuring devices mean that the listener, for whom the instrument is ultimately intended, is more and more ignored? Winckel has stated that electronic measuring devices can plot the structure of musical sounds, "making them visible much more clearly than they could be perceived by the ear." This makes the value of electronic measuring devices suspect: is it useful for a player to own a violin, the quality of which is judged by criteria the listener is unable to recognize? Leipp, too, is on shaky ground when he establishes scientific criteria for the evaluation of instrumental sounds: to substitute a mechanical device for the player's bow; a completely "dead" recording studio for an auditorium, and a recording device for the listener. In real life, a violin must pass muster under exactly opposite conditions.

VIOLIN MAKING SINCE 1800

The great art of eighteenth-century violin making resulted in the wide distribution of master instruments, at first within Europe and later elsewhere, especially in the United States. But with the gradual decline of this art the situation changed materially. The demand for new instruments lessened, and buyers were reluctant to pay high prices. Selling and repairing existing instruments moved into the foreground, so that there are now many luthiers who do only repair work, including rehairing bows, making bridges, and replacing soundposts that have fallen down. They sell instruments, including inexpensive student violins, along with strings, rosin, violin cases, and music stands. Only rarely do they make instruments. Most of their customers don't even know that they *are* makers, or that violin making formed part of their training. If occasionally they do build an instrument, this is apt to be a labor of love, or to satisfy themselves that they still know how to do it.

In spite of this, the average level of violin making is quite high, and many luthiers have risen considerably above the average. Violins one buys today are much the same, whether the luthier lives in Toronto, Buenos Aires, Tokyo, or Vienna; national differences have become negligible, for everyone follows the Strad and Guarneri models. Most professional luthiers believe that these two masters represent the last word—that one must follow their models as closely as possible, and that any attempt to deviate from them would have negative consequences. The lack of success of those who have tried to break away from their models confirms this belief.

Around 1800, for a number of reasons, the care and maintenance of instruments became a new and extremely important task. Shortly before 1700 Stradivari, anxious to make violins with a large sound, went to extremes, perhaps moving ahead of his time. As he developed his definitive model he had to retreat somewhat from those extremes, eventually reaching a compromise between his own large model and the Amati model. As far as tone volume is concerned, del Gesù went even farther than Stradivari. Instruments by both makers show characteristic differences. Guarneri's violins show evidence of intensive use during the eighteenth century, which is rarely true of Stradivari's. This suggests that Guarneri's violins were bought chiefly by professional musicians and played daily, while Stradivari's more typically were acquired by amateurs and collectors and soon ended up in the instrument collections of the nobility.

Guarneri's violins did not respond easily. Rather thick strings and a strong bow arm were needed to achieve optimal vibration. It soon became customary to "scrape" Guarneri violins, that is, to reduce the wood's thickness so that the violin would speak more readily. The brothers Carlo, Pietro Giovanni, and Francesco Mantegazza, luthiers in Milan, made excellent violins in the Amati manner. They were experts at this scraping, so that Cozio di Salabue repeatedly sang the praises of these "adjusters." In his book he refers to a "violin by Petrus Guarnerius, one of this master's strong instruments with an even tone, adjusted in the modern fashion by the Mantegazza brothers." He also refers to a 1730 Strad as having been "made thinner by Guadagnini." I already mentioned that Stainer violins were not spared. Simoutre (1886) was outspoken: "The repairer's vandalism was inflicted with special violence on Stainer's instruments."

Fortunately, the scrapers did not get their hands on all Guarneri violins, or similarly built ones. Those that were spared forced violinists to adopt a radically different manner of bowing. Cozio observed that a well-versed professional Italian violinist would know how to use the bow properly. Around 1800 a new manner of bowing was adopted in France. The bow stick was firmly grasped, exerting greater pressure, which seemed to be appropriate for the style of the classic symphony and for the larger orchestras, first used in Mannheim and then especially in Paris. As the middle class assumed a more important place in musical life, the aristocracy played a correspondingly diminished role. Larger concert halls required larger sound, especially from the orchestra's string section, a development which began with the Concert Spirituel in Paris (1725 on); the Leipzig Gewandhaus concerts (1781); the gigantic Handel commemorations in London (1784); performances of Haydn oratorios (composed in 1799 and 1801) and of Beethoven symphonies; and the concerts of the Paris Conservatoire (1828 on). The gradual rise in concert pitch was a byproduct of this development. Along with these changes came a change in public taste: instead of the Amati and Stainer violins, those made by later Italians were preferred. As early as 1803, F. J. Schubert recommended Stainer and Mittenwald violins for small spaces, but Cremona violins for large ones.

Most violins made before 1750, and many later ones based on the same measurements, had been intended for different situations: smaller halls, thinner strings, a lighter, more elegant style of playing, and a lower concert pitch. To cope with the new conditions required a fairly substantial change: the violin's short neck gave way to the new, modern dimensions:

short-neck violin

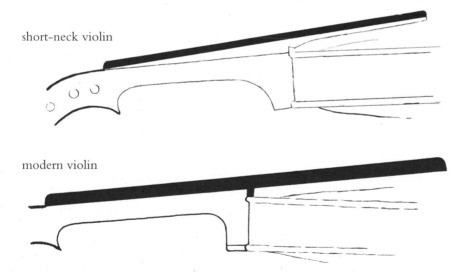

modern violin

This rebuilding of old master violins soon became customary, with Paris leading the way in the metamorphosis. According to Cozio, officers of the French army of occupation in the Cisalpine Republic ca. 1800 bought many old Italian instruments, especially Amati violins, to have them remodeled "all'uso di Parigi" (in the Paris manner).

Before this, the violin's neck and body lay in the same plain. Up to the time of Stradivari, the neck was fastened to the body with three metal nails, driven from the violin's inside through the upper block. To place the fingerboard at the proper angle a wedge was inserted, rising from the saddle and supporting the entire length of the fingerboard. The fingerboard was very thin, due to the high price of ebony wood. The demand for a louder sound at first led to using thicker strings and increasing the length of their vibrating portion, and then to retaining the length of the violin body while slightly increasing the neck's length. To avoid having the strings touch the fingerboard, a higher bridge was needed, but this resulted in increased pressure exerted by the strings. This rendered the traditional method of attaching the neck inadequate. It was now mounted at an angle, so that the scroll was in a lower position than before. Glue was used instead of the nails, which had impeded vibration. Since the neck was now at an angle, a wedge no longer was needed, and the substantially thicker fingerboard was placed directly on the neck. The fingerboard's length had gradually been increasing, for composers such as Vivaldi and Locatelli required playing in the high positions. In 1790, Viotti advocated adding several millimeters to the fingerboard's length, thereby bringing it up to current dimensions.

In order to effect all these changes, the old neck had to be removed and replaced, and a stronger bass bar was called for. Very few old master instruments remain in their original condition, for by 1840 virtually all violins made before 1750 had undergone these modifications. French luthiers who had dealt directly with Tarisio were among the last to have handled fairly large numbers of classic Italian violins in their original condition.

Cozio di Salabue relates interesting details about the evolution of the bridge after 1750. Those made by Stradivari and his contemporaries no longer were usable; their feet were too thick, the indentations excessive, and the bridges in general were too low (see illustration on p. 19). They produced a tone that was light and silvery but somewhat nasal and weak. In Cozio's day, therefore, bridges were made 1) alla Tartini, 2) in Mantegazzi's manner, or 3) in the Paris style. The Paris style resulted in the brightest and strongest sound which, however, was somewhat piercing and "not pleasing to the Italians' pure ears."

The various modifications to which the violin was subjected required replacing the original bass bar with a somewhat longer and thicker one. The fate of Stradivari's "Messiah" violin illustrates this development. In 1855, when Vuillaume purchased it from Tarisio's estate, he replaced the original bass bar. Later, when the Hill brothers acquired it, they substituted an even heavier one. Stradivari's original bar has been preserved in the Ashmolean Museum. Abbé Sibire (1806) clearly recognized the close connection between musical changes and changes in instrument making: "Music has been revolutionized; the changes inevitably are reflected in violin making."

To reconstruct so many different models of old instruments required great sensitivity and manual skill. Not many early nineteenth-century luthiers were qualified; as a result, many valuable instruments were ruined and are now to be looked at rather than played. Still, a number of outstanding luthiers who became expert repairers emerged in many countries. They were and are in great demand by virtuosos to care for their instruments and also to act as appraisers. Often, for obvious reasons, they spent much of their time buying and selling violins. Some large firms came into being, their names known all over the world, and their expertise was passed on within the family from generation to generation.

ITALY

Despite the systematic acquiring of Italian master instruments by clever violin merchants abroad, a sufficient number remained in Italy, so that nineteenth- and twentieth-century Italian luthiers, having studied the old violins' acoustic qualities, were inspired to build new violins according to the old traditions. In many cities the old tradition was maintained, even if the high standards of the Stradivari-Guarneri era may not have been matched in every case, and the Gagliano and Guadagnini dynasties continued their activity, even to our own time.

Turin became the most important center, due perhaps to the tradition established by the Guadagninis. Gian Francesco Pressenda (1777–1854) was a pupil of Lorenzo Storioni in Cremona. For a while he was a jeweler, but in 1820 he established himself as a luthier in Turin and was the chief transmitter of the old tradition. For a long time his violins were considered to be "mere" Strad copies, but when the great German violinist Wilhelmj began concertizing with a Pressenda, the value of that maker's instruments rose steeply. (Before this, Wilhelmj had had the foresight to buy eighty Pressenda violins at low prices, along with a large number of instruments by G. A. Rocca.) Henley has predicted that Pressenda's violins will become *the* master instruments of the future, a view shared by some leading virtuosos. Other makers who built high-quality violins were Pressenda's pupils Alexandre Despine (D'Espine; d. 1842); Gioffredo Benedetto Rinaldi (d. 1888) and his son Marengo Romano Rinaldi; and the Malegari brothers, of whom Enrico Clodovic Malegari (d. 1888) was one of the best Italian luthiers of the nineteenth century. The Rocca family also contributed outstanding luthiers, beginning with Giovanni Domenico Rocca, active in Turin since 1800. Giuseppe Antonio Rocca (d. 1865) had learned his craft from Pressenda; his best violins equal those of his master. His son Enrico Rocca (d. 1915) became famous for his fine copies of old Italian violins, many of which received prizes at exhibitions. Instruments made by members of the Rocca family bring ever higher prices since they are increasingly in demand by professional violinists. The Turin tradition of fine violin making was continued in the early twentieth century by Carlo Giuseppe Oddone (d. 1936) and Annibale Fagnola (d. 1939).

The influence of the old traditions continued in Cremona as well. Giambattista Ceruti (d. 1817), a pupil of Lorenzo Storioni, took over his master's shop after Storioni's death. His son Giuseppe Ceruti (d. 1860) built

Violin by Giovanni Francesco Pressenda, Turin 1837
(Roger and Max Millant collection)

fine instruments in Mantua; Enrico Ceruti (d. 1883), representing the third generation, again worked in Cremona. The Antoniazzi family also contributed three generations of luthiers. Gaetano (d. 1897), given to imaginative experimentation, worked in Cremona and Milan, where he was highly regarded; his sons Riccardo and Romeo continued the tradition. Antoniazzi's pupil Giuseppe Pedrazzini (d. 1958) also came from Cremona. He moved to Milan, where he was in charge of instruments at the conservatory and La Scala. Astride Cavalli (d. 1931) founded the Officina Claudio Monteverdi in Cremona; it was continued by his son, the physicist and mathematician Lelio Cavalli. New life was imbued to violin making in Cremona by the great exhibition of 1937, commemorating the bicentennial of Stradivari's death. Since then, much has been done to atone for the city's lack of interest during the nineteenth century. A museum, at first part of the violin making school, now has its own quarters. Among the exhibits are the tools and other materials with which Stradivari worked. The school, the Scuola Internazionale di Liuteria, was directed by Pietro Sgarabotto (b. 1903), the son of one of Italy's foremost modern luthiers. Several of his own instruments are on display at the school, showing him to be a first-rate maker. In Cremona's city hall two Strads are exhibited, including the magnificent "Il Cremonese" of 1715 (see frontispiece).

Nineteenth-century Brescia produced few above-average violins. Only the Scarampella family can be credited with superior work, beginning with Paolo Scarampella (d. 1870), who began as a carpenter. His son Giuseppe (d. 1902) became the curator of the famous instrument collection at Florence's Istituto Musicale; his other son, Stefano (d. 1927), settled in Mantua and became one of the leading turn-of-the-century luthiers. The municipal music school in Brescia now sends instruments to Cremona to be repaired. Times have changed!

The Degani family came from Montagnana near Padua; its members worked in many locations. Domenico Degani (d. 1887) had a shop in Padua. His son Eugenio (d. 1915) settled in Venice; his instruments are distinguished by beautiful, yellowish golden varnish, which he prepared himself according to a closely guarded formula. Grandson Giulio Ettore emigrated to Cincinnati, where he became one of the most successful modern American luthiers.

In Milan, the aforementioned Mantegazza family, thoroughly familiar with valuable violins, passed on their expertise, in an unbroken tradition, to the nineteenth century. In 1834 Giacomo Rivolta earned a gold medal for "having resurrected the school of the famous Stradivari." More recently, Leandro Bisiach (d. 1945) of Milan, a very capable orchestra violinist, was much in demand for making copies of historic instruments. As a luthier he was assisted by his sons Andrea, Giacomo, and Leandro Jr. His varnish is based on a recipe dated 1704, allegedly by Stradivari, though its authenticity has been questioned. Another son, Carlo Bisiach (d. 1908), worked in Florence. Celeste Farotti (Farotto; d. 1928) received many prizes for his work. Together with his brother Salvatore Farotti (d. 1942) he founded a violin shop that became world famous and was taken over by his nephew Celestino

Farotti (b. 1905). They made excellent violins based on models by Stradivari, Rocca, and Pressenda.

Other master luthiers anxious to return to the old traditions included Lorenzo Arcangioli of Florence (first half of the 1800s); Antonio Comuni (d. 1825) of Piacenza; Giuseppe Dall'Aglio (d. 1840) of Mantua; Giuseppe Baldantoni (d. 1873) of Ancona; and Nicolò Bianchi (d. 1881) of Genoa, an expert repairer who worked in Paris and eventually settled in Nice. Giovanni Dollenz (d. 1856) worked in Storioni's shop in Cremona before settling in Trieste, where he made good violins in the Stradivari and Guarneri manner. Francesco Maurizi (d. 1903) and his son Giovanni (d. 1922) were active in Appignano.

Henley's dictionary includes no less than nine luthiers by the name of Fiorini, but some were the invention of the London violin dealers Beare & Son, able businessmen (the name occurs only on labels that were inserted in good-quality violins). Raffaele Fiorini (d. 1898), on the other hand, was a highly talented luthier whose violins in the Cremona manner approach their models tonally. His son Giuseppe, trained in his father's shop in Bologna, has been rightly called one of the best luthiers of recent times.

Giuseppe Fiorini worked in Munich until the outbreak of World War I, moved to Zurich and Rome, and finally returned to Munich, where he died in 1934. A co-founder of the Society of German Luthiers, he also developed the plan to establish a school for luthiers in Cremona, a project that was realized only after his death. He has a special place in the history of violin making; he located Cozio di Salabue's estate and purchased it, thereby safeguarding it. It included not only the documents later published as the *Carteggio* but also materials with which Stradivari worked. In 1930 Fiorino donated these to the City of Cremona. Among his many pupils, Augusto Pollastri (d. 1927) deserves mention. He excelled at making copies of old master violins.

In the mid-nineteenth century, Naples became a major center of violin making in which the Ventapane family figures importantly. Most talented was Lorenzo Ventapane (d. 1843), who followed the Gagliano model. Vincenzo Jorio (d. 1849) also belongs here. Vincenzo Sannino (b. 1879), who began his career as a violinist, accompanied Fridolin Hamma on his Italian journeys as an interpreter. A self-trained violin maker, he produced instruments in the best Gagliano tradition, achieving such mastery that even connoisseurs mistook his copies for authentic Gaglianos. Their tone quality made them much in demand by soloists. Sannino later worked in Rome; he is said to have produced more than eight hundred instruments.

Antonio Gibertini (d. 1866), active in Parma and Genoa, made fine Guarneri copies but was best known as a good restorer, looking after Paganini's instruments. Gaetano Sgarabotto (d. 1959), one of the best luthiers of his age, had a good artistic education and won his first gold medal at the age of twenty in Turin, followed by others at practically all major international exhibits. He worked in Milan and Vicenza. In 1928 he succeeded in founding a luthier class at the Parma conservatory. His excellent reputation as a repairer gave him access to many valuable violins, details of which he recorded in drawings and plaster casts. This unique collection, now owned by his son, is available to students at the Cremona violin making school. As a builder, Gaetano followed the best traditions, succeeding in combining the practices of several major luthiers of the seventeenth and eighteenth centuries.

Several generations of luthiers belonging to the Averna family were active in Sicily, especially in Palermo. Their chief representatives were Gesualdo Averna (b. 1875) and Alfredo Averna (b. 1905). A female member of the family also participated in making instruments, as is indicated by labels reading "Alfonso e figlia."

FRANCE

Changes in what was considered the ideal sound caused the turning away from the highly arched Stainer model to the flatter and louder-sounding model used by later Italian makers. Outside of Italy, this change first affected violin making in France. As a result, French luthiers for a long time held a position of leadership, reflected most clearly in instruments by Nicolas Lupot, whose instruments and those of his school are characterized by a beautiful, brilliant red varnish. Many aspiring violin makers sought to train in his shop; among these were several members of the Gand family of Mirecourt. Charles-François Gand established himself in Paris and bought Koliker's shop. He became Lupot's successor and married his daughter, thereby following a longstanding tradition among luthiers; at times marrying a violin maker's daughter was even a condition of being accepted as his apprentice. Gand's large firm employed many highly skilled workers and became a major trading post for Italian master violins. Its importance was reflected in the appointment of Gand's son Charles-Adolphe as "luthier du Conservatoire de Musique." In all, the Gand family produced five master luthiers, most of whom built violins in Lupot's manner.

Charles-Nicolas-Eugène Gand, who studied violin with Baillot, displayed organizational and business talent, and after his brother's death he joined the outstanding Lupot pupil Auguste Sébastien Philippe Bernardel (d.

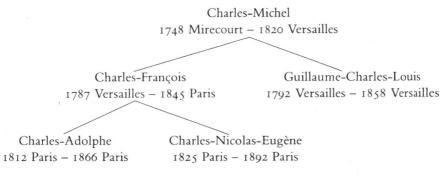

Charles-Michel
1748 Mirecourt – 1820 Versailles

Charles-François
1787 Versailles – 1845 Paris

Guillaume-Charles-Louis
1792 Versailles – 1858 Versailles

Charles-Adolphe
1812 Paris – 1866 Paris

Charles-Nicolas-Eugène
1825 Paris – 1892 Paris

Genealogy of the Gand Family of Luthiers

1870) of Mirecourt in founding the firm of Gand et Bernardel. For a long time they were entrusted with the care and maintenance of instruments in the court chapel and the Conservatoire. The Bernardel family produced a number of distinguished luthiers, preserving the reputation of the founders through four generations, into the twentieth century.

The studio of Jean-Baptiste Vuillaume (1798–1875), one of the most interesting figures in the history of violin making, was a gathering place for traveling virtuosos and amateurs. Born into a well-known Mirecourt family, Vuillaume obtained his training in his father's shop. At the age of nineteen he went to Paris, where he worked for two years with the inventive Chanot. He was an assistant to the organ builder Lété; at the age of twenty-seven he became his partner. Lété also repaired string instruments. Since 1828 Vuillaume was an independent luthier, showing great interest in Savart's work and becoming perhaps the first luthier to combine an artisan's skill with a knowledge of history and an understanding of the laws of physics, especially acoustics. Much in demand as a restorer (and later because of his association with Tarisio), he was in a position to examine fine Italian violins in their original condition. The knowledge thus gained enabled him to make copies that even experts could hardly distinguish from the originals. Because of his "Tieffenbrucker violins" he acquired a reputation as an unscrupulous forger, which indeed he was at times. But his actions are perhaps understandable when one considers the situation in which a luthier then found himself. When he first offered his own violins to the public, despite their good quality, few people took notice, for at the time many buyers had their eyes on old master violins. Prices were largely determined by the snobbism of collectors with lots of money and little expertise. In a sense, Vuillaume's forgeries were his way of getting even with this segment of the violin-buying public, which included many would-be experts. His tricks included aging the wood artificially by subjecting it to high temperatures, though this usually destroyed the wood fibers. Flesch (*The Art of Violin Playing*, vol. 1) commented on this practice:

> It is due to J.-B. Vuillaume that we have so few perfect concert instruments, for he rendered some three thousand violins unfit for concert purposes by "baking" them. "Baking" is an artificial preparation of the wood, which consists of exposing it to high temperature, which kills the wood fibers, a process taking place *naturally* only after a very long period of time. If the same number of violins "baked" by his emulators and admirers be added, we have at least six thousand admirably built examples, captivating in appearance, which have been withdrawn from artistic use owing to Vuillaume's obsession, and which are greatly missed.

A prize specimen of Vuillaume's skill at making copies is an instrument that for a century was believed to be a Strad and acquired worldwide fame as the "Balfour" Strad. It brought a remarkably high price at a pre–World War I auction by the London firm of Puttick & Simpson.

Copy of a Stradivarius violin by Jean-Baptiste Vuillaume

Vuillaume continued his shady practices for many years. He became very successful, won many prizes, and made much money. At that point he could afford to stop making copies and now sold instruments that were "genuine Vuillaumes." These are considered outstanding examples of French violin making, appreciated by soloists for their superb tonal characteristics. Vuillaume only used wood of the best quality, which he acquired on extended journeys through Switzerland, the Tyrol, and Dalmatia. Mailand examined his varnishes closely and found that they were equal to those of the old Italians.

Vuillaume's brothers Nicolas (d. 1871) and Nicolas-François (d. 1876) were also highly talented luthiers. Nicolas was active in Mirecourt; Nicolas-François worked with Jean-Baptiste in Paris before settling in Brussels.

Instruments by Jean-François Aldric (d. 1843), who like most of his Paris colleagues hailed from Mirecourt, were equal to those of the best Paris luthiers. His grandfather, Jean Aldric, had built fine violins in the Italian manner, and Jean-François followed Stradivari's model. His instruments were so much like Lupot's that some were sold (and no doubt continue to be sold) as genuine Lupots. Paul Bailly (d. 1915), a Vuillaume pupil, traveled widely before settling in Paris. Among his two thousand violins are fine copies of instruments by top Italian makers and by Vuillaume. His shop was taken over by his daughter Jenny Bailly, a highly qualified violin maker.

Expert luthiers continued to work in Mirecourt, resisting the temptation to make more money through mass production, or at least devoting some of their time to making superior instruments. Among these were Dominique Peccatte (d. 1874); Jean-Joseph-Honoré Dérazey (d. 1883) and his son Juste Dérazey (d. 1890); members of the Brugère family; and more recently, Georges Apparut (d. 1948).

Excellent luthiers could also be found in smaller French cities. In Lyon were the brothers Pierre (d. 1859), Hippolyte Silvestre (d. 1879), and Paul-François Blanchard (d. 1912), who cared for instruments belonging to the conservatory. Pierre Pacherle (d. 1871), a Pressenda pupil, worked in Nice, as did Augustin Blanchi (d. 1899) and his son Alberto Blanchi (d. 1948). The family tradition was successfully maintained by Alberto's nephew Pierre Gaggini (b. 1903). Georges Chanot II (d. 1883), the experimenter's brother, worked in Courcelles; Pierre-Joseph Hel (d. 1902) and his son Pierre Jean Henry Hel (d. 1937) made violins in Lille. Several of these master builders came from Mirecourt and worked in well-known Paris ateliers before establishing their own shops, such as Joseph Aubry (d. 1937), who won prizes at various exhibitions before he settled in Le Havre.

Many top luthiers were active in Paris during the second half of the nineteenth and into the twentieth century. Among them was Claude-Augustin Miremont (d. 1887) of Mirecourt, who worked at various times in New York before opening his own Paris establishment. Télesphore Amable Barbé (d. 1892) had a career that seems strange but was not uncommon among luthiers. He worked for virtually all the major French makers of his time, yet in spite of being an excellent worker he never was able to establish himself independently. The label in one of his violins reads "Télesphore Barbé / Expremier ouvrier de J.-B. Vuillaume / Médaillé à l'Exposition de 1867 / Paris" (Formerly the principal worker for Vuillaume, awarded a medal at the 1867 exposition).

Marcel Vatelot (d. 1970) also came from Mirecourt. After working for several masters he became an independent luthier. His violins are among the finest produced in modern France. His son Étienne Vatelot (b. 1925) took over the shop. Léon Fischesser–Chollet (d. 1937) for some time attracted attention with his fine violins. Together with Lucien Greilsamer he developed a varnish that approaches that of the old Italians. Charles Enel (d. 1954) of Mirecourt traveled widely abroad before opening his shop in Paris. He soon enjoyed an excellent reputation. His violins display great artistry and good tonal qualities. To this group of superior luthiers belongs Émile Marcel Français (b. 1894). His father, Henri Français (d. 1943), also was a very fine repairer. Émile's masterpiece was a copy of the "Khevenhüller" Strad for Menuhin. In 1929, the San Francisco banker Goldman had given the real Khevenhüller to Menuhin. In order not to put too much strain on it, Menuhin at first practiced only on his Grancino; he then had Français make the Khevenhüller copy for him. "This proved such a good instrument," Magidoff says, "that when Menuhin uses it at times in the concert hall not even critics are aware of any difference in quality."

For a long time, touring violinists who stopped in Paris would entrust their violins to Roger (b. 1901) and Max Millant (b. 1903), the grandsons and pupils of Sébastien Auguste Deroux (d. 1919), one of the best French makers of the nineteenth century. The Millant brothers published a fine manual on violin making, based on their experiences.

Pierre Audinot (b. 1893) came from an old family of violin makers in Mirecourt. He worked at first for his father, Nestor Dominique Audinot (d. 1920), then for the Millant–Deroux brothers. Another well-established family were the Bazins, going back to François Bazin (d. 1865), a bow maker in Mirecourt. Gustave Bazin (d. 1920) was one of the foremost French luthiers around the turn of the century. The war had a curious effect on the life of his nephew Charles René Bazin (b. 1906): after working for Dieudonné (Mirecourt), Vatelot (Paris), and Darche (Brussels), he became a German prisoner of war and was assigned to work in the Hamma shop. His "captivity" in the Stuttgart atelier does not appear to have been too unpleasant, for he rejoined it in 1951 and stayed until he established his own shop in Munich in 1957.

ENGLAND

At the beginning of the nineteenth century, England's musical life offered relatively few opportunities for the sale of new string instruments, little doubt the reason for the small number of above-average English luthiers. But before long, London became one of the leading cities, next to Paris, for selling and repairing violins.

One of the best luthiers of the time was Thomas Perry (d. 1830), who made more than three thousand violins, mostly following Amati. Thomas Dodd (d. 1823), from the well-known family of bow makers, made fine violins in the Italian style, but some instruments with his labels were probably made by Fendt and J. Fr. Lott (d. 1853), who worked in his shop. Lott, originally from Germany, began his career as a furniture maker; he later became famous for his cellos and basses. His two sons, George Frederick Lott (d. 1868) and John Frederick Lott (d. 1871) were highly regarded repairers and appraisers. Members of the Furber family (late 1700s and early 1800s) built good violins after Stradivari and Guarneri.

Good reputations were also enjoyed by eight luthiers named Hardie, belonging to several families. Most accomplished was Matthew Hardie (d. 1826 in Edinburgh). For his outstanding violins in the Cremona manner he became known as "the Scottish Stradivari." James Hardie II, who died in 1916 at the age of eighty, also worked in Edinburgh. In all he has more than two thousand instruments to his credit; he said that he built them entirely by himself.

Vincenzo Trusiano Panormo (d. 1813) was born in Sicily and worked in Cremona, Turin, Paris, and other places before the French Revolution caused him to move to London. Highly esteemed, especially for his violins after Stradivari, Panormo was ably assisted by William Taylor (d. 1820). Three sons and two grandsons carried on Vincenzo's tradition with varying degrees of success. Richard Tobin (d. 1841), who worked from time to time in the Betts atelier, may have been the most talented English luthier of all time. He never succeeded in establishing his own shop—a genius who never received the recognition he deserved. Quite likely some of his Strad copies are owned by proud collectors who believe them to be originals. Often the scrolls of his violins were removed to serve as the starting point for "old Italian violins"; some violin bodies were similarly treated.

George Craske (d. 1888) worked as a repairer in the firm established by Muzio Clementi, the piano virtuoso and composer. He then started his own shop, and during the course of his ninety-one years made 2620 violins, violas, cellos, and basses, all in the tradition of the best Italian masters.

The Fendt (Fent) family played an important part in the history of English violin making. The founder, Bernhard Fendt, born in Füssen, reached London by way of Paris in 1798. There he worked for Thomas Dodd and John Betts. His sons Bernhard Simon (d. 1852), Martin (d. 1845), and Jacob (d. 1849) were also highly gifted luthiers. They made amazingly good Stradivari and Guarneri copies that no doubt deceived many collectors who would never have thought of buying a "merc" Fendt.

Members of the famous Chanot family achieved similar importance in England. George III (b. 1830 in Paris) founded the English branch of the ancient Mirecourt family. He opened his own atelier in London in 1858 and soon attracted very skillful workers. His sons also made fine instruments and were widely known as first-rate repairers. A grandson, Alfred Ernest Chanot, was still active in London ca. 1980.

George Hart & Son was another London firm that at various times had a superior reputation. John Thomas Hart (d. 1874), the family's first luthier, did not excel at making violins but did excellent repairs and was a capable dealer. His son George (d. 1891), a fine musician (violin and piano), soon established himself as one of the world's foremost experts. His books on the violin are among the best. George II, the grandson, received his training in Paris. He was able to develop the family business to become an international gathering place for violinists, violin lovers, and collectors. Instruments with the label "Hart & Son" were for the most part made by capable workers found and trained by George II. One of the firm's specialties was making copies of specific master violins; they would have labels such as "Exact copy of 'The d'Egville' / Guarneri, date 1735 / Hart & Son / Makers / 28. War-dour Street. W / 18 London 99."

London shops also specialized in holding auctions at regular intervals. According to Starcke, the Puttick & Simpson firm auctioned off two to three thousand instruments annually, including some very valuable ones.

The making, repairing, and selling of violins was dominated by a few large London firms, including (aside from Hill) Dykes & Sons and Edward Withers & Sons (founded in 1765). As a result, even very good luthiers were increasingly reluctant to incur the risk of opening their own shops, preferring the security—and anonymity—of being an employee. Nevertheless, some small ateliers satisfied the modest demand for individually made violins. David Arnot (d. 1897), who had earned many prizes and was a fine violinist himself, made very good instruments in the Italian tradition. George Darbey (d. 1920) was active in Bristol. Both Sarasate and Wilhelmj played his violins. Walter H. Mayson (d. 1905) of Manchester was fond of giving names to his best instruments such as "Ethelberta," "Sarasate," and "Alfred the Great." Robert Alton (b. 1882), a luthier in Bootle, also became known as the author of several good books on violin making.

William Atkinson (d. 1929), one of the best turn-of-the-century luthiers, was also knowledgeable about acoustics. He produced a very good oil var-nish, claiming to have rediscovered the secret of the old Italians. After apply-ing fifteen to twenty layers he air-dried his instruments. When he noticed that the climate of Tottenham, his residence, was detrimental to the drying process, he moved his shop to Essex. Instruments he built after having devel-oped his own varnish he called "Cremonides." Jeffery James Gilbert (d. 1942) at first was discouraged by his father, an amateur violin maker. Because of this he entered the profession rather late but in time developed a distinctive per-sonal style. He lived to be ninety-two years old, continually experimenting with varnishes. During his last years he claimed finally to have discovered the Cremona secret.

In 1885 William, Charles, and Arthur Voller opened a successful shop in London. As specialists in making copies, their reputation was somewhat dubious. Instruments they acknowledged as their own they labelled "Voller fratelli / Londra."

THE AMERICAS

Not a single American luthier is mentioned by Fuchs, who was chiefly con-cerned with higher-priced instruments and their builders. Vannes, on the other hand, includes the names of more than six hundred luthiers in North and South America, 107 of whom worked in New York, forty-five in Buenos Aires, and ten in Toronto. James Juhan, of French ancestry, may have been the first violin maker in America. He was a genius who, during the second half of the eighteenth century, was active in Philadelphia as a composer, teacher of music and dance, and maker of violins and bows. Noah Allen was an early nineteenth-century luthier in Chicago. Gradually others opened shops in the larger cities; most had immigrated from Italy, France, and Germany, and in some cases came from well-known European families of violin makers. No doubt some of them changed their names to imply being related to the great Italians of the past. Joseph Amato in New York may be one of these, while Rovatti, a Buenos Aires maker of Italian descent, gave himself a middle name and accordingly used the label "Thomas Stradivari Rovatti / fece in Buenos Aires." A New York manufacturer of strings advertised his company as "The Cremonese." Like American skyscrapers, business-minded luthiers also "reached for the sky": Joseph Pepin founded "The Pepin Perfect Tone Violin Company," while another, actually quite good maker used the label "Joseph Bohrman, the World's Greatest / Musical Instrument Maker / 276 W. Madison Street / Chicago."

In the second half of the nineteenth century luthiers settled in all larger American cities, the increase reflecting a flourishing musical life based on European traditions. Symphony orchestras were founded, and music played an important part in education. With the rise of capitalism, more Americans bought Italian master violins, which created a need for qualified repairers and merchants. Good luthiers can now be found in every major American city, while stores such as Lyon & Healy in Chicago employ experts whose opinions carry a lot of weight in the European market as well. Rudolph Francis Wurlitzer (d. 1914) founded the firm that at one time had offices in sixty U.S. cities. Wurlitzer came from an old family of luthiers in Markneukirchen. His son Rudolph Henry (d. 1948) received his training at August Riechers's in Berlin; he also studied with Helmholtz and Spitta at the university, obtaining a Ph.D. Rembert Wurlitzer, of the third generation, visited the major European centers of violin making during his training period. The family's instrument collection is one of the world's best.

As in Europe, some independent luthiers were able to succeed, making instruments of above-average quality. Carl B. Ackley of Ohio was one of these; his violins were much in demand during the first half of the twentieth century. August Martin Ludwig (d. 1895) and Georg Gemünder (d. 1899) had come from Germany. Gemünder worked for Vuillaume in Paris, making Italian-style violins and providing them with excellent varnish in the French manner. In 1880 he published his study *Georg Gemünders Fortschritte im Violinbau sowie interessante Aufklärungen über die Violinmacherkunst, deren Kritiker und über Violinen im Allgemeinen* (Gemünder's innovations in violin making, along with interesting information about the art of making violins, its critics, and about violins in general). Published in English the following year, it contains some worthwhile material, but also amounts to some not-so-subtle advertising for his enterprise. Heron-Allen called it "a complaint about the juries at exhibitions who refused to recognize him as the new Stradivari, and a diatribe against all other luthiers."

Charles Fr. Albert (d. 1901), of Freiburg (Breisgau) originally, worked in both New York and Philadelphia. He showed great imagination, introduced improvements in string and rosin making, designed an unusual chin rest, and constructed a practice violin. His brother Eugen John Albert (d. 1902) built violins based on a design developed by their father John Albert (d. 1887) that was endorsed by many. Labels read "The John Albert / American / Concert Violin / manufactured by / E. J. Albert / Philadelphia Penna."

Ignatz Anton Lutz (d. 1927), born and trained in Vienna, worked in San Francisco. He made superior copies and other violins that were played by major soloists. Henry Bentin (d. 1928 in New Orleans) was from Poland. He attracted much attention with a perfect copy of the "Emperor" Strad, made for Kubelik. John Friedrich (d. 1943), born and trained in Germany, built attractive violins on Cremona models. The violins of Ole H. Bryant (d. 1943) were modeled on del Gesù. He founded a violin making school in Boston.

René Aerts (d. 1942) of Mirecourt went to Germany and England, then for some time was in charge of instruments at the Brussels conservatory; he finally settled in Los Angeles. His outstanding copies of Italian masters were played by the Pro Arte Quartet. His son Marcel (b. 1910) worked in Long Beach. George M. Anderson, an individualist with much imagination, lived in Glendale, Calif. Ernest Adam (b. 1891) was active in St. Louis, chiefly as a repairer. J. H. Abernethy (b. 1886) made violins in Virginia. Carl Becker (b. 1887 in Chicago) enjoyed an excellent reputation, supplying instruments to players in major symphony orchestras and chamber music groups. His association with the famous firm of William Lewis & Son is representative of an important trend among modern luthiers. Such an arrangement meant a luthier could concentrate on his craft, leaving the sale of his instruments to a well-established house.

A leading maker in Canada was Rosario Bayeur (d. 1944 in Montreal), who experimented successfully with native types of wood.

THE IBERIAN PENINSULA

For a relatively brief period during the eighteenth century violin making flourished on the Iberian Peninsula, influenced by Italian practices, but only the emergence of a highly developed concert life in the late nineteenth century created employment possibilities, in the larger cities, for good luthiers. Now they are found everywhere. For the last two hundred years Vannes lists forty makers in Lisbon alone, thirty-five in Barcelona, and thirty-three in Madrid. Among these we should mention José de Hierro (d. 1905) of the Madrid conservatory, and the three brothers Manuel, Bienvenido, and Ignacio Fleta of Barcelona, whose cellos won the approval of Casals. Antonio Joseph da Cruz-Mura was the best Portuguese maker. Domingos Capela (b. 1904), also from Portugal, was a cabinetmaker before he turned to instrument making, succeeding with violins based on Italian models. Jacques Camurat (b. 1927 in Madrid) had a shop in Bilbao, then moved to Paris. He competed successfully in international shows.

BELGIUM AND HOLLAND

Violin making was well developed in eighteenth-century Belgium and Holland, supported by the nobility. But the changes brought about by the rising importance of the middle class resulted in a crisis lasting several decades. The situation improved, at first in Belgium, when Nicolas-François Vuillaume (d. 1876), Jean-Baptiste's brother, settled in Brussels. The three Darche brothers from Mirecourt followed him as co-workers and apprentices; of these, Charles Claude François Darche (d. 1874) founded his own establishment. His much-admired masterpiece was the repair of a genuine Andrea Amati cello dated 1547, which had belonged to Charles II of France and had been completely destroyed before being handed over to Darche. Hilaire Darche (d. 1929), a nephew, together with a brother, a piano maker, founded the firm of Darche Frères. Hilaire became the official luthier of the Brussels conservatory, which meant that he was also the curator of that institution's magnificent instrument collection. His own violins are among the twentieth century's best.

The Liège conservatory, so important in the history of violin playing, had on its staff Emile Heynberg (d. 1939), whose instruments were based on Stradivari and Guarneri models as well as on those by J.-B. Vuillaume (this was becoming a trend). His son Georges Heynberg (b. 1901) successfully carried on the shop, its specialty being a "vernis Crémonais" (Cremonese varnish), as its labels indicate. André Bernard (d. 1959), trained in Paris, founded an atelier in Liège and around the turn of the century received many prizes. He was especially interested in what was then becoming an important aspect of musical life: the making of replicas of early string instruments, an activity that was carried on by his son Jacques Bernard (b. 1919).

In Amsterdam, brothers Johann Warnaar (d. 1889) and Gerrit Kok (d. 1899) brought in Paul Kunze (d. 1957), a luthier from Markneukirchen, to take over their atelier. Later, Kunze established himself in The Hague. Another builder from Markneukirchen, Max Möller (d. 1948), came to Amsterdam by way of Berlin and St. Petersburg. Before opening his own shop he worked for Karel van der Meer (d. 1932). Möller's son Max (b. 1915) successfully carried on his father's work. Eugène I Eberle (d. 1936) was a leading violin maker in Rotterdam; his brother Eugène II Eberle (b. 1915) was trained by Möckel in Berlin. All these master luthiers (especially Max Möller I) made outstanding instruments and were reliable repairers and expert appraisers.

SCANDINAVIA AND FINLAND

During the seventeenth century, when the Swedish court chapel for the first time included violinists, these, along with their instruments, were imported from Italy. For a long time Italian, Austrian, French, and German violins were prevalent in the Scandinavian countries. In Norway, however, the Hardanger fiddle soon became widely used in folk music. This instrument, using drone

Hardanger fiddle by John Erichsen Helland, 1834
(Copenhagen, Music History Museum)

strings, required a special playing technique and was chiefly used for dancing. These fiddles were often homemade or built by village carpenters.

The first Scandinavian violin makers of record included Arefroid Romegren (d. 1737) and Johannes Georg Mohte (d. 1765), both of Sweden. Copenhagen soon became a center of violin making with luthiers including Johan Helwich (d. 1770), Ole Dreier (d. 1810), Niels Jensen Lund (d. 1858), and Thomas Jacobsen (d. 1853), who trained in Germany and worked for Vuillaume in Paris before establishing himself at home.

The Hjorth family of luthiers was founded in Copenhagen by Andreas Hansen Hjorth (d. 1834), who built fine violins in the Amati style and looked after the instruments at the Danish court. Emil Hjorth (d. 1920) was his grandson. He learned the craft from his father, Johannes Hjorth, and spent several years gaining experience in Vienna, Paris, and London. Arne Hjorth (b. 1910), a fifth-generation luthier, was trained in Paris. He maintained the high family standards making excellent Guarneri copies. He also took a lively interest in Telmányi's experiments with a Bach bow.

German makers have continued to settle in Denmark right up to the present, including Karl Heinel (b. 1907), a Paulus pupil, who came from a well-known family in Markneukirchen. He settled in Copenhagen, working at first for the Paul Merling firm; he opened his own shop in 1951.

A certain Johan Lett (1600s) seems to have been the first Stockholm luthier. During the eighteenth century Elias Carlander (d. 1784), a violinist in the royal chapel, attracted attention with his excellent instruments. One of his labels reads "Elias Carlander / Königl. Hofmusicus / J. Stockholm A. . . ." Johan Öhberg (d. 1779) was a leading maker, best known for his cellos. His pupil Erik Sandberg (d. 1800) produced a veritable flood of instruments, including 300 violins, 270 violas, 50 cellos, 200 guitars, and 120 harps, all of above-average quality, though they may not be altogether his own handiwork.

Alfred Nilsson Brock (d. 1935) was court luthier in Stockholm and also had charge of instruments at the royal conservatory. His successor Otto Sand, originally an orchestra violinist, established himself as a Stockholm luthier in 1922. A high level of violin making is represented by the work of Sven Alfred Ronnel (b. 1877), the winner of many international prizes, and of Bengt Lindholm (b. 1917), trained in Markneukirchen and New York. The Norwegian Sveinung Andersen (b. 1908) was another outstanding luthier. The first Finnish violin was made in 1756 by Johan Granqvist (d. 1788); the first professional luthier there was Johan Lindström (d. 1828 in Turku). Anti Niklander (d. 1951) of Helsinki had an international reputation, in part due to his excellent bows. The violinist Juka Bergman (b. 1896) was an Auer pupil before he turned to violin making. His son and pupil Carlo Bergman (b. 1938) spent four years at the violin maker's school in Cremona. He specializes in preserving and restoring old instruments. Next to him, Martti Piiponen (b. 1931) and Ristto Vainio (b. 1930) are among the leading Finnish luthiers. Since the mid-nineteenth century, it is characteristic of the nordic countries that instrument makers have worked in small towns and villages. Perhaps in the days before phonograph and radio, music making in the home was of special importance, especially during the long winter evenings of the polar regions. No doubt many a villager attempted to make his or her own instrument, and some may have gained enough proficiency to become professionals. Others remained enthusiastic amateurs yet at times succeeded in making remarkably good violins.

GERMANY

German violin makers were late in changing over to the flatter and tonally stronger Italian eighteenth-century models. Moreover, there was increasing emphasis on industrial production. As a result, nineteenth-century Germany was late in catching up to international standards. In the first half of the nineteenth century, French craftsmen excelled in making copies of old masters; after that the skill was more often found in Germany. As Drögemeyer jokingly phrased it, "Most old Italian master violins are found in Germany, the homeland of such instruments." The bon mot supposedly originated with an English luthier.

Jacob Augustus Otto (d. 1829) came from the eighteenth-century tradition. In his youth he had studied mathematics and physics, including acoustics. He worked in Weimar, Halle, Leipzig, Magdeburg, Berlin, and Jena. His excellent book on violin making was reprinted several times until 1886; an English translation had gone through five printings by 1875. Jean Cornelius Vauchel (d. 1856), the son of a political refugee, was born in Germany, then trained by Tourte in Paris. An influential figure in German violin making, he worked in several German cities, making instruments approximating in quality those of the best Italian masters.

Important centers of violin making were slow to emerge. Very good luthiers came from the Diehl family; during the eighteenth and nineteenth centuries they could be found in many locations. The most prominent member was Nicolaus Diehl (d. 1851 in Darmstadt), luthier to the court of the Grand Duke of Hessia. His grandson August Diehl (d. 1922) made a name for himself in Hamburg with various experimental bows.

Martin Baur (d. 1875), a trumpeter in military bands before receiving training as a violin maker, was instrument maker to the royal court in Stuttgart, where he came under the tutelage and protection of Molique. His son Adolf Baur (d. 1873) for a while worked under Vuillaume. Like some of his colleagues, he spoiled many instruments by subjecting the wood to artificial aging before using it. The Baur shop nevertheless enjoyed a good reputation. It was continued by Anton Sprenger (d. 1900), whose experiments with improving tone attracted attention. His son Adolf (b. 1872), after training with Zach in Vienna, worked in New York and Stuttgart. His fine work as a builder and repairer brought international recognition to the family. Anton's second son, Eugen (d. 1953), gained experience in Switzerland and England before opening his shop in Frankfurt, which enjoyed an equally good reputation.

Ludwig Christian August Bausch (d. 1871), a superior bow maker, was also known for his violins. Möckel, however, reports that the wood in some Bausch copies of old master violins was artificially (chemically) aged; even now such instruments can be recognized by their acrid smell. August Riechers (d. 1893), a Bausch pupil, after years as a journeyman settled in Hanover, his hometown. In 1872 Joachim engaged him to care for instruments at the Berlin Hochschule für Musik. About two thousand violins and cellos, built after Stradivari and Guarneri, came from his shop. He repaired more than three hundred Strads, thus becoming one of the best connoisseurs of classic Italian violin making. His book about the violin is most valuable.

Nicolas Darche (d. 1873), a member of the famous family of luthiers from Mirecourt, pursued his profession in Aachen (Aix-la-Chapelle). Petrus Schulz (d. 1871) spent some years abroad before establishing himself in Regensburg. He too knew the Italian masters well, making copies of Maggini, Stradivari, and Guarneri violins that are well above the average German production of the time. Instruments by Ludwig Neuner (d. 1897), a member of the famous Mittenwald family, stand out above much that was produced there, which, as we have seen, included everything related to the violin, including instrument cases. Neuner had been Engleder's apprentice in Munich, where he also studied the cello at the conservatory. He then became an assistant at Lemböck's in Vienna and later also worked with Vuillaume in Paris, and in London. He made use of the time in Paris by taking cello lessons from Franchomme. Having established his own atelier in Berlin, Neuner gave it up in order to take over the father's firm of Neuner & Hornsteiner in Mittenwald. A good organizer, he expanded it to the point where he employed two hundred workers.

The Rieger family of Mittenwald produced many competent luthiers—sixteen, according to Henley. Of these, Joseph Rieger (d. 1837) was most successful, to judge by the steadily rising prices commanded by his instruments. Rieger & Fiorini, a Munich firm, marketed not only violins but also guitars and zithers. Vincenz Beck (d. 1862) of Glatz operated a true family enterprise, employing at times three sons and nine daughters!

The imaginative luthier Carl Schulze (d. 1903) of Berlin, thoroughly trained in acoustics, has already been mentioned in connection with the innovations in violin making described in his book. Oskar Bernhard Heinel (d. 1931) worked in Dresden and Hamburg before establishing himself in his hometown Markneukirchen. Both the construction and the varnish of his instruments were first-rate. Leipzig instrument maker Wilhelm Hermann Hammig (d. 1925) was also from Markneukirchen. Henley said of him, "Future buyers will have to pay high prices for his violins." Even in his own time Hamming enjoyed a fine reputation, having been put in charge of instruments of the Gewandhaus Orchestra and the Leipzig conservatory.

Apparently it was the custom among German luthiers to spend long years "on the road," as journeymen, thereby widening their horizons and acquainting themselves with techniques used elsewhere. Georg Winterling (d. 1927), whom Fuchs calls one of the best modern masters, produced instruments with outstanding tonal properties; he worked in Frankfurt, Dresden, and Vienna before opening shops in Hamburg and Munich. Likewise Albin Wilfer (d. 1939), whose forebears were amateur violin makers, was active in Markneukirchen and Moscow before establishing an atelier in Leipzig. Michael Dötsch (d. 1940) did not make the permanent move to Berlin until he had gained experience abroad. His detailed studies of Italian instruments resulted in fine copies after Stradivari, Guadagnini, Nicolò Gagliano, Lupot, and Vuillaume.

In 1864 Fridolin I Hamma (d. 1892) founded the firm of Hamma & Co., which was continued by his son Emil I Hamma (d. 1928). Their own expertise coupled with their talent for attracting superior workers made the company an international success; Henley considered the well-connected organization "one of the most important, if not *the* most important firm in all of Germany." The brothers Fridolin, Franz, and Albert lived in Italy; they were very good at scouting out old instruments. In the twentieth century Emil Hamma's sons Fridolin II (d. 1964) and Emil II (d. 1958) raised the firm's reputation even higher, in part because of Fridolin II's important publications. Walter Hamma (1916–1988), Fridolin II's son, had similar talents.

The Padewet brothers came to Germany from Vienna. Karl Padewet (d. 1896), known for his outstanding Strad copies, settled in Munich. Johann I Padewet (d. 1872), after working in Budapest and Basel, became court luthier to the grand duke of Baden in Karlsruhe. The shop then went to his son Johann II Padewet (d. 1902), and Johann Karl Padewet (b. 1887) successfully represented the third generation. Eugen I Wahl (d. 1961) began as a woodcarver, then studied theology and worked in the Karlsruhe city mission. During his leisure time he made a few violins that turned out surprisingly well. He changed his vocation and passed the master luthier's exam in 1913. His son Gerhard Wahl (b. 1908) learned the craft from him, then worked for Hjorth in Copenhagen. From 1933 to 1943 Gerhard had his own atelier in Stockholm, after which he took charge of his father's shop, in place of his brother, Eugen II, reported missing in the war. The family string quartet played remarkably well.

Max Schäffner (d. 1948) reached Hamburg by way of Leipzig and Nuremberg. Together with his brother Paul (d. 1949) he operated a very fine shop, making distinctive violins with a special varnish. After schooling in Frankfurt, Berlin, and Leipzig, Eduard Adler (b. 1865) established himself in Grünberg, Silesia. His very useful book on the care of violins went through three printings. The Stuttgart luthier Eugen Gärtner (d. 1944), a student of Anton Sprenger and Simoutre, was one of the best turn-of-the-century German luthiers. His labels refer to him as "luthier to the royal court of Württemberg and supplier of instruments to the prince of Hohenzollern." Johann Evangelist Bader (d. 1960) worked in Karlsruhe, Würzburg, Koblenz, and Munich before opening his shop in his hometown of Mittenwald, where he taught from time to time at the local school of violin making.

Heinrich Bartsch (b. 1910), trained by J. E. Bader in Mittenwald, took over the shop of his father Albert Bartsch (d. 1928) in Essen. During World

War II he became a Russian prisoner of war and for five years built makeshift instruments for the prison camp.

Olga Adelmann (b. 1913) earned a master luthier's diploma in 1945. She worked as an expert repairer for the state collection of instruments in Berlin.

SWITZERLAND

The first Swiss luthiers of note were Hans Krouchdaler in the seventeenth century and Jean Emery who, in the early eighteenth century, was a "maître Luthié" in Geneva. In Neufchâtel Charles Frédéric Borel (d. 1824) and his son Jérôme Emanuel (d. 1837) worked as both "ébénistes" (furniture makers) and luthiers. Franciscus Maria Pupunatus (d. 1868), as he called himself on his labels, was "maître ébéniste." After some initial success at violin making he turned entirely to that profession. Gustav Methfessel (d. 1910), son of a composer-conductor, was a pupil of Schulz in Regensburg and Lemböck in Vienna. He made fine violins, was very successful as a repairer, and became an expert on Italian masters.

Because of its geographic location and political stability, Switzerland always attracted makers from abroad, for shorter or longer stays. Outstanding among them was Giuseppe Fiorini and the German Georg Ullmann (d. 1946); both worked in Zurich.

Fritz I Baumgartner (d. 1976), established in Basel since 1920, and his son Fritz II (d. 1975) were among the leading Swiss luthiers. Both made excellent Strad and Guarneri copies. Gustav Senn (d. 1980) and his son Paul (b. 1919) also worked in Basel. Ulrich W. Zimmermann (b. 1934) was the successful director of the violin making school in Brienz, in which position he succeeded Adolf Heinrich König (b. 1908). Members of the Werro family earned international recognition. Jean Werro (d. 1938) worked in England for a while before settling in Bern. His son Henry (b. 1896) took over the shop and earned many prizes. Henry Jean Werro (b. 1930) successfully represents the third generation.

AUSTRIA

In Austria too the Stainer tradition remained strong for a long time, even though the aristocratic amateurs of Beethoven's time had Italian master violins brought to Vienna, inviting comparisons. Ambros Joseph Bogner (d. 1816) was one of the first to change over to the modern model. Johann Georg Staufer (d. 1853), an outstanding luthier, began as a furniture maker and then became a pupil of Geissenhof. His early violins demonstrate the changeover from the Stainer to the Strad model. Inventive and given to experimentation he produced the arpeggione, a guitar-cello, which is remembered only because of the sonata Schubert wrote for this instrument. Later Staufer experimented with modifying various parts of the violin. Probably inspired by Chanot he developed a "patent violin" and later a "guitarre d'amour." With all these experiments and inventions he seems to have neglected his professional work, for he ended his days in the poorhouse.

Mathias Daum (d. 1855) was more successful, eventually establishing his own atelier in Wiener Neustadt. Anton Hofmann (d. 1871), pupil of and successor to J. Martin Stoss, built very distinctive violins and succeeded in obtaining an appointment as luthier to the imperial-royal Austrian court. David Bittner (d. 1887), a pupil of W. Rupprecht and "Geigenmacher des K. K. Hof. Op. Th. in Wien" (luthier for the imperial-royal court opera in Vienna), made very fine instruments in the Cremona style. The Vienna shop of Gabriel Lemböck (d. 1892) of Budapest was an important gathering place for students of the craft, including foreigners. He made good copies of Maggini, Stainer, and del Gesù; he also worked on modifying bass bars so that they stood up to the acoustical requirements of the day. He reportedly repaired Paganini's "Cannon" and then made a copy of it, for which he provided a rather pompous-sounding label: "Gabriel Lemböck fecit secundum / Josephi Guarneri Cremonensis originale / ex Nicolai Paganini Concertuosa Violina, / Viennae Anno 1852. J.H.S."

Thomas Zach (d. 1892), an excellent violin maker, was schooled in Prague, then worked in several Hungarian towns and in Bucharest before settling in Vienna. His son Carl (d. 1918) took over the shop but led a restless existence, moving around a great deal. Together with Prof. Ernst Fleischer he invented a procedure intended to improve the wood to be used in violins by impregnating it with resin, but the attempt was a failure. Anton Jirowsky (d. 1941), a Thomas pupil, carried on the Zach tradition in Vienna. Instruments by members of the Hamberger family were highly regarded by orchestra players and lovers of chamber music. Joseph I Hamberger (d. 1864) was born in Vienna and settled in Pressburg (Bratislava), as did Ferdinand Hamberger, his oldest son. Joseph II Hamberger (d. 1904), the second son, became court luthier in Vienna. Josef Krenn (d. 1962) was much in demand for repairing and maintaining instruments.

Vienna attracted a strong influx of outsiders, especially from the countries of the Austro-Hungarian empire. Wilhelm Joseph Jaura (d. 1908) came from Znaim; he was the first of a family of luthiers, the most distinguished member of which was Wilhelm Thomas Jaura (d. 1922). He owned one of Vienna's foremost violin shops, rose to the position of court luthier, and indicated opus numbers on his instruments' labels. Carl Hermann Voigt (d. 1925), from a large Markneukirchen family, was initially a bow factory worker. After schooling in Budapest and with Lemböck, he became instrument maker to the court in Vienna and enjoyed a fine reputation as an appraiser and entirely honest dealer. Franz Angerer (d. 1924), a good violinist and guitar player, also won prizes as a maker of these instruments. His son of the same name (d. 1938) continued the shop.

Good luthiers in the Austrian provinces included Joseph Böllinger (d. 1819) of Steyr; Alois Maximilian Palfner (d. 1947) of Graz, who made fine Strad and Vuillaume copies; Franz Fuchs (d. 1950) of Linz, who acquired intimate knowledge of Italian masters from Hamma in Stuttgart; and Karl Lang (b. 1907 in Schönbach), whose work was much in demand in Salzburg.

During his youth Carl Flesch became well acquainted with Austrian violin making and thought very highly of it. In his opinion, early nineteenth-century Viennese violins had not yet been "discovered" but would be all the more valued in the future.

CZECHOSLOVAKIA AND HUNGARY

As members of the Austro-Hungarian empire, luthiers in Vienna, Bohemia, and Hungary were close to and influenced by each other. In time the traditionally high level of musicianship found in Bohemia, and in talented Hungarian gypsy musicians, also affected instrument making. Caspar Strnad (d. 1823), one of the first Prague violin makers to turn away from the Stainer model, was a pupil of Hulinzky, known especially for his fine violas. Johann Kulik (d. 1872), an important Prague luthier, based his instruments on Italian models. On some of his labels he indicated in German that the violin was an exact Strad copy; only after the emergence of strong Czech nationalism did he word his labels in that language. His pupil Jan Baptiste Dvořák (Dworak; d. 1890) worked in Budapest and Vienna before returning to Prague. He was the first of a family of excellent luthiers among whom his sons Karel Borromäus (d. 1909) and Jaroslav Anton (d. 1921) were most notable. Along with his brother Ferdinand Joseph I (d. 1862), Emanuel Adam Homolka (d. 1849) represents another family of superior luthiers. He made very distinctive violins based on Stradivari models. His son Ferdinand August Vincenz (d. 1890) did so well that he became known as "the Prague Stradivari"; another son, Vincenz Emanuel (d. 1861), also worked at various times in Budapest and Vienna. In all, Henley has identified nine luthiers belonging to the Homolka family.

Three generations of fine violin makers belonged to the Špidlen family. For a while František F. Špidlen (d. 1916) worked in Kiev; he then took over Salzard's shop in Moscow and became the luthier of the Moscow Conservatory. Eventually he returned to Prague. His son Otakar Špidlen (d. 1958) and his grandson Přemysl Otakar Špidlen (b. 1920) were later in charge of the shop; their Italian and French style instruments acquired an international reputation.

Johann Nepomuk Bina (d. 1897), a fine Prague luthier, pursued his craft in several towns within the Austro-Hungarian empire before establishing himself in his hometown. On his labels he also referred to himself as a certified appraiser.

Anton Sitt (d. 1897) was born in Hungary; at first he worked for his father in Budapest and later for Johann Kulik in Prague, whose daughter he married. He was the father of the violinist Hans Sitt. His very good copies of Italian master violins have labels such as "Antonius Sitt / ad formam G. Guarnerii fecit Pragae 18—." Franz Böhm, an early nineteenth-century luthier from Budapest, also made such outstanding copies that some of them were sold as genuine Italian master violins. The two Schunda brothers, Joseph (d. 1871) and Wenzel Josef (d. 1923) of Bohemia, ran one of the finest Budapest ateliers for more than a half century, the younger Schunda having learned his craft from his brother. Johann Baptist Schweitzer (b. in Vienna, d. 1865) was a pupil of Geissenhof before setting up shop in Budapest, where his fine work brought him great financial success. He built for his retirement a residence that included a laboratory dedicated to varnish research; not surprisingly his instruments are particularly valued for their fine varnish. Samuel Felix Nemessányi (d. 1881) was trained by Schweitzer, worked for Sitt in Prague, and then opened a shop in Budapest. Though he ended his days as an alcoholic street vendor, his excellent Italian-style violins bring good prices in the current market. After working for Zach in Vienna, Béla Szepessy (d. 1925) emigrated to England, where his work was highly valued. Other Budapest luthiers who made violins in the Italian manner were Andreas Bergmann (d. 1934) and János Michelberger (d. 1935)

POLAND

Not surprisingly, violin making in Poland flourished early. Perhaps the popularity of the "Polish violin" (which, although not yet a true violin, fed speculation that Poland was the violin's land of origin) as a folk instrument led to the violin's early and widespread acceptance in that country. The close political ties between Poland and Saxony also figured: for some time the Polish king was also the elector of Saxony and in that role maintained a "Polish court chapel" in Saxony.

Among the earliest important Polish violin makers were Mateusz Dobrucki (d. 1602 in Cracow) and Baltazar Dankwart (d. ca. 1622), a Warsaw master. Martin Groblicz (d. 1609) learned his craft in Italy, but eighteenth-century Polish luthiers consistently followed the Stainer model. One of the best was Carl Nicolaus Sawicki (d. 1850) of Lemberg. He moved to Vienna, where he was known for his excellent copies, especially of Strads. An instrument he dedicated to the Austrian emperor Ferdinand bears this label: "Smae C. R. Apostolicae Maiestati / Ferdinando Imo Austriae imperatori / dedicavit in signum Venerationis et Submissionis / Carol Nicol. Sawicki Leopolitanus Viennae A. 1837" (Dedicated to His Imperial and Royal Apostolic Majesty Ferdinand I by Carl Nicolaus Sawicki of Lemberg as a token of his veneration and deep respect. Vienna 1837).

Vannes lists nineteen luthiers active in Lemberg, forty-six in Posen (Poznan), forty-nine in Cracow, and sixty-eight in Warsaw, indicating an unbroken tradition from the sixteenth century to the present. Tomasz Panufnik (d. 1951), father of the composer, was a major Polish luthier. He was the director of a string instrument factory in Warsaw, designed two violin types that he named "Antiqua" and "Polonia," and wrote two important books on violin making. Andrej Bednarz (d. 1967), though self-taught, rose to become a special instructor at a luthiers' school in Zakopane. Eugeniusz Arnold (b. 1912), one of the best Polish luthiers, was the son and grandson of very good violin makers of German extraction.

RUSSIA

The musical life of Russia's upper class was dominated, well into the nineteenth century, by artists from abroad. They, of course, brought their instruments with them, which meant that few native makers existed. Even during the second half of the nineteenth century many Russian luthiers were German-born; many of them had left Markneukirchen, attracted by the opportunities created by musical activities related to the conservatories in St. Petersburg and Moscow, founded in 1862 and 1866 respectively.

Ivan F. Arkhusen (d. 1870) of Copenhagen established himself in St. Petersburg, as did Moritz Paulus (d. 1896) of Markneukirchen; Anton Jaudt (mid 1800s) and Ernst Geisser (d. 1929) of Munich; and Ludwig Otto (d. 1887) of Jena, who first worked in Erfurt and Cologne. The German Nikolaus Kittel (d. 1870), known for his excellent bows as "the Russian Tourte," rose to the position of court luthier, which he indicated on his labels: "Nicolaus Kittel / faber instrumentorum caesarianus / Petropoli Anno. . . ." Max Möckel, having worked in Warsaw and Moscow, benefited from a stay in St. Petersburg, where together with the chemist Golonin he developed a varnish closely resembling the varnish of the old Italians; he then moved on to Berlin. Radivanowsky, a staff officer of Czar Alexander III, also undertook thorough researches into the Italian manner of varnish making.

In 1876 Julius Heinrich Zimmer, a clever German businessman, founded a publishing house in St. Petersburg, to which his son added a luthier's shop, establishing branches in Moscow, Riga, London, Berlin, and Leipzig. By hiring able assistants and perfecting mass production processes, he could sell relatively good instruments at affordable prices. Prior to his retirement he moved the firm's headquarters back to Markneukirchen. Otto Felix Wunderlich (d. 1925), also of Markneukirchen, went to Moscow by way of Cologne, Amsterdam, and Karlsruhe; his good reputation was in part due to his excellent bows.

For a long time Russian violin making was restricted to rustic instruments for country dancing. The first known Russian luthiers in the eighteenth century were Saves Kiapone and Ivan Andreyevich Batov. Batov, a serf, made instruments as a pastime at first; he was then trained at the expense of his master, for whose orchestra he made instruments. When serfdom was abolished, Batov settled in St. Petersburg, where he died in 1841. Like other Russian violin makers he also made good guitars, balalaikas, and other Russian national instruments.

Anatol Ivanovich Leman (d. 1913), a man of many talents, made more than two hundred outstanding violins. To his patriotic friends he presented his achievements as the beginning of a specifically Russian school of violin making. They referred to him as "the Messiah of the violin," a title he gladly accepted and used on his labels: "Anatole le Léman / Messie du Violon / St. Petersburg." His more than twenty-five essays in Russian, French, and German indicate that he did not suffer from excessive modesty. Henley quotes one sentence: "If Stradivari were living today, I would be his teacher." One

Russian luthier, L. Dobrianski (b. 1865) of Odessa, did completely master Stradivari's style—so much so that many of his instruments appear in collections as true Strads.

Many French luthiers worked in nineteenth-century Moscow. Ernest André Salzard (d. 1897) came from a Mirecourt family of luthiers. After learning his métier in France he went to St. Petersburg and then to Moscow, where he became court luthier and had charge of instruments at the opera and conservatory. He achieved distinction both as a builder and repairer. Among his longtime co-workers were Edouard Arnould (d. 1895), a fine repairer who later worked independently in Moscow, and Auguste Didelot, who worked in Moscow until 1900, and then in St. Petersburg.

After the Revolution, Moscow became the center of violin making. Timofej Philippovich Podgorny (b. 1873) was a carpenter before becoming a successful luthier; late in life he held leading positions in the state-supervised training program for instrument makers. Nicolai Mikhailovich Vrolov (d. 1896), a cellist, attended the state school in Moscow and became a highly regarded repairer. The current importance of repairing (rather than making) violins is demonstrated by the figures given by Vannes for Alexander Silvain Wichnygorsky (d. 1932 in Moscow). He made 236 violins, violas, cellos, basses, and viole d'amore, but he repaired and maintained no less than ten thousand instruments. Georg Alexevich Morosov (d. 1970) was another such luthier; his work as a restorer and curator were central to his activities. A violin maker for the conservatory intermittently, he was later put in charge of the state collection of ancient instruments in Moscow. Vladimir Oberberg, a luthier of the earlier twentieth century, also investigated Italian violin making and made outstanding copies after Stradivari and Guarneri.

THE BALKANS

Violin making was not a major activity in the Balkans; for the most part, instrument makers here produced the plucked instruments used in national and folk music, such as the tamburitza. One of the better luthiers in Yugoslavia was Adolf Beuthner (d. 1917) of Markneukirchen; he settled in Üsküb. Karlo Parik (d. 1887), a bank employee and amateur violin maker, eventually became a professional. He made fine Strad copies and taught at the luthiers' school in Belgrade. E. Kosovel (b. 1902) and Franjo Schneider (b. 1903) worked in Belgrade and Zagreb respectively; they also were known for their Strad copies. For a long time István Vasváry (d. 1894) of Arad was Romania's leading luthier.

TURKEY

According to Vannes there were twenty-one makers of bowed and plucked instruments in Constantinople (Istanbul), but most of them devoted their considerable skills almost exclusively to the making of folk or national instruments. Two true violin makers were Georges Papagorgliu (b. 1896) and

Vahakin Nikogresyan (b. 1911), who studied with Vatelot in Paris before setting up shop at home in 1936.

JAPAN

Japan, like other countries with a strong indigenous musical heritage, did not become exposed to European music (and therefore violin making) until relatively late. In his youth, Masakichi Suzuki (d. 1944) made Japanese string instruments. He was immediately interested when he saw his first violin at age twenty-five and, in 1884, built the first violin ever to have been made in Japan. Suzuki's firm, begun with two branches in Nagoya, soon employed more than a thousand workers and mass produced violins of relatively good quality, made of Japanese woods. By making inexpensive instruments available he had a strong influence on the spread of violin playing in Japan. The company was continued by his son Shiro Suzuki, brother of the famous pedagogue. The Kyoyeki Shosha Company in Tokyo, a similar enterprise, is also given to mass production.

AUSTRALIA

During the second half of the nineteenth century, music in Australia developed along European lines, chiefly in the large cities of Sydney, Melbourne, and Adelaide. Early violin makers were immigrants, such as Henry James Shrosbree (d. 1908) of London, who also worked at times as a taxidermist. His instruments were awarded prizes at the Adelaide exhibition of 1900. The Scottish luthier William Henry Dow (d. 1928 in Melbourne) made a name for himself with good Strad and Guarneri copies. Arthur Edward Smith (b. 1880 in England) was self-taught. He began working in Melbourne in 1909, later moved to Sydney, and for a long time was much in demand as a teacher. Thomas Baldwin Jaffrey (d. 1933 in Sydney), a very fine luthier, tried to use native woods—unsuccessfully, due to their high resin content. The German William Paszek (d. 1888) enjoyed a fine reputation in Sydney.

The next generation of luthiers included some native Australians, among them Howard F. Sleath (b. 1899 in Brisbane), the son of a cellist-luthier. He was known for his Guarneri copies and later was responsible for the upkeep of instruments in leading Australian orchestras. Kitty Deneraz Smith studied violin at the Sydney conservatory and violin making with her father, A. E. Smith. In 1949 her excellent instruments earned her a prize at an exhibition in The Hague.

NEW ZEALAND

Luthiers here registered some notable accomplishments, but as in almost all non–European countries, the use of native wood proved unsuccessful, so that one gradually returned to imported wood. New Zealand's climate encourages rapid tree growth, resulting in wood with wide annual rings and excessive resin content. Stephan Savage (b. 1874), a civil servant before turning to professional violin making, built good instruments following Italian models. The Auckland luthier George Nicoll (b. 1880) spent years trying to detect a mathematical basis for the construction of classic violins, but though he produced fine instruments he failed to find the secret. Laurence Day (b. 1896) also engaged in much research and experimentation. He developed a fine varnish, and his more than two hundred violins have excellent tonal characteristics.

SOUTH AFRICA

The first important South African luthier was the Englishman Henry Humphrey Saby (d. 1930), who settled in Cape Town in 1890 and became very successful. He also assembled a collection of valuable old violins. Adam Mackie (b. 1871), also from England, began his career as a carpenter. Having received training as a violin maker, he traveled extensively before settling in Johannesburg, where he made fine copies of Italian instruments. His small, very good book, *The Secret of Italian Tone*, is based on his long experience as a luthier. Amon Bilmark (b. 1894 in Copenhagen) was schooled in Rome. In 1929 he established himself in Durban; he too succeeded with good Strad copies.

A survey of violin making since 1800 must be incomplete, given the abundance of masters who worked not only in major music centers but also in small towns. The purpose of our survey was not to come up with the largest possible number of names, but to establish the chief lines of development as represented by leading luthiers, and also to name those who went their own particular ways. The survey is least comprehensive for the late twentieth century. Violin making is different from many crafts but similar to much art: value judgments of a given time seldom coincide with those of later generations. Carl Flesch (1934) aptly described the problem as it relates to violin making:

> It seems hardly possible for me to express an opinion as to the art of violin making of our time and tonal results gained through same. Assuredly there must be new violins the tonal properties of which can also satisfy discriminating violinists; the lasting tonal value of an instrument, however, depends less upon momentary impression than upon its tonal properties which it may develop in the course of years. The "baked" Vuillaume violins, for example, were noble sounding instruments directly after their completion; only after a number of years it became apparent that the artificial drying of the wood-fibers had simultaneously caused a gradual drying up of the tonal spirit as well. In judging new instruments, the consideration of what the future may have in store for them is of greater importance than present impressions; therefore the uncertainty of trying to express an opinion about modern instruments.

To make a selection, based on quality, from the thousands of luthiers currently working is a virtual impossibility, all the more so because available information on contemporary violin making varies greatly. Shops that publish the most beautiful and impressive brochures do not always produce the finest violins, nor does an instrument that looks beautiful in the prospectus necessarily sound good. Violin making is a profession in which we still find, as in times past, many humble, quiet, hard workers who derive their inner fulfillment from their work, who do not enter competitions, and who shun publicity. Thus in spite of excellent accomplishments they are hardly known except to their immediate customers.

Some countries have not been mentioned specifically, but that does not mean that no violins were made there. Rather, they made no significant contributions to the craft's general development. One can now meet luthiers in all countries in which Western music is played. When speaking of violin making one would not normally think of Iran, Egypt, or Algeria. Yet the luthier Sourène Arakélian (b. 1890 in Tiflis) trained in Prague, Berlin, and Moscow before pursuing his craft in Tehran; he experimented with varnishes based on resins from Asia Minor and wrote an interesting small book on violin making. Marco Dobretsovich (b. 1891 in Alexandria) received his master's diploma in Italy and made good violins based on Italian models. Jean Pico (b. 1880) trained in Paris and made and sold violins in Algiers. René Marichal (b. 1903) trained in Mirecourt and settled in Algiers in 1926, after having gained experience in Paris.

Virtuosos on the international circuit at times need help from a capable repairer, even in out-of-the-way places. They frequently have been impressed by the existence of fine luthiers all over the world. New, good-quality instruments can be purchased and reliably repaired almost anywhere.

The violin has been widely accepted in the folk and art music of many non-Western countries. A well-known leader of a string quartet, on a concert tour in Marrakesh, Morocco, thought he heard some interesting sounds of folk music in the distance. When he investigated he came upon a group of Berber musicians who were playing Mirecourt violins, holding them like cellos. The strings turned out to have been made by the Thomastik firm of Vienna!

VIOLIN MAKING AS A HOBBY

There is no reason why the conscientious worker who is possessed of ordinary acquaintance with edge tools should not, with a little practice, become a skilled fiddle maker.   ROBERT ALTON,
VIOLIN AND CELLO BUILDING AND REPAIRING, 1946

In his book *British Violin Makers* (1904), W. Meredith Morris described the state of violin making in England:

There are fifty to sixty professional luthiers now living and working, and at least ten times that number of amateur and occasional makers. This number is exclusive of dealers in factory fiddles, foreign makers living in this country, and firms who employ mere repairers.

These figures for England, which even boasts a British Amateur Violin Makers' Association, are probably more or less true for other countries as well.

Musical instruments, and especially those played with a bow, seem to have a magical attraction for amateurs, inspiring them to build their own in hopes of discovering the secrets that account for the violin's beautiful sound. Names such as Amati, Stainer, Guarneri, and especially Stradivari seem to have a truly demonic effect on thousands of violin lovers who, hoping to accomplish what those masters did, devote all their free time, and often considerable money, to reaching this goal, undaunted by any failures. Ole H. Bryant (d. 1943), a fine American luthier, gave summer courses in violin making that were open to amateurs. In the United States, the Bretch School of Violin Making also offered courses, including correspondence courses, for amateurs.

No clear distinction can be made between professional and amateur violin makers. Quite a few recognized luthiers at first had other professions and made violins strictly as a hobby. Later they may have entered the field on a part-time basis before they turned to violin making as their true calling, often rather late in life.

One frequent station along this road was work as a carpenter. Furniture makers and restorers of antique furniture develop specialized knowledge that, one might say, predestines them for violin making. Once they turn to that occupation, an amateur stage often follows, initially. Joseph Aubry serves as an example. He was born in Mirecourt, where his father was a guitar maker. Until the age of eighteen he trained as an artisan carpenter and woodcarver; only then did he set out to learn violin making, a field in which he achieved great expertise. Knute Reindahl, for many years president of the American Guild of Violin Makers, was a woodcarver who made violins as a hobby before he opened shops in Chicago and Madison. Antonio Pedrinelli (d. 1854), an outstanding Italian luthier, made coffins before he discovered his true vocation. The Canadian Rosario Bayeur began as a construction worker and then for many years turned to carpentry, all along making violins as a hobby. He then underwent professional training as a luthier, and at thirty-two years of age opened his atelier in Montreal. Twelve years later, despite his success and record for making excellent instruments, his desire to learn more sent him to the Paris shop of Emile Germain. Similarly the Italian Carlo Pizzamiglio (b. 1914) was a carpenter before taking up violin making. As a prisoner of war he made forty violins using makeshift tools. Some of his labels read "C.P. / Sesto ed Uniti / Cremona Italia—Fece in Egitto / L'anno 1942. Camp 309 P.O.W." The Finnish luthier Väinö Kanu (b. 1893) also had a multifaceted career. He began as a baker's apprentice, but in turn became a cast-metal worker, farrier, orchestra musician, and painter, before taking up violin making.

Many aspiring luthiers encountered great hardships before entering the profession. As the parents of Willy Berndt (d. 1876) were too poor to buy him a violin, the boy made one himself, and since there was no luthier in Stettin (Szczecin) to whom he might have been apprenticed, Berndt became a furniture maker; only later did he become a Pfretzschner pupil. Johannes Theodorus Cuypers, a well-known Dutch maker, worked in Paris as a carpenter. He supposedly became Guersan's apprentice only because he was unable to find work in his own trade.

Yet there were also those whose careers developed in the opposite direction. Benvenuto Botturi, a professional luthier, made more than one hundred violins and two hundred bows before being named the administrative director of a lumber company.

Henley tells a fascinating tale about Job Anderu (b. 1826). Anderu spent most of his eighty-six years as a village carpenter, but also made more than five hundred violins. He was so fond of them that parting with them was out of the question, so that in the end every nook and cranny of his home overflowed with violins. After Anderu's death, Hill bought them all—a purchase the firm surely did not regret. The violins, based on Amati models, are not quite up to the requirements of virtuosos, but they have pleased orchestra and chamber music players.

Not all newcomers to violin making were from the fields of carpentry and related crafts. Other callings are related to violin making because they require special manual skills or a well-developed sense of formal perfection. Thomas Baldwin of Birmingham was a jeweler; the Swiss Emil Baltensperger, a painter, made more than three hundred violins based on very individual concepts. Hans Bosch, quite a good luthier, had been an architect. Other amateur luthiers made their living as watchmakers, mechanics, or turners. For some, varnish was the attraction that led them to violin making, which may explain why many amateur violin makers can be found among chemists, pharmacists, and related professions. One even used his labels to show this: "The Chemist's Violin / Made by A. Barlow / Braunton. N. Devon / 19—." Henley said that the quality of Barlow's work reflected the work of an enthusiastic amateur.

J. Edwin Bonn (d. 1927 in Brading, Isle of Wight) had a fascinating career. He studied medicine but did not complete the course and worked instead in a chemistry laboratory. A passionate violinist, he also conducted an amateur orchestra. Occasionally he would buy, sell, and repair instruments, which led him gradually to violin making, though he never had any formal training. He built his violins following good models and made his own varnish. Hoping to obtain equally good sound from all four strings he devised a bridge with four feet, and in 1885 described his experiments in a small book entitled *Technical Notes on the Choice, Keeping, and Preparation of Violin Strings: With an Account of the Chemical Methods Employed in Their Production and an Analysis of Their Ultimate Composition*. Bonn also made a widely used oil-based cleaning preparation. Similar versatility was demonstrated by David Jones (d. 1840), who succeeded in all his endeavors: he made clocks, mechanical toys, dentures—and violins.

Bonn's great variety of pursuits tells us something about differences between amateur and professional violin makers: amateurs are more inclined to experiment, something already touched on in our chapter on innovations in violin making. A professionally trained luthier, responsible for a shop, tends to be far more influenced by tradition when faced with a work-related problem. He or she is not likely to question certain proven work processes or building methods. Dilettantes, on the other hand, not constrained by technical knowledge, are apt to be fascinated by any possibility (and sometimes impossibility!). A new idea appeals to their inborn urge to experiment, and so they try it out. Above all, the hobby instrument maker has time—his leisure time is not money. The professional, however, used to thinking in terms of hourly wages, is less likely to waste his working hours on experiments. Often he is very busy and needs to devote all his energy to the financial success of his work.

Prisoners of war and internees at times made instruments under primitive conditions, to avoid boredom and to please their fellow inmates. For some, such a pastime later turned into a profession, as it did for Luigi Agostinelli. During World War II he was interned in Kenya, made some instruments for the camp, and after the war built some very good violins. Francesco Ponzo did the same during his time in a camp. Later he became a pupil of Professor Pasqualini in Rome and eventually became a professional luthier in Buenos Aires.

Some researchers took up violin making for different reasons, for instance, the physicist Karl Fuhr. When he became involved in research, he wanted to carry out his experiments himself, which forced him to acquire some knowledge about violin making. To remain free from bias, he purposely avoided receiving any instruction. The engineer Léon Mordret also took up violin making in order to prove his theories.

Quite a few amateur violin makers came from the ranks of professional musicians, and some professional luthiers began their careers as orchestra players. The stagione system in Italian opera encouraged the double profession of "liutaio-violinista." Such a combination is natural because a luthier ideally should have some serious experience with violin playing, at least for a time. In their youth, some luthiers graduated from a conservatory having majored in violin playing; they then continue to do some playing while working as professional instrument makers. A professional violinist who lives in a place where there is no luthier is at an advantage if his hobby is violin making, or if he at least knows how to make minor repairs and adjustments, such as fitting a bridge or positioning a soundpost. A violin teacher who can do these things for pupils will be greatly valued.

In 1866 Victor Grivel, a first violinist in the Grenoble orchestra, published his study *Vernis des anciens luthiers d'Italie, retrouvé par Victor Grivel*, adding his name to the list of those claiming to have rediscovered the secret of the old Italian varnish. Frederick Drennan Barry (d. 1926) was a professional violinist, cellist, and harpist before he trained to be a luthier. He became known for a varnish he prepared himself. Carl Grimm (d. 1855), a Berlin trumpet virtuoso, began making violins out of pure curiosity. By dint of serious study and much experimentation he became an accredited master luthier, making up to thirty instruments a year in his own shop. At his death he was instrument maker to the court.

Whether an amateur decided to turn professional may have depended on how successful his first violins turned out to be. Noël Bénard (early 1800s) was modest enough to refer to himself on labels as "luthier dilettante." A certain Herr Schmidt, a member of the royal orchestra in Kassel, also was a fine luthier. The *Allgemeine Musikalische Zeitung* of 1809 wrote about him thus: "It is unfortunate that instead of devoting himself entirely to the luthier's craft he must spend most of his time sitting at his music stand, for which he is paid a pittance." Accidents and other injuries at times caused an instrumentalist to turn to violin making. Similar physical limitations may also be responsible for others who left other occupations to become amateur luthiers. The large instrument collections of the Paris and Brussels conservatories contain violins made by a butcher's apprentice who had been inspired by Chanot's ideas. The label in one of his violins tells us that this was "the second violin made by Belleville, butcher, anno 1812." Among the many other amateur or semi-professional violin makers I found bakers, dentists, engineers, schoolteachers, photographers, tailors, hairdressers, lawyers, foresters, insurance agents, postmasters, a customs official, a policeman, a secular priest, a prison guard, a Franciscan pater, a member of an opera chorus, a metallurgist, a maker of reeds for bagpipes, and a professional football player. Some turned to professionals for instruction, but others proudly called themselves self-taught and avoided all contact with professionals. One such hobbyist even eschewed the use of traditional violin makers' tools, preferring to do all his work with a primitive carving knife. No doubt there were and are other rugged individualists, some more peculiar than others. One Irishman used this label: "Made by John Delany / in order to perpetuate his memory in future ages. / Dublin, 1808. / Liberty to all the world, black and white." A Mr. Slaughter, an American globetrotter, made only one violin, using a pocketknife and chisel. In all he used 150 pieces of wood, collected during his far-flung travels. The violin's back was made of wood that was more than two hundred years old, taken from an abandoned building at Howard Payne College; the back contained two inlaid pieces of wood from the Holy Land, one from the Garden of Gethsemane!

Naturally, most of these more or less talented hobbyists were anxious for recognition. The American Henry W. Beeman, a capable amateur luthier, was happy to give away his instruments to friends. Others made presents to music students and young beginners. The Scottish tax collector Peter Davidson hit upon an unusual way to dispose of violins he made. He also was an amateur violinist and composer of dances, and in 1871 published a book, *The Violin: A Concise Exposition of the General Principles of Construction, Theo-*

retically and Practically Treated; Including the Important Researches of Savart, an Epitome of the Lives of the Most Eminent Artists and an Alphabetical List of Violin-Makers. It went through no less than four printings in ten years. Whoever subscribed to the collections of dances composed by him would receive one of his violins, gratis.

At times, when a hobbyist succeeded especially well, he or she turned to a well-known virtuoso for an endorsement. Kindhearted performers such as Kreisler may have agreed to furnish such support, but it is doubtful that they went so far as to play on such an instrument in public.

Some amateur violin makers came to their hobby quite late in life. James Bernard, a hairdresser by profession, was fifty-seven years old when he made his first violin; E. Crooke began at seventy-two, J. B. Copping at seventy-five, and F. Grant Ball, watchmaker and jeweler, at eighty. During the six following years he made twelve instruments! Not to be confused with dilettantes are those makers who, for whatever reasons, had a second profession. We know of many luthiers from southern Germany, Austria, and Italy who were farmers as well, often to keep food on the table. They worked their fields in the summer and made violins during the winter months. Alexander Smillie, an amateur turned professional, was a dealer in antiques specializing in oriental rugs, which gave him some financial security.

Returning to Morris's observation that in England there were ten times as many amateur makers as professionals, one wonders about the ratio of success. Here, the "pros" surely win out by better than a 10:1 ratio, for success depends on many factors, not talent alone. Manual dexterity, acquired through years of practice, is one requirement, and few amateurs can devote entire years to their hobby. Still, it is only fair to point out that some amateurs achieved distinction. Henley judged that violins made by the English amateur John Jeffrey (d. 1918) were as good if not better than many Italian ones that did not come from Cremona. Franklin De Haven, a member of the National Academy of Design in New York, competed with one of his violins against a Strad in 1924. Both instruments were played behind a curtain. The Strad received 38 points; De Haven's violin was accorded 58 points!

Nor did professional standing guarantee good workmanship. Concerning the work of B. L. Scholte, active in Amsterdam ca. 1800, Max Möller (1955) could only say, "When examining his work, one cannot help wondering whether he has, perhaps, had training as a carpenter instead of as a violin maker."

THE HISTORY AND MAKING OF VIOLIN BOWS

The early history of the violin bow needs to be rewritten.
DAVID D. BOYDEN, *THE HISTORY OF VIOLIN PLAYING*, 1965

A true violin did not exist before the early sixteenth century. Indeed, even during the first decades of the violin's development, no violin bow as we know it existed; only gradually did the tonal properties of the new instrument suggest the need for a bow specifically suited to it. Those who at first played the violin also continued to play the established instruments: fiddle, viola da bracchio, lira da bracchio, and gamba, depending on what their employers demanded. They may have preferred for a long time to use bows with which they were familiar, even after taking up the new violin. Existing sources, at any rate, reveal nothing about a bow intended specifically for the violin.

The oldest preserved violin bows date from the early seventeenth century; until then, pictorial representations and some references in theoretical works are our only meager sources of information. As to works of art, a caveat is in order, concerning the bow and the instrument. Not all painters were knowledgeable about playing instruments, nor were they necessarily concerned about realistic representation. A painting intended for a church altarpiece, for instance, may include many figures, among them a little angel fiddling away in a corner. Most likely the artist was not concerned with precisely representing bow and violin in relation to other persons included. Nevertheless, enough paintings of this kind have come down to us that we can arrive at some tentative conclusions.

Most noticeable are the greatly differing bow sizes, and this probably cannot be attributed to the painters' carelessness. No standard length had been set; it was largely up to the player's preference and to the musical task at hand. In a Paris woodcut of 1516, for instance, we see Galenus play a violinlike instrument with an unusually long and thin bow. Such bows are frequently encountered in paintings showing fiddle playing. Bows of medium length are seen in paintings by Gaudenzio Ferrari. A much shorter bow with a sturdy stick also is found; in earlier times it may have been used with the rebec, especially for dancing. Illustrations 8 and 11 in Boyden's book show details of paintings by Gentileschi (b. ca. 1565, d. ca. 1638) and Caravaggio (1573–1610). They reveal rather heavy types of bows reminiscent of today's string bass bows, which hardly could have been suitable for playing elegant, embellished high lines in polyphonic music.

Klaus Marx (*Die Entwicklung*, 1963) believes that no organological difference between bows for the violin and gamba existed during the sixteenth and seventeenth centuries. This may be true in regard to their basic structure but not to the sounds they could produce. The two bows shown in Boyden's illustrations certainly could not create the delicate, floating tone of a gamba, nor would a gamba bow satisfy a dance fiddler. The two bows had to differ in weight, details of construction, and amount of bow hair.

As to the bow's curvature, virtually all writers claim that up to Tourte it had a convex, outward curve, but this too must be qualified. Here again illustrations tell us that in the course of the sixteenth century bows became straight—but only gradually. Boyden reproduces another painting, this one from the end of the fifteenth century, in which we see a bow with a straight stick. It may have been exceptional, or it may have been in existence for some time.

Making a serviceable bow involved the following special operations:

1) Fastening the hair at the tip
2) Fastening the hair at the lower end
3) Providing tension for the hair, so that one could play on a single string—a change from polyphonic to melodic playing
4) Providing enough clearance between bow hair and stick, especially after the adoption of the straight stick

In early bows, the hair was attached to the tip with a loop which, when tightened, contracted into a kind of knot. Werner Bachmann includes several illustrations of twelfth- to fourteenth-century instruments showing this stage (ills. 65, 69, 73, and 87). This primitive attachment did have the advantage that the hair could be tightened if necessary. A bow now in the Kunsthistorisches Museum in Vienna, probably from the sixteenth century, shows an interesting device representing an early state of development, even if (being a homemade, rather folklike piece of work) it actually was made later (see photograph). In the loop, the bow hair is divided by a wire pin, then gathered again and fastened to the stick's tip. This may represent an early attempt at varying the tension quickly by turning or compressing the pin. A mortise in the bow's tip soon served as the place for fastening the hair, making it possible to spread the band of hair evenly. Up to then it had been gathered together at the tip, ropelike.

Illustrations showing musicians in action rarely let us see the way in which the hair was attached at the stick's lower end since the player's hand

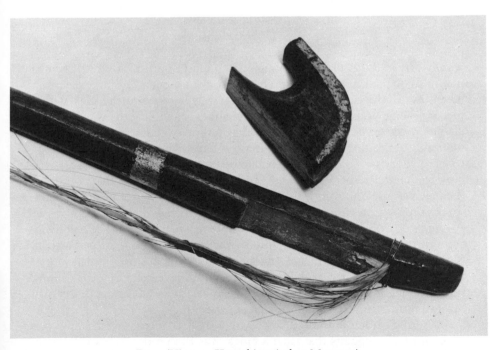

Bow (Vienna, Kunsthistorisches Museum)

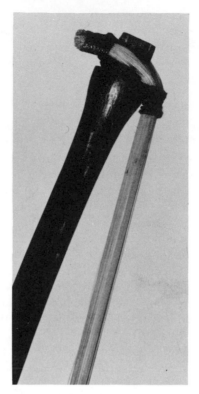

Bow with the earlier ropelike hair

usually covered this place. Virdung's 1511 illustration of bows for tromba marina and small fiddle ("Trumscheit und clein Geigen") is an exception. The bow on the right shows that the hair was fastened to the stick with a piece of string wound around both, in a manner resembling the way in which clarinet reeds are now fastened. A similar method of attaching the hair is recognizable at the tip, but it had two serious flaws: 1) every time one wanted to increase the tension, the string had to be unfastened, and 2) the hair was so close to the stick, especially near the place of attachment, that that portion of the hair was useless, even if the stick was quite curved. Villoteau noticed a similar type of fastening in a seventeenth-century drawing of an Arabic bow. A simple device, however, made it possible to keep the band of hair away from the stick's lower end, and also to vary the tension. This was a small block of wood, varying in size and adjustable in its position. Small forked branches were similarly used. Such devices must have been in use for a long time; a small board of this kind can be seen clearly in a fourteenth-century Spanish illustration (Bachmann 1969, ill. 75).

Virdung's other illustrated bow, with a small triangular wedge between stick and hair, suggests that such a block was the predecessor of the frog, with the wedge representing an intermediate stage. It was not firmly attached

but wedged in. If a player had several sizes available, the tension, even in early sixteenth-century bows, could be changed quickly. It has often been claimed that during the first century of its existence the violin bow could not be tightened, but this is wrong, at least for this type of bow. One should therefore be careful about drawing conclusions about the lack of bow tension (and therefore tone volume) that could be achieved at this time.

Early makers were also concerned with the problem of obtaining adequate distance between stick and hair at the bow's tip. A fifteenth-century solution is shown in the drawing reproduced in Boyden (1965, p. 47). Illustrations from the following centuries occasionally show, if not very clearly, an early form of the tip, somewhat beaklike and sometimes referred to as "duck bill." Taking the ribbon of hair as the horizontal plane, this kind of tip lay considerably lower than the frog, meaning that it kept the hair completely away from the stick. This was the customary shape until the mid-eighteenth century. The stick was quite straight, with a slight curvature at the tip caused by the pull of the hair. The tips of some bows are somewhat thicker and point downward, probably to facilitate attaching the hair. Fétis (ills. 1–6) shows such forms.

Still during the sixteenth century it became customary to carve out a mortise at the stick's lower end, to insert the band of hair, and to have it wind around the wedge in a channel provided for that purpose. By then the wedge had assumed an elegant shape, and the place to accommodate the thumb had been fully developed. It was left up to the player whether to place the thumb there or on the hair, or to hold the bow higher up on the stick, as seen in many illustrations. The wedge was not firmly attached to the stick but was positioned in a small indentation in the stick. Pressure from the hair kept it in place. A similarly wedged-in and therefore exchangeable frog belongs to a bow in the Ashmolean Museum; it is dated ca. 1700. According to Mersenne (1636–1637), bows were provided with eighty to a hundred hairs.

All the methods of tightening bow hair described so far were slow and imprecise. As violin playing technique developed, these deficiencies were removed in two ways, both of which took place during the seventeenth century. Around 1650, someone invented a way to refine an earlier, primitive way of attaching the hair. For this, a metal loop was hooked over one of several cogs fastened to the top of the bow stick (see photograph on p. 234). The frog moved in a groove or rail in the stick's underside. Once a mortise in which to hang the band of hair had been carved out of the frog, the bow tension could be changed quickly. Since the cogs or ratchets were close together, different degrees of bow tension were possible. The French word "crémaillère" was generally adopted for this kind of bow.

Crémaillère bow (Vienna, Kunsthistorisches Museum)

By the end of the seventeenth century the adjusting screw had been invented, threaded through a screw-eye in the frog, and except for minor improvements, the frog mechanism has remained the same since. A bow in the Hill collection dating from 1694 is the earliest known bow with this hair-tightening mechanism. Pictorial sources are of no help with detailing this, for long before this time it had become customary to decorate the stick's end with a buttonlike ornament. During the seventeenth century a longer bow often was used for chamber music and a shorter one for dance music, to the extent that ca. 1700 the longer bow was called "sonata bow."

We are not sure about the various stages of the next innovation, which affected the bow stick's curvature. In the appendix of his book about Stradivari (1856), Fétis outlined these developments in a series of eight illustrations, bows from Mersenne in 1620 to Viotti in 1790. These drawings have often been reproduced, usually without indicating the source, up to and including Boyden and the German music encyclopedia *MGG*. They were actually taken from the 1798 violin method by Michel Woldemar, who had a collection of bows that allegedly had been owned by great violinists. Fétis's series deserves mention as the first attempt to outline the bow's development, but the names, dates, and early bow shapes he gives are inaccurate, and those after Tartini definitely wrong or misleading. We do not know that Corelli had any influence on bow making; Woldemar's mention of his name merely indicates him as the possible owner of the bow in question. Yet the entire literature on bow making, following Fétis, refers to Corelli as one of the key figures in improving the bow. The bow stick attributed to him has the same shape as the one reproduced by Boyden (1965, p. 47).

An interesting detail about Tartini is revealed by Gian-Rinaldo Carli in a 1744 letter that was published in 1786. Carli had studied at the University of Padua from 1739 to 1743, after which he taught there for some time. He therefore appears to have been in contact with Tartini for several years. In this letter, Carli praises Tartini for his experiments with acoustics, which led Tartini "to use thicker strings and a longer bow, thereby producing more regular vibrations and a sweeter, more colorful tone." Fétis (1856) further commented that Tartini greatly improved the bow ca. 1730, using lighter wood for a straight, shorter stick, which also provided a better grip, so the bow would not turn between the fingers. Fétis was referring to Woldemar's Tartini bow. It is possible that three stages of it are visible in 1) a portrait of the young Tartini, ca. 1715 (Milan catalog, plate 26), 2) a later portrait (Capri 1945, p. 16), and 3) a bow that had belonged to Tartini (Milan catalog, plate 27). The bow in 1) shows a decidedly convex curvature; 2) shows the usual bow, with a slightly convex curve, due to the lower position of the tip. The Milan bow, with its slightly concave shape and steeply inclined tip, already represents the modern type. As described in the catalog, this bow, at the point of contact, shows considerable wear "from the master's sinewy fingers," clearly shown in the photo. After an accident in 1740, Tartini rarely played the violin, so the bow may have been made ca. 1725–1730. If this is the case, based on Tartini's suggestions, a bow maker in Padua or Venice may have made the first modern bow of the kind required for playing Tartini's *L'arte dell'arco*. According to Vidal, Tartini's experiments with bows go back to 1725; more generally 1730 has been mentioned. An indentation at the frog (for a better grip) and the octagonal shape of the stick resulted in weight reduction while maintaining the same tension.

The most important innovation visible in Tartini's Milan bow, credited to him, is the stick's concave shape. It gives to it the elasticity, the spring, that responds to pressure from fingers and wrist, making various kinds of bouncing and other bowings possible. As a result, violin playing (and with it, composing) has been enriched by a wealth of articulation possibilities that characterize Mozart's violin concertos, Haydn's string quartets, and the symphonies of both masters. The innovation, however, was necessitated by changes in musical style. It may have emerged independently in France and perhaps also in England from the Dodd family.

The shape of the bow head or tip is closely related to the stick's concave bent. Earlier, the duck bill bow head resulted in a soft, gentle end; its structure absorbed bow pressure, which is quite different from what the concave stick requires. In order to respond, with a bounce, to every pressure exerted on the bow, it needed a hard, angular end. Realizing this, many makers of early concave bows terminated the bow head abruptly, and later artisans often chose a similar shape, though it lacks grace.

Perhaps deferring to tradition, or responding to a customer's wish, some bow makers stayed with the duck bill tip. More commonly a compromise was adopted, preserving the general appearance of the steep, angular head for the tip's inside while imparting a more or less elegant incline to the outside.

Tip of bow made by Tourte le père

The first master exclusively devoted to bow making was Tourte le père (so called to distinguish him from his son, also a bow maker). Before him, bow making was a sideline of luthiers; even Stradivari made some. Most likely workers in some of the larger violin shops, even before Tourte, specialized in bow making. Tourte worked in Paris from 1750 to 1785; his birth and death dates are unknown. His son, François Xavier Tourte (1750–1835) became the most famous bow maker of all time. Some of his fame was transferred back, so to say, to his father, who seems to have been credited retroactively with whatever could not be dated or properly ascribed to others, such as the invention of the screw, the concave stick, and the steep angle at the tip. Though the screw-and-nut mechanism existed before Tourte, it is possible that the stick's modern shape goes back to him, and that Tartini learned about it from French pupils. But it is impossible to assign priorities as there are no reliably dated bows. Dating usually is attempted on the basis of the very characteristics that still need to be dated. Be that as it may, Tourte le père was an outstanding bow maker who also excelled in metal work and introduced minor improvements in the frog's mechanism.

François Xavier had been intended for the watchmaker's profession, which he pursued for eight years before turning to bow making. He soon experimented with the stick. According to Vidal he created ca. 1780–1790 the type that then became the ideal to which bow makers have aspired ever since, just as luthiers aspired to the Stradivari ideal. Viotti is said to have been Tourte's advisor; he had come to Paris in 1781 and reaped sensational successes at the Concert Spirituel during the 1782/83 season, after which he decided to live in Paris. Most likely Viotti counseled Tourte at length, in addition to putting his experiments to the test of performance. Only a violinist whose style of musical interpretation puts great demands on the bow would have been able to identify the needed structural changes.

François Tourte was an artisan without equal; he had the uncanny ability to identify all kinds of subtle details of which only an artist would be aware. Riechers described the Tourte bow as follows:

The length of the stick, from its [lower] end to the head's end is 73–74 cm. The hair length, from the lower part of the tip to the ferrule at the frog, is 63–64 cm. The height of the head, from the stick down to the tip liner and plate, is 23 mm, the height of the frog, from the stick to the outer ferrule where the hair begins, is 26 mm. The ribbon of hair at the frog is 11 mm wide, at the tip, 10 mm. Tourte's bows had 80–100 hairs; today 150–160 are used. . . . Tourte never varnished or polished his bows but only cleaned and smoothed them with pumice and linseed oil. If varnish or polish are found on his bows, they were added by others.

A painstaking bow maker, Tourte chose only the best materials, devoting great care to selecting bow hair and spreading it out evenly. Innovations in woodwork have also been ascribed to him, but most likely he only refined existing techniques. If the concave bow is to have great tensile strength it must be cut exactly with the grain. To be bent, the stick must be warm, but it is not enough to warm the outer layer. In that case the inner fibers will tend to resume their original form, and the bow will gradually lose its elasticity. François Tourte may have been the first to fully comprehend these matters and to take them into account in his bow making. But his major achievement was a new distribution of weight that imparted to the bow both firmness and elasticity, along with that seeming weightlessness without which virtuoso playing is impossible.

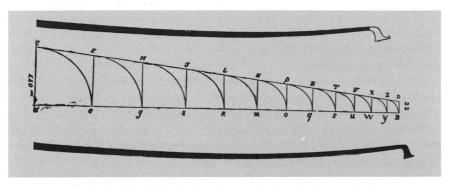

(read "K" for what looks like an "R" in the bottom line)

Vuillaume closely examined many Tourte bows and developed a graphic procedure for establishing the stick's measurements. Fétis (*Antoine Stradivari*, 1856) published this procedure (see above). Line a–B is 70 cm long—the bow's length. Two vertical lines are drawn, a–C and B–D; they are 11 cm and 2.2 cm long respectively. The connecting line C–D is then drawn. The distance a–C is transferred to line a–B; this establishes point E. A vertical line on E will fix F at the intersection with line C–D. Continuing this procedure we obtain the ten measuring points G, I, K, M, O, Q, S, U, W, and Y. After each of these, the stick's diameter decreases by .3 mm. Fétis continued these calculations to define the stick's curvature.

After Tourte, Möckel also found a regular procedure to establish the stick's curvature. He divided his line a–b into eight equal segments and established certain distances at each point:

Tourte worked up to his eighty-fifth year, when failing eyesight forced him to lay down his tools. By his death, the violin bow essentially had been given its present form. Later modifications affected length and weight only, not the proportions. Violinists belonging to the circle of Viotti and Baillot used a relatively heavy bow to produce a large tone. After them, lighter bows were popular, especially those made by Voirin. The generation of Vieuxtemps and Ysaÿe again favored heavier bows, aware of the requirements of Wagner and Strauss orchestral parts and of larger concert halls. These changes, however, did not bring about any essential modification of Tourte's bow. Some inventions involving materials, such as Vuillaume's metal bow, or gadgets that were meant to enable players to rehair their own bows, never caught on, but these did not affect the bow's dimensions or tension.

In time it became the highest ambition of bow makers to emulate Tourte's work, just as all violinists were eager to own a Tourte bow, and thus a flourishing trade in "genuine" Tourte bows sprang up. Markneukirchen in particular became a center for producing "old French bows." Retford relates that large numbers of these were made and circulated. Some of the copies are so good that even experts have a hard time distinguishing the genuine from the imitation. If they succeed, it is because of details that have no bearing on the bow's playing quality.

Edward Dodd was the first maker to imprint his name on his bow sticks, but it is very easy to forge such a brand. It also became customary to use a brand name merely to indicate the model or type used by a bow factory, so a name no longer was a guarantee of quality. Before this happened, good but inexpensive mass-produced bows were exported from Markneukirchen to England, where they were stamped "Dodd" or "Tubbs." They were then returned to Germany, where dealers made a profit far beyond the shipping costs. But some makers were honest, such as Weichold, who stamped his bows "Imitation de Tourte."

So many outstanding bow makers followed Tourte and Dodd that it was unnecessary to spend good money on forgeries. Peccatte, Voirin, Bausch, and Pfretzschner, to name a few, made bows acclaimed by the greatest virtuosos, suitable for playing music requiring the most advanced bowing technique. Bows by these masters differ only in minor details. Thus Retford on the differences between German and French bows:

> A characteristic of the German head is the polished surface of the ivory face—the French being usually matte finished. The finish of the bottom plate of the nut also differs from the French, the present-day German being secured by nonferrous screws.

Discussion of such minutiae goes beyond the scope of this book, which deals with the violin as a musical instrument.

A list of major bow makers in France, England, and Germany follows. It is noteworthy that Italy has produced few outstanding makers; the modern bow emerged at a time when the golden age of Italian violin making was past. Aside from Paris bow makers, Cozio praised bows made by the Mantegazza brothers, who worked during the second half of the eighteenth century.

LIST OF BOW MAKERS

FRANCE

Tourte le père, d. after 1785
Maire, Michel, late 1700s
Eury, Nicolas, d. ca. 1830
Baroux, d. after 1830
Lafleur, Jacques, d. 1832
Tourte, François Xavier, d. 1835
Lupot, François II, d. 1837
Pajeot (Pageot), Simon, d. 1849
Schwarz, Georg Friedrich, d. 1849
Persoit (Persois), R. S., d. 1850
Maline, Guillaume, d. after 1850
Peccatte, François, d. 1855
Adam, Jean-Dominique, d. 1864
Bazin, François, d. 1865
Fonclause (Fonclauze), Joseph le
    Mayeux, d. 1864
Voirin, Joseph, d. after 1867
Adam (Grand-Adam), d. 1869
Henry, Jacques, d. 1870
Husson, Charles-Claude I, d. 1870
Lafleur, Joseph-René, d. 1874
Peccatte, Dominique, d. 1874
Vuillaume, J.-B., d. 1875
Maire, Nicolas, d. 1878
Simon, P., d. 1882
Voirin, François Nicolas, d. 1885
Thomassin, Louis, d. 1904
Vigneron, Joseph-Arthur, d. 1905
Bazin, Charles, d. 1915
Husson, Charles-Claude II, d.
    1915
Lamy, Alfred-Joseph, d. 1919
Peccatte, Charles, d. 1920

Poirson, Justin, d. 1925
Fétique, Victor, d. 1933
Sartory, Eugène, d. 1946
Bazin, Louis, d. 1953

ENGLAND

Dodd, Edward, d. 1810
Tubbs, Thomas, early 1800s
Dodd, John, d. 1839
Panormo, George Louis, d. 1842
Brown, James II, d. 1860
Tubbs, William, d. 1878
Duff, William, d. 1882
Tubbs, Alfred, d. 1911
Allen, Samuel, b. 1858
Tubbs, James, d. 1921
Acton, William John, d. 1931
Retford, William Charles, d. 1970

GERMANY

Strötz, Joseph, d. 1760
Herrmann, Johann Gottfried, d.
    1817
Knopf, Christian Wilhelm, d.
    1837
Herrmann, Heinrich Wilhelm, d.
    1848
Knopf, Karl Wilhelm, d. 1860
Herrmann, Friedrich Alexander, d.
    1867
Nürnberger, Karl Gottlob, d. 1868
Kittel, Nikolaus, d. 1870

Bausch, Ludwig Christian August,
  d. 1871
Knopf, Heinrich I, d. 1875
Knopf, Heinrich II, d. 1885
Pfretzschner, Richard, d. 1893
Nürnberger, Franz Albert I, d.
  1895
Herrmann, Christian Friedrich, d.
  1896
Knopf, Christian Friedrich
  Wilhelm, d. 1897
Süss, Johann Christian, d. 1900
Weichold, Richard, d. 1902
Nürnberger, Adolph, d. 1914
Knopf, Johann Wilhelm, d. after
  1914
Pfretzschner, Hermann Richard,
  d. 1921

Prell, Hermann Wilhelm, d. 1925
Nürnberger, Karl Albert I, d. 1931
Nürnberger, Franz Albert II, d.
  1931
Prager, Gustav, d. 1931
Nürnberger, Philipp Paul, d. 1931
Knorr, Ernst Robert, d. 1932
Herrmann, Karl Ludwig, d. 1945
Herrmann, Friedrich August, d.
  1945
Prager, Max, d. 1948
Rau, August, d. 1951
Prager, August Edwin, d. 1956
Herrmann, Albert Franz, d. 1960
Nürnberger, Suess August, b. 1875
Wunderlich, Friedrich, b. 1878
Knorr, Arthur, b. 1886
Herrmann, Edwin Otto, b. 1893

[For listings of American violin and bow makers, the reader may wish to consult the membership directory of the American Federation of Violin and Bow Makers, Philadelphia. See also *The Violin Makers of the United States* by Thomas James Wenberg (Mt. Hood, Ore., 1986), *German and Austrian Violin-Makers* by Karel Jalovec (London 1967), and similar specialized studies. Particularly useful is *The Strad Directory*, edited by Marianne Reeve (Harrow, Middlesex, England); published annually, its coverage is international, listing violin and bow makers, violin dealers, violin making schools, competitions for violin makers and players, exhibitions, and festivals. *Strings*, a bimonthly magazine published by The String Letter Press (San Anselmo, Calif.) issues an annual resource guide that also lists violin and bow makers internationally. *Ed.*]

SUMMARY AND PROJECTIONS

The current situation of violin makers, viewed in the context of history, occupied us earlier. It may be helpful to summarize and to arrive at some conclusions.

After a relatively brief early history, the violin assumed a leading position in the musical life of Europe. The sudden and steady demand for instruments defies our imagination. Because of it, luthiers from the time of Andrea Amati and Gasparo da Salò to Antonio Stradivari and the Guarneri family honed their skills to the high degree of mastery associated with these names. Contributing to the high level of craftsmanship were the princely patrons. Their largesse made possible, and indeed demanded, that only the best materials be used, including superior varnish, carefully applied. According to Henley, the outstanding luthier Angelo Bertolini (b. 1881) made about thirty-five violins during his active professional career. When we compare this with the old masters who made approximately twenty instruments *per year*, a real change is evident. No one, no matter how gifted and well trained, will become a modern Stradivari with a lifetime production of thirty-five violins. Stradivari probably made about seven hundred instruments before he was fifty-six years old, at which time he began making those instruments that established his fame.

A saturation point was reached during the mid-eighteenth century. When high-quality violins became more difficult to sell, changes in production methods resulted—methods that required less time and therefore made lower prices possible. To care for and to repair the vast number of instruments became the primary task of luthiers after Stradivari. At the end of the eighteenth century, a veritable run set in on valuable old Italian violins, with the result that selling violins became a lucrative business. A new kind of luthier now appeared on the scene. If he had good business sense (and perhaps not too many scruples), he became the owner of a firm, with an attractive store facing the street and a shop in the back, where he employed apprentices and other workers. He did some work himself but mostly minded the store, waiting on customers who were good prospects. He talked shop with experts, attended to his extensive business correspondence, and went on business trips, mostly to scout for valuable instruments. Having little time to make instruments, he supervised the work of others, as Morris said of Richard Davis, who in 1816 had taken over the Norris & Barnes firm. In the early nineteenth century, Salle le père in Paris made few violins but was much in demand as a repairer. Often the business included selling and distributing cheap instruments as well. Léon Bernardel, one of the directors of the Paris firm Couesnon & Co., was careful to distinguish between these two types of activities, as shown by his labels: "Fait sous la direction de / Léon Bernardel, Luthier / à Paris" and "Choisi par . . ." [selected by].

In the twentieth century, renewed interest in early music caused some luthiers to devote more time to making historic or period instruments. One of the first to specialize in historic string instruments was Rudolf Eras (b. 1904) of Markneukirchen. There have been many others since, in many countries.

A growing interest in collecting also had ramifications for violin making and selling. Collectors were less interested in buying instruments in order to play them themselves. Rather they bought old violins to display them (thereby displaying their wealth) and as investments. Under these circumstances, sound became a secondary concern. Because of the collecting mania, many luthiers no longer viewed supplying good instruments for professional players as their main task. More money was to be had in catering to well-to-do collectors. This led to a rise in prices for old violins, but also to a trend among buyers to look down on new violins—a prejudice that remains. Such buyers cared little whether a new violin sounded good, a situation that would have been incomprehensible in Stradivari's day.

Max Möckel (*Das Konstruktionsgeheimnis*) aptly described these changing criteria:

At the time of the old classic Italians, an instrument above all had to sound good; if it was beautiful, that was a welcome additional attribute. Today there are many who will buy a good-looking copy with poor sound, and there are few connoisseurs who refuse to be seduced by an attractive appearance in the absence of tonal beauty.

Customers will pay steep prices for attractive-looking old violins, but they balk at fair prices for fine new ones. Naturally, luthiers see little incentive in making such violins, given the buyers' resistance. Moreover, there are those who make deprecating remarks to prospective buyers of a fine new violin, which Konrad Leonhardt (1969) saw clearly:

Soloists at times would concertize on violins made by contemporary luthiers. They would win praise until those who had an axe to grind would put down the new violins, hoping thereby to prevail on performers to buy an old instrument by a prestigious maker, investing a small fortune in it. Today, if a famous violinist is asked to perform on a new violin, thereby endorsing it, he most likely will make excuses, blaming his refusal on the public's attitude.

Problems of this kind are partially to blame for the decline in the number of violin makers. In 1926–1927 there were fifteen violin shops in Mirecourt; in 1965 there were but five! Later this shrank to three, plus a few independent luthiers and bow makers. In all, only about a hundred people are employed there in violin making and auxiliary enterprises. At a convention of French luthiers not long ago it was announced that France's fifty-five master luthiers have two apprentices among them. Others are deterred by the long training period of six years, three of which must take place abroad. During the 1980s, five schools of violin making still existed: in Brienz (Switzerland, since 1944), Cremona, Mittenwald, Novi Targ (Poland, since 1954), and Mirecourt. This last opened in 1970, with five pupils; there is hope that it will revive violin making in Lorraine. In 1965, ten pupils were enrolled at Cremona's school, eight of them foreigners.

Many more schools existed in the past, such as one in Schwerin, Germany, founded in 1887, and a well-established school in Schönbach. The Bretch School of Violin Making was founded in the United States in 1910; it also offered correspondence courses. Another school was founded in Los Angeles in 1920. During World War I, the British Violin Makers' Guild offered courses for disabled soldiers, and at the Music Training Centre the handicapped made violins. Paris boasted an excellent school during the 1920s, directed by Léonidas Nadegnini; a Cremona School offered instruction in Amsterdam ca. 1933, and after World War I, the Scuola Superiore di Liuteria Gasparo da Salò operated in the town of Salò.

The current emphasis on visual rather than tonal qualities is reminiscent of attitudes found in other arts and crafts: people will buy a valuable Renaissance armoire regardless of its usefulness as a piece of furniture. During the first elimination round at competitions, instruments are typically judged strictly according to craftsmanship. Only later do juries consider tonal criteria. An instrument possessing superior tone may therefore be eliminated at the beginning—something that has happened and will happen, again and again. Many of Stradivari's instruments would not have found a jury's favor, to say nothing of those by del Gesù, because the *f* holes were cut freehand and often are asymmetrical. (Conceivably, the same jury members, when trying to *sell* a Strad, might praise these personal touches as particularly attractive, and raise the asking price accordingly!)

Judging string instruments in contests is problematic in many ways. Casals once said that in order to become really familiar with a cello, one has to play on it for ten years; Cassadò considered this somewhat exaggerated but basically true. We know of many instances where juries listened to a Strad, compared it with another violin, and gave a higher rating to the other violin, which over time turned out to be a disappointment. Leonhardt took a dim view of such contests and made a plea for impartiality by the judges. The instruments should be played behind a screen; the general public (including music students and teachers, and professional players) should be the jury; and decisions should be made purely on the basis of an instrument's sound, not its appearance. To demonstrate a violin's tonal quality, scales, arpeggios, and short pieces in which all four strings are used are best; long concert pieces or concerto movements are not suitable. Leonhardt's demand that the violin maker have complete freedom in regard to the violin's size and appearance is largely ignored.

Questionable priorities of this kind can also be found in books and articles about violin making. Many pages have been devoted to descriptions of the scroll, though it has virtually no influence on sound. It was given its shape largely to protect the instrument's extremity; it also was convenient for hanging up the violin when not in use. As to varnish, writers have waxed poetic in describing its beauties. Glowing accounts of this kind may then end with a brief sentence about the violin's sound. Morris's remark about James Banks should give us pause: "He occasionally succeeded in making a good instrument with a fine varnish. The tone is never good." In other words, there are "good" instruments that have a "bad" sound! Max Möller (*The Violin Makers*) aptly though harshly describes this situation as it developed during the last hundred years:

> In the early twentieth century we find a curious admiration for technique, i.e., for manual dexterity in making violins. One now sees violinmakers in the Low Countries who produce instruments with a painfully correct finish. This technique was made particularly popular by Eugen Gärtner, of Stuttgart, and is called "Gärtnerism."

Möller then points to Guarnerius del Gesù, whose instruments in some ways are technically less than perfect; evidently he was more concerned with their sound.

All this does not add up to a rosy picture, and indeed, a feeling of resignation has crept over many professional luthiers. Again and again they say that with Stradivari's death the art of violin making came to a close, so that luthiers since have no other option than making as faithful a Strad copy as they can—if there is any point in making violins at all. Franz Anton Ernst was a musician endowed with many talents: concertmaster, luthier, and composer. In 1804, having experimented for twenty years, he declared that it was impossible to improve on the old Italian violins. In our own time Rödig expressed similarly pessimistic views. The profession is at a virtual standstill.

But new paths can be forged by continuing developments, the most important of which is the gradual tonal deterioration of the great violins of the golden age. (Many of the greatest ones have been spirited away into museums, display cases, and bank vaults.) Many were so damaged by excessive scraping and other repairs that they no longer stand up to the requirements of contemporary soloists. But even those pre-1750 instruments that are still in use sooner or later will have to be retired, simply because even the best wood has a limited lifespan, no matter how well it has been cared for. This was already clear in 1867 when Hanslick, the Viennese music critic, wrote, "Many of the best Cremona violins played by our virtuosos are already showing signs of deterioration."

A plea for greater care of valuable old violins was made by the Hills (*Antonio Stradivari*, 1902):

> One more earnest word. Instruments by continual use are apt to become weary. They may even virtually be killed. Give them rests. We feel it a duty to urge most strongly that fine instruments should not be brought to premature death by ceaseless use.

Carl Flesch (*The Art of Violin Playing*, vol. 1) advises concert violinists to use a second instrument for practicing, preferably one that is a copy, in terms of measurements, of their concert violin. He also recommends that, if the latter sounds tired and weak, this might be remedied by lowering the tuning of all four strings for twenty-four hours.

The steadily rising pitch to which orchestras have tuned for some time is death to string instruments. A tuning fork used by Handel gives A = 392 vibrations per second, which is approximately today's G; our standard A is 440. In 1788, pitch in Paris was 409; the old so-called Mozart pitch was 421. By 1850, the Vienna and Berlin pitch had already risen to A = 442; as a result, the Paris Commission of 1858 and the Vienna International Conference on Pitch established an official pitch of 435, to prevent further rises. At the London conference of 1939 it rose to 440, but some orchestras now tune A to 450. By our standards, Beethoven would have heard his Fifth Symphony played in approximately B-flat minor!

This trend to ever-higher pitch is led by our major orchestras and their conductors, who seek by it to impart greater stimulus and excitement to listeners, who in turn supposedly perceive in this new pitch a special tone quality. They ignore the fact that Antonio Stradivari built his violins for approximately A = 404, which means that all tensions, measurements, wood thicknesses, and the like were calculated with this pitch in mind. Some relief is possible by providing a heavier bass bar and making a few minor adjustments, but there is a limit to this. In the long run, even the best instrument will not stand up under pressures and tensions for which it was not built.

To be sure, there is still great publicity value in announcing that a soloist is going to perform on a Strad, and there are still those in the audience who are impressed by the name rather than the sound. But in time we will no longer hear violins by the old Italian masters in the concert halls—they are gradually wearing out. Some artists now prefer a healthy-sounding nineteenth-century violin—for instance, by Pressenda or Vuillaume—to an Italian violin afflicted with symptoms of old age. This trend is beginning to be reflected in prices; violin dealers often are the first to sense such changes.

Pre-1800 instruments were not only built with a lower pitch in mind; they were meant to be heard in smaller spaces. The Concert Spirituel in Paris, the Gewandhaus concerts in Leipzig, and similar institutions were harbingers of change, reflecting the participation of a large middle class in concert life. Larger halls became necessary to make this financially feasible. The seating capacity of new concert halls and opera houses is largely determined by administrators, based on expected income and expenses. In orchestras, one can add string players if the string section's sound is too weak, but this is no solution for a string quartet performing for an audience of two thousand. Therefore the trend toward instruments with a large, even robust tone is not represented only by the concert violinist whose rendition of the Brahms Concerto must penetrate to the last row of seats; nor is it restricted to orchestra players who are expected to "give," ever more, in works by Wagner, Bruckner, and Strauss. It affects performers of all kinds of chamber music.

The decline of old master violins is gradual. For the last 150 years, Stainer violins have rarely been played in public. As early as 1806, Sibire declared, "The world's best Stainer violin is more suited to the chamber than to the concert hall." Instruments of the Amati family were the next to go, and it seems that soon it will be the turn of those of the great eighteenth-century luthiers. To replace them, instruments that are up to the demands of our concert life (exceedingly high tuning, huge concert halls, and compositions in which the percussion section is most prominent) are needed. We may regret this development and retreat to our homes, to enjoy the sound of a quartet of Amati instruments—but the sound of an amplified harpsichord will remind us that even concerts of early music at times capitulate to commercial considerations.

What, then, are the tasks of violin makers, to correctly interpret current trends and to provide instruments that fill the needs of today and tomorrow? The question has no simple answer, but one thing seems to be certain: we will have to free ourselves from the traditional concepts and restrictions of form. To continue to build the best possible copies of old masterworks will inevitably result in instruments that reflect the needs and conditions of a bygone age. Designing violins that can withstand our modern pitch and produce the sound volume we expect may result in violins that collectors and amateurs will reject. At that point we may have to ask ourselves: is the violin primarily a musical instrument, or an object to be seen? As Leipp (*Le violon*) said, "The violin is above all a machine to produce sounds." In a sense, the visual appearance of a modern symphony orchestra is strange if not grotesque: a modern auditorium, often with a modern organ gracing the back of the stage; eighty musicians in modern evening dress sitting at ingeniously designed modern music stands. We see woodwinds, timpani, vibraphone and other highly developed, sophisticated precision machines, and in the middle of all this a few dozen ancient instruments or copies of these. It is conceivable that some day violins such as those designed by Savart will be seen and heard as being more appropriate.

Though there are those who advocate looking for new directions in violin making, professional luthiers inevitably point out that the many previous experiments never brought lasting results. This claim needs to be more thoroughly investigated. Certainly, many experimenters have been disappointed, but that in itself means little. Countless inventions in other, technical fields have been granted patents, but an amazingly small part of these proved feasible, and not always due to an inherent flaw. Whether or not an invention succeeds also depends on its timeliness, that is, whether it is needed, and whether there is venture capital to explore it commercially. Luthiers have come up with all kinds of abstruse ideas; a few promising ones ought to be pursued further, if only to establish the reasons for their failure if indeed they were failures. In the case of some innovations, violinists refused to play on instruments that had no aesthetic appeal, which was the real reason for the experiment's so-called failure. In 1869, in the second edition of his book, *Manuel du luthier*, Maugin noted this lack of enterprise by recalling Savart's trapezoid violin, which failed because of its unattractive appearance.

Modern research should reexamine previous experimental violins, asking the following questions:

1) Was the experimental violin carefully made by a first-rate luthier?
2) Was it made of superior wood?
3) Did the luthier build an adequate number of instruments representing the same experiment, that is, was he able to gain enough experience with the type, so that he could learn from it and combine the many factors that would result in a successful instrument?

Usually, if a master was willing to devote time and skill to experimentation, he would not have complied with the third question, primarily due to economic considerations. To make two or three dozen instruments in order to carry through a certain experiment is something no luthier could afford to do; for this he would have to give up his normal work for several years, devoting himself entirely to research. Moreover, for such basic research, to create the violin of the future, a team would be needed.

How and where might this be possible? One thinks of an institute devoted to violin research, associated with a technical university, in a large music center where historical and acoustical research could be combined. Supported with public funds and by private foundations, such an institute might attract outstanding luthiers, along with nonprofessional researchers, who would work there for a limited period. The institute would have to have the most up-to-date technical equipment, and the research results would be continually subjected to impartial testing.

Some day this might lead to the creation of violins that can produce superior tone volume without sacrificing any of the tone quality of the traditional instrument. In that situation we might witness the emergence of two branches of violin making: a historical branch that continues to provide copies of the old Italian masters, chiefly for amateurs and collectors, and a modern branch that produces instruments with which the professional player will succeed. Certainly no modern flourishing of violin making is conceivable without close contact with acoustical research.

PART THREE

PERFORMANCE, PEDAGOGY, AND COMPOSITION

T o play the violin, to teach violin playing, and to write music for it all formed part and parcel of a musician's activities well into the eighteenth century, whether or not the player had any special talent for composing. Corelli, Vivaldi, Tartini, and many others were equally esteemed for their contributions in all three areas; what they accomplished in one tended to influence what they did in the others. They composed great music for their instrument, all the while relying on their experience as performers; they were good teachers because they could base their teaching on what they had learned and practiced daily on their instrument. Beyond the purely technical aspects, their teaching dealt with matters of compositional style as represented in their own works.

Playing a string instrument was part of a musician's basic training right up to the time of the young Mendelssohn. It would have been unusual for any musician to write for the violin without firsthand experience with it. Many great composers played string instruments during their youth, at least for a time. Monteverdi, Bach, Handel, Mozart, and Beethoven knew well how to write idiomatically for at least violin and viola.

In the nineteenth century, this close connection between playing, teaching, and composing is exemplified by Louis Spohr, and later by Enesco; for the piano by Chopin, Schumann, Liszt, Brahms, and later, Bartók.

To account for closely related developments in the three fields presents a problem. It might have been clearer to deal with each in a separate part of the book, but this would have obscured the close relation between them. Numerous cross-references would be required, which could easily prove tiresome for the reader. To repeat some of the same material under different headings also would have been undesirable.

In dealing with playing, teaching, and composing, our emphasis varied. In some instances it was the virtuosos who chiefly affected developments, in others cases, the composers. Emerging and changing musical forms may have influenced violin writing, or developments in one nation may have inspired composers in others. To give an account of all this we chose to do so in separate sections, their content and length determined by the nature of the subject matter. If dates are given here and there they are intended to help, in a general way, to clarify major developments. To delimit these by precise dates never has been meaningful.

Major books on the history of violin playing were written by Wilhelm Joseph von Wasielewski (1869) and Andreas Moser (1923). Since then, researchers have provided a wealth of new material, and this continues to the present day, enlarging our knowledge of violin playing, pedagogy, and composition. Computers tend to make such material more readily available than ever before. It is not my intention to overwhelm the reader with this mass of information; rather, I hope to outline the most essential developments, occasionally using charts and tables to provide an overview of a complex subject.

VIOLIN PLAYING AND TEACHING IN THE SIXTEENTH CENTURY

The wedding of Ferdinando de Medici, grand duke of Tuscany, and Christina of Lorraine, was celebrated in Florence in 1589 with elaborate festivities. Among the theatrical offerings were six intermezzos inserted in the comedy *La pellegrina* by Girolamo Bargagli. These little dramatic sketches included music and dance. Three composers contributed music: Malvezzi, Marenzio, and Cavalieri. As was the custom at the time, the musical numbers were varyingly and colorfully scored; a violin was heard in some of them. The instructions for one work read, "This piece is to be performed by one harp, two liras, two bass gambas, four lutes, one bass trombone, one cornetto, one violin, and twelve singers." A sinfonia for Cristofano Malvezzi's fifth intermezzo included the following remark: "One violin, played excellently by Giovanni Battista Iacomelli, known as 'Il Violino.'" Peri, in the preface to his *Euridice* (1601), lavishes great praise on Iacomelli; other sources call him "Giovanni Battista del Violino." It was customary in Italy to refer to an outstanding virtuoso simply by the name of his instrument. It is, however, hard to understand how in a polyphonic movement in six parts the player of a top line such as the one given here could have greatly distinguished himself.

"Il violino," to be sure, did not restrict himself to playing the notes written in his part. He would fill in large skips with passing tones and would improvise ornamentation on long notes. What a composer wrote down indicated only the general course of the melody; individual notes were merely the important fixed points, necessary for establishing the harmony with the other instruments. Ganassi and Ortiz provide copious examples for this kind of improvising on the basis of a melodic skeleton; this was an important skill that every musician had to acquire. Some compositions from ca. 1600 were intended to demonstrate how to embellish a melody. One of these is Giovanni Bassano's *Ricercate, passagi et cadentie . . .* (Ricercars, melodic passages, and cadences, to practice closing embellishments on all kinds of instruments . . . by Giovanni Bassano, player in the service of the most illustrious *Signoria* [city government] of Venice, newly composed and published in Venice 1585). The work was reprinted in 1598, demonstrating that such instruction books were popular and needed. Riccardo Rognoni acknowledges the importance of such works in his own publication, *Passagi per potersi esercitare nel diminuire* (Venice 1592). In his preface, Rognoni specifically mentions the "violino da brazzo." He demonstrates how a basic melody can be embellished in many ways, from using minor ornaments to improvising passages of great rhythmic complexity.

Both singers and instrumentalists were expected to do this—a tradition of performance practice that lasted into the late eighteenth century. In the sixteenth century, however, when bowed instruments chiefly played vocally conceived lines in the first position, listeners were most interested in what a player could do with this simple raw material. Many aristocratic listeners also were amateur players, well acquainted with the practice of diminution; they did not expect to hear the notes played as written. If they heard several performances of a piece by the same player, what they relished was not a literal repeat but a new version, improvised on the spot. If a piece was rendered by different players, each would be evaluated on the basis of each musician's improvising skill.

Diminution also led to excesses. If a performer lacked creative ability, he or she was likely to "obscure the music with too much busy coloration," as one contemporary put it. Composers sometimes tried to prevent this by inserting appropriate warnings in their scores. F. M. Veracini, for instance, marked certain passages in his op. 2 violin sonatas "come sta" (play as written). A century earlier, Quagliati (*Sfera armoniosa*, 1623) inserted this warning to the violinist: "In ensemble pieces with violin, the player must play exactly what has been written. He may use trills for ornamentation, but must not add passage work."

We cannot fully evaluate sixteenth-century violin playing on the basis of those few instrumental parts that were specifically written for the violin. Actually, much music making dispensed altogether with written or printed music. Pictorial documents showing dancing never include sheet music, music scrolls, or music stands. Dance music was played by ear, even if the music was taken from printed collections such as the four-part *Livres de danceries* by Claude Gervaise, published in Paris around the mid–sixteenth century. Jacques Cordier, called Bocan, was active at the court of Lorraine since 1580. Later he was a violinist, dance master, and choreographer at the French and English courts. We know that he could not read music (nor do all current players of popular music read music), but this did not prevent him from becoming a violinist in the king's private chapel ("violon du cabinet du roi"), and from being called a perfect violinist by Mersenne.

Written or printed violin music by sixteenth- and seventeenth-century composers falls into the following categories:

1) Vocal music known to have been played by violinists
2) Instrumental music not scored for specific instruments, but known to have been played by violinists or by a string orchestra including violins
3) Works that, according to title or preface, can be played *ad libitum*, but specifically mentioning instruments of the violin family
4) Works in which some parts are assigned to an instrument that actually may have been today's violin
5) Works definitely intended for the violin and written idiomatically for that instrument

Vocal music formed part of the repertory of early violinists. Choral works, especially chansons, were played entirely by instruments, or choral parts could be doubled, or instruments could replace missing singers. Massimo Troiano, a court singer in Orlando di Lasso's circle in Munich, described the festivities that took place in 1568 for the wedding of Duke Wilhelm V of Bavaria. On that occasion a string orchestra, led by concertmaster Antonio Morari, played chansons, motets, and madrigals for the banquet. Troiano mentions a six–part motet by Cipriano de Rore, scored for six "viole da brazzo," which probably meant two violins, two violas, a cello, and a violone, the latter then meaning a bass gamba rather than a string (double) bass.

An example of 2) is the ballet *Circe, ou Le balet comique de la Royne,* performed in 1581 for the wedding of the Duc de Joyeuse (a favorite of Henry III) and the queen's sister. The libretto was by Le Chesnay, the royal almoner, the music by Lambert de Beaulieu and Jacques Salmon. Beaujoyeulx, violinist and maître de chapelle, directed the performance and also provided the choreography; costumes and scenery were designed by court painter Jacques Patin. The elaborate production, intended to demonstrate the sovereign's power, made quite a stir. A contemporary account included details about the music: "The ballet's first *entrée* was played by ten violins, five on each side. The players were dressed in white satin decorated with gold and with silver egret feathers." This may have been an orchestra of ten string players; those playing bass instruments probably remained in the orchestra space or pit. The score does not mention any specific instruments. Boyden considers this to be the earliest printed violin music known, but the dances in question do not specify ten violins, and the score does not refer to a string orchestra. The music, in five parts, is quite typical of dance music of the time:

Such a score could be played by gambas, instruments of the violin family, wind instruments, or any combination of these; it is typical *ad libitum* music. Though the top part is instrumentally conceived, it does not suggest any specific instrument. In order to attract players of as many instruments as possible as buyers, publishers used titles such as *Pavans, Galliards, Almains, and other short Aeirs, both grave and light in five parts for viols, violins, and other Musicall Winde Instruments* (A. Holborne, 1599). This custom lasted into the eighteenth century and was revived in the twentieth century with the new interest in baroque practices, leading in Germany to a category known as Spielmusik (music for playing).

Giovanni Gabrieli's *Sonata pian e forte* (1597) is the first work to include specific references to violins in a score. The work, for double choir, is scored for violin and three trombones in Choir I and cornetto and three trombones in Choir II. This might be considered the first piece of music calling for a violin, but the part marked "violino" goes lower than the open G string, so that it probably was intended for the viola. "Violino" here refers to an instrument of the violin family, a meaning then customary in Venice. Nor is this unequivocally a viola part. All Gabrieli may have had in mind was an instrument in the high range that had a more robust sound than other string instruments in use at the time.

Thus we have no sixteenth–century music written idiomatically for the violin. Composers still wrote, predominantly, "per cantar e sonar" (for singing and playing), or as Heinrich Finck phrased it in a Nürnberg edition of 1536, music that was "pleasant to sing, and suitable for all kinds of instruments." Even typically instrumental genres in use ca. 1600, such as canzona (derived from the vocal chanson) and ricercar, include music that could easily be texted. Strictly instrumental phrases and formulations appear gradually, but during the next few decades these do not yet represent true string writing.

The list that follows includes the more important events documenting the gradual rise of the violin up to ca. 1600. It does not repeat previously mentioned dates documenting the use of the term "violin" before 1500, nor does it include examples from the fine arts during the first two decades of the sixteenth century.

1523   At the court of the duke of Savoy in Turin, a honorarium is paid for "trompettes et vyollons" from Vercelli.

1529	Altarpiece *La Madonna degli Aranci* by Gaudenzio Ferrari in the S. Cristoforo church in Vercelli includes a violin-playing putto.
	A French court account book refers to "6 viollons." A list of those obligated to pay taxes includes one Giovanni Battista d'Oneda; his profession is given as "fa di violini" (violin maker).
	Instruments heard at a state banquet in Ferrara include a rebecchino (probably a violin).
1530	Andrea Borgo, acting in Rome for Bernardo Clesio, recommends four musicians who are adequate players "da violini grandi," perhaps referring to violas or cellos.
	Messer Albert, a violinist, is hired by the French court.
1532	The first documented violin, labelled "Peregrino Zanetto fecit Brixiae (made it in Brescia) 1532." It was repaired by G. Sgarabotto in 1907.
1533	Among the retinue of the Venetian ambassador to France are "Thimodio de Luqua et ses compagnons, joueurs de viollons."
	The treatise *Scintille di musica* by G. M. Lanfranco published in Brescia. It refers to "violette da arco senza tasti" (small bowed arm viols without frets).
1533/34	Violinists accompany the French king Francis I on his travels. The account book detailing his personal expenses ("dépenses sécrètes") contains this entry, dated 23 June: "Lyon. A gift for [eight names], all players of violins and other instruments for the King, the sum of eight times twenty écus, i.e., 20 écus for each, to help each with the purchase of a horse."
1534	The exchequer at the Piedmont court pays 2 testoni to the "Taborins et Viollons de Thurin."
	Mengin, oboist at the court of Lorraine, is instructed to buy four violins.
1535/36	Frescoes in the cupola of the Saronno cathedral, painted by Gaudenzio Ferrari, include angels playing violin, viola, and cello.
1538	At a meeting of Charles V with Pope Paul III in Villafranca (Villefranche) near Nice, the pope's entourage includes "violinists from Milan."
1540	The registry of births in the Salò parish lists, on 20 May, Francesco Bertolotti, the father of Gasparo, and Sanctino Bertolotti, Gasparo's grandfather, as violinists and violin makers.
1541	An entry, dated 1 January, in the account book of Prince Emmanuele Filiberto: a payment of 4 scudi "for the violinists who played for the Prince" in Nice.

1542	The first violin known to have been made by Andrea Amati. The birth certificate of Francesco Bertolotti's oldest daughter refers to her as "filia Maestri Francisci violini" (daughter of Maestro Francesco, violin maker or violinist).
1542/43	Ganassi's *Regola rupertina*, printed in Venice, refers to the "viola da brazzi senza tasti" (arm viola without frets), tuned in fifths.
1543	French court documents mention violinists who accompanied Francis I on his travels.
1543/45	Account books of Prince Emmanuele Filiberto of Savoy list amounts paid for "viollons" who played at banquets or in the prince's chambers. Among places mentioned is Milan, where "16 viollons" played.
1546	Andrea Amati's second authentic violin. Rabelais contrasts the courtly instruments that have a pleasant sound—lute, rebec, and violin ("violons auliques," or courtly violins)—with peasants' bagpipes.
1547	Six violinists participate in the funeral music for Francis I.
1548	Violinists are heard at the court of Modena. Violinists participate in festivities in honor of the visit of Henry II in Lyon.
1550	François Massi, a violinist in the court chapel of Charles V in Brussels. On 1 and 2 October in Rouen, festivities in honor of Henry II and Catherine de Medici. A description mentions "nine muses, dressed in white satin, who together played magnificent music on their resplendent violins."
ca. 1550	Violinists are heard for the first time in the castle of Turku, Finland.
1551	A group of violinists plays in Trento for Emmanuele Filiberto of Savoy.
since 1551	Violins are included in the inventories of French instrument makers.
1551/52	Violins are mentioned in two works by Antonio Francesco Doni, printed in Venice.
1552	A letter refers to the sale of a violin by Peregrino, known as Zanetto de Montechiaro.
1553	Estienne Loré plays the "taille de violon" (viola) at the French court. *Tratado de glosas sobre cláusulas* (Treatise on ornamentation) by Diego Ortiz is published in Rome.
1554	Italian violinists play in the Swedish court orchestra, German and Italian violinists play in the Munich court chapel.
since 1554	The street in Salò on which the Bertolotti family lives is called Contrada Violinorum (street of the violinists or violin makers).

1555	Ambrose Lupo "de Myllan," since 1540 gamba player in The King's Musick in London, is mentioned as a violinist. Other violinists from Venice, Cremona, and Milan are hired.
	Hondré Castelan at the Paris court is referred to as "violon de la chambre de Henri II."
	Georges Le Moyne is "joueur de violon en l'hôtel de Monseigneur" (the duke's private orchestra) in Nancy.
	Jacopo da Ponte's painting *The Wedding in Cana* includes violins.
	In his *L'antica musica*, printed in Rome, Nicolò Vicentino mentions "viole d'arco con tre corde senza tasti" (three-string bowed violas without frets).
	Matteo Besuzio is a violinist in the Dresden court chapel.
	Baldassare da Belgioioso is engaged by the French court, along with a group of Italian violinists. He soon calls himself Baltazarini de Beaujoyeulx.
1556	*Épitome musical* by Philibert Jambe-de-Fer is published in Lyon. It contains the first precise account of the violin.
1557	The Brussels town band's "violons" play for Emmanuele Filiberto of Savoy.
	Mathieu Le Saulvage, Alan Moureau, and Giles Harent are violinists at the court in Nancy.
1558	Three "vyalls" and six "violins" participate in the coronation festivities for Queen Elizabeth of England.
	Lejeune, an instrument maker in Lyon, is known to have made violins.
	The military band in Nancy includes violins, pipes, and drums, and continues thus during following years.
1559	The Utrecht town council purchases five violins from Pietro Lupo in Antwerp.
1559/60	In a surveillance list ("registro delle custodie") Zanetto da Montechiaro (b. ca. 1520) is identified as a maker of violins.
1561	The play *Gorboduc* is performed at the English court with "Musicke of Violenze."
	Queen Mary is greeted in Edinburgh with a serenade played by "wretched violins and small rebecs."
	On his journey to Germany, the duke of Lorraine is accompanied by five violinists from the ducal chapel.
1562	Date of the first authentic violin by Gasparo da Salò.
	In a register of those required to pay taxes, Giovanni Battista da Brescia is listed as a violin maker ("che fa violini").
1563	Veronese's painting *The Wedding at Cana* includes violins.
	Francesco de Venetia is mentioned as a violinist at the English court.

The court chapel in Lorraine acquires violins.

1565   The intermezzo *Psyche e Amor* by Striggio and Corteccia is performed on the occasion of the wedding of Francesco de Medici and Johanna of Austria. The orchestra includes a rebecchino (probably a violin).

Dance music is played for the visit of Catherine de Medici to Bayonne. Instruments include a "dessus de violon," perhaps a violino piccolo.

1565/70   Hans Mielich's illustration *The Bavarian Court Chapel under Lassus* (in a sumptuous illuminated manuscript of Lassus's [=Orlando di Lasso's] *Penitential Psalms*) shows a violin, a viola alta, and a viola tenore.

Charles IX of France is reported to have ordered from Andrea Amati twelve large and twelve small violins, six violas, and eight basses (probably cellos).

1566   An inventory of instruments belonging to Raimund Fugger the Younger lists several violins made in "Bressa" (Brescia).

Two violinists, Alberto Ardesi and Maurizio Sinibaldi, both from Cremona, are employed at the court in Vienna.

1567   The violinists Claude and Nicolas from Florence are engaged for the court in Nancy.

1568   At the Munich wedding of Wilhelm V and Renée of Lorraine, six "viole da brazzo" participate, led by the violinist Antonio Morari.

The brothers Matteo and Zerbonio Besuzio are engaged as violinists for the Munich court chapel.

1571   The chapel of Queen Elizabeth of England includes seven violinists.

Giovanni Battista Giacometti "del violino" is active in Rome.

1572   Sir Thomas Kytson buys a "treble violin" for 20 shillings.

The French king provides funds to Delinet, a court musician, for the purchase of a Cremona violin.

Another court musician, Baptiste Delphinon, is sent to Italy to hire eight violinists.

1573   Catherine de Medici entertains the Polish ambassador with a *Ballet polonais* in which thirty "violons" participate, meaning a string orchestra of thirty players.

1577   Paris luthier Nicolas Aubry receives an order for four violins, "with inlay, made in the Cremona manner."

1579   Court of Lorraine pays 3000 francs for the purchase of instruments for the "six violons du Monseigneur."

1580   Christoph Harant, a page boy at the court of Archduke Ferdinand in Innsbruck, is given violin lessons.

Montaigne reports about a mass celebrated in Verona in which violins were heard.

Alessandro Orlogio is a violinist in the chapel of Rudolf II in Prague.

1581   Performance of the Ballet Comique de la Royne.

Date of a violin made by Ventura Linarolo in Venice.

1583   The inventory of the Earl of Leicester in Kenilworth lists a "chest of five violens."

Camillo Cortellini, called "Il violino," becomes a member of the Bologna municipal orchestra.

1584   Violins participate in church music in Genoa.

1585   French music inventories list violins "de Bresse" (from Brescia).

The Norwich town band includes violinists.

A motet is performed at the opening of the Hungarian parliament in Medgyes; an Italian violinist employed by the Polish court participates.

"Maestro Santino, the violinist" participates "with his ensemble" in a Genoa church procession.

1586   Antonio Beltramin, violinist, is hired by the Padua cathedral.

1588   In a statement to tax collectors, Gasparo da Salò points out that the wars have caused his instrument trade with France to suffer.

1589   In an intermezzo given in Florence the following instruments participated: sopranino di viola, soprani di viole, violino, una violina.

The French queen Catherine de Medici has a violinist play for her on her deathbed.

1590   At the court of Queen Elizabeth of England, almost all violinists are Italians.

Town musicians in Chester play "violons."

1592   The instruction book *Prattica di musica* by Lodovico Zacconi, printed in Venice, includes information about the violin.

In his treatise on vocal and instrumental ornamentation, Riccardo Rognoni specifically includes "il violino da brazzo."

1594   Henry IV of France sends to his mistress Gabrielle d'Estrécs "une assez bonne bande de violons pour vous réjouir" (a very good string orchestra, to give you pleasure).

1597   Giovanni Gabrieli's *Sonata pian e forte* for double choir. One choir includes a "violino" and three trombones.

1599   A. Holborne's collection of dances for "viols, violins, or other Musicall Winde Instruments."

Who, then, were the first violinists—or, more correctly, the first musicians who, while also playing other instruments, now turned to the so-very-useful "sopranino di viola"? No doubt most of them were rebec players, for the fingering and general manner of playing the two instruments are very similar. The rebec's bridge had to be quite flat for playing drones. Since the violin bridge is more curved, a somewhat refined technique was needed to facilitate playing on single strings. To play both violin and gamba must have been rare. The statement that Norwich town musicians played "viol or violin, or both" may only have meant that this was a mixed ensemble. There was a great deal of difference between soprano and alto gamba on one hand, and violin and viola on the other, particularly in regard to strings, so that it was unlikely for one musician to play both. Ganassi was aware of this; he reported that players of instruments from the viola da brazzo family modified gambas by mounting only three strings and tuning them in fifths. Conversely in England ca. 1560, gambists played on violins that were tuned in fourths and held between the legs. Quite likely many gamba players switched over to the violin as the instrument that offered greater opportunities, including better pay, to professional musicians. This applies to Ambrose Lupo, a Milan musician at the English court. Around 1600, Alessandro Striggio is referred to as a player of both lira and violin.

The rebec and fiddle were gradually outclassed by the continued structural improvements of the violin. By 1550 the violin was the leading instrument in the soprano register. The first anonymous violinists came from "Verceil" (Vercelli), Turin, and Milan; the first players whose names we know came from the same region in northern Italy. Baldassare, from the small hamlet Belgioioso in Lombardy, was hailed as "the best violinist in Christendom," showing that a brilliant career was already possible; his successes at the French court have already been noted. Many European courts copied French ceremonial and other customs, but they prided themselves on having Italian violinists in their service.

Nevertheless, there is no documentation that would cause us to speak of violin technique as such, let alone Italian technique. Ganassi gives fingerings for an instrument tuned in fifths that show that lute and gamba fingerings at first were tried on the violin by violinists who had played those instruments: 1, 3, 4 on the G string; 1, 2, 4 on the D and A strings. These fingerings were necessary on the cello, with its large distances, but they fail to take advantage of the smaller distances on a soprano-range fingerboard. They were adequate for playing dance music and vocal parts, and advantageous for the low register of the viola. The body of one viola preserved from this time is no less than 480 mm long.

Greatly varying sizes of da bracchio instruments also affected the manner of holding them, which was by no means uniform. Pictures show all kinds of positions for holding fiddle, rebec, viola da bracchio, and violin. Most frequently they were held firmly against the chest or clavicle, but not held under the chin, probably because at that time a singer might still accompany himself on a string instrument. Still, some illustrations show the chin hold, including a well-known Paris print of 1516. Another shows the player's chin on the right side of the tailpiece. The larger the instrument, the more necessary it was to hold it against the neck rather than the chest. The chest position was customary when playing for dancing and other social occasions, perhaps because it facilitated a more robust bow stroke, perhaps too because it freed the upper torso to engage in dancelike motions, urging the dancers along.

There is a close connection between holding the violin and playing in the higher positions, especially the shifting down to lower positions. If the left hand must not only play but at the same time must press the instrument against the body, it may still be possible to shift up. Shifting down, however, will result in the violin's moving too, unless it is held in place by the chin. Ganassi's fingerings require playing in higher positions, but his instruction applies only to the gamba, all sizes of which were held on or between the legs. But the manner of holding violin and viola, as shown in contemporary illustrations, suggests it was rare to change positions. In many illustrations the player's left hand is in a higher position than the first (as in the case of the viola-playing angel in Saronno), but this is no contradiction. Depending on the key, higher positions were used; the hand was then kept in that position for an entire piece or section of it. The gamba, tuned like the lute, required a partly chromatic fingering; the fingering of the violin, tuned in fifths, is best for playing diatonic melodies within the compass of an octave.

A basic difference between violin and gamba bowing soon evolved. Some of Ganassi's general rules apply to both instruments, for instance, that the bow should move at a right angle to the string, and that the correct point of contact between bow and string must be observed. Ganassi was also aware of basic differences in bowing as related to weight. Keeping the hand above the bow stick is physiologically correct for fiddle, rebec, lira da bracchio, and violin; underhand bowing is right for the gamba. As a result, a down bow played on instruments of the first group carries the weight of the entire hand; the up bow is relatively weightless unless the index finger compensates by exerting pressure. There are also basic differences in weight and pressure at the bow's tip, middle, and frog. Greater possibilities to vary these gradually helped the violin to become the favored instrument. Underhand bowing keeps the right hand approximately in one plane. A down bow requires pulling rather than applying weight; an up bow requires pushing rather than pressure. Realizing this, a gamba player plays accented notes with an up bow while instruments of the violin family require a down bow, as had been true of fiddles and rebecs. At first, players may have bowed that way instinctively, but then it became so consistent that L'Abbé le fils, in his violin method of 1761, simply advised gambists who wanted to use his book to reverse all bowing instructions. In *Traité de la viole* (1687), Jean Rousseau said the same. Ganassi's work, by the way, makes no reference to tied notes but does mention playing two detached notes, *portato*, on one bow, to prepare for an upcoming accented note.

Pictures provide good information about holding the bow. Index, middle, and fourth finger usually rest on the stick or at times are extended above it; the little finger often is stretched out—something that some current players seem to think of as very elegant. The thumb rests on the bow hair (as in the painting by Palamedesz), but even in early illustrations it can be seen in

A. Palamedesz, *Merry Company* (Amsterdam, Rijksmuseum)

the position that later became normal, alongside the stick. To some extent the thumb could vary the tension by exerting pressure on the bow hair. This, however, would result in a tighter grip and more clumsy bowing. Such robust bowing suited dance music, which, to make itself heard in an often noisy environment, required vigorous, short, accented notes.

Italian violinists early on practiced the other technique, keeping the thumb alongside the stick. This facilitated greater nuances in bowing, appropriate for secular, text-related music. Violinists may have used both manners depending on the type of music played. Though pictorial evidence is limited, one surmises that placing the thumb along the stick became the general practice in Italy, while the other was viewed as typical of French violin playing.

Illustrations of sixteenth-century music making show bows of greatly varying length, perhaps reflecting regional traditions, but also individual preferences. This may also indicate that longer bows were favored for participating in vocal music with long, sustained notes and ligatures, while a short, robust bow stroke was best for lively, accented dance music.

At this early stage, treatises on violin pedagogy were not yet needed. Books of this kind intended for other instruments provided violinists with sufficient information on improvisation and some aspects of playing technique. A 1582 reference to the possibly first (anonymous) violin teacher is so brief that we cannot be sure whether instruction indeed took place, or what was taught.

EARLY SEVENTEENTH-CENTURY DEVELOPMENTS

Vocal music dominated sixteenth-century musical life; there was far less purely instrumental music, much of it dance music, and it played a generally less significant role. In the course of the seventeenth century this changed greatly, to the extent that ca. 1700 we find composers who wrote hardly any vocal music, and publishers who almost exclusively printed instrumental chamber music and orchestral works. Bel canto came to the fore—vocal music that expressed personal feelings in colorful, varied ways. The new orchestral instruments not only provided harmonic background but eloquent, expressive music that vied with the singers. Because it could supply volume, tone quality, subtle dynamic shading, and much color, the violin outshone all other instruments and soon became the bel canto instrument par excellence. Giovanni Battista Doni (*Annotazioni sopra il compendio de' generi*, Rome 1640), a widely traveled scholar, enthusiastically praised the violin:

> Among all musical instruments, the violin stands out as a true wonder. No other instrument, so small in size and with so few strings, can produce such a variety of tones, harmonies, and melodic graces. . . . In the hands of an experienced player it combines the lute's gentleness, the gamba's sweetness, the harp's majesty, the trumpet's force, the fife's vivacity, the flute's melancholy, and the cornetto's pathos.

Doni expressed the prevailing sentiment of his contemporaries. They realized, of course, that when it came to expressing personal feelings, no instrument could equal the human voice. But when composers wrote for these instruments idiomatically, making full use of their expressive potential, this instrumental language exceeded by far what the voice could achieve. When voices and instruments collaborated, the result was the resplendent sound, so richly articulated, that we encounter in Monteverdi's music.

Though purely instrumental music was still young, it displayed much variety, including intimate works intended for the chamber. On the other end of the spectrum we find lavish, large works for grand, festive occasions, combining and contrasting the new instrumental resources in small and large ensembles. Thus we have the early "sonada," as distinct from the "cantada," but we also marvel at the grand polychoral compositions by Giovanni Gabrieli and his contemporaries.

In this development the violin soon played the leading role, due to its distinctive, idiomatic language. Nevertheless, we continue to find works such as Giovanni Battista Fontana's of 1641 that were intended "for violin or cornetto," that is, the melodic line respected the more limited possibilities of that woodwind instrument.

Different attempts to define the violin's characteristic idiom are best seen and heard in the music of three major composers. Claudio Monteverdi, the great dramatist, explored the violin's potential for dramatic expression; Biagio Marini, violinist-composer, sought new approaches based on his own daily contact with the instrument; and Carlo Farina experimented end-lessly—though the results at times were odd and extreme, he helped to extend the violin's expressive range.

MONTEVERDI AND THE VIOLIN

During the early decades of the seventeenth century, opera was the leading genre, attracting the greatest interest of avant garde composers, first in Italy, and soon throughout Europe. Strong emotions were expressed in moving recitatives and flowing ariosos, resulting in works such as Monteverdi's "Lamento di Arianna," which served as the model for countless early seven-teenth-century works.

Operas at first were written for the aristocracy, commissioned for impor-tant events in princely families, such as weddings. Opera therefore was per-formed for a small, select audience. The degree of lavishness reflected the event's importance; financial considerations did not govern the size and makeup of the orchestra. If the occasion warranted it, professional musicians from near and far were engaged, and qualified amateurs joined them. Such were the conditions surrounding the premiere of Monteverdi's *Orfeo* in 1607. It was not the first opera, but the first by a major composer.

Claudio Monteverdi (b. 1567 in Cremona) was a pupil of Marc Antonio Ingegneri, known not only as a composer but also as a "violino da grido" (famous violinist). Monteverdi at first earned a living playing the violin and viola bastarda, meaning that he played the then–customary orchestral string instruments whenever his services were wanted. His instrumental writing was governed by the aesthetic principle, established during the renaissance, that instrumental as well as vocal parts should express the meaning of the words. In many of his works the violins do not merely double the voice parts, or carry the top line in polyphonic movements, but take an active part in dramatic situations. In his *Orfeo* the orchestra consists of a number of self-contained groups, participating as the onstage events require it and accord-ing to each group's expressive possibilities.

The multicolored orchestra includes two "violini piccoli alla francese" and ten "viole da bracchio." According to the custom of the time, the sec-ond group most likely was a five-part string orchestra with two players on each part. The makeup of the two "violini piccoli alla francese" has been widely discussed and variously interpreted, especially since at one point in the score the words "violini ordinarij da bracchio" appear. Boyden, who has investigated the problem in detail, believes that the "violini piccoli" were *pochettes* or kits—the small pocket violins used by dance teachers, tuned an octave higher than violins. Praetorius mentions such small violins, saying that they existed with two tunings: the "small discant violin," tuned c' g' d'' a'' and the "very small, three-string violin" tuned a' e'' b'' or g' d'' a''. Using these small violins made it unnecessary for the regular violins to play in high positions. In *Orfeo*, Monteverdi's violin parts do not rise above the first position. A few bars from the third-act aria "Possente spirto" show how Monteverdi's writing for obbligato violins reflects the spirit of the text:

Monteverdi's later works increasingly exploit typically violinistic writing. A Magnificat of 1610 (without violini alla francese) displays characteristic figuration, taking the violin up to the fifth position. The seventh and eighth books of madrigals (1619, 1638) bring the traditional choral madrigal to the new concertato style, with violins participating prominently; the highly dramatic cantata *Il combattimento di Tancredi e Clorinda* of 1624, which uses pizzicato and tremolo among other special effects, is most representative of this. Monteverdi explains pizzicato: "Here one puts down the bow and plucks the strings with two fingers," possibly alternating fingers, as on the lute. Later he writes, "Here one again picks up the bow." Monteverdi claimed tremolo was his own invention, but in fact tremolo appears in a work by Marini printed in 1617, and repeated notes had been used for decades in "battle pieces," to represent warlike din. Monteverdi, however, was the first to use it as a dramatic device in the *stile concitato*, to express strong emotion. In the preface to *Il combattimento* he explains,

> I thought it prudent to state that I was the one who first used this device, so necessary in the art of music, which up to now had been incomplete without it. . . . At first, those who played the basso continuo thought it laughable rather than laudable to bow back and forth on the same string, sixteen times in one measure. They therefore played only one note, . . . thereby eliminating the effect of excited speech.

The creation of musico-dramatic effects must be recognized as a significant ingredient in the development of typically violinistic writing. In describing the history of violin playing, more obvious characteristics, such as the exploration of ever-higher positions on the fingerboard, are too often stressed, while the desire to find new expressive means has been largely ignored. Monteverdi held a key position in this development, and during the first half of the seventeenth century three leading instrumentalists, in addition to Farina, played violin in Mantua under Monteverdi's direction: Salamone Rossi, Giovanni Battista Buonamente, and Biagio Marini.

BIAGIO MARINI

Marini (b. ca. 1597 in Brescia) was brought up in the stimulating environment of Gasparo da Salò and Maggini, which led him to become one of the best violinists of his time. His teacher probably was Giovanni Battista Fontana, also from Brescia, a virtuoso violinist also highly gifted as a composer, who in 1631 fell victim to the plague in Padua. Only one of Fontana's works was published, posthumously, in 1641; it consists of eighteen compositions including six solo sonatas. In Mantua, Marini may also have studied composition with Monteverdi; certainly he was inspired by him. His interest soon turned to writing for the violin, especially in the then-new form of the sonata. Formal models were the first printed sonatas for violin and figured bass by Gian Paolo Cima (Milan 1610) and others, such as the Sonata for three violins and basso continuo by Giovanni Gabrieli, published posthumously (Venice 1615). For the violinistic writing, Monteverdi may have been the model.

Marini's *Affetti musicali* was published in 1617 as his op. 1 in Venice, where he was a member of the municipal orchestra ("musico della serenissima signoria"). It contains a great variety of pieces that at the time were deemed useful for chamber, church, or other venues—specifically, according to the work's subtitle, "sinfonias, canzonas, sonatas, balletti, arias, branles, gagliards, and correntes in one, two, or three parts, and to be played on the violin, cornetto, or any kind of instrument." Of the twenty-seven compositions, eleven are for two and fourteen for three instruments; the scores mention violins, trombones, and bassoons. The term "affetti" signified trills, tremolos, or similar embellishments; as a title it was meant to inspire the player to add expressive ornamentation. The collection contained much that was new and different; it may have led to Marini's appointment in 1623 to the Wittelsbach court in Neuburg. After return trips to Italy, Marini went to Düsseldorf in 1640; he died in Venice in 1665. His *oeuvre* consists of no less than twenty-three printed editions, not all of which have been preserved. New concepts of violin technique are shown in his op. 8 (Venice 1629): "Sonatas, sinfonias, canzonas, passamezzi, balletti, correntes, gagliards, and ritornellos for one to six parts for all sorts of instruments. A four-part capriccio for two violins, an echo for three violins, and several sonate capricciose in two and three parts, with a solo violin, and other curious and modern inventions."

Marini's position as a composer and violinist in Germany reflects the changes that had taken place since the sixteenth century. Some sixty to eighty years earlier, Italian violinists went abroad to introduce the "barbarians" to the wonders of a new world of sound. Now they encountered in many music centers significant national or regional styles, inspired by Italy but showing local features. No doubt Marini contributed to German music but also learned from it. His op. 8, the preface of which he wrote while still in Neuburg, is particularly rich. It includes a sonata "in ecco" for three violins, two of which are to be invisible. In the sonata "per il violino d'inventione" one movement calls for the E string to be tuned down to C, then to be brought up again. A capriccio "for playing in three parts, in the manner of the lira" contains three-part chords, evidently to imitate the then-very-popular lira da gamba. Notable is the consistent use of the lowest string, for because of its poor sound it was largely avoided until wound strings had been invented. A. Heuss (*Sammelbände der Internationalen Musik-Gesellschaft*, Leipzig 1899–1914, vol. 4), however, believes that the G string was used more frequently than generally assumed by other scholars and states, "Violinists are not likely to have mounted a G string merely for luxury or prestige."

To write for the violin polyphonically, in two or more parts, was probably an idea derived from lute playing. Lutenists for some time had transcribed polyphonic choral pieces, notating them in tablature; gamba players then adopted the practice. Both lute and gamba were limited in the execution of polyphony; the violin even more so, having fewer strings. Attempts to overcome these limitations, however, greatly advanced violin technique. One of the most remarkable manifestations of this is a work by Ottaviomaria Grandi, organist at the cathedral and the Servites' church in Reggio, and a professional violinist. It was published in Venice in 1628 and was discussed by Moser. Many passages in Marini's works prove that there are substantial differences between the notation of polyphonic writing and its realization on a violin:

In such a passage, anyone used to listening to polyphonic music will mentally complete the melodic line in spite of the rest. The composer could assume that the listener could and would do this, but for reasons of musical logic he wrote certain note values "for the eye," knowing that they could not be heard. This discrepancy between notation and actual sound exists in much violin music; it has at times puzzled both publishers and interpreters of Bach's sonatas and partitas for unaccompanied violin.

It may seem strange that Italian composers after the mid-century wrote little violin music in a polyphonic idiom. Italians, as true practitioners of bel canto, treated the violin increasingly as a melody instrument, wisely leaving polyphony to the keyboard instruments for which it was intended.

FORMS OF SEVENTEENTH-CENTURY VIOLIN MUSIC

Music by Marini and his contemporaries forms part of a large violin repertory, using various scorings, which represents one aspect of the general development of instrumental music and its forms. The French vocal chanson was a point of departure. Its form is governed by the treatment of each line of text as an entity, ending with a cadential formula. Musical motives related to the text's meaning were treated in imitation by the several voices. This formal structure led to the instrumental chanson (canzona) and the closely related ricercar, characterized by a succession of thematically independent fugal expositions. Gabrieli's Sonata for three violins and figured bass exemplifies the nature of such motives and the manner in which they were treated in the several voices:

This work is a one-movement canzona. The title "sonata" has no formal meaning but was then merely a general term indicating an instrumental piece; the word continued to be used that way for many decades. In 1613, the title of one of Stefano Bernardi's works advises that it includes several "canzoni per sonare" (instrumental canzonas), but then refers to the individual works as "sonata prima," and so forth. Around 1650 the term "sonata" was generally employed, but even in 1645 Marco Uccellini used such titles as *Sonata over [=or] Toccata*, and in 1649 *Sonate over Canzoni*.

In time, composers tended to set the individual sections of a ricercar as separate entities, including different tempo and time signatures, which led to cyclical arrangements: the formerly distinct sections of a ricercar now became the movements of a larger composition. At the end of this development, what with the predominantly sacred use of canzone and ricercar, the term "sonata da chiesa" (church sonata) was adopted. Tarquinio Merulo's op. 12 (Venice 1637) is called "Canzoni ovvero Sonate concertate per chiesa e camera" (for church and chamber). The distinction set off the church sonata from the customary group of dances (usually four) that in Italy became known as "sonata da camera," in France as "suite," and in Germany as "partie" or "partita." Marini's works belong to both categories, da camera and da chiesa.

These two differed not only in content and formal arrangement; they also called for different violinistic interpretation. Though chamber sonatas became increasingly stylized, being less and less intended for actual dancing, their mood nevertheless was dancelike, requiring short, accented bowing and emphasizing down bows. The church sonata, especially in the slow movements, required broad, cantabile bowing, taking advantage of the bow's full length. Allegro and presto movements, usually fugal, required a supple wrist in order to bring out the rapid contrapuntal lines. To hold the bow with the thumb alongside the stick thus became a musical necessity, as did the long and light bow itself.

FARINA AND VIRTUOSO PLAYING

The violinist Carlo Farina (b. ca. 1600 in Mantua) began his career under Monteverdi. He then spent several years as concertmaster in Dresden under Heinrich Schütz, after which he went to Danzig. With his *Capriccio stravagante* he ushered in a genre that became highly significant for the violin, though it often had little musical substance: the virtuoso showpiece. The Capriccio is scored for string orchestra, but the top line is treated soloistically, apparently to be performed by only one player. The work forms part of a collection of thirty individual pieces, described in the title thus: "Pavanes, galliards, courantes, French airs, and an entertaining *quodlibet*, with all kinds of curious inventions such as have never before been seen in print. Also some German dances, all to sound good on the violin. In four parts, created by Carlo Farina of Mantua, violist in the service of the Elector of Saxony. Dresden . . . 1627." The "curious inventions" were programmatic pieces. It is interesting to note that in the title Farina calls himself a violist, a usage still extant in German music of Bach's day, meaning violinist.

Tone painting in violin music was inspired by earlier program music. Imitating the sounds of the hunt, battle, and other noises had attracted composers for centuries (the clumsy changing of positions by violinists reminded Rabelais of caterwauling). Farina's famous Capriccio gave the composer a bad reputation among those espousing "noble" violin playing, but as an outstanding virtuoso he apparently had fun exploring all the sounds he could extract from his instrument. Some indeed were new at the time and no doubt amused his listeners in a harmless way. Farina imitates instruments such as timpani, military drums, Spanish zither, and "pifferino della soldatesca" (a small military fife), as well as hens cackling, dogs barking, and cocks crowing:

He also gave precise verbal instructions to the violinist:

For caterwauling, gradually move the finger down from the written note. For the sixteenth notes, play as loud and fast as possible on either side of the bridge. This is how cats [sound], after they have bitten each other, and are quickly running away.

Farina indicated special effects that have since become routine, such as portamento, glissando, and sul ponticello. He was quite familiar with col legno playing, an effect that as late as 1819 was considered indecent by one writer in the *Allgemeine Musikalische Zeitung*, who urged it not be produced "in front of members of the nobility." Farina's instructions appear in both German and Italian, advising the violinist to "beat with the wooden part of the bow." He prescribes exactly how to obtain certain coloristic effects, as shown by his explanation of *flautando* playing: "A lovely flute sound can be produced near the bridge, about a finger's width away from it—a quiet sound as on the lira. The sound of a soldier's fife can be created by playing louder and nearer the bridge." These may be the earliest references to the proper place of contact between bow and bridge, such an important factor in tone production in general.

Farina's works are also informative because of their notation. The Kassel copy of the Capriccio print of 1627 includes double stops that were added by hand. Printed editions of his sonatas contain only one-line writing, but in some places numerals are added to indicate double stops. Studying violin music from this period, Beckmann noted that while printed editions do not include double stops, they are frequent in manuscript copies. He probably was right in concluding that printing techniques of the time could not adequately reproduce simultaneously sounding notes, especially if they were close to each other. It follows that printed editions do not fully inform us of the state of violin playing at the time.

STANDARDIZATION OF THE ORCHESTRA

CATEGORIES AND FORMAL DESIGN IN ORCHESTRAL MUSIC

Early opera did not require a standard, set orchestra; its makeup was determined by the dramatic requirements of individual scenes, including any tonal symbolism involved. But a trend toward standardization soon set in, as it did in other categories of music. Instruments of the violin family were not yet represented in sufficient numbers to produce large effects. They formed a small group next to the many winds, gambas, and continuo instruments. We are surprised by the variety of timbres and by the imbalance of instruments in the scoring of early Italian orchestral compositions. Gabrieli's *Sonata pian e forte* is a good example. According to a contemporary, a six-part sinfonia by Malvezzi called for "a harp, played by Giulio Caccini; a chitarrone, two archlutes, two small lutes, two liras, a psaltery, a violin played by Alessandrino, a transverse flute, and a bass viola bastarda played by Duritio Isorelli, who is a master of that instrument." Nor did early ballets call for any standard orchestration. A description of the Ballet Comique de la Royne (1581), published a year after the performance, states, "Ten separate groups of players were installed in the orchestra box."

In 1626 Louis XIII of France established the permanent group known as the Vingt-quatre Violons du Roi (royal string orchestra of twenty-four players), a milestone in the history of orchestra playing. They functioned independently of the court chapel and had been preceded in 1609 by a group of twenty-two players, including violas and cellos, known as the Violons Ordinaires de la Chambre du Roy. The Vingt-quatre Violons continued as a group until 1761. The king had good reasons for establishing such an elite group: these violin, viola, and cello players, using instruments from Cremona, were superior to gambists and woodwind players in regard to intonation and volume and brilliance of sound. Uniting them in a special ensemble was bound to bring outstanding results, which explains Mersenne's enthusiastic account (*Harmonie universelle*, Paris 1636–1637):

> Those who have heard the 24 Violons du Roi swear that they never have heard anything more enchanting and magnificent. No group is better at inspiring dancers, as has been done in ballets, but it excels equally at all other musical occasions. They produce an exceedingly beautiful and graceful sound, preferable to that of any other ensemble. Their bowing is so attractive that one hates to have them stop, especially when the bowing is enhanced by all kinds of left-hand embellishments. All listeners gladly will admit that the violin is the queen of instruments.

Members of this orchestra enjoyed important new social benefits. They were well paid and entitled to a pension; they paid no taxes and had free board at court; and they wore a special uniform in keeping with the festive occasions at which they performed. Here again, the term "violons" included the entire violin family. Mersenne gives the exact composition of the group, which consisted of five sections:

Dessus (violin): 6
Haute-contre (viola, also called haute-contre-taille): 4
Taille (viola): 4
Quinte (viola, also called cinquiesme, quinte de viole): 4
Basse (cello): 6

The groups of violas had the same tuning but differed in size, according to which they played in higher or lower ranges. Later, Lully changed the distribution of players, assigning three rather than four to the fourth group and using only five cellos, but adding two double basses, thus bringing the ensemble closer to the modern string orchestra.

Most seventeenth-century European rulers modeled life at their courts on French customs. Thus in 1661 Charles II of England instituted the Twenty-four Violins of the King with the distribution given by Mersenne. A similar string orchestra had been formed at the English court in 1631, made up of fourteen players (3 / 2 / 2 / 3 / 4).

New orchestras of this kind were characterized by a gentle, velvety sound, producing volume that would seem small by today's standards, due to the prominence of violas and the absence (at first) of double basses. When the then-new mutes were used, an even gentler sound resulted. Mersenne first described the mute in 1636; Lully first called for it in a 1686 score. Courtly audiences in France and England apparently liked this sound, but in the long run the constant five-part texture (which in France lasted into the early 1700s) proved somewhat heavy and tiresome. Other influences affected the orchestra's later development.

While at first opera, as a courtly entertainment, had not been open to the public, this changed when, in the 1630s, regular opera seasons ("stagioni") were offered, at first in Rome and Venice; at various times Venice supported ten theaters in which operas were staged, exclusively so in seven of these. The Teatro Grimani in Venice, near the San Cassiano church, opened its doors in 1637, the important innovation being that tickets could be purchased by anyone. Noble families continued to be the chief supporters, renting boxes on a permanent basis, but now an impresario rather than a prince was financially responsible. The impresario signed contracts with librettists, composers, singers, musicians, and other personnel. Since he invested his own money in the undertaking ("impresa"), he was well motivated to recoup his investment and make a tidy profit.

This change from a patronage to a business system had far-reaching consequences. Above all, the profit motive suggested a reduction of musical forces to a minimum. Lavish orchestras such as played in Monteverdi's *Orfeo* were now out of the question; instead, a fairly small, standard orchestra emerged. The violin family formed its nucleus, but in contrast to French five-part scoring, only two violins, viola, and cello were the norm. At first a bass gamba, later a double bass might reinforce the cello line, while a harpsichord provided the basso continuo, which was especially important during the recitatives. The nucleus could be augmented as needed by oboes (interchangeably with recorders and transverse flutes), bassoons, horns, trumpets, and timpani. This remained the customary orchestra up to the time of Haydn's and Mozart's early works and still forms the backbone of orchestras of our own day. Many seventeenth- and eighteenth-century opera scores require only strings and a few winds *ad libitum*; if necessary, a string quartet (playing wind cues when needed) and harpsichord suffice. As yet there was no conductor in our sense; direction came from both harpsichordist and concertmaster, who approached the maestro di cappella, or director, in rank. The concertmaster was also expected to be a capable soloist.

Such economies resulted in a less colorful orchestral sound, necessitated by the absence, as a rule, of wealthy patrons. For the next 150 years, orchestras of this general makeup were the rule in churches, in the palaces of nobility, in the collegium musicum of students and/or townspeople, in ensembles supported by municipalities, and wherever Italian opera was performed. Consequences for the status of musicians and for composing were far-reaching, as orchestras provided a living for many string players. With so many players needed, violin pedagogy as a discipline got its true start.

Now composers could create an orchestral sound based on the instruments' characteristics, for they could be reasonably sure of finding this four-part string orchestra and its few wind players everywhere. Although aiming, naturally, for the most effective results, composers still found it necessary to write nonspecific orchestra parts ca. 1600, leaving the choice of instruments to the maestro. Publishers gradually became interested in printing orchestral music because potential buyers could be found throughout Europe. This promoted the emergence of specific forms of orchestral music and the adoption of forms that had proved successful in other categories of instrumental music.

For opera, instrumental pieces cast in various formal arrangements—or sinfonie, as they were chiefly known—were heard at the opera's beginning, during scene changes and processions onstage, and as background music for scenes without singing. Outside of opera, the orchestra suite was popular, featuring dance types that changed according to fashion. For the church, the sonata da chiesa was especially useful because its individual movements could be played at certain points during mass or for festive processions. Cathedral orchestras, such as the one established at San Petronio in Bologna in 1657, included only a few highly qualified professionals, joined by amateurs for high holidays. This led to a particular way of scoring solo passages. Echo effects; varied (embellished) repeats of sections, especially in dance movements; and technically difficult passages were played by the professionals, which was not necessarily indicated in the music.

The concerto grosso was a product of this manner of performing. Alessandro Stradella (d. 1681), Jean-Baptiste Lully (d. 1687), and Arcangelo Corelli (d. 1713) were the greatest composers to pit small groups of soloists

against the whole (tutti) orchestra. The term "concerto grosso" does not refer to a form; it means "large body of sound," while the solo players are the
"little concerto," or concertino. The concertino, perhaps influenced by the
trio sonata, favored an ensemble of two violins and figured bass (cello and
harpsichord). This style of composing and playing was applied to many genres; it is found in the suite, chamber sonata, and opera sinfonia, as well as in
instrumentally accompanied church music. Formally speaking, what came to
be called a concerto grosso usually amounted to a church sonata, sometimes
interspersed with dance movements.

CHAMBER MUSIC AND ORCHESTRAL MUSIC BEFORE CORELLI

Among the three aforementioned pioneers of violin playing, Marini exerted
the strongest influence, with many works specifically intended for the violin.
He became the model for generations of violinist-composers, many of
whom, in court chapels and cathedral orchestras, were eager to write string
music for their own daily use, based on their practical playing experience.
Such works at first were published in large collections (parts only, no scores),
but eventually an edition contained twelve works typically. Early editions
included variously scored works, as shown by these representative titles:

1650   Andrea Falconiero, *Il primo libro di canzone, sinfonie, fantasie,*
             capricci, brandi, correnti, gagliarde, alemane, volte per violini, e viole,
             overo altro stromento à uno, due, e trè con il basso continuo, Naples
1651   Massimiliano Neri, *Sonate da sonarsi con varii stromenti a trè sino a*
             dodeci op. 2, Venice
1663   Giovanni Legrenzi, *Sonate a 2, 3, 5 e 6 istromenti* op. 8, Venice
1667   Giovanni Maria Bononcini, *Sonate da camera e da ballo a 1, 2, 3, e*
             4 op. 2, Venice

The collection by Neri contains:

> 3 Sonate a 3
> 2 Sonate a 4
> 1 Sonata a 5
> 2 Sonate a 6
> 1 Sonata a 7
> 1 Sonata a 8
> 1 Sonata a 9
> 2 Sonate a 10
> 2 Sonate a 12

The instruments specified are violino, viola, fagotto, basso, viola da brazzo,
cornetti, tromboni, violetta, teorbo, and flauti.

Later buyers preferred a volume of sonatas, all for the same instrument. Titles, however, were slow in indicating this, often referring to *ad libitum* (optional) parts, as in D. Marco Uccellini's *Sinfonie boscarecie a violino solo e basso, con l'agiunta di due altri violini ad libitum, per poter sonare à due, à trè, e à quattro conforme piacerà* op. 2 (Antwerp 1669). Most favored was the trio sonata, which Schenk (1955) called "the genre of baroque music most often played today." In his introduction Schenk offers an extensive list of such works by Italian composers. It is significant that titles indicated the scoring, but not the contents, for this music appealed chiefly to the consumer's needs. If he regularly played trio sonatas at home, he wanted to know from a collection's title whether it was appropriate for his group. The custom was kept up during the classic and romantic periods, when sonatas were designated not by form but by the instruments needed: string quartet, piano trio, and so on.

Designations found in baroque music may need some explanation. "Sonata a violino solo" normally did not refer to an unaccompanied work, but to a sonata for violin and basso continuo. Customary instruments were as follows:

1) For the top (melody) part: violin, but also other instruments having approximately the same range, such as, at first, the cornetto, and later the recorder, transverse flute, or oboe. If double stops (for the violin) occurred, one note would be omitted; if out of the instrument's range, a note might be transposed an octave up or down.
2) For the figured bass: a melody instrument (cello, bass gamba, bassoon) and a harmony instrument (harpsichord, organ, lute, and others). Ideally, both were (and should be) used, so that the harmonies called for by the figures will be realized, and the bass line (played by a melody instrument) will have the necessary weight.

Accordingly, for a good performance of a violin "solo" sonata, three instruments were desirable. Violin, cello, and harpsichord are now most common, but many options existed, based on what instruments were available in a home. Even the harmony instrument alone would do for the continuo, just as it is possible to play such a sonata using only violin and cello, without a chord instrument.

For a trio sonata ("sonata a tre") the composer provided three parts: the two upper voices and the figured bass. What was just said about the bass applies here as well, so that normally four instruments would play a trio sonata. Again, any melody instruments of the appropriate range could play the upper parts; combinations such as oboe and violin or flute and violin were frequent.

Only rarely was the second melody part intended for the gamba or cello. This may have led to the practice of cellists playing the second part, transposing it down an octave. Such a use of three instruments anticipates the later piano trio.

Trio sonatas could also be played with several players on a part, as long as the work was structurally simple and did not require very advanced violin technique. Italian composers especially wrote great quantities of trio sonatas, often publishing them in groups of twelve. It appears that the viola had lost some of its importance, especially in music making in the home. Few amateurs at the time played the viola.

In works for more than three voices the titles do not tell us whether they refer to a chamber group or orchestra. Giovanni Battista Vitali's op. 11 is a case in point: *Varie sonate alla francese, & all'itagliana à sei stromenti* (Modena 1684). These include violins 1, 2, and 3; alto viola; tenor viola; and small harpsichord ("spinetta") or bass. Fully scored works such as this one were primarily intended for public or festive occasions, which suggests orchestral doubling. Scoring was determined by the occasion and venue. Muffat relates that such works could also be heard at home, presumably with a less-full-sounding complement.

GERMANY AND AUSTRIA IN THE SEVENTEENTH CENTURY

Because of their geographical and political situations, coupled with inter-marriages between ruling families, both Germany and Austria were strongly affected by influences from abroad. Important ancient trade routes connected them, by way of the Brenner and Loibl Passes, with Lombardy and the Veneto. Ever since the days of Hassler, Schütz, and others, a period of study in Italy had been imperative for young composers from the north. As a result, new ideas about music quickly found their way back across the Alps.

In their writings, which reached many, Praetorius and others described these innovations in great detail. When Italian opera conquered all Europe, Munich, Vienna, and Dresden became important centers for the cultivation of Italian music.

As early as 1554, German violinists are known to have joined their Italian colleagues in Munich and soon became eager students. Versatility in matters of style was a must, for French dances were performed in addition to Italian music and even English music, such as William Brade and others had imported, especially to northern Germany. Brade was a Danish court musician before he worked in various north German cities, usually for the town council. He exerted considerable influence on German violin playing, excelling not only at dance music (the usual fare of town bands) but also in virtuosic displays, as required in his sets of variations.

A preface by Schütz (*Symphoniae sacrae*, part 2, 1647) informs us about the level of accomplishment of German musicians. He was not entirely satisfied with his violinists in Dresden. Among other admonitions, he urged them (timeless advice!) to "practice their parts before a performance, especially rapid passages and broad bow strokes, for these are not sufficiently known among us Germans."

The compositions of Nicolas Bleyer (ca. 1590–1658), a Brade pupil, and of the South German Johann Schop, give us an idea about the state of soloistic violin playing in early seventeenth-century Germany. Those works of Bleyer that have been preserved require a well-developed technique for bowing and double stop playing. Schop, the leader of the Hamburg town musicians, composed suites ca. 1640 that also reveal advanced violinistic features.

Johann Heinrich (von) Schmeltzer (b. ca. 1623, d. 1680 in Vienna), a leading Austrian musician, was first violinist in the imperial chapel in Vienna ("primo violinista della Capella Caesarea"), active at court since 1649. Of special significance are his sonatas for one violin and continuo (Nuremberg 1664), which demonstrate a degree of technical accomplishment that puts him on par with Italian composers.

Thomas Baltzar (b. ca. 1630, d. 1663) was a fourth-generation member of a family of organists and town musicians. A highly talented violinist, he was appointed to the orchestra of Queen Christina of Sweden when he was twenty years old. In 1655 he went to England, where he attracted attention with his new way of holding the violin under his chin, by playing in the highest positions then possible (the fingerboard still being shorter), by skillful use of double stops, and by his bowing technique. Works in variation form were much in vogue then in England; Baltzar's show well his command of technique (see example). Unfortunately, excessive drinking forced him to cede the concertmaster's position of the Twenty-four Violins of the King to Banister. His vice "took him to the grave," as a contemporary chronicler put it, bringing to an end the career of a promising composer.

A major figure in seventeenth-century German music was Nicolaus Adam Strungk (b. 1640 in Braunschweig), the son of Delphin Strungk, composer and organist. Mattheson relates that at the age of seventeen he went to Lübeck where, under the tutelage of N. Schnittelbach, a then-famous violinist, he developed an uncommon talent. He was employed in Wolfenbüttel, Celle, Hamburg, and Hanover, and undertook successful journeys to Vienna. In Italy he met Corelli, who is said to have been amazed by Strungk's double stop playing and frequent use of *scordatura* (special tunings). His successful career ended in Dresden in 1701. Operas, church music, and instrumental works are all part of his *oeuvre*, but unfortunately the work that would be most interesting for violinists has not been preserved: his *Musicalische Übung auf der Violin und Viola da Gamba* (Dresden 1691).

New heights of violin playing and composing were reached in Austria by Heinrich von Biber (1644–1704) and in Germany by Johann Jacob Walther. Biber came from the hamlet of Wartenberg near Reichenberg in Bohemia. He may have been a pupil of Schmeltzer in Vienna, then worked in Olmütz and Kremsier before settling in Salzburg, where he rose to the positions of kapellmeister and steward. The emperor ennobled him in 1690. Biber was in contact with Jacobus Stainer, arranging for the sale of some of Stainer's instruments to the bishop of Olmütz. In a letter Stainer stressed that the outstanding virtuoso, Herr Biber, "surely would vouch" for the instruments' quality.

Biber's chief contribution to the violin repertory are fifteen sonatas with continuo "in honor of the fifteen mysteries in the life of the Virgin Mary," published ca. 1674. Some of these are one-movement sonatas; the set ends with a passacaglia for unaccompanied violin.

This is absolute, non-programmatic music, though every sonata has a title, such as "The Archangel Gabriel Announces Christ's Birth to Mary," "The Shepherds at the Cradle," "Christ's Suffering and Struggles on the Mount of Olives," "Christ Crowned with Thorns," "Christ's Ascension," "Mary's Ascension," and "The Coronation of the Virgin." The work was inspired by the celebrations of the rosary, held in October. As Beckmann (1918) explained it, "The number 15, and the subjects of the fifteen pictures, correspond exactly to the . . . prayers of the rosary. Five are joyful, five sorrowful, and five . . . glorious." Technical requirements go far beyond those of contemporary Italian works such as Corelli's. Positions up to the seventh are called for, along with effects hardly heard before:

10. Sonate, 4. Variation

Skordatur

Biber loved to experiment with *scordatura*, which practice was not new (Marini used *scordatura* in his op. 8). Sympathetic strings in particular were usually tuned according to the requirements of the passage or composition in question; standard tunings were only gradually introduced. At times Biber's tunings are quite ingenious (example a). *Scordatura* normally used a "finger" rather than an actual pitch notation, making it unnecessary for the player to transpose. [For a more detailed explanation, see, for instance, the article "Scordatura" in the *Harvard Dictionary. Ed.*] Thus fifths become octaves and sevenths become tenths (example b). To indicate this finger notation, special key signatures are provided (example c).

a

b

c

Scordatura makes possible special arpeggio and bariolage effects in a particular key, but the unusual tunings present problems to the performer. Our strings are manufactured for specific pitches; they stay reasonably well in tune if always tuned to those pitches. If tuned higher, they may break, if tuned lower, tone quality suffers. When normal tuning is resumed, it usually takes several days before the strings again stay in tune. If the player is required to change the tuning during a concert, or especially within one piece, poor intonation inevitably results. For this reason players now resort to a second instrument that is tuned to the special pitches several days before the concert. Actually, Biber's tuning (example a) is impractical today, for the D string will not tolerate the excessive tension when tuned up to g′, while the A string's sound, if tuned down to d′, is completely unsatisfactory. Most likely Biber exchanged the D and A strings; in that case he only had to tune the A string down to g′. In all these situations it is best to use a specially prepared violin, just as concertmasters now do for playing the *scordatura* solo in the Scherzo of Mahler's Fourth Symphony. In his "Rosary" or "Mystery" Sonatas, Biber uses sixteen different tunings:

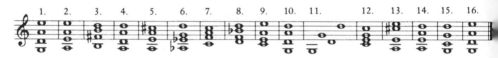

Some of this may seem like playing games, but it does not detract from Biber's significance as a composer. The passacaglia for solo violin that ends the "Mystery" Sonatas is a remarkable work; its form and exploration of the violin's possibilities point to Bach's famous Chaconne. A descending bass figure (G–F–E-flat–D) is repeated sixty-five times. In some statements it moves to the top line, sometimes it is varied. While there is no tempo indication, the insertion of an Adagio followed by Allegro suggests an Allegro moderato tempo for the opening. It is a work for a player with well-above-average technique.

Johann Jacob Walther (ca. 1650–1717) carried virtuosity to even greater heights. Born near Erfurt, he is said to have learned violin playing "from a Polish gentleman whom he served," largely by watching him, as J. G. Walther, his namesake, said in his lexicon. He may have studied in Florence and Rome; at the age of twenty-three he became "primo violinista di camera" at the Dresden court. In 1681 he went to Mainz, where he held a secretary's appointment to the bishop-elector and rose to the rank of *canonicus*. Walther's contributions to violin playing consist of two major works, the *Scherzi da violino solo con il basso continuo* (Frankfurt or Mainz 1676) and the collection *Hortulus chelicus* (Mainz 1688), which deals with playing "on two, three, and sometimes four strings at the same time." Both works were soon reprinted.

Perhaps inspired by Farina, Walther composed some programmatic works and also attempted to have the violin imitate other instruments. In the *Hortulus*, entire pizzicato movements are intended to sound like harp, lute, guitar, and even timpani. The cellist is instructed to play the basso continuo pizzicato. Walther may have been the first composer to call for left-hand pizzicato. What he thought he could have his listeners hear is revealed in the curious title of one of the works in the *Hortulus*: "Serenade for a solo violin, representing a chorus of violins, an organ playing tremolo, a small guitar, a shawm, two trumpets and timpani, a German lira, and a muted harp." Walther must have had an amazing bowing technique, to judge by thirty-second-note passages executed with rapid saltato (bouncing) arpeggio bowing. He also called for staccato extending over thirty-two notes—presumably our "flying" staccato. His typically German fondness for polyphonic playing, at times in three or four parts, points to Bach.

Johann Paul von Westhoff (1656–1705) was an important and in some ways strange figure. He was not strictly a violinist by profession, but at various times held positions as court secretary and diplomat. He lived in Dresden when Walther resided there, took part in a campaign against the Turks in Hungary, then spent time in Italy and Paris, where he successfully played for Louis XIV and published some works. Later he went to Weimar. J. S. Bach probably knew him personally when for a short time Walther was violinist and violist in the ducal chapel of Johann Ernst of Saxony-Weimar. The acquaintance is significant because polyphonic violin playing was one of Westhoff's special interests. A *Sonata senza basso*—that is, truly unaccompanied—was published in Paris in 1693. It is one of his best works, a variations suite consisting of Prelude, Allemande, Courante, Sarabande, and Gigue (with "autre Gigue"). In it, the violin's possibilities are very imaginatively explored. Bach may have remembered Westhoff's works when he wrote his six sonatas and partitas for unaccompanied violin.

Mattheson (*Grundlage einer Ehren-Pforte*, 1740) relates an unusual example of improvisational skill by Nikolaus Bruhns (1665–1697), organist in Husum and a Buxtehude pupil. Bruhns was a fine violinist who continued Baltzar's tradition of polyphonic playing. He occasionally improvised on the violin while seated on the organ bench, providing a pedal bass line for the violin part. Bruhns, however, left no violin compositions.

FRANCE AND ENGLAND IN THE
SEVENTEENTH CENTURY

The violin had been introduced to France early and quickly. [See Anthony 1997, ch. 1. *Ed.*] Given Baltazarini's influential role at the French court, and in view of the founding of the Vingt-quatre Violons du Roi in 1626, one might expect that France played a leading role in seventeenth-century violin playing. For a number of reasons, however, France (and also England, culturally rather dependent on France) gradually lost touch with the main trends. For dancing, an art in which the French traditionally excelled, the bright sound of the violin was thought to be particularly inspiring, and the French imported Italian violinists along with the instrument. France also adopted a cautious stance toward opera and for a long time preferred ballets, somewhat operatic though some of them were. String players often participated in costume. We know of a ballet performance in 1628 during which violinists wore face masks on the back of their heads and moved backward. Spectators thus were given the impression that the musicians played with the instruments behind their back.

The development of the sonata in Italy was tied to a new technique of playing, using long and elegant bow strokes quite different from the short, rhythmic, dancelike strokes. The stylistic, formal differences were conscious and aesthetic and led to extensive polemic writing. True, Fontenelle's famous saying "Sonate, que me veux-tu?" (what do you mean to me?) was not coined until the eighteenth century, but the thought behind it characterizes seventeenth-century French thinking about music. It expresses a mentality that found music incomprehensible except in connection with actions and words. At any rate, French violin playing for a long time did not advance very significantly beyond its state of development in the second half of the sixteenth century. The bow continued to be held with the thumb on the bow hair, which promoted a strong but heavy, cumbersome stroke. Left-hand technique seldom went above the first position.

The creation of the royal string orchestra did little to raise the mediocre level of French violin playing, for the technique needed for playing the top line in five-part dances did not go beyond what has just been described. In 1639 André Maugars, a well-known French gamba player who trained in England, reported on his visit to Rome. Though he did not hear any outstanding gambist, he was impressed by the high level of violin playing, especially of rapid notes.

Mersenne had words of high praise for French violinists, but his judgment may have been clouded by a lack of opportunity for making comparisons and was likely based on French musicians' playing dance music, a field in which they specialized.

At the age of twelve, Lully (1632–1687) left Florence for Paris, where he was employed at court. He quickly rose from the post of composer of instrumental music to "surintendant (supervisor) de musique" and "maître de la musique de la famille royale." Lully was not satisfied with the Vingt-quatre Violons. When they objected to his orders, he (being the king's favorite) succeeded in having them reduced in importance, for Louis ordered him to form a small, elite orchestra, Les Petits Violons de Lully. At first it consisted of sixteen, later twenty-one players. In 1702 its official title became Violons du Cabinet, the king's private orchestra. As such it satisfied the king's musical needs, including playing for dinners and dances and providing music in the royal chambers. The select group included strings (6 / 2 / 3 / 2 / 4), two soprano cornettos, and two bassoons. With it, Lully established the high standards that later called forth Georg Muffat's glowing description, but their playing with such perfection hardly extended beyond dancelike music.

Among the reasons for Lully's difficulties with the Vingt-quatre Violons was their being conditioned by age-old traditions of guild membership, still typical for seventeenth-century French musicians. In 1321, following the example of artisans, Paris musicians organized a guild that a few years later became known as the Confrérie de St. Julien des Ménétriers (musicians' brotherhood of St. Julien). Having been granted royal privileges, the organization soon extended to all France, though it encountered some resistance. Members jealously guarded their prerogatives, prohibiting nonmembers from playing in public. Their leader originally was known as "roi des ménétriers" (king of the musicians), a title that in the sixteenth century changed to "roi des violons," reflecting the violin's rise to prominence. In 1590 Claude Nyon (Nion), a member of the royal orchestra, became the guild's head. The position paid 40,000 francs annually, which made it very desirable. It usually went to a member of the royal chapel.

The guild operated, basically unchanged, until 1773. It was important to be a member because being a professional musician usually was combined with the very lucrative position of dance master. Thus in 1742 François Hanot, composer of six published violin sonatas, was "maître de danse et de violon" in Tournai. In 1612 Michael Praetorius said of his own collection of dance tunes that they were composed by French dancers, "most of them also excellent violinists or lutanists." His collaborator in Wolfenbüttel was the French violinist Caroubel. In Paris, according to Praetorius, were some three hundred dance masters, some of whom also composed.

Every dance teacher was expected to play the *pochette*, a small, very flat violin that comfortably fit into a pocket on the right trouser leg. This requirement lasted into the early nineteenth century. In his book *Notes sans musique* [1949, Engl. trans. 1952] Darius Milhaud recalls that his first music teacher in Aix-en-Provence was the son of a dance teacher who accompanied his pupils on a miniature violin.

The guild statutes of 1658 are quite informative. A normal period of apprenticeship was four years, three at the least. A master who disregarded this rule was fined 150 livres, with equal amounts going to the state, the guild, and the roi des violons. A fee was paid at the beginning, a signed contract was deposited with the guild, and the apprentice was required to live in the master's house. At the end of the course of instruction an examination took place in the presence of the roi who usually was assisted by twenty masters—only ten if the candidate was a master's son. The master's diploma was issued on payment of 60 livres into the guild's treasury; for masters' sons the fee was reduced to 25 livres. Masters were always eager to marry off their daughters, as is implied in paragraph 5: "If the husband of a master's daughter aspires to become a master himself, he may enroll as a master's son and will be treated as one."

Unlawful competition by nonmembers resulted in severe fines: 100 livres and confiscation of the instrument at the first infraction, corporal punishment for repeated ones.

A roi des violons had the right to appoint a lieutenant or deputy in every town, ensuring ruthless enforcement of all privileges. Many legal disputes resulted from this. In 1662, however, the king permitted thirteen Paris dance

LE MAITRE DE DANSE

Maitre habile en cet art, qui plait tant au bel âge ,
  N'es-tu point gagé par l'Amour ,
Pour que la jeune Iris ait la puissance un jour
De mettre tous les cœurs dans un doux esclavage ?

Ah ! pour un tel dessein tes soins sont superflus :
  Sans l'orner de graces nouvelles ,
Par les seules beautez qui lui sont naturelles ,
Tous ceux qui la verront, seront bientost vaincues .

Moreau?

Paris chez J.P. Le Bas graveur du Cabinet du Roy, dans la porte cochere au bas de la rué de la Harpe, Avec Privilege du Roy.

Engraving by Le Bas, 1745, after a painting by Ph. Canot
(Berlin, Kupferstichkabinett)

teachers to found the Académie de Danse, which succeeded in gaining independence from the guild—the first breach in the guild's stranglehold. Ten years later Lully, armed with a royal privilege, founded the Académie Royale de Musique. Its statutes specify its function: "To train pupils in the art of good singing and acting, also to form orchestras of violins, flutes, and other instruments." For all practical purposes this ended the guild's monopoly on instrumental instruction as well. In 1728, members of the opera orchestra were granted permission to use their free time for any musical activities whatever, even if they did not belong to the guild, an edict that further eroded guild membership. After ca. 1750, no restrictions of any kind were enforced; as a result, the guild was dissolved in 1773, the position of roi des violons abandoned, and all guilds were dissolved in 1776. On 1 April 1791 complete freedom to pursue any trade was proclaimed.

We know few details about the training of aspiring professional musicians except that during the seventeenth century it was conducted in a master-pupil arrangement. Quite likely the emphasis was not on acquiring highly developed mastery of one instrument but on acquiring a working knowledge of several, such as professionals were likely to need. Instruction in the rudiments of fingering and bowing led to practicing the contents of the standard collections of dances. As soon as he was ready, the apprentice was taken along on engagements, which added to the income of the master, who was responsible for the apprentice's room and board. In this way the student might acquire basic skills but hardly any artistic perception or expertise. Some masters, of course, may not have been eager to train apprentices so well that they became competitors.

Few seventeenth-century French court violinists were above-average performers; the exceptions were Lazarin (d. ca. 1653), Louis Constantin (d. 1657), and Guillaume du Manoir (d. 1697). According to an old story, if a dance tune went up to a high C ("ut"), violinists would alert each other by calling out, "Gare l'ut!" (watch out—a high C!), but this may just have been an "in" joke among orchestra musicians. There are reports, however, that even in the early eighteenth century French players were greatly challenged by Corelli's trio sonatas. Though the skills of French players may have been below those of their Italian and German colleagues, the gradual decline of the guild's power had a favorable result: the number of players grew, so that every nobleman was in a position to have his own small orchestra. A few professional players formed the nucleus; members of the household personnel supplied the rest. Some servants were hired primarily for other tasks because they also played the violin; others received on-the-job training.

Given the French specialization and excellence in dance music, and the widespread imitation of French court ceremonial, this repertory and manner of playing were heard everywhere. Georg Muffat (b. 1653 in Savoy) has provided much information on Lully's improvements in orchestra playing and on the interpretation of French ballet music. Muffat was educated in Paris. After appointments in the Alsace, Vienna, and Prague, his career took him to Salzburg, where he was court organist. Later he was employed as kapellmeister by the archbishop of Passau. A scholarship provided by his Salzburg employer enabled him to visit Rome from 1681 to 1682; there he studied with Bernardo Pasquini and came in close contact with Corelli. He then made it his principal task to inform his colleagues in Austria and southern Germany about performance practices in France and Italy.

The prefaces to Muffat's collections of dances entitled *Florilegium musicum* (part 1, Augsburg 1695; part 2, Passau 1698) are the most valuable source of information about stylistic matters. They are written in Latin, German, Italian, and French. Chapters on "how to perform ballets in the Lullyan-French manner" are clearly organized; they deal with fingering, bowing, tempo, and orchestral conventions, including embellishments. Muffat's advice about bowing is especially important. He not only clarifies the differences between the Italian and Franco-German manner of holding the bow, but with copious music examples clarifies details of the Lully style with which we are no longer familiar. About the example given here Muffat says, "At a fast tempo, on the second and third beats one uses a bouncing up-bow," that is, lifting the bow rather than playing staccato or portato.

A light, springy sound would result at a moderate to fast tempo. "If the speed permits it," even notes should be played as dotted notes. About the following two examples he says that the first sounds "tired, plump, and unpleasant," while the second represents "the modified, nobler manner"—the *notes inégales*.

Muffat's explanations are all the more important because German suite composers during the first half of the eighteenth century completely adopted the French style, not only in the choice and formal treatment of the dances but also in the manner of performing them. Bach called attention to the special situation of German musicians, who had to be familiar not only with the French style but with the style of other nations as well. In his famous memorandum of 23 August 1730, addressed to the Leipzig city council, he said, "Truly, it is amazing that one expects German musicians to play at sight all kinds of music, whether of Italian, French, English, or Polish provenance." For the study of French style, Muffat's *Florilegium* is the best source of information.

Soon after 1700 the violin's position in society changed radically. In 1705, *Le Cerf de la Viéville* reported that few members of the nobility played the violin. Yet by 25 November 1728, when Guignon was to perform the first concerto of Vivaldi's *Four Seasons* for the king, members of the high nobility filled in for missing orchestra members.

At the beginning of the seventeenth century, English violin playing displayed few indigenous traits. Light French court music served as the model; later some aspects of Lully's orchestra discipline were adopted. When Thomas Baltzar arrived from Germany (ca. 1655) and Nicola Matteis from Italy (ca. 1672), their playing caused a sensation, which throws some light on the standards of the English court chapel. Matteis, who was also a guitar virtuoso, was chiefly responsible for introducing the new Italian style of violin playing to England. His own compositions show that he had observed something of the German tradition. He also may have imitated English gamba playing on the violin, both of which are reflected in double stop playing. Some movements carry titles such as "Fuga à due corde" and "Giga à due corde difficile." An extended "Fantasia a violino solo senza basso" comes close to Bach's works in that genre, displaying concentrated motivic writing.

Davies Mell (1604–1662), at first a watchmaker, was one of the major English violinists of the time, but not quite the equal of his colleagues from abroad. John I Banister (d. 1679) succeeded Mell as concertmaster of the royal chapel. In 1672 he began offering public concerts at his home in White Friars, London; they were continued until his death, giving an impetus to English instrumental music. Thomas Britton, a coal merchant, also organized concerts that often included violin music. John Banister II (ca. 1663–1735) studied with his father. He is credited with having introduced Corelli's op. 5 to England.

Though the purchase of two Cremona violins for the chapel of Charles II is documented, it took the English a long time to warm up to violin playing. An entry in Ecelyn's diary (21 December 1662) reflects this:

> One of the royal chaplains preached. Following this, instead of the venerable, serious, and solemn wind music with organ accompaniment, we heard, during every interval, 24 violins. They played in the eccentric, frivolous French manner that is more suitable for tavern and theater than for the church.

CORELLI AND VIOLIN MUSIC AT THE END OF THE SEVENTEENTH CENTURY

Quite likely Corelli was not the greatest violinist of his time. He did not follow in the footsteps of Farina and others who had succeeded in gradually exploring the highest regions of the fingerboard, nor did he experiment with *scordatura*, like Biber, or with polyphonic writing as cultivated by the German school. Nevertheless ca. 1700 he was Italy's foremost violinist-composer, whose works were more often performed throughout Europe than those of any others. The explanation is this: among violinists he was the best composer, and among composers he was the best violinist. This balance of talents, combined with a quiet, harmonious personality, resulted in a slow but steady development that reached a high point in works written late in his life.

Arcangelo Corelli was born in 1653 in Fusignano near Faenza, where he received his first musical instruction. At the age of thirteen he was taken to Bologna, where the orchestra at the San Petronio cathedral was becoming an important center of instrumental music. Ercole Gaibara was the founder of the Bologna school of violin playing; among his pupils were Giovanni Benvenuti, Leonardo Brugnoli (famous for his improvisational skill), and G. N. Laurenti. These three are said to have been the teachers of Corelli, who later in Rome was called "Il Bolognese."

Corelli is known to have been a church violinist in Rome since 1675; he soon acted as concertmaster in opera performances. On one such occasion the Abbé Raguenet heard him, along with Pasquini (harpsichord) and Gaetano (theorbo), remarking in 1702 that they were "the world's best players of violin, harpsichord, and theorbo or archlute." He further noted that each of the three was paid the extraordinary fee of 300 to 400 pistols for a stagione no longer than six weeks.

In 1681 Corelli published his op. 1, dedicated to Queen Christina of Sweden. She had abdicated the throne, converted to Catholicism, and after 1655 lived in Rome, where her palace became a major artistic and scientific center. In 1687 Cardinal Benedetto Panfili appointed Corelli as his maestro di musica; eventually Pietro Ottoboni, who was a cardinal at the age of twenty-two and a nephew of Pope Alexander VIII, became Corelli's patron. The composer was a member of several artistic academies and directed Ottoboni's musical events. Up to his death in 1713 Corelli was one of Rome's leading musicians. His estate included not only valuable instruments and considerable funds, but also 136 paintings and drawings by artists of his acquaintance and major figures such as Breughel and Poussin. Among his violins were one each by Albani and Andrea Amati. Corelli was buried in the Pantheon next to Raphael; the inscription on his marble tombstone refers to him as one who will be among the immortals.

Corelli's works with opus numbers are as follows:

1681   (12) Sonate a tre (church sonatas), op. 1, Rome
1685   (12) Sonate da camera (2 vns and b.c.), op. 2, Rome
1689   (12) Sonate a tre (church sonatas), op. 3, Rome
1694   (12) Sonate a tre (chamber sonatas), op. 4, Rome
1700   (12) Sonate a violino, op. 5, Rome
1714   (12) Concerti grossi, op. 6, Amsterdam

These collections met with tremendous success, attesting to a great demand for music in an age when violin playing and the cultivation of chamber music were more than merely fashionable. The op. 1 sonatas were reprinted twelve times in the decade following their publication; op. 2 seventeen times. Even greater was the success of op. 5: these twelve sonatas were printed in Amsterdam and London within the year of their Rome publication. By 1815 there were forty-two editions. The op. 6 concerti grossi became the standby of all string orchestras; even now hardly a collegium musicum or school orchestra gets along without them. Countless arrangements of Corelli's music were made. Geminiani transformed the violin sonatas into concerti grossi, and Pepusch added a viola to the three solo instruments of op. 6. (Schoenberg made a similar arrangement of a baroque concerto grosso.) Some of Corelli's *oeuvre* belongs to the small body of baroque music that survived the great style change ca. 1750 and has never been completely forgotten.

The secret of Corelli's success can be seen in his trio sonatas, which met the need of his age for solid string music—music that grew out of the spirit and expressive potential of the instruments. It is music of high quality, yet it offers no insurmountable hurdles to any violinist who has practiced diligently for a few years.

The op. 5 sonatas go considerably beyond that. Sonatas 1–6 are church sonatas, nos. 7–11 are chamber sonatas. No. 12 consists of a set of variations on a melody known as "La Follia," or "Folies d'Espagne" (Follies of Spain). The tune, in saraband rhythm, goes back to the fourteenth century. Some movements in op. 5, especially in the church sonatas, require virtuoso skills for both left and right hands. The second movement of the Third Sonata, for instance, is a kind of written-out closing cadenza over a pedal point on the dominant:

Such movements provided excellent study material; some definitely convey the impression that they were written for pedagogical purposes. The third movement of the Fourth Sonata, for instance, provides practice material for fourth-finger extensions or for second-position playing:

It is no surprise that Giuseppe Tartini, the eighteenth century's leading violin pedagogue, made Corelli's op. 5 the basis of his teaching program; every one of his many students was expected to practice it. Corelli's fugal movements no doubt inspired many later composers of violin etudes, especially Fiorillo and Kreutzer, and indeed much later polyphonic writing for the violin. They demonstrate that musical-formal considerations were foremost, that violin technique served musical ends.

An edition of these sonatas published by Estienne Roger (Amsterdam 1710) shows how players would breathe life into the bare notes of a slow movement by adding ornamentation. The title page refers to this as a "new edition, enlarged by embellishments of the Adagio movements as played by Corelli." Certain movements also exist in another version by the English violinist Dubourg, published as "Corelli's Solos: grac'd by Dubourg." It is instructive to compare the original text with the embellishments of the Amsterdam print (quite certainly by Corelli, as Pincherle proved in his Corelli biography) and with those by Dubourg.

Corelli's op. 6 concerti grossi represent the prototype of a genre that goes back to Alessandro Stradella. In 1682, when he attended rehearsals in Corelli's residence in Rome, Georg Muffat had occasion to observe the delightful interaction between a three-part solo group and the full orchestra. The works in question may have been from op. 6. These concerti grossi greatly advanced the development of string playing. The three soloists' parts are challenging but generally do not go beyond what was customary at the time, while the orchestral parts, the "grosso," could be handled by players of moderate accomplishment. Structurally, these works were not yet entirely idiomatic; the number of players could be greatly varied without affecting the sound adversely. In 1687 Corelli was commanded by Queen Christina to provide music for a festive event honoring Pope Innocent XI. On that occasion he conducted an orchestra of 150 string players, probably performing his own church sonatas and orchestral works.

Corelli's concerti grossi are characterized by rather short groups of motives, usually two to four measures long, shared by and alternating between solo and tutti sections. In the dance movements (whether or not they are designated as such) the repeats of eight-measure phrases sometimes bring changes in instrumentation. Movements in which the solo violin dominates or has long passage work are rare; during his late years Corelli does not seem to have been influenced by features of the emerging solo concerto.

As Corelli's fame as a composer spread, he became increasingly sought after as a violin teacher. Among the more important students were Geminiani, Locatelli, Mascitti, and Somis. Others are now little known since they did not distinguish themselves as composers. Most of them eventually developed their own style as violinists, but they all received a thorough grounding in technique that predestined them to become interpreters of the best repertory. Corelli also taught many amateur violinists, most of them members of the nobility. Their love of chamber music partially accounts for the many printed editions of the master's works.

SEVENTEENTH-CENTURY
VIOLIN INSTRUCTION BOOKS

During the first century of the violin's development, most players had come to it from another string instrument. They simply transferred their earlier experience with bowed instruments to the violin. As yet instruction books meant specifically for the violin were not needed. More important than playing technique was the skill of ornamentation, especially for those playing upper-range melody instruments. As a result, the first instructional works in which the word "violin" appears in the title are those acquainting the player with "passagi," meaning runs, passage work, ornamentation, and diminution. Executing some of these required considerable skill and velocity, which suggests that such models also were used for developing technique. Exercises intended for singing could also be studied by instrumentalists, for instance, the *Regole passagi di musica: Madrigali, e motetti passegiati* (Rules of diminution: Ornamented madrigals and motets) by Giovanni Bovicelli (Venice 1594), a singer in the Milan cathedral. He instructs singers on how to "fill in" the interval of a fifth, which example could also be used for elementary fingering and bowing exercises.

Instruction books that later would be called violin methods or tutors appeared only slowly during the seventeenth century, but information about violin playing often can be found hidden away in more general musical treatises, in prefaces to compositions, and even in handwritten notes. Tablatures, as "finger" notation, can provide insights into the state of violin technique and pedagogy. Therefore the following list of the more important seventeenth-century pedagogical works includes some that deal with violin playing but are not primarily instruction books.

1601	Scipione Cerretto, *Della prattica musica vocale et strumentale*, Naples (rpt. Bologna 1969)
1614	Francesco Rognoni, *Aggiunta del scolare di violino* (lost)
1620	Francesco Rognoni, *Selva de varii passaggi secondo l'uso moderno*, Milan (rpt. Bologna 1969)
1621/29	Dario Castello, *Sonate concertante in stile moderno*, Venice
1623	Daniel Hitzler, *Extract Auss der Neuen Musica Oder Singkunst*, Nuremberg
ca. 1630	Anonymous, *Principia sopra'l violino*, along with another manuscript in the Breslau Municipal Library, mus. mss. 115 and 113
1636/37	Marin Mersenne, *Harmonie universelle* (2 vols.), Paris (Engl. trans. The Hague 1957)
ca. 1640	Pierre Trichet, *Traité des instruments de musique* (manuscript) Ms. 114 in the Breslau Municipal Library
1642	Johann Andreas Herbst, *Musica practica, sive instructio pro symphoniacis*, Nuremberg
1645	Gasparo Zanetti, *Il scolaro per imparar a suonare di violino ed altri stromenti*, Milan
1658	John Playford, *A Briefe Introduction to the Skill of Musick for Song and Viol . . . Second Book, Directions for the Playing on the Viol de Gambo and also on the Treble Violin*, London (12th ed. 1694; rpt. New York 1972)
1659	Christopher Simpson, *The Division Violist, or An Introduction to the Playing upon a Ground*, London (a later edition contains "instructions for the treble-violin, several lessons for the violin, both by notes and letters"; facsim. rpt. London 1978)
1669	Matthias Kelz, *Epidigma harmoniae novae*, Augsburg
ca. 1669	John Playford, *Apollo's Banquet for the Treble-Violin . . . to which Is Added the Tunes of the French Dances also Rules and Directions for Practitioners on the Treble-Violin*, London

ca. 1672	Thomas Salmon, *Essay to the Advancement of Musick*, London
1676/85	Nicola Matteis, *Ayres of the Violin*, London (books 1 and 2, 1676; books 3 and 4, 1685)
1678	John Jenkins, *New Lessons for Viols or Violins*, London
1682	Anonymous, *Ductor ad pandorum, or A Tutor for the Treble Violin*, London
1684/85	John Playford, *The Division Violin*, London
1687	*Clark's Introduction to the Violin*, London
	Johann Wilhelm Furchheim, *Auserlesenes Violin-Exercitium aus verschiedenen Sonaten, Arien, Balletten, Allemanden, Couranten, Sarabanden und Giguen von fünf Partien bestehend*, Dresden
	Daniel Speer, *Grund-richtiger kurtz leicht und nöthiger Unterricht der musicalischen Kunst*, Ulm
1688	Georg Falck, *Idea boni cantoris*, Nuremberg (rpt. Kassel 1990; Engl. trans. Baton Rouge, La., 1971)
1690	Johann Adam Reincken, *Hortus musicus*, Hamburg
1693	John Lenton, *The Gentleman's Diversion, or The Violin Explained*, London
1695	Anonymous, *The Self-Instructor on the Violin, or The Art of Playing on That Instrument*, London
	Anonymous, *Nolens volens, or You Shall Learn to Play on the Violin Whether You Will or No*, London
	Daniel Merck, *Compendium Musicae Instrumentalis Chelicae, das ist: Kurtzer Begrif, welcher Gestalten die Instrumental-Music auf der Violin, Pratschen, Viola da Gamba und Bass, gründlich und leicht zu erlernen seye*, Augsburg
1698	Georg Muffat, *Florilegium secundum*, Passau (rpt. Graz 1959)
1699	John Banister, *The Complete Tutor to the Violin*, London

Cerreto was a composer, theoretician, and lutanist as well as the author of several teaching methods, some of which exist only in manuscript. His 1601 publication is a general compendium of musical practices, most of it concerning composition and the art of embellishment. Instruction about playing a string instrument does not go much beyond Ganassi.

A work that is significant for both violin playing and more general musical matters is the *Nürnberger Tabulatur*, thirty-seven pages in length and described in detail by Beckmann. Johann Wolff Gerhard, probably an amateur violinist, began writing it on "26 September a.[nno] 1613." It contains both sacred and secular songs, along with dances. Each melody is followed by a variation; in multisectional melodies every section is varied immediately. All music is written in tablature, a manner of notation that fiddlers adopted from lute music and with which string players were familiar. On a four-line staff the lines represent the strings; the numbers indicate fingers. Note values are given above the staff; beams indicate tied notes. Several tablatures of this kind were in use. They resemble each other, though in Italian tablatures the E string is represented by the lowest line and the G string by the top line.

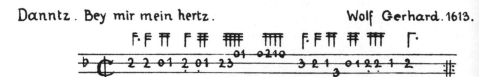

modern notation:

Francesco Rognoni's instruction book, in two parts, deals mostly with diminution. He discusses individual instruments in the second part and remarks that, unless it is carefully bowed, "the arm viol, especially the violin, has a rough, piercing sound." Rognoni recommends legato playing, tying together the notes in up to half a measure. For this he uses the term "lireggiare" (playing in the manner of a lira). Such legato playing no doubt was based on singers' vocalises. Rognoni's remark is of interest because of his aesthetic reservations about the violin, though he admits that these reservations would be modified by a refined bowing technique.

Dario Castello, Monteverdi's concertmaster in Venice, deemed it necessary to provide in a postscript explanatory commentary about his compositions, works that displayed quite an advanced violin technique. Such explanations are often found in seventeenth- and eighteenth-century publications.

Daniel Hitzler was a theologian and teacher of religion. His treatise *Neue Musica* (ca. 1615) has not been preserved, but an excerpt, published later, includes some instruction about violin playing.

The three manuscripts in the Breslau (now Wroclaw) Library, like Gerhard's tablature, represent efforts of the time to assemble material for teaching and practicing at home. According to its title, ms. 115 is decidedly a violin method, albeit rather elementary. Ms. 114 consists of sixty-eight pieces, most of which have titles such as "ricercare," "fantasie," "toccata," and "capriccio." They are technically more challenging, calling for double stops and playing up to the fifth position. According to Beckmann this manuscript dates from shortly before 1650. It is not a violin method as such but a collection of pieces for practicing, taken from well-known repertory. We learn that the Bergamasca no. 49 "came from Nuremberg," suggesting that an effort was made to locate music of this kind.

The title of Mersenne's famous work, "containing both the theory and practice of music," indicates its scope. Book 4 includes advice for violinists who wish to study "without the help of any teacher." There are no music examples.

Pierre Trichet showed even less concern with technique and pedagogy. His remarks deal with details of organology and music history.

Johann Andreas Herbst (d. 1666) was an efficient organizer of municipal music activities in Frankfurt on the Main. For major concerts he relied on an assistant kapellmeister to direct rehearsals. He provided a comprehensive pedagogical treatise, including a section on violin playing based on "the outstanding Italian authors." An enlarged second edition appeared within a few years; it amounts to a complete compendium of choral and orchestral practices of the time.

Gasparo Zanetti's 149-page book represents the first true instruction method, not only for the violin but for all instruments of the violin family. He used a sensible didactic approach, providing all music examples in two kinds of notation: normal notation on the left side, violin tablature on the right. This provided fingerings throughout, so that the player, whenever encountering difficulties with the normal notation, would find solutions on the right page. Fourth-finger extensions are occasionally called for; they are indicated by the numeral 5, a custom still used in the nineteenth century. The work consists of four sections:

Per la chiave maestra (for the principal clef): 13 exercises for playing in the G clef
Per la chiave in basso: 16 exercises in the bass clef, to be played on the cello
Per la chiave alta: 21 exercises in the alto clef
Balletti: 38 dances for four parts, scored for violin, two violas, and cello

In addition to the fingerings provided in the tablature, Zanetti supplies precise bowing instructions, using the letters T ("tirare"; down bow) and P ("puntare"; up bow). These show that all down beats call for down bows unless musical reasons dictate otherwise. Thus in triple meter, two measures often form a motivic and rhythmic unit, so that a real accent occurs only in every other measure. Often two notes are played on one bow, probably in a portato style, where meter and accent suggest this. Zanetti's instructions lead us to believe that at the time in Italy a less accented manner of bowing was also in use, especially in church sonatas, and that this manner soon found its way into the playing of the stylized dance movements of the sonata da camera.

The oft-quoted instructional works by John Playford (d. 1686) clearly show the gradual change from the gamba to the violin as the preferred instrument. Playford, both composer and publisher, had a keen instinct for noting trends in public taste. His first work deals with the gamba exclusively; only in its second edition did he add the short chapter "Direction for Playing the Viol de Gamba and Treble Violin." The latter term means "soprano of the violin family," that is, our violin. Beginning in 1651 Playford published collections of dances and other social music, some of which went through many editions. The *Briefe Introduction* is essentially this kind of collection, with little pedagogical value, but by 1730 it had gone through nineteen printings. Playford recommends that beginners use violins with frets that later could be discarded. He also considered tablatures merely an aid to beginners.

Christopher Simpson (d. 1669) was an outstanding player and teacher of the gamba. His instructional work *The Division Violist* includes examples on how to play divisions (variations) over a given bass, then a very popular practice. Simpson was not without business acumen. The great success of his book caused him to follow it up with *The Division Violin*, a collection containing chiefly sets of variations by leading English composers and by foreign violinist-composers active in England. Included are twenty-six pieces, mostly for violin and figured bass, by Mell, Baltzar, and Banister, among others. Most pieces consist of a clearly defined motive followed by one variation. A set thus resembles a succession of short etudes. Baltzar's contributions in particular demand a well-developed technique, not so much in the higher positions as in double stops and rapid passage work.

Matthias Kelz (d. ca. 1694) of Augsburg's collection of fifty pieces for violin and gamba may be the first volume to include true violin etudes. The subtitle ("exercitionum musicarum") indicates further that they were "intended to help those who are successful violinists and wish to make further progress." Seven pieces are called "capriceti," twelve others "capricioso," pointing to the later equating of capriccio and etude. Kelz's material chiefly develops technique; it has less musical importance. Polyphonic parts for the outer voices had already been provided in sixteenth-century solo writing for the gamba and were developed further in the early seventeenth century. Kelz's use of polyphony prepared the way for similar writing by Bach.

Up to this time, English publications such as those by Salmon and Jenkins could be used for both gamba and violin, but *Ductor ad pandorum* (1682) set off a veritable landslide of violin tutors, the first ones specifically for that instrument. We know of some of these only through newspaper advertisements; a few copies of others have been preserved. Such volumes may have deteriorated under heavy, prolonged use by families, or they may have been discarded as being too primitive when in 1751 Geminiani's well-planned, methodical tutor, *The Art of Playing on the Violin*, appeared. Works of this kind were widely announced as "self-instructors" and were organized as follows: a few, rather sketchy instructions for beginners, followed by short pieces taken from dance collections then in vogue, or from popular operas. Later printings (the fourteenth edition of *Nolens volens* appeared in 1723!) often substituted different selections in order to include the public's current favorites. In some cases, new editions were given a new title, probably to cause potential customers to assume that these were entirely new publications. Such practices were frequent ca. 1700. In two studies Boyden established a genealogy of these works, from at least 1695 to Prelleur (1731).

Johann Wilhelm Furchheim (d. 1682) was a member of the Dresden court chapel, where he rose from the rank of ripieno player to vice-kapellmeister. Of his two published works only the titles have been preserved. The title of the first collection of 1687 clearly indicates its purpose: to provide sonatas and suites as study material for violinists. Most likely explanatory material was restricted to the preface.

Daniel Speer's comprehensive violin tutor offered little more than general remarks, but the tutor of Georg Falck (d. 1689), the cantor in Rothenburg on the Tauber, went far beyond. In 1688 he published his treatise with the subtitle "Getreu und gründliche Anleitung." The volume deals with practical music in general. For his musically gifted Latin students he requires instruction in "violin, gamba, violone, bassoon, flutes, lutes, and figured bass playing." One chapter is entitled "Violin Playing for Beginners." It is worth noting that before the age of tempered tuning he disapproves of the customary tuning in pure fifths, beginning with the D string, because it would result in too high a pitch for the heavily used E string. He therefore recommends using the A string as the point of departure, believing that an out-of-tune G string is less disturbing. Some of Falck's instructions are surprisingly modern. He recommends a relaxed position for the left hand to facilitate changing positions and warns against keeping the arms close to the body because they should be able to "move freely."

Daniel Merck also deals with the entire violin and gamba families, but the part devoted to the violin is so extensive that his *Compendium* can be considered the first German violin school. His valuable remarks on fingering are based on the principle of the supporting finger. He takes up the advantages of remaining in a given position rather than shifting and makes references to works by Biber, Walther, and Westhoff, which he evidently knew. Up and down bows are indicated by the letters A and N ("Niedergang"); like Walther he uses the letter M to indicate vibrato. Boyden surmises that vibrato was always used in connection with *messa di voce*.

In prefaces to his compositions, composer Georg Muffat provided remarks on violin playing, which comments show him to be very knowledgeable about violin technique. Two of his sons entered the imperial court chapel in Vienna as violinists.

TORELLI AND THE BEGINNINGS OF THE SOLO CONCERTO

Giuseppe Torelli (b. 1658 in Verona, d. 1709 in Bologna) may have received his early training in Bologna among the capable string players of the San Petronio orchestra. At the age of twenty-six, after composition studies with Giacomo Antonio Perti, he was granted membership in the Accademia Filarmonica, the highly prestigious association of Bolognese artists that admitted members only after a rigorous examination. In 1686 he became a viola player in the Bologna orchestra; he left it in 1698 to become concertmaster in the court chapel of the margrave of Brandenburg in Ansbach. From 1699 to 1700 he was active in Vienna, returning to Bologna in 1701. A violinist and composer, he left eighty-four works that were published and grouped under seven opus numbers. About fifty other works are preserved in manuscript form.

His *oeuvre* is important. The first movements of his op. 6, the *Concerti musicali a quattro* of 1698, can be viewed as the first solo concerto movements in regard to form and instrumentation. His earlier chamber and orchestral music follow traditional formal designs. Around 1700, music for a solo violinist with orchestra represented a great step forward from the concerto grosso, offering greater possibilities for artistic expression to the soloist. No doubt the operatic aria served as a model. A hundred years before the solo concerto's appearance, the aria with ritornello represented an interesting cooperation between a solo singer and an orchestra. An orchestra ritornello served as introduction, interlude, and postlude for the aria, the text of which usually had three stanzas. The singer was accompanied by basso continuo only; the ritornello was in the principal key. Typically, it was written out only once, to be played by the orchestra as needed. In the fully developed solo concerto the ritornello's appearance (four times in the same key) was felt to be tiresome and therefore was avoided. It was repeated in different keys and also in varied or abbreviated form, the better to hold a listener's attention. Presenting the two types in two columns will indicate similarities and differences (rit. I, II, and III may be identical or modified; arrows indicate modulation).

Ritornello Aria			*Solo Concerto*		
rit.	orch.	tonic	rit. I	orch.	tonic
1st section	voice + b.c.	tonic	solo I	solo instr. + b.c.	tonic → dom.
rit.	orch.	tonic	rit. II	orch.	dominant
2d section	voice + b.c.,	rel. min. or maj.	solo II	solo instr. + b.c.	dom → rel. min. or maj.
rit.	orch.	tonic	rit. III	orch.	rel. maj. or min.
3d section	voice + b.c.	tonic	solo III	solo instr. + b.c.	tonic
rit.	orch.	tonic	rit. IV	orch (usually same as rit. I, as *da capo*)	→ tonic

Between the earlier ritornello aria and the solo concerto movement we find intermediate phases of development, chiefly in music from Bologna. The favored solo instrument in public performance ca. 1650 was not yet the violin but the trumpet, which symbolized princely power and the glorification of God. One of the most important musical genres to add musical splendor to major church holidays was the trumpet sinfonia, also called sonata. We have more than thirty such works by Torelli, for up to four solo trumpets, mostly with string accompaniment. Given the small number of notes playable on the natural (valveless) trumpet, movements in rondo form are prominent; trumpet and strings alternate, with the strings providing the harmonically richer sections. In works of this kind the solo trumpeter had to be extraordinarily skilled, playing in the very high (clarino) register. If an adequate trumpeter was not available, an oboist or violinist might substitute. A collection by the Bolognese composer Giovanni Battista Bononcini was published in 1685 with the title *Sinfonia a 5, 6, 7 e 8 instrumenti, con alcune a una e due trombe* (some for one or two trumpets), op. 3. Not surprising is its subtitle, "servendo ancora per violini (may also be played by violins). In other words, the composer himself thought such a substitution possible. The trumpet part is designated "tromba prima o violino" (first trumpet or violin). In a sense, this could be regarded as the birth of the violin concerto.

Other developments led to concertante works with solo violin. On high holidays it was customary in Bologna to call on amateurs to reinforce the small group of "professori" (professional musicians). The amateurs would not play during the more difficult passages "per evitar maggior confusione" (to avoid great confusion), as Torelli stated in the preface to his op. 8. For instance, in the first movement of the Concerto for string orchestra in G major, op. 6, no. 1, in ritornello form, the opening section (see example) moves mostly in quarter notes, appearing four times, in the keys of G, D, G, and G major. The interludes (allegro, alla breve) are technically difficult—probably too difficult for most ripieno players. If therefore measures 8–14 (and similarly challenging measures later) were played by the concertmaster alone, the movement from a concerto for strings had been changed into a typical one for a solo concerto. By ca. 1700, composers were incorporating such practices as they wrote out concerto movements, so that they formed part of the work's structure.

The concerto grosso type developed by Corelli continued to have a strong influence, but the solo concerto emerged as the favored type. As a result, the solo concerto form was also adopted for works calling for several soloists; they are properly called double, triple, or quadruple concertos. Bach's Brandenburg Concertos include masterpieces of this kind. In spite of the popularity of the solo concerto, the Corelli type continued to exist. The greatest master of the concerto grosso after Corelli was Handel.

ANTONIO VIVALDI AND THE SOLO CONCERTO

To a certain extent, the history of violin playing can be studied by examining the major composers and their writings, but it would be wrong to focus on them exclusively without paying attention to the environment and traditions that affected their lives and from which they received inspiration. The life and work of Antonio Vivaldi (b. 1678) demonstrates how one such person, however great a genius, is inseparable from the environment that nurtured him, in this case the city whose musical life had grown through many generations.

Vivaldi—virtuoso, composer, teacher of violinists and orchestras, maestro di cappella, and opera impresario—by the age of thirty had become one of the most famous musicians of the Western world. His father, a barber and amateur violinist, had moved from Brescia to Venice. He turned his hobby into a profession, becoming a member of the orchestra of St. Mark's cathedral. Hairdresser-violinists were fairly customary in Italy, as dance master-violinists had been in France. Barber shops would make waiting more pleasant by supplying instruments to customers. Membership lists of church orchestras in Genoa often list a member's occupation as "garzone del barbiere" (barber's assistant).

Father Giambattista Vivaldi, known as a capable orchestra violinist, probably was his son's first teacher. Antonio was soon able to substitute for his father in the church orchestra, acquiring not only orchestral experience but also becoming familiar with works of the great masters. Antonio may have studied composition with Giovanni Legrenzi (d. 1690), the maestro di cappella at St. Mark's. He was ordained a priest in 1703, but due to a congenital condition of angina pectoris he was soon excused from celebrating mass. That same year he was appointed violin teacher at the Ospedale della Pietà, one of the largest Venice orphanages that offered musical training to talented girls. Vivaldi soon advanced to the rank of resident composer and leader of the institution's orchestra, which meant that he supplied most of the music needed for ordinary Sundays and holidays, and prepared and conducted performances. He made good use of the opportunity to work regularly with an orchestra and its individual players. The quality of performances by the Pietà orchestra soon made it famous; the concerts ranked among Venice's chief tourist attractions.

Vivaldi's talent revealed itself early on; his first two sets of compositions, twelve trio sonatas, op. 1 (Venice 1705) and twelve violin sonatas, op. 2 (Venice 1709), already show him to be a mature composer. His compositions attracted the attention of the capable publisher Estienne Roger, so that beginning with the twelve concertos of op. 3 (the famous *L'estro armonico*) all Vivaldi's works were published by Roger in Amsterdam; they were issued shortly after in London and Paris as well. Within ten years, an unknown violin teacher had become one of Europe's leading maestros! Many composers studied his works and modeled their own compositions on them, above all Johann Sebastian Bach. Bach's arrangements for organ or harpsichord of ten Vivaldi concertos may have served study purposes; certainly the Italian's music exerted a lasting influence on the German composer. If at this time the solo concerto entered a period of great vogue, this is due less to Torelli than to the veritable flood of concertos by Vivaldi, who prided himself on composing so rapidly that copyists could not keep up with him.

Approximately 450 solo concertos by Vivaldi have been preserved or are known to have been written, among them 228 for violin. In thirty-six others the violin is one of several other solo instruments. An early account of Vivaldi's violin playing was given by Johann Friedrich Armand von Uffenbach, a German music lover and son of a Frankfurt patrician, who later became mayor of his hometown. In his travel diary for 4 February 1715 he describes an opera performance he attended at Venice's Teatro San Angelo:

> Toward the end, Vivaldi played an accompanied solo, admirably. He ended with a fantasy that really frightened me, for nothing like it can ever have been played, nor will it be in the future. His fingers came within a hair's breadth of the bridge, so that there was no room for the bow. This he did on all four strings, playing fugues, all incredibly fast.

During the opera's intermission, Vivaldi played a violin concerto, a practice still observed in Mozart's time. In the improvised cadenza he introduced technical feats unheard-of before. Uffenbach's description may well be exaggerated, but he conveys a lively picture of the impression Vivaldi's playing made on an astute observer who himself played the violin and lute.

We cannot form an accurate opinion of the master's violin technique on the basis of printed editions of the music, for the technically more demanding concertos were not published during his lifetime, as the market for them among amateurs was judged to be insufficient. Vivaldi rarely used double stops and wrote few polyphonic passages for the solo violin. In this he followed the Italian rather than German tradition. He was fond, however, of writing chords, which he arpeggiated in various ways. The solo portions usually pick up a distinctive head motif from the ritornello and treat it in an improvisatory manner, leading into variously arranged chords. Passages like these are typical:

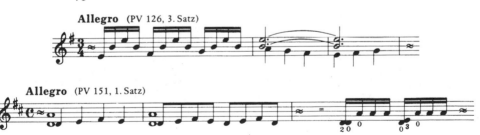

He used bariolage effects liberally, not only in the solo portions but also in the orchestra ritornello and at the beginning of a movement, producing the same note on both an open and stopped string:

At that time the strings were called, in ascending order, Basso, Tenore, Canto, and Cantin(o). For the following example the E string had to be tuned up to F-sharp:

The complexity of an excerpt from the first movement of the D major Concerto (PV 200) suggests something by Paganini:

Vivaldi seems to have been able to execute large left-hand stretches. He made use of this in his own compositions, where the stretch usually involves the first finger. Only in that way are great stretches like these possible:

His well-developed bowing technique, evidenced by his fondness for bariolage and arpeggios, is further demonstrated by staccato passages for twenty-four notes and frequent leaps crossing two strings. Such leaps occur in one of the famous concertos from *The Four Seasons* (op. 8, nos. 1–4), where they suggest the staggering of a drunk.

Vivaldi figures most importantly in the development of violin technique beyond Corelli, a development the beginning of which was seen in the first decade of the century in works by Torelli and in soloistic violin parts in operas by A. Scarlatti and Aldrovandini. This is directly attributable to Vivaldi's own violin playing and to his compositions, which every aspiring violin virtuoso soon practiced. Franz Benda, longtime concertmaster for King Frederick the Great, recalled that in his youth, ca. 1720, "I played the viola in Dresden, where the choirboys arranged their own concerts. I also practiced the violin, playing Vivaldi's concertos from memory." Countless other professional and amateur violinists improved their playing by studying Vivaldi's concertos. Others, such as Guignon in Paris in 1728, successfully performed them in public. Few of Vivaldi's personal pupils, however, reached prominence. Most of the female violinists he trained remained anonymous, for in the eighteenth century they had few professional opportunities. The well-brought-up girls in the orphanages were desirable candidates for matrimony and soon vanished from public life. His known pupils include already accomplished violinists who visited Venice and perhaps took some lessons, but who came chiefly to hear Vivaldi and to observe his interpretive style. One was Johann Georg Pisendel, concertmaster in Dresden, who in 1717 traveled to Venice in the entourage of the prince-elector of Saxony. Pisendel studied with Vivaldi for a few weeks, establishing a cordial relationship with his teacher that found expression in a number of concertos and sonatas "fatto per il Sig. Pisendel." These are now in Dresden. Vivaldi also provided ornamented adagios for this advanced pupil. It has been said of a number of well-known eighteenth-century violinists that they were Vivaldi pupils (Somis, for instance), but we know no details. In most cases the contacts must have been brief. Vivaldi's influence on violinists of his day was exerted chiefly through his compositions.

THE ORIGIN OF THE SOLO CADENZA

Many works in the concerto form developed by Torelli and Vivaldi feature a solo cadenza. To understand its evolution we must clear up a widespread misconception, namely that a cadence (in harmony) and a virtuoso cadenza are two entirely different things. The end of a melody, or part of a melody, may contain a slight embellishment of the leading tone, thereby emphasizing its "pull" to the octave. Here we already have the germ of what later developed into a full-fledged cadenza that could last several minutes.

It is difficult to establish just how much violinists might have embellished this leading-tone–to–octave progression through improvisation, thereby providing a small cadenza. Such things were never written down, and neither printed nor manuscript sources give us any clues. Only toward the end of the seventeenth century are there written-down indications—or at least instructions on what to play, if not the cadenza itself. In a sinfonia (1688) by Pietro Sammartini, maestro at the Florence cathedral, players of the upper parts are instructed to improvise a capriccio over the written-out basso continuo.

The first notated instrumental cadenzas appear to be those by Torelli, but these postdate a long period of improvised cadenzas. In three Torelli pieces for two violins over a sustained bass note, preserved in manuscript, the word "perfidia" appears at the beginning. The term indicated short soloistic passages, excited in mood, usually based on a single musical idea. The sustained bass is reminiscent of organ music, where such a "pedal point" customarily brought free, cadenzalike improvisation. Pincherle (*Feuillets*) has quoted a remarkably early example of a written-out cadenza over a figured bass. Its writer was Roman Weichlein, a composer born in Linz, Austria, who was a Benedictine monk in Lambach and Innsbruck. Around 1700 we encounter many such soloistic cadenzas, especially in opera arias with obbligato instruments.

Vivaldi, who soon after 1700 wrote many concertos, may have been inspired by this. Several sources attest to the existence of many fully developed cadenzas during the first decades of the eighteenth century. Quantz (1752) declared, "The cadenzas that are customary today, in which the bass must stop, came into vogue around 1710–1716." If Vivaldi appeared as soloist, as in the performance described by Uffenbach, he would improvise a cadenza as a matter of course, merely indicating the place for it in the written or printed music. Often the words "qui si ferma à piacimento" (stop here if desired) appear, while the concluding tutti is indicated by the words "poi segue" (then follows). Just as in an opera aria the main cadenza is sung before the last sung text word, the violinist would improvise a cadenza just before the last ritornello.

It is fortunate for us that as a pedagogue Vivaldi found it necessary to write down model cadenzas for his students, perhaps to help those girls who had little talent for improvisation. We should not think that all baroque musicians were experts at this. Many traveling opera singers would carry their long, carefully memorized cadenzas in their baggage, as Benedetto Marcello ironically described in his satire, *Il teatro alla moda*.

Nine cadenzas composed by Vivaldi have come down to us, enabling us to note some structural principles. They begin with an improvisatory elaboration of several motives; motives used for the last movement's cadenza may be taken from the first movement. An elaborate, arpeggiated passage might follow, and just before the concluding trill the pace slows down to a broadly conceived adagio, at times leading into distant harmonic regions. A typical cadenza occurs in the third movement of the C major Concerto for two violins (PV 23):

The D major Concerto (PV 165), "Fatto per la Solemnità della S. Lingua di S. Antonio in Padua," is more advanced in its treatment of themes from the first and third movements, even requiring changes in time signature. This work is of special importance for the history of the solo cadenza because we know that it was performed in 1712. It calls for the use of the twelfth position, leading us to assume that Vivaldi required a special fingerboard that was longer than then customary. Such cadenzas were not in general use then, but a violinist of Pisendel's stature took seven Vivaldi cadenzas with him to Dresden. Another was found in Paris; they apparently were widely known and invited imitation. Locatelli's example shows how quickly such ideas were adopted. As the improvised cadenza developed into a self-contained unit within a movement, the term "capriccio" was gradually adopted for it. Tartini (*Regole*) wrote,

> This type of cadenza today [1752–1756?] is known as capriccio, rather than cadenza, for today every singer or instrumentalist takes the liberty of prolonging it and expressing in it so many different moods that one cannot rightly call it cadenza but is forced to call it "capriccio."

This is an apt definition of the term. Later authors equated it with "etude," while in 1768 J.-J. Rousseau still defined it as "sorte de pièce . . . composition" (a piece of music, a composition).

ITALIAN VIOLIN PLAYING AFTER VIVALDI

GEMINIANI, SOMIS, VERACINI, LOCATELLI

Some of the great violinists of Vivaldi's generation were also major composers, including Geminiani, Somis, F. M. Veracini, Tartini, and Locatelli. They influenced eighteenth-century violin playing through their pupils and their compositions.

Francesco Saverio Geminiani (b. 1680 in Lucca), the son of a court musician, studied with Lonati in Milan and Corelli in Rome. Alessandro Scarlatti instructed him in composition, after which he entered the court chapel in Lucca. In 1714 he went to England, where as an outstanding soloist he soon was one of the leading musicians of Handel's time. Geminiani had good business sense; he organized subscription concerts, which were well attended. In conjunction with some highly successful concerts in a Dublin hall, he used adjoining rooms for the exhibit and sale of paintings from his own collection. He journeyed to Paris chiefly to look after the printing of his own compositions. After many years of concertizing and teaching he died in Dublin in 1762.

Aside from his sonatas for one or two violins with basso continuo, his concerti grossi are important for violinists. Acceding to his contemporaries' preference for a fuller sound, Geminiani added a viola to the solo trio scoring used by Corelli. Concerto grosso performances were very popular in England from ca. 1725 on; after that Geminiani wrote virtually no other music. His very fine Sonata "a violino solo senza basso" is the first such multi-movement work by an Italian composer. His greatest significance, however, lies in the field of pedagogy. His violin teaching was much in demand among members of London and Dublin society, so that he contributed materially to the forming of the English public's taste.

Burney reported that in Naples, Geminiani's rhythmically free style of playing so confused the orchestra's other violinists that he was assigned to play tenor viola. Stories of this kind abound in eighteenth-century writing on music, often undoubtedly the creation of a lively imagination. If Geminiani was "demoted" to the viola, the real reason may have been that the older musicians, used to the earlier concerto grosso style of playing, could not relate to the new interpretive manner coming from the solo concerto. Since the solo portions were accompanied by basso continuo only, the soloist could perfectly well use rubato and other liberties. Geminiani seems to have been one of the first (perhaps somewhat ahead of his time) to strive for a new, expressive manner of playing. His failure in Naples bears a striking resemblance to the young Kreisler's unsuccessful audition for the Vienna Philharmonic.

Giovanni Battista Somis (b. 1686 in Turin, d. 1763) was the son of a musician and an unusually gifted child. He was accepted into the ducal chapel at the age of ten; at seventeen he was sent for three years to Rome to study with Corelli. He then returned to Turin, where he remained as concertmaster until his death, having acquired great fame as a soloist. Charles de Brosses, endeavoring to favorably describe an outstanding singer in one of his letters from Italy, said that undoubtedly she had swallowed Somis's violin.

Much of Somis's large *oeuvre* has been lost. He wrote 150 concertos (142 for the violin) and about a hundred trio sonatas. His published sonatas show him to be a tasteful composer, a link between the Corelli tradition and the early classic style. He too made his greatest mark as a teacher, again forming a link between his own teacher and the later French school of violin playing. On an Italian journey in 1726, Quantz made a stop in Turin solely to hear Somis, an indication of the violinist's European renown. He attracted many young pupils, especially from France; Pugnani and Leclair were outstanding among them, but Guillemain, Guignon, and Chabran also turned out to be important in French musical life as influential teachers, preparing the rise of the French school of violin playing on the solid base of Corelli's style.

The rather eccentric personality of Francesco Maria Veracini (d. 1768) may have affected his interpretation, as had been true of Geminiani. He came from a highly regarded Florentine family of musicians. His grandfather was the proprietor of a conservatory; his uncle Antonio was a competent violinist who also composed for his instrument. Francesco Maria was trained in Florence and Rome; he may have been a Corelli pupil. A great urge to travel put him in the company of modern touring virtuosos. We know only some of the stops during his many travels. In 1711 he played a violin concerto of his own composition during a solemn mass in Frankfurt, on the occasion of the emperor's coronation. Other concerts took him to London (1714), Düsseldorf (1715), and Venice (1716), where he played for the Saxon prince-elector. He dedicated his first twelve sonatas (without opus numbers) to him and was appointed Saxon court composer in Dresden. In 1722 he seems to have returned to Italy; the following year he participated in Prague in the gala performance of the opera *Costanza e fortezza*, which formed part of the festivities surrounding the coronation of Charles VI as king of Bohemia. From 1735 to 1738 and again in 1744 he reaped successes in England as an opera composer; in 1750 he concertized at the Turin court. The last years of his life were spent in Florence.

From Francesco Maria Veracini's *Sonate accademiche* op. 2
(London and Florence 1744)

Important contributions to the repertory are his twelve violin sonatas
op. 1 (Dresden 1721) and especially the twelve *Sonate accademiche* op. 2, for
violin and figured bass (London and Florence 1744), which are solidly composed and conceived on a gigantic scale, tapping the instrument's virtuoso
possibilities. In all, these sonatas represent a high point of late baroque violin
music, surpassed only by Bach's contributions, which, however, represent an

entirely different approach. For his op. 2 Veracini supplied a preface with much information on performance practice. He explains the meaning of frequently used signs:

◆ = a long bow stroke, beginning *piano*, increasing to *fortissimo*, leading back to *pianissimo*
▲ = beginning *forte*, ending *piano*
▼ = beginning *piano*, ending *forte*
⊔ = up bow
⊓ = down bow
m^r = mordent

Pietro Antonio Locatelli (b. 1695 in Bergamo, d. 1764 in Amsterdam) studied in Rome with Corelli. His first compositions were published when he was twenty-six years old. In 1725 he became concertmaster in Mantua; later he entered the service of August the Strong of Poland and Saxony. After 1729 he lived in Amsterdam, where he was much in demand as a teacher. He published his own music and also had a business selling strings. His estate included 150 paintings and engravings, a library consisting of nearly a thousand volumes, including many historical and philosophical studies, and a large collection of music. Among the instruments were violins by Stainer (1667), Techler (1724), and Antonio and Hieronymus Amati (1618).

Locatelli was forty-two years younger than Corelli and seventeen years younger than Vivaldi. His early work is founded on those masters, but he soon acquired his own style, which displayed a greatly advanced playing technique. As a composer he spoke the highly expressive, intense language of the high baroque. His music must have made a profound impression on his contemporaries. In Diderot's satirical novella *Le neveu de Rameau* (Rameau's nephew) Rameau remarks, "The first one who played Locatelli was the apostle of the new music."

A milestone in the history of violin playing is Locatelli's op. 3, *L'arte del violino: XII concerti, cioè violino solo con XXIV capricci ad libitum* (Twelve violin concertos with twenty-four cadenzas *ad libitum*, Amsterdam 1733)—a landmark in the development of violin technique from Corelli to the French school, by way of Vivaldi. Locatelli's debt to Vivaldi is clear in many details, particularly in the arrangement of orchestra ritornellos, whose movements follow the traditional fast-slow-fast sequence. Locatelli's language, however, is more gentle, containing hints of romanticism, announcing and anticipating later developments. His tempos are nontraditional; in some concertos we find no really fast movements:

No. 2: Andante, Largo, Andante
No. 3: Andante, Largo, Vivace
No. 4: Largo/Andante, Largo, Andante
No. 5: Largo/Andante, Adagio, Allegro

The sequence of tonalities is also less traditional; submediant relations are frequently found:

No. 1: D—B-flat—D
No. 4: E/E—C—E
No. 9: G—E-flat—G
No. 11: A—F—A

The twenty-four solo capriccios go beyond Vivaldi. They occur in the two outer movements (not counting the Largo introductions) before the concluding ritornello and amount to composed, written-out cadenzas. Curiously enough, Locatelli repeats the word "cadenza" at the capriccio's end, which may mean no more than a final, leading-tone trill. Some of these cadenzas have little if any connection with the preceding movements and may even be in another key. Others are directly derived from the concerto movement in question. Capriccio no. 20 involves the exploration of very high positions:

segue

Dittersdorf judged these works "fine exercises, but not good for performance," in the nature of etudes. Significantly, violinists continued to practice them long after the twelve concertos had fallen into oblivion, as had so much baroque music after the mid-eighteenth century. Locatelli's op. 3 greatly influenced Paganini, and even today the capriccio-cadenzas are considered excellent preparatory studies for Paganini's famous twenty-four Caprices op. 1.

Further compositions by Locatelli include twelve concerti grossi (six each in the second parts of opp. 4 and 7), ten trio sonatas (six in op. 5 and four in op. 8), and eighteen violin sonatas (twelve published as op. 6 and six in op. 8). These do not call for the advanced technique required by op. 3, which was intended for teaching, but they do include elaborate passages in double stops, more elaborate than what is found in concertos of the period. Some of the sonatas have slow movements with a wealth of ornamentation and passage work; one gets the impression that Locatelli wanted to provide models for his students.

Among the composers born shortly before 1700 we should include Tartini, but due to his long life and the major style changes reflected in his late works, he really belongs to another epoch. He will therefore concern us later, in connection with the changes that occurred ca. 1750.

JOHANN SEBASTIAN BACH'S COMPOSITIONS
FOR VIOLIN

We normally think of J. S. Bach as the cantor of St. Thomas's in Leipzig—a church musician, as were many other members of that far-flung family. Because of this association most people tend to overlook that Bach's father was a town and court musician whose principal instrument was the violin. Johann Sebastian's first musical instruction was on the violin; no doubt it was thought that he would one day follow in his father's footsteps. After the father's early death the boy was brought up by his brother Johann Christoph, organist in Ohrdruf, so that keyboard instruments figured more prominently in Sebastian's musical training. He did not, however, altogether neglect the violin. In 1703, at the age of eighteen, he was employed as a string player in the Weimar music establishment of Duke Johann Ernst, brother of the reigning duke. During this brief appointment, Bach met Christoph Eibenstein, a fine violinist who worked as a valet. Johann Paul von Westhoff also lived in Weimar; quite likely Bach was acquainted with him.

Having held several positions as an organist, Bach returned to Weimar in 1714 as court organist and chamber musician. His professional activities acquainted him with Vivaldi's opp. 3 and 4 concertos, which had appeared in Amsterdam ca. 1712. Familiarizing himself with Italian concerto forms and with the new concertante style turned out to be of profound significance for Bach's further development. He arranged twenty-two concertos, ten of them by Vivaldi, for harpsichord or organ, incorporating the solo parts. Such studies influenced Bach's own composing during his next period of employment, from 1717 to 1723 as court kapellmeister in Köthen, where he worked closely with members of the prince's orchestra, some of whom were outstanding players. For the local concertmaster Meinrad Spiess Bach wrote his two violin concertos, in A minor and E major, the Double Concerto in D minor, probably all eleven sonatas for violin and harpsichord, and a sonata for two violins and harpsichord.

Bach did not slavishly imitate the Italian concerto form but developed it in his own creative way. We note this chiefly in the interaction between solo and tutti portions, a characteristic the beginnings of which can be seen in Vivaldi's op. 3. The resulting formal arrangements largely do away with the contrast between solo and tutti portions. Solo passages occur in the ritornello, and the orchestra figures importantly in accompanying the soloist. Intensive collaboration of this kind was called for in part by the small size of the Köthen orchestra, which was at its best in works with a chamber music texture. Compared to these conditions, orchestras that play Bach's concertos today are far too large, requiring the soloist to produce an extremely large volume in order to be heard over the orchestra.

In 1721, while in Köthen, Bach dedicated six concertos to Christian Ludwig, margrave of Brandenburg. We know that the last of these (for two violins, two gambas, two cellos, and continuo) could be played in Köthen only if Bach played one of the viola parts and the talented prince participated as gambist. In the Third Concerto, in G major (three violins, three violas, three cellos), all nine players have important solo parts; in concertos nos. 2, 4, and 5, the solo violin parts demand much technical skill in passage work, double stops, and arpeggios. The F major Concerto calls for a violino piccolo tuned to B-flat–F–C–G, a minor third higher than normal tuning. This instrument was no longer in general use in Bach's time; we do not know why Bach included it.

Structurally the Concerto in A minor for transverse flute, violin, harpsichord, and string orchestra belongs with the Brandenburg Concertos. It represents a masterful return to an older compositional style.

Johann Nikolaus Forkel, the author of Bach's first biography (Leipzig 1802), left us an account of the mature Bach as a string player:

> At musical gatherings, when quartets or larger instrumental compositions were performed in which he was not professionally involved, it was Bach's pleasure to join the musicians playing the viola. This placed him in the middle of the harmony, a position from which he could best hear and enjoy the upper and lower voices.

Bach's abilities as a violinist may not have been quite up to performing his six sonatas and partitas for unaccompanied violin, written ca. 1720. Though we know of no dedicatee, it is quite possible that Bach wrote them with Pisendel or the Dresden concertmaster Volumier in mind. He had been on friendly terms with both. The sequence of these works is as follows:

Sonata no. 1 in G minor: Adagio, Fuga Allegro, Siciliana, Presto
Partita no. 1 in B minor: Allemande (Double), Corrente (Double),
   Sarabande (Double), Bourrée (Double)
Sonata no. 2 in A minor: Grave, Fuga, Andante, Allegro
Partita no. 2 in D minor: Allemande, Courante, Sarabande, Gigue,
   Chaconne
Sonata no. 3 in C major: Adagio, Fuga, Largo, Allegro assai
Partita no. 3 in E major: Preludio, Loure, Gavotte en Rondeau, Menuet
   I, Menuet II, Bourrée, Gigue

The partitas (suites) are clearly based on the traditional framework of the four basic dances—allemande, courante, sarabande, and gigue—to which composers added as they saw fit. The fourth work features the monumental Chaconne, which demands artistic mastery and a superior command of the bow. For 250 years it has been every violinist's endurance test, the ultimate challenge in regard to playing double stops and chords. Flesch has called attention to the curious fact that in the entire gigantic movement there is not a single rest during which the player might make a quick adjustment to the tuning, though a violin may need some retuning after only a few measures. In other words, the performer not only must be able to play the Chaconne in tune on a well-tuned violin but may have to provide flawless intonation on an out-of-tune violin!

In June 1877 Brahms, in a letter to Clara Schumann, commented on the Chaconne:

> For me it is one of the most wondrous, incomprehensible works of music. On one staff, and on a small instrument, [Bach] expresses a world of most profound thoughts and strongest feelings. If I had been inspired and able to write this piece, I would have been so greatly excited, so profoundly moved, as to lose my sanity.

A simple ground bass, used by many baroque composers, serves as the foundation for thirty-two double variations. The Chaconne bass consists of a sequence of four bars, built on the descending line D–C-sharp–B-flat–A. For larger formal units, Bach usually (as at the beginning) combines two such four-bar units in the manner of antecedent and consequent phrases. At times the line is modified; beginning in bar 32 it includes chromatic progressions. By presenting the middle section (bars 132–207) in D major, Bach adds harmonic interest.

Even more challenging than the Chaconne (and dreaded by some players) are the fugues in the sonatas, which in some ways represent the last, most profound utterances in violin playing, even though violin technique continued to develop after Bach. The incredible compositional achievement they represent was pointed out by Kurth in his detailed analysis of the C major fugue in *Grundlagen des linearen Kontrapunkts: Bachs melodische Polyphonie* (Foundations of linear counterpoint: Bach's melodic polyphony). In 1855 Joachim wrote to Brahms thus: "Yesterday I played the great C major fugue for the first time, not without some trepidation, but well just the same."

Bach's violin works have had an interesting history. Neither the chamber music compositions with violin nor the concertos became known beyond the master's immediate circle. When he directed a Leipzig collegium musicum for students, he arranged the violin concertos for harpsichord and orchestra since he needed works of that kind, but because of the limited range of the harpsichord he transposed both concertos down a step, to G minor and D major. After Bach's death the concertos and sonatas were largely forgotten by the public, but this was not the fate of the works for unaccompanied violin. In 1802 Forkel noted, "For many years the greatest violinists considered them to be the best study material for those eager to master the instrument." They were circulated in manuscript copies and were among the few Bach works that lived on, at least among professional musicians.

Nardini is said to have prepared a shortened version of the Chaconne. Gaviniès owned a copy of all six sonatas and partitas; from that copy Jean-Baptiste Cartier obtained the C major fugue, which he included in his *L'art du violon* (Paris 1798), rendering at least one movement generally accessible in printed form. Johann Peter Salomon of Bonn, who later organized Haydn's concerts in London, was an avid Bach player. He may have brought the sonatas and partitas to the attention of Simrock, a fellow player in the orchestra and later a publisher; in 1802 Simrock published the first complete edition. In 1814 Georg Pölchau, a devoted collector of Bach's music, found Bach's autograph of the six in St. Petersburg and barely rescued it from being used to wrap cheese. In 1829 Zelter's interest in Bach's work enabled Mendelssohn to direct the first modern performance of the *St. Matthew Passion*, inaugurating a Bach renaissance that, over the next hundred years, brought all Bach's music back to life.

Mendelssohn invited Ferdinand David, concertmaster of the Gewandhaus Orchestra, to perform the Chaconne during the 1839/40 season in a historical concert, but David declined, saying that he would feel ridiculous stepping up to the concert platform all by himself! Only after Mendelssohn wrote a keyboard accompaniment for the Chaconne was David willing to perform it. We now tend to put down Mendelssohn's accompaniment as a romantic aberration, but actually it was a pioneering undertaking, as was Schumann's masterly piano accompaniment to all six sonatas and partitas, published in 1854. Schumann took his task very seriously; an *Urtext* (based on the original source) version of the violin part was published with the Schumann edition.

Basically, these works for unaccompanied violin were then considered to be studies, as implied by the subtitle of David's edition of the six: "For use at the Leipzig Conservatory, supplied with fingering and bowing indications and other editorial markings." Nevertheless, David's edition is exemplary by modern standards. The music is printed on two staves, the upper staff reproducing the original source, the lower staff containing David's suggestions for performance. He indicated on the title page, "Those who want to provide their own markings may use the original text, which has been carefully reproduced from the composer's autograph in the Berlin Royal Library. It is printed in small type." Apparently the practice of going back to an *Urtext* is not an achievement of our own time!

The young Joachim was the first to perform the Chaconne in public, unaccompanied, in Leipzig. He repeated the feat in Paris. Since then the Chaconne has fascinated nonviolinists as well. Brahms prepared a version for piano left hand, saying, "Joachim doesn't come here very often." Busoni's arrangement is for two hands, broadly conceived in a very individualistic manner that has horrified some musical purists. There is an edition for cello, and even one for zither, which is actually quite carefully crafted. Spitta writes about the Chaconne's sound qualities in his Bach biography (vol. 2):

> The spirit of the master urges the instruments to incredible utterance; at the end of the major section it sounds like an organ, and sometimes a whole band of violins might seem to be playing. This Chaconne is a triumph of spirit over matter such as even he never repeated in a more brilliant manner.

Spitta's remarks led to further arrangements for string quartet and for orchestra, by composers from Raff to Casella. Wilhelmj even provided a version for violin and orchestra.

The violin concertos were long in receiving general public recognition. Spitta blamed this on what he considered their lack of easily appreciated melodic lines. He also believed that the concerto's form no longer was familiar. Even Leopold Auer (1921), one of the leading pedagogues in the early twentieth century, had reservations:

> With regard to J. S. Bach's two concertos for violin, I have never given them to my pupils to study because, from my point of view, only the two slow movements in them are musically valuable and really worthy of their composer; while the first and last movements of each concerto are not very interesting, either musically or technically. This, of course, is my own humble opinion.

Such opinions no longer prevail. Every serious violinist who wishes to acquire a comprehensive command of technique and style will want to study at least one of Bach's concertos. They occupy a secure place on our concert programs and have even entered the world of ballet. The Double Concerto has greatly succeeded in such a production, entitled *Concerto Barocco Balanchine*.

The solo sonatas and partitas are of foremost importance among Bach's violin music and call for intensive study. All great violinist-teachers have been aware of this, and as a result many editions have been published, ranging from facsimiles of Bach's autograph, to free personal interpretations, to those giving extremely detailed advice to the player. Chief among the many problems encountered in performing Bach's music for unaccompanied violin are the discrepancies between the notational picture and its possible realization in sound. Weighty questions are raised by the Chaconne's very opening bars. What Bach wrote cannot be realized exactly in sound—but what did the composer have in mind? One can think of two possibilities:

Yet a stickler will point out that, strictly speaking, the first chord will sound in one of two ways:

Generations of violinists have struggled with these questions, and the published editions reflect this combat between the ideal sound and the limitations of reality, in this case, the four strings of the violin. In *La technique supérieure de l'archet* (Paris 1916), Lucien Capet went further than anyone else in providing bowing instructions, as for instance for the second measure of the Adagio from Sonata no. 1:

To understand this complex picture one must refer to the table of signs and abbreviations in Capet's preface, reproduced here, which accordingly translate Capet's bowing instructions: whole bow, upper third, sixth eighth of the bow near the tip, the same again, then fifth eighth, second quarter, then first quarter (always figured from the frog). Many violinists may be horrified by such detailed instructions. On the other hand, one frequently hears the criticism that performances of Bach's solo violin works are marred by incorrect accentuation and unintended dynamics due to incompetent, unplanned bowing. Players therefore might well profit from giving some thought to Capet's edition.

EXPLICATION DES SIGNES ET ABRÉVIATIONS

MAIN GAUCHE

I. II. III. IV. V. VI. VII. Positions.
S corde sol.(ou 4me corde) **R** corde ré (ou 3me corde)
L corde la (ou 2me corde) **M** corde mi (ou 1re corde).
⟶ Déplacement expressif d'une position à une autre, sans changement de doigt.
o— Changement de position par l'intermédiaire du du doigt placé sur la corde. *Ex.*
xx Vibrato très expressif.
⌣ Souplesse générale de la main gauche donnant une expression moins violente.
⌐o Ne pas vibrer.

MAIN DROITE

⊔ tirez ∨ poussez **T** talon **M** milieu **P** pointe.
— Appuyer profondément l'Archet au commencement de chaque note.
, l'Archet légèrement au dessus de la corde.
+ Arrêter l'Archet sans le soulever.
o Reprendre l'Archet.
▭ l'Archet posé, préparant l'accentuation.
A Tout l'Archet.
B La moitié.
C Le quart.
D Le huitième.
E Le tiers.

Figure explicative des divisions de l'Archet

Players may decide against an editor's suggestions and look for their own solution to a problem; it is wise, in such cases, to consult several editions, to see what has worked well for others. Flesch (*The Art of Violin Playing*, vol. 2) provides very helpful suggestions on interpretation, especially for the Chaconne. His advice is well worth considering, even if the player will decide not to use it all. Finally, other editors after David have accepted the format of juxtaposing *Urtext* and edited text so that, if questions arise, players can easily go "back to Bach."

THE "BACH" BOW

All polyphonic violin music represents a discrepancy between notational appearance and sound. This is particularly true in Bach's works and, since the advent of the Bach renaissance, has increasingly concerned performers and scholars. It was widely thought that Bach surely would not have written music details of which are impossible to render in sound. This line of thinking led Arnold Schering to investigate the special "baroque" bow that (he believed) must have existed to execute three- and four-note chords without arpeggiating them.

It is true that the bow of Bach's age, that is, the pre-Tourte bow, did not yet have a concave curvature, and that the hair had less tension than what we are now accustomed to. With a looser band of hair, three-note chords were played more easily. Schering further noted that in eighteenth-century Germany and France the bow was normally held with the thumb on the hair. Before the invention of the screw, the thumb regulated the tension to a certain extent, applying more or less pressure. But even after the end screw's invention it took some time for it to come into general use.

Schering (1904) published two articles in which he described a Bach bow he believed to have been used at that time to play the sonatas and partitas. The thumb, he argued, would relax hair tension for playing chords and increase it for playing normal melodic lines.

Albert Schweitzer at once took up Schering's theory and tested it in collaboration with Ernst Hahnemann, a violinist of his acquaintance. As a result of the publication of Schweitzer's widely read Bach book (Paris 1905), the standard violin bow, including the one used in the eighteenth century, became virtually discredited for playing Bach among many professionals and amateurs. Beckmann (1918) considered Schering's idea untenable, citing pictorial evidence and theoretical treatises. Andreas Moser (1920) an expert, also denied, using valid arguments, that such a Bach bow ever existed, but to no avail. Even though Schering, in a footnote to Moser's article, revised his earlier position, the tale of the Bach bow refused to die. Schering had to experience how fascinating and persistent falsehoods can become if they support a concept that seems to be in the air at the time.

For some fifty years many violinists, working with bow makers, busily reconstructed a bow that never existed. Very few of these attempts went beyond experimentation, among them Berlin luthier Hermann Berkowski's "polyphonic bow," which featured a mechanism that made it possible to vary bow hair tension while playing. In 1925 Hans Baumgart patented two improvements. Rolph Schröder revived the subject with an experiment in 1930, while Hellwig's "polyphonic baroque bow" constituted another effort. Georges Frey and Rudolf Gutmann followed; Gutmann provided a kind of rubber spring between bow hair and stick.

Finally the violinist Telmányi took up Schröder's idea and had the luthiers Arne Hjorth and Knud Vestergaard of Viby, Denmark, construct the "Vega bow" [see Boyden 1965, p. 435. Ed.]. Its stick had an enormous

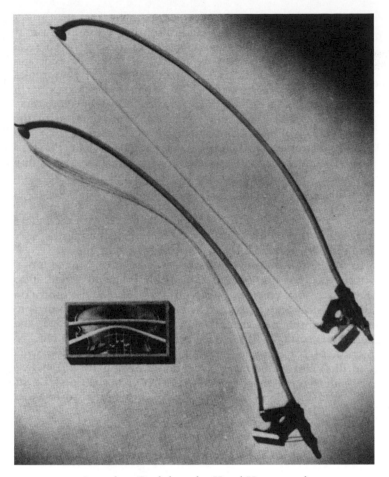

A modern Bach bow by Knud Vestergaard
(from *The New Grove Violin Family*, New York 1989)

convex curve so that even under great pressure it would not touch the strings. The thumb rests in a metal ring, which regulates tension as desired. The resulting sound was strange, somewhat accordionlike. Three- and four-part chords could indeed be played simultaneously, but the sound suggests three or four individual violinists playing. It is weak, so that there is no way to play chords to intensify expression.

In 1950 the aged Schweitzer still vigorously defended Schering's phantom bow, but the following arguments speak against it:

1) Not a single such bow is known, though many other eighteenth-century bows have been preserved
2) No illustration of such a bow is known
3) No treatise includes a description of the bow, or how it is to be used, nor is there any other reference to it in the relevant literature

The most persuasive argument, however, exists in certain passages of Bach's music, passages to which neither Schering nor Schweitzer seem to have paid any attention. Eduard Melkus (1963) mentions two of these (see examples). If, in the first case, the first finger remains on A and the second on C-sharp, then G, F, and F-sharp in the upper line are impossible to play. Melkus also points out other examples that might barely be playable with extremely complicated fingerings, but not up to tempo. The original purpose of the Bach bow had been to render faithfully Bach's music for unaccompanied violin, but as it turns out, important voices in these polyphonic works remain unplayable.

Two years after Bach's death, Quantz (1752) expressed his views on playing chords on the violin. He differentiated between chords followed and not followed by a rest.

If [the chord] is not followed by a rest, the bow remains on the top string. In either case the lowest strings must be released, at a slow or fast tempo. They must be touched quickly, one after the other, lest the sound is that of a chord broken [arpeggiated] in triplets.

A 1968 German radio program showed how errors tend to persist. The commentator cited these lines from an essay by Schweitzer:

Did violinists in Bach's day play better than our great virtuosos? No! But they used a different bow. On this round bow the hair, if sufficiently loose, can set all four strings into motion simultaneously without having the stick get in the way. Thus nothing interferes with polyphonic playing. . . . Otto Büchner further developed the historic round bow revived by Schweitzer; he adapted it to the modern violin so that it would produce the big tone needed for our concert halls. He improved the frog's mechanism and, most importantly, gave a larger curvature to the stick, adapting it to today's more arched bridges.

There has been no end to the concerns about the round bow. Rudolf Gähler plays Bach solo sonatas and partitas with a bow with variable hair tension. His playing so impressed Helmut Bornefeld that in 1978 he composed a sonata for unaccompanied violin, taking into account Gähler's ideas.

INSTRUCTION BOOKS FROM THE FIRST HALF
OF THE EIGHTEENTH CENTURY

Violin pedagogy took an upswing during the last decades of the seventeenth century, hand in hand with the violin's rising popularity, especially among English amateurs. The development was soon felt in France as well, where teachers felt called upon to satisfy a demand for instructional works. As in England, publishers often took the initiative. A chronological table outlines the trend:

1701	Anonymous, *Musical Recreations, or The Whole Art and Mastery of Playing on the Violin*, London
1704	Anonymous, *The Compleat Musick-Master*, London
1709	Anonymous, *Book of Instruction for the Violin*, London
	Anonymous, *The New Violin-Master, or The Whole Art of Playing on that Instrument*, London
1711/12	Michel Pignolet de Montéclair, *Méthode facile pour aprendre à jouer du violon avec un abrégé des principes de musique nécessaires pour cet instrument*, Paris
ca. 1712	Sébastien de Brossard, *Fragments d'une méthode de violon*, manuscript at Bibliothèque Nationale, Paris
1712	Giov. Antonio Piani, *Twelve Sonatas for Violin and Figured Bass*, Paris
1718	Pierre Dupont, *Principes de violon par demandes et par reponse par lequel touttes personne pouront aprendre l'euxmêmes à soner dudit instrument*, Paris
	Johann Graff, *Sei soli a violino solo e cont.*, op. 1, Bamberg
ca. 1721	Anonymous, *Books for Learners on the Violin*, London
ca. 1730	Robert Crome, *The Fiddle New Model'd, or A Useful Introduction for the Violin*, London
1731	Peter Prelleur, *The Modern Musick-Master, or The Universal Musician*, London (facsim. rpt. Kassel and London 1965)
1732	Joseph Fr. B. C. Majer, *Museum Musicum Theoretico Practicum, das ist neueröffneter Theoretisch- u. Practischer Music-Saal*, Schwäbisch Hall (facsim. rpts. Kassel 1954, 1968)
1733	Pietro Antonio Locatelli, *L'arte del violino: XII concerti, cioé violino solo con XXIV capricci ad libitum*, op. 3, Amsterdam
1734	Carlo Tessarini, *Il maestro e discepolo, divertimenti da camera a due violini*, op. 2, Urbino
ca. 1735	Jean-Joseph Cassanéa de Mondonville, *Les sons harmoniques, sonates à violon seul avec la basse continue* op. 4, Paris
1738	Michel Corrette, *L'école d'Orphée: Méthode pour apprendre facilement à jouer du violon dans le goût français et italien*, Paris (facsim. rpt. Geneva 1973)
	J. P. Eisel, *Musicus Autodidaktus*, Erfurt

1740–	Franz Benda, *101 caprices*, manuscript copies in several libraries
1741	Carlo Tessarini, *Grammatica di musica: Insegna il modo facile e breve per bene imparare di sonare il violino sù la parte*, Rome
ca. 1745	Francesco Geminiani, *Rules for Playing in a True Taste on the Violin, German Flute, Violoncello and Harpsichord*, London
	P. Pinelli, *Nouvelle étude. . .* , Paris (together with a portion of Tartini's *L'arte dell'arco*)
	Carlo Tessarini, *Grammatica per i principianti di violino*, Rome

As we see, English publications were in the forefront. Some authors/publishers preferred to remain anonymous, probably in order to conceal the fact that they had copied from each other liberally. Some of these schools succeeded well; *Musical Recreations* published by Walsh & Hare reached a fourth printing within seven years. In 1704, the London publisher John Young came out with *The Compleat Musick-Master*, a truly comprehensive tutor that included a section on voice teaching along with others devoted to violin, flute, oboe, and the gamba family. It tells us little about the violin except for the usual basic instruction, but it is interesting that the author lamented the gradual demise of the gambas. A third printing of Young's tutor appeared in 1722. In addition to new treatises, many old ones were reprinted, often with new music examples taken from what was then popular. All this points to the enormous demand for such tutors at the time.

Montéclair's publication (2d ed. 1720) was the first real violin school published in France—a remarkable state of affairs, considering that by then violins had been played in France for almost two hundred years. It was clearly meant for beginners and contains some sound advice, advocating, for instance, a relaxed position of the left hand, with the elbow directly under the violin, a relaxed right hand (with the thumb on the bow hair), and a loose wrist and elbow. Montéclair's music examples are notated in the French violin clef, with G on the first rather than the second line. This reduced the need for ledger lines when playing above the first position on the E string. At the bottom, however, an additional line is needed for notes on the G string, which is confusing. The author therefore recommends using the C clef on the first or second line. He also points out that in Italian violin music the G clef on the second line is used, so that one should familiarize oneself with that clef also.

In an age when Italian violin music was beginning to make inroads in France, a French violinist had to be able to read four clefs, of which the French violin clef was the most important. It appears in all Lully's scores. Moreover, it was expected that violinists and violists could read the bass clef. If in the accompaniment to a solo concerto their part became the lowest one, it was customarily written in the bass clef in order to indicate to the players the importance of their line. Such a part was called bassett(o). To be able to read the bass clef was generally useful, especially for music making in the home. It made it easy to play a sonata with basso continuo as a duo for two violins.

The knowledgeable and versatile Brossard never completed his *Méthode*, which is unfortunate because Dupont's method addresses itself only to the "maître de musique et de danse," while Montéclair instructs beginners and also dance fiddlers. This applies especially to what they say about bowing, based on Lully's orchestral practice as described by Muffat. In 1740, Dupont's school also appeared in a second printing.

Piani's and Graff's compositions are particularly informative. Since they provide precise fingerings throughout, they tell us much about playing in the higher positions. We learn that the old method (using higher positions only on the E string and returning as quickly as possible to the first position) was gradually discarded. Instead, position playing on all strings was increasingly favored, using whatever position seemed logical for a given passage, and remaining in that position as long as possible. Some authors of the time used an asterisk to mark the return to the first position.

Prelleur was a French organist, harpsichordist, and composer who worked in England. His book, in six parts, amounts to a compendium of practical music, followed by "a brief history of musick" and "a dictionary explaining such Greek, Latin, Italian & French words as generally occur in musick." The six parts are entitled, in order, "An Introduction to Singing," "Directions for Playing on the Flute [recorder]," "The Newest Method for Learners on the German Flute [transverse flute]," "Instructions on the Hautboy," "The Art of Playing on the Violin," and "The Harpsichord Illustrated & Improv'd." Instructions on gamba playing are no longer included. The violin section is forty-eight pages long; a collection of minuets and other dances, some "by M*r* Handel," begins on page 10. Most require the first position only, but one group goes up to the third position. What few instructions on playing there are were taken from *Nolens volens* of 1695, and the sections on other instruments are not original either.

Majer contributed a work on general music and instruments. Its second edition appeared in 1741. On the three pages devoted to the violin, like Prelleur, he did not offer anything original. His source was Falck's *Idea boni cantoris* (1688).

In a wider sense, Locatelli's op. 3 also belongs among the instruction books. He undoubtedly intended the twenty-four capriccio-cadenzas that form part of it to be practicing material for very advanced violin students. After 1800, the caprices were frequently published separately from the concertos.

Like other authors of instruction books before him, Eisel was basically a compiler rather than an expert on the instruments he describes. Noteworthy is his emphasis on using the whole bow, thus going beyond the practice of players of dance music and advocating the Italian manner of playing sonatas.

Michel Corrette's *School of Orpheus* owed its title to the many illustrations since the Renaissance that depict Orpheus playing a fiddle or violin. Corrette, a capable and industrious musician, had been a Paris organist since 1726. He published another violin tutor in 1782. Eighteenth-century students of virtually any instrument were bound to encounter one of Corrette's teaching methods, for he also authored later tutors for soprano gamba, transverse flute, harpsichord, voice, guitar, mandolin, harp (with or without pedal), oboe, bassoon, viola, and hurdy-gurdy, most of which went through many editions. Corrette could not have been an expert on all these instruments as his methods were hardly adequate for advanced pupils. This prompted the violinist Gaviniès to coin a malicious play on the word "anachorète" (hermit, anchorite): ânes à Corrette (Corrette asses).

But most likely Corrette did play the violin, for much of what he says goes far beyond earlier sources and deals with important technical details of violin playing. As to holding the instrument, his advice is this: "To change positions it is absolutely necessary to rest the chin on the violin. This frees the left hand, especially when one needs to return to the first position." He states this clearly, while Montéclair and Dupont barely mention the problem. He also goes into detail about holding the bow: the French keep three fingers on the stick, the thumb rests on the hair, while the little finger rests "a costé du bois" (on the stick's side). The Italians keep all four fingers on the stick, the thumb lying against its lower side. They grasp the bow higher, approximately up a quarter of the bow's length, while the French, according to Corrette, hold the bow at the frog.

In Corrette's work, as in other tutors, pieces for practicing take up most of the space. Their headings indicate the technical problems they are meant to address, such as "Menuets pour apprendre à jouer par accords" (for learning how to play chords). L'école d'Orphée also gives advice on many aspects of general performance practice, such as embellishments and dynamics. Corrette recommends,

> In sarabandes, adagios, largos, and other expressive movements, whole, half, and quarter notes must be played with a lot of bow. The volume must increase toward the note's end. Especially in cantabile melodies the last note must begin with a delicate sound that grows toward the middle and then dies away. This kind of bow stroke creates a beautiful effect.

In all, Corrette's school is superior to all previous violin tutors. Gaviniès's malicious remark probably means that he could not resist a clever play on words; it does not imply serious criticism of his colleague.

During the first half of the eighteenth century, Carlo Tessarini was the most important violin pedagogue. An outstanding violinist and good composer for his instrument, he was active in Venice, Urbino, and Brno. He also concertized in Germany and Holland. His 1734 duets for two unaccompanied violins made teaching materials available for ensemble playing. The duets consist of six sonatas and six canons, all highly instructive. The title of Tessarini's major publication is misleading; only the subtitle clarifies the work's purpose. It represents a major contribution to the study of violin technique and performance practice. These are short, cadenza-like exercises in all major and minor keys, in that sense remininscent of Bach's Well-Tempered Clavier. For beginners, they provide a kind of foretaste of or guide to how one improvises cadenzas. Andreas Moser cites some examples from the *Grammatica*, which show Tessarini to be an imaginative musician who also provides exercises in the second position, so important for certain keys. The work's success led to French and English translations. By its title, the French edition points ahead to the promotional announcements and claims of our own age: *Nouvelle méthode pour apprendre par théorie dans un mois de tems a jouer du violon* (A new methodical approach to learning how to play the violin in one month).

Benda's *101 Caprices* was not conceived as a self-contained compendium but grew out of his teaching experience and was probably begun soon after 1740, when he instructed his brother Joseph. Additional material was written for his sons Carl and Friedrich. The collection was not published during his lifetime, but circulated in manuscript copies among his students. The pieces, compiled over a period of forty years, vary greatly; some of the shorter ones provide models for improvisation, while others are typical etudes. Some contain quite complex writing, making it likely that Benda was well acquainted with Bach's music for unaccompanied violin.

MID-CENTURY STYLE CHANGES

JOHANN STAMITZ

Bach's death in 1750 has been generally held to mark a turning point in music history. It may be a convenient date to remember, but if one delves further into musical developments from about 1720 on, it is soon apparent that there was no real break. Early classicism, rococo, *empfindsamer Stil*, or whatever terms have been used in connection with this period, were developing for some decades before the deaths of Bach and Handel. To a significant extent this gradual change is reflected in violin and orchestra music. The *espressivo* quality of string sound mentioned before may have contributed to this development.

A melodic style that was less severe but lighter and more rococo-like can already be detected here and there in music by Vivaldi, Veracini, and Geminiani. Certain works by Locatelli exhibit an expressive force that is almost romantic; it can also be found in the six *Concertini per 4 violini, alto, violoncello, basso continuo* (The Hague 1740), variously attributed to Handel, Pergolesi, Ricciotti, Chelleri, and Birckenstock but believed to have been "written by a noble gentleman." Pergolesi, who died in 1736 at the age of twenty-six, certainly was not the composer, though his *La serva padrona* was ahead of its time and not far removed from Mozart's world.

Next to this group of Italians (which also included Giovanni Battista Sammartini), the composers around Johann Wenzel Anton Stamitz, known as the Mannheim School, may have had the strongest influence on mid-century musical life. The rise and fall of this center of music is typical for the age of absolutism. In 1720, the Palatine elector Karl Philipp moved his residence from Heidelberg to Mannheim, where he assembled an group of outstanding musicians. Karl Theodor, who succeeded him in 1743, continued this intensive cultivation of music, and Mannheim became one of Europe's foremost musical cities. In 1778 Karl Theodor, having inherited the office of elector of Bavaria, moved with his court to Munich, leaving only a handful of musicians in Mannheim.

Stamitz (b. 1717 in Bohemia) was trained as a violinist. He went to Mannheim, probably in 1741, and a year later performed in Frankfurt during the festivities surrounding the coronation of Charles VII. On that occasion he was heard on violin, viola d'amore, cello, and contrabass. In 1743 he advanced to the position of first concert violinist or concertmaster of the fifty-piece orchestra, which during the summer months was in residence at Schwetzingen castle. Later Stamitz became the director of instrumental music, in which capacity he hired many outstanding players. Young Mozart was delighted by what he heard in Mannheim. Stamitz had molded many capable individuals into a highly disciplined, homogeneous orchestral ensemble. Uniform bowing was used in the string sections, and dynamic contrasts as well as subtle nuances were observed.

Stamitz's orchestral and chamber music compositions, representing new stylistic concepts, attracted much attention and elicited invitations for two lengthy stays in Paris. During the 1754 Concert Spirituel he performed one of his own symphonies, followed during the next season by a violin concerto and a sonata for viola d'amore. La Pouplinière, a great patron of music, engaged him as kapellmeister and resident composer in Passy. By performing his own works he not only influenced French composers but also affected the quality of French orchestral playing, bringing to Paris practices and standards he had established in Mannheim. By the time Stamitz died at the age of forty, the Mannheim style had been firmly established, making it possible for others to continue and develop it further. These included his two sons and the composers Ignaz Holzbauer, Christian Cannabich, and Franz Xaver Richter.

Johann Stamitz's seven violin concertos and his sonatas are significant for our purposes. Many of their details are harbingers of Mozart's idiom, but when Haydn and Mozart wrote their first masterworks, Stamitz's music for a long time was forgotten. In 1799 a violinist performed Stamitz in public, but the reviewer from the *Allgemeine Musikalische Zeitung* was not impressed, saying that he had "extracted a concerto by the old Stamitz from the dustbin of oblivion." Later in the nineteenth century, in line with a general revival of interest in music of the past, Stamitz was rediscovered, leading to a new appreciation of his music not only for its historic significance but for its purely musical attractiveness. Since then it has received much attention, especially in amateur circles.

Carl Stamitz (1745–1801) began as a second violinist in the Mannheim orchestra. He later lived in Paris, whence he undertook long concert tours through Germany, England, and Holland. He died in Jena, Germany. His brother Anton (b. 1754, d. ca. 1809), also an orchestra member, concertized especially as a player of viola and viola d'amore. He later lived in Paris, where he became Kreutzer's teacher. Both brothers, but especially Carl, included among their many works concertos for several soloists, for which the term "sinfonia concertante" was coined. It constitutes a combination of the new classical concerto form and the old concerto grosso. Aside from fifteen violin concertos, Carl Stamitz wrote thirty-eight such works, among them thirty for two, four for three, two for four, one for six, and one for seven soloists. From Anton Stamitz's pen we have fifteen violin concertos and six double concertos.

GIUSEPPE TARTINI

Aside from the Serenade, what shall we program on our concert? I request Tartini.

So wrote Brahms, in a letter of 12 March 1859 to Joachim. The work in question was Tartini's "Devil's Trill" Sonata, one of Brahms's favorites.

Giuseppe Tartini (1692–1770) still belongs to the generation that was directly influenced by Corelli and Vivaldi; his life bridges two epochs and reflects the gradual change from baroque to early classic style with regard to both composing and performing works for the violin. He was born in Pirano on the Istrian peninsula and studied law in Padua. Little is known about his period of violin study, but biographers, lacking factual information, supplied romantic details, including his alleged abduction of a young girl. In 1714 he went to Ancona as a musician in the local theater; in 1721 he became concertmaster in Padua. The famous pilgrimage church there supported a choir of sixteen professional singers and an orchestra of twenty-four. Tartini's duties included playing violin solos at designated places during mass. In 1717, Francesco Montarini was similarly employed at St. Peter's in Rome.

By 1723, Tartini's reputation evidently spanned Europe, for he was invited to participate in the coronation music for Charles VI in Prague. He remained in Bohemia for several years; after that, until his death, he lived chiefly in Padua. He had always been much in demand as a teacher and ca. 1727 founded a school for violinists and composers. An arm injury suffered in 1740 curtailed his playing but increased his teaching activities. Tartini, the "maestro delle nazioni" (teacher of the world), had more than seventy pupils. Of these, Nardini, Pugnani, and De Tremais were best known as violinists while J. G. Graun, Manfredini, Johann Gottlieb Naumann, and Friedrich Wilhelm Rust acquired greater fame as composers.

Tartini's aim was to train violinists to be well grounded in both technique and interpretation with special emphasis on bowing. He is said to have used two bows for practicing, divided by chalk marks into thirds and quarters respectively. Leopold Mozart said of Nardini, "No one bests him for beauty, purity, and evenness of tone, nor in tasteful cantabile playing." Such praise applies to Tartini's students in general. His teaching maxim was "Per ben sonare bisogna ben cantare" (to play well one must sing well). A contemporary described him thus: "He does not play the violin, he sings it."

Tartini's letter of 5 March 1760 to his pupil Maddalena de Sirmen gives details about his teaching approach, as do several of his pedagogical writings. In the letter he stresses the importance of bowing exercises to achieve a relaxed yet intensive stroke. The tone must "breathe" or speak immediately, regardless of which part of the bow makes contact with the string. An hour a day should be devoted to bowing exercises, "some of it in the morning, some in the evening." One should practice long bow strokes leading gradually from *pianissimo* to *fortissimo*, using both up and down bows. An allegro from a Corelli sonata is good for practicing martellato bows, at first at the tip, then elsewhere. All allegro studies should be done with both up and down bows. Exercises for string changing that require skipping over one string are "truly useful." To develop facility in position playing and especially to improve sight reading, orchestra parts should be practiced using the second, third, and higher positions. Trills also require diligent practice; begin slowly and gradually increase their speed. "The fourth finger requires extra attention [for trills] because he is smaller than his brothers." No doubt there were other such letters, but they have not been preserved. Tartini's set of variations entitled *L'arte dell'arco* demonstrates his systematic approach to developing bowing technique.

To learn the art of diminution or ornamentation was an important requirement for eighteenth-century violinists. Probably for his students, Tartini provided a set of seventeen variations on the Adagio from his own Violin Sonata op. 2, no. 5. Cartier published it in 1798 in the appendix of his *L'art du violon*. Another pedagogical work is Tartini's *Regole per arrivare a saper ben suonar il violino*, a thorough, systematic compendium on the skill of diminution. It also describes his own manner of playing and his expectations of his students.

Tartini may have turned to composition relatively late. His *Sei concerti a cinque* (Six concertos for violin and four-part orchestra) were published as op. 1 by Le Cene in Amsterdam. In 1733 a competing Amsterdam publisher brought out *Sei sonate a violino e violone o cimbalo*, also as op. 1. Those who know the habits of publishers of the time will not be surprised to learn that two years later yet another op. 1 appeared in print.

Both form and melodic style put these early works in the neighborhood of Vivaldi; the concertos especially follow that popular model. Yet soon certain style elements begin to emerge that point toward early romanticism. These were the qualities that impressed mid-century musicians and raised Tartini to the forefront of music developments of the day.

His best-known composition is the "Devil's Trill" Sonata, a work that is masterful in concept, execution, and exploration of the violin's possibilities. Tartini said that in 1730 he had a dream in which the devil appeared to him and played a sonata. On awakening he tried to play and commit to paper what he had heard, but what he was able to write down was but a faint recollection. The story has been discredited as a romantic fantasy, invented for the sake of publicity, but why doubt it? What Tartini requires the violinist to play is indeed devilish:

The colorful story gave rise to some other much admired compositions. Around 1830, Auguste Panseron, a French composer of romances, wrote *Le songe de Tartini, grande scène vocale avec violon obligé*; it became a favorite of Mme Viardot. A ballet by Cesare Pugni, *Le violon de diable*, was given at the Paris Opéra in 1849. Charles-Victor Saint-Léon was choreographer, solo dancer, and violinist, having written the violin music for it.

Around 1735–1740, Tartini's concerto style underwent a profound change toward the light and pleasantly expressive, characterized by such themes as the beginning of the Concerto in G major, Dounias catalog no. 76:

Continuing in this direction, Tartini increasingly turned to themes made up of liedlike periods. The overall form of a movement also changed. Instead of the conventional ritornello–solo sequence we have what amounts to ternary form. The orchestral introduction and first solo are repeated, which is indicated by the repeat sign. In general, we notice a gradual approach to the first-movement form of the classic concerto.

His was a keen, speculative mind. In 1714, according to his own recollection, he discovered the terzo tuono, or combination tone, a low pitch that becomes audible when a higher double stop, such as a major third, is played in pure intonation. Tartini made use of this discovery as a teaching aid in controlling intonation. In all, Tartini, as violinist, teacher, and composer, was one of the eighteenth century's outstanding musicians. His *oeuvre* includes 175 violin sonatas with basso continuo, 150 concertos, forty trio sonatas, thirty violin sonatas without (or with optional) basso continuo, and fifteen works for string orchestra. These numbers are approximate: the authorship of some works is uncertain, and previously unknown ones continue to be found.

Soon after Tartini's death, rapid changes in taste caused his music to be seen as old-fashioned. In 1768, Maddalena Lombardini de Sirmen successfully performed a Tartini concerto at the Concert Spirituel. Seventeen years later, in May 1785, when she again appeared in Paris, the Mercure de France commented,

We cannot deny that she created a less favorable impression this time. Mme Sirmen's playing continues to reflect the principles of Tartini's excellent schooling, somewhat forgotten today. Her tone has magic beauty; her technique is fine. Her charming and graceful playing is perhaps enhanced by her attractiveness—but her style is the same she displayed seventeen years ago: it is completely outdated. . . . Since this manner no longer is fashionable, we feel impelled to advise her to perform more modern concertos.

THE CLASSIC SOLO CONCERTO

The essential formal principle of mid-eighteenth-century music was the emerging use of contrasting thematic material, of concise thematic germs. Monothematic writing, typical of baroque music, had lent cohesion to fugal structures but also to concerto movements based on one orchestral ritornello. Independently of each other, many composers seem to have felt the desire for expressive contrast, among them Domenico Scarlatti, Johann Stamitz, and Sammartini. Contrast was brought about by the introduction of a second theme, or contrasting tonality. In Haydn's early works such a second theme amounted to little more than a variant of the first theme, but it gradually acquired more independence. Such formal arrangements later gave rise to the term "sonata (or sonata–allegro, or first-movement) form." In broadest outline, it is organized as follows: the movement's first section (exposition) presents the two contrasting themes, the second appearing, after a modulating passage, in a new key, often the dominant. The exposition is then repeated. In the movement's second large section, the thematic material is modified and developed (hence the term "development" for this section), while the third section, the reprise or recapitulation, brings back the exposition, but now stressing the principal key. This formal arrangement is found in the first movements of most three- or four-movement sonatas, at times also in the slow movement, somewhat more often in the finale. The term "sonata form" similarly applies to orchestral and chamber music works. Formally speaking, a symphony of this age might be seen as a "sonata for orchestra," a piano trio is a "sonata for violin, cello, and piano," and so forth.

During the classic/romantic age these structural concepts also apply to the solo concerto, a "sonata for solo instrument and orchestra." Given the division into solo and orchestra portions, the sonata–allegro form was modified in various ways. In one frequent design, the orchestra presents both (or even more) themes, which results in a far longer orchestral introduction than what we found in the ritornello of the older solo concerto type. The soloist then may present both themes, and this exposition is not repeated. A close integration of solo and tutti parts characterizes the development, and the recapitulation brings a shortened orchestral exposition. Immediately before the concluding tutti we arrive at a cadence, the place for the soloist's cadenza, which up to Liszt's time was often improvised. The final tutti usually is quite short, strong, and affirmative in mood. Coming immediately after the soloist's brilliant cadenza it led directly to audience applause. (Up to the time of Bruckner's symphonies it was customary to applaud after each movement.)

This basic formal concept was subject to much variation. Often the soloist would be heard during the orchestral exposition, at which time new thematic material might be introduced, combined with themes in the orchestra to become double themes.

A concerto's middle movement normally was in A-B-A form, with some modification of the opening section. Rondo form was popular for the last movement, the recurring statements of the main theme suggesting virtuosic variation by the soloist.

The cadenza's traditional place was immediately before the orchestral conclusion, at the point where the orchestra had reached a I_4^6 chord that normally would resolve, by way of the dominant, to the tonic. Composers left the cadenza to the soloist's discretion and imagination, though there was at least a possibility that he or she might improvise a cadenza that was not organically related to the movement itself. The public, of course, was curious about just what the soloist would come up with, and a skillful improviser might fascinate the audience. This atmosphere of expectant tension is hard for us to imagine today, when soloists perform cadenzas, usually composed by someone else, that they have carefully memorized, with the composer duly mentioned on the concert program.

Violinists in the age of Kreutzer and Baillot did indeed improvise their cadenzas. In the performance of a quintet for piano and wind instruments, Beethoven, the pianist, annoyed the other players when, in an improvised cadenza, he repeatedly reached what they believed to be the final trill only to go on with more improvisation—causing the others to raise their instruments to the playing position only to have to put them down again. No doubt the public was greatly amused. When, at a concert in Mainz, the pianist Joseph Wölfl played his cadenza, an approaching marching band could be heard outside. With great presence of mind Wölfl modulated to the key in which they were playing, embroidered the march with elaborate passage work and, as the band disappeared into the distance, returned to his own cadenza. Frenetic applause ensued.

Problems could arise if the soloist, overly anxious to display all technical prowess, embarked upon an endless cadenza. At an already long concert in Lille the violinist Alexandre Boucher treated his audience to such a never-ending, improvised cadenza. Without his noticing, one orchestra player after another stealthily left the platform. When he finally reached the concluding trill he had to laugh: no musicians remained for the final tutti.

MOZART'S COMPOSITIONS FOR VIOLIN

At the age of eighteen, Leopold Mozart, the son of a bookbinder, left his native Augsburg to study philosophy at the Salzburg university. Soon his love of music won out over academic pursuits and he entered the archbishop's musical establishment. He rose to the post of chamber composer and eventually vice kapellmeister. Displaying a decided talent for teaching he became one of Salzburg's most sought-after instructors of violin and pianoforte. His well-known pedagogical work, the *Violinschule*, grew out of his experience. It was published in 1756, the year his son Wolfgang Amadeus was born.

Wolfgang grew up in an atmosphere saturated with music and was exceptionally well cared for and guided in that field. The piano became his principal instrument, but from his fourth year on he also played the violin. No wonder, then, that everything he wrote for the violin seems to fit just right. We may think of Mozart only as a composer and keyboard player and tend to ignore that he was also an excellent violinist, especially during his years of employment in Salzburg. Systematic violin lessons began in his seventh year. A lively report of his amazing talent for that instrument has come down to us from Andreas Schachtner, family friend and court trumpeter; it has often been quoted [as in Heartz 1995. *Ed.*]. As early as June 1763 Wolfgang was able to play a violin concerto with improvised cadenzas for the elector of Bavaria. From then on a violin was his constant travel companion. As a child prodigy he was presented to an amazed public playing both piano and violin, as he did in Frankfurt in August of the same year. He performed on a Mittenwald violin labeled "Jacobus Stainer, Absam, 1659." Later he gave it to his sister; it is now on exhibit in the Salzburg Mozarteum.

His many travels provided frequent opportunities to meet violinists and to acquaint himself with their ways of playing. This affected his own playing style and also his composing for the violin. In Munich, the seven-year-old boy heard Luigi Tomasini, Haydn's concertmaster, which gave Wolfgang a taste of the Italian style. Tartini had a strong though indirect influence as he had many pupils throughout Europe; their paths frequently crossed those of the young composer from Salzburg. In 1763 in Ludwigsburg he made the acquaintance of Pietro Nardini who, seven years later, "accompanied" Mozart in Florence (where he was court kapellmeister) in a sonata for piano and violin. When the Mozart family, on their extended journey to England, spent almost a year in Paris, Wolfgang, at the Concert Spirituel, repeatedly heard violin concertos composed and performed by Gaviniès. Somewhat later the French school of violin playing would affect the style of Mozart's own violin concertos. Other violinists he heard in Paris were Horand, Besson, and Nicolas Capron; in Brussels, Friedrich Schwindel, "virtuoso di violino." In London it was the French violinist Barthélémon. Adam and Georg Kreusser, both concertmasters in Amsterdam, were among the Mozarts' acquaintances.

In 1769, just before the first tour of Italy, the thirteen-year-old was appointed the archbishop's concertmaster. It was agreed that his salary would not be paid until after the Mozarts' return (1772), when Wolfgang would actually assume the position. Thus Mozart, like Beethoven, earned his first regular salary as a string player. Again and again in his travel diaries and letters from Italy we come across the names of well-known violinists: Locatelli in Verona; Lucchini, Boroni, Pasqualini, and Vinacchini in Milan; Monigi in Parma; Gaetano Pugnani in Turin; Nazari, Colonna, and (on the second journey) Antonio Lolli in Venice. These artists represented strong competition, as did some of their outstanding students, such as Nardini's pupil

Thomas Linley. In view of this Mozart no longer played in public but did not neglect the violin entirely, thinking ahead to his Salzburg appointment. On his return to that city, his duties as concertmaster included participation in evening performances such as serenades, and in cathedral services.

But the violin for him was not merely a way to earn a living. Having received recognition abroad he also wanted to prove himself as a violinist in front of his Salzburg colleagues. His first soloistic work for violin is a "concertone" for two solo violins, two oboes, two horns, two trumpets, and strings, dated 3 May 1773 and evidently intended for his own use. No high position playing or complex bowing is required. The other violinist was the Italian Antonio Brunetti, who normally shared the first stand with Mozart and in 1777 moved up to his position. Brunetti was not without influence on the composer. When he found the slow movement of Mozart's A major Violin Concerto (K. 219) "too learned," Mozart obliged with a substitute, the Adagio K. 261. Other pieces for his Salzburg friend followed, including the Rondo for violin and orchestra K. 373, performed on 8 April 1781 in Vienna. A violin sonata was also heard on that occasion. Mozart improvised the piano part, having run out of time to write it down.

Brunetti gladly acknowledged his younger colleague's genius. He may have provided the stimulus for Mozart's composing the five famous violin concertos, between 14 April and 20 December 1775, a period in Mozart's life of felicitous inspiration. They are the concertos in B-flat major K. 207, D major K. 211, G major K. 216, D major K. 218, and A major K. 219. Except for the first, all are written in keys that sound good on the violin, making use of the sympathetic vibration of open strings that also favor the sound of certain double stops and chords.

This is social music, but written for a highly cultivated society that appreciated musical achievement due to their own involvement in music as amateurs. Mozart's concertos were heard on various occasions at court and also in the theater. In a letter to his son (6 October 1777) Leopold Mozart had this news for him:

> On Saturday I went to the theater. Since there also was a French play, requiring costume changes, Brunetti had to play a concerto; it was your own Strassburg Concerto [K. 218]. He played quite well, but there were some mishaps in the two allegro movements, and once in a cadenza he almost couldn't find his way back down.

Soloistic music also occurs in the serenades, usually forming part of a larger work. The serenades for orchestra K. 185, 203, and 204, written at about the time of the violin concertos, all feature a solo violin, as does the famous "Haffner" Serenade K. 250. Its movements consist of an Allegro maestoso/Allegro molto; Andante (with solo violin); Menuetto (solo violin in the trio); Rondeau (with solo violin); Menuetto galante; Andante; Menuetto (with two trios); Adagio; and Allegro assai—amounting to a three-movement violin concerto inserted in an orchestra serenade. We can imagine Mozart playing the solo violin, surrounded by music-loving citizens, in a palace or the house of a patrician. Such movements with solo violin sometimes were published separately. In his *Hohe Schule* Ferdinand David took the Andante, Menuet, and Rondo from K. 204 and assembled them into a short concerto. The autograph of another D major concerto, K. 271a is lost; it supposedly was dated 16 July 1777. The solo part is extremely brilliant but differs so much from the 1775 concertos that it may well be an arrangement by an early nineteenth-century virtuoso.

Marius Casadesus published another "Mozart" concerto in 1933 under the title "Adelaide." Experts have never believed it to be authentic. The story goes that on 26 May 1766 in Versailles the ten-year-old Mozart dedicated it to Princess Adelaide who in 1791, before her flight to Trieste, supposedly entrusted it to Laval de Montmorency. His descendants then kept the precious manuscript until it was published. But on the day in question Mozart was not in Versailles, and the Montmorency family died out in 1851. Walter Lebermann proved that this concerto (like others, among them the viola concerto allegedly by Handel) was fabricated by Casadesus, who in this regard may have been inspired by Kreisler (see p. 473). He may also be the composer of some melodies that Stravinsky believed to be by Pergolesi. In July 1977 Casadesus finally admitted to having written the "Handel" concerto. Nor is the Violin Concerto in E-flat major K. 268 by Mozart, at least not in its preserved form.

Lebermann also believes on good evidence that a violin concerto in D major, published by Schott in 1924 as being by Boccherini, is a forgery. Samuel Dushkin received the manuscript (a twentieth-century copy) from Nonnel, Diaghilev's secretary. Its close resemblance to K. 218 caused some Mozart experts to reluctantly concede that it might be a Mozart "adaptation." An autograph has never been located.

Mozart's authentic violin concertos amount to the high point, both in musical substance and violinistic writing, between Bach's two concertos and the only one by Beethoven. Written during the decade after Tartini's death, they make the vast concerto repertory before Tartini seem antiquated. Nor do concertos by Kreutzer, Baillot, Rode, Viotti, and others live up to the quality of Mozart's works. It therefore seems all the more strange that after Mozart's death the concertos of these violinists were performed everywhere, while Mozart's violin concertos (unlike his piano concertos) were seldom heard. They now have a secure place in the education of all violinists, while even the greatest virtuosos perform them and continually ponder questions of their interpretation.

Among Mozart's violin compositions the sonatas for piano and violin occupy an important place. We are likely to call them violin sonatas, but they are far removed from baroque violin sonatas in which the melody line was the chief interest, supported by a bass providing the harmonic foundation. (Contrapuntally conceived fugato movements are the exception.) The classic violin sonata developed out of the harpsichord sonata, to which a violin part was added for melodic and expressive reinforcement. A 1707 collection entitled *Sonates de clavecin avec violon facultatif* (Harpsichord sonatas with optional violin part) provides the earliest known examples. In the *oeuvre* of some composers the changeover from the basso continuo sonata to the accompanied harpsichord sonata took place within a short time span. Mondonville's op. 1 of 1733, for instance, is entitled *Sonates pour le violon avec la basse chiffré*, while his op. 3 (ca. 1734) appeared as *Pièces de clavecin en sonates, avec accompagnement de violon.*

While in Paris and London, Leopold Mozart wanted to introduce little Wolfgang to this genre, for which purpose he took the boy's keyboard sonatas K. 6–9 and added a violin part, probably of his own. The results were printed as *Sonates pour le clavecin qui peuvent se jouer avec l'accompagnement de violon*, indicating the *ad libitum* nature of the violin part. There is therefore a distinction between these pieces and a set of three sonatas by Saint-Georges, *Trois sonates pour le clavecin ou fortepiano avec accompagnement de violon obligé*, making it clear that in these the violin part was essential.

Mozart's next sonatas, K. 10–15 of 1765, were dedicated to the queen of England and engraved in London as op. 2. A cello part *ad libitum* was added, and the melody line could be played by either violin or flute. In all, Mozart wrote thirty-eight violin sonatas and two sets of variations. In these the violin gradually emerges as the piano's equal. In essence, Mozart prepared the way for the true duo, as represented by Beethoven's ten sonatas. Yet even then it was customary to speak of the violinist as the accompanist, and early editions of Beethoven's sonatas refer to them as "for piano and violin."

Compared with Mozart's violin compositions, those of Haydn are less significant. This is surprising, for in his string quartets Haydn provided much idiomatic writing for the violin, showing (as he did in the symphonies) that he knew well how to write for it. According to Pohl, Haydn wrote nine violin concertos; other sources mention twelve. Of these, four have been preserved, in C, B-flat, A, and G major; the attribution of five others is problematic. There is also a piano concerto in F major with a solo violin part. All these were written in Eisenstadt for Haydn's concertmaster Luigi Tomasini; in his *Entwurfskatalog* Haydn refers to one of them as "concerto per il violino fatto per il luigi." Concerning the sonatas for violin and piano Hoboken says, "We are not certain that Haydn composed piano duos." Most of the works under consideration are arrangements of divertimentos or keyboard sonatas with added (not by Haydn) violin parts, and one of them is a piano trio from which the cello part has been omitted.

Some duets can be played by two violinists standing across from each other and playing from the same part, placed on a table between them. They have been called "mirror" or "upside down" duets and have been ascribed to both Haydn and Mozart. Listeners and onlookers are always intrigued by these, but the compositional process involved is actually fairly simple. (A mirror duet allegedly by Mozart is reproduced on p. 332.)

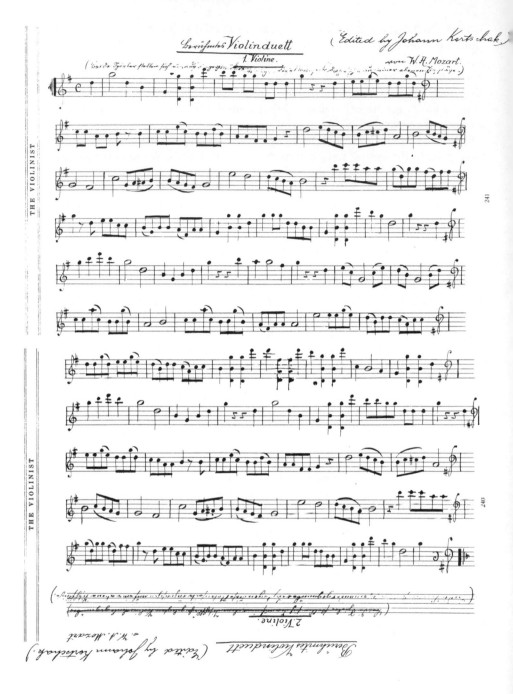

Berühmtes Violinduett
1. Violine.

(Edited by Johann Kortschak.)
von W. A. Mozart.

241

243

2 Violine.

THE ORIGINS OF THE STRING QUARTET

QUARTETS BY HAYDN AND MOZART

During the late eighteenth and the nineteenth centuries, piano sonatas, lieder with piano accompaniment, and string quartets were among the most favored genres for informal music making in the home and among friends. A rich repertory attests to this, such as Schubert's six hundred lieder and Haydn's "eighty-three" string quartets, seventy-two of which are now considered authentic. (At least some of the six string quartets of op. 3 are now believed to have been written by Roman Hoffstetter.)

Compositions for two violins, viola, and cello, without basso continuo, began to appear ca. 1750, but even in the 1600s it was not uncommon to play in similar ensembles, also without continuo, with string bass rather than cello. Muffat relates that five-part works (which we normally consider orchestral music) could also be played with one player on a part and without figured bass. When, as he continues, the second or tenor viola part also could be omitted, we actually have a description of string quartet playing. The many four-part suites by Schein, Scheidt, Peuerl, Franck, and others, according to their titles and the general custom of the time, were playable "on all sorts of instruments." In practice, performances by a string quartet were among the options. This still does not represent writing specifically intended for a string quartet but simply for four parts, as indicated by titles such as "sonata a quattro," "concertino a quattro," or "quadro." Also pointing in the direction of the later string quartet was the custom, even in the early 1700s, to add a viola to the solo trio of the concerto grosso. The leading string players of an orchestra often worked together as the concertino group, helping to create a demand for true string quartet music.

One step had yet to be taken: to turn away from the traditional concept of the figured bass and its function, replacing it by true four-part texture in which the second and third parts (the inner voices) did not merely complete the harmony but became nearly equal partners. Such a trend was increasingly noted ca. 1730, and in time the keyboard instrument as a supplier of harmonic support became superfluous. Tradition caused it to be included for another half century or even longer, but not in an essential way. Instead, composers gave more importance to the middle voices. We can trace this development in the music of Stamitz and his circle, and in works by C. P. E. Bach and John Christian Bach, Sammartini, and others.

Soloistic music making by the four-part concertino group came to appeal to amateurs as well, and composers were quick to fill the need for appropriate music. Georg Matthias Monn (1717–1750) must have been one of the first to do so. His *Six quatuors* for two violins, viola, and cello were not published in Vienna until 1808, but their composition antedates Haydn's earliest quartets. When Luigi Boccherini published his *Six quatuors, opus 1, dédiés aux véritables dilettantes et connaisseurs en musique* (Paris 1761), he no doubt thought about amateur performers as well as listeners. Haydn's first quartet, dated 1750 by Griesinger and 1755 by Pohl, also owed its origin to a group of amateur players. An excerpt from Franz Joseph Fröhlich's long encyclopedia article about Haydn, written in 1828, follows:

> At this time he wrote his first quartet for Baron Fürnberg, who occasionally invited friends for a pleasant get-together to make music: his parish priest, his administrator, Haydn, and Albrechtsberger (the brother of the excellent composer and organist), who plays the cello.

This well describes the kind of social setting for which composers wrote quartets. Such a "pleasant get-together" of five people was typical. Haydn's twelve quartets of opp. 1 and 2 were also published with a continuo part and were probably played that way with Fürnberg. Soon after 1760, quartets by Sacchini, Pugnani, Vanhal, Boccherini, and Gassmann were published in Paris; some with, others without continuo. At these sessions with Baron Fürnberg, Haydn (who as an adolescent had earned a living as a dance fiddler) probably played viola. Like Mozart's violin concertos, Haydn's quartets were based on firsthand experience with the instruments.

Haydn wrote more quartets during his years in Eisenstadt, though at first his duties there required him above all to compose symphonies. Luigi Tomasini was the accomplished concertmaster of the prince's orchestra; he may also have played chamber music with his kapellmeister. A new wave of string quartets followed between 1769 and 1772, those of opp. 9, 17, and 20. Like the symphonies and sonatas, these display clearly differentiated themes and elaborate development sections. They stand far above run-of-the-mill works by others that were intended for enthusiastic amateur players.

Mozart wrote his early quartets without any knowledge of Haydn's accomplishments in that genre. Wolfgang's first quartet dates from his second journey to Italy and was written in Lodi in 1770; three others were added in Salzburg in 1772. During that same year, having again set out for Italy, he wrote another quartet "in miserable Bolzano, out of sheer boredom." This was the first of the six "Milan" quartets K. 155–160. Their style points to Tartini, Sammartini, and Boccherini, suggesting that they were inspired by what Mozart was hearing in Italy. The six quartets K. 168–173 were written within a few weeks of each other in Vienna. Their style, and their dedication to Haydn, are evidence of Mozart's involvement with the venerated master's music. The title "Haydn" quartets, however, has been given to six later quartets, K. 387, 421, 428, 458, 464, and 465, written in Vienna between 1782 and 1785. This cycle, among Mozart's masterworks, also was dedicated to Mozart's "dear friend Haydn" who, between 1778 and 1781, had raised string quartet writing to new heights. Haydn's op. 33 quartets have become known as the "Russian" quartets because of their dedication to Grand Duke Paul of Russia.

Mozart was inspired not only by these and other Haydn compositions. Through contact with the Viennese Baron Gottfried van Swieten, a great

Bach admirer, he had become familiar with Bach's music. But beyond all these studies and sources of inspiration it was Mozart's unique genius that led to the creation of his masterful and supremely individualistic music. We need only listen to his great C major Quartet which, because of the remarkable successive entrances of the four parts, has acquired the title "Dissonant" Quartet. Certainly, remarkable heights were reached by both Haydn and Mozart. One can indeed speak of a dialogue, especially when we consider their personal contacts at gatherings in Mozart's quarters, where the latest string quartets would be read through by this remarkable ensemble: Johann Baptist Vanhal, first violin; Joseph Haydn, second violin; Wolfgang Mozart, viola; and Karl Dittersdorf, cello. It was a source of great satisfaction for Leopold Mozart that shortly before his death he could hear his son's great quartets played by such a distinguished group.

In all, Mozart wrote twenty-three quartets. The last of these, K. 575, 589, and 590, were commissioned by King Friedrich Wilhelm II of Prussia, a fine cellist and devoted quartet player. Mozart made sure that the cello parts offered the king ample solo passages.

Haydn, too, was approached with commissions for quartets. Johann Tost, a former member of the Eszterháza orchestra and a fine violinist, was now a well-to-do merchant eager to play Haydn quartets written expressly for him. Two groups of six quartets each, opp. 54 and 64, were the result; they represent a transition to Haydn's mature masterworks in that genre, which he would write for the Apponyi, Eröly, and Lobkowitz families, members of the Austro-Hungarian nobility. Later, Haydn personally supervised a complete edition of his quartets and prepared a string quartet arrangement of his *Seven Last Words*. There are other quartet arrangements and, as mentioned before, quartets of doubtful authenticity. His Quartet in C major, op. 76, no. 3, became famous as the "Emperor" Quartet. It includes a set of variations on the hymn to the emperor that Haydn had written a few months earlier. The melody then became the Austrian national anthem; later it was similarly used in Germany.

In 1793, when Haydn wrote the opp. 71 and 74 quartets, the young Beethoven had already arrived in Vienna from Bonn to study with Haydn. Beethoven's mentor Count Waldstein and Haydn himself introduced him to the Viennese nobility, circles in which the most recent quartets were likely to be played even before they were published. Some of these aristocratic families maintained their own quartets of professional players. Family members might also participate, playing on fine instruments that had been in the family for generations.

In his youth, and especially after his arrival in Vienna, Beethoven, as a composer in many genres, intended to follow in Haydn's and Mozart's footsteps. His op. 18 quartets, written between 1798 and 1800, represented important milestones in Beethoven's development. Sketches for some of these may go back to his Bonn years. In these six quartets Beethoven's strong ties to Vienna's string quartet tradition are evident, as is his own individuality and ever maturing artistic personality.

Aside from Haydn's and Mozart's masterworks and Beethoven's early contributions, the turn-of-the-century period provided an abundance of quartets by somewhat lesser masters, such as Boccherini (ca. ninety quartets), Bruni, Cambini (144 quartets), Danzi, Dittersdorf, Dotzauer, Fesca, Fraenzel, Gyrowetz, Haensel, Hofmeister, R. Kreutzer, Krommer, Pleyel, Reicha, Rode, A. Romberg, B. Romberg, Vanhal, Viotti, ·and A. Wranitzky, to mention some of the most productive talents of the second and third magnitude. Similar works of chamber music for different groups of instruments include string quintets (usually for two violins, two violas, and cello) and string trios, the latter sometimes jokingly referred to as string quartets with a missing second violin. (To this day, amateur quartet players may turn to string trios if one of the violinists fails to show up!) Mozart's string quintets K. 174, 515, 516, 593, and 614 are among the best of the kind. No doubt the composer often participated as a violist, as he did in the premiere of the "Kegelstatt" Trio K. 498 for clarinet, viola, and piano.

Most of Haydn's trios, whether authentic or not, are for two violins and cello, a popular combination during the early days of the string trio because there were more violinists than violists. In time, violin, viola, and cello became the favored scoring. Again Mozart's contribution to the genre, the Divertimento in E-flat major K. 563, is outstanding. It makes great technical demands on all three players. This work, and Beethoven's Serenade op. 8 for string trio, through the titles and their multi-movement form, represent an Austrian tradition of chiefly outdoor music making. Serenades and divertimentos were cherished entertainments for important family events, such as birthdays, name days, engagements, and weddings, especially during the summer.

Popular chamber music categories included the piano trio (piano, violin, cello), piano quartet (with added viola), and piano quintet (usually piano and string quartet). As discussed earlier, the piano sonata stood at the beginning of these genres. C. P. E. Bach's piano trios, published 1776 and 1777 in Leipzig, were called "sonatas for the clavier with the accompaniment of a violin and a cello." Haydn's thirty-one trios, and Mozart's eight, indicate the genre's popularity in middle class and aristocratic circles.

Chamber music composing and violin playing affected each other in important ways. In late eighteenth-century society, violin playing was widespread and the level of accomplishment often astonishingly high. Playing chamber music in the home, with family and friends, was a well-established custom that inspired composers and publishers. A rich, often high-quality repertory offered motivation and incentive for violinists to play their instruments well enough so that they could tackle the great contributions of Haydn, Mozart, and Beethoven. Haydn's first violin parts at times are extremely challenging. That chamber music of this kind was attempted and enjoyed by amateur players gives us an idea of the level of violin playing reached in at least some circles.

ORCHESTRA PLAYING IN THE EIGHTEENTH CENTURY

THE CLASSICAL SYMPHONY

Music held an important place in eighteenth-century court life, with Versailles serving as the model. Lesser princes may not have been able to maintain "vingt-quatre violons," but they were eager to reproduce at least some of the Sun King's splendor. Having a music ensemble may simply have have been a matter of prestige for some rulers; others were motivated by a true love of music. Members of the nobility often received good music training as part of their general education, including learning to play an instrument and rudiments of harmony and composition.

During the seventeenth century, court orchestras were well established in Vienna, London, Versailles, and Dresden; many lesser ensembles were founded in the early eighteenth century. Size depended largely on the ruler's means, though it was not uncommon for him to exceed them, ever eager to impress his peers and his subjects. When Mozart was born, the Mannheim orchestra had forty-two members, to which trumpeters and timpanists from the military band were added as needed. The Salzburg archbishop, Leopold Mozart's lifelong employer, maintained an orchestra of twenty-five, including ten violinists. As the century progressed, a trend to enlarge such orchestras is documented in account books, budgets, travelers' reports, and musicians' letters.

This tendency corresponds with the scoring of classic orchestra music, from Haydn's youth symphonies (strings, two oboes, two horns) to his and Mozart's late works. In 1773 at the Concert Spirituel one might hear thirteen first and eleven second violins, four violas, ten cellos, four basses, nine woodwinds (including four bassoons!), two horns, two trumpets, and timpani. In the Paris Concert des Amateurs the players at times included as many as forty violins (probably including violas), twelve cellos, and eight basses. The San Carlo Opera in Naples employed eighteen first and eighteen second violins; La Scala in Milan used fourteen of each. Monster orchestras were assembled for special events such as the 1784 Handel celebrations in London with forty-eight first and forty-two second violins, while in a 1786 event in Berlin, thirty-eight first and thirty-nine second violins participated. An orchestra of 160 played for Haydn's *Creation* in Prague in 1807.

In Berlin, in addition to the royal court orchestra, small ensembles were maintained by the princes of Prussia for their private use. In 1754 Prince Carl employed five violins plus one player each for the other string parts, along with one flute, three oboes, one bassoon, and two horns. Prince Heinrich's group consisted of only nine players, including four violins. Both were flexible and could be enlarged.

In general, wind players played several instruments: flute players doubled on oboe, and some wind players could also hold down string parts. Someone looking for court employment as a secretary, valet, kitchen overseer, or hunter's apprentice was likely to succeed if he played an instrument and could serve as an auxiliary orchestra member. Town musicians and local organists might also be recruited, and for special occasions one could borrow musicians from a nearby princely establishment. Military bands also expected members to be versatile. From a small book by H. Fleming entitled *Der vollkommene teutsche Soldat* (The perfect German soldier, 1726) we learn the following:

> Every morning, the oboists will play a song in front of the colonel's quarters: perhaps a favorite march, an *entrée*, and a few minuets. . . . The same will happen in the evening. When the colonel entertains, they will play on violins and basses, also on recorders and other instruments. Their leader must also know something about composing.

In eighteenth-century Germany, church orchestras, so common in Italy, were seldom found. The court orchestra would play for religious services; in larger episcopal residences such as Salzburg (where the archbishop also was the secular head of state) the same orchestra served him in his palace and in the cathedral. In the "free" cities, musicians employed by the town council also supplied music for the churches. Bach was not happy with the quality of those in Leipzig. But what they lacked in expertise they made up for in versatility; "with strings and with brass" they accompanied a burgher's life from the cradle to the grave—string music at the christening and brass music at the funeral.

With so many orchestras large and small, supported by nobility and municipalities, there was ample employment for trained eighteenth-century violinists. Professional players like Leopold Mozart were also teachers of their instruments and were likely to perform chamber music at private gatherings, so that each orchestra tended to promote violin playing. We have already noted the increase in instrument making, even on a large industrial scale, and the growth of music publishing.

The first serious setback to all this growth was related to the wars following the French Revolution. In 1799, a reporter for the *Allgemeine Musikalische Zeitung* wrote thus:

> The [Frankfurt] orchestra for the most part consists of players from the former chapels in Cologne, Mainz, Trier, Zweibrücken, and Saarbrücken. Due to present conditions, princely employers have been forced to furlough their personnel until times again will be more propitious.

Another setback followed, namely the devaluation of currencies, which forced many noblemen to dissolve their orchestras.

To judge by contemporary accounts, the level of competency in orchestras, from Corelli to Beethoven, varied greatly. Again, much of this depended on a prince's artistic ideas and the means at his disposal. Outstanding players sold their services to the highest bidder, and Italian concertmasters were especially expensive. In the long run, an orchestra's accomplishments largely were governed by the leader's standards. Often musicians of modest gifts would move up to such positions; with advancing years their ability to enforce high standards might decline. Top orchestras existed only where a top artist was in charge and was given the opportunity to realize his artistic aims. This was the case in Venice at Vivaldi's Ospedale della Pietà. His student Pisendel took back to Germany what he had learned and observed there. In his *Briefe eines aufmerksamen Reisenden*, J. F. Reichardt describes what he saw:

> Pisendel spared no effort. For each opera or sacred work he would carefully mark the dynamics in all the orchestra parts, even minute shadings, and would also mark all bowings. As a result, performances of the Dresden orchestra, a very select group, displayed utmost order and precision.

Even more renowned, as we learned, was the Mannheim orchestra, carefully supervised by Johann Stamitz. That group was famous for the execution of a gradual crescendo, from a barely audible *ppp* to *fff*. The poet Christian Friedrich Daniel Schubart provided this oft-quoted description:

> There is no orchestra in the world that surpasses the Mannheimers. Its *forte* is like thunder, its crescendo, a downpour; its diminuendo a gentle river disappearing in the distance, its *piano* a breath of spring. The wind instruments are used to best advantage; they uplift and carry, they reinforce and give life to the storm of the orchestra.

Such high achievements must have been noted by other court orchestras, even if emulating them was beyond their reach.

The post of kapellmeister was frequently held by a virtuoso violinist. In an age when orchestras were "conducted" from the concertmaster's stand and from the harpsichord, the surest way to rise to the top position was to excel as a violinist. It was the best way to train and lead an orchestra. Many an eighteenth-century kapellmeister was a composer but also a good or excellent violinist. In 1752, Gluck led his orchestra violin in hand or, as the saying then went, "He conducted his symphony on the violin." (Many famous conductors also began their careers as violinists, including Spohr, Damrosch, Lamoureux, Nikisch, Monteux, Maazel, and Kertész; for seven years Charles Munch was the Leipzig concertmaster under Furtwängler.) If a kapellmeister also composed, regular association with good performers was apt to inspire him. Haydn's early employment was with Count Morzin in Lukavec, later with several Esterházy princes in Eisenstadt. He reminisced, "As the orchestra's conductor I was able to experiment. . . . I was isolated from the world at large . . . and had to become original." His orchestra was far above average and not without influence on Vienna's music scene. Many a musician who later became a kapellmeister began as a violinist in Eisenstadt, among them Paul Wranitzky, the eventual kapellmeister at the Vienna court.

Lukavec was a small country estate; there, in 1759, Haydn wrote his

First Symphony, inspired and governed by the resources available to him. Eighteenth-century society and its musical culture always had a bearing on his work. The old complete edition of his works included 104 symphonies; that number has been revised. Some symphonies are of uncertain authorship, others are outright forgeries, for claiming Haydn as the composer always helped sales.

Mozart began writing symphonies in London, at the age of nine. They were inspired by works of John Christian Bach, which were close to the Italian opera sinfonia or overture, an approach to the symphony quite different from young Haydn's. Bright, spirited outer movements are typical of these early works, featuring first violin parts with brilliant passage work. Mozart's later activity as Salzburg concertmaster has left its trace in symphonies from that period. When in 1781 he left Salzburg for Vienna he had composed more than forty symphonies. His final ones are closer to Haydn's manner; works of great depth that represent high points in symphonic literature, notably the last three in E-flat major, G minor, and C major (the "Jupiter").

An article in the *Allgemeine Musikalische Zeitung* of 1799 conveys a lively picture of the kind of setting in which symphonies were then performed.

> During the year's pleasant season, Herr Schuppanzigh presents twelve to sixteen concerts in the great hall of the Augarten. They begin at the unusual hour of seven a.m. and last about two hours. Many amateur players participate except in the string bass and wind sections. Herr Schuppanzigh directs the music with great precision and much fire, giving the best possible rendition of each composition. His work serves as a model for all other such events and for their directors. Here one can hear the most difficult symphonies by Haydn and Mozart, played with a precision and clarity that brings out all the beauty with which the composers have endowed every instrumental part. There never is a lack of an audience, though here as elsewhere people want to hear good music but hope to pay little or nothing. Herr Schuppanzigh is mindful of these folks: a subscriber pays only 4 florins 30 kreuzer for four concerts, but in return is given twenty-four tickets. This very low price of admission brings in lots of listeners, always eager to hear new music and new virtuosos. They seldom are disappointed, for few virtuosos stay in Vienna for any length of time without appearing here, and few composers live in our city who would not let us hear their symphonies even before they have been published.

Many symphonies of this period made substantial demands on string players, especially on those in the first violin section. We can assume fairly high standards of orchestra playing, though rehearsals were few and somewhat casual by our standards. This repertory did much to raise the quality and spread of violin playing in general. It is of course true that the technical requirements are even higher for playing violin parts in Wagner, Bruckner, and Strauss, but eighteenth-century symphonies present their own, very special challenges: every note will be heard—especially every wrong note! Many a seemingly harmless Haydn symphony contains treacherous passages about which players may worry more than about some major nineteenth-century symphonies.

INSTRUCTION BOOKS, 1750–1800

As violin music developed beyond Corelli, Vivaldi, Locatelli, and Bach, encompassing Mozart's concertos, Haydn's quartets and symphonies, and music by the violinist-composers Gaviniès and Viotti, violinists coped with new technical challenges. Numerous pedagogical works were written to fill this need; the most important are listed here.

ca. 1750	[Bordet?], *Méthode raisonnée pour apprendre la musique d'une façon claire et plus précise à laquelle on joint l'étendue de la flûte traversière, du violon*, Paris
	Robert Bremner, *The Compleat Tutor for the Violin*, London
	Carlo Tessarini, *Nouvelle méthode pour apprendre par théorie dans un mois de tems à jouer du violon*, Liège
1751	Francesco Geminiani, *The Art of Playing on the Violin*, London (facsim. rpt. 1952)
1752	Johann Joachim Quantz, *Versuch einer Anweisung die Flöte traversière zu spielen*, Berlin (rpt. Kassel 1992; Engl. trans. New York 1966, 1985)
ca. 1754	Giuseppe Tartini, *Regole per arrivare a saper ben suonar il violino*, Bologna (eds. in English, French, and German as *Traité des agréments de la musique*, Paris 1771, Celle and New York 1961)
ca. 1755	[Georg Chr. Wagenseil?], *Rudimenta Panduristae oder Geig-Fundamente*, Augsburg
1756	José Herrando, *Arte y puntual explicaciòn del modo de tocar el violon*, Paris
	Leopold Mozart, *Versuch einer gründlichen Violinschule*, Augsburg (Engl. trans. London 1948, 1985)
1757	Wenceslaus Wodiczka, *Instructions pour les commençans*, Amsterdam (trans. from German)
1758	Giuseppe Tartini, *L'arte dell'arco, ou L'art de l'archet*, Paris
1761	L'Abbé le fils, *Principes du violon pour apprendre le doigté de cet instrument et les différends agréments dont il est susceptible*, Paris (facsim. rpts. Paris 1961, Geneva 1976)
1762	Carlo Zuccari, *The True Method of Playing an Adagio Made Easy by Twelve Examples . . . Adapted for Those Who Study the Violin*, London
1763	E. C. R. Brijon, *Réflexions sur la musique et sur la vraie manière de l'exécuter sur le violon*, Paris (facsim. rpt. Geneva 1971)

Ignatz Franz Xaver Kürzinger, *Getreuer Unterricht zum Singen mit Manieren, und die Violin zu spielen*, Augsburg

1766   Anonymous, *Tablature idéale du violon, jugée par feu M. le Clair l'Aîné être la véritable*, Paris

ca. 1767   Stephen Philpot, *An Introduction to the Art of Playing on the Violin, on an Entire New Plan*, London

1770   Valentin Roeser, *Méthode raisonnée pour apprendre à jouer le violon*, Paris

1774   Georg Simon Löhlein, *Anweisung zum Violinspielen, mit pracktischen Beyspielen und zur Uebung mit vier und zwanzig kleinen Duetten erläutert*, Leipzig

Jean-Théodore Tarade, *Nouveaux principes de musique et de violon*, Paris

ca. 1775   Antonio Lolli, *École du violon avec alto et basse*, op. 8, Paris

1776   Joh. Fr. Reichardt, *Über die Pflichten des Ripien-Violinisten*, Berlin

1777   P. Signoretti, *Méthode contenant les principes de la musique et du violon*, The Hague

ca. 1780   Anonymous, *The Compleat Tutor for the Violin*, London

Vanheck, *Méthode de violon et de musique*, Paris

1782   Anonymous, *La parfaite connaissance du manche du violon*, Paris

Michel Corrette, *L'art de se perfectionner dans le violon*, Paris (facsim. rpt. Geneva 1973)

1783   Leoni, *Méthode raisonnée pour passer du violon à la mandoline*, Paris

ca. 1783   [Francesco Geminiani?], *The Entire and Compleate Tutor for the Violin*, London

[Francesco Geminiani?], *New and Compleat Instructions for the Violin*, London

[Francesco Geminiani?], *The Compleat Tutor for the Violin*, London

1784   [I. Astachofi], *Ecole de violon*, St. Petersburg

ca. 1784   Antonio Bartolomeo Bruni, *Nouvelle méthode de violon*, Paris

1784–   Bornet l'aîné, *Journal du violon*, Paris

1785   Ignaz Schweigl, *Grundlehre der Violin*, Vienna

1786   Joseph Gehot, *The Art of Bowing the Violin*, London

Ignaz Schweigl, *Verbesserte Grundlehre der Violin*, Vienna

1787   A. B. Bruni, *Caprices et airs variés en forme d'étude pour un violon seul*, Paris

Ferdinand Kauer, *Kurzgefasste Violinschule für Anfänger*, Vienna

Johann Anton Kobricht, *Geig-Fundament*, Augsburg

1788   Bornet l'aîné, *Nouvelle méthode de violon et de musique, dans laquelle on a observé toutes les gradations nécessaires pour apprendre ces deux arts ensemble*, Paris

ca. 1790   Jean-Joseph Cambini, *Méthode de violon*, Paris

	Federigo Fiorillo, *Étude pour le violon, formant 36 caprices* op. 3, Paris
	Frédéric Thiémé, *Principes abrégés de musique à l'usage de ceux qui veulent apprendre à jouer du violon*, Paris
	Anton Wranitzky, *Violinfundament*, Vienna
1791	Francesco Galeazzi, *Elementi teorico-pratici di musica*, Rome (part 2, 1796)
ca. 1792	Joseph Schmidt, *Principes de violon*, Amsterdam
1792	Johann Adam Hiller, *Anweisung zum Violinspielen, für Schulen, und zum Selbstunterricht; nebst einem kurzgefassten Lexicon der fremden Wörter und Benennungen in der Musik*, Leipzig (rpt. New York)
1793	Nicolo Mestrino, *Fantasie et variations pour violon seul*, Paris
ca. 1793	J. B. Labandens, *Nouvelle méthode pour apprendre à jouer du violon et à lire la musique*, Paris
ca. 1795	Alday l'aîné, *Nouvelle méthode de violon*, Lyon
	Jean-Joseph Cambini, *Petite méthode de violon*, Paris
1796	M. Durieu, *Méthode de violon par demandes et réponses*, Paris
1797	Bartolomeo Campagnoli, *Metodo per violino* op. 21, Milan (rpt. 1945)
1798	Antoine Bailleux, *Méthode raisonnée pour apprendre à jouer du violon*, Paris (facsim. rpt. Geneva 1971)
	Jean-Baptiste Cartier, *L'art du violon, ou Collection choisie dans les sonates des écoles italiennes, françoises et allemandes*, Paris (facsim. rpt. New York 1973)
	Bernard Lorenziti, *Principes ou nouvelle méthode de musique pour apprendre à jouer facilement du violon*, Paris
	P. Vignetti, *Études pour le violon* op. 2, Paris
	Michel Woldemar, *Grande méthode ou étude élémentaire pour le violon*, Paris
ca. 1798/99	Rodolphe Kreutzer, *40 études ou caprices pour le violon*, Paris
1799	Peter Fux, *Caprice pour un violon seul*, Vienna
1800	Pierre Gaviniès, *Les vingt-quatre matinées*, Paris
ca. 1800	Jean-Joseph Cambini, *Nouvelle méthode théorique et pratique pour le violon*, Paris (facsim. rpt. Geneva 1971)
	Ferdinand Kauer, *Neuverfasste Violinschule nebst Tonstücken zur Übung*, Vienna
	Ferdinand Kauer, *Scuola prattica oder 40 Fantasien und Fermaten für eine Violine*, Vienna

Aside from his activities as performer and composer, Francesco Geminiani was increasingly popular as a violin teacher, in time becoming English society's most fashionable instructor. Aware of a multitude of teaching materials that were second-rate or worse, he gave thought to providing his own, based on his experience. He must have taken his task very seriously, for he did not write, or at least publish, his tutor until he had reached the age of seventy. His objective is defined in the preface: he was not concerned with feats of tone painting "and all other such tricks," but with genuine means of expression. For that reason he considered his work suitable for cellists as well, and "in some sort" even for aspiring composers. The study, sixty pages in length, consists of the text, twenty-four music examples (most of which are subdivided several times), and twelve "composizioni" for violin and basso continuo, resembling sonata movements.

Geminiani begins with a diatonic fingering chart and advises the beginner to transfer it to and mark it on the fingerboard. He then shows how to place the fingers on the four strings (see above). He goes on to say that if one then lifts the fingers slightly off the strings, the hand is in the proper playing position. One should hold the violin with the E string lying slightly lower than the G string, so that the latter can be reached more easily by the bow. Bowing instructions are detailed and include important advice.

> One of the principal Beauties of the Violin is the swelling or encreasing and softening of the Sound; which is done by pressing the Bow upon the Strings with the Fore-finger more or less. In playing all long Notes the Sound should be begun soft, and gradually swelled till the Middle, and from thence gradually softened till the End.

Exercises for fingering and position playing should at first be practiced without the bow, in order not to compound difficulties. Some excellent exercises are included:

His scales for two fingers have become standard practicing material. He gives very modern fingerings for scales in which chromatic and diatonic steps are mixed, for he does *not* derive the fingering for the altered note from the basic note:

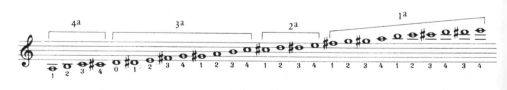

Rhythm training, neglected in most tutors, is provided in example 8 with twenty scale exercises. In example 9 Geminiani shows how a basic succession of tones (a theme) can be varied, introducing the student to the subject of diminution. Yet each of the twenty variations also deals with a problem of technique or rhythm.

Geminiani appears as a true baroque master when he turns to ways of breaking chords, a subject already taken up by Vivaldi. Geminiani provides eighteen possible ways of elaborating a sequence of eight chords. Eight other exercises deal with scales in double stops including unisons, seconds, fourths, and sevenths. Example 24 consists of thirty-two bowing studies on open strings, some of which were mentioned earlier in his book, to be practiced as needed. Again Geminiani shows what a fine pedagogue he is: just as he had wanted the first exercises to be practiced without bow, he now directs the pupil to try all difficult bowings on open strings, from string changes at quarter-note speed to complex arpeggios. An excerpt from the last variation is reproduced here.

Geminiani's *Art of Playing on the Violin* is the first modern tutor. It covers too much ground in very little space. After beginning with a fingering chart and instructions on how to hold the violin—material for the very beginner— he offers on nine pages of text and fifty-one pages of examples material that even today would be appropriate for virtuosos. His methodical approach, such as dealing separately with left-hand and right-hand problems, affected violin teaching well beyond his time. After his death, a flood of instruction books appeared, some of them with his name, others partly attributed to him. Still others plagiarize him so much that they really are his intellectual property. In the preface to the facsimile edition, Boyden tried to sort these all out.

An unusually large number of instruction books for various instruments appeared during the decade after Bach's death. Perhaps a need was seen, at the end of a major musical epoch, to preserve and describe its performance practices in general, for the benefit of a younger generation exposed to new style concepts. A more cogent reason may have been the dramatic growth of instrumental music in the fifty years since Corelli's op. 5, music that made greater technical demands than earlier tutors treated. The demands went beyond matters of technique; they included style and performance conventions. In that area, special conditions existed in Germany, well known to musicians there. Strong Italian and French influences gave rise in Germany to what Quantz called the "vermischte goût" (mixed style or taste). To explain it and to apply it to the ways of playing various instruments seemed important. Four treatises appeared within the span of ten years:

1752   C. P. E. Bach, *Versuch über die wahre Art das Clavier zu spielen* (part 1), Berlin (trans. as *Essay on the True Art of Playing Keyboard Instruments*, New York 1949)
Johann Joachim Quantz, *Versuch . . .*

1756   Leopold Mozart, *Versuch* . . . (trans. as *A Treatise on the Fundamental Principles of Violin Playing*, London 1948, 1985)
1762   C. P. E. Bach, *Versuch* . . . (part 2), Berlin

For the development of violin pedagogy, Leopold Mozart's work is the most important of these, but all three have much in common. Quantz in particular says much that applies to violin playing. He points this out in the preface, explaining that what he has to say about good taste in music can be useful for all instrumentalists and singers. "Whoever is so inclined can extract what applies to his voice or instrument and benefit from it." Quantz begins with questions of general and musical pedagogy, taking up the "qualifications of a master, if he wants to produce good students." Most of his treatise, however, deals with ornamentation and diminution, with allegro and adagio playing. In part 2 he turns to practical music in general terms. For Quantz, a member of the court chapel of Frederick the Great, this means above all orchestra playing. Twenty pages are devoted to the duties of a ripieno player, the first such account in any pedagogical treatise. Quantz was very familiar with matters of violin bowing. His instructions almost duplicate those given by Tartini to Madame Lombardini de Sirmen, whom he hardly could have known. He recommends the violinist "practice up bows as well as down bows."

Quantz had traveled through Italy from 1724 to 1726, was in Paris in 1726 and in London in 1727. He was familiar with national styles and points out the difference between the "short, articulated bow strokes of the French, far more effective than the long, dragging Italian strokes." His *Versuch* is a compendium of musical practices of his day. No earlier work gave such detailed information on instrumental technique and performance practice.

Tartini's *Regole* (Rules) had a curious history. They first appeared in Paris in 1771, after the author's death, translated by P. Denis as *Traité des agréments de la musique*. The original had been considered lost; for decades, violin researchers and specialists in performance practice had been on the lookout for it. Then, in 1957, two very similar manuscript copies in Italian appeared, entitled *Libro delle regole, ed esempi necessari per ben suonare*. Actually, the French title describes the work's content better than the original one, which suggests a comprehensive work on violin instruction. Erwin Jacobi, who edited the 1961 publication, dated the original fairly accurately on the basis of its contents, placing it between Quantz and Leopold Mozart. Boyden (1965) favors a less precise attribution.

Tartini provides few specific details about violin playing; he deals chiefly with ornamentation, including vibrato. Grace notes are taken up first, followed by trills, tremolo, and mordents. One must be able to play trills at slow, moderate, and fast tempos. Slow trills are required for "serious, pathetic, and melancholic pieces; moderate trills for those that are somewhat subdued but cheerful; fast trills for merry, witty, and rapidly moving pieces." Tartini includes vibrato in his definition of tremolo, saying that it is more suitable for instruments than voices. Vibrating harpsichord strings with their bell–like sounds serve as models; they are imitated by vibrato on violin, gamba, and cello. Vibrato can be slow, gradually accelerating, or fast.

The work's second part deals with manners ("maniere"), which Tartini divides into natural and artificial, referring to the ornamentation of basic melodic formulae. His examples show how typical melody patterns first used by the Mannheim composers actually derive from the ornamentation practices of the time. Apparently the composers wrote down what had customarily been played for some decades. The most important "artificial [or artful] manner" is the cadenza. Starting with a basic form, Tartini advances to ever more complex patterns, up to what the French called a "point d'orgue" (pedal point) since they were improvised over a sustained bass note, the dominant (see example). This section forms the conclusion of the *Regole*, a treatise that in many details resembles those by Geminiani, C. P. E. Bach, Quantz, and Leopold Mozart. This does not suggest that these writers depended on each other, but that they described situations and practices with a common stylistic background.

Leopold Mozart's *Violinschule* (1756) is the first comprehensive work of its kind in German. He must have written the book before Geminiani's had become known in Germany, for an observation by Marpurg, who "regretted that there still was no violin method," caused him to have it published. "For many years I have written down the present rules for those whom I instructed in playing," the author says in his preface. "I hope to convert all those who, by their bad instruction, have ill served their apprentices." Evidently the elder Mozart was writing for violin teachers as well as pupils. Being methodical in his approach, Mozart includes a historical introduction that also deals with violin making. A general introduction to music follows, including a glossary of musical terms. The second section explains the proper ways to hold violin and bow. Here and later Mozart uses illustrations to demonstrate good and bad positions. He strongly recommends holding the violin under the chin, but to the right of the tailpiece, "on the E string side." He was familiar with the physiologically correct manner of bowing, with little shoulder motion, more from the elbow, and free, natural wrist motion, "without ridiculous and unnatural twists or excessive outward curvature." For down bows the wrist should be kept low; for up bows it should be bent naturally and without strain. Tone is chiefly controlled by hand and wrist motion.

Mozart's remarks on playing in the higher positions are of interest, especially about "half" and "whole" positions. The half are what we call the second, fourth, and sixth positions; the whole positions are our first, third, and fifth.

half position   whole position   half   whole

To use the half positions "sometimes is necessary, sometimes convenient." Changing positions, from half to whole, is governed by similar considerations. Mozart was familiar with changing positions by finger extensions (see below). From the ninth section on, he deals in great detail with grace notes, trills, and other embellishments, and with "tremulo," his term for vibrato.

the third finger reaches down

Leopold Mozart's violin school goes far beyond Geminiani's treatise, not only in length. Tartini's influence is evident. It is a well-organized violin method, intended to be supplemented with practicing material taken from violin music currently in vogue. Several subsequent editions attest to its wide distribution and to the profound influence it had; the second edition appeared in 1769–1770, followed by other editions by the same publisher in 1787 and 1800. Pirated editions appeared in 1791, 1801, and 1804 in Frankfurt, Vienna, and Leipzig. The Vienna print was edited and arranged by J. Pierlinger. There is a Dutch translation (Haarlem 1766) and a French one entitled *Méthode raisonnée* (Paris 1770). Leopold wrote in a vivid, down-to-earth, southern German style that makes enjoyable reading even in translation. At the book's end he refers to plans for a sequel, intended for "our esteemed concert artists," but this did not materialize. It is typical for the publishing world of the time that the author had to pay the publisher 300 gulden to help defray printing costs.

Tartini's *L'arte dell'arco* (Paris 1758) most likely was written many years before publication, for use by his students. The work consists of thirty-eight variations on the gavotte from Corelli's Sonata op. 5, no. 10. It had been published thirteen years earlier in abbreviated form, as an appendix to Pinelli's little-known violin school. Twelve years after Tartini's death it was published in Naples as *L'arte dell'arco o siano cinquanta variazioni* (apparently the master had intended to provide fifty variations). The set is a magnificent example of an old tradition: to illustrate various technical problems through variations on a memorable theme. No written commentary is included. A few excerpts (see opposite) show Tartini's imaginative approach to problems of violin technique. Actually, the title is somewhat misleading, for Tartini, in addition to bowing problems, takes up trills and double stop playing.

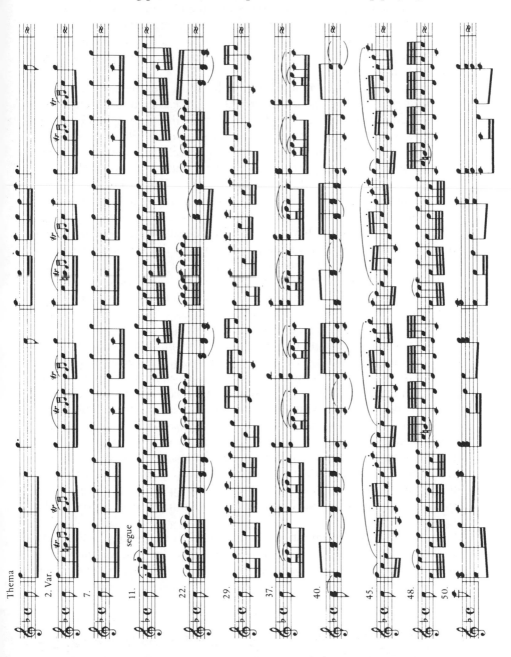

The author of *Principes du violon* was Barnabé L'Abbé le fils (the son, to distinguish him from his father, who was the solo cellist of the Paris Opéra orchestra). Aristide Wirsta (*MGG*) considers the *Principes* to be the "third–

best violin tutor of the time, after Geminiani's and Leopold Mozart's." The author was an excellent violinist, a pupil of Leclair, and for many years a member of the Opéra Comique orchestra. Like Geminiani, he begins with advice on how to hold the violin and continues with detailed instruction, leading all the way to virtuoso level. His method could conceivably accompany above-average violinists from their first lessons to the highest development of their technique.

L'Abbé's remarks on holding the violin show that he was au courant with most recent practices not described in any earlier tutor. "The violin must rest on the clavicle so that the chin is near the G string." This is our modern way of holding it. It may already be shown in earlier paintings, but probably as the result of an artist's imagination rather than observation. Similar details about left-hand position also are new, such as his demand that the thumb "must rest opposite the A on the G string." This makes for a relaxed left hand, needed for the execution of the later examples in his work.

L'Abbé's advice concerning bow position describes modern practices by Leclair and his pupils that have become prerequisites for producing a large tone. They are related to early attempts, by Tourte father and son, to improve the bow itself. L'Abbé recommends that the second joint of the index finger have contact with the bow stick. "In order to exert more force it must be at a slight distance from the others. . . . The tip of the little finger must be placed on the part of the bow that is connected to the frog." That way the little finger provides the balance needed for delicate bowings (such as those in *L'arte dell'arco*); it also adds strength to bow motion. This amounts to discarding the elegant manner of holding the bow so frequently depicted in illustrations well into the second half of the eighteenth century, in favor of one providing great drawing power. Yet the fingers of the right hand must remain flexible, for they make subtle, "invisible motions" that affect the tone. The bow is "the soul of the instrument," and L'Abbé's advice to "filer le son"—to draw or spin from the violin an intense tone of great beauty—was to become one of the most important concepts in the language of French violinists.

L'Abbé also discusses the use of our half position, reflecting the requirements of mid-century violin music. He uses the quaint term "doigts d'emprunt"—fingers "borrowed" from the first position where they would play different notes.

While what he says about ornamentation does not go beyond the customs of the time, his advice about fingering is entirely modern. Many notes can be played with stretches and extensions without changing position. He gives examples that might have been provided by a violinist of our time.

Two scale studies remain valuable,

as do these bariolage passages:

At the end, L'Abbé takes up natural and artificial harmonics and up and down bow staccato, thus covering virtually all aspects of mid-eighteenth-century technique. In the appendix he provides a small selection of quite attractive etudes, summarizing the technical problems covered in the body of his work. Without a doubt, *Principes* is the best French treatise on violin playing up to the time. It is more detailed and precise than contemporary works and requires technique far beyond Geminiani and Leopold Mozart.

Löhlein, for many years a conscripted soldier in Potsdam, went into music as a profession. He became music director in Jena and eventually went to Leipzig, where he had a leading position under Hiller at the Grosse Konzert. Having a fine reputation as a music teacher, he published a piano tutor that was widely used and went through many printings. In his violin method, citing Quantz and Leopold Mozart, he explains what caused him to write it.

> Quantz fails to include the basics of violin playing, and Mozart's treatise also omits much that a beginner needs to know. Both works are expensive and hard to find. This moved me to publish the present little treatise, encouraged by some of my friends who were kind enough to applaud my piano method.

Löhlein delivered what he promised—an inexpensive version of Leopold's *Versuch*—but not much more. Admittedly, many interesting details about musical practices in general are offered, but there is no methodical approach. The first thirty-eight pages take up general matters, followed by scales in all keys up to the fourth position, with all fingerings provided. A section on ways of playing ("von den Spielmanieren") is immediately followed by duets for which no preparatory exercises are given. His last chapter, about various bowings and fingerings, includes brief remarks about certain aspects of virtuosity. About a succession of six intervals of a tenth Löhlein observes, "These are measured by the yardstick." Nevertheless, his method was reprinted in 1781 and again in 1791.

Michel Corrette's 1738 treatise has been mentioned earlier. His *L'art de se perfectionner*, written at the age of seventy-three, goes far beyond the earlier work. As the title implies, it takes the student up into the realms of virtuoso playing. Corrette addresses the capable orchestra violinist who wants to perfect himself as a soloist. He cites Locatelli, Tartini, and "Le grand Claire" (the great Leclair). He wisely decided not to compose the music examples himself but instead extracted them from mostly Italian masterworks, thereby imparting a timeless quality to his tutor. He pays special attention to playing in the higher positions, with examples up to the eleventh position, and he acquaints his students with playing octaves and tenths as well as with up bow and down bow staccato.

More and more pedagogical works of varying quality appeared ca. 1800. Those by Bornet l'aîné (the elder, to distinguish him from his brother, also a violinist) best represent these. He joined the Paris Opéra orchestra in 1762 and quickly established himself as a violin teacher. In 1784 he began publishing *Journal du violon*. His 1788 violin school (2d ed. 1799) is of special interest because of his intention, indicated by the title, to deal with violin playing *and* music, emphasizing that both must be taught together. To us this may be an obvious approach, but many later methods neglect one in favor of the other.

Ferdinand Kauer (d. 1831) of Moravia in some ways resembles Corrette. Active as a violinist and orchestra conductor in Vienna, he also was an incredibly industrious composer, having brought out seven stage works in the year 1811 alone. Responding to the bourgeoisie's widespread interest in music, Kauer provided tutors for flute, piano, clarinet, cello, and voice, in addition to three separate violin methods. He may have been the first to compose student violin concertos with piano accompaniment.

Galeazzi's contribution strictly speaking is not a violin tutor but incorporates a teaching concept that seems to have been ignored by others at the time. Well into the nineteenth century, instrumental methods start out with the key of C major, supposedly the easiest to learn. This means that beginning violin students are immediately confronted with three different finger positions: 0–1–1–½ on the G string; 0–1–½–1 on D and A, and 0–½–1–1 on the E string where, for the interval F–B, a large stretch (tritone) is required. For the small hands of many young beginners this is apt to lead to poor intonation, because the first finger—and with it the entire hand—may be pulled upward. Galeazzi advocates beginning with G major, which avoids the tritone and requires only two finger positions. Moreover, tonic and dominant are open strings, which facilitates checking intonation.

Hiller's *Anweisungen* are rather modest when compared with some earlier treatises, but in a way are typical for their age. The author was from a poor family; laboriously he moved up from being a student and steward at an estate to the post of director of the Leipzig Grosse Konzert, and of a boys' singing school. At the outbreak of the French Revolution, when he was sixty-one years old, Hiller became cantor at St. Thomas's. A versatile and well-educated person (he translated works by Rousseau), he was eager to provide popular music education. For this purpose he issued a journal, *Wöchentliche Nachrichten . . . die Musik betreffend* (Musical Weekly), published his *Lebensbeschreibungen berühmter Musikgelehrter und Tonkünstler neuerer Zeit* (Lives of famous music scholars and artists of our time), and wrote various instructional manuals. Typical for the tendencies of this period is his *Kurze und erleichterte Anweisung zum Singen für Schulen in Städten und Dörfern* (Short and simple singing tutor for city and country schools, 1791). Such pedagogical projects especially flourished in areas less affected by revolutionary upheavals.

Hiller's violin school was primarily intended for training teachers; its requirements were geared to what was realistic within that framework. It should be noted that Hiller was the first to use our system of numbering the positions.

Only a few eighteenth-century methods have maintained their place in modern violin teaching; Fiorillo's op. 3 is one of these. Published in Paris in 1790, its immediate success caused it to be reprinted in Vienna in 1798. Fiorillo had appeared successfully as soloist at the Concert Spirituel. After that he seems to have lived in Paris for a few years, coming in contact with representatives of the French school of violin playing. His *Étude* is more comprehensive than Gaviniès's and requires more virtuosity than Kreutzer's. Each caprice ends in a key other than the tonic, usually in the dominant, leading directly into the following caprice. The entire work apparently was conceived as a unit, to be played daily from beginning to end, for constant repetition of basic material. This approach, combined with the creativity of the violinist-composer, caused his caprices to enjoy a permanent place in the repertory. Most likely, however, they were and are seldom used as intended.

Fiorillo was a fine composer—tasteful and imaginative, never repeating ad nauseam a motif that is intended to deal with a technical problem. Thus each caprice serves several purposes and sustains the student's attention. In Caprice no. 9, for instance, a new motif, introduced in the third measure, gradually gains in importance and dominates from measure 21 on. In measure 25 the original thought returns, somewhat modified, and is again freely developed. In measure 33 a new motif is derived from the descending passages of the last two measures and then carried through to the end. All these changes continually force the player to face new problems.

Contrast within one caprice also is often provided by dividing it into two parts, such as Largo/Allegro (Caprice no. 1) or Grave/Moderato (Caprice no. 29). Special attention is given to the playing of octaves and tenths, and to large stretches, also in the lower positions. His own double stop studies (which include double trills) suggest that, while in Germany, Fiorillo became acquainted with manuscript copies of Bach's works for unaccompanied violin. Caprice no. 4 in particular seems to have been directly inspired by that master; all make excellent preparatory studies for Bach.

Bartolomeo Campagnoli (1751–1827) was an orchestra violinist for many years before beginning studies with Nardini. His most important pedagogical work was *Metodo per violino* (1797). A French edition may have been published in 1791; English and German translations followed. This method might be seen as the last didactic manifestation of classic Italian violin playing of the eighteenth century, distinguished by the systematic arrangement of its contents. Double stops and trills are thoroughly explored, further developing the "Geminianian grip," using twenty-three four-part chords applied to trill exercises.

Other publications by Campagnoli take up special problems. His *Thirty Preludes* op. 12, moving through all keys, call for playing in two to four parts. Together with his six fugues for solo violin, op. 10, they serve well those players who want to go on to Bach's solo violin compositions. A pedagogical approach also characterizes Campagnoli's seven sonatas in four movements: each is to be played in one position throughout. They make up his op. 18, entitled *Divertissements pour l'exercice des sept principales positions* (to study the seven principal positions). His op. 17 provides models for improvised cadenzas; it contains a total of 246 fantasies and cadenzas, constituting an important contribution to soloistic violin playing of his age.

At his death Michel Woldemar (1750–1815), who taught violin in Paris at various times, was maître de chapelle in Clermont-Ferrand. In his method he incorporated the style of his teachers Lolli and Mestrino, requiring much of his students, who must have been outstandingly gifted. He favored exercises on one string, intended to develop great facility in changing positions and using stretches. His double stop exercises anticipate Ševčík's. As a composer he displayed moderate talent, demonstrated by three violin concertos and other works for both violin and viola. He provided separate sets of embellishments, which show that virtuoso practices at the end of the century were even more extreme than those displayed by Tartini.

Woldemar had an inquisitive, inventive mind, though not all his ideas came off. He also wrote methods for viola and clarinet, invented a "Violon-Alto," a five-string instrument combining the range of both, and published a *Tableau mélo-tachigraphique*, a kind of music shorthand system. Among his compositions is a group of four *Sonates fantômagiques* with the titles "L'ombre de Lolli" (The ghost of Lolli), "L'ombre de Mestrino," "L'ombre de Pugnani," and "L'ombre de Tartini"—all clever copies of the styles of these composers. Woldemar claimed that the music had been communicated to him through direct contacts with the spirits of the four great violinists.

Another major instructional work was written at the very end of the century: *L'art du violon* by Jean-Baptiste Cartier (1765–1841). He was a pupil of Viotti in Paris, second concertmaster of the Paris Opéra since 1791, and much in demand as a violin teacher. His pedagogical intent is clarified by the subtitle: "To present forty-nine compositions in progressive order, amounting to a history of the development of style."

Cartier knew violin music well and for a long time had collected examples from various periods. He succeeded in making available in print for the first time such now famous works as the fugue from Bach's C major Sonata for unaccompanied violin and Tartini's "Devil's Trill" Sonata. Cartier's work succeeded quickly; a second edition was needed in 1801. It was officially adopted at the Paris Conservatoire as a supplement to the violin school by Rode, Kreutzer, and Baillot. The opening section ("Principes abrégés pour le violon"), however, is disappointing, relying heavily on standard eighteenth-century treatises.

Les vingt-quatre matinées can be regarded as the concluding chapter of eighteenth-century violin pedagogy, written by the aged Gaviniès (1728–1800), who had been appointed to the Conservatoire at the age of sixty-seven. These "morning studies" have musical value and deal intelligently with matters of technique. They are more successful than Locatelli's caprices because of their fine workmanship. The *Matinées* for a long time formed part of every serious violinist's training. Carl Flesch, however, no longer granted them that standing, considering them "one-sided, antiquated, overly florid and somewhat exaggerated in the manner of Locatelli." The reference to Locatelli is appropriate, who, however, had moved technique so far ahead of his contemporaries that study material was needed to bridge the gap between the technique of an average violinist and that required by Locatelli's caprices. Gaviniès filled that need very well, and we should not blame him if a flood of later studies rendered his *Matinées* less essential. Contemporary teachers use them selectively.

Surveying teaching materials from the second half of the eighteenth century it is evident that a decisive change had taken place. It no longer was enough to provide young violinists with the most basic instruction. A systematic plan, well thought out in all details, was needed to equip them for playing the music of the great masters up to Mozart and Haydn. Teachers like

Geminiani and Tartini provided the intensive kind of training we see re-flected in the pedagogical works of their time.

Italians admittedly played a leading role in this, but it is to be noted that Fiorillo's caprices were first published in Paris. The French capital had be-come a center of violin playing, including amateurs, and of professional train-ing leading up to virtuoso level. Those who appeared as soloists in the Con-cert Spirituel, or were members of the royal chapel, or played in the Opéra and Opéra Comique orchestras, were highly accomplished musicians who had to maintain their standing in the face of tough competition. In earlier times one had to travel to study with Somis or Tartini, but with Leclair, Gaviniès, and others now resident, it was possible to receive excellent train-ing at home. The Paris Conservatoire, founded shortly before the end of the century, became the official center for this. Quite logically all these devel-opments led to a flourishing of music publishers. From mid-century on, more and more of the chief works of violin literature were printed in Paris, and translations of important new foreign publications were quick to appear there. Tartini's *Traité* was published only in French, reflecting the emer-gence of France as the hub of violin pedagogy.

THE ETUDE'S ORIGIN

The title of Fiorillo's method, *Étude pour le violon*, suggests a look at the mean-ing and origin of that term. "A piece for practicing" might do for a short working definition. In German, a distinction between "Übung" (exercise) and "Etude" gradually came to be made. A one-measure bowing or finger-ing exercise by Ševčík would not be called an etude, a term that suggests, for one thing, greater length. Yet some "etudes" by Baillot really amount to lit-tle more than such an exercise, drawn out by sequential repetition. Such material, without any musical substance, would not yet be called "etude"; it does not amount to a "piece." The definition of an etude implies its having some musical form and regularity which, of course, can change with the conventions of the time. A somewhat broader definition of "etude" therefore might be this: a composition, primarily for purposes of study and chiefly concerned with technical problems.

"Exercises" are as old as violin playing itself. Many basic diminution pat-terns of the sixteenth century were invented to improve a player's technique. Such exercises are found above all in gamba methods, which were also used by violinists. No additional study material was needed because much of the violin music of the seventeenth and early eighteenth centuries is based on violinistic patterns. Fast sonata movements, for instance, provided excellent study material. The Allegro of a violin sonata by Johann Christian Pepusch (see opposite) begins with a triadic motif that then is further developed.

This anticipates a formal aspect of the later etude: a technical concept (in this case a broken triad) is varied and made into a composition. When the player has studied it thoroughly, various applications of the concept have

Allegro

been mastered. If we omit from the earlier broader definition the words "primarily for purposes of study," it includes virtually all violin music of the baroque period. We know that Tartini used fast movements from Corelli's violin sonatas as etudes, for studying all aspects of technique. We can assume that Corelli considered his violin compositions entirely suitable for study purposes.

Variations on a theme filled that need especially well, including such variation forms as passacaglia and chaconne. Keyboard players especially fell back on variations to develop their technique. Corelli's "La Folia" Variations can be considered a succession of short violin etudes, and Tartini's variations mentioned earlier were intended to improve bowing technique. As late as 1776 an advertisement was published in the Paris *Almanach musical*: "Twenty-four New Variations on the Song "Ah! vous dirai-je maman," for Solo Violin, for Practicing All Bowings and Different Motions, by M. C. C. de Bar of the Académie Royale de Musique. Available from the Author." In the seventeenth and early eighteenth centuries violinists had ample study material of this kind at their disposal. A course of instruction might begin with the rudiments of violin playing, based on the standard tutors, and proceed to sonatas and sets of variations then in vogue. Further instruction would include violin concertos by Torelli, Vivaldi, and others, the solo sections of these consisting to a large extent of typical violinistic passage work and formulae. Locatelli's publications prove that such a course of study could lead to the most advanced level.

During the second half of the eighteenth century a gradual change took place, away from music that was primarily conceived in terms of the instrument itself. It is a development that might be compared with the change from the baroque sonata for violin and continuo to the piano sonata with violin accompaniment. These new works chiefly explored the idiomatic-technical resources of the keyboard instrument. The violinist, being the "accompanist," contributes very little that explores the violin's possibilities. In symphonic and chamber music a melodic style emerged (strongly influenced by vocal music) that, though generally instrumental, did not display the characteristics of specific instruments. This increasingly affected violin music as well. A violinist therefore faced new technical challenges no longer satisfied by earlier study material. Violin methods of the later eighteenth century take this into account; they increasingly include study material that points to the later type of etude. For this kind of material, designations such as cadenza, cadenza artificiale, exercise, esercizio, Übung, studio, lesson, and capriccio were used. If they were very short, they did little to advance a violinist's general level of accomplishment. As time went on, however, the term "capriccio" referred to fully developed pieces that both in length and design come close to the later etude.

We are not certain just when the term "etude" was first used for a piece for practicing, but it apparently was in France, in connection with violin music. Many printed editions did not give a publication date, and in some cases the word "etude" appeared only in a later edition or printing. The matter is complicated because the word, a singular noun, originally meant "study" in general (as in "the study of medicine"), applied to a publication in general rather than to a single piece. The title of Fiorillo's method therefore might be translated as "a compendium of violin study through thirty-six caprices." Vignetti may have been the first to use the word, in its plural form, in a title. His op. 2, published by Sieber in Paris without a date (probably 1798), is entitled *Études pour le violon avec le doigté indiqué pour en faciliter l'exécution, composées par P. Vignetti* (Violin etudes with fingerings given to facilitate their playing). His six etudes are well constructed, in two sections or consisting of two or three movements. In content they are close to Fiorillo's caprices. Actually it is not very important who first used the term. Fiorillo's caprices represent the type of the later etude so well that one can regard them as the first etudes, even though he did not yet use the term in our sense.

Rodolphe Kreutzer has generally been considered the creator of the violin etude, but the exact year of publication of his forty etudes has not yet been determined. The earliest date is given by Gerber (*Neues historisch-biographisches Lexikon der Tonkünstler*, vol. 3, 1813). But Gerber's dates are generally unreliable, especially for France, so that neither title nor year of publication are necessarily correct. His reference reads thus: *Etudes de violon ou caprices, recueil [vols.] 1 et 2, Paris, bei Imbault, auch Offenbach, 1796.* No copies of these two volumes are known. Ganz called attention to the announcement of the Kreutzer etudes in the "Intelligenz- Blatt I" (col. 2) of the *Allgemeine Musikalische Zeitung* (vol. 2, 1799–1800), where they are listed as *Etude ou caprices pour le violon, recueil 1.* This suggests a publication date of 1798–1799. The use of the singular form, "etude," implies that, as by Fiorillo, the term was not yet used for a single piece. The title given here is more likely to be more accurate than that cited by Gerber. There is a "Nouvelle édition revue et corrigée par l'Auteur" with the title *40 études pour le violon, dédiées à Monsieur le Comte de Bondy par R. Kreutzer, premier violon de la chapelle du roi et professeur de l'Ecole Royale de Musique.* The publisher is given as "Frey, Artiste de l'Académie Royale, Editeur de Musique." This would place it after 1816 because Frey did not join the opera orchestra as violist until then. The first of these two editions was still issued in two volumes. Between the two editions, reprints by Breitkopf, André, Haslinger, and Artaria appeared, as well as an edition published ca. 1807 by the Magasin de Musique, a publishing house affiliated with the Conservatoire. The 1807 edition differs from Kreutzer's revision, for he had replaced two etudes (nos. 1 and 2 in A minor) with new ones, a trill etude in dotted rhythm and an etude in octaves. Vieuxtemps was the first to publish all the etudes, arriving at the total of forty-two with which we are familiar. Later, Kreutzer published another collection of nineteen etudes; others have never been published.

Having been appointed professor of violin at the Conservatoire in 1795, Kreutzer began assembling instructional materials for his students and then selected appropriate studies for publication. Like Czerny, he had a special talent for isolating a specific technical problem and treating it in accordance with laws of musical form, including conventions of harmony. He used both primary and secondary chords, imparting harmonic variety to the violinistic phrases.

In his day Kreutzer was much acclaimed as a composer of operas and chamber music. His imaginative approach is exemplified by Etude no. 17 in B-flat major. The principal idea, half a measure long, takes up two technical problems: the mordent-like rapid trill and martellato bowing involving string crossing. These problems are dealt with in their basic form through measure 11, with emphasis on the string-crossing motif. In any etude there is the danger that, in spite of the best pedagogical intentions, such a motif might be used to excess, so that the player's concentration will suffer. Kreutzer tries to avoid this. Beginning in measure 12, he expands the half-measure idea to a whole measure by repeating the string-crossing motif three times while enlarging the octave interval to a tenth. He returns to the original idea in G minor (measure 18), and by emphasizing the second motif he avoids belaboring the first. When the first motif again is stressed, from measure 28 on, it has that much more impetus. Meanwhile a series of modulations has led to the key of D minor. After the recapitulation in measure 36 the material is developed further, for too much literal repetition would not be economical in teaching. After both themes have been treated in some depth, a new technical problem, double stop playing, is introduced in measure 44, so that the player is challenged to the very end. At the same time the parallel minor mode, not previously encountered, presents new challenges in regard to intonation.

Analyses of this kind demonstrate the vitality of Kreutzer's etudes. He knew how to present basic musical procedures in an effective violinistic way, and how to carry them through an entire etude without losing momentum. His ideas are never trivial; he never stoops to the sentimentality of second- or third-rank composers of his day and avoids the banalities provided by so many composers of "études characteristiques."

Ever since they appeared, Kreutzer's etudes have occupied a central position in violin pedagogy. Much has been written about them, beginning with C. Hering's small book of 1858 *Concerning Kreutzer's Etudes, a Systematic*

Manual for Violin Teachers. In 1903 Benjamin Cutter's *How to Study Kreutzer* was published, and Ševčík's op. 26 is an annotated four-volume edition of the etudes. Alberto Bachmann published *1000 coups d'archet . . . sur la deuxième et la huitième étude* (Paris 1938), of which 474 are based on the second etude and 526 on the eighth. A volume entitled *The Staccato* (London 1925) by Demetrius Dounis is based entirely on Kreutzer etudes. They have also been adopted for other instruments, completely or selectively, including editions for viola, cello, string bass, flute, oboe, clarinet, saxophone, and bassoon.

There are countless editions for violin. The Ricordi catalog, for instance, lists three editions, by Abbado, Polo, and Principe. The title of Henry Petri's publication describes it as an "instructive edition, copiously annotated." Similarly M. L. Goldis added a subtitle ("edited, arranged progressively, and supplied with analyses") but what he calls analyses are little more than brief preparatory exercises for the more difficult portions. Maxim Jacobsen added similar good preparatory studies to his edition. He also was the author of *One Hundred Technical Paraphrases on the Kreutzer Etudes, for Left-Hand Development* and a corresponding volume of 120 paraphrases for the right hand. He may, of course, have introduced the danger that Kreutzer so effectively avoided: the tiring of the student's mind by an excess of repetitive material. Almost all editors added bowings to those etudes where they considered it appropriate.

Strangely enough, a small publication by Kreutzer's pupil Massart, *L'art de travailler les études de Kreutzer,* has been overlooked completely, though it informs us as to the exact manner in which Kreutzer wanted his etudes to be practiced. The editor points out, "Massart was Kreutzer's favorite pupil who lived in his home. He was moved to write down the many valuable comments continually made by the master." For Etude no. 1 in C major (traditionally included as no. 2), 150 different bowings are provided. Kreutzer also wanted it to be practiced in octaves, as he did with no. 3 (4) and several others. Massart edited one of these so heavily that it amounted to a new etude. Kreutzer also wanted the E major Etude (position changes) and the A major Etude (arpeggios) to be practiced an octave higher. He indicates that the double stop Etude in F major, no. 31 (33), should be practiced up an octave, and be transposed to C, D, and E major. With all these additions, the Kreutzer etudes, which are often given to students two to three years too early, amount to an advanced course in violin technique. Joachim once met Wieniawski when that virtuoso was practicing Kreutzer's etudes and remarked, "They are much more difficult than most violinists think." Andreas Moser remembered that Joachim practiced them throughout his life.

The last group of the Kreutzer etudes calls for highly advanced technique. This inspired a number of violin teachers to fill in the levels between the usual method books and Kreutzer's etudes. Some good publications resulted, including Blumenstengel's op. 24, with such subtitles as "Préparatoires aux études de Kreutzer."

THE DEVELOPMENT OF VIOLIN PLAYING IN THE PRINCIPAL COUNTRIES OF EUROPE DURING THE EIGHTEENTH CENTURY

ITALY

In the early eighteenth century, Italy excelled in music, producing a host not only of composers but also of vocal and instrumental performers who held most of the important positions throughout Europe, a state of affairs that lasted until Beethoven's youth. During the seventeenth century, Germany and Austria produced what might be considered a national school of violin playing, stressing, unlike the Italians, multiple-stop playing; Walther, Biber, and Westhoff were of this school. Corelli, however, was the leading figure in early eighteenth-century violin playing, and his compositions were performed everywhere. Other great violinist-composers included Vivaldi, Geminiani, Somis, Veracini, Locatelli, and Tartini. With all these, Italy's leading role was clear. As a result, serious students from many countries flocked to these masters and endeavored to improve their playing by studying Italian compositions. After Tartini's death, Italy's dominant position gradually declined, though he had established a tradition that was still to influence Paganini in important ways.

Pietro Nardini (1722–1793) was Tartini's foremost pupil. Upon completing his studies (begun at the age of twelve) he returned for some time to his hometown of Livorno. In 1762, after concert tours to Austria and Germany, Nardini became concertmaster at the Stuttgart court under the orchestra's leader, Jomelli. At various times Lolli and the Tartini pupils Pasqualino Bini and Domenico Ferrari were also employed there. Schubart called Nardini a "violinist of love, raised by the Graces," praising especially his sensitive performing of adagios, which moved stern princes and ladies at court to tears. "Often while playing, he himself would shed tears on his violin." The Mozart family visited Ludwigsburg in 1763, and father Leopold reported that Nardini's tasteful cantabile playing strongly impressed seven-year-old Wolfgang. From 1769 to 1793 Nardini was concertmaster and leader of the orchestra at the grandducal court in Tuscany. As the leading Italian violinist of the day, he attracted many students. Among his compositions the many violin sonatas are particularly valuable. They still call for basso continuo in the baroque tradition, but their musical content relates them to *Empfindsamkeit* and early classicism. His six violin concertos display the "singing allegro" manner at its best; their influence on the young Mozart is unmistakable. A sonata "enigmatica" for unaccompanied violin and unfigured bass, to be played on one violin, is of special interest because of its notation. It is written on two staves, the lower one using the bass clef, which part must be played an octave higher than written.

The Berlin National Library has in its collecion two volumes containing fifty and sixty caprices for violin. Nardini's authorship has not been definitively established but is highly probable for stylistic reasons. These caprices display great formal variety. Many are extremely challenging, pointing ahead to Paganini's Caprices. Some well-written fugues are included; their compositional style and idiomatic writing for the violin caused Andreas Moser to assume that Nardini must have known Bach's works for unaccompanied violin.

Antonio Lolli (ca. 1730–1802) of northern Italy was another fine violinist. From 1758 to 1774 he was a member of the Stuttgart musical establishment. Numerous concert tours took him to Vienna, Paris, many German cities, Holland, and Italy. Lolli is said to have taken a year off from all other activities to devote himself to practicing, hoping thereby to prove himself Nardini's equal. As the chamber virtuoso of Empress Catherine II of Russia he lived in St. Petersburg, whence he went on extended tours. Upon quitting his Russian post he toured England and Spain, traveling, it is said, in his own four-horse coach accompanied by his servant. Lolli died in Palermo after having served as concertmaster to the Neapolitan king.

Lolli may have been the greatest virtuoso before Paganini. Audiences admired him but also were critical, depending on whether they were impressed by his dazzling technique or expected him to be a composer of substantial music. In 1772, Claudius said of his playing, "That man has ten fingers on his left hand and holds five bows in his right hand." He wrote approximately two dozen concertos and numerous sonatas, writing out only the solo part, which bristled with difficulties, and leaving the rest to more experienced colleagues. It comes as no surprise that this procedure did not result in well-designed, coherent works. Paganini may have heard him on several occasions; that Paganini was influenced by Lolli in several ways is clear. For instance, Lolli was fond of playing in the highest positions on all strings, including the G string; substantial portions of some compositions, especially some variations, are to be played on the G string exclusively. He also specialized in artificial harmonics. École du violon en quatuor contains studies with trio accompaniment, testifying to Lolli's teaching activities. Caprices for the violin have been preserved in manuscript form.

In Russia, Lolli found out how eighteenth-century court musicians could be subjected to a ruler's whims. Felice Giardini, a Somis student, at various times was employed by the empress, who decided that he was a better player of adagios than Lolli. She therefore ordered that in concerto performances Giardini was to play the slow movements, leaving the outer movements to Lolli. One of Giardini's talents, it has been claimed, was to produce a beautiful tone even on cheap violins. He would play such "matchbox" violins in public, then sell them for good money.

Researchers have established what we might call pedagogical family trees for Nardini and Lolli, chiefly going back to Tartini, with occasional crossovers. Thus Campagnoli at first studied with Dall'Occa, a Lolli pupil who also was a virtuoso on the double bass, but later studied with Guastarobba, a Tartini pupil, and also with Nardini. Campagnoli held posts in Freising and Dresden and in 1797 became the highly esteemed concertmaster of the Leipzig Gewandhaus Orchestra; his last appointment was as court kapellmeister in Neustrelitz. Like Lolli, he used these positions chiefly as bases of operation for extensive touring. In all, he succeeded as soloist, composer, and pedagogue. Giulio Gaetano Pugnani (1731–1798) was the third major Italian violinist of the time. He was born and died in Turin. Under Somis's instruction he matured early. After studying counterpoint with Ciampi in Rome he returned to Turin, where he advanced from leader of the second violins to concertmaster and to the post of "direttore generale della musica strumentale." Concerts in Paris and a stay of several years in London, where he succeeded as a composer of operas, further advanced his career. Pugnani was an excellent teacher who did much to advance the art of violin playing. His many students included Bruni and Viotti, with whom he undertook a concert tour of Russia. Boris Schwarz (article "Viotti" in *MGG*) pointed out that Viotti was instrumental in developing a new school of violin playing that indirectly goes back to Pugnani. Unfortunately Pugnani did not leave a written record of his pedagogical knowledge. He composed much, including very fine chamber music that represents the transition from late baroque to early classic style.

Nicolo Mestrino (1748–1789) was one of many Italians who spent a portion of their careers in Paris. Born in Milan, he belonged for several years to the Eisenstadt orchestra under Haydn, then entered the service of Countess Erdödy in Pressburg (Bratislava). A concert tour took him to Belgium and on to Paris, where Viotti appointed him leader of the orchestra at the Théâtre de Monsieur. An early death ended his promising career, during which he had composed twelve violin concertos and some etudes. As a performer he was fond of using glissando, especially in slow movements, so much so that Woldemar referred to this as "coulé à la Mestrino."

Antonio Bartolomeo Bruni (1759–1823) was another product of Pugnani's teaching in Turin. In 1780 he too went to Paris, where he succeeded at various theaters and as a composer of many works including operas. For some time he was Mestrino's successor at the Théâtre de Monsieur. During 1794 and 1795 he served on a government art commission. There, together with Sarrette, he endeavored to preserve sheet music and instruments that had been left behind by emigrating aristocrats. From 1806 to 1814, and permanently after 1820, Bruni returned to Italy. In Paris he enjoyed a fine reputation as a teacher; his instructional works are still used.

Giovanni Battista Viotti's life saw many changes, largely due to the turbulent events of the French Revolution. He was born in Piedmont. Noble patrons in Turin supported his training as a violinist, first by Antonio Celionat, a Somis pupil, then by Pugnani. While a member of the royal orchestra he was granted a leave to tour with Pugnani, performing in Switzerland, Dresden, Berlin, Warsaw, St. Petersburg, and finally in Paris. His appearance there in 1782 was a sensation, leading to twelve successive performances at the Concert Spirituel. He remained in Paris, active as a soloist, performer in chamber music, and director. He also was very productive as a composer. For several years he directed performances for Marie Antoinette. In 1788 he established the Théâtre de Monsieur, directed it successfully, and later moved it to the Théâtre Feydeau, which he had constructed. The premiere of Cherubini's opera *Lodoiska* (1791) was one of the most notable events under Viotti's direction.

In 1789 Viotti joined the National Guard as a noncommissioned officer, and in 1792 a Paris newspaper referred to him as "the Jacobins' violinist." Nevertheless, the revolutionary events gradually made further work in Paris impossible, especially since Viotti was accused of being a turncoat who had been on good terms with the aristocracy before joining the revolutionaries. He went to London, where he appeared in the same series of concerts, organized by Salomon, during which Haydn directed his own symphonies. He also became active in the theatrical world. Together with Rode he was accused of spreading revolutionary ideas; he was forced to leave England in 1798. Not until 1801 was he allowed to return, having spent the interim in Hamburg.

In Paris, Viotti had been considered the greatest violinist of his time, praised for his secure technique combined with depth of feeling and good taste. A number of talented young players gathered around him, to take lessons and to derive inspiration from his playing. When Viotti performed his Violin Concerto no. 29 in E minor, listeners were so greatly moved that a Viotti pupil was heard sobbing soon after the master began playing. Viotti himself was moved to tears. Such intense reactions by listeners were not uncommon in those days.

In both Paris and London Viotti was much in demand as a teacher. When, at the age of seventeen, Spohr was urged and supported by his employer to continue his studies, Viotti was the obvious choice. To Spohr's great disappointment, Viotti refused to take him on—he had become a wine merchant. (Viotti was not the first violinist to make such a career change; Stefano Carbonelli, a Corelli pupil who had lived in London since 1720, gave up a concertmaster's position for the same purpose, eventually becoming the wine supplier to the royal family.)

On the occasion of an 1801 Viotti appearance in Paris, a reviewer for the *Allgemeine Musikalische Zeitung* made an interesting comparison of Rode's and Viotti's playing. Rode, he claimed, always had complete control but less inspiration, while the vehement Viotti "occasionally played wrong notes. Inspiration will outshine mistakes, but inspiration is no substitute for the art of avoiding mistakes." Viotti continued to be an excellent performer even in his old age. After the Restoration he was called back to Paris to become the director of both the Opéra and the Théâtre Italien, but he was not successful with either. He died in London in 1824.

Viotti composed more than 150 works, almost all for the violin. Chief among these are his twenty-nine violin concertos some of which, of excellent quality, have exerted great influence on violin composing in general. In time, however, they were replaced by the Beethoven, Mendelssohn, and Brahms concertos. No. 22 in A minor is now only occasionally heard in public, but still serves for the study of various aspects of technique and interpretation. His duos for two unaccompanied violins occupied an important place in teaching and ensemble playing; they are valuable preparation for advanced chamber music and orchestra playing. Viotti published sixty-two such duos, standard repertory until they were partially eclipsed by a growing interest in baroque duos. Viotti did not write a teaching method or violin tutor as such; on 27 May 1800 the *Hamburger Zeitung* reported that he was engaged in writing such a work, but most likely it was never achieved. An existing manuscript, only a few pages long, entitled *Mon opinion sur la manière d'enseigner et d'apprendre à jouer du violon* (My thoughts on teaching and learning violin playing) may have been the beginning of such a project.

During the late eighteenth and early nineteenth centuries, many Italian violinists less famous than Nardini, Lolli, Fiorillo, Pugnani, Campagnoli, and Viotti held positions at European courts. Nardini's pupil Filippo Manfredini appeared in concerts with Luigi Boccherini and was soloist at the Spanish court in Madrid, where he died in 1780. Gaetano Brunetti, another Nardini pupil, also was active in Madrid. He was a prolific composer whose tours took him to Mannheim, where he received valuable impressions. He died in Madrid in 1798. Lolli's pupil Giuseffo Festa conducted an orchestra in Naples, where he died in 1839.

Alessandro Rolla (1757–1841) achieved fame as the teacher of Paganini. To be sure, he soon had to tell his pupil that there was nothing more he could teach him. Rolla was one of the early concertizing violists and wrote much for that instrument. As a violinist he served as concertmaster in Parma, from 1803 to 1833 he directed the orchestra of La Scala in Milan, and at various times was soloist for Viceroy Eugène de Beauharnais. As teacher at the recently opened Milan conservatory he was an influential pedagogue. Among his many compositions are seven violin concertos and several valuable instruction books.

His son and student Giuseppe Antonio Rolla was a talented violinist and composer. He soon rose to leading positions, first in Bologna and after 1822 as concertmaster in Dresden, where he died in 1837 at the early age of thirty nine.

Though born in Brunswick, Federigo Fiorillo (b. 1755, d. ca. 1823) also belonged to the world of Italian musicians. His father, Ignatio Fiorillo, was a successful opera composer employed as court kapellmeister in Brunswick and Kassel. The son began as a performer on the mandolin, toured Russia and Poland as mandolin and violin soloist, and for a short time was music director in Riga. He then settled in London, where he was the violist in Salomon's string quartet. Fiorillo wrote more than seventy works, including a fair amount of chamber music. His duos for two violins or violin and viola chiefly serve teaching purposes; contemporary violinists know only his caprices.

Giovanni Jarnovic (Giornovichi; ca. 1740–1804) also belonged to the Italian school. He became a Lolli pupil and went on to reap spectacular successes, performing at the Concert Spirituel in 1773. Six years later we meet him as concertmaster in Berlin. He toured extensively and spent several years at the court of Catherine II in St. Petersburg, where, after stays in Hamburg and England, he died. Though one of the most talented violinists of his day, his restless life kept him from maturing as a person and artist. Death came while he was playing billiards, an activity from which he at times derived his living.

The ranks of eighteenth-century virtuosos included two women. Maddalena Lombardini de Sirmen (b. 1735 in Venice) is still known because of the letter Tartini wrote to her. She trained at the Ospedale dei Mendicanti; her successes included appearances at the Concert Spirituel. Regina Strinasacchi (b. 1764 in Mantua) was also educated in Venice, at the Ospedale della Pietà. Mozart wrote the Violin Sonata in B–flat major, K. 454, for her; together they premiered the work in Vienna in 1784. After a period of touring in Germany and France she married Johann Konrad Schlick, principal cellist in Gotha, where she also played in the orchestra. Spohr met her when he assumed the directorship of the Gotha music establishment. In 1822 she sold him her magnificent Strad. In 1785, Leopold Mozart praised her sensitive playing:

> Every note she plays shows depth of feeling; even in a symphony her playing is expressive. There is no one who can render an Adagio with more delicate sentiment, for she puts her heart and soul into every melody. Her tone is beautiful and forceful. In general I would say that a talented woman plays with more expression than a man.

In a letter of 24 April 1784, Wolfgang Mozart also had words of high praise for her.

Regina Strinasacchi, silhouette by an unknown artist, 1795

During the late eighteenth century many outstanding Italian violinists continued the tradition of Geminiani, Locatelli, Tartini, and others, forming a bridge to Paganini, yet strangely enough, writers on the eighteenth-century Italian violin school have often referred to a decline. According to Boyden (1965), this decline began in 1761, the year L'Abbé le fils published his violin school: "It is a date which also serves to mark the gradual decline of the Italian school of violin playing and the gradual assumption of leadership on the part of the French."

FRANCE

In the early eighteenth century, French music underwent changes that can be related to the different views of older and younger generations, but also to national differences between the French and Italians. The traditional gentle sound of the gamba had been so long favored by the French that the "pardessus de viole" (sopranino gamba) for a while offered serious competition to the violin. Since Mersenne's time the violin had been favored for dance music, including Lully's ballets. Italian instrumental music represented progress, and the violin was its chief manifestation, but resistance to this progress was at least in part due to national pride. The *Parallèle des Italiens et des François* (1702) by the Abbé Raguenet and similar writings found aesthetic-philosophical reasons for these contrasts, and patriotically inspired polemic essays on art were published into Rousseau's time.

Attitudes, however, were beginning to change ca. 1700, in part due to the wider acceptance of Corelli's works. François Du Val (Duval), a violinist in the court orchestra, was the first to play them in France. Along with Duval's own compositions in the Italian manner they paved the way for the acceptance of Italian music. It is true that Corelli's opp. 1–3 were not published in France until the first decade of the new century, and op. 4 not until ca. 1720, but it is significant that the op. 5 sonatas, so important for the evolution of violin playing, were issued by Faucault in Paris in 1701, only a year after they had been published in Rome. Massard de la Tour and Ballard, other Paris publishers, soon followed suit.

Corelli's pupil Michel Mascitti (b. ca. 1664 in the kingdom of Naples) concertized widely and then settled in Paris in the service of the duke of Orléans. His sonatas for one or two violins and basso continuo appeared in Paris in 1704. Additional suitelike works, many of only moderate difficulty and intended for amateurs, helped to attract French violinists to Italian music.

More Italian violinists came to Paris around the turn of the century, such as Giovanni-Antonio Guido, who became "maître de la musique du Duc d'Orléans" and as a violinist and composer played a leading role for several decades. The Neapolitan Giovanni Antonio Piani (Des Planes) made his mark by introducing crescendo and decrescendo signs that anticipate those in use today. In his op. 1 sonatas (Paris 1712) he explained these signs in detail, clarifying for French violinists subtleties of Italian interpretation of which they had been only vaguely aware.

An early attempt by a French composer to write sonatas based on Italian models was made by François Couperin le jeune. When in 1692 he performed a trio sonata of his own composition he used the pen name Couperroni, fearing that as a French composer he might be ridiculed for writing in this style. He was followed by Jean-Féry Rebel (d. 1747), Lully's pupil and later a court composer, who in 1695 wrote twelve sonatas for one or two violins and basso continuo. They were not published until 1713. After 1700 more and more violin music by French composers was printed, including Dandrieu's trio sonatas (1703) and violin sonatas with continuo (1710). In 1707 Joseph Marchand, violinist in the royal chapel, published in Paris his *Suites de pièces meslées de sonates pour le violon et la basse, qui ont esté exécutez plusieurs fois devant Sa Majesté* (Suites and sonatas for violin and bass that have been performed several times for His Majesty). Having found favor at court, sonatas were accepted by the general public. A group of French violinists began to distance themselves from the very limited manner of playing that went back to Lully, turning instead to the kind of virtuosity that had long been cultivated in Italy.

Best known in this group are Jean-Baptiste Anet (1676–1755), a Corelli pupil, and Anet's pupil Jean-Baptiste Sénaillié (1687–1730), whose five books of sonatas containing ten works each require considerable skill in position playing. During a journey to Italy Sénaillié learned much about both playing and composing. He was a member of "la musique du Duc d'Orléans," later of the royal chapel, and was much in demand as a teacher. Guillemain and Guignon were his best students. The two Francoeur brothers, Louis le fils aîné and François le cadet, were prominent in Paris music circles. Their complex multiple-stop writing points to Bach. Andreas Moser has cited examples that are playable only with very intricate fingering.

Two events heralded the coming of a French school of violin playing: the publication in 1723 of the *Premier livre de sonates a violon seul avec la basse continue composées par Mr Leclair l'aîné. . . Paris chez le Sr Boivin* and, in 1725, the founding of the Concert Spirituel by Anne Danican Philidor (1681–1728). A year earlier, Pietro Crozat had inaugurated the Concert Italien.

Philidor, a member of a prominent Paris family of musicians, was a flutist and court composer. During Lent, all theaters were closed for about five weeks—a lean season for professional musicians. It was Philidor's idea to offer concerts of sacred music to circumvent the edict. The first concert took place on 18 March 1725 in the Swiss Hall of the Tuileries, whose amphitheater-shaped podium accommodated sixty musicians. The program consisted of two motets by Delalande, Corelli's "Christmas" Concerto (op. 6, no. 8), and several "soli de violon," probably sonatas with basso continuo. Instrumental music thus was included from the start, and soon violin concertos occupied a regular place on the programs.

The first concert was a great success among members of society, and the ensuing series of concerts was popular with the Paris public. To appear on these programs became a must for career-minded violinists, and high performance standards improved the quality of French instrumental playing and composition in general. Here Jacques Aubert (1684–1753), a Sénaillié pupil, performed one of his own violin concertos, the first by a French composer. There was no better endorsement for a work than its having been heard in a Concert Spirituel. As late as 1783 the *Almanach Musical* announced the publication of the "Septième Concerto de Lolli, tel qu'il a été joué au Concert spirituel, par M. Jarnovik. Chez M. Sieber" (Lolli's Seventh Concerto, which was performed at the Concert Spirituel by Jarnovik. Published by Sieber). In 1775, no fewer than twenty new violin concertos were presented at these concerts. All famous violinists from abroad were among the soloists, raising standards to international levels and widening the public's musical horizon.

Philidor also was in charge of the business side. To obtain from the opera the right to put on these concerts he had to pay 6000 francs yearly. From 1755 to 1762 the violinist Mondonville was the entrepreneur; Gaviniès, Leduc, and Gossec managed the concerts. The valuable institution disappeared during the upsets of the French Revolution in 1790–1791.

Like his father, Jean–Marie Leclair (b. 1697 in Lyon) began as an amateur violinist. Together with his wife he belonged to the ballet of the Lyon opera, then in 1722 joined the Turin opera as solo dancer and ballet master. His op. 1 was published in Paris in 1723. While he was still living in Turin (until 1728), his talent as a violinist was discovered by Somis who became his teacher. After 1728 Leclair made a name for himself as a soloist at the Concert Spirituel, which caused him (along with Jean-Pierre Guignon, another Somis pupil) to be appointed to the Musique Royale. He lived in Amsterdam from 1737 to 1743, later in Chambéry, then returned to Paris. On 23 October 1764 he was found murdered in his apartment; the identity of the killer has never been established.

Leclair's *oeuvre* includes fifteen printed editions of works, made up of forty-nine sonatas for violin and continuo, twelve sonatas for two violins without bass, twenty-five trio sonatas for two violins and continuo, and twelve violin concertos with string orchestra. Except for one opera, he wrote for violin exclusively. His style—of thematic invention, form, and treatment of the violin—was based on Corelli, Vivaldi, Tartini, and his teacher Somis. His violin compositions and probably also his playing were even more strongly affected by Locatelli's virtuosity. His left-hand stretches must have been amazing, to judge by passages like these:

Double stops and ingenious broken chords show Leclair to have advanced considerably beyond his Italian models. Surprising, in view of such

highly developed technique, is his use of the thumb ("le pouce") in one of his
op. 1 sonatas, for the entire passage could be played in half position:

At first Leclair's playing and composing were thought to be Italian; later,
people were proud that a Frenchman could do all this, and eventually they
contrasted Leclair with the Italians. He had a lasting effect on French violin
playing in the late eighteenth century, even though only a few important
violinists were among his students: L'Abbé le fils, Saint-Georges, and probably Gaviniès. Young students were seldom able to pay the fees commanded
by great teachers, which may explain this. Yet many were affected and
inspired by his playing and by studying his works, including the suggestions
for performing them included in the prefaces. Authors of early nineteenth-
century violin tutors continued to recommend the study of his music, and
Cartier included three entire sonatas and two single movements in his compilation.

Among Leclair's students, L'Abbé le fils (d. 1803) was known chiefly for
his violin school. He first appeared at the Concert Spirituel at the age of
fourteen, performing with Gaviniès one of his teacher's trio sonatas. He was
engaged by the Paris Opéra in 1742. In his late sonatas he did not carry on
Leclair's virtuoso tradition, but he may have been the initiator of "jolis airs
ajustés et variés pour un violon seul" (pleasant melodies arranged and varied
for solo violin). This genre of variations on folk songs or fashionably popular tunes with a didactic message remained popular well into the nineteenth
century.

The Chevalier Joseph de Saint-Georges (d. 1799 in Paris) had most likely
also studied with Leclair. Born in 1739 in Guadeloupe, he was the son of a
count and a native mother. When in 1769 Gossec founded the Concert des
Amateurs, Saint-Georges became its concertmaster and later also directed
the concerts. After busy years composing he participated in the revolutionary wars as a high-ranking officer. Originality and imagination characterize
his violin concertos and *symphonies concertantes*; they anticipate much of the
brilliance of romantic violin music.

Jean-Joseph Cassanéa de Mondonville (1711–1772) began his career as a
first violinist in Lille. He debuted at a Concert Spirituel at the age of twenty-
three and settled in Paris a few years later. At first a member, he gradually rose
to directorship of the royal orchestra. His stage works and oratorios have
fallen into oblivion. Most valuable are his op. 4 sonatas, *Les sons harmoniques*
(The harmonics, ca. 1735), in which he used simple and double stop harmonics (the first in France to do so), providing an explanatory chart in the
preface. The manner of playing the tromba marina may have inspired him to
exploit harmonics. In the printed music they are indicated by a short wavy

line above the note, similar to a mordent sign. A group of his works for violin and voice seems to be lost, including a concerto "de violon avec chant" (1747) and another "avec voix, orchestre et choeurs" (1752). Some pieces for harpsichord and voice or violin (1740) have been preserved.

After 1750, many fine violinists played in the orchestras of the Paris theaters or were employed by the nobility. Among them were Pierre Lahoussage, De Tremais, Jean-Baptiste Dupont, and Marie-Alexandre Guénin. [Very little is known about De Tremais, who composed chiefly violin sonatas and duets. *Ed.*] Outstanding among them was Pierre Gaviniès, the son of a Bordeaux luthier. He may have studied with Leclair; at the age of thirteen he debuted at the Concert Spirituel. Acclaimed as a soloist there for decades, he eventually became their conductor. He also wrote operas. His work at the Paris Conservatoire may have inspired him to write *Les vingt-quatre matinées.*

Simon le Duc (Leduc) l'aîné was one of his talented pupils. He died in 1777 before he had reached the age of thirty. Together with his brother Pierre le Duc le jeune he founded a publishing house that still exists.

Two other brothers, Alday l'aîné (b. 1763) and Alday le jeune (b. 1764), were fine violinists who composed for their instrument. Alday l'aîné became a music dealer in Lyon and published a very useful violin method; Alday le jeune studied with Viotti before fleeing to England to avoid the Revolution. He wrote very good etudes.

Alexandre Boucher (1778–1861) was a strange, talented violinist, a shady individual who may have strayed from the straight and narrow path during the turbulent events of the Revolution. As a child prodigy he played for Marie Antoinette, then studied with Gaviniès. When the Bastille was taken he is said to have fought in the front line but then went to Spain as concert-master to the royal court. He returned to Paris and embarked upon tours that took him all the way to Russia. He attracted attention with his acrobatic violin playing and his resemblance to Napoleon, whom he imitated by adopting his haircut and gestures. For different movements of a concerto he would use different violins, and for *fortissimo* passages he used a special bow with black hair. Up to his death at the age of eighty-three, still an able performer, he called himself "doyen des musiciens connus d'Europe" (the oldest of Europe's famous musicians).

Paris offered ample professional opportunities, and with such great masters as Leclair and Gaviniès as models, the French school of violin playing flourished at the end of the century, headed by Rode, Baillot, and Kreutzer. Their teaching activities were closely related to the founding of the Paris Conservatoire.

GERMANY AND AUSTRIA

A distinct style of violin playing developed in seventeenth-century Germany and Austria, quite apart from the Italian manner; it is reflected in Westhoff's turn-of-the-century compositions. During the first decades of the new century, however, Italian violin music and violin playing strongly asserted themselves, evident in the success of Corelli's music and, later, of Vivaldi's concertos, which affected virtually all major composers. The resulting flourishing of violin playing, both as to quality and quantity, was not, however, closed to French influences. It was an age of great variety in interpretation, a variety that made it difficult for some of the lesser composers to develop a personal style.

Johann Georg Pisendel (1687–1755), a Torelli pupil, rose to the position of Dresden concertmaster in 1728. Journeys to Paris and Italy (including study with Vivaldi) and a stay in Vienna greatly widened his horizons. Stylistically, his Sonata for unaccompanied violin (ca. 1716) is surprisingly close to Bach, whom he had met in Weimar in 1709, and again, probably on several occasions, in Dresden. The sonata's slow introduction is highly ornamented, with many double stops in the Bach manner, followed by a single-line Allegro and ending with a Gigue and Double that again are rich in chords.

Johann Adam Birckenstock (1687–1733), a Volumier pupil, was a member of the Kassel court chapel; his employer arranged for his further study with François Duval in France, and he eventually became kapellmeister in Eisenach. A virtuoso, Birckenstock toured abroad. His own violin sonatas offer great technical challenges.

Eighteenth-century musicians were generally expected to have some knowledge of violin playing, without necessarily advancing very far. Georg Philipp Telemann (1681–1767), to judge by his 1718 memoirs (published in *Denkmäler deutscher Tonkunst*, vol. 28, Leipzig 1892), was no great admirer of violin concertos:

> Most concertos I have seen display many difficulties and awkward leaps, but also poor harmony and worse melodic writing. I hated the former, for they did not fit my hand and bow, and I could not warm up to the latter. Having developed an ear for French music I did not care to imitate such writing.

Nevertheless, he wrote "quite a few" concertos himself —twenty that have been preserved, according to E. Kross. They are ably written but rather routinely conceived, with technical demands that do not go beyond what was customary in courtly entertainment of the day. Telemann did write well for unaccompanied violin, as shown in his *XII fantasie per il violino senza basso* (1735). The term "fantasy" is misleading, for most of them are in three short movements, comparable to what later would be called a sonatina.

During the first half of the eighteenth century, German violin playing reflected first French, then Italian influences. This changed with Johann Stamitz's appointment in Mannheim and Franz (František) Benda's appointment to the court of the Prussian crown prince Frederick. Also at that court was Johann Gottlieb Graun (1703–1771), the composer of more than sixty violin concertos and ninety-seven symphonies.

Like Stamitz, Franz Benda (1709–1786) came from Bohemia; with the king's help he soon brought his parents and other family members to Potsdam. There, among C. P. E. Bach, Quantz, and the Graun brothers, he affected stylistic developments at least in regard to violin playing. Benda was soon viewed as the representative of German, as opposed to Italian violin playing, a situation comparable to France, where the Somis pupil Leclair was regarded as the proponent of French vs. Italian style. Benda's manner of playing probably was not specifically Bohemian; it was admired for its *empfindsam* quality, so different from the classic Italian manner that was already considered old-fashioned. Listeners waxed poetic over his playing; as Schubart described it, "It came from the heart and went to the heart. . . . When Benda played an Adagio, people often were moved to tears." In 1819 Benda's son Carl, in his only publication (*Remarks on the Playing and Interpretation of Adagios*), described some characteristics of German violin playing ca. 1760–1770, with specific references to his father. A player must find the exact mood called for by a piece or section of a piece. Once he has detected these, "he will hardly need the expression marks printed in the music, which often are very unreliable." The exact sentiments to be expressed "cannot be described; they must be felt."

Franz Benda attracted many students, including his three younger brothers Johann, Georg, and Joseph. These, along with his sons Friedrich and Carl, became capable members of the Potsdam orchestra and helped establish the reputation of a Benda school of violin playing. Franz Benda was fond of playing Bach's music; he had met him in Leipzig in 1734. According to Forkel, Bach highly esteemed Benda, who probably was present when Bach visited Potsdam in 1747. Two of Benda's best pupils were Friedrich Wilhelm Rust (1739–1796), music director in Dessau, and Johann Peter Salomon (1745–1815), later Haydn's London impresario. They played a major part in keeping the Bach tradition alive. Rust wrote sonatas for unaccompanied violin in the Bach manner. His grandson made a name for himself as editor of Bach's music. Salomon performed Bach's works for solo violin at a time when they had become virtually forgotten. Leopold August Abel (1718–1794), also a product of the Benda school, was the son of Bach's gamba player in Köthen, Christian Ferdinand Abel, and the brother of the famous gamba player Karl Friedrich Abel. Leopold August held concertmaster positions at several courts, the last one at Ludwigsburg, where his two sons were orchestra violinists.

Violin playing in Germany was also greatly affected by the work of Johann Stamitz who, to be sure, performed less as time went by. When the Mannheim court and its orchestra moved to Munich, that city became the center of south German violin playing, affecting what took place in many smaller residences. Among violinists in Mannheim/Munich were Ignaz Fränzl (1736–1811) and his son Ferdinand (1770–1833), appointed Munich kapellmeister in 1806. In his autobiography Spohr repeatedly commented on Ferdinand's playing. Friedrich Wilhelm Pixis (1786–1842), a child prodigy, had studied with Ignaz Fränzl and with Viotti in Hamburg. His tours with his brother, a pianist, caused much excitement. After years in Vienna he headed the advanced class in violin playing at the Prague conservatory.

Johann Anton André (1775–1842) began his career at the age of sixteen at the Mannheim court theater. He too concertized extensively before heading the Offenbach publishing house founded by his father, turning it into one of the foremost firms of the time, partly as the result of acquiring Mozart's estate from his widow.

Johann Friedrich Eck (1766–1810) also came from the Mannheim tradition; his Bohemian father had played French horn under Stamitz. Johann Eck went to Munich, where he taught his brother Franz Eck (1774–1804), who became Spohr's teacher. The Eck brothers played impressively, producing a large tone, in the French manner. In the review of a concert in Munich (late October 1802), a critic pointed this out: "[Mr. Eck's] playing can be heard in spacious halls. He creates a large effect, carefully calculated, and bound to please the listener."

Two other Mannheim violinists were Christian Cannabich (1731–1798), who settled in Munich after studies in Italy, and Wilhelm Cramer (1745–1799), who made a name for himself in London. He was the father of the famous pianist Johann Baptist Cramer.

The life of the violinist Bernhard Hupfeld (b. 1717 in Kassel) typifies the German situation at that time. He began as a choirboy, with early violin study, then traveled in the service of a count to Hungary and Vienna; he directed a regimental wind band and participated in several military campaigns. In 1749 he studied violin and composition in Italy; in 1753, as director and concertmaster for Prince Ludwig Ferdinand Sayn-Wittgenstein, his specific duties included training and supervising musicians and "busying himself as a composer." He was dismissed in 1755 because of a retrenchment at court. His next post was concertmaster at Marburg University, where he offered "to instruct all lovers of music in composition, violin, thorough bass, flute, and singing . . . to organize and direct any music for festive occasions at the university." This changeover—from employment by a gradually declining nobility to employment by the rising middle class—is characteristic for the age.

Heinrich Weissenburg von Biswang (active ca. 1700) was a Swiss composer whose violin music reflected German technique. Having studied music he embarked upon a military career in Holland. Italianizing his name to Henrico Albicastro surely helped sales of his violin compositions, which were published in Amsterdam.

Italian musicians held leading positions at the imperial court in Vienna, among them Nicola Matteis (Mathys; d. 1737) and Giovanni Antonio Piani, the concertmaster, who previously had lived in France. Matteis (the son of an English violinist of the same name) worked under Fux in Vienna, "in charge of the emperor's twenty-three violinists," according to Walther's lexicon. He also succeeded as a composer of ballet music. The Italian Aloisio Luigi Tomasini (1741–1808), Haydn's concertmaster in Eisenstadt, studied in Venice and also for several years in Salzburg under Leopold Mozart. At the age of sixteen he had become a valet to Prince Paul Anton Esterházy. A contract of 1801 stipulated that he was to instruct members of the prince's orchestra. His sons Luigi and Antonio had their start in the Eisenstadt orchestra.

It took some time before German-Austrian violinists could hold their own against Italian virtuosos. One of them was the Viennese Joseph Starzer (1726–1787), whom Burney described as playing adagios with special, deep feeling. Starzer also spent some time in Russia. Though writing ballet music was his chief interest, he maintained his position as concertmaster of the court chapel for many years. Karl Dittersdorf (1739–1799), also of Vienna, at first excelled as a violinist and at various times belonged to the imperial opera orchestra. Later, composing and directing absorbed his interest. Karoline Bayer (d. 1803 in Vienna), the daughter of a Viennese court trumpeter, attracted a good deal of attention as a traveling virtuosa.

In 1740 the administration of the court theaters inaugurated a series of concerts, held every Friday and on holidays. Modeled on the Concert Spirituel, the concerts, which included oratorios, cantatas, orchestral music, and concertos in their programs, were an important medium for the cultivation of instrumental music in the city. When they were discontinued in 1772, Florian Gassmann instituted benefit concerts for the society supporting widows and orphans of Viennese court musicians. The intensive practice of instrumental music in Austrian monasteries also affected violin playing. High masses with full orchestra were celebrated on major feast days. Biographies of many violinists stress the thorough instruction in violin playing offered in the monasteries' boarding schools, a basis on which many a violinist's career was founded.

In Vienna as in Germany, Bohemian musicians were increasingly evident after the mid-eighteenth century. Bohemia, "Europe's conservatory" as Burney called it, produced many more musicians than could find employment there. Members of the Bohemian aristocracy customarily spent summers on their country estates but resided in Vienna during the winter. Quite naturally then, Bohemian musicians flocked to the capital—actually a migration within the confines of the Hapsburg monarchy. Those who began as violinists might also compose and advance to kapellmeister posts. Wenzel Pichl (d. 1805), the composer of violin concertos and valuable studies, was one of these Viennese Bohemians. After years in Italy he came to Vienna as kapellmeister; he died while performing a violin concerto in the Lobkowitz palace. Another Viennese Bohemian was Paul Wranitzky (d. 1808), first violinist in Eisenstadt and later violinist and director of the two imperial-royal court theaters in Vienna.

Johann Baptist Vanhal (Wanhal; d. 1813 in Vienna) enjoyed a fine reputation as a composer of instrumental music. At times he joined Haydn and Mozart to play string quartets. Anton Wranitzky (d. 1820 in Vienna), for many years kapellmeister for Prince Lobkowitz, directed several orchestras (as did his brother Paul) including the orchestra at the Theater an der Wien. Andreas Moser called him "the true founder of the Viennese school of violin playing." Finally we should mention Wenzel Krumpholz (d. 1817 in Vienna), Beethoven's friend and occasional violin instructor, who began as a violinist in Eisenstadt and then served Prince Kinsky and the imperial court orchestra. Ignaz Schuppanzigh, Wranitzky's student, was a strong representative of the local school of violin playing. Most of these players were also capable and industrious composers, though little of their *oeuvre* has come down to us.

Compared with Vienna, Salzburg and other Austrian provincial cities did little to develop a characteristic Austrian style of violin playing, in spite of Biber's and Leopold Mozart's contributions. The significance of the elder Mozart, a pedagogue but not a first-rate performer, cannot be compared with Tartini's.

ENGLAND AND OTHER EUROPEAN COUNTRIES

During the late seventeenth century amateur violin playing had made great strides in England, but the professional players of above-average talent were Italians. Aside from Geminiani and Veracini, many other Italians could be heard in London's theater orchestras and those of the nobility, such as Corelli's pupils Pietro and Prospero Castrucci (the former was Handel's London concertmaster). Others included Felice Giardini, a Somis pupil, and Gasparo Visconti from Cremona, who is said to have advised Stradivari for some time. Aside from teaching wealthy amateurs, they affected violin playing in England through some truly talented pupils, chief among them John Clagg (Clegg), a pupil of Dubourg and Bononcini, whose brief life ended in an asylum. Thomas Linley was a promising Nardini student, known through his association with Mozart. At the age of twenty-two he met his death in a boating accident. Another talented English violinist, John Henry Eccles, went to France, became one of the Violons du Roi, and in 1720 published a fine sonata collection entitled *Douze solos de violon*.

Michael Christian Feisting (d. 1752), of German origin but trained in London, was a Geminiani pupil. He led the orchestra of the Italian opera, composed valuable concertos and chamber music, and eventually rose to the rank of royal music director.

Geminiani's best-known pupil was Matthew Dubourg (1703–1767). The son of a dance master, he appeared at the age of nine in the concerts arranged by Thomas Britton, a coal merchant, which series occupied an important place in London's musical life. He succeeded Kusser as concertmaster in Dublin, then directed the London Royal Opera. Once while Handel's concertmaster, Dubourg improvised a seemingly endless cadenza that took him to the most remote keys. When he finally returned to the tonic, Handel greeted him with these words: "Welcome home, Dubourg!" His grandson George Dubourg was the author of a small book, *The Violin* (London 1836), which went through five editions.

During the eighteenth century, England witnessed the development of a vigorous concert life, supported by individuals and organizations. The Academy of Ancient Music was founded in 1710; three years later public concerts began in Hickford's Room, and the Castle Society began operations in 1724. Later the Hanover Square Room Concerts (1775) and the Professional Concerts (1785) provided events comparable in quality to what was offered in France, apparently the model. Public and private music making attracted Italians and other foreigners. François Hippolyte Barthélémon (d. 1808) was a career officer before he settled in London as concertmaster and soloist. He became one of Haydn's friends. Salomon, the talented German impresario, did much to further orchestra playing in London during an age of transition from aristocratic to middle-class patronage. When the Reign of Terror swept France, England became a haven for many musicians, including Viotti.

Any account of eighteenth-century violin playing in England would be incomplete without considering Handel. Though primarily a keyboard player, he played the violin well enough in his youth to join the Hamburg opera at the Gänsemarkt in 1703, playing second violin. In his concerti grossi he provided challenges not only for the orchestra but also for the solo group (two violins and continuo). His trio sonatas, and especially his op. 5 sonatas for violin and continuo, remain in the standard violin repertory.

Other European countries experienced a similar shift: a preponderance of Italian influence early in the eighteenth century followed by the gradual emergence of talented local violinists who moved up into leading positions. The region of the Low Countries that later would become Belgium was affected by developments in France, while many virtuosos from central Europe concertized in Holland on their way to London. Violin making flourished in Holland, supported by much amateur music making that also affected the success, early in the century, of the Roger music publishing firm. Locatelli had lived in Amsterdam since 1729; Leclair resided there from 1737 to 1743; Vivaldi concertized in Amsterdam in 1738. Peter vom Laar (d. ca. 1674), a painter, was the first major Dutch violinist. He studied both art forms in Rome and upon his return worked in Amsterdam and Haarlem. Ernst Schick (d. 1815) at first followed his father's profession of dance master, at the time a desirable combination with violin playing. Inspired by Lolli's playing he devoted himself entirely to music and became concertmaster in Mainz and Berlin. Willem de Fesch (d. 1757 in London) composed attractive sonatas and concertos; his work eventually took him to England.

The political upheavals in the region that later became Belgium had both positive and negative effects. After the battle of Höchstädt in 1704 the Bavarian elector Max Emanuel went into exile in Brussels, taking along his musicians, among them Evaristo Felice dal'Abaco (1675–1742), a violinist, cellist, and composer. Other fine violinists at the Brussels court, such as Pierre van Maldere (d. 1768) and Henry Jacques de Croes (d. 1786), also distinguished themselves as composers. Some violinists from the country's south went to Paris, including François Cupis de Camargo (b. 1719 in Brussels), a member of the Paris Opéra orchestra. François Joseph Gossec (1734–1829) also hailed from the later Belgium. A choirboy in his youth, he was trained as a violinist and eventually became an outstanding composer in Paris.

The importance of Bohemia in eighteenth-century string playing has already been pointed out, as well as the great festivities in Prague accompanying the coronation of Charles VI in 1723. Anton Kamell (d. ca. 1788) was sent by a local benefactor to study with Tartini in Padua; on his return he emigrated to England. Ever since the 1730s, musicians of the stature of Benda and Stamitz, as well as lesser talents, had left their native Bohemia to find work with the German and Austrian nobility. Burney attributed the high standards of Bohemian violin playing to musically well-trained schoolteachers in town and country, who usually gave private lessons on several instruments and on every Sunday provided orchestras for high mass, with violins forming the backbone. Many gifted Bohemian violinists were members of the clergy, and monasteries there were known for their active cultivation of music. As mentioned, many violinists went from Bohemia to Vienna, but other countries also benefited from the abundant supply. Johann Baptist Neruda and his sons Georg and Anton held prominent places in the Dresden court chapel, as did the violinist Anton Giranek (d. 1761). In 1758 Stamitz brought Georg Czarth to Mannheim, and Ernst Haveck was a fellow violist of the young Beethoven in Bonn. Haveck's father had gone to Bonn after a stay in Munich.

THE FOUNDING OF THE PARIS CONSERVATOIRE

THE BEGINNINGS OF MODERN MUSIC EDUCATION

In the early eighteenth century, the road to a professional music career contained many obstacles, and success involved a certain amount of good fortune. It was a smooth road at the outset if a young boy had a good voice, which would help him to be accepted in a boarding school for choirboys. For large families, such as the Haydns and Schuberts, this meant one less mouth to feed. Basic instruction in violin playing was part of the curriculum, training that came in handy during the often-lean years after a boy's voice changed. To play at weddings, fairs, and other festive occasions provided the adolescent Haydn and other ex-choristers with a minimal livelihood. Good fortune could also appear in the person of a patron who would pay for further training with a fine teacher or even for study abroad. Such a benefactor usually hoped to keep the well-trained young musician in his service. To apprentice oneself to a town musician was another road, often arduous, to professional standing.

Once a certain competence had been achieved, employment in an aristocratic family, usually a combination of musical and other duties, was fairly easy to find. Tomasini began as a valet in Eisenstadt; eventually Haydn was able to free such an outstanding violinist from nonmusical assignments.

The Neapolitan and Venetian conservatories provided music education at its most intensive. Outstanding maestros formed their teaching faculties. Burney (1773) described the S. Onofrio conservatory in Naples, which in 1770 had ninety students:

> The only vacation in these schools, in the whole year, is in autumn, and that for a few days only: during the winter, the boys rise two hours before it is light, from which time they continue their exercise, an hour and a

half at dinner excepted, till eight o'clock at night; and this constant perseverance, for a number of years, with genius and good teaching, must produce great musicians.

It was customary to "farm out" students to play in churches, theaters, and for special music occasions—a way to have them earn virtually their entire keep. Though this gave them practical experience, some of the energy and time no doubt would have been better spent on their real training. Aside from a few private schools, such as Tartini's in Padua, these conservatories then were the only institutions coming close to what we would call music schools. Though first proposed by Plato, the idea that it was the state's responsibility to provide a general education that included music had not yet been realized.

Broad public education was one of the tenets of the French Revolution; it led to the foundation of a school, open to all and state-supported, that would offer the best possible professional training in music. The opening ceremonies of the Paris Conservatoire de Musique took place on 22 October 1796; the preceding developments are worth reviewing in some detail. On the day before the taking of the Bastille, Bernard Sarrette, a music enthusiast in the military administration, assembled forty-five volunteer musicians to play for parades and celebrations. This band of the National Guard attracted good musicians formerly employed by the nobility and now without work. The establishment of an "école de musique militaire" had already been proposed in 1791; the following year the Paris city council voted to found it. In it, 120 students were to be taught, free of charge, with admission restricted to the sons of National Guard members. Each of the sixty battalions was entitled to nominate two students. The curriculum included two hours weekly of solfège, three hours of instrumental instruction, and band practice. One of the objectives was to ensure a supply of players for the regiments departing for the front. At this time the composer Gossec served as lieutenant and bandmaster, while Devienne, a well-known flutist and composer for his instrument, was a master sergeant. In 1793 Sarrette began to make plans for an "institut national de musique," its faculty to be augmented by composers Lesueur and Méhul and violinists Rodolphe Kreutzer and Pierre Rode. An enlarged curriculum resulted, especially in the area of opera, furthered by the inclusion of the old École Royale de Chant et de Déclamation.

In 1795, plans for the Conservatoire were complete: 115 professors were to instruct six hundred students, the faculty to include four teachers for violin, three for cello, and one for string bass. Before all this became an accomplished fact, two other momentous developments took place: instruments, libraries of sheet music and books on music, confiscated from emigrés and dissolved monasteries, were "stored" in the Conservatoire—where they remained permanently, forming the nucleus of the magnificent Conservatoire library (much of it now housed in the Bibliothèque Nationale) and instrument collections.

The other development was the founding of a state publishing house,

initially to make available song sheets and instrumental parts for national celebrations. Quite appropriately its name was Le Magasin de Musique à l'Usage
des Fêtes Nationales et du Conservatoire. On Gossec's initiative instructional
works were also to be edited and published, making available the important
methods of Kreutzer, Gaviniès, Rode, and Baillot. Quite likely some instrumental works were written for the emerging Conservatoire. A *symphonie
concertante* for two violins and string bass was performed on 30 October 1794,
with Kreutzer and Rode as violin soloists.

What happened in Paris led to comparable developments elsewhere.
During the following decades major conservatories were founded in Milan,
Prague, Vienna, and Graz. In Milan the conservatory enjoyed the protection
of Viceroy Eugène de Beauharnais, Napoleon's son by his first marriage; its
planning committee had requested that Sarrette provide them with a copy of
the Paris statutes, to serve as a model. In 1805 Karl Konrad Cannabich, son
of the well-known Mannheim kapellmeister, student of Eck and music director at the Munich court, was sent to Paris to study the Conservatoire's organization. Unfortunately this study bore no results because upon his return to
Munich Cannabich suddenly died. A curriculum in use in Vienna as late as
1835 listed as obligatory the study materials and methods used in Paris.

A national school of violin playing, going back to Leclair and Gaviniès,
was thus put on a sound, central basis, enhanced by the teaching of leading
violinists. All talented students regardless of means were eligible for admission—a broad foundation for the development of excellent violinists. Habeneck eventually had at his disposal an outstanding Orchestre du Conservatoire, which established nineteenth-century standards for interpreting
Beethoven's music. Wagner was greatly impressed by its playing; it affected
the orchestral writing in his own music dramas.

BEETHOVEN'S COMPOSITIONS FOR VIOLIN

As the grandson of a court kapellmeister and son of a singer in the court
chapel who also played several instruments passably well, Beethoven seemed
destined for a court musician's career. He had early lessons on harpsichord
and violin; basic familiarity with these was a must for anyone aiming at court
employment.

Ludwig showed above-average talent, which his father hoped to put to
good use, as Leopold Mozart had done with young Wolfgang. Franz Anton
Ries, a pupil of Salomon and a Bonn court musician, for a while gave violin
lessons to young Ludwig. In his own youth, Ries's concert tours had taken
him all the way to Vienna. He became a fatherly friend of his student, whose
family situation left much to be desired, and he also provided him with sufficiently solid training such that at the age of twelve Ludwig joined the court
orchestra as a violist. This offered him an excellent opportunity to acquire
firsthand knowledge of an orchestra's workings, knowledge that no doubt
affected the development of the later composer of symphonies.

After his arrival in Vienna, Beethoven continued occasional violin study with Krumpholz and Schuppanzigh, in addition to taking horn and clarinet instruction. He had access to Vienna's nobility, such as the Lichnowsky and Lobkowitz families, who maintained their own string quartets. From this frequent contact with first-rate string players, Beethoven learned what sounded well and what some of the technical challenges were.

It is important to remember this, if only because of an incident in Beethoven's later life that has often been misinterpreted. Schuppanzigh, Beethoven's true, artistic friend, unselfishly premiered virtually all Beethoven's chamber music. Once at a rehearsal, however, Schuppanzigh lost his temper. Frustrated by a seemingly unplayable passage, he threw his music on the floor. Beethoven, equally ill-tempered, lit into him: "Do you believe that when the Muse speaks to me I think of your miserable violin?" His words became famous, often quoted out of context by composers who lack a working knowledge of instrumental technique and who leave it up to the poor performer to cope with the unidiomatic things they have written. Conversation within Beethoven's circle was cordial but at times also rather rough. Schuppanzigh probably considered the uncouth remark about his "miserable violin" a momentary explosion, coming as it did from the greatest musician of his time, one who had been wracked by various strokes of fate and intensive creative work. Beethoven never disregarded the realities of instrumental technique.

Among his works for the "miserable violin," the Concerto for violin and orchestra op. 61 is foremost. It was written in 1806, shortly before the Fifth Symphony, during a period of felicitous creation when Beethoven's style, though viewed as novel and highly personal, still was understood and accepted by Vienna's musical elite. The concerto apparently was written for the fine Viennese violinist Franz Clement, twenty-six years old and at the time director of the orchestra at the Theater an der Wien. He had requested it for a concert that took place on 23 December. It was not Beethoven's custom to compose on short notice, but according to Czerny the concerto was "performed only two days after its completion and was a great success." The score is inscribed "Concerto par Clemenza pour Clement primo violino e direttore al theatro a Vienna" (Concerto written out of clemency for Clement).

It is instructive to examine the program in its entirety, for the curious variety of its offerings is not unusual for the time. It consisted of "a grand new overture by Méhul"; "a new violin concerto" by Beethoven, played by Clement; a Mozart aria; overture and chorus from Handel's *Ode for St. Cecilia's Day*, orchestrated by Mozart; and a new overture and a new vocal quartet by Cherubini. Following this, according to the announcement, "Herr Clement will improvise on the violin; he will also play a sonata on one string while holding the violin upside-down." The concert concluded with another grand chorus from the *Ode for St. Cecilia's Day*. What is perhaps arousing our curiosity, is Clement's contribution to the concert's second half. We may wonder what the public admired more: Beethoven's concerto or Clement's circuslike display.

Heute Dienstag den 23. Dezember 1806

Wird in dem k. k. priv. Schauspielhaus an der Wien
gegeben

Eine große

musikalische Akademie

mit Verstärkung des Orchesters

Zum Vortheil des Franz Klement,

Musikdirektor dieses Theaters.

Erste Abtheilung.

1. Eine grosse neue Overture von Herrn *Mehul.*
2. Ein neues *Violin-Concert* von Herrn Ludwig van Beethoven, gespielt von Hrn. Clement.
3. Eine *Aria* von Herrn W. Mozart, gesungen von Mad. Campi.
4. Eine *Overture* samt einem grossen *Chor* von Herrn *Hendel,* aus der *Ode auf St. Cæcilia,* instrumentirt von Herrn W. Mozart.

Zweyte Abtheilung.

1. Eine neue *Overture* von Herrn *Cherubini.*
2. Ein neues *Ouartetto* von Herrn *Cherubini,* gesungen von Mad. Campi, Hrn. Ehlers, Herrn Meier und Herrn Winkopf.
3. Wird Herr Clement auf der *Violine phantasiren* und auch eine *Sonate auf einer einzigen Saite* mit umgekehrter *Violin* spielen.
4. Ein grosser *Chor* von Herrn *Hendel,* aus der *Ode auf St. Cæcilia* instrumentirt von Herrn W. Mozart.

Die Logen und gesperrten Sitze sind in seiner Wohnung beim
schwarzen Bären an der Wien Nro. 456 im 1ten Stock,
von 9 Uhr früh bis Nachmittag um 5 Uhr zu haben.

Der Anfang um halb 7 Uhr.

Announcement of the concert in which Franz Clement appeared as violin soloist,
23 December 1806

Beethoven's Violin Concerto was slow in gaining the popularity it now enjoys. It was heard again in 1834, when Beethoven's friend Holz was most anxious to have Vieuxtemps play it, resulting in a great success for composer and soloist. Paganini is said to have attempted it once, and Ferdinand David gave it some early hearings. Joachim first played it in Hamburg in 1848. His interpretation caused it to be viewed as the prototype of a classical violin concerto. Joachim's sponsoring of the work is also significant because of a remark made by no less a composer than Spohr. After Joachim had played the concerto for him, Spohr reacted by saying, "Well, dear Herr Joachim, that was rather nice, but now I'd like to hear you play a *real* piece for the violin!"

Though the Beethoven Concerto makes considerable demands on the soloist's virtuosity, its musical substance outweighs any technical display. It is organically conceived; the orchestra is the soloist's equal partner. It has sometimes been called a "symphony with solo violin," not without some justification. Beethoven established a standard that has been observed, consciously or not, by those who have had the courage to write violin concertos after him. Brahms and Alban Berg may have come closest to this type in terms of quality.

Those who believe that the concerto's violin part represents ideal writing for that instrument may be surprised to learn that the composer, in the year following the first performance, arranged the work as a piano concerto, at the request of Clementi, who had visited Beethoven during a business trip to Vienna. Surprisingly, the concerto sounds quite good in this version, which includes no essential changes. To be sure, the pianist's first entry comes as something of a shock to listeners accustomed to the violin, but the piano arrangement offers a special bonus: Beethoven composed cadenzas for it. The one for the first movement is of special interest because (referring back to the opening tutti) Beethoven included two timpani. At the change of time signature a new motif is introduced, joyful and marchlike, quite different from our usual concept of a cadenza as being organically related to the movement itself. Based on Beethoven's piano cadenza, a number of attempts have been made to derive from it a cadenza for the Violin Concerto. Vieuxtemps was the first to do this; Wolfgang Schneiderhan's version has been published. Many violin virtuosos have provided their own cadenzas. Those by Joachim and Kreisler have become best known. Busoni also honored the composer by writing cadenzas for the concerto, and a fairly recent one was contributed by Max Rostal.

Beethoven's Triple Concerto, op. 56, for violin, cello, piano, and orchestra does not quite reach the level of the Violin Concerto. The original edition was entitled *Grand concerto concertant*. Both title and scoring relate this work to the category of sinfonia concertante which, however, by 1800 had tended to be lighter in substance, while the concerto, having symphonic proportions, was increasingly intended for the concert hall. The Triple Concerto's piano part was written for the young Archduke Rudolph and was designed not to be too difficult, which may have inhibited Beethoven's imagination. In a letter to Mendelssohn (16 February 1844), Ferdinand David reported, "Yesterday we played the Triple Concerto with Hiller and Rietz. To our surprise the audience liked it very much, but in the last movement we tried all kinds of tricks to make it come across."

Along with the fragment of a concerto movement dating from Beethoven's Bonn years, the two romances for violin and orchestra in G major (op. 40) and F major (op. 50) are among his earliest concerted works for that instrument. They are seldom heard in the concert hall but are assiduously played by students, though they are by no means easy.

A major component of the violinist's repertory are the ten violin sonatas, as we call them. That this was not the case at the time is shown by the original title of the great Ninth Sonata, op. 47: *Sonata per il pianoforte ed un violino obbligato, scritta in uno stile molto concertante, quasi come d'un concerto. Composta e dedicata al suo amico R. Kreuzer. Membro del Conservatorio di Musica in Parigi, primo violino dell'Academia delle Arti, e della Camera imperiale.* (Sonata for pianoforte and violin, written in a concertizing style approximating a concerto. Composed and dedicated to his friend R. Kreutzer, member of the Paris Conservatoire, concertmaster of the Academy of the Arts and of the Imperial Orchestra).

Bridgetower was the original dedicatee; Kreutzer had come to Vienna in 1798 in the entourage of the French ambassador, General Bernadotte. As an enthusiastic supporter of the French Revolution, Beethoven moved freely among those connected with the embassy and came to be on very friendly terms with the famous violinist. Strangely enough, Kreutzer never played the sonata in public. Later in the nineteenth century, the work acquired a somewhat dubious reputation because of Tolstoy's short story, but this did not directly involve Beethoven's music. The sonata makes great technical demands, beginning with the unaccompanied opening measures, difficult and exposed. In this sonata the violin is often the leader; in others, both instruments share more or less equally, except in some variation movements. The title "Spring" for the Sonata in F major no. 5, op. 24, is not Beethoven's but was coined by amateurs who liked the light and gentle quality of its themes. Some of the sonata's popularity is due to the title; it may be Beethoven's most often played violin composition.

Together with the great Fugue in B-flat major, the sixteen string quartets constitute a musical universe of their own. The first six, op. 18, might be seen as important steps on the road to the First Symphony, op. 21. The next group consists of the three op. 59 quartets and the following two, op. 74 and op. 95. Ambitious foursomes of amateur players have tackled them all, aware of the considerable technical challenges. Of the last group of quartets, beginning with op. 127, three were commissioned by the Russian Prince Galitzin, the enthusiastic cellist and chamber music player who organized the first performance of the Ninth Symphony in St. Petersburg. During his last years, Beethoven's search for ever greater expressive intensity gave rise to large and complex formal structures, straining the possibilities of the quartet medium. The last quartets demand from players not only sovereign command of their instruments but also the subordination of individual virtuosity in service to the work as a whole.

There are parallels in the development of Beethoven's symphonic writing. Beginning with the "Eroica" (op. 55), a work of unheard-of length at the time, the symphonies received mixed receptions, in part because orchestra players had not faced such challenges before. Nor did customs of the time allow for sufficient rehearsal time. To perform his symphonies well requires a highly disciplined orchestra made up of capable players, conditions that only gradually came to exist in the nineteenth century, and only in cities with a strong musical heritage.

In a discussion of Beethoven as a composer for violin, mention should be made of the great violin solo in his *Missa solemnis*. In high masses with orchestra accompaniment it was traditional to feature solo instruments to interpret certain text passages. Violin solos occur in many masses, from the Salzburg Festival Mass (1682), formerly attributed to Orazio Benevoli, to Bach's Mass in B minor and to many "solemn" or "long" masses of the eighteenth and nineteenth centuries. In the *Missa solemnis* the violin solo occurs in the Benedictus. It is connected to the preceding Sanctus by a thirty-two measure introduction, played by divided violas and cellos, and low-register winds. Over this velvety soft background, the solo violin enters on a high G; the gradual descent to the G string symbolizes the Son of God coming down to mankind. A broadly conceived section of 124 measures follows (12/8 time, Andante molto cantabile e non troppo mosso) during which the solo violin floats above the vocal solo quartet, at times rising to the fourth octave above middle C. Beethoven's expressive writing has inspired similar dispositions of timbres in later symphonic writing, in oratorios, cantatas, and other sacred music.

TRAVELING VIRTUOSOS

Musical migratory birds, that is, vagrant fiddlers and pipers, these days can be heard everywhere in our Holy Roman Empire. It seems as though charlatans from the north and south had agreed to draw the money out of the pockets of our honest German citizens, in return for foisting on them the foolish tricks that they claim to be incredible artistry. A true artist rarely is found among them.

BERLINER MUSICALISCHE ZEITUNG, 30 NOVEMBER 1793

As we read the biographies of great musicians of the seventeenth and eighteenth centuries, we note that traveling assumed an increasingly important role in their careers. It is true that in earlier times musicians from the Netherlands could be found throughout Europe, but these were not touring performers. Rather, they sought and held on to employment, chiefly at court. This applies even to Veracini's extended travels, always punctuated by long stays in one location, but the tours Leopold Mozart undertook with his son already served different purposes. They were in the first place educational, intended to lead the young genius out of the confining Salzburg environment and to introduce him to new developments in the major European music centers. In addition concerts, it was hoped, would produce income, sufficient at least to cover the substantial travel expenses. If they also brought honor and fame, all the better. Leopold hoped that in time they would help Wolfgang obtain a well-salaried court position.

In the decades following Mozart's astounding appearances as a child prodigy, hundreds of parents subjected their specially talented children to ruthless regimes of practicing, hoping to turn them into similar little wonders and to exploit them financially. A critic of the time wrote that ca. 1790 more than half of all soloists appearing in Vienna were less than fourteen years old. In order to succeed as a performer, he continued, one had to be "blind, good looking, or six to eight years old."

Leopold and Wolfgang's letters provide lively pictures of this aspect of an artist's life; in those days travel was far from pleasant. It took Wolfgang seven days to go from Mannheim to Paris. In frigid winter weather a fur-lined sack was the only way to protect one's feet from freezing. Roads were often terrible; wheels broke, and the coach might get mired in the mud, making it necessary to find a peasant whose help cost good money. Good horses to replace those with which one had started out were hard to find en route. Highway robbers were a constant threat, especially in southern Italy, but Germany was not safe either. In 1803, upon his arrival in Göttingen, Spohr noted that his Guarneri violin, which had been secured to the back of his coach, had disappeared. Customs officials, far more numerous then than now, always gave musicians a hard time. An exception was made at one of Vienna's gates, when the six-year-old Mozart charmed an inspector by playing a minuet for him, causing him to forgo a luggage search. Endless red tape at the border has been known to cause misery in our time as well. In 1949, when an instrumental ensemble traveled from Innsbruck to Zurich, officials insisted that all instruments, with their cases, be weighed. The list included violins (19 kg), violas (8 kg), cellos (11 kg), and a double bass (15 kg). By the time it had been compiled, the train had left. In 1969 the Bulgarian State Orchestra was delayed for seven hours at the Bavarian frontier because "importing" an entire symphony orchestra was *verboten*. Even in the early nineteenth century local governments were quick to realize that money could be made by taxing the receipts of traveling musicians.

When Mozart was young, concert organizations and managers were just beginning to appear on the scene, so that arranging public appearances was left to an artist's personal initiative. When the Mozarts arrived in a town, Leopold would first deliver as many letters of recommendation as he had been able to take along. Following this, it was important to obtain invitations to influential families, hoping that his son would become the talk of society. A concert at court, of course, was most desirable, but often there were obstacles: a period of official mourning, diplomatic complications, the ruler's absence, or other major entertainments, such as hunting parties. Arranging a public concert entailed risk, for expenses often exceeded what was taken in at the box office, even with good attendance, and it was easy to cheat a visiting artist, who usually departed the next day. A concert reviewer in 1803 complained, "Only one-third of the audience paid for their tickets; the rest managed to get in through a back door." Paganini had learned this the hard way. As a result he manned the box office himself and would lock all doors before going onstage. At times several virtuosos playing the same instrument would arrive in a town in close succession, meaning that one of them would have to wait, sometimes several weeks. All this cost time and money, and some performers were forced to explore other sources of income. They might sell instruments and strings, market their own compositions, or solicit subscriptions for their forthcoming publications.

Even in the nineteenth century, well-known artists were approached about endorsing commercial products. Joachim received a letter from a wine merchant suggesting that (since Joachim moved among persons of rank and wealth) he might recommend the firm's red wines, and offering him a 25 percent commission on each sale. On a less mundane level, amateur players often took advantage of an artist's presence in town by taking lessons. Spohr (1865) experienced this in London:

> I was running or driving about all day in huge London, and frequently right weary of it; for the greater part of my pupils had neither talent nor application, and took lessons of me merely to be enabled to say that they were pupils of *Spohr*.

In all, the life of a concert artist well into the nineteenth century was difficult and hazardous. Few were able to save much for their old age by touring. The chief incentive was that it helped an artist become known, thereby making a well-paid court appointment more likely.

Things improved somewhat in the larger cities with the establishment of concert societies, supported by the educated middle class. Such groups (philharmonic societies, music clubs, and the like) organized concerts on a regular basis, thus relieving the virtuoso of that chore. Often they could assure the performer of an audience as well. An article in the *Berliner Musicalische Zeitung* of 4 January 1794 gives interesting details on how an organization of amateurs in Stettin arranged concerts and how they tried to protect the public from charlatans.

> The traveling virtuoso is offered a guaranteed fee of 32 to 34 Rhtl. which, in special cases, may be augmented by the association. This is not a fortune, but at least an assured fee. Moreover, he incurs no expenses, has no legwork to do except to contact music director Haak, and is assured of the best obtainable accompaniment. . . . If the visiting virtuoso's excellence is not known, he must first audition for the music club, either in a private recital or, if time does not permit, at a specially arranged meeting. The club members then vote; a two-thirds majority is required for sponsoring him.

In 1804 a music society in Frankfurt also established a fund for hiring traveling artists.

The great socio-economic changes that resulted from the French Revolution and the Napoleonic wars profoundly affected musical taste. The Viennese nobility, Beethoven's patrons, friends, and students for the most part, were highly educated music lovers and occasionally capable instrumentalists. Eager to become acquainted with the newest compositions, they were ready to pay for them and wanted to understand them. But those who now flocked to public concerts, as a rule, lacked the general and musical education of those in the salons of the aristocracy. Resident music leaders tried to raise the general level by teaching and by conducting choruses and orchestras, but the traveling virtuoso was eager to appeal to the less developed knowledge and taste of the largest possible audience. This gave rise to a repertory that required little effort on the listener's part; rather, attention was focused on the player's dazzling technique. Certain terms began to appear on programs and in publishers' catalogues, such as "rondo brillant," "grande polonaise brillante," and "grande exercise di bravura en forme de rondeau brillant." Sets of variations were especially in vogue; each successive variation might display increasingly brilliant fireworks. The variation form, of course, was not new, but it flourished under the conditions of early public concerts. Variations on themes from current operas were especially popular, as were (to please audiences in a particular country) variations on national anthems or on well-known regional folk songs. Typical is a work entitled *Introduction, Variations, and Rondo on Two Favorite Styrian Alpine Airs*. Aside from variations, works with a graphic program were likely to appeal to less discriminating audiences. About a concert by the violinist Scheller in Schwerin, the critic of the *Allgemeine Musikalische Zeitung* (1800) reported, "The representation on the violin of the famous revolutionary march of the fishwives on Versailles greatly delighted the audience." Two years later the family Bohdanowicz appeared in Vienna, "performing a sonata, on one ordinary violin, but played by three persons with twelve fingers and three bows."

Local conditions influenced what kind of orchestral accompaniment awaited the virtuoso and his concerto. Normally he had to hire the orchestra out of his own pocket, an orchestra that in small towns was apt to be very weak. To cut down on expenses a small (early) classic orchestra was indicated. In Viotti's early concertos, for instance, the oboe and horn parts are optional. Soloists also considered it prudent to simplify orchestra parts, so that one quick rehearsal would suffice. For the solo portions the accompaniment was kept as simple as possible, so that the soloist would not have to deal with problems. It is quite instructive to examine the original orchestration for Paganini's violin concertos, for in modern recordings we hear greatly enlarged versions. On 4 March 1829 the great man performed in Berlin for an audience of nine hundred, accompanied by an orchestra of only twenty-five, a number he rarely exceeded. Before a rehearsal he handed out the parts personally and collected them again at the end, thus assuring that no unauthorized copies were made—again, a lesson he had learned the hard way.

Concert conditions gradually improved. With the help of local concert organizations it was possible to plan tours far ahead. Successful soloists employed a secretary who accompanied them on tour, sometimes acting as an advance detail. In time this kind of division of labor gave rise to the profession of concert agent, with all its advantages and disadvantages. Certain menial tasks might also be assigned to the accompanying pianist, who was required by some virtuosos to carry the performer's violin and sheet music.

With better education and much cultivation of music in the home, the general and musical taste level rose. In a letter to Mendelssohn (31 May 1839), Ferdinand David wrote from London:

> I was delighted to notice that harmonics and pizzicato no longer are fashionable here. Even the least perceptive listeners realize that they are mere charlatanry. Some performers, however, will have to do without their most effective tricks. It's strange that the Germans always are the last to catch on to such things.

Some great artists, such as Joachim and Hans von Bülow, made it their task to educate the public's taste by programming music of the highest quality. Nevertheless, a kind of standard format for violin recitals maintained itself well into our own time. One began with a Handel sonata, "to warm up," followed by something more "artistic" such as Beethoven's "Spring" Sonata; the program's first half concluded with something like Saint-Saëns's *Rondo capriccioso*. A similar piece opened the second half, followed by Sarasate's *Gypsy Airs* and a group of shorter "crowd pleasers," be they brilliant display pieces or sentimental schmaltz. Willy Burmester was a violinist–composer who specialized in this kind of repertory. In defense of our fathers and grandfathers, however, it must be said that such pieces often were "tossed off" with great élan, and that many great violinists of the early twentieth century, especially Fritz Kreisler, played these miniatures masterfully. Even Enrico Toselli's Serenade was impressive when played with the violinistic perfection of an artist such as Váša Příhoda.

Around the mid-nineteenth century, concertizing could still be quite casual. Dancla recalls an occasion in 1845 when he was scheduled to give a recital in Lyon. It so happened that at the last minute Liszt also arrived in town. Dancla immediately invited him to join him, and Liszt accepted. Without any rehearsal they played two movements of the "Kreutzer" Sonata, followed by the "Tell" Variations by Osborne-Bériot. In that piece Liszt, on the spur of the moment, added an improvised piano variation. The concert concluded with Liszt improvising on a theme handed to him from the audience.

NICOLÒ PAGANINI

When Paganini walked along the street, people eyed him closely, wondering whether they might detect his cloven foot—a mark of the devil. Once, shortly before he was to go onstage, he felt a nail in his shoe, which caused

Nicolò Paganini

him to limp slightly as he arrived on the podium. Some members of the audience looked at each other knowingly, for it was widely believed that there was something mysterious, supernatural about his playing. Even people who did not believe in the devil were convinced of it. Ever since they have tried to discover his secret. For almost a year, an Englishman followed him on his tours, taking an adjoining hotel room and listening constantly. While on the road, however, Paganini hardly ever practiced, and when he briefly warmed up before concerts, he used such a heavy mute that no one could hear him.

Countless books and pamphlets have been written about the secret of his practicing and about other, hitherto unknown, explanations of his virtuosity. Much has been brought to light that is interesting and informative, but no secrets have been revealed. Paganini's accomplishments must be attributed to a handful of quite understandable factors, as is true of above-average achievement in any field. In his case we are aware of great musicality; a distinct talent for the violin that included certain physiological characteristics; a strict practicing regime supervised by his father, who soon noted the unusual gift; and a highly developed desire to excel as an artist. All produced astonishing results.

Paganini was born in Genoa in 1782, the son of a dockworker whose hobbies included fortunetelling and playing the violin and mandolin. He taught Nicolò both instruments. "It would be hard to imagine a stricter father," the boy recalled. Further instruction by two orchestra violinists led to lessons by Giacomo Costa, music director at the cathedral, whose pupil soon performed solos there. This was a customary eighteenth-century venue, as it had been for Tartini, and such appearances in church were occasionally reviewed in the press. On 31 May 1794 a notice was printed in *Avvisi*, a Genoa newspaper: "[During high mass] Nicolò Paganini, a highly gifted eleven-year-old boy, performed a concerto, for which he was greatly admired."

Encouraged by such successes, the father entrusted the thirteen-year-old Nicolò to Alessandro Rolla, then teaching in Parma. Though Rolla declared that there was nothing he could teach him, he gave his young student a solid foundation in music theory and probably good advice as well. While in Parma, Nicolò also studied counterpoint with Ghiretti and Paër, for whom he wrote, among other exercises, twenty-four fugues in four parts. Years of intensive practice under the father's strict supervision followed his return home. During this period he acquired the phenomenal command of the violin that amazed musicians and music lovers everywhere.

Paganini stands at the threshold of a new era in violin playing. If later in life he referred to himself as self-taught, this does not imply a lack of gratitude to his teachers. He developed his very individual style of playing on his own, during his up to twelve hours of daily practice, as he recalled. In 1801 he freed himself of his father's relentless supervision by joining the orchestra in Lucca as a first violinist. Five years later he moved on to the court of Napoleon's sister Elisa Bacciocchi, then princess of Lucca. He remained there until 1809, active as a soloist, music director, orchestra member, and chamber music player. His career as a touring virtuoso did not begin until 1813 when, thirty-one years old, he reaped such spectacular successes in Milan that the world took notice.

Spohr met Paganini in Venice in 1816, an occasion he recorded in his diary on 17 October 1816 and in his autobiography (1865):

> He called on me this morning, and so I have at last made the personal acquaintance of this wonderful man, of whom since I have been in Italy I have heard some story or other every day. No instrumentalist ever charmed the Italians so much as he, and although they are not very fond of instrumental concerts, yet he gave more than a dozen concerts in Milan and five here. On making nearer enquiry as to how and with what means he actually fascinates his listeners, one hears from the nonmusical portion the most exaggerated encomiums—that he is a complete wizard, and brings tones from his violin which were never heard before from that instrument. Connoisseurs, on the other hand, say that it cannot be denied he certainly possesses a great dexterity with the left hand, in double-chords and in passages of every kind, but that the very thing by which he fascinates the crowd debases him to a mere charlatan, and does not compensate for what he is utterly lacking—a grand tone, a long bow-stroke, and a tasteful execution.

Paganini visited Spohr on 20 October to congratulate him on his first concert. Spohr urged Paganini to play for him, but Paganini made excuses, saying he had recently hurt his arm. He further explained that his manner of playing was calculated to appeal to a large audience and did not suit an intimate setting. This is a characteristic picture of Paganini, as seen through Spohr's eyes, who stood for a completely different concept of playing, a view shared by the public. Paganini's feats of technique amazed many Italian listeners—even as they realized that this was the end of the classical school of violin playing represented by Tartini, Nardini, and Pugnani.

Paganini's confidential remarks to Spohr about his playing show how candid he could be to one of his peers. He knew the secret of his own success, the limits of his playing, and what went over with the public. When his Paris performances of concertos by Kreutzer and Rode were only mildly successful he decided henceforth to play only his own compositions. He once said to Harrys, his manager, "I have my own method; my compositions are based on it. If I were to play music written by others, I would have to modify them first. Therefore I prefer writing my own pieces in which I am completely free to express my own feelings."

Paganini was a compulsive gambler who at times came close to being sent to debtor's prison, and who once had to use his violin to pay his debts. In this dilemma, someone presented him with a Guarneri violin so that he could play a concert that had already been scheduled.

The sensational aspects of Paganini's public appearances were heightened by a wealth of freely invented stories, such as the one about his prison sentence, for which there is absolutely no foundation. While he played the violin in prison, it is related, three strings broke, one after another, until only the G string remained, so that he was forced to develop his uncanny ability to play on one string alone. (The later "Moses" Fantasy is one of his compositions demonstrating this skill.) According to another wild story he strangled his wife (in fact, Paganini never married) and used her intestines as raw material for strings. Such stories may have been inspired by the virtuoso's fondness, reminiscent of Don Giovanni's, for the fair sex, which indeed accounted for many romantic adventures in his youth. Stories persisted, even late in his life, about wealthy countesses and others who offered him their money and their everything—stories that of course were good publicity. It is a fact that his profoundly melancholic appearance and his haggard, mephistophelian figure held a strong fascination for women, which he did not mind at all.

Behind the virtuoso facade he cultivated, there was another Paganini—the one who in private gatherings played Beethoven quartets well and with great enthusiasm, including the late quartets. When on tour, he missed no opportunity to hear *Fidelio* or *Don Giovanni*. He also was quite fond of older vocal music, especially Palestrina's.

Paganini's fame was restricted to Italy until 1828, when, at the age of forty-six, he traveled to Vienna for his first engagement abroad. The impression he made there defies imagination. The first recital took place on 29 March in the Redoutensaal, filled to capacity. All local violinists were there, along with Schubert, the poet Grillparzer, the Esterházy family, and everyone who was anyone in the arts and in society. Thirteen more concerts followed, all equally crowded. A veritable Paganini mania broke out. Strauss wrote a "Paganini Waltz," merchants offered Paganini schnitzel, cravats, and haircuts. When Paganini's good business sense led him to raise the price of admission to one gold florin, that coin became known as a "Paganinerl." There were poems of fulsome admiration, and the critics outdid each other writing hymns of praise. Rellstab later called the great man "the Chimborazo of violin playing," while Mayseder was quoted as saying, "We have never heard anything like it, and we never shall. Let us destroy all our violins."

Until 1831, Paganini chiefly concertized in Germany, residing in Frankfurt on the Main. Some during this period refused to be caught up in the delirious adulation and were all the more critical of the violinist and his mesmerized public. They expressed reservations about his rather small tone, and about his compositions, which bristled with technical difficulties. Above all they objected to his excessive use of glissando, which "threaten[ed] to transform a harmonious composition into the sound of wailing infants or meowing cats." Those adhering to traditional aesthetic norms considered glissando an abomination, so much so that in 1811 Salieri, head maestro of the Vienna court theaters, posted a notice forbidding its use, calling glissando "a declaration of love among cats."

Others were more insightful and understanding of the changing times. Following a concert in Stuttgart, the *Morgenblatt* of 12 December 1829 ran a short essay on the history of violin playing, leading up to this observation: "Now, with Paganini, a new epoch of the art of violin playing has dawned."

In 1831 the great virtuoso finally decided to go to Paris. By that time the years of newspaper reports, the first-person accounts by those who had heard him, and last but not least the many persistent rumors about his private life had aroused immense curiosity. Paganini cashed in on this; he waited two weeks and did not announce the concert (with the opera orchestra conducted by Habeneck) until the day before it took place. Nevertheless, all Paris was there, including Rossini, Delacroix, and George Sand. As in Vienna, the event was a tremendous success. "You cannot imagine what kind of a triumph it was," Paganini wrote to a friend. More concerts followed in quick succession. Programs were carefully planned, including the premiere of "La campanella," the *Variazioni sulla preghiera del Mosè* ("Moses" Fantasy on a theme by Rossini), and the Concerto no. 4 in D minor.

All kinds of writers turned to the subject of Paganini. One small volume has a characteristic title: *Nicolò Paganini, sa vie, sa personne, et quelques mots sur son secret* (his life, his personality, and a few remarks about his secret). Another was written by his manager Georg Harrys: *Paganini in seinem Reisewagen und Zimmer, in seinen redseligen Stunden, in gesellschaftlichen Zirkeln und seinen Concerten* (in his traveling coach and room, in a conversational mood, among society, and at his concerts). Paganini was even the subject of a play, given on 10 April 1831 at the Théâtre des Nouveautés: *Paganini en Allemagne, a-propos anecdotique en un acte* (a one-act play with couplets).

Among those who heard Paganini in Paris was the twenty-year-old Liszt, who had just undergone a severe psychological crisis. Impressed by Paganini's playing he embarked on a regime of practicing technical exercises for four to five hours daily, in addition to his repertory studies. He wrote to a friend, "Unless I go insane, I shall be an artist when we meet again." Liszt advanced to the highest level of his artistry, establishing modern standards of piano technique. These accomplishments were soon reflected in his *Six études d'exécution transcendante d'après Paganini*.

In 1834, after a journey to England, Paganini returned to Italy. He concertized little after this. His health, never good, deteriorated more and more. Death came in Nice on 27 May 1840. Intolerant clergymen cast a pall over his last weeks and refused him a Christian burial. Not until 1896 were his remains properly interred in Parma.

Serious scholars, eccentrics, journalists, and charlatans ever since have tried to discover the miracle of his playing and its effect on audiences. Some significant details were established, but anyone who tried to build an entire system on such discoveries, even a philosophy of violin playing, lost their credibility. They sought to give credence to all kinds of theories and fantasies of their own by somehow connecting them with Paganini. Jarosy even mentioned an essay by a Russian virtuoso and conservatory professor: *Paganini's Secret, Applicable to All String Instruments, Piano, and Small Drum*. Such writings gave a bad name to more serious attempts to analyze and explain Paganini's playing. As Flesch (*The Art of Violin Playing*, vol. 2) said, "A publication whose title uses the name Paganini as a sales placard impresses one at once as a mere advertising puff."

Without a doubt, Paganini's physique was extremely well suited to violin playing, yet his left hand was no larger than average. The Paris physician Dr. Bennatti confirmed this in an article submitted in 1831 to the French Academy of Sciences, entitled "Notice physiologique sur Nicolò Paganini." He noted the violinist's remarkable ability to stretch muscles and tendons in both shoulders, those connecting wrist and lower arm, and those within the hand. "Without changing hand position, Paganini can flex laterally the joints of left-hand fingers, those that touch the strings, at a right angle to the normal direction. He can do this with great ease, precision, and speed." Goethe, who was familiar with this article, opined to Zelter that both men and animals receive direction from their organs, but that man has the additional ability to train his organs. Also in 1831, Carl Guhr published *Über Paganinis Kunst die Violine zu spielen, ein Anhang zu jeder bis jetzt erschienenen Violinschule nebst einer Abhandlung über das Flageoletspiel in einfachen und Doppeltönen. Den Heroen der Violine Rode, Kreutzer, Baillot, Spohr zugeeignet von Carl Guhr, Director und Kapellmeister des Theaters zu Frankfurt a/M.* (Concerning Paganini's art of violin playing; an addendum to all previously published violin schools, along with a dissertation on playing single and double stop harmonics. Dedicated to the heroes of the violin . . . by Carl Guhr, director and kapellmeister of the Frankfurt on the Main theaters). Guhr had been on friendly terms with Paganini for several years. His remarks are professional and sound.

What Paganini accomplished required thin strings; they made possible the harmonics and left-hand pizzicato, and they facilitated the raising of a string's pitch as required in several of his compositions. The strings were positioned as low as possible, and the bridge was quite flat, to make playing three-part chords possible. Guhr also mentioned the remarkable left-hand stretches, which enabled Paganini to play the four-part chord of c (first finger), c′ (second), c″ (third), and c‴ (fourth). Guhr includes many music examples, one of them of special interest: Paganini's *Introduction et variations sur "Nel cor più non mi sento"* (Guhr, after repeated hearings, was able to write it down from memory). In closing he states, "Everything in Paganini's playing that is soulful, enthusiastic, and unique comes from his innermost being. The emotions he wants to kindle in the listener are his own."

Paganini's left-hand stretches go far beyond those required to play Vivaldi, Locatelli, Leclair, Gaviniès, and others; he spanned intervals and created effects unheard-of before. He was comfortable playing in several positions at the same time without moving his hand. This enabled him to play, effortlessly, the fingered octaves found everywhere in his works, combined with octave half-step trills, as in the Eighth Caprice. Sivori, one of Paganini's few pupils, claimed that fingered octaves were his real secret. A hand that had been trained to play fingered octaves, legato, could play virtually anything.

Paganini systematically explored artificial harmonics everywhere on the fingerboard, to the public's great admiration. He used them in his compositions, and he developed other aspects of technique to previously unknown heights: double stop playing, changing positions over great distances, staccato, and other feats of bowing. Listeners obtained an impression of perfection bordering on the miraculous, reinforced by a tone that was sweet though not large, and a performance manner that went beyond the written notes. His talent for improvisation was highly developed, coupled with ornamentation based on late baroque practice, a gift Liszt also possessed. This ability impressed those who heard Paganini play several times; to them his relatively limited repertory sounded different every time. When he played Beethoven quartets, he had to use great restraint not to add embellishments. Once he appeared in Milan together with the excellent violinist Charles Philippe Lafont; in the performance of a Kreutzer *symphonie concertante* Paganini played rings around his partner, improvising all conceivable left-hand and right-hand fireworks.

We tend to forget that in addition to being such a dazzling performer, Paganini was also a superb musician. His hearing was phenomenally keen, often astounding orchestra players at rehearsals. He was a fine sight reader, proving his mettle once in Naples, where a colleague had written a piece full of traps, especially planned to do him in. He was an outstanding guitar player, the instrument on which he did much of his composing and that accompanied him to the end of his days.

In 1832, Paganini, who had always been interested in the instrument, bought a viola made by Stradivari, and the next year he commissioned Berlioz to write a virtuoso piece for him, a kind of symphonic poem entitled *The Last Moments of Mary Stuart*, which was to include virtuoso variations for the solo viola. Instead, Berlioz wrote *Harold in Italy*, including a solo viola part, but it did not appeal to Paganini, who never played it. Unlike Spohr, Berlioz had a high opinion of Paganini the musician, formed in part during conversations that were "illuminated by the kind of radiance that emanates from certain select individuals. It seemed to surround Paganini with a kind of poetic aura."

Paganini's many compositions include six quartets for violin, viola, cello, and guitar, and nineteen pieces for solo guitar. His musical estate, which included numerous unpublished pieces, was kept intact until our own era; some years ago it was offered at auction.

Paganini published his twenty-four Caprices for solo violin in 1820 as his op. 1, dedicating them to "the artists," but they were by no means his first compositions. Rather, he followed the convention of counting only works that had been printed. Only four other sets of works were published, among them twelve sonatas for violin and guitar. Except for the variations written down by Guhr, and a few small pieces, nothing was published during his lifetime, even though the master (who had the reputation of being a tightwad) could have reaped handsome profits. Six violin concertos have been preserved (according to Schottky, Paganini wrote ten); of these only two were printed—in Paris, and not until 1851.

Paganini, of course, knew full well that he was most successful performing his own works. By holding on to them he did not have to worry about competition. For some pieces, such as the *Sonata amorosa e galante*, the orchestra parts have been preserved, but the solo part is missing. Quite likely Paganini never wrote it down, to avoid unauthorized copying.

Paganini's talent as a composer is perhaps best revealed in his Caprices op. 1, which represent a felicitous combination of technical and musical invention. At first people were dumbfounded by their previously unheard-of technical requirements. According to Fétis, violinists in Paris found them enigmatic, were even mystified, but word soon got around that there was a violinist in Italy for whom these pieces were child's play. In time they came to fascinate not only violinists but also other composers; aside from Liszt, Schumann (who had heard Paganini repeatedly and even had followed him on one of his journeys) was inspired by them. He had first heard Paganini in Frankfurt in 1830, an occasion that influenced him decisively to pursue a professional career in music. Schumann soon began a work for piano and orchestra, *Introduction and Variations on a Theme by Paganini*; unfortunately it was never finished. Two years later came *Etudes after Paganini*, op. 3. Brahms too was an admirer, using the twelve-bar theme of the Twenty-fourth Caprice for his op. 35, entitled *Studies for the Pianoforte: Variations on a Theme by Paganini*. (Paganini himself provided eleven variations on his theme.) Brahms practiced this set of variations whenever he prepared for one of his occasional appearances as a pianist. Alfredo Casella made use of less well-known Paganini themes when he was commissioned to write an orchestral work for the centennial of the Vienna Philharmonic in 1942. The title is *Paganiniana: Divertimento for Orchestra Based on Themes by Nicolò Paganini*.

Paganini did not relish teaching, in part, perhaps, because he did not want to share his accomplishments with others. Some claim that in his early days he coached a cellist from the Parma orchestra so well that he shortly was the solo cellist; others report that a string bass player benefited from Paganini's lessons. Karol Lipinsky, a Polish violinist and member of the Dresden court chapel, was twenty-seven and already an accomplished virtuoso when he visited Paganini in Italy; he established a cordial relationship with him and received many suggestions from the master. Paganini also gave lessons to Ernesto Sivori, a child prodigy. Fétis reported that Paganini had plans for establishing a conservatory in Italy after he concluded his extended tours. It might have provided fertile ground for the growing art of violin playing.

Paganini must be credited with inaugurating a new era, not only for violin playing but for instrumental accomplishment in general. The standards he set are still valid in our time. Liszt, a genius, was able by virtue of great effort and superhuman concentration, to adapt Paganini's technique to his own piano playing. It took violinists almost a century to accomplish this for their instrument and to develop pedagogical methods based on Paganini's achievements. Many authors have tried to explain his work, among them R. Sabatini (*L'arte di studiare i 24 caprici di Paganini*) and E. Kross, in a work the lengthy title of which can be translated thus: "How to study Paganini's twenty-four caprices, and how small hands can master them by using Paganini's hand and arm positions." There also continue to be those who have discovered Paganini's "secret," including *Le secret de Paganini: Méthode des méthodes de violon par R. Mantovani du Conservatoire de Parme* (Paris 1922); Joseph B. A. Klein, *Paganinis Übegeheimnis* (The secret of Paganini's practicing, Leipzig 1934); and J. Marcelli, *Petit traité de violon pour le développement rapide de la technique et de la sonorité par l'application du secret de Paganini et l'art de travailler* (Croix 1935).

NINETEENTH-CENTURY VIOLIN PLAYING

First, a caveat: it has become customary to speak of various nineteenth-century national schools (Franco-Belgian, Russian, Hungarian, and so on). Such groupings are sometimes based on national characteristics, at other times on aspects of playing such as bowing and vibrato, or on the strong personality of a teacher who had special influence in a given country. One is tempted to see decisive factors in a teacher's effect on his students, passing on to them distinctive features. Pedagogical family trees have been prepared that way, but the experience of the eighteenth century proves that such influences (as exerted by Tartini, Somis, and Nardini) seldom affect more than one generation, after which other factors enter the picture, having to do with period conventions and national styles. Among violinists, every strong personality gradually develops an individual style, thereby transforming what had been typical of a given school or tradition. Such a violinist will also be exposed to influences that may differ greatly, or indeed may contradict each other. Nor must we forget that most violinists are products of several teachers and have been exposed to various, often conflicting schools.

Violinistic and pedagogical family trees that go back more than one or two generations yield some strange results. In *Grosse Geiger unserer Zeit* (Great violinists of our age), Joachim Hartnack drew up four such genealogical tables, some going back three hundred years, in spite of reservations he expresses elsewhere in his book. He includes a "Toscana school" that includes Padua, its ancestor being Antonio Veracini; Schuppanzigh, Vieuxtemps, Sarasate, and Marteau, among others, belong to it. He speaks of a "Lombardy-Venetian school that includes elements of the Franco-Belgian, Hungarian, Russian, and Berlin schools." Its ancestor was Gian Battista Pagani [active in Cremona 1735–1747, according to Bachmann 1906. *Ed.*]; it extends by way of Corelli and Joachim to the present time and includes Heifetz, Huberman, Kulenkampff, Strub, Varga, Zimbalist, and many others. Ferras, Odnoposoff, Peinemann, Stern, and Szeryng are seen to go back to the "Mannheimers." This kind of forced pigeonholing makes one wonder about the supposed common ancestry of Corelli and Heifetz: are there really common characteristics to their playing except that they bow parallel to the bridge and treat E to F-sharp as a whole step? Nineteenth-century musical life and intellectual life in general was much affected by national traits, which suggests viewing the development of violin playing according to national groupings, and within these to concentrate on individuals.

FRANCE AND BELGIUM

During the early decades of the nineteenth century, violin playing in France and Belgium still felt the effect of earlier strong personalities, such as Gaviniès and Viotti. Kreutzer, Baillot, and Rode were their immediate pupils or were at least much influenced by their playing. Through the recently founded Conservatoire, these three teachers strongly affected the future direction of violin playing.

Rodolphe Kreutzer (1766–1831) was born in Versailles of German parents. His father was a band musician in Saxony before the French king authorized the Swiss guards in Versailles to form a band of sixteen musicians; he taught Rodolphe on the basis of Leopold Mozart's violin school. Later Rodolphe became a pupil of Anton Stamitz and then Viotti. He was thirteen years old when he successfully performed his own violin concerto at a Concert Spirituel; a year later he played a concerto by his teacher. In 1783 he became a member of the royal chapel, in 1790 he played first violin at the Paris Théâtre Italien, and in 1795 received a teaching appointment at the Conservatoire. In 1806, after tours abroad, Napoleon appointed him imperial chamber virtuoso. He became a conductor at the Opéra Comique in 1815 and eventually the music director of that house, a position that reflected his success as a composer of light operas. Neither these nor his chamber music (fifteen string quartets and fifteen string trios), however, stood the test of time. Only a few of his violin concertos, including the last one in D minor, are still used in teaching; they are hardly ever heard in public. His forty etudes have established and maintained his reputation to this day, at least among violinists. Among his students, Rovelli and Massart were outstanding.

At the age of eleven, François de Sales Baillot (1771–1842) became Viotti's pupil and also studied counterpoint and composition with Reicha and Cherubini. He too was called to the Conservatoire in 1795 and took his teaching duties very seriously, in spite of many concert tours of Russia, England, and Italy. As concertmaster of the royal chapel, conductor, and quartet player he was an important figure in the musical life of Paris. One observer decribed his bowing thus: "He played with a bow of cotton, guided by the arm of Hercules." No doubt he was one of the violinists who cultivated a large tone suitable for modern concert halls. In 1804 the Paris correspondent of the *Allgemeine Musikalische Zeitung* remarked that Baillot "was known for having developed a vigorous, aggressive manner of playing, introduced to Germany by Kreutzer and especially Rode. . . . His tone is large and borders on being rough." A tour of Germany in 1810 elicited similar comments. His nine violin concertos are forgotten, but his pedagogical works contain much that remains valuable. It was Baillot who, on 23 March 1828, gave the Paris premiere of Beethoven's Violin Concerto.

Pierre Rode (1774–1830), from Bordeaux, became Viotti's pupil at the age of thirteen. A few years later he premiered two of his master's violin concertos. He played in several Paris orchestras and toured extensively before being called to the Conservatoire in 1798; from 1804 to 1808 he was at the Czar's court in St. Petersburg. Napoleon installed him as concertmaster of his chapel, causing Rode to call himself "le premier violon du premier consul." In Vienna on 29 December 1812 he premiered Beethoven's Sonata op. 96 in G major, in the residence of Prince Lobkowitz, then played it in public a few days later. Some called Rode Europe's foremost violinist, in part because of his large tone. The reviewer of an 1803 concert in Leipzig noted that his tone was "vigorous, full, and well developed," that he "used his instrument to fullest advantage, especially the bow. . . . We should add that in the most fiery passages, and in the highest register . . . his tone at times is a little too incisive, no doubt because he is used to performing in the vast theaters found in Paris" (*Allgemeine Musikalische Zeitung*, 22 February 1803). Poor health greatly diminished his later playing career, but as a composer he was superior to Baillot. While his thirteen violin concertos (the first written in 1794) were esteemed and influential at the time, Rode is remembered chiefly for his caprices.

Well-developed bowing and a healthy, vigorous, noble tone character-ized the playing of Kreutzer, Baillot, and Rode. Their left-hand technique did not match Paganini's but included much playing of double stops, octaves, and trills. Apparently the aim was to have sure execution without incurring undue risk. All three violinists possessed fine musicality and refined taste, qualities that made them excel as chamber music players.

Like Kreutzer, François Antoine Habeneck (1781–1849) was the off-spring of a German military bandsman. He studied with Baillot, then played in various orchestras. In 1806, as an assistant to his teacher, he was entrusted with the Conservatoire's student orchestra, with which he performed Bee-thoven's "Eroica" in 1811. Later he divided his time between violin teach-ing at the Conservatoire and conducting. In 1828 he was instrumental in inaugurating the Société des Concerts du Conservatoire, whose orchestra was only loosely connected with the institution. In all, Habeneck gave 184 concerts with this ensemble. Beethoven occupied the central position in the repertory, including the first Paris performance of the Ninth, in 1831. Habe-neck's intensive rehearsal manner yielded a highly disciplined orchestra, unusual at the time, which caused a veritable Beethoven cult in France.

Ever since the Conservatoire's founding, French violin teaching aimed primarily at producing skillful orchestra musicians who could sight read well. As a boy, Dancla auditioned for Rode, who asked him to sight read manu-script music. Later, when playing for Cherubini and Baillot, he was given the tutti of a Viotti concerto to read. Good musicianship and quick comprehen-sion of written or printed music were of the utmost importance for violinists.

Famous teachers in Paris soon attracted students from Belgium, which neighboring country had achieved independence in 1830–1831. Liège had boasted a music school for some time; in 1831 it became the Conservatoire Royal de Musique, known for its thorough training of violinists. Among the first major Belgian violinists to arrive in Paris was Charles Auguste de Bériot (1802–1870), who by then was a mature musician. After a brief period of study with Baillot he toured the major European music centers, together with his later wife, the famous singer Maria Felicità Malibran. He succeeded Baillot at the Conservatoire, but in 1843 returned to Brussels to teach violin at that city's conservatory. An eye disease that eventually led to blindness forced him to resign his teaching position in 1852.

Most of Bériot's violin compositions, including ten concertos, were written for his own use. They reflect his style of playing: brilliant technique, tasteful execution of elaborately ornamented melodic lines, and a tone that was beautiful but not large, which qualities appealed to the public of this era. His special interest was writing teaching materials, an activity encouraged by his highly talented older son, who died at an early age. Bériot performed his Violin Concerto no. 2 in E-flat major on a violin that was tuned a half step up [i.e., playing in D major, a more resonant key on the violin. *Ed.*].

Belgian child prodigy François Prume (1816–1849), a student of Habeneck, performed Rode's Seventh Concerto in public at the age of seven and became a teacher at the Liège conservatory when he was seventeen.

Lambert-Joseph Massart (b. 1811 in Liège, d. 1892) was especially important to the French tradition of violin playing. A Kreutzer pupil, he soon succeeded as a performer, at times with Liszt. In 1843 he joined the Paris Conservatoire faculty. He was one of the first to play Beethoven string quartets in public, but his increasing inhibitions about solo performing eventually led him to devote all his time to teaching. Among his students were Wieniawski and Kreisler.

After studying in Liège, Hubert Léonard (1819–1890) went to Paris, where Habeneck became his teacher. He toured extensively and taught at conservatories in Brussels and Liège before returning to Paris, where he concentrated more and more on playing chamber music. Léonard's development and activities represent a change characteristic of the second half of the nineteenth century: pure virtuosity was of secondary importance; impeccable technique remained a must, but only in the service of interpreting music of the highest quality. A violinist must be a pioneer, championing the newest compositions for his instrument. Léonard premiered works by Fauré and introduced French audiences to the chamber music of Brahms. He was also an advocate of good but less-well-known works, as his editions of music by earlier composers such as Corelli, Bach, and Tartini show. In large part, Corelli's "La Folia" Variations owe their popularity to an arrangement by Léonard. Forgotten are his five violin concertos and (unjustly so) his pedagogical works; his fine cadenzas for Beethoven's Violin Concerto are still heard occasionally.

Henri Vieuxtemps (1820–1881) was the best-known virtuoso of the Belgian group. At the age of six he played Rode's Fifth Concerto in public. A year later he studied with Bériot; Paris first heard him in concert when he was eight. Beginning in 1831 he undertook many tours, three of which took him to America. It was his habit in every city he visited to establish contacts with violinists and composers: Spohr in Kassel, Molique in Stuttgart, Schumann in Leipzig, Paganini in London, and Reicha in Paris. He studied counterpoint with Sechter in Vienna. In 1846 he began a five-year position at the Czar's court and taught in St. Petersburg; in 1871 he joined the faculty of the Brussels conservatory, but a stroke ended this assignment after a few years.

In his day the composer Vieuxtemps was almost as highly regarded as the violinist. In fact, he was one of the best nineteenth-century violinist-composers, though his seven violin concertos and pieces such as *Ballade and Polonaise* are now chiefly used in teaching. His concert etudes are extremely difficult, which we can understand if we remember that Hubay and Ysaÿe were his students. He insisted that his pupils understood the music they studied. No composition was played until it had been thoroughly analyzed.

Jacques-Féréol Mazas (1782–1849), a student of Baillot, had a lasting effect on violin teaching through his pedagogical works. After a short tenure as a violinist at the Théâtre du Palais Royal, Mazas concertized throughout Europe; he later held positions in Orléans and Cambrai.

Delphin Alard (1815–1888), a pupil of Habeneck, was Bériot's successor at the Conservatoire. He also toured widely. Like Léonard he made it his task to prepare modern editions of neglected violin music of the past, especially of the eighteenth century. Since early music usually contained very few performance indications, Alard communicated his own intentions, as in his edition of a Nardini sonata "avec le style, le phrasé, l'expression, les doigts et les coups d'archet" (with information about style, phrasing, expression, fingering, and bowing). He too was devoted to quartet playing. One of his partners, with whom he performed much Beethoven after 1837, was Jean-Baptiste-Charles Dancla (1817–1907), a soloist and orchestra player who for more than thirty years was a highly regarded professor at the Conservatoire. The many works he wrote for teaching purposes made him one of the foremost pedagogues of his time and have kept his name alive to the present.

Martin-Pierre-Joseph Marsick (1848–1924) was another excellent soloist and quartet player, a pupil of Massart in Paris and Joachim in Berlin. His teaching career at the Conservatoire was brief but eminently successful: Flesch, Enesco, and Thibaud were members of his class.

Since Paris attracted many violin students, and since France and Belgium are neighbors, the term "Franco-Belgian school" may be justified, even though over time the differences were such that one can hardly speak of a uniform style. But it is curious that during the second half of the century many of the features usually associated with a Paris tradition were represented in the playing of Belgian violinists.

César Thomson (1857–1932) of Liège was considered by some to be one of the greatest virtuosos since Paganini. As a child prodigy he was a pupil of Léonard and Dupuis, then went on to concertmaster posts in Berlin and other cities and taught at the conservatories in Liège and Brussels. He possessed a splendid technique, playing fingered octaves as easily as his colleagues would play regular octaves, which made him a Paganini player par excellence. When audiences became accustomed to his feats of fingers and bow, he did what Burmester and Kubelik would do after him: he concentrated on teaching, finally in Italy and Switzerland.

Émile Sauret (1852–1920), by his life span and especially his manner of playing, represents the transition to the twentieth century. As a pupil of Bériot, Vieuxtemps, and Wieniawski he absorbed important traditions, but in his expressive, very intense style (including his distinctive vibrato) he anticipated many details of Kreisler's style and strongly influenced the coming generation through his activities in Berlin, London, Chicago, and Geneva.

VIENNA

Some readers may be surprised that a single city will be the subject of a separate discussion. But the name Austria then meant Austria–Hungary, an area that for our purposes is too vast, for in the nineteenth century, developments took place in Prague and Budapest must be examined separately. Moreover, Viennese violin playing followed a path of its own.

Around 1800, several orchestras in Vienna provided a living for violinists who were interested in solid orchestral and chamber music playing and less eager to follow a virtuoso career. Outstanding among them was Ignaz Schuppanzigh (1776–1830), who played first violin in several quartets. At the age of sixteen, he led Lichnowsky's boys' quartet; he spent twenty years in Prince Carl Lichnowsky's group, and then went to Prince Andreas Rasumowski's quartet. After concert tours that took him as far as Russia he gave quartet recitals in Vienna, directed an orchestra, and was a member of the imperial court chapel. He knew Haydn's and Mozart's chamber music intimately and premiered most chamber works by Beethoven and Schubert, at the same time inspiring those composers by his playing.

Schuppanzigh was the first representative of a certain type of Viennese violinist. In his youth he often played in local dance bands and at the "Heurigen" wine taverns, still known for the somewhat sweet and sentimental but charming music one can hear there. Under the supervision of capable teachers he acquired a well-grounded technique, broadening his interpretive skills by playing symphonic and chamber music. Violinists with this background would often join one of Vienna's larger orchestras eventually. The Viennese style was thus perpetuated (for the concertmasters of these orchestras also held the more important teaching posts), while Bohemian and Hungarian influences helped prevent violinistic inbreeding.

It is a characteristic of these Viennese players that they were not consumed with acquiring the kind of virtuosity that led to success on the international concert circuit. It has been claimed, somewhat maliciously, that this was due to a certain easygoing Viennese view of life, the same attitude that so annoyed Beethoven.

Viennese dance music of Beethoven's time is well represented by works by Michael Pamer, music leader at a local dance hall. He published a collection of "new, brilliant solo *Ländler* for violin, accompanied by a second violin and bass," pieces that contain characteristic passages for the solo violin.

Paganini may have heard and enjoyed such music when patronizing Viennese Heuriger establishments. (The fingerings, by the way, are original—they could be by Flesch!)

In 1813 Johann Felix Knaffl, a Styrian official, made some perceptive comments about typical folk dance melodies and the manner of playing them. To find the right national-regional flavor, a certain manner of bowing is called for, somewhat heavy and ponderous rather than elegant and dainty. To give appropriate weight and accent to a note, unusual position changes and phrasing may also be in order. "Nothing is more distasteful than to see and hear an *a la camera* virtuoso play dances from Upper Styria." Such popular violin playing gave rise to the art of the "standup" violinists of the Strauss family. It is worth noting that Johann Strauss, Sr., first earned a living by playing viola in Pamer's orchestra.

Franz Clement (Klement; 1780–1842) was an important representative of artistic violin playing in Vienna, known to posterity for having given the first performance of Beethoven's Violin Concerto. At the time, Vienna's concert life was flourishing, to judge by a review in the *Allgemeine Musikalische Zeitung* of 1806: "Clement gave two performances in one evening, in two different theaters, earning great applause for both."

Joseph Mayseder (1789–1863), a pupil of Wranitzky and Schuppanzigh, joined the latter's quartet at an early age as second violinist. Frequent musical contacts with Beethoven and Schubert strongly influenced young Mayseder's development. As a popular teacher he was able to pass on to the next generation the authentic interpretation of their music. Later, Mayseder became a member of the court chapel as the imperial-royal chamber virtuoso. He also wrote a number of compositions for violin in the Viennese idiom.

Among Hungarians who flocked to Vienna was Joseph Böhm (b. 1795 in Pest, d. 1876 in Vienna). He studied with Rode, probably while the latter was in Vienna in 1812. In 1819, after concertizing successfully in Vienna and Italy, he headed the newly established conservatory of the Gesellschaft der Musikfreunde. In that capacity he trained many outstanding violinists including such virtuosos as Dont, Ernst, Georg Hellmesberger, Joachim, and Reményi. Their personalities and their backgrounds were quite different: Dont and Hellmesberger were Viennese, Ernst came from Brno, Joachim from Kitsee near Bratislava, and Reményi from Miskolc in Hungary. Again we realize that just because a number of violinists studied with the same teacher in the same city does not justify our referring to them collectively as a "school." Böhm stopped appearing in public rather early, as he had problems with stage fright, and concentrated on teaching. He remained a distinguished player of chamber music in a domestic setting. Duet playing had an important place in his teaching.

When he was fourteen years old, Heinrich Wilhelm Ernst (1814–1865) was so impressed by Paganini's Vienna appearances that he continued to look for opportunities to hear him play, hoping to discover his secret. He must have had a fine reputation, for he was not afraid of performing publicly in Frankfurt at the same time Paganini was appearing there. Having often heard the piece, he memorized his hero's *Introduction et variations sur "Nel cor più non mi sento"* and performed it in Frankfurt, no doubt to the composer's irritation. Ernst's own compositions, such as his Violin Concerto in F-sharp minor, bristle with technical difficulties and for a long time were considered the ultimate tests of a virtuoso's capabilities.

Ede Reményi (1828–1898) is chiefly remembered for his association with Brahms, who for some years was his accompanist. The acquaintance inspired Brahms to write his *Hungarian Dances*. Having studied in Vienna, Reményi became concertmaster in London, but in 1848 he participated in the Hungarian Revolution. His later concert tours took him all the way to America. Playing in a gypsy style, even in classical compositions, seems to have ensured his public success. Gypsy airs as a genre flourished in nineteenth-century virtuoso salon music, largely because of Reményi.

Jacob Dont (1815–1888) was another fine violinist who never quite conquered his stage fright and renounced a solo career, finding satisfaction in teaching and chamber music playing. He was a member of the court chapel; late in life he held a professorship at the conservatory. Among his many teaching materials the op. 35 etudes are still considered basic.

Georg Hellmesberger the elder was the founding father of a dynasty of Viennese musicians that lasted into the twentieth century. Georg the elder, Schubert's fellow choirboy, played the violin for the emperor as a six-year-old prodigy. After years of study with Böhm he became his assistant; at the age of thirty-three he was promoted to professor, in charge of his own class. He was also a member of the opera orchestra; when it became the Philharmonic Orchestra in 1842, giving more concerts, Hellmesberger became its first director. As a teacher and admirable quartet player he had a strong impact

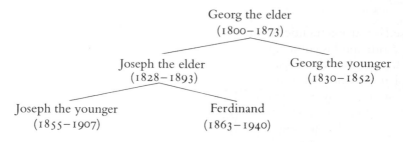

Georg the elder
(1800–1873)

Joseph the elder
(1828–1893)

Georg the younger
(1830–1852)

Joseph the younger
(1855–1907)

Ferdinand
(1863–1940)

Genealogy of the Hellmesberger Family of Luthiers

on Vienna's musical life. Georg the younger, highly gifted as a violinist and composer, became court kapellmeister in Hanover but died at the age of twenty-two.

Joseph the elder continued the traditions of his Viennese family. In 1848, aged twenty, he became the artistic director of the Gesellschaft der Musik-freunde and its conservatory. A fine, versatile artist, he put his stamp on Viennese music of his time. The quartet he founded in 1849, and in which his sons also were to play, championed the late Beethoven and Brahms and even the Quintet of the controversial Bruckner. For a few years Joseph the elder conducted the society's orchestra concerts; in 1860 he became concertmaster of the court opera orchestra. Countless capable orchestra musicians graduated from his class, but also major soloists such as Auer and Brodsky. We can tell something about the quality of orchestra training at the conservatory when we note that they performed Brahms symphonies under Hellmesberger's direction with his eleven-year-old pupil Georges Enesco in the concertmaster's chair! Given his many responsibilities it is amazing that Hellmesberger found time for ca. 250 compositions, including studies for the violin. He was famous for his aphorisms on many subjects including violin playing. He once said that octaves must be played "slightly out of tune, or the public won't realize that they are octaves."

Joseph the younger was as versatile as his father: professor at the conservatory, concertmaster of the court opera, successor to his father in the string quartet, court kapellmeister, and at times conductor of the philharmonic concerts. In spite of all this his true calling was composing. His stage works, mostly operettas, were very successful around the turn of the century. Ferdinand, the youngest Hellmesberger, was a cellist and conductor.

Leopold Jansa (1795–1875) of Bohemia also made important contributions to violin playing in Vienna. In 1834 he became director of music at the University of Vienna. He continued Schuppanzigh's tradition of giving public quartet recitals. While in London, Jansa participated in a benefit concert for Hungarian refugees, an incautious action that cost him his position and made it impossible for him to return to Vienna for twenty years. His compositions, mostly violin and chamber music, are forgotten, but his violin duos were used in teaching for a long time.

ITALY

Based on strong traditions, nineteenth-century violin playing as represented by Viotti and his contemporaries continued to flourish, reaching its apogee with Paganini. But Paganini did very little teaching, which may partially explain why no significant school of violin playing existed in Italy after him. It is strange, however, that he did not become a model. A combination of artistic, political, and economic factors may account for this situation. Ever since the mid-eighteenth century many important musical developments took place in countries to the north, and Italian musicians, eagerly imported in earlier times by many European countries, were less in demand. Politically Italy was fragmented into many small territories, which worked counter to the rise of major cultural centers. During the classic period Italy, except for Turin, boasted no court opera or other significant court-supported music activities that would compare with those in France, Austria, or some of the smaller German courts.

During the ascent of the middle class as a main supporter of cultural life, no Italian city had concert institutions such as then existed in Paris, Vienna, or Leipzig. Italy was the land of the great bel canto tradition; as such it showed no interest in the rise of classic-romantic instrumental music, an attitude that lasted into the late nineteenth century. In 1842, four original compositions for the violin and six arrangements were printed in Italy, as compared with sixty-five in Germany. Even a musician of Verdi's stature repeatedly stated that the cultivation of instrumental music was not an Italian task, though he was probably comparing voice-oriented Italian opera with Wagnerian symphonic opera. Until ca. 1870 symphony concerts and public performances of chamber music were relatively rare in Italy, so that the musical climate offered few incentives for nurturing superior violin playing.

In Paganini's day, only Rolla in Milan had established what might be called an Italian school of violin playing. Antonio Bazzini (1818–1897), who as a young man benefited from Paganini's advice, gave concerts throughout Europe, partly from a base in Paris. He then turned exclusively to composing and in 1873 began teaching composition at the Milan conservatory, later becoming its director. The few outstanding Italian violinists found ample room abroad for their activities, as they had in the eighteenth century.

Pietro Rovelli (1793–1838) studied with Kreutzer in Paris, concertized widely, and became concertmaster of the Munich court orchestra. He then returned home and accepted a minor post in Bergamo. His well-written caprices have kept his name alive. Rolla's pupil Luigi Arditi (1822–1903) had a career as concertmaster, conductor, and composer that took him to Havana, New York, Constantinople, and London. The sisters Teresa (d. 1904) and Maria Milanollo (d. 1848), acclaimed as sensational violinists, received their training in Paris and Brussels, showing how the focus of instruction had moved away from their homeland. Their playing exhibited different strengths, so much so that at times they were billed as "Mlle Adagio" and "Mlle Staccato."

Ernesto Camillo Sivori (1815–1894), who studied with Paganini's teacher Costa in Genoa, was the only violinist to have had any sustained contact with the great virtuoso. Allegedly born on 25 October in Genoa's Teatro S. Agostino, during one of Paganini's concerts, Sivori was nine years old when the master took an interest in him, composing music for violin and guitar to be played by both of them. At the age of twelve Sivori performed with success in Paris and London; he eventually became one of the greatest violinists in the period following Paganini, giving concerts in many countries. Inspired by his teacher he was always striving for perfection as a soloist and quartet player. He participated in the world premiere of Verdi's String Quartet with Marsick playing second violin. Sivori's instrument was the famous copy of Paganini's "Cannon," made by Vuillaume, which the maestro had left him in his will.

GERMANY

Germany had no cultural center comparable to Paris, with its opportunities for healthy competition and concertizing. At the beginning of the nineteenth century, although court chapels in Germany employed many capable orchestra violinists, few of them, if any, reached the level of French violin playing of that time. Most German violinists were influenced directly or indirectly by Benda in Berlin or by the Mannheim players who had moved on to Munich.

The musician who rose above the generally good level of German concertmasters was Ludwig (Louis) Spohr (1784–1859). We are well informed about his career through his detailed autobiography, which fascinating picture of cultural life is recommended reading for all violinists. Spohr was introduced to music by a French immigrant. He was only fifteen years old when he became a Braunschweig court musician, but soon his employer, an amateur violinist, provided funds for his further training while accompanying Franz Eck on a concert tour to Russia. Rode was Spohr's idol, however, and in his youth he referred to himself as Rode's "true copy." At the age of twenty he performed at the Leipzig Gewandhaus, about which event Friedrich Rochlitz wrote an enthusiastic review.

The following year Spohr became concertmaster in Gotha; from 1812 to 1815 he served as kapellmeister at the Theater an der Wien and made Beethoven's acquaintance. After employment in Frankfurt and Dresden he went to Kassel in 1822, as court kapellmeister. There he became an advocate of Wagner's early works. Conducting assignments loomed large in his career, ever since he directed the first German music festival in Frankenhausen (Thuringia) in 1810. One of the most successful composers of the time, he wrote operas, oratorios, and symphonies. Fifteen violin concertos (including three concertinos) are of interest to violinists, as are his fine duets. The concertos (including the excellent Seventh, in E minor) are now rarely performed.

Spohr's violin playing was distinguished by a large, warm tone; by a completely reliable left-hand technique, including double stop playing; and by his

Ludwig (Louis) Spohr, self-portrait in pastels, ca. 1807
(Braunschweig, Landesmuseum)

brilliant staccato, which he often put to good use in his own compositions. A decided talent for teaching showed itself early in his career, and students flocked to him even during his years in Gotha. Spohr's observations about his students make interesting reading. After the master's death, Alexander Malibran compiled a list of no fewer than 187 Spohr students. Of these, 150 were German, indicating how strong his impact on German violin playing must have been. Admittedly the list includes few above-average violinists; Saint-Lubin and Ferdinand David were the only ones to achieve international standing. Spohr's objectives in teaching were probably to produce good orchestra and chamber music players, for during the first half of the nineteenth century, Paris and Brussels appealed more to prospective virtuosos.

We gain insight into Spohr's aesthetic beliefs through a quotation from his *Violin School* (1833):

> The abovementioned harmonics, as not materially differing in sound from the natural notes, have at all times been used, in conjunction with the natural notes, by all good Violinists. All others, however, and particularly the so-called artificial harmonics, must be rejected as useless; because they so totally differ from the natural notes of the instrument. It is, indeed, a degradation to this noble instrument, to play whole melodies in such childish, heterogenial sounds. A great sensation has been created by the celebrated Paganini in recent times, by the revival of the ancient and wholly forgotten harmonic playing and by his eminent perfection therein; however alluring such an example may be, I must nevertheless seriously advise all young Violinists not to lose their time in such a pursuit, to the neglect of that which is more important. In support of this view of the matter I may quote the greatest performers of every age, as Pugnani, Tartini, Corelli, Viotti, Eck, Rode, Kreutzer, Baillot, Lafont et cetera: not one of whom has played in harmonics after the manner of Paganini. Indeed, if harmonic playing were even found to be of benefit to the art and an improvement in Violin playing, such as good taste might justify, it would, in sacrificing a full, round tone, be nevertheless purchased at too high a rate; for with this it is incompatible, as the artificial harmonics only come out on very thin strings, from which it is impossible to draw a full tone.

Bernhard Molique (b. 1802 in Nuremberg, d. 1869) was a pupil of Rovelli in Munich and for a brief period also studied with Spohr. For twenty-three years he served as royal music director and concertmaster in Stuttgart. After many successful appearances abroad he turned entirely to composing, a subject he eventually taught at the Royal Academy of Music in London. His six violin concertos, very popular at the time, are now forgotten.

The career of Ferdinand David (1810–1873), one of Spohr's pupils in Kassel, was important for the development of violin playing in Leipzig. At the age of twenty-six he became concertmaster of the Gewandhaus Orchestra, the same ensemble that had accompanied him when, at fifteen years of age, he performed Spohr's Concerto no. 8 ("in modo d'una scena cantante"). A "model concertmaster" according to Schumann, David rounded out that side of his talent in his six years as first violinist in a private string quartet. When, at Mendelssohn's instigation, the Leipzig conservatory was founded in 1843, David and Spohr both taught there.

David's interest in violin music of the past followed a trend of the time. Many professional and amateur violinists had their introduction to this music through David's collection, *Hohe Schule des Violinspiels*, which contains works by Biber, Geminiani, Veracini, Vitali, and others. Ten groups of preliminary studies, intended to serve as preparation to the *Hohe Schule*, are based mostly on Corelli and Leclair. David's editions do not measure up to our concepts of authenticity as represented by *Urtext* editions, but they served an important purpose in their day. His violin tutor and his five violin concertos are now forgotten.

Léon de Saint-Lubin (1805–1850), though born in Turin of French parents, belongs here because of his training and career. He grew up in Hamburg, was taught by Spohr in Kassel, played in the Josefstadt Theater in Vienna while still a pupil of Böhm, and for twenty years served as concertmaster in Berlin. That he was also talented as a composer is demonstrated in his *Six grands caprices* op. 42.

We noted before that it is problematic to group outstanding violinists in "schools," and that during the nineteenth century one encounters not only significant national tendencies but also supranational ones. A case in point is Joseph Joachim (1831–1907), who was born near Bratislava yet became a major representative of German violin playing. His first teacher was Stanislaus Servaczynski, concertmaster of the Budapest opera. Later in Vienna Joachim studied with Georg Hellmesberger the elder and with Böhm. When he was twelve years old he graduated from the Vienna conservatory by performing Vieuxtemps's E major Concerto. Joachim then wanted to enter the new conservatory in Leipzig, but Mendelssohn announced that the boy needed no more formal training as a violinist. Mendelssohn, however, did take a personal interest in young Joachim's musical growth. On 27 May 1844, with Mendelssohn conducting, Joachim for the first time performed Beethoven's Violin Concerto; a year later in Dresden, under Schumann's direction, he was the soloist in Mendelssohn's Violin Concerto. At age sixteen, he was associate concertmaster of the Gewandhaus Orchestra and taught at the conservatory, where he was younger than any of his pupils.

Concertmaster appointments followed in Weimar (where he was in contact with Liszt) and Hanover. During this period a close friendship developed between Joachim and Brahms, expressed in much music making and in reviewing each other's counterpoint studies. Somewhat later, Joachim gave Brahms valuable advice while the composer worked on his Violin Concerto, and before Brahms sent one of his string sextets to the publisher, Joachim provided fingerings and bowings.

In 1869 Joachim received a call to Berlin to head the new music academy—an important milestone in Joachim's career and in Berlin's rise as a major music center. The year also marks the founding of Joachim's string quartet. Though the membership of that group changed, its interpretations, especially of Beethoven and Brahms, were considered exemplary. As a soloist, Joachim's reputation was similar, for the clean technique and great spiritual depth of his interpretations of the Beethoven Concerto and works by Bach were for a long time considered definitive. Many accomplished players emerged from his class, and under his direction the conservatory orchestra soon provided impressive performances. In 1899 Joachim celebrated the sixtieth anniversary of his first appearance as a concert soloist, an event that had taken place in Budapest when he was eight years old. A gigantic orchestra was assembled for the celebration; every one of its forty-four violinists and thirty-two violists had been his student.

In his teaching, like Spohr, he put less emphasis on developing virtuosity than on purely musical matters. As a result, though the general level of accomplishment of his students was very high, few truly outstanding virtuosos emerged from his class. Auer, who was seventeen when he began studying with Joachim, recalled that his teacher showed little interest in a student's technique; it was up to the pupil to acquire it. Joachim always taught with violin in hand and played everything for his students, without explanation. "This is the way you should do it" was his constant remark. Depending on the student, such teaching may have been effective, but often it was not. In 1905 Szigeti, a highly trained child prodigy, played for Joachim in Berlin. By that time, Joachim's pedagogical approach had changed greatly, as Szigeti (1947) recalled:

> At Joachim's invitation I attended one of his lessons at the Hochschule, saw the master seated alone on a little platform in the middle of the room, no violin in his hands, listening, criticizing—but not demonstrating. This lack of interplay, this lack of kindling the pupil's enthusiasm through actual example, made for a certain remoteness in their relationship, or so I thought. It was as if the little platform symbolized the absence of flow between the two.

Szigeti did not become Joachim's pupil. Joachim might have made the Berlin academy an important center of violin teaching had he appointed some first-rate faculty members, but this did not happen, as Flesch (1957) noted with regret:

> As the head of an institution he seems to have been too easily swayed by the advice of others. There can be no other explanation for the circumstance that around 1900 such teachers as Hess, Petri, Eldering, and Wendling were all employed in smaller institutes somewhere in Germany, while the education of the young generation in Berlin was entrusted to Wirth, Moser, Markees, and Exner. As a result, in the last seventy years the Franco-Belgian and the Russian schools have achieved an indubitable superiority over the German in world opinion.

Joachim also composed, which side of his talent impressed Brahms greatly, but probably because of his responsibilities in Berlin he gradually gave up writing music. Flesch considered his *Concerto in the Hungarian Manner* one of the best works "ever written by a violinist for his own instrument." In 1854, Joachim admitted in a letter to Liszt that he continued to have fond feelings for Hungary and its music:

> How beautiful is the Danube as it flows past Pest! And the gypsies continue to play with abandon, from the heart to the heart, as you know. There is more rhythm and sentiment in their bowing than in that of all North German orchestra players, including those in Hanover.

Joachim's cadenzas for some of the major violin concertos are especially inspired, among the best of their kind. In editions of the Bach unaccompanied sonatas and of Beethoven's violin sonatas, Joachim committed to paper his ideas on interpretation, and his experiences as a teacher led him to write a violin method.

Critics were concerned when Joachim's violin playing began to decline, but everyone, friend or foe, agreed that he was a master of planning programs. Working in the environment of Mendelssohn, Schumann, and Brahms he consistently championed the best repertory, both as soloist and quartet player, and in so doing he helped form the public's taste. In 1863 he reached an understanding with his colleagues in Hanover not to appear on any program "unless every part of it was entirely dignified." He even spoke of forming a "league against musical trash." In time he succeeded in establishing his standards of what constituted good music, so that those who stooped to a lower level were seen as belonging to a different class of violinists.

A significant amount of music was inspired by Joachim. Moser (1901) drew up a list of some thirty works dedicated to Joachim, including concertos by Brahms, Bruch, and Dvořák. Joachim also conducted the premiere of Brahms's Piano Concerto no. 1, with the composer as soloist.

Compared with Joachim's mature musicianship, August Wilhelmj (1845–1908) is a lesser figure. After successes as a child prodigy he studied for three years with David in Leipzig, toured extensively, and participated as concertmaster in the first Bayreuth festival in 1876. Later he had only limited success as the founder of a private academy of violin playing. He died in London, where he had taught at the Guildhall Music School. Quite a few arrangements (some rather arbitrary) were published by him, including one of Paganini's D major Concerto. His "Wagner Paraphrases" were often performed in his day, with the master's complete approval. Similar Wagner arrangements by Seybold maintained their popularity into the twentieth century.

BOHEMIA

In Prague's inns and taverns one often hears fiddlers who are decent
enough to find employment in good orchestras.

ALLGEMEINE MUSIKALISCHE ZEITUNG, VOL. 2, 1800

Bohemia, a small crown land in the Hapsburg empire, had an important
place in eighteenth- and nineteenth-century violin playing. One key factor
was Bohemia's generally gifted populace, from which came the Stamitz and
Benda families, and many others who moved to Vienna. The importance of
music teaching in the schools has already been noted, as has the 1811 foundation of the Prague conservatory, modeled on the Paris Conservatoire curriculum. Friedrich Wilhelm Pixis of Mannheim directed the first class of
advanced violin students, helping to establish Prague as a major training center. Johann Wenzel Kalliwoda (1801–1866), Pixis's pupil, became court
kapellmeister in Donaueschingen; his violin duets maintained their popularity for a long time. Pixis's successor at the conservatory was Moritz Mild-

ner (1812–1865). Many outstanding concertmasters were products of his teaching, as was Ferdinand Laub (1832–1875), a virtuoso who taught in Moscow, having previously held positions in Weimar and Berlin.

Mildner's student and successor was Anton Bennewitz (1833–1926), an outstanding teacher who directed the Prague conservatory for almost twenty years. Otakar Ševčík (1852–1934) was his most famous pupil. Franz Ondricek (1857–1922) studied with Bennewitz and then with Massart in Paris. Though one of the best violinists of the time, he turned to teaching early in his career and published several works based on his teaching experiences in Vienna.

Wilma Neruda (1839–1911), a Jansa pupil, belongs among the leading Bohemian violinists. She married the Swedish conductor Norman and taught in Stockholm. Her second marriage was to Charles Hallé, which led to her continued activities in London.

HUNGARY

In his 1859 book *Des Bohémiens et de leur musique en Hongrie* (About the gypsies and their music in Hungary), Liszt described the playing of major gypsy violinists, basing his account on what he had learned from others but also on playing he had heard firsthand. The gypsy János Bihari (1764–1827) particularly impressed the young Liszt. Only later did the researches of Kodály and Bartók clarify the differences between gypsy music and true Hungarian folk music. Nevertheless, close ties existed between Hungarian popular music and gypsy music, ties that contributed materially to the development of violin playing in Hungary. Liszt also mentions two Hungarian violinists, Ľavatta and Csermák, who had adopted the gypsy style. Acquiring the appropriate technique and style was sometimes a problem for Hungarian violinists who wanted to pursue a career playing classic-romantic repertory. Reményi never quite succeeded in this. "Tonight I'll give them the Kreutzer Sonata," he said in his heavy Hungarian accent. "Just watch their eyes pop out!"

At the time, Pest was far from being a center of violin study. Talented violinists from the Hungarian realm (which then included Bratislava) preferred going to Vienna, among them Miska Hauser (1822–1887), who studied with Mayseder and Böhm before he becoming Kreutzer's pupil. Joachim, Auer, and Flesch also began their studies in Vienna. The real founder of a Hungarian school of violin playing was Eugen Huber (1858–1937), who later assumed the name Jenö Hubay.

POLAND

For several hundred years popular Polish dance music favored the violin, which was played in a characteristic manner that included stopping the strings with the fingernails, perhaps in playing harmonics. In his autobiography Telemann recalls hearing such groups in Upper Silesia and in Cracow. Their playing had a "barbaric beauty" of its own, on violins tuned a third higher than normal. These fiddlers could "outplay half a dozen others" and improvised skillfully together with bagpipes. "An attentive listener might gather enough ideas for a lifetime [of improvisation]."

Political alliances brought periods of close contact between Polish musicians and those at the Dresden court, then under strong Italian influence. As a result, Polish string players found employment in the royal chapel, and Polish folk features soon turned up in art music. Adam Jarzeleski (b. ca. 1590, d. ca. 1649) was the first Polish violinist known in western Europe. He belonged to the orchestra of Elector Johann Siegmund von Brandenburg. After a journey to Italy he went to Warsaw, where he occupied a leading place in the court chapel. Other Polish violinists of note include Johann Hübner (b. 1696 in Warsaw), who trained in Vienna and was later active in Russia, and Felix Janiewicz (1762–1848), who on several occasions appeared as soloist at the Concert Spirituel in Paris. Like Chopin, Auguste-Frédéric Duranowski (ca. 1774–1834) was of partly French extraction. Prince Oginski arranged for him to study with Viotti in Paris, where he developed into a remarkable virtuoso. While in Italy he is said to have influenced even Paganini. His life was restless and varied, including years as an army officer. Eventually he joined a theater orchestra in Strasbourg.

Karol Josef Lipinski (1790–1862) was among the outstanding virtuosos of the time. He was self-taught. After serving as concertmaster, then conductor at the theater in Lemberg, he went to Italy, always anxious to improve himself, and studied there for several years, perhaps attracted by Paganini's fame. Lipinski became acquainted with his idol and received valuable advice from him for further intensive study. That he accomplished much is suggested by his joint appearances with Paganini, performing double concertos. The Polish violinist took his Italian studies quite seriously and eagerly explored the Tartini tradition that then was on the wane. Wasielewski (1869), whose information came firsthand from Lipinski, tells of the latter's meeting an old gentleman in Trieste who had been a Tartini student.

> When Lipinski asked how Tartini had played some of his own compositions, the Italian gentleman handed him a poem, asked him to read it, and then to play an adagio by Tartini. This was by way of explaining how the master had prepared himself for performing it. He further recalled that Tartini had had the habit of copying poems by his favorite writers on the bottom of a violin part, so that the poem was his guide to its proper interpretation.

According to Moser, Lipinski was admired for his performing Bach's music. After successful concert tours of Russia and England he concluded his career as concertmaster of the court orchestra in Dresden.

Around the mid-nineteenth century, Polish violinists usually went to Paris for their training. Among them, Henri Wieniawski (1835–1880) was outstanding. Massart taught the child prodigy at the Conservatoire; the boy was only eleven years old when he won a premier prix. He then toured, with Anton Rubinstein as his partner, and at the age of twelve became chamber virtuoso at the imperial court in St. Petersburg. He taught off and on at the Brussels conservatory. With Paganini he not only shared exceptional talent but also an addiction to gambling, causing him serious financial problems during the years preceding his fatal heart disease. In spite of his illness he was forced to give concerts until the end. At a concert in Berlin he attempted Bach's Chaconne but had to stop after a few measures. Joachim, who was in the audience, rushed to the podium and completed the piece on Wieniawski's violin.

In his prime, Wieniawski's left-hand technique was effortless. He was also known as someone who could play trite melodies (which occur in his own works) in an inimitable and convincing manner. Andreas Moser had heard him perform several times. About Wieniawski's playing of his own *Légende*, Moser (1967, vol. 2) said, "The piece is of little musical significance, but when he performed it, even some blasé members of the audience would soon have tears in their eyes."

RUSSIA

A Russian national school of violin playing was late in developing, for foreigners, mostly Italians, had held the principal musical posts since the eighteenth century. Ivan Khandoshkin (1747–1804) was the first Russian to make a name for himself, as a violinist and composer. He studied with Tito Porta, the Italian concertmaster in St. Petersburg. The first to find international recognition was Adolf Brodsky (1851–1929), a pupil of J. Hellmesberger the elder in Vienna. He also played in his quartet. Later Brodsky taught at the Moscow and Leipzig conservatories. After a stay in New York he became director of the Manchester College of Music.

While we do speak of a Russian school of violin playing and of a characteristic Russian style, Russians actually had little to do with it. Nor is it true, as some have claimed, that such a school came about by sheer accident. It was no accident that Auer was appointed to teach at the St. Petersburg conservatory; rather, it does credit to those who found him.

Leopold (von) Auer (1850–1930), a Hungarian, studied with Dont in Vienna and completed his training with Joachim in Hanover. He held posts in Düsseldorf and Hamburg before becoming solo violinist at the imperial court in St. Petersburg and heading the violin department at the local conservatory. A great success, he was ennobled in 1895. In 1918 he went to New York. He taught extensively, in New York and at Philadelphia's Curtis Institute, until his death.

Auer was many things: outstanding virtuoso, quartet player, and fine conductor. But above all he was an unusually gifted and devoted teacher. World-class soloists such as Elman, Zimbalist, and Heifetz were among his pupils, along with many other well-trained players who distinguished themselves as concertmasters and pedagogues. Flesch attributed Auer's results to the above-average talent of Russian-Jewish violinists and claimed that while in entrance exams at the Berlin academy about 10 percent of applicants were better than average, the percentage in St. Petersburg and Moscow was 90 to 95! According to Flesch, most of these already had received such thorough training that the academy merely provided the final touches.

In his memoirs, Flesch (1957) recalls that Auer pupils typically produced a round, mellow tone, probably the result of a special bowing style. Upon close examination he noted that on the bow stick, Russian violinists place the index finger about a centimeter closer to the lowest joint (the one closest to the hand) than do players of the Franco–Belgian school. He supposed that this might be related to the introduction of steel strings. In the coauthored *Graded Course of Violin Playing* (8 vols.), Auer used fifteen photographs to demonstrate various ways of holding the bow. The one of Auer playing in the middle of the bow, on the D and A strings, reveals his manner of holding the bow particularly well.

Leopold Auer

UNITED STATES

In the early nineteenth century, a growing number of European virtuosos came to the United States. For a long time the vast country did not offer enough opportunities to support an American tradition of classical violin playing, but conditions changed rapidly with the founding of the New York Philharmonic Society in 1842 and the New York Symphony Society in 1878, whose early players were mostly foreign-born and prominent in the developing concert life; they tended to occupy the principal chairs as other

American orchestras were founded. Gradually the number of American-born violinists grew, many of whom had studied in Europe, Sam Franko (1857–1937) and Charles Loeffler (1861–1935) among them. The American-born Amadeus von der Hoya (1874–1922), who studied with Joachim, Sauret, and Halir, became concertmaster in Weimar, then taught many students in Linz, Austria.

Four major waves of immigration impacted cultural life in the United States, the first after the French Revolution, the next after the revolutions of 1848, the third after the Russian Revolution of 1917, and the fourth after Hitler came to power in 1933. The last two upheavals not only brought world-class performers (or their parents) to the New World, but also pedagogues of similar stature. [Concerning violin playing in America during the late nineteenth and early twentieth centuries, see Schwarz 1983, "The Older Generation," with sections on Maud Powell, Franz Kneisel, David Mannes, Louis Persinger, and others. *Ed.*]

ENGLAND

Nineteenth-century England continued to attract foreign violinists but did not produce much native talent. The London Philharmonic Society, founded in 1813, and the Royal Academy of Music, an institution that welcomed all, were central to the city's concert life; both advanced the level of English violin playing. Henry Gamble Blagrove (1811–1872), a child prodigy and student of the Royal Academy, sought further coaching with Spohr, who enjoyed a fine reputation as a soloist in England. Blagrove then stayed in London for several decades, a well-known concert artist, quartet player, and concertmaster. The brothers Alfred (1837–1876) and Henry Holmes (1839–1905) toured France, Greece, and Austria, establishing fine reputations on the Continent.

The training of young English violinists by foreign pedagogues such as Brodsky in Manchester and Wilhelmj in London did much to enhance London concert life by providing qualified players for the city's orchestras as well as for new orchestras in other cities.

SCANDINAVIA

In the nordic countries, as in Poland, Russia, and Hungary, violin playing based on folk traditions existed side by side with aristocratic traditions imported from England, Germany, and Italy. The Norwegian Hardanger fiddle, a national folk instrument, was played following well-established rustic traditions, especially as an accompaniment to folk dancing. Drone basses and nonstandard tunings were characteristic features (see illustration on p. 211).

Baron Ludvig von Holberg (1684–1754) was a fine Norwegian violinist, writer, and theologian, and Waldemar Thrane (1790–1828), who studied with Baillot and Habeneck in Paris, was also quite gifted, but Ole Bull (Bornemann; 1810–1880) was undoubtedly the greatest Norwegian violinist of the nineteenth century. Trained in Bergen in a rudimentary fashion, he was forever striving to develop his remarkable talent in original, unusual ways, which brought him admiration from some and criticism from others; many of his contemporaries saw him as controversial. By using a very flat bridge and thin strings he could play three- and four-part chords, his purpose being to retain the sound of Norwegian folk music while playing classical art music; he compensated for the small resulting tone by playing with an unusually long bow. After initial successes at home Bull went to Kassel, hoping to become Spohr's pupil, but Spohr was not impressed, and nothing came of the plan. Bull then followed Paganini on his tours. A talented performer, Bull was able to incorporate in his own playing many details gleaned from observing the great Italian's technique.

Some of Bull's far-flung concert tours (throughout Europe, and several to America) were extremely successful financially. Like Paganini, he was given to include in his programs showy pieces that were bound to impress an unsophisticated public. One such piece was *Capriccio extravagante*, a musical representation of an ox being devoured by a tiger. Bull's repertory was somewhat limited. He admitted that he had tried several times to add Spohr's concertos to his programs, but they "simply didn't fit" his technique. His one attempt to perform Spohr's Concerto no. 8 met with so little success that he did not repeat the experiment. Joachim, however, in a letter to Clara Schumann (12 December 1860) had some positive things to say:

I found [Bull] more interesting than I had expected. He has an unusual command of his instrument, playing animatedly, with a beautiful tone. Of course, I only heard him play various excerpts, in a room, along with pleasant little and very simple Norwegian folk songs.

Johan Severin Swendsen (1840–1911), one of Norway's leading composers, was a more substantial musician; perhaps for that reason he attracted less attention. After studies with David in Leipzig he became concertmaster there, followed by a kapellmeister position in Copenhagen. The Romance in G major, op. 26, his most famous though not his best work, for a long time was a standard repertory item for any self-respecting violinist.

Sweden's Johan Helmich Roman (1694–1758) was an above-average violinist and composer. He studied in England for a while, and traveled there as well as in France and Germany, the representative of a national tradition of violin playing. His *Assagi a violino solo* are among the best works for unaccompanied violin that make full use of the instrument's possibilities.

Johann Friedrich Berwald (1787–1861), a child prodigy, wrote valuable symphonic music that straddles classicism and romanticism. After concertizing abroad he returned to Stockholm for almost fifty years, first as concertmaster, then as court kapellmeister. Following study in Berlin, Tor Aulin (1866–1914) succeeded him as concertmaster; he too composed for his instrument.

Claus Schall (1757–1835) represented a high level of violin playing in Denmark. He made a name for himself on concert tours abroad before becoming concertmaster of the Danish court orchestra. He taught many students, preparing them for membership in his orchestra. Famous Danish composers such as Niels W. Gade (1817–1890) and Carl Nielsen (1865–1931) began their careers as violinists. Gade, the son of a carpenter who also made violins, played in the royal orchestra in Copenhagen before becoming the conductor of the Leipzig Gewandhaus Orchestra; he returned home as conductor and director of the conservatory.

SPAIN

Violin playing on the Iberian peninsula went through the same stages we encountered in other regions on the perimeter of central Europe: positions in court and other orchestras supported by the nobility were filled at first by a preponderance of Italian players, supplanted gradually by their Spanish pupils. Philippe Libon (1775–1838), born in Cádiz of French parents, studied with Viotti in London, where he earned his first successes as a soloist. Libon also distinguished himself as the leader of a string quartet, playing works by Haydn for the master himself. Further concerts took him to Lisbon, Madrid, and Paris. Among his compositions, the thirty caprices of op. 15 are still played.

A remarkable child prodigy, as violinist and especially as composer, was Juan Crisóstomo de Arriaga (b. 1806), who died before his twentieth birthday. He studied with Baillot. Most important for the development of violin playing in Spain was Jesús de Monasterio (1836–1903), a pupil of Bériot in Brussels. After some touring he became concertmaster and professor at the Madrid conservatory, eventually serving as its director. Many fine violinists graduated from this institution.

The name, however, that first comes to mind in connection with Spanish violin playing is Pablo de Sarasate (1844–1908), who achieved immortality with his *Gypsy Airs*. The son of a military bandmaster, Sarasate went to Paris to study with Alard on a scholarship given him by Queen Isabella. By the age of thirteen his technique was well established, and he set out on a career that was the most brilliant after Paganini. Completely reliable intonation and flawless tone quality made him the idol of the public and of the younger generation of violinists. Flesch (1957) said, "From [Sarasate], in fact, dates the modern striving after technical precision and reliability, whereas before him a somewhat facile fluency and brilliance were considered the most important thing." Violinists who have struggled to develop a true staccato may be consoled with the knowledge that neither Joachim nor Sarasate had one, according to Flesch. Fortunately a vast, magnificent violin repertory does not require it!

Many composers, inspired by Sarasate's playing, dedicated works to him, including Lalo's *Symphonie espagnole*, Saint-Saëns's *Rondo capriccioso*, and the second concertos of Wieniawski and Bruch. He excelled as the interpreter of his own very unostentatious settings of Spanish dances (fourteen collections). Knowing the limits of his interpretive gifts he programmed accordingly. Moser (1923, vol. 2) tells of Sarasate's statement about the Brahms Violin Concerto, a remark made during a spirited discussion: "Do you really think

I would have the bad taste to stand on a concert platform, holding my violin, and listen while in the Adagio the oboe plays the only real melody in the
entire concerto?"

I am grateful to Hans Bunner for pointing out that Sarasate collected
material for his *Gypsy Airs* from Hungarian sources he found in Budapest
during a concert tour in 1877 (*Frankfurter Allgemeine Zeitung*, 16 August
1971). The tunes occur in a collection of *Verbunkos*, which include melodies
by Bihari, the famous gypsy violinist. Joan Manén (1883–1971) carried the
Sarasate tradition into the twentieth century. He also appeared as a child
prodigy pianist and published his memoirs in a valuable small book (*El violin*,
Barcelona 1958).

NINETEENTH-CENTURY VIOLIN MUSIC

The abundance of nineteenth-century violin music is closely related to other
developments of the era: an increasing number of public concerts, an intensive cultivation of family music making, and the founding of a variety of
music schools, open to the public. Compositions range from great masterworks to the modest, often short casual works that appealed and were accessible to the amateur. This enormous repertory, only a small portion of which
is now generally familiar, can be divided as follows:

1)   Works for violin and orchestra, including double and triple concertos
2)   Works for one or several violins and piano
3)   Works for unaccompanied violin
4)   Duets for two violins, violin and viola, violin and cello, and so forth

The chronological lists are not limited to works by the great composers.
Also included are pieces that, although virtually forgotten, are significant for
the development of violin literature, as well as a few compositions by major
violinists that reflect their own style of playing and other works that are mere
curiosities but typical for their period. Works such as string trios, piano trios,
and larger combinations are excluded from this overview. [For available
modern editions of violin music in all categories, see Margaret K. Farish,
String Music in Print, 2d ed. New York 1973, and 1984 supplement. *Ed.*]

WORKS FOR VIOLIN AND ORCHESTRA

Only first-rate concertos tend to last. Others often feature the kind of
passage work typical for that time, and because of that they sooner or
later will be considered old-fashioned, unless a piece is particularly rich
in musical substance. Because of this, the younger generation no longer
plays my concertos.

FERDINAND DAVID, QUOTED IN JULIUS ECKHARDT,
FERDINAND DAVID UND DIE FAMILIE MENDELSSOHN, 1888

1802   Beethoven, romances in G major, op. 40, and F major, op. 50

Kreutzer, *Symphonie concertante* for two violins and cello (or viola)

1803   Spohr, Violin Concerto no. 1 in A major, op. 1

1804   Beethoven, Triple Concerto in C major for piano, violin, and cello, op. 56

Rode, violin concertos nos. 7 (A minor) and 8 (E minor)

1805   Hummel, Concerto in G major for piano, violin, and orchestra, op. 51

Viotti, Violin Concerto no. 22 in A minor, op. 124 (composed 1793 in London)

1806   Beethoven, Violin Concerto in D major, op. 61

1808   Spohr, *Grande polonaise* in A minor, op. 40

1810   Kreutzer, violin concertos nos. 18 (E minor) and 19 (D minor)

1811   Paganini, Violin Concerto no. 1 in D major, op. 6

1815   Baillot, *Air varié "Vive Henri IV,"* op. 27

1816   Spohr, Violin Concerto no. 8 in A minor, "in modo d'una scena cantante," op. 47

1822   Mendelssohn, Violin Concerto in D minor

1823   Mendelssohn, Concerto in D minor for piano, violin, and string orchestra

1829   Molique, *Fantaisie sur les airs suisses pour le violon avec grand orchestre ou le pianoforte*

1834   Saint-Lubin, *Divertissement*, op. 34

1837   Maurer, Sinfonia Concertante for four violins and orchestra

1839   Ernst, *Fantaisie brillante sur la Marche et la Romance d'*Otello *de Rossini*, op. 11

1840   Habeneck, *Symphonie concertante* no. 1 for two violins and orchestra, op. 6

Vieuxtemps, "Norma" Fantasy on the G string, for violin and orchestra (or piano), op. 18

1844   Mendelssohn, Violin Concerto in E minor, op. 64

1845   Spohr, Concerto in A minor for string quartet and orchestra, op. 131

1853   Schumann, Violin Concerto in D minor

Schumann, Fantasy in C major for violin and orchestra (or piano), op. 131

Wieniawski, *Souvenir de Moscou*, op. 6

Wieniawski, *Polonaise de concert* in D major, op. 4

Wieniawski, Concerto no. 1 in F-sharp minor, op. 14

1856   Ernst, Concerto in F-sharp minor in one movement, op. 23 (composed 1844)

Wieniawski, *Scherzo-Tarantelle*, op. 16

1857   Joachim, *Concerto in the Hungarian Manner*, op. 11

1860   Vieuxtemps, Violin Concerto no. 5 in A minor ("Grétry"), op. 37

Wieniawski, *Légende*, op. 17

1861	Vieuxtemps, *Duo brillant* for violin, cello, and orchestra, op. 39
1862	Wieniawski, Concerto no. 2 in D minor, op. 22
1863	Saint-Saëns, *Introduction et rondo capriccioso*, op. 28
1867	Bruch, Violin Concerto no. 1 in G minor, op. 26
1868	Saint-Saëns, Violin Concerto no. 1 in A major, op. 20 (composed 1859)
1870	Wieniawski, *Polonaise brillante* no. 2 in A major, op. 21
1873	Lalo, *Symphonie espagnole*, op. 21
1877	Goldmark, Violin Concerto in A minor, op. 28
1878	Brahms, Violin Concerto in D major, op. 77
	Tchaikovsky, Violin Concerto in D major, op. 35
1880	Dvořák, Violin Concerto in A minor, op. 53
	Saint-Saëns, Violin Concerto no. 3 in B minor, op. 61
1882	R. Strauss, Violin Concerto in D minor, op. 8
1883	Lalo, *Concerto russe*, op. 29
1884	Cui, *Suite concertante*, op. 25
1885	Mackenzie, Violin Concerto in C-sharp minor
1886	Rimsky-Korsakov, *Fantasy on Russian Popular Themes*, op. 33
1887	Brahms, Concerto for violin, cello, and orchestra in A minor, op. 102
1888	Saint-Saëns, *Havanaise*, op. 83
1891	Chausson, Concerto for piano, violin, and string quartet in D major, op. 21
1896	Chausson, *Poème*, op. 25
1897	Busoni, Violin Concerto in D major, op. 35a

By the time Beethoven and Spohr wrote their works for violin and orchestra, most of Viotti's compositions had been published and were performed in public, studied by violinists, and used as models by other composers. Viotti wrote his twenty-nine violin concertos (including two he transcribed from his own piano concertos) for his own appearances at the Concert Spirituel. He also played them on tour, in private recitals, and on other occasions. They are scored for small orchestra except for those written in London, for the Salomon concerts in Hanover Square, where more players were available. This "Haydn" or "small Beethoven" orchestra remained fairly constant for nineteenth-century accompaniments, although early in the century, during the war years, more powerful orchestras were occasionally heard; a review of a Munich concert appeared in the *Allgemeine Musikalische Zeitung* of 1803:

> Tonight Director Cannabich, together with Herr Bohrer, performed a violin [sinfonia] concertante composed by himself. Such a din, reminiscent of cannibals, may never before have been heard in a concert hall. All instruments had solo passages, including the bass drum, a small drum that played its rolls *fortissimo*, timpani, three trombones, trumpets, four horns, and so on. To these were added the thin sounds of the solo violins.

Another report from Munich in the same journal of 1809 dealt with an unusual type of violin composition:

> On this occasion, Director Fränzl once more presented his concerto, accompanied by choruses, harps, and other sounds. How nice, how thoughtful! But this is nothing new for us, for we have heard such violin concertos in church, while the text of the mass was being recited, for some time.

In France especially, Viotti as a composer was the model for the younger generation of violinists. Kreutzer's and Rode's concertos show his influence in regard to form and violin technique. Kreutzer wrote a concerto that amounts to a curiosity: it is based on themes by Haydn and was written for a memorial service in Paris in 1806. As it turned out, news of Haydn's death was "greatly exaggerated," for the master lived three more years.

It has often been noted that concertos by Viotti, Kreutzer, and Rode have very "meager" adagio movements. One must remember, however, that the practice of embellishing melodies (a tradition going back to the baroque) had not yet disappeared, so that performers rarely played only what was written or printed, especially in slow movements. Cartier and Baillot, for instance, devote a substantial portion of their instructional works to the art of ornamentation, as does Labarre's 1844 harp method.

Spohr was nineteen years old when he wrote his first violin concerto. In those days a violinist with any talent for composition would as a matter of course write concertos to acquaint the public with his abilities in that field as well. Most of these works are no longer played, but they remain interesting because they tell us something about the composer's violin playing. Certain violinistic phrases or patterns tend to find their way into such compositions almost automatically, or they may be included intentionally, to show off the composer-performer's particular strengths as a virtuoso.

So many traveling artists and resident concertmasters presented themselves to the public with their own creations that at least one critic (*Allgemeine Musikalische Zeitung*, 1804) had to vent his exasperation:

> As we know, most concertos are composed by virtuosos who write them out of sheer necessity, though they may not even know how to resolve a seventh properly. By dint of great effort they may manage to cobble together their own part, never failing to include the kinds of fireworks at which they excel. They then try to provide some kind of accompaniment, based on what their intuition and ears tell them, and with the help of a piano they somehow put it on paper. Composers of this kind are called naturalists, but the term is used in its low, vulgar meaning.

Rode turned to experienced orchestrators for help with his accompaniments.

During this age of traveling virtuosos, the sinfonia concertante gradually went out of favor. It lasted longer in Paris than elsewhere because at the

Conservatoire it was a convenient medium for presenting several professors or student soloists at one time—a way to impress the authorities that provided funding by showing off the quality of work accomplished at that institution.

Beethoven's first works for violin and orchestra were written beginning in 1802. Although one might think that the two romances and the Triple Concerto were preliminary studies for it, we know that the Violin Concerto came about almost by accident. With this work, which provided such close interaction between solo violin and orchestra, Beethoven created the symphonic violin concerto. It served as a model, intentionally or otherwise, for other composers who were not primarily violinists and who had a symphonic concept of concerto form.

Paganini's Concerto no. 1, written a few years later, represents the opposite approach in regard to form, virtuosic shaping of the solo part, and orchestral accompaniment. As mentioned earlier, the orchestra parts are written in E-flat major, the solo violin part in D major, to be played on a violin tuned a half step above normal, so that the famous D major Concerto really is an E-flat major concerto. The opus number six is not to be taken as an indication of its chronological place in the composer's *oeuvre*. Its dating by Fétis was approximate and arrived at rather casually. By then Paganini had written dozens of other works. Schottky refers to ten concertos and Fétis to eight, but only six have been authenticated:

> Concerto in E minor (ca. 1815, published 1973)
> Concerto no. 1 in D (E-flat) major, op. 6 (ca. 1817)
> Concerto no. 2 in B minor, op. 7 (1826)
> Concerto no. 3 in E major (1826)
> Concerto no. 4 in D minor (1830)
> Concerto no. 5 in A minor (1830)

The first modern performance of the Concerto no. 3 was given by Henryk Szeryng in London on 10 October 1971. Up to that time, Paganini's heirs had refused to make it available. According to press reports it was "discovered" in Milan. In modern editions the orchestra tuttis are usually shortened and the instrumentation is heavier. Paganini scored most of his compositions (currently available only in editions for violin and piano) with full orchestral accompaniment, for he concertized only that way.

Spohr wrote his Concerto no. 8 in A minor ("in modo d'una scena cantante") for his Italian journey of 1816–1817. This accounts for its unusual form (indicated in the title), which includes sections in recitative and arioso style. In his 1865 autobiography Spohr describes the 27 September 1816 premiere, in Milan:

> Last evening we gave our concert in the *della Scala* theater. The orchestra kept its usual place, but the female singers, and Dorette and I, for our performances, took our places under the Proscenium, between the curtain which remained down, and the orchestra. The house, although favorable for music, requires nevertheless, on account of its immense

size, a very powerful tone, and a grand but simple style of playing. It is also very difficult, in a place where people are accustomed to hear voices only, to satisfy the ear with the tone of a violin. This consideration, and uncertainty as to whether my method of playing and my compositions would please the Italians, made me somewhat nervous on this, my first *début* in a country where I was as yet unknown; but as I observed that my playing was listened to with attention after the first few bars, this fear soon left me, and I then played without any embarrassment. I also had the satisfaction of seeing that in the new concerto I had written in Switzerland, which was in the form of a vocal scena, I had very happily hit upon the taste of the Italians, and that all the cantabile parts in particular were received with great enthusiasm. Gratifying and encouraging as this noisy approbation may be to the Solo-player, it is nevertheless exceedingly annoying to the composer. By it, all connexion is completely disturbed, the *tutti* so industriously worked out, are wholly unheeded, and people hear the Solo-player begin again in another tone without anyone knowing how the orchestra has modulated with it. Besides the Concerto, I played with Dorette the new Pot-pourris for piano and violin, and another with orchestral accompaniment. The latter, by general request, I was obliged to repeat.

Spohr's diary is a valuable source of information, telling us much about performing practices involving solo concertos.

Given the wealth of nineteenth-century violin concertos one wonders why so few have survived. Apart from those by Beethoven and Paganini, we have no truly "immortal" violin concertos until Mendelssohn's Concerto in E minor, in 1844. Though generally he composed quickly and easily, Mendelssohn experimented with the concerto form, gaining experience; he devoted six years of careful work to this concerto, from the first sketches to the completed piece. He was averse to interpolated cadenzas; he considered them foreign bodies, not organically related to the whole, and therefore wrote his own cadenza, building it into the first movement—a felicitous idea, imitated by other composers. Correspondence between Mendelssohn and his friend Ferdinand David reveals that the composer received a good deal of advice from the performer. David premiered the concerto on 13 March 1845, in the Leipzig Gewandhaus.

In 1837, at the age of seventeen, Vieuxtemps wrote the first of his seven concertos, which were frequently played at the time. Bériot's ten concertos, which followed soon after, reflect his own violin playing and also the taste of the mid-century public. They continue to be worth studying, both for their elegant style and their technical requirements, and they are useful for a general loosening-up of a violinist's playing apparatus.

Also popular in its day was Maurer's Sinfonia Concertante. For an 1840 performance in Vienna, the soloists were Joachim, Simon, and the brothers J. and G. Hellmesberger. At the time all four, aged nine to eleven, were pupils of Georg Hellmesberger the elder. Ernst, Bazzini, David, and Joachim have also performed the work, as have Marsick, Massart, Thomson, and Ysaÿe. It is now completely forgotten.

Fantasies on well-known operatic melodies were an important part of the lighter repertory. The genre goes back to the custom of pianists improvising in public, at times on themes given them by members of the audience. Variations on themes from operas were especially popular as shown by many written by Beethoven. If several themes from the same opera were freely varied, the work was usually called "fantasy." Many were composed with orchestra accompaniment but published in editions for violin and piano. At a time when operas were chiefly heard in larger cities or princely residences, fantasies enabled violinists to become acquainted with operatic melodies; such works could also remind listeners of operas they had seen and heard. "Réminiscences d'opéra" was a title used by Liszt for this genre, which is now looked down upon, unjustly. In degree of difficulty they range from the "Norma" Fantasy by Vieuxtemps and the fiendishly difficult "Otello" Fantasy by Ernst (played by the young Joachim at his debut), from the "Faust" fantasies by Sarasate and Wieniawski, to the series edited by Jean-Baptiste Singelée, which was also published in a simplified student edition. These creations are not far removed from the true "potpourri," a type of still lighter music, to which even Spohr had contributed.

Many sets of variations and fantasies are based on folk tunes, a reflection of the nineteenth century's intense interest in nationalism, which included the musical past of one's own people. Especially popular were folkloristic materials from the Tyrol, Russia, Poland, and Hungary, and later Spain. Political events in one country, and important personalities associated with them, sometimes helped such music to become fashionable, at least for a while. This applies to the Tyrolean hero Andreas Hofer, to Kosciuszko in Poland, and Kossuth in Hungary. Traveling virtuosos also found that they could endear themselves to the public by performing variations on songs from the host country. But as early as 1799 the oversupply of such variation works caused a writer in the *Allgemeine Musikalische Zeitung* to sigh, "In Germany there seems to be no end to the writing of variations."

Strange circumstances surround Schumann's Violin Concerto, written in 1853 in an incredibly short time, a few months before the composer's collapse. Schumann began it on 21 September; on 3 October he declared it finished, "including the instrumentation." He then immediately sent it to Joachim, who was to give the premiere, asking him to look it over. Joachim felt that, though it contained some original ideas, it showed Schumann's declining creative powers, and he never performed it. Clara Schumann made a gift of the manuscript to Joachim, in whose estate it was found with the stipulation that it was not to be performed until a hundred years after Schumann's death. Joachim's heirs, however, revoked that clause, and in 1937 Kulenkampff gave the eagerly awaited first performance. The concerto has not become part of the standard repertory. Occasional performances seem like noble attempts to rescue a work that does not quite deserve it. Aside from its weak formal organization, it gives the impression of having been

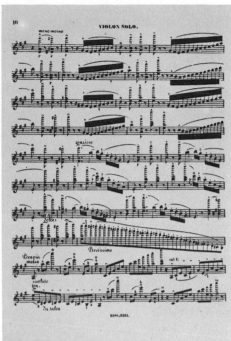

Title page of Delphin Alard's *Concert Fantasy on Themes from Gounod's Opera* Faust, op. 47 (1869), and a page from the violin part of Henri Wieniawski's *Fantaisie brillante sur des motifs de l'opéra* Faust *de Gounod*, op. 20

written with the piano, rather than the violin, in mind. As a result it contains little that is rewarding for violinists. The solo part is often covered by the orchestra and not sufficiently differentiated from it. Schumann's other work for violin (or piano) and orchestra is the Fantasy in C major op. 131, which Joachim premiered in Düsseldorf in 1853; it too is seldom heard. Adolf and Fritz Busch were the only ones who repeatedly opted for the version with orchestral accompaniment. Kulenkampff called it a "noble but thankless" composition, while Flesch considered it "very valuable," but "torture for the violinist." Joachim and Hellmesberger once discussed it with Brahms in the presence of the young Kreisler. Brahms thought that it needed to be "freed from all the underbrush." Kreisler attempted to do this, but his edition did not succeed either.

While these violin works are among Schumann's weaker ones, two other composers who are much less known were quite successful with just one of their violin concertos each. Among Bruch's many compositions, the Violin Concerto no. 1 is virtually the only one now heard regularly. Likewise Lalo is chiefly known (except in France) for his *Symphonie espagnole*.

While in Hanover, Max Bruch (1838–1920) had close contacts with Joachim, whose playing soon inspired him to write his Concerto in G minor op. 26. It is "dedicated to Joseph Joachim in friendship" and was first performed by him in 1868. The work is well designed, in cyclical form. The first movement amounts to an introduction or prelude, free and improvisatory, and the Finale is especially effective for the violin. This concerto, originally entitled "Fantasy," has a secure place in the repertory and is largely responsible for keeping the composer's name alive, along with the *Kol nidrei* for cello and orchestra. Bruch's other two violin concertos (op. 44 and 58, both in D minor) have suffered from comparison with the ever-popular G minor Concerto, as has his *Scottish Fantasy*, dedicated to Sarasate.

Victor Antoine Edouard Lalo (1823–1892), a student of Habeneck, became one of France's leading chamber music players as a member of the Armingaud Quartet. Of his five works for violin and orchestra, only the *Symphonie espagnole* has maintained itself on concert programs. It was dedicated "to my friend Sarasate," who premiered it in 1875. Spanish folk elements permeate this work, which is effectively written for the violin and competently composed and orchestrated, all of which explain its great popularity with performers and public alike.

A banner year for violin concertos was 1878, which saw the birth of those by Brahms and Tchaikovsky, both in D major, a most effective key for the violin. Brahms's Violin Concerto was written at Joachim's request; as early as September 1864 he had urged his friend to "write! And especially: write a violin concerto!" Brahms's integration of solo and orchestra goes even further than Beethoven's. Though Joachim gave an impeccable first performance (Leipzig, 1 January 1879) he was not satisfied with some of the details. For months he corresponded with the composer, taking up basic concepts such as idiomatic differences between violin and piano music. The concerto's solo part was scrutinized with a view to obtaining optimal sound.

It took some time for both the Brahms and the Tchaikovsky concertos to establish themselves, but for different reasons. Brahms was not primarily interested in violinistic effects to impress audiences; as a result, some of the top virtuosos did not find his concerto gratifying. When Joachim performed it in Berlin ca. 1880, accompanied by the academy orchestra, he encountered heavy criticism in the press for forcing students to play "such questionable stuff" (*unqualifizierbares Zeug*).

Tchaikovsky's Violin Concerto was written during March and April, months the composer spent in Clarens on Lake Geneva. Joseph Josefovich Kotek, a talented young Russian violinist and sometime pupil of Joachim, was visiting there and counseled the composer regarding the solo part. The concerto was originally dedicated to Leopold Auer, but that great teacher found it too difficult and too modern. Auer also advised Emile Sauret against playing it. Finally Brodsky took an interest and premiered the concerto during a Vienna Philharmonic concert on 4 December 1881, three years after its completion. Eduard Hanslick, the famous-infamous Viennese critic, tried mightily to deliver a death blow to Tchaikovsky's creation. His review in the *Neue Freie Presse* is a classic example of late nineteenth-century journalism, which aimed to be clever rather than factual and informative:

For a while, the sound is restrained, musical, and not without imagination, but soon coarseness gains the upper hand and maintains it to the end of the first movement. This is not violin playing, but violin yanking, tearing, pummeling. I don't know whether it is humanly possible to conquer the hair-raising difficulties with good intonation, but certainly Herr Brodsky, in trying, tortured us as much as himself. The Adagio, expressing gentle, Slavic melancholy, is about to appease us, but very soon it gives way to the Finale that takes us to a Russian country fair, with a mood of brutality and of merry-making with a sad undertone. We see nothing but wild, common faces, we hear vulgar curses, and we smell the schnapps on their breath. In discussing lascivious renderings, Friedrich Vischer once claimed that there are "pictures that reek." Tchaikovsky's Violin Concerto is the first to suggest the frightening thought that there might also be compositions in which one can hear the stench.

Admittedly Hanslick put his finger on certain weaknesses, but he completely ignores the fact that this virtuoso concerto, with its many characteristically Russian features, hangs together extremely well, and in spite of Hanslick, it has remained popular with violinists and audiences. Though Auer's intrigues worked against the concerto's Russian premiere, he later made peace with it, performing it himself in a memorial concert shortly after the composer's death and devoting an important place in his teaching to its interpretation.

Two other Tchaikovsky compositions for violin and orchestra might be considered important preparatory studies for the concerto: the *Sérénade mélancolique* op. 26 and *Valse Scherzo* op. 34.

Having been a violist in the Prague theater orchestra for many years, Dvořák (1841–1904) was familiar with the violin's possibilities as well. Brahms had taken an interest in him ever since 1878, and probably on his recommendation Dvořák also approached Joachim for advice. Dvořák dedicated his Violin Concerto to Joachim who, however, never played it. It was premiered by Ondricek in 1883. In conception it lies somewhere between Brahms's symphonic and Tchaikovsky's more virtuosic approach, and it can be counted among the few timeless works for solo violin and orchestra. Slavic violinists, especially Váša Příhoda, excelled in interpreting it. Dvořák too preceded his concerto by two smaller works: the Romance in F minor op. 11 and the *Mazurek* op. 49.

No great nineteenth-century concertos followed the three just discussed. Neither Richard Strauss's nor Busoni's concerto has become standard repertory, nor has Chausson's *Poème*, for a long time a favorite of French soloists. Camille Saint-Saëns (1835–1921) wrote three concertos that used to be heard more frequently, along with his *Introduction et rondo capriccioso* and *Havanaise*. Nor did Lalo's effective incorporation of folk elements inspire other works with lasting appeal.

Brahms's Double Concerto, however, has maintained its success. Its scoring for violin and cello perhaps was suggested by the *Duo brillant* by

Vieuxtemps. As usual, Brahms made many refinements after it had been completed. Its premiere in Baden-Baden, with the very capable local orchestra, established its success.

When we consider the vast number of concertos written at the time of Vivaldi and Tartini, the nineteenth-century repertory seems limited indeed. While violinists still composed for their own use, concertos were now written more often by composers who perhaps had had some acquaintance with the violin in their youth but were not fully conversant with all its technical possibilities and subtleties. For them, writing a violin concerto was a musical, compositional challenge above all; they were far less concerned with practical matters of violin technique. To consult a violin virtuoso therefore became increasingly necessary, lest a "concerto against the violin" might result—a term maliciously applied by some to Brahms's contribution.

Concertos by the great baroque masters practically disappeared as styles changed after 1750. During the nineteenth century, however, a body of standard violin concertos evolved that has hardly changed since. It begins with those by Mozart and Beethoven, even though they were rarely heard immediately after the composers' deaths. Later composers had to match and reckon with their standard of quality—the chief reason for the steadily declining number of major nineteenth-century violin concertos. It was a golden age of violin playing, yet 80 to 90 percent of the then-popular violin concertos are completely forgotten.

WORKS FOR VIOLIN AND PIANO (OR HARP)

The late sonatas of Mozart and Beethoven had established the equality of the violin and piano parts, but in titles the older custom prevailed for some time: "for piano, with violin accompaniment." The following list includes some of the more important compositions, along with a few curiosities.

ca. 1800	Boieldieu, *Ouverture du calife de Bagdad, arrangé pour le piano avec accompagnement de violon obligé par l'auteur*
1800	Beethoven, *Deux sonates pour le pianoforte avec un violon* opp. 23 and 24
1802	Beethoven, *Trois sonates pour le pianoforte avec l'accompagnement d'un violon* op. 30, nos. 1–3
1802/03	Beethoven, *Sonata per il pianoforte ed un violino obbligato* op. 47
1805	Spohr, Sonata in C minor for harp and violin
ca. 1806	Kreutzer, *Trois sonates faciles pour le violon avec accompagnement de basse*
1812	Beethoven, Sonata for pianoforte and violin op. 96
1814	Baillot, *Charmante Gabrielle, air varié,* op. 25
1816	Schubert, Three Sonatinas op. 137
	Spohr, Potpourri in G major
	Viotti, *Trois sonates pour le violon avec accompagnement de forte-piano,* opp. 151–153

ca. 1817	Romberg, *Potpourri sur des mélodies de l'opéra* Don Juan *de Mozart* op. 49
1817	Schubert, Duo in A major, op. 162
1817/18	Beethoven, Six Themes and Variations for piano with optional accompaniment of a flute or violin, op. 105
ca. 1820	Mazas, *Fantaisie sur la quatrième corde,* op. 20
1823	Mendelssohn, Sonata in F minor for violin and piano, op. 4
ca. 1825	Hünten, *Variations concertantes pour piano forte et violon sur le motif de l'opéra* Der Freischütz *"Durch die Wälder, durch die Auen,"* op. 18
1826	Schubert, *Rondeau brillant* in B minor for violin and piano, op. 70
1827	Schubert, Fantasy in C major, op. 159
1831	Herz and Bériot, *Variations concertantes pour piano et violon sur la tyrolienne favorite de* La fiancée *d'Auber,* op. 56
	Paganini, *Les charmes de Padue, divertimento per violino e piano concertante*
1836	Spohr, *Souvenir d'un voyage à Dresden et dans la suisse saxonne. Duo concertant pour pianoforte et violon,* op. 96
1838	Mendelssohn, Sonata in F major for violin and piano
ca. 1840	Heller and Ernst, *Pensées fugitives* for violin and piano
1841/44	Vieuxtemps, five duos concertants: opp. 13, 14, and 20 with E. Wolff; op. 23 with Kullak; op. 26 with A. Rubinstein
1846	Spohr, Six Salon Pieces, op. 135
1851	Schumann, Sonata no. 1 in A minor, op. 105
	Schumann, Sonata no. 2 in D minor, op. 121
1853	Dietrich/Schumann/Brahms/Schumann, *Sonate F.A.E.* ("frei, aber einsam"; free, but lonely)
1865	Grieg, Sonata in F major for violin and piano, op. 8
1867	Grieg, Sonata in G major for violin and piano, op. 13
1876	Fauré, Sonata in A major for violin and piano, op. 13
1878/79	Brahms, Sonata in G major for piano and violin, op. 78
1880	Dvořák, Sonata in F major, op. 57
1885/87	Grieg, Sonata in C minor, op. 45
1886	Brahms, Sonata in D minor for piano and violin, op. 108
	Franck, Sonata for piano and violin or cello
1887/88	R. Strauss, Sonata in E-flat major for violin and piano, op. 18
1890	Busoni, Sonata no. 1 in E minor, op. 29
1891	Reger, Sonata in D minor, op. 1
	Reger, Sonata in D major, op. 3
1893	Dvořák, Sonatina in G major, op. 100
1894	Fitelberg, Sonata, op. 2
1897	Enesco, Sonata, op. 2
1898	Busoni, Sonata no. 2 in E minor, op. 36a
1899	Enesco, Sonata, op. 6
	Reger, Sonata in A major, op. 41

A number of Beethoven's masterworks date from the turn of the century, the first three having been written in 1797 and 1798. Of the ten sonatas for violin and piano, nine were written within the short span of six years. Opus 96 followed in 1812 after a pause of several years, and Beethoven wrote none after that, which relates to his activities as a pianist. Around 1800, as one of Vienna's leading pianists, he needed works for his own appearances with violinists in public and private concerts. When Kreutzer declined to perform the Sonata op. 47, Beethoven premiered it in May 1803 with Bridgetower. A partial autograph, acquired by the Beethoven-Haus in Bonn in 1965, carries the inscription "Sonata mulattica." As Beethoven's hearing deteriorated he no longer performed in public, which caused him to lose interest in the genre. His last sonata was occasioned by Rode's visit to Vienna. Archduke Rudolph was the famous violinist's partner in the premiere, an indication of the high quality of amateur music making in Vienna.

Schubert was inspired by Beethoven's works for violin and piano. His three sonatinas are masterworks. They require less technique than Beethoven's sonatas, for which reason they are studied by less advanced students and are beloved by amateurs. Professional violinists rarely include them in recitals. Schubert's *Grand duo* and the Fantasy in C major, a late work, belong among his many unjustly neglected creations. Bad luck seems to have pursued the latter ever since its premiere, upon which occasion a Viennese critic wrote, "[It] somewhat exceeded the amount of time the Viennese are prepared to devote to spiritual delights. More and more members of the audience left, and this reviewer must confess that he cannot report anything about the work's end." Another critic even believed that "the popular composer in this instance has miscomposed." If the Fantasy in C major is seldom heard, this may also be due to the orchestrally conceived piano part. In 1853 Joachim was inspired to provide an orchestral version of the accompaniment.

It is curious that while Beethoven and Schubert wrote duos for two equal partners, sonatas for violin and figured bass continued to be composed. Kreutzer's six sonatas of this kind are not the sole examples, especially in France. For some violin teachers this may have been a convenience. They might have found it difficult to play a complex piano accompaniment for their students but could manage a basso continuo, especially since it could be realized on a violin, playing double stops, which Eugène Sauzay advocated as late as 1889.

Boieldieu's opera *Le calife de Bagdad* was a great success at its premiere in 1800. Following the custom of the time, the composer provided various arrangements of its most popular melodies, suitable for music making in the home. He made it a point to include the overture which, with its catchy tunes, remained a standby for all kinds of small and large groups into the 1920s. Arrangements of this kind also served as study material for prospective orchestra players. An incredible number of opera excerpts has come down to us in this manner. In the simpler arrangements the violin merely reproduces the vocal line, but others display all degrees of virtuosity, including free paraphrases in Liszt's manner. Top performers wrote them, carefully including the kinds of fireworks guaranteed to amaze their listeners. Paganini's fantasies and variations with orchestra accompaniment gave rise to comparable pieces published with piano accompaniment, which of course were easier to sell. Arrangements of this kind, by Romberg, Pixis, Hünten, and others, became bestsellers.

At times, two virtuosos might collaborate, so that we have duets by Herz/Bériot, Heller/Ernst, and other piano/violin teams. Following tradition, the pianist's name usually was given first. Even great masters did not consider it below their dignity to provide such arrangements. Franchomme and Chopin wrote duets for violin and piano on melodies from Meyerbeer's *Robert le diable*.

Several decades passed before substantial sonatas followed those by Mozart, Beethoven, and Schubert. (Spohr's only violin sonata calls for harp accompaniment.) Not until 1851 do we have comparable masterworks: the violin sonatas by Schumann, written shortly before his creative powers declined. Joachim, whose violin playing had inspired them, first performed them with the composer, after whose death Joachim and Clara Schumann added them to their repertory. In 1853 Schumann composed a violin sonata together with Albert Dietrich and Brahms. In 1956 Eduard Melkus called attention to additional movements for this sonata, written later by Schumann, adding up to a third Schumann violin sonata.

Few compositions for violin and piano issued from Paganini's pen. Most of those published in that form were originally conceived with orchestra accompaniment. But the great virtuoso did write for violin and guitar, including a "duetto amoroso," a "sonata concertata," a "gran sonata," and a sonatina. There are also quartets for violin, viola, cello, and guitar.

Virtuoso writing is also found in chamber music. Many a work entitled "quatuor concertant" really amounts to a violin concerto accompanied by string trio, with the "soloist" also playing in the "tutti" sections. Early nineteenth-century titles often included the word "brillant," indicating that virtuoso playing was an important ingredient. Spohr used the title "duo concertant" in place of "sonata"; many composers, especially lesser ones, followed his example. Spohr also contributed to the genre of "salon music" for violin and piano, which was amazingly popular in the nineteenth century, if publishers' catalogs and advertisements on the back pages of printed violin music are any evidence. Albert Tottmann's *Führer durch den Violin-Unterricht* cautions against including too much of this repertory, especially during the first few years of violin instruction, and urges that students should soon give preference to concertos.

Thousands of violin teachers and minor composers felt compelled to provide music of this type for players at all levels, for example, Karl Henning's *Die ersten Freuden des jungen Violinspielers* (The young violinist's first pleasures) op. 49; Ludwig Jansa's *Der junge Opernfreund* (The young opera lover) op. 75 (in *sixty* issues!—they must have had fantastic sales, for Jansa added a "New Series" of twelve issues); Ferdinand Magerstädt's *Des Violinspielers Erheiterungen* (The violinist's pleasures) op. 34; Josef Nesvadba's *Paraphrase on Silcher's*

Loreley op. 17; and August Siede's *Goldenes Melodiealbum für angehende Violinisten* (Album of golden melodies for beginning violinists; two sets with six parts each) opp. 1 and 2.

An avalanche of often trivial compositions resulted, with titles such as "character pieces," "romances," "elegies," and "Hungarian airs." [An oft-quoted bon mot: What is a character piece? A piece without character. *Ed.*] To be sure, some of these compositions were inspired and were attractive to violinists. Some, such as Raff's *Cavatina*, François Schubert's *The Bee*, and Rimsky-Korsakov's *Flight of the Bumble Bee*, provided excellent material for practicing specific technical problems or challenges. They were more palatable for young violinists than etudes. Such pieces tend to be looked down on by those who will settle for nothing less than original compositions of greater substance. As a result, some attractive material from the nineteenth century, an age when virtuoso playing flourished, is disappearing.

Grieg's three sonatas follow the great tradition of Schumann's. Two of them are dedicated to his fellow composers Gade and Swendsen. Grieg's talent was largely lyrical, shown best in smaller pieces that have gone out of fashion. Even his three substantial sonatas are frowned upon by some, which is unfortunate. Certainly the C minor Sonata is a mature masterwork. With the renewed appreciation of much nineteenth-century music, perhaps the other two may again come into their own.

Few French composers wrote duos for violin and piano, those by Viotti, Baillot, Lalo, and a few others being exceptions. The genre did not figure prominently in French concert life—surprisingly, for string quartets gave many public performances. Things changed in 1871 with the founding of the Société Nationale de Musique, which promoted recitals of chamber music with piano, as did its rival Société Moderne. Fauré's A major Sonata (1876) may have resulted from these efforts. It is still labeled a work for piano and violin, whereas the title of Fauré's Second Sonata (1916) lists the violin first. César Franck's Violin Sonata undoubtedly represents the high point among French contributions to the genre. Ysaÿe premiered it in Brussels two months after its completion; it has remained a favorite among violinists.

Since Brahms and Joachim frequently performed together, it is not surprising that some violin sonatas resulted. An early Brahms sonata in A minor, mentioned by the composer in an 1853 letter to Joachim, has been lost. Impressed by Beethoven's and Schumann's masterworks, Brahms took a long time before he returned to the medium, a characteristic trait of the composer who so often was critical of his own writing. The results were well worth the wait: within a few years Brahms wrote the three sonatas that are masterworks worthy of continuing the great tradition.

While Brahms's sonatas were the product of a long period of maturation, those by Max Reger stand at the beginning of his career. Frau Riemann did not think much of his opp. 1 and 3 sonatas: "If one wants to improve upon Beethoven and Brahms, this is the kind of stuff that results!" Indeed, the sonatas caused widespread dismay, and Reger later distanced himself from the works of his youth. Nevertheless, among his nine sonatas for violin and piano, these early ones are important, indicating his beginnings and early development.

WORKS FOR UNACCOMPANIED VIOLIN

It is widely held that composing for a melody instrument without accompaniment was in vogue during the baroque era, went out of fashion after 1750, and returned during the nineteenth-century revival of interest in earlier music that in turn introduced neobaroque features. This is true as far as the great masters are concerned, but the generation of violinists after 1750 knew more of the baroque repertory for unaccompanied violin than is generally assumed. With their technical challenges, these works continued to exert some influence on players. The Mendelssohn-Schumann circle's championing of Bach's solo violin writings therefore did not really amount to a rediscovery. After Cartier published the C major Fugue, Simrock was enterprising enough to bring out an edition of all the sonatas and partitas, published in Paris in 1804 as *Sonates d'étude*. It is true that for a long time they were more appreciated as study material than for their intrinsic musical value. Tottmann placed them on level VIa as "etudes for unaccompanied violin," while Ludwig Abel (d. 1895), concertmaster and professor at the Munich academy, included individual movements in his publication *Collection of Studies for Violin Alone*, along with etudes by Gaviniès, Rode, and Kreutzer. On the other hand, Kreutzer's last etude is so different from the usual ones that one might rather call it a "composition." Quite a few nineteenth-century violinist-composers set their own works apart from typical etudes by calling them "concert etudes," "études caracteristiques," or "caprices." There are no clear lines of demarcation between all these.

1801	Pichl, *6 fughe con un preludio fugato per un violino solo*
1802	Campagnoli, *6 fughe per violino solo*, op. 10
1804	Campagnoli, *20 Präludien in allen Dur- und Molltonarten* (in all major and minor keys), op. 12
1808	W. Krumpholz, *Abendunterhaltung für eine Violine* (Evening entertainment for one violin)
ca. 1809	Bruni, *Six duos à violon seul*
1813	Campagnoli, *L'art d'inventer à l'improviste des fantaisies ed cadences*, op. 17
	Campagnoli, *Sept divertissements pour violon*, op. 18
1834	Chélard, *Duettvariationen mit Doppelgriffen für Violine ohne Begleitung* (with double stops, for unaccompanied violin)
ca. 1840	Ernst, *Grand caprice solo pour violon sur "Le Roi des Aulnes" de F. Schubert*, op. 26
1852	Deldevez, *Six études caprices*, op. 13
ca. 1855	F. David, Suite in G minor for unaccompanied violin, op. 43
ca. 1860	Kayser, *75 kurze Passagenübungen und Präludien* (short exercises for passage work and preludes), op. 68 (3 vols.)

1860   Dancla, *Vingt études brillantes et caractéristiques*, op. 73
1892   Barth, Partita in F minor, op. 10
              Elgar, *Cinq études caractéristiques*, op. 24
1899/1900 Reger, Four Sonatas, op. 42

Pichl and Campagnoli wrote their solo works under the influence of the baroque tradition. It is wrong, however, to compare them with those by Bach, a composer of far greater stature. At any rate, they show that Bach's spirit and manner of writing for solo violin were still alive more than half a century later.

Of interest are the many efforts to provide students with models for improvising, a tradition that was becoming lost during the nineteenth century. These efforts continued to Kayser's time. Also based on baroque tradition and technique are several attempts to create, on one violin, the impression of a duet. Biber had already done this successfully in his 1681 composition *Gara [competition] di due violini in uno*. Later bravura pieces such as Ernst's arrangement of Schubert's *Erl King* (see illustration) no doubt helped stimulate the public's interest in works for unaccompanied violin. A new impetus was provided by David's Suite op. 43, which quite likely grew out of his Bach interpretations and his teaching in Leipzig. Another violinist-composer was Richard Barth, a Joachim pupil, a concertmaster and conductor, and one of the rare violinists who bowed with his left arm.

Opening page of Ernst's *Grand caprice*, op. 26

For a long time, major composers showed no interest in the genre. This changed with Max Reger and his Four Sonatas, op. 42. At the turn of the century it was no longer considered daring to perform Bach's solo works in public, for there were now many appreciative listeners. Reger dedicated these sonatas to Burmester, hoping (in vain) that he would perform them. Their baroque ancestry is obvious; by building on Bach's polyphonic movements, but by also using his own brand of chromaticism, Reger provided great technical challenges in these four sonatas. They stand at the beginning of Reger's *oeuvre* for solo violin, which includes eleven sonatas, thirteen preludes and fugues, and a chaconne, inspiring much writing for solo violin in the twentieth century.

DUETS

When I was almost nine years old I began composing short pieces for two violins, and later longer pieces as well. . . . I used to play with my teacher or with one of my cousins. Having practiced violin duets by Viotti, Pleyel, and others, I imitated their style. In that way my composing progressed as my playing did. I eventually reached the point where I could write a kind of symphonic poem, based on Schiller's play *Die Räuber* (The robbers). I called it the *Räuber-Phantasie*.

ARNOLD SCHOENBERG IN 1959, QUOTED IN WILLI REICH,
SCHOENBERG ODER DER KONSERVATIVE REVOLUTIONÄR,
VIENNA 1968

The quantity of duets for string instruments written from the late eighteenth century on defies our imagination, for the genre is now nearly defunct. Antoine Vidal's book *Les instruments à archet* (String instruments, 1876–1878) has statistics: in his third volume the list of duets for two violins fills forty-one pages, that for two cellos is nine pages long. Pleyel is represented by 135 violin duets, Dotzauer wrote more than twenty six sets for two cellos, and Jacques Offenbach, famous for his operettas but also an important cellist, is credited with twelve duets for violin and cello and thirty-nine for two cellos.

The great demand for duets is related to a widely accepted manner of teaching that tests whatever level a pupil has reached by applying it immediately to duet playing, with the teacher or with another student. Many violin teachers wrote such duets, based on their own experience and requirements. As composers they may seldom have risen very high; on the other hand, by basing their compositions on classic models they rarely fell below an acceptable level. These duets typically featured attractive melodies in one part and standard accompaniment patterns in the other. Development sections involving dialogue between the two instruments were apt to be modest in length and invention. Nevertheless these duets pointed to what students would encounter in orchestra and chamber music.

One source of violin duets was the baroque sonata for violin and figured bass. As mentioned earlier, a teacher might play the bass part on the violin by transposing it up an octave, as is still done. Duets by Telemann, Tessarini, and Leclair were probably inspired by this practice. Some trio sonatas by Vivaldi carry the remark "may also be played without the bass."

Guignon and Mondonville performed duets as early as 1745, at a Concert Spirituel, but more typically duet playing formed part of instruction and music making in the home. A letter from Viotti to his colleague Baillot invites him for a meal of chops, to be followed by duet playing. More recently Menuhin and Schneiderhan met occasionally to play Bartók's duets, "just for fun."

Much operatic and symphonic music was arranged for two violins. Immediately after its premiere in 1794, the overture to Bruni's Singspiel *Claudine* was published in two editions: for violin and piano, and for two violins. Patriotic music was no exception, such as a 1799 collection of *Music Written on the Occasion of the General Mobilization in Vienna* for two violins or two flutes. A few years earlier, Cartier in Paris had published his *Fourth Patriotic Potpourri* for violin and viola, including the famous song of the Revolution, "Ca ira." Violinists were even expected to depict battle scenes. In 1801 the *Allgemeine Musikalische Zeitung* announced the publication of *La battaille de Marengo: Pièce militaire pour 2 clarinettes. La même pour 2 violons* (The battle of Marengo: Military composition for two clarinets, also arranged for two violins).

Some further statistics illustrate the incredible amount of published duets. Viotti wrote fifty-one duets, five preludes, and six serenades for two violins. (One of his partners was the famous string bass virtuoso Dragonetti, who played the second violin part in the original violin register!) Kalliwoda published sets of duets as opp. 20, 50, 70, 116, 152, 178, 179, 180, 181, 213, 234, and 243. He was outdone by Jansa who contributed sixteen sets, and by Dancla with twenty-three, ranging from "très facile" to "brillant." Given the great demand it is not surprising that many works by Bach, Haydn, Mozart, and Beethoven were published in arrangements for two violins. Léonard and Vieuxtemps found a collaborator for some of their violin and cello duets in Adrien-François Servais (1807–1866).

NINETEENTH-CENTURY VIOLIN PEDAGOGY

TEACHING AS A SCIENCE

There are some teachers here who hardly seem capable of *taking* lessons.
MENDELSSOHN, WRITING TO FERDINAND DAVID,
BERLIN, AUGUST 1826

Teachers really are spiritual counselors who, more than anyone else, are responsible for maintaining the great spiritual, uninterrupted tradition of their art. They are the crucial, most important link in the hierarchy of violinists.   CARL FLESCH, *THE ART OF VIOLIN PLAYING*, VOL. 2, 1923

With the rise of the natural sciences during the nineteenth century, strong tensions developed in many fields. On the one hand there was the emphasis on romantic feeling and thinking, on the other, scientific approaches. Even in the realms of art and creativity, which had always been the domain of romantic intuition, thought processes derived from the natural sciences tended to encroach upon what had been considered to be beyond the realm of the intellect. It is noteworthy that during the height of musical romanticism we also encounter ever-growing research in the field of acoustics. This research, based on Chladni's discoveries, increasingly dealt with artistic questions. Savart, Chanot, and many others applied new discoveries in acoustics to violin making, encountering stubborn resistance from those who believed that violin making was an art based on intuition and experience. To many, a luthier with training in science, who worked according to rational considerations, represented a danger.

Likewise violin playing was, in the belief of many, a talent bestowed by God—or in the case of Paganini, by the devil—a gift that simply had to be developed and nurtured by diligent practicing. Since, from Corelli to the nineteenth century, violin music had become technically ever more difficult, the time violinists spent practicing increased steadily, at least during a student's formative years and when preparing for concerts. In Paganini's and

Ysaÿe as a teacher

Spohr's time, this meant ten to twelve hours daily, though the average was probably much less. Whatever problems were encountered, the solution always was practicing, and more practicing. Flesch (1957) recalled how things were during his student days in Vienna ca. 1880:

> The running sore of teaching at that time was the complete ignorance of rational methods of study. After inadequate performances the remedy was always "try again" or "more" study, without any discussion of the whys and hows. The *quantity* of practice was regarded as the criterion of virtue. Apparently nobody knew that logical analysis of the task would yield twice the result in half the time.

To find the best ways to practice is not merely a matter of method, of pedagogy; it requires a good understanding of the complex motions involved in playing an instrument, which were known at the time of which Flesch speaks. Around 1800 the maverick Galeazzi already had clear notions about the mechanical aspects of violin playing, and during the following decades many voices advocated applying scientific methods to these aspects. These tendencies gained momentum in connection with attempts ca. 1830 to explain the phenomenon of Paganini. It comes as no surprise that a physician was involved. Ole Bull also attracted the interest of physicians. In 1877 Alpheus B. Crosby, professor of anatomy at Bellevue Hospital Medical College in New York, wrote a book, *The Art of Holding the Violin and Bow as Exemplified by Ole Bull*. Related to these interests we encounter a new trend in the literature on violin pedagogy. In Baillot's *L'art du violon* (1835) the text portion already is long, but some later books separate the part containing substantive discussions from the music examples or exercises. Books were now written *about* violin playing, books that would have been unthinkable at the time of Geminiani's or Leopold Mozart's practical treatises. They approach the subject from the point of view of psychology or methodology; they analyze complex problems by isolating their components; they provide thorough analyses of a specific issue. The following three publications are typical of the trend:

1864   C. W. Henning, *Practical Instructions for the Violin on Scientific Principles*, Boston

1888   Hermann Schröder, *Untersuchungen über die sympathetischen Klänge der Geigeninstrumente und eine hieraus folgende Theorie der Wirkung des Bogens auf die Saiten* (Researches concerning the sympathetic sounds of instruments of the violin family, leading to a theory about the bow's effect on the strings), Leipzig

1909   Ondricek and Mittelmann, *Neue Methode zur Erlangung der Meistertechnik des Violinspiels auf anatomisch- physiologischer Grundlage* (New method to acquire mastery of violin playing, based on anatomical-physiological concepts), Vienna

Admittedly all books on violin playing share a common problem. The physical motions involved in playing are extremely complex, so that describing them precisely with words is extremely difficult, if not impossible. Books of this kind therefore are fully intelligible only to the person who has already studied for some time, with a good teacher. Violin teaching traditionally has consisted chiefly of the student following and imitating the teacher, a procedure that can be clarified only to a certain extent by written instruction. Let me give an example of the insufficiency of written instructions. Adrian Rappoldi (in his *10 Dresdner Etüden*, Hamburg 1957) prefaced one of the etudes as follows: "To be played at the tip of the bow. Hold the bow lightly between the fingers and throw it with a wrist motion." Having read this, few players would suspect that the author is referring to ricochet bowing, nor would they master that bowing on the basis of the written description.

Many books on violin pedagogy contain very broad statements that, while not exactly wrong, tell the reader-player very little. To continually bid a student to be "loose and relaxed" while playing is not going to do much for someone who tends to tighten up. Actually, it is impossible to play the violin in a completely "loose and relaxed" manner, but aside from that, only the reader who has already learned to play with a minimum of exertion will understand what the author is trying to say. Similarly, to demand that before playing a work, the violinist must "explore it mentally" will accomplish little unless the player has already learned how to analyze a composition, a skill acquired only with much time and effort.

Many books on violin playing have been written by those who have not played the instrument for some time, or have no concertizing experience. They are responsible for that cruel saying, "Those who can, do; those who can't, teach." Too often theories expounded in such books are not validated by practical artistic experience. Flesch, a professional performer, agreed, and regretted that so few of the great nineteenth-century violinists gave us the benefit of their experiences. Moreover, some writers have resorted to esoteric pronouncements to make their statements seem all the more profound. In his own books Flesch attempted to write as clearly as possible, using only those technical and foreign terms that were absolutely necessary.

By ca. 1870–1880 it had become imperative for violinists to give serious thought to their playing mechanism. Earlier the playing of even the greatest violinists, such as Paganini, had been characterized by a thin tone that was, however, conducive to elegant bowing and also facilitated complex special bowings. Thin strings with low tension also produced a small tone, but they spoke readily and favored a flexible, virtuosic manner of playing. Piano sound had already changed due to the invention and improvement of the cast-iron frame after ca. 1825. Larger concert halls required larger sound. A related development was the growth of the symphony orchestra, especially of the brass section as needed in works by Wagner and others. String players found it difficult to cope with such volume. Mention of a large string tone usually referred to the way some violinists played on the great instruments of the past. Wilhelmj, the first Bayreuth concertmaster, enlarged his tone by frequent bow changes, an approach typical for his time.

The relatively small tone produced by earlier players was due to several factors, some of which have already been mentioned. Chief among them was the way one held the bow, using the first joint of the index finger, and the excessive importance attributed to wrist motion, while the upper and lower arm participated no more than absolutely necessary. Illustrations in many violin methods, along with early photographs and paintings, show players holding the upper arm close to the body. Menzel's well-known 1854 charcoal drawing of Joachim and Clara Schumann playing together (partially reproduced here) shows this well. Most teachers of this period demanded that a player should be able to wedge a book between upper arm and body and play all kinds of bowings that way. This supposedly ensured that the wrist executed all necessary motions. String changes were to be made with wrist motion only. As late as 1905, Richard Scholz recommended that the upper arm and elbow be fastened to the torso with a piece of string in order to keep them close to the body while practicing. A position that at first was advocated solely for practicing gradually became the standard for all playing.

To free oneself from this straitjacket became a necessity by the end of the nineteenth century. In *Conversations with Casals*, J. Corredor relates how the twelve-year-old cellist solved the problem for himself, against his teacher's instruction. In 1910 Enesco created a sensation in Paris by playing with complete ease and freedom, adjusting his right arm's position to the requirements of the moment.

The physician Friedrich Adolf Steinhausen (1859–1910), an enthusiastic amateur violinist and pianist, systematically investigated the physiological bases of playing both instruments. He played the violin well enough to analyze the motions involved in his own playing and to correlate them with the sounds produced, publishing the results of his investigations in two basic works: *Die Physiologie der Bogenführung* (The physiology of bowing, Leipzig 1905) and *Die physiologischen Fehler und die Umgestaltung der Klaviertechnik* (Physiological errors and changing piano technique, Leipzig 1905; Engl. trans. Rochester, N.Y., 1963). At about the same time Marie Jaëll, formerly Liszt's assistant, similarly researched piano playing in collaboration with

Charles Féré, an expert physiologist; their work led to the publication of *La musique et la psycho-physiologie* (Paris 1896).

Steinhausen's book on bowing caused a sensation of enthusiastic endorsement and strong opposition as soon as it was published. Its lasting impact is documented by the appearance in 1907 of a second enlarged and thoroughly revised edition, third and fourth editions by Schering (without changing the text of the second edition), and a 1928 fifth edition by Florizel von Reuter, who incorporated some additions. Steinhausen's systematic approach gave rise to a large number of similar investigations; some authors followed him closely without giving him credit.

In the preface to his first edition Steinhausen outlines his basic tenets and his approach, pointing out that a reliance on basic natural laws has become generally accepted procedure, not only in traditional branches of science but even in the more complex aspects of artistic work. Such investigations may lead to progress in technical matters, including bowing technique. Proceeding methodically will prove superior to the haphazard and laborious trial-and-error approach of earlier times. "I have critically and analytically examined the mechanical workings of joints and muscles and how these affect bowing. I began by carefully scrutinizing the playing of today's artists, and I tried to apply the results to perfecting my own tone production. In doing so I encountered a number of problems with which I shall deal in the following." His investigations led Steinhausen to the following conclusions:

No. 137: The upper arm provides strength; it leads in all bowings.
No. 146: Mechanical components of bow motion are involved in giving life and inspiration to the sound, for everything to which the soul aspires can be traced to brain stimuli and external motion, hence also to the bow's motion.
No. 154: The arm leads and the hand follows, not vice versa.

In his summary Steinhausen reiterates that the former practice of developing wrist motion exclusively is flawed and full of contradictions, and that a new approach and methodology must be developed by those who will teach succeeding generations of string players. "The aim must be threefold: to perfect sound production, to simplify and facilitate technique, and to establish the proper relationship between technique and artistry." Following Steinhausen, Strub came up with this extreme statement: "Technique is the avoidance of all unnecessary motions."

In some ways Steinhausen's enthusiasm carried him too far. He may have been so delighted with the novelty of his findings that he ignored what others had discovered before him. Some of his statements are exaggerated and one-sided; they were attacked by pedagogues, including those who were annoyed by a nonprofessional's "butting into" their field. Others feared that an overemphasis on movement analysis might harm a player's natural impulses in artistic expression. No doubt there were and are violin teachers and performers who, concealing a lack of artistic ability behind an excess of intellect-driven obsession with analysis, may have been encouraged (and in some cases adversely affected) by the writings of Steinhausen and his followers. Steinhausen was aware of the dangers and always stressed that artistic concerns must come first. One of his most severe critics was Andreas Moser, who felt that some of Steinhausen's broad generalizations represented an attack on Joachim, Moser's idol. He also feared that Steinhausen's statements amounted to criticism of the violin school on which he and Joachim were then working. (It appeared two years after Steinhausen's book.) But many of Moser's reservations are well founded.

G. Demeny's book *Le violoniste* appeared in Paris in the same year as Steinhausen's. The book formed part of the series *Physiologie des professions*. Demeny was a teacher of physical education; his title page (see illustration) indicates something of the new approach. Studies such as Steinhausen's are important (even if not correct in every detail) because they add a new dimension to the complicated subject of how the violin is played. They form part of a general trend represented by other studies listed in his bibliography. These deal with the physiology of muscles, the mechanisms of joints and elbow muscles, the physiology of coordination, physiological psychology, and similar topics.

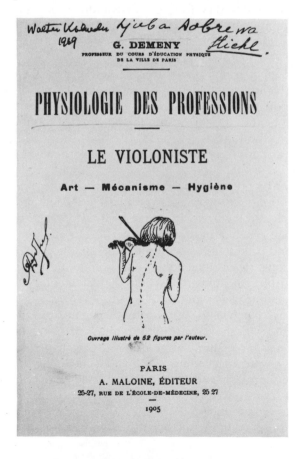

Other basic studies followed Steinhausen's. Some are independent, others are influenced or inspired by him. Many of his conclusions concerning bowing were now extended to left-hand technique and to the entire playing apparatus. The activities of Carl Flesch reflect the basic changes in viewing violinistic problems. The son of a physician and therefore well equipped to investigate the psycho-physiological bases of violin playing, Flesch was one of the first pedagogues whose insights into these aspects of violin playing were combined with sensitivity to its musical and spiritual or aesthetic aspects. In his teaching Flesch never ignored one at the expense of the other. His pupil Max Rostal recalled that Flesch was fond of referring to himself as "doctor [physician] of violin playing."

One of Steinhausen's immediate successors was Wilhelm Trendelenburg, an M.D. and professor of physiology at the University of Tübingen, whose book *Die natürlichen Grundlagen der Kunst des Streichinstrumentenspiels* (The natural foundations of string instrument playing) was published in 1925. As an expert physiologist Trendelenburg went far beyond Steinhausen, especially in his experiments. He analyzed all motions involved in playing, including those that applied specifically to viola, cello, and string bass. He commented on the connections between the conscious and subconscious processes and advocated that their connections must be explored. This did not cause him to fear that such investigations would result in unartistic playing. "Once the technical workings have been fully explored they will recede into the realm of the only vaguely conscious, providing the perfect basis for artistic creativity."

Books of this kind can be problematic because of discrepancies between the author's scientific findings and actual artistic experience. Trendelenburg, for instance, has this to say about the aesthetic aspects of changing positions:

> If a very large move to a higher position is called for, it is best to stop the bow during the move [of the left hand]. Though this will result in a break, this will not be noticed—at least much less than the unpleasant sound of the supporting finger's slide upward while the bow continues to move.

Such statements might make us wonder whether the author is qualified to write on the subject of violin playing. Other books, such as the one by Heinrich Kosnick (1927) are so full of medical jargon and terminology that they are unlikely to improve anyone's bowing technique. As Flesch (*The Art of Violin Playing*, vol. 1) put it, "To pull the wool over the reader's eyes by using Latin terms gleaned from anatomy books only serves to cover up a book's lack of substance and an author's failure to prove his points."

Nineteenth-century violin pedagogy also benefited from the results of acoustic research, especially to document or confirm details of playing that violinists previously executed instinctively. Helmholtz (*Die Lehre von den Tonempfindungen*) contributed significantly, discussing, for instance, the proper point of contact between bow and string.

If in bowing one comes too close to the fingerboard (the end of which lies a fifth of the string's length from the bridge), the sound will lack the fifth or sixth partial that normally is clearly heard. The resulting sound will be somewhat hollow.

Some writers, having read specialized treatises on acoustics, tried to impress their readers by including mathematical formulas that they most likely hardly understood themselves:

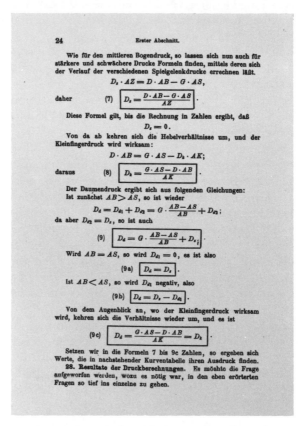

A page from Arthur Jahn's *Die Grundlagen der natürlichen Bogenführung auf der Violine* (The foundations of natural violin bowing, Leipzig 1913)

Physiological considerations have also led to a reexamination of how to teach beginners, keeping in mind anatomical conditions, especially of the left hand. Teachers gradually realized that it was best to begin with scales and exercises in G major, which had been advocated since Galeazzi and Viotti. Bériot was the first to introduce the principle in his violin tutor, though not consistently. But the tradition of beginning with C major died a slow death, especially in Germany. Opposing this, Wassmann, in his 1889 method, began with the flat keys, believing that the left hand was more firmly positioned by having the first finger close to the saddle. Violin methods by Halm (1916) and Kromp (1931) followed Wassmann's idea which, however, has the disadvantage that the open strings cannot check a player's intonation. In the major tetrachord the first and third fingers span a major third, a large stretch for children. Others recommended beginning with the third position, an experiment that found few imitators but at least shows the general concern with instruction for beginners. Most modern teachers believe that the sequence of open string–whole tone–whole tone–half tone corresponds best to the hand's anatomy. Use of the open strings also facilitates good intonation. The sequence works on all strings in the keys of G, D, and A major. Whether to teach the third position before the second position is a question on which pedagogues disagree; Hiebsch (*Methodik des Violinunterrichts*) takes the negative view.

As violin technique developed during the nineteenth century, various mechanical devices were proposed to adapt the human physique, the playing apparatus, to the instrument's requirements. Paganini's concertizing stimulated some of these experiments, for his sensational successes were rightly related to his extraordinary capacity for left-hand stretches. Schumann's misfortunes along these lines are common knowledge; induced by the forced immobilization of individual fingers, an incurable finger paralysis put an end to his career as a pianist. Mechanical devices were designed to ensure straight bowing and to keep the left wrist in the correct position. Other contrivances intended to increase stretches and to strengthen the player's fingers. One of these involved wearing lead rings; another consisted of a wrist brace claimed to improve staccato playing. Dumas invented a movable weight (5 g) to be fastened to the bow stick; he claimed it would increase the player's strength and lightness of bowing—and eliminate nervous disorders! Equally absurd was M. Tabuteau's invention (Paris 1849) of a wooden contraption for the right arm. The upper arm, elbow, wrist, and hand were tied to it, and it was to be worn at night until it no longer caused pain. It was touted to lead to Paganini's "pearllike" bow stroke—but we have no record of any violinists who succeeded that way. Commenting on the absurdity of these devices, Diestel (1912) said that all such instruments of torture were evil and likely to have the opposite effects from those desired. They could even put an end to the victim's ability to play the violin: "Violin technique does not require artificial contortions and distortions, nor the strength of an athlete. It needs free, natural motions. . . . Instead, violinists should take good general care of their bodies through physical activity."

A "factory owner and amateur violinist" in Stockholm was one of many dilettantes ready to reveal the innermost secrets of violin playing (see illustration on p. 450). Olsen extended a special invitation to foreign violinists, urging them to feel free to call on him, hear him play, and benefit from his advice.

Since 1800, violin pedagogy frequently took a wrong turn. Often the necessary unity or balance of innate musicality and physical disposition was upset. All kinds of "systems" interfered with normal instincts and urges to

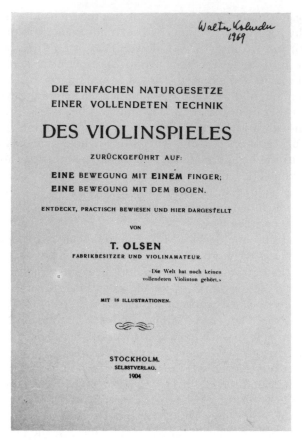

Olsen's title page, announcing "basic natural laws
leading to a perfect technique of violin playing,
based on *one* motion with *one* finger, *one* motion
of the bow"

make music. It is sad to think how many talented students were sent down a
dead-end road—losing out on years so important to their development—
before returning to the road that led ahead.

INSTRUCTIONAL WORKS

The development of nineteenth-century violin playing received stimuli from
two very different sources early on: Paganini and Beethoven. Later, violinists such as Joachim and Ysaÿe provided much inspiration to composers, as
did quartet playing by Joachim, Rosé, and others. Interest in Bach's works for
solo violin was another contributing factor, leading to Reger's early works in
that genre. Kreisler's different concepts also affected styles of playing. The

many innovations were bound to be reflected in violin teaching and indeed brought forth a flood of violin methods, etudes, and special studies. The titles that follow therefore represent only the most significant contributions, those that have stood the test of time or were at least highly influential in their own era. Again, some are included as mere curiosities. [Stowell 1985 lists instruction books from ca. 1760 to ca. 1840. *Ed.*]

1802/03	Baillot, Rode, and Kreutzer, *Méthode de violon*, Paris (facsim. rpt. Geneva 1973)
1803	Baillot, *Douze caprices* op. 2, Paris
	Fenkner, *Anweisungen zum Violinspielen*, Halle
1804	Bruni, *Méthode pour le violon composée sur l'alphabet musical de Mme Duhan*, Paris
1807	André, *Anleitung zum Violinspielen*, op. 30, Offenbach
	Bornhard, *Violin Journal* (issued in installments), Paris
1808	Lottin, *Principes élémentaires de musique et de violon*, Paris
1810	Hering, *Praktische Violinschule*, Leipzig
1810/11	Fröhlich, *Violinschule* (extracted from *Die Allgemeine Theoretische und Praktische Musikschule*), Bologna and Bonn
1811	Jousse, *The Theory and Practice of the Violin*, London
ca. 1812	Kreutzer, *Dix-neuf études ou caprices pour le violon seul*, Paris
ca. 1813	Rode, *Vingt-quatre caprices en forme d'études . . . dans les vingt-quatre tons de la gamme*, Paris
1816	Keith, *A Violin Preceptor on an Entire New Principle Calculated to Lay a Regular and Stable Foundation for Young Practitioners*, London
1818	Baillard, *Méthode de violon, adoptée pour les pages de la Musique du Roi de France*, Paris
ca. 1818	Rolla, *50 petits exercices progressifs*, Leipzig
1820	Libon, *30 caprices*, op. 15, Milan
	Paganini, *24 capricci*, op. 1, Milan
	Rode, *Douze études pour le violon avec accompagnement de piano ad libitum* op. posth., Paris
ca. 1820/22	Rovelli, Twelve caprices, opp. 3 and 5
ca. 1820	Cobham, *Harmonic System for the Violin: A Treatise in Single and Double Harmonics*, London
	Mazas, *Méthode de violon suivie d'un traité des sons harmoniques en simple et double chordes*, Paris
	Saint-Lubin, *Six caprices ou études*, op. 42, Leipzig
1822	Macdonald, *A Treatise on the Harmonic System Arising from the Vibrations of the Aliquot Divisions of Strings*, London
ca. 1825	Turbry, *Méthode de violon sympathique*, Paris
1829	Blumenthal, *Abhandlung über die Eigenthümlichkeit des Flageolets . . . auf der Violine*, Vienna
1832	Spohr, *Violinschule. In drei Abtheilungen. Mit erläuternden Kupfertafeln*, Vienna

1835	Baillot, *L'art du violon*, Paris (Engl. trans. by Louise Goldberg, Evanston, Ill., 1991)
	Barnbeck, *Theoretisch-praktische Anleitung zum Violinspiel für Dilettanten, namentlich auch Schullehrer, Seminaristen . . .*, Stuttgart
1837	Bergerre, *Méthode de violon adoptée par le Conservatoire de Paris*, Paris
pre-1840	Hamilton, *A Catechism for the Violin*, London (19th printing 1889!)
ca. 1840	Hohmann, *Praktische Violinschule*, Nuremberg
1840	Ries, *Violinschule für den Anfangs-Unterricht. Mit besonderer Berücksichtigung für den Gebrauch an Seminarien, Musikschulen etc.*, Leipzig
1842	Habeneck, *Méthode théorique et pratique*, Paris
	Loder, *For the Violin: The Whole of the Modern Art of Bowing*, London
1843	Anonymous, *The Hand-book of the Violin: Its Theory and Practice*, London
	Mazas, *75 études mélodiques et progressives*, op. 36 (vol. 1: *Études spéciales*, vol. 2: *Études brillantes*, vol. 3: *Études d'artistes*), Leipzig
pre-1844	Straub, *Kurze Anleitung zum Violinspielen für Lehrer und Lernende*, Stuttgart
	Zimmermann, *Praktische Violinschule* (46 booklets), Dresden
1846	Vieuxtemps, Six Concert Etudes, op. 16, Leipzig
ca. 1846	Alard, *Ecole du violon*, Paris
pre-1848	Dont, *24 Vorübungen zu Kreutzers und Rodes Etüden*, op. 37, Vienna
1848	Kayser, Thirty-six Etudes, op. 20, Leipzig
1849	Dont, *Etüden und Kapricen*, op. 35, Vienna
1850	Le Dhny and Blumer, *Petite encyclopédie instrumentale*, Paris
	Dont, *Theoretische und praktische Beiträge zur Ergänzung der Violinschulen und zur Erleichterung des Unterrichts* (8 parts), Wiener-Neustadt
	Léonard, *La gymnastique du violon*, Mainz
1854	Wieniawski, *L'école moderne*, op. 10, Leipzig
1855	Dancla, *Méthode élémentaire et progressive du violon*, op. 52, Paris
1856	Wälder, *Violinschule zum eigentlichen Hausgebrauch, oder zum Unterricht für Zöglinge für Stadt und Land*
1858/60	Bériot, *Méthode de violon*, op. 102 (3 vols.), Paris
	Meyer, *Schule der dritten Lage*
1859	Dancla, *Ecole du mécanisme*, op. 74, Leipzig
	Lvov, *Méthode de violon*, St. Petersburg
	Panseron, *L'art de moduler au violon* (with examples by Dancla), Paris

1863	David, *Violinschule* (part 1: *Der Anfänger*, part 2: *Der vorgerückte Schüler*), Leipzig
	Sattler, *Chor-Violinschule, zunächst für Präparanden- Anstalten*
	Wieniawski, *Études-caprices avec accompagnement d'un second violon*, op. 18, Leipzig
1864	Burg, *Das Büchlein von der Geige, oder die Grundmaterialien des Violinspiels*, Leipzig
1867	Bériot, *Ecole transcendante du violon, annexe de la méthode*, Mainz
	Kayser, *Neueste Methode des Violinspiels*, op. 32, Hamburg
1869	Meerts, *Le mécanisme de l'archet*, Mainz
1870	Ludwig Abel, *6 grosse Etüden nach Motiven aus Wagners* Der fliegende Holländer *und* Tannhäuser, Berlin
1873	Courvoisier, *Die Grundlage der Violintechnik*, Berlin
1874	Tottmann, *Führer durch den Violin-Unterricht*, Leipzig
	Wohlfahrt, *60 Etüden*, Leipzig
1875	D'Este, *The Violin in Class: Complete Graduated Guide to the Art of Playing*, London
	Mukhopadhya, *Bahoolina Tatwa, or A Treatise on Violin*, Calcutta 1281 (=1875)
	Schradieck, *Die Schule der Violintechnik*, Hamburg
1878	Courvoisier, *Die Violintechnik*, Cologne
	Jesùs de Monasterio, *20 Et. art. de Concert*, Madrid
ca. 1880	Anonymous, *The Art of Playing the Violin without a Master*, Glasgow
1880	Schröder, *Preis-Violinschule für Lehrerseminarien*, Cologne
1881	Ševčík, *Schule der Violintechnik*, op. 1 (4 vols.), Leipzig
1882	Mitchell, *How to Hold a Violin and Bow*, London
1883	Moret, *Le secret du violon, ou L'art de bien travailler*, Paris
1886	Sauret, *20 grandes études*, op. 24, Leipzig
1887	Hiebsch, *Methodik des Violinunterrichts*, Wiener-Neustadt
1888	Scholz, *Die Violintechnik in ihrem ganzen Umfang nach neuestem System dargestellt*, Hanover
1889	Sauzay, *Le violon harmonique: Ses ressources, son employ dans les écoles anciennes et modernes*, Paris
1890	Ysaÿe, *Exercices et gammes* (published 1967 by Szigeti, ed.)
1892	Kross, *Die Kunst der Bogenführung*, Leipzig
	Lippich, *Über die Wirkungsweise des Violinbogens*, Leipzig
1893	Viardot, *Neuf études-caprices*, Paris
1895	Ševčík, *Schule der Bogentechnik*, op. 2 (6 vols.), Leipzig
	Ševčík, *Lagenwechsel- und Tonleitervorstudien*, op. 8, Leipzig
1896	Sauret, *Gradus ad Parnassum du violiniste*, op. 36 (5 vols.), Leipzig
1898	Hoya, *Die Grundlagen der Violintechnik*, Leipzig (part 2, *Die Grundlagen der Technik des Violinspiels*, 1904–1905)
	Viardot, *L'archet* (twenty etudes), Paris
pre-1900	Scholz, *Das Staccatostudium*, op. 11, Leipzig

By decree, one of the principal tasks of the Paris Conservatoire's faculty was to prepare teaching materials, which were to be published by the Conservatoire's Magasin de Musique. Music education was to be made available to the people. On 13 April 1801 a committee of eleven members was appointed; it commissioned Baillot, Kreutzer, and Rode to create a violin method to be officially adopted by the Conservatoire. The three composers were to establish its basic principles and organization; Baillot served as editor.

Completed by 14 February 1802, the manuscript was thoroughly examined by the committee and approved for publication. A slightly abbreviated German edition was issued by Diabelli in Vienna, consisting of sixty-five pages. Actual music for practicing does not appear until page 26. The pedagogical text therefore seems disproportionately long, but it is highly interesting. It describes the then-current state of violin playing and teaching very well. The introduction includes the following observations:

> By nature, this instrument is destined to hold the highest rank in concerts, adapted to all flights of genius. Its character has varied according to the great masters who played it: simple and melodious in Corelli's hands, rich and harmonious, moving and graceful under Tartini's bow, lovely and sweet when played by Gaviniès, noble and fiery in Pugnani's performances, lofty and sublime in Viotti's hands. He knew how to have the instrument express strong and noble feelings, as is proper, considering how powerfully it affects the soul.

In the following pages we are introduced to what amounts to the music aesthetics of Beethoven's time, with thoughts about the concepts of genius, classic musical sentiment, and enthusiasm for philanthropy. General remarks on pedagogy precede more specific advice on violin playing.

> The violin is difficult to play, for slight lapses produce grave mistakes. Beginners therefore are urged to study the violin's mechanics thoroughly. If they practice according to the principles set forth in this violin school they will overcome all difficulties . . . and make their playing highly expressive. Before they think about expression they must dedicate themselves completely to the technical aspects of playing. Once they have mastered these, they will not have to give any further thought to them.

The work's second part deals with matters of style. It reveals a consciously historical perspective that was new ca. 1800. Excercises then take the student through all scales (up to D-sharp and A-flat minor) in the first position. A second-violin part is provided, written by Cherubini. Scale studies in double stops (including fourths) follow, moving through all positions. The work ends with three arpeggio etudes by Kreutzer that cover the entire fingerboard.

It is unlikely that the authors of this *Méthode du Conservatoire* intended to provide progressive studies that would take the beginner up to the level of a competent orchestra player—that would hardly have been possible in such a short compendium. On the other hand it includes double stop exercises in tenths in the first to third positions, and others in parallel unisons. In other words, we proceed from open-string exercises to rather challenging material, all within relatively few pages. It therefore seems that the authors intended to provide little more than a general pedagogical outline, which would also explain the lengthy text portion. Duets and etudes provide progressive materials for each level.

Bruni's violin school is interesting for several reasons. In the first part he takes issue with the French use of too many clefs, believing that the G clef on the second line is all a violinist needs. His remarks about holding the violin and bow show him to be far ahead of his time. While others continue to demand that the right arm must be pressed against the body, he advocates a "somewhat higher" position for the elbow. He also considers it important to cultivate playing near the frog, and he takes up finger extensions ("allonger les doigts"). The book, very well organized, consists of 107 pieces in the manner of etudes and includes a second-violin part. It is useful for developing technique and musicianship, including ensemble playing.

An unknown musician compiled an unusual collection of etudes by assembling solo passages from the then-popular violin concertos of Nicola Mestrino (d. 1789). These "concerto studies" did not find imitators, though there are violin schools that include individual concertos in an appendix. The idea of publishing difficult excerpts from orchestral works (and to a lesser extent from chamber music) eventually caught on.

Rode's etudes, which resemble solo compositions, in some ways correspond to Kreutzer's but deal less with basic technical matters. Bach's plan to provide material in all keys seems to have been Rode's model. Etudes in specific positions are valuable: no. 3 is to be played in the second position, the Allegretto of no. 9 in the fourth, and no. 10 in the third position. Rode's etudes, in regard to their musical content, are representative of their era, more so than Kreutzer's; nevertheless they have retained a secure place in violin teaching. They are dedicated to Prince de Chimay, a good violinist who employed a small resident orchestra.

Baillot's *L'art du violon*, Habeneck's *Méthode*, and similar publications have not enjoyed lasting success, probably because of the extensive text portions. Teachers, as a rule, don't think that they need them; pupils are not interested yet have to pay for them. Nor is the layout of Spohr's *Violin School* entirely satisfactory. No doubt it was written by an artist of stature, but like most of his great colleagues Spohr was not an experienced teacher of beginners. The work, 250 pages long, begins with exercises on the open strings and an introduction to the rudiments of music. It progresses all the way to the solo sections of Rode's seventh and Spohr's own ninth concertos. These normally require eight to twelve years of study, yet exercises nos. 13–29 already contain material that ordinarily would not be mastered in less than two to three years. Playing in the higher positions is dealt with on thirty-six pages; exercise no. 49 introduces playing tenths, without any preparation. All music examples are by Spohr, restricting the student to one musical style. The examples, however, are of more musical substance than what one finds in violin schools by many others.

Nevertheless, we should not ignore the positive aspects. Spohr's pedagogical observations are fairly concise and valuable, describing the state of violin playing during the first half of the nineteenth century. The comments on vibrato are helpful, and the chapter on embellishments and ornamentation has lost none of its significance. Etudes such as nos. 37ff (positions) are excellent; it is regrettable that they, along with the rest of the *Violin School*, are known to few students today.

Spohr wrote no other etudes. If any collections are offered for sale, the contents either are extracted from his *Violin School*, or they contain concerto excerpts published by Nadaud as *Premier (deuxième) livre d'études*.

If the overall organization of Spohr's *Violin School* is not altogether satisfactory, this may be due to its origin. For some time Spohr's main publisher had asked him for some etudes. The composer had almost completed a collection when the publisher died, whereupon Spohr offered it to Haslinger in Vienna. That publisher, however, wanted a violin school. Spohr hastily complied with the request; as a result the balance between text and music is somewhat flawed.

Most studies written by Lambert Joseph Meerts have been unjustly forgotten. His *Études rythmiques*, based on excerpts from Beethoven's chamber music arranged for two violins, represent a concept not taken up by other writers.

Violin methods serving a variety of purposes appeared ca. 1850, all the result of dissatisfaction with previously published material. In the preface to his collection Dancla gave credit to his teacher Baillot and his *L'art du violon*, which he felt needed additional material for practicing. But probably the most important method of the time is Bériot's *Méthode*, 254 pages long. It resembles Spohr's in that it covers the spectrum from exercises for beginners to the interpretation of concertos. More than others Bériot paid attention to the needs of beginners, though he too moves quickly on to the study of higher positions. His thirty years of teaching experience, referred to in the preface, is evident in many practical suggestions. For instance, Bériot provides preparatory exercises for playing octaves. They consist of scales on one string, at first played with the first finger only, then with the fourth. He devotes an entire section to the diminished fifth, a difficult interval for intonation. For playing chromatic scales he provides not only the standard fingering, derived from the diatonic scale, but also the important alternative 0 1 2 3 1 2 3 0 1 2 3, and so on, that later teachers claim to have "discovered." The subject matter taken up toward the end of part 2, with its many details, prepares the student for the kind of technique that came into use with Paganini; in fact, one can consider that portion of Bériot's *Méthode* a preparation for Paganini's Caprices.

Part 3 deals with compositional style. The examples chosen go beyond concerto excerpts; they include operatic arias (with texts!) in order to clarify matters of expression and dynamics. The headings of two sections demonstrate this: "De la prononciation de l'archet" (How the bow speaks) and "De la prosodie de l'archet." To indicate nuances of bowing Bériot employs signs similar to those introduced by Veracini more than a hundred years earlier. He also relates his discussion of glissando to singing, using the term "port-de-voix," borrowed from vocal technique. For Bériot this is one of the most important devices for obtaining a "singing" quality on the violin, but he cautions against its excessive use and gives examples of bad execution. Vibrato, he continues, must express strong emotion and must not suggest the "bleating of goats, or nervous trembling." It is appropriate only when the dramatic context requires it. He mentions violinists who in his opinion misuse vibrato. In all, Bériot's *Méthode* is a major artistic and pedagogical accomplishment, recommended to all contemporary teachers, even though as a teaching tool it did not have a long life.

Few outstanding instructional works existed in the mid-nineteenth century, but there were many that were bound to lead to mediocre, amateurish violin playing. As yet there was no solid, middle-of-the-road violin school. This may account for the worldwide success of Christian Heinrich Hohmann's contribution. He was not an outstanding performer but a solid pedagogue who knew what was needed, especially on the elementary level. In addition to his violin school he published similar works for piano and for organ, as well as a textbook on composition. All were intended to provide a solid foundation for country schoolteachers. His violin school is in five volumes, arranged methodically and progressively. From the very beginning it stresses ensemble playing, including second-violin parts that are instructive and competently written. The work, which met with spectacular success, was subjected to arrangements by Schmidt, Ambrosio, Bostelmann, Heim, Dessauer, Demuth, Wohlfahrt, and others, and was translated into many languages. An edition published by Tonger in Cologne states that 766,000 copies were in print; another edition, by Gabriel, proclaims, "Almost two million copies are used in teaching."

In German-speaking countries violin teaching not intended to lead to a professional career flourished when violin study became a required subject for grade school teachers, part of a plan to raise the level of music teaching. As early as 1793, free instrumental lessons had been offered in grade schools in Nördlingen. Quite a number of pedagogical works were published specifically for use in teacher training institutions. Reviewing one of these, Tottmann (1874) says that it was intended to bring pupils up to the level of accomplishment required by standards established by the Prussian ministry of education.

Not that this kind of group instruction was perfect. Leoš Janáček, who for some years taught violin in the teacher training institute in Brno, recalls that this kind of instruction was "sheer torture," and one of his students remembered having to supervise forty violinists "of varying degrees of unaccomplishment" as they played Pleyel duets. Nevertheless, though some of this kind of teacher training was primitive, it was the only way to provide violin teachers for even the smallest village schools. More than one great violinist later gratefully recalled that this had been his first introduction to the violin.

Vienna, with its long tradition of excellence in orchestra and chamber music playing, saw the publication of an abundance of teaching materials. In 1806–1807 the Kreutzer etudes appeared there, in two editions. *Scale Studies* by J. Hellmesberger, Sr.; Dont's opp. 39 and 60; and similar collections by Maxintsack and Adler confirm that intensive scale practice was a peculiarly Viennese characteristic. According to Hiebsch (1887), Dont's pedagogical works approached intonation and bowing exercises in a new manner. Dont also introduced new symbols to indicate sections of the bow (instead of using the terms "upper half" and the like), but these were not generally accepted.

Many volumes of etudes were published. For beginning and intermediate students, the material was preparatory to the Kreutzer etudes; other studies addressed those who had already mastered them. Contributions by the French teacher Mazas (op. 36) are noteworthy, as well as those by Kayser (Thirty-six Etudes op. 20; also opp. 31, 50, and 53, the Paganini studies). A repertory of instructional materials was thus created, one that has seen few changes since, despite the many changes in musical style that by rights should have led to new etudes.

Materials contributed by Ferdinand David amount to a self-contained course of study, the result of his extensive teaching experience at the Leipzig conservatory; these include a violin school with supplementary etudes and other publications, leading up to his *Concert Studies*, which introduces the student to the classic French concert repertory. David's *Hohe Schule des Violinspiels* (1867–1872) was also highly influential. Similar anthologies published by Wittig and Alard made a valuable repertory, particularly from the early eighteenth century, accessible to students.

Violin pedagogy took on a new dimension with the appearance, beginning in 1881, of Ševčík's works. His insights into the physiological aspects of violin playing and his concerns with analyzing the elements of playing technique led him to write very detailed, specialized studies. Ever-rising expectations of performers during the last decades of the century necessitated such works, which in turn contributed to advanced technique and thus higher violinistic accomplishments. The danger of such an approach, however, was that highly specialized exercises might cause teachers to disregard the working together of the individual components of playing. This awareness brought about a synthesis between the specialization of Ševčík's method and the concern with artistic aspects of playing. Violin pedagogy at the beginning of the twentieth century encompassed these two seemingly conflicting—but actually quite complementary—tendencies.

Excerpts from the symphonic repertory also served as instructional materials. Conscientious orchestra players had always copied out difficult passages, for home study before performances. Some players accumulated thick volumes of such excerpts, which they in turn loaned to their students, in preparation for auditions. Over time, such collections were assembled for every instrument, and it seemed logical to publish them. Although Bériot and other authors had included excerpts in their violin schools, the first to offer excerpts alone, in printed form, was Ferdinand Hüllweck (1824–1887), concertmaster in Dresden since 1844. Other compilations supplemented Hüllweck's four volumes of excerpts, such as the twenty volumes issued by Richard Hofmann in Leipzig.

Of course, the "standard" repertory continued to change, and it was necessary to update such volumes from time to time. There are now so many collections that the prospective orchestra player is assured of being thoroughly prepared. Some of the new collections deal with works of single composers, or even specific groups of works; other volumes, such as those by Ludwig Bus, include excerpts from very recent compositions. Unfortunately they are not as widely used as they should be. Too many violin teachers seem to believe that all their students are prospective young Menuhins, while students dream of nothing but a soloist's career and look down on the study of orchestra parts. By the time they fail an audition they realize, belatedly, their mistake.

OTAKAR ŠEVČÍK, OR THE PERFECT METHOD

The publication of Ševčík's studies had far-reaching consequences. All violinists who use them properly can improve their technique and solve difficult technical problems. Up to that time, few violinists could accomplish this.   CARL FLESCH, *THE ART OF VIOLIN PLAYING*, VOL. I, 1923

When Ševčík applied for admission to the Prague conservatory he failed the entrance exam three times; he was finally admitted by a special dispensation granted by the director. Perhaps the quality of other applicants at the time was unusually high, or perhaps Ševčík did indeed show lack of talent, which the jury recognized. On the other hand, juries, at all times and places, have been known to come up with faulty verdicts by failing to give consideration to the applicant's character; too often the most "showy" applicant has the best chances. In any case, at an early stage, Ševčík decided that violin playing was his destiny, and with stubborn determination he prevailed in spite of the jury's evaluation, well founded though it may have been.

Ševčík's failure did not undermine his self-confidence; rather, it made him all the more determined to show what he could do. Like Casals, he embarked on his own course of study, in addition to the prescribed curriculum. By establishing habits of very concentrated practicing he advanced as rapidly as his more gifted fellow students. Most likely he developed the basic concepts of his system while still a student, so that in a way he was his own teacher as well as a student.

Ševčík's basic pedagogical premises are quite simple and generally valid:

1)   Any accomplishment may be broken down into partial accomplishments. To develop the resources for the whole, one must isolate its

components and master them. For the violin these include trills; double stops; bowing technique; and position changes or shifting. All can be isolated to a high degree, if not entirely.

2) Any complex, difficult task, and every part thereof, is based on elementary playing functions. Any task and its components can be carried out if preceded by exercises of gradually increasing difficulty. If done systematically, the desired result will occur almost by itself, unnoticed.

3) If the ultimate result is not achieved, the partial tasks may have been poorly coordinated, or the student tried to reach the result without gradual preparation. Repetition will not correct mistakes that are due to faulty playing motions or procedures; they may become all the more firmly ingrained. Rational practicing therefore requires analysis and slow, patient mastery of the partial tasks.

Theories of this kind, of course, existed before Ševčík. His merit was to apply them consistently to violin playing and to codify and explain them, with admirable logic, in his publications. A specific example of his procedure can be found in exercise 38 from the sixth volume of his bowing studies. This exercise consists of 726 different bowings, not including the additional variants introduced by playing the bowings in the upper or lower half of the bow, or at the frog, middle, or tip. Increases in tempo are also called for, with precise metronome marks given. The basic exercise is written in whole notes, in four-part chords, followed by the variants.

In Ševčík's method all bowing exercises are to be played from memory, so that the eyes can continually control the bow's point of contact with the string. Whoever has the patience to spend several months practicing such an etude and all its variants—not only as a daily duty, but with great concentration and good sound quality—will find the results worthwhile, even students with only average talent. Ševčík supposedly said, "Any idiot who follows my system can acquire a good technique." His detractors were fond of varying this statement, which reflects a mixture of irony and justified pride: "Only an idiot can acquire a good technique following his system; a normal person couldn't stand it." But the real question is, how much? Many prescriptions are fatal if an overdose is taken; likewise in sports a thin line separates excessive, specialized training from failure. Ševčík's numerous critics, while acknowledging the merits of his system, worried about a one-sided application that neglected musical matters.

Max Strub, at one time Flesch's assistant and the leader of a well-known string quartet, occasionally spoke of Ševčík's system as a "method for fools." During the war, Strub lost all his music. One day he came to me, happy and excited because he had been invited to perform the Beethoven Concerto, and asked to borrow—several volumes of Ševčík. I asked him whether he had now joined the fools, to which he answered, laughing, "I'm not such a fool that I *don't* practice any Ševčík!"

The *Violin School* is probably Ševčík's least successful publication. It puts the beginning student, eager to play some "real" music, into a merciless practicing routine. Flesch (1957) remembers how he failed in his first attempts to teach violin by imposing excessive amounts of Ševčík on his students. To lighten things up a little, Ševčík inserted "melodies" here and there in his *School*, but they are rather dry. How strange that a compatriot of Dvořák produced such concoctions!

Ševčík's systematic approach gradually developed into an obsession, as in his preliminary studies for Tchaikovsky's Violin Concerto. A student who cannot properly execute a first-finger shift from A to C-sharp should stay away from that concerto and practice the appropriate shifting exercises as provided elsewhere by Ševčík.

It was Jan Kubelik who established Ševčík's worldwide fame as a teacher—Kubelik, who perhaps was the greatest virtuoso after Sarasate. Other famous twentieth-century violinists who were Ševčík pupils, at least for a while, were Kocián, Moodie, Morini, Ondricek, Schneiderhan, and Zimbalist. In his 1948 book about Ševčík's life and works, Viktor Nopp lists 370 of his students. Their playing was consistently clean and brilliant, though they were not necessarily the best interpreters of great music (unless they had acquired that talent elsewhere).

Ševčík's vision was limited. He did not realize that technical perfection is only part of the goal. A violinist cannot concern himself exclusively with it and turn to music only when perfection has been reached. Instead, at every stage of a player's development, technique must be meaningfully related to music. Failure to recognize this has been the downfall of many violin teachers, before and after Ševčík.

THE VIOLINIST'S PHYSICAL AND MENTAL HEALTH

TWENTIETH-CENTURY PROBLEMS

The fairly common notion, especially in the arts, that the human soul or spirit exists separately from the body, is particularly senseless in musical performance. In instrumental, and even more in vocal music, all spiritual, artistic expression is closely related to and dependent on physical matters. The opposite is also true: the physical activity involved in producing musical sounds is affected or controlled by mental, emotional impulses. It is only for clarity of presentation in the following remarks that physical and mental health are treated separately. In effect, we are viewing the same matter from two different sides.

It has long been known that only a healthy body can produce a successful and lasting vocal or instrumental achievement. Hours of daily physical exercise were part of the regime of castrato singers, including breathing exercises, horseback riding, fencing, and ball games. Although the references to this in the literature on instrumental music are few, there are early remarks that sensible finger gymnastics can render that part of the playing apparatus supple. In his 1716 harpsichord tutor Couperin advised that "those who have received a late start on the instrument, or who have been poorly taught" should do finger stretching exercises, by themselves or with the help of others.

Telemann must have known something about inflammation of the tendons, for he describes how several days before a concert he would apply ointments to his left arm. Others tried more drastic remedies. In a letter to Mendelssohn, Ferdinand David describes how on some days he "worked like a horse," playing in an orchestra for ten hours. To cure his "bad arm" he applied ten leeches, "and now things are better again."

In modern times, violin music presents ever greater technical demands, which bring on more health problems. Ambitious young players are most vulnerable. In their eagerness to excel they are likely to overtax their bodies. Flesch (*The Art of Violin Playing*, vol. 1) believed that hand injuries are likely to occur when the player views fatigue as "a weakness that must be overcome, rather than interpreting it as a warning signal from the body. Fatigue calls for letting the arm rest, if only for half a minute. Frequent or persistent muscular arm pains may be treated with heat applications or massage. One should not hesitate to consult a specialist."

Spohr also tried to anticipate physical problems. He was aware of his basically excellent health and knew how much practicing his body could take. He was fond of physical exercise, swam well, and counseled his students to exercise regularly. For his private violin students in Pisek, Ševčík prescribed carefully planned walks. When during these they noted poor circulation in their fingers, they devised a system of putting an arm in a sling, in front of the body, so that they could resume practicing immediately upon returning home.

We have little information about physical problems of violinists before the mid-nineteenth century, probably because real specialization in violin playing began only then. Almost all famous violinists before Wieniawski, Ysaÿe, and Kreisler were all-around musicians who not only played the violin but also composed. When, early in the nineteenth century, the conductor in our sense emerged—standing in front of the orchestra, wielding a baton—many great violinists also conducted. Spohr was such a musician. His generation of violinists did not encounter physical or mental health problems, thanks to the variety of their musical activities. A musician like Spohr could "recover" from one kind of strenuous work by turning to another.

What medical problems violinists from earlier periods did encounter may have been caused less by the exercise of their profession than by excessive sensitivity. Music exerted a powerful emotional fascination for them; they lived for nothing else. Later, many violinists, in their eagerness to reach the top, fell by the wayside. Not that the general level of talent was lower; rather, the ever-increasing intensity of practicing exerted more physical, mental, and emotional pressure than some players could take. Physical and mental health were unfamiliar fields, and violinists had no appropriate way to cope with these strains. Moreover, travel was strenuous, many aspects of daily life were still primitive, and people knew little about personal hygiene. All this rendered artists vulnerable to increased expectations and challenges.

It is no accident that the careers of an increasing number of violinists were interrupted, if not destroyed, by music-related illnesses. Bériot's nervous disorders most likely were induced by his wife's fatal riding accident soon after their wedding. After several years of complete apathy he was able to manage a single concert tour. Health problems forced him to retire from teaching when he was fifty; a few years later blindness and paralysis set in. At the age of fifty-three, Vieuxtemps gave up performing and soon after had to resign from his teaching position at the Brussels conservatory. A stroke had caused partial paralysis of the left side of his body. After a brilliant beginning, Ysaÿe's career floundered due to a variety of health problems (discussed by Flesch 1957).

As one reads Flesch's memoirs one notes with dismay how many crises can threaten a violinist's existence and how seldom a career develops steadily, onward and upward. This has been especially true since about 1900. Ever since Paganini our ideas of violinistic perfection have undergone drastic changes; as a result, time and intensity devoted to practicing have increased. International standards of virtuoso performance require such specialization, leaving no time for other activities that might serve as a counterbalance. An extremely versatile, multitalented violinist like Enesco would not have been unusual in the early nineteenth century; in our day he was an exception.

High-speed travel has made more closely spaced concerts possible, and the resulting pressure on performers often goes beyond what they can easily manage in terms of physical and mental strain. As far back as 1912, Kreisler played thirty-two American concerts in thirty-one days. Once, at the height of their fame, the Busch Quartet appeared twenty-seven times in one month. At the end of that time the players' nerves were so much on edge that they were unable to play a *piano* entrance with a down bow without their bows shaking; they had to begin with an up bow! Magidoff tells us that during the war, Menuhin gave some five hundred concerts for the armed forces, necessitating much travel, often under front line conditions. Obviously the nervous system of a sensitive artist might suffer.

For some time orchestra players and singers have been subjected to an additional strain: the current mania for festivals. Until the 1920s, artists vacationed during the summer, when their institution was not in session; hardly any concerts were scheduled during the summer. In the fall they returned, fully rested, to rehearsals for the new season. Auer recalled that Sarasate did not practice at all during the summer months, while Davidov, a well-known cellist and a member of Auer's quartet, put his Strad cello in the safe until rehearsals resumed in the fall. Nor did he play any other instrument during the interval.

Kreisler (quoted in Lochner 1950) was famous for his aversion to practicing:

In the eight weeks I have been in Maine, I have not once taken my violin out of the case, except to clean it. If I played too frequently, I should rub the bloom off the musical imagination. I should drag my melodies like shackles. I prefer to be always thrilled by my interpretations of great music, and so it is well for me not to be always fiddling. . . . My craftsmanship loses nothing if I stop playing for a summer; it has been too long building. The intricate human machinery of playing is governed by a kind of directing ecstasy that takes its rise in the intellect and flies to the fingers. The fingers in time come to have little intellects in their tips; let them have their vacation.

Now things are quite different; summer festivals everywhere require orchestra players and virtuosos to be in top form. [A German government publication, *Music in Germany 1996*, lists more than forty-five summer festivals in that country alone, not counting opera seasons or regular concert series, nor concerts presented by radio stations. *Ed.*] Often players return from the summer season physically and mentally tired. All this is aided and abetted by "festival freaks," for whom summer festivals are the place to be, and who snobbishly spurn whatever their hometowns have to offer during the regular season.

Constant practicing, to keep in shape through the entire year, can easily lead to health problems. In his book *Fifty Years as a Concert Violinist* (Berlin 1926) Burmester tells his own story. He retired early from a successful career as a concertmaster to have more time for study, hoping to gain instant fame by performing a series of Paganini concerts in Berlin. He describes his practicing regime thus:

On some days I practiced from six a.m. to eleven p.m. with very few interruptions. I thrived on working fourteen to fifteen hours a day for five months. . . . I added to my repertoire one of Paganini's sets of variations and five of the most difficult caprices. As to those five, I kept close track, like a bookkeeper. For instance, I wanted to play the C major Caprice in thirds as fast as others play simple scales. During those five months I practiced it 4276 times! After that, I could not merely "play" it; I tossed it off like a juggler tosses balls!

Thousands of violinists since then have tried to outdo Burmester, thinking that they could figure out just how often even a less talented violinist would have to "rattle off" such a show piece before he or she could play it at virtuoso level. An American violinist is said to have practiced twelve hours a day à la Burmester, preparing himself for *the* great recital in Paris. When his right shoulder hurt he would lie down and practice left-hand pizzicato! Unfortunately, the concert turned out to be less successful than he had hoped and he suffered a nervous breakdown. A long period of recovery in a sanitarium followed, after which he was able to hold down a chair in the first violin section of an American orchestra, all the while mourning his failed virtuoso career.

Flesch (*The Art of Violin Playing*, vol. 1) made sensible recommendations about practicing, pointing out that the amount of time spent is less important than the quality of the work. Three hours of rational, purposeful practice are adequate for most students. "Violinists who work eight-hour shifts, like a factory worker, seldom succeed."

A typical daily schedule of violinists in a major orchestra explains a good deal about health problems they are likely to encounter: leave home in the morning by car (that is to say, no exercise) for a rehearsal, back home for lunch, afternoon teaching at a music school, home again, then drive to the auditorium for an evening performance. A soloist's life is not much different, for intensive practicing may take the place of orchestra rehearsals. Year after year fingers, arms, shoulders, and wrists are taxed to the limit, interrupted at times by twenty-four hours of complete inactivity. Sooner or later such irregular demands are bound to lead to physical problems.

Remedial exercises including gymnastics have been advocated. Demeny devotes an entire chapter to correcting posture with the help of daily exercises. Reading a book, of course, will accomplish little unless it leads to a regime of appropriate exercises. We know that Stravinsky and Karajan practiced yogalike gymnastics daily. Magidoff (1955) describes how Menuhin dealt with such problems:

> As he was tucking the violin under his chin, he became aware of the familiar tension across the back, a heavy weight in his limbs, and resistance in the joints. Obeying an impulse, he put the instrument aside, lay down on the floor and began exercises in search of basic positions of body relaxation and muscle control. Breathing in and out deeply and evenly, he improvised progressively elaborate motions. This relaxed him enormously, and as he developed the habit of these exercises, he found that if he added concentration on some abstract thought, were it musical or philosophical, it greatly enhanced the effect. Years later, chancing upon a book on yoga during a sojourn in New Zealand, he discovered to his surprise that he had instinctively developed some of the methods leading toward bodily well-being and inner peace that had been devised by Indian sages thousands of years ago.

Vieuxtemps too practiced a kind of violinist's yoga. Before a concert appearance he went through concentration exercises during which, for several minutes, he executed up and down bows above the string, always at a constant distance from it, and never touching it.

Flesch deals with different crises, those encountered by most child prodigies. Their spectacular early successes are due to manual dexterity, above average musicality (though often one-sided), a certain mental makeup, and early rigorous training supervised by outstanding teachers. Particularly important is a decided ability to imitate, which usually disappears during puberty. At that point a strong, personal creative talent must evolve; if it doesn't, little will remain of the Wunderkind but a facile technique. That may be enough only for a short virtuoso career, for in the long run the public demands more, and soon the bright light of the child's comet will fade, while another, more brilliant star appears in the sky.

Franz von Vécsey at the time of his first
great successes in Berlin, 1903–1904

Menuhin faced many crises, but he coped with them all. At the age of seventeen, his career as a child prodigy at an end, he stopped performing and spent the next one and a half years broadening his general education. This is not to say that one becomes a better violinist by studying Latin, logarithms, and history, but undoubtedly a liberal education forms one's mind, if only through the intellectual rigor involved. Years of one-sided drill, to the exclusion of everything else, tragically ends the careers of many child prodigies. Once such a young player has mastered everything related to technique, he faces a veritable void. Often he is not even aware of what he lacks, for early successes have turned his head. At the age of fourteen, Szigeti, a highly trained racehorse out of Hubay's stable, had reached such a point. Thanks to his own instinct and to the guidance of thoughtful persons he made the transition from narrowly taught prodigy to well-educated, mature artist. He described this road in his book, *With Strings Attached*. Eventually the world's museums and art galleries were as familiar to him as the fingerboard of his violin.

Kato Havas at her first public appearance,
aged seven

Child prodigies as a rule know only a limited repertory, which affects their technique accordingly. Early successes on the concert stage force them to concentrate on a few compositions and master their technical requirements. Although young Menuhin earned spectacular acclaim with Lalo's *Symphonie espagnole*, when he played for Ysaÿe he had trouble with simple arpeggiated chords, and Ysaÿe lost interest in the child.

An all-around command of technique, however, is a must for all virtuosos. It must be based on the repertory, so that even when a player is not feeling well, or is undergoing some sort of crisis, a performance will not fall below an acceptable level. Flesch (1957) reported on the musical maturity a child prodigy had to acquire:

[Josef Wolfsthal] was ten years old when I took over his training. When he was sixteen, I released him and let him play a few times in public, but thought it wiser to put him into an orchestra for the time being in order to widen his musical horizon. In quick succession he sat at the first desk in Bremen, Stockholm, and Berlin, and became a teacher at the Berlin Hochschule at the early age of twenty-six, but died at thirty-one from the after-effects of influenza. He was already considered one of the finest violinists of Germany; his bowing particularly was near absolute perfection.

Strangely enough, many talented string players take a dim view of joining an orchestra, fearing that it will result in coarse and generally careless playing. But this is only a matter of personal standards and discipline. Before embarking on virtuoso careers, such great violinists as Paganini, Ysaÿe, Thibaud, Busch, Kulenkampff, and Schneiderhan spent years as concertmasters, learning much about repertory, sight reading, group discipline, and interpretation—knowledge that remained with them for life.

Menuhin clearly understood the problems inherent in the transition from child prodigy to mature musician (discussed by Magidoff in chapter 7). The transition involves the change from instinctive playing to a rational, thinking approach to musicianship. At that critical juncture a crisis is likely to occur, often between the ages of thirty and forty. Huberman (1912) described it precisely, referring to the danger of "burnout" due to the excessive performance of a limited repertory. He made it a point to add new works frequently, and he also found it imperative to rest completely after a tour that involved playing the same pieces over and over again. "After a pause of four to six weeks I would be incapable of giving a recital. To regain my full potential I would have to relearn everything. . . . That is a lot of work, but from it I gained new energy and new perspective."

For many violinists, quartet playing is a kind of self-medication, a relief from the strain of performing the same repertory and strenuous concert routine; when he turned thirty, Elman frequently played quartets. Some great violinists became alcoholics at the height of their careers, likely a symptom of some crisis they were otherwise unable to handle. Wilhelmj enjoyed a brilliant career up to the age of forty; alcohol then allegedly became his undoing. Other virtuosos at the peak of their success found satisfaction in teaching, a blessing for their mental health. Ondricek gave up concertizing at an early age, turned to teaching, and wrote about his teaching experiences.

Critics and the public have come to expect perfection on recordings, an extremely important part of a concert violinist's life, for financial and other reasons. Around the time of World War I, primitively produced recordings were viewed as curiosities, since the repertory committed to disks was often less than substantial. Pieces could last no longer than three to four minutes, and the "talking machine" companies selected little gems that were likely to sell well. In our time, however, making recordings has become serious business for violin virtuosos, often requiring months of preparation. A performer who plans to record a work from the standard repertory knows that twenty or more disks of the same work exist, and that some record buyers will be hypercritical, comparing every note with other interpretations, by violinists past, present—and future. This awareness can produce tensions that interfere with a spontaneous, personal interpretation, although there is slight comfort in knowing that blemishes can be removed, and corrections spliced in, resulting in a "perfect" version.

Recordings, radio, and television have raised the public's expectations to a level that has profoundly affected the concert artist's situation. Back in the 1920s, even a moderately accomplished violinist could give a solo recital in a small city. Not much risk was involved because there was little chance that a better performer had appeared there before. Today, in every community, there are those who have heard top-drawer virtuosos, or have seen them on television. As a result, every note a violinist plays in public is compared with the playing of the stars.

Violin playing and teaching have continually evolved since the days of Tartini and Viotti. The shifts are closely related to general and musical developments, to writing for the violin, and to social and technological changes. Demands and expectations have changed accordingly, requiring both specialization and a general musical education unheard-of in earlier times. Career-minded violinists must recognize the dangers confronting them and must take measures to ensure their physical and mental health. This applies even to their earliest lessons. It is not (and never has been) enough to simply give the assignment for the next lesson and bid the student, "Practice well." He or she must be shown how to practice rationally. Siegfried Eberhardt put it clearly and succinctly: "To practice carefully means to listen carefully."

Again, teaching and practicing cannot ignore physical and mental health. Too many promising violinists have failed due to too much or mindless practicing, or too much physical exertion, just as others have failed because of too little practicing, lack of concentration, or unhealthy lifestyles. Many orchestra players will never become concertmasters because nervousness would cause their bows to shake if they were required to play even a short solo passage. Others had to abandon their studies due to illnesses of all kinds, or had to resign from professional playing, or were never able to live up to their potential. They remind us of Max Strub's remark, exaggerated though it may seem: "A violinist who practices four hours and plays soccer for two hours will do better than the one who practices six hours." Auer, perhaps the greatest mentor of early twentieth-century violinists, recommended never to practice more than thirty to forty minutes without taking a ten- to fifteen-minute break. Daily practicing should not exceed a total of four to five hours, spread out over six to seven hours.

FRITZ KREISLER AND MODERN VIOLIN PLAYING

VIBRATO

Kreisler has been the most important figure for us violinists since Ysaÿe's decline; he has fundamentally influenced the development of our art as no other violinist of his time has done.   CARL FLESCH, *MEMOIRS*, 1957

Kreisler: remember that name! He is the teacher of us all.
JACQUES THIBAUD, TALKING TO MARC PINCHERLE, CA. 1910.

Fritz Kreisler died in New York, four days short of his eighty-seventh birthday. Even during his last years he improvised on the violin daily. His wife was not allowed to let anyone listen, but at least once she ignored his order, for which we must be thankful: in an adjoining room she recorded his improvisation on tape. If we hear this recording, not knowing who was playing or at what age, we would assume that this was one of the great violinists of our time, at the peak of his performing career, playing a beautiful, virtuosic solo composition from the romantic repertory. We hear a tone that is forceful and luminous, impeccable technique, and virile, attractive bowing. The improvisation contains a wealth of ideas; many a fine composer might wish to write that well for the violin. That tape recording is the last artistic manifestation of a violinist who (with the possible exception of Paganini) was the most distinctive phenomenon in the history of violin playing, which he influenced decisively at an important stage of its development.

Kreisler was born in Vienna in 1875, the son of a physician who had moved there from Poland. His father was an enthusiastic amateur violinist; he instructed young Fritz so well that at the age of seven the boy was accepted by Joseph Hellmesberger, Jr., as a pupil at the conservatory. When Fritz was ten years old, his father arranged for him to study with Massart in Paris; two years later he left the Conservatoire with a premier prix that he had won playing on a quarter-size Amati. As a special gift he obtained a full-size Gand et Bernardel.

The thirteen-year-old then went on a successful American tour, accompanied by Moriz Rosenthal. Thanks to his father's guidance he was able to avoid the crisis of transition from child prodigy to adult performer. In spite of tempting offers, Kreisler finished his secondary education, studied medicine, and did his military service. Flesch, a lifelong friend, has commented on Kreisler's bohemian lifestyle, but also recalled that one of his most profound violinistic experiences was to hear Kreisler play Thomé's "Adagio religioso."

Kreisler received a rude awakening from his easygoing ways when, at his father's urging, he auditioned for the court opera orchestra. He failed the audition, and the reason given was—unsteady rhythm! Much has been written about this audition. Perhaps the vacancy had already been promised to another young violinist who had the right connections—it would not have been the first time. Perhaps it was due to Kreisler's not altogether good reputation, about which his rivals may well have spread rumors. It is more likely that Kreisler's playing was somewhat undisciplined, and that by that time he had developed his very distinctive, individual manner of playing, with a very intense *espressivo* and sustained vibrato. Those who auditioned him may have worried about his fitting in with the rest of the players.

After this failure Kreisler decided to resume his virtuoso career by giving a recital in Berlin. This time he was well prepared. An 1899 performance of the Mendelssohn Concerto, accompanied by the Berlin Philharmonic under Nikisch, marked the real beginning of his career as a soloist. The concert was a decided success, but it was another ten years before critics and the public fully accepted Kreisler, though the quality of his playing changed little in the interval. As Flesch said, he was ahead of his time; the public was not yet ready for his style of playing. But what distinguished his playing was more than a matter of fashion. Changes in nineteenth-century violin playing had chiefly to do with sound volume and intensity. Steinhausen and others tried to change an outmoded manner of playing by dealing with its physiological aspects. In Kreisler's case, the change was effected by an urge to find a new kind of expression. In a way, he could be called one of the "fauves" of violin playing, a term that in composition might apply to Reger. At first his expressive style shocked rather than fascinated the public, but with some modifications, it has become *the* accepted way of playing the violin. Its chief characteristic was a continuous vibrato, even during passage work.

Contrary to the belief of some early music disciples, players of string instruments have used vibrato for a long time, even before violin playing as such existed. It was an important expressive device, one of the ways to embellish a sustained tone, as were trill and mordent. In the eighteenth century, vibrato was used similarly to the *Bebung* on the clavichord; employed sparingly, it must have been all the more effective. On the violin, applied only to important notes, it was produced with the finger only. Leopold Mozart described it clearly, saying that it was slow and of small amplitude in soft passages, and somewhat faster for a loud tone. He disapproved of excessive vibrato: "There are players who tremble on every note, as though they were plagued by a perpetual fever." As late as 1889 Sauzay used the term "vibrato épileptique," and in a 1904 letter to Franz von Vécsey, Joachim warned against "excessive vibrato and slow finger-wiggling during a cantilena; it is actually a finger weakness that reminds us of old women wailing."

It is not true that before 1900 all vibrato was finger vibrato. In his *Violin School* Spohr specifically mentions hand vibrato and gives his opinions about it. Bériot may have based his ideas about vibrato on the singing of his famous wife, Maria Malibran. A more intense vibrato coming from the wrist, characteristic of the Belgian school, may have been introduced by Bériot; it became one of Ysaÿe's characteristics. Sauret, a Bériot student whose successes date from the 1870s, also cultivated a very intense vibrato that distinguished him from other violinists of his day, while Sarasate used a rather wide vibrato. Massart is said to have taught a kind of constant vibrato to his students at the Paris Conservatoire, as had Marsick. Massart in turn was the teacher of Ysaÿe's teacher, Wieniawski. The young Kreisler may have learned it from Massart.

Detailed proof that seemingly new expressive devices were developed and passed on from generation to generation is hard to come by. In July 1799 the Hamburg correspondent of the *Allgemeine Musikalische Zeitung* reported that Viotti, according to his friends, "was an outstanding player, except for his strong *tremulando*." In the same year, "viprato" was mentioned as a special characteristic of the playing of Johann Georg Schetky, a cello virtuoso.

At any rate, continuous vibrato must have been widespread during the late nineteenth century. But Kreisler's extremely intense vibrato, which shocked so many, must have been more than something he was taught. Nor was he the only one to play with such intense expression. Thibaud's rise as a soloist took place at about the same time; his playing showed similar characteristics. Auer's playing reflected the older tradition. He admitted that he found it difficult to restrain his young charges from using too much vibrato for expressive purposes. Continuous vibrato found its way even into twentieth-century quartet playing, so that "non vibrato" playing became a novel and admired effect. Bartók specifically marked it in his scores, and in *La technique supérieure de l'archet* (Paris 1916), Lucien Capet introduced the ∽ sign to indicate "no vibrato." Sustained vibrato was characteristic of Furtwängler's orchestral sound and became part of modern orchestra timbre in general. Some conductors call for especially strong vibrato with a shaking motion of their left hand.

Once vibrato became a permanent feature in violin playing, teachers had to concern themselves with it. At first it was believed that, like staccato, a good vibrato was something that could not be taught. Nevertheless, teachers were faced with the challenge of correcting a poor vibrato. According to Flesch, Thomson was the first to try to do this with gymnastic exercises. A really well-executed, continuous vibrato is rare, even among concert violinists. Changing fingers tends to inhibit vibrato: the vibrating finger stops, and the next finger is placed without vibrating immediately, resulting in an unintended interruption. Kreisler succeeded in developing a consistently pulsing, living sound that others, for lack of adequate training, could only imitate poorly.

Much of what young Kreisler accomplished affected the violin playing of his era, including quartet and orchestra playing. His fine reputation, firmly established ca. 1910, was lifelong, even though there were other brilliant violinists whose technique perhaps was more reliable and whose training had been more thorough. Aside from the vibrato, his playing was characterized by a great economy in bowing, which nevertheless produced an intense sound. Kreisler claimed that economic bowing was necessary for him because of a short right arm. Above all, he charmed his audiences with his warm, radiant personality—spontaneous, sincere, and not only displayed on the concert platform. Many have attested to his generosity, demonstrated by his many benefit concerts especially after World War I when, from the United States, he was able to contribute substantial amounts to relieve suffering in Europe. Similar largesse continued after World War II, often anonymously, and revealed only after his death. He once was told that there was no point in sending CARE packages to Europe since the contents often were stolen en route. He replied, "Well, thieves also have children they must feed."

A section on Kreisler would be incomplete without mention of his compositions. As a boy he had studied harmony under Bruckner at the Vienna conservatory, but Kreisler's works do not reflect that teaching. Beginning ca. 1900 he occasionally performed a C major violin concerto by Vivaldi, a pleasant enough work that seemed a little suspicious to some listeners, including Marc Pincherle, a French musicologist who was anxious to see the original. His requests to Kreisler went unanswered, however, and library research turned up nothing. Gradually it became clear that not only this concerto but quite a few other pieces by "old masters," such as the *Preludium and Fugue* by

Pugnani-Kreisler, were not arrangements but composed in their entirety by Kreisler. For several decades he had been able to pull the wool over the eyes (and ears) of public and critics alike, but in the spring of 1935 Kreisler admitted to his fakes. Inevitably, the public's esteem of Pugnani declined, and Kreisler's publisher, somewhat bashfully, henceforth printed these works as "classical manuscripts." The eighteen pieces, published by Schott, sold seventy thousand copies within six months!

As the composer of sentimental Viennese songs, tinted with a dash of melancholy, the great violinist was in his element—no need to add any "baroque" flavor there. Pieces such as *Liebesfreud* and *Liebesleid* reached tremendous popularity between the two world wars, encouraging the great interpreter of classical violin concertos to make further excursions, this time into the world of sentimental operetta (*Apple Blossoms*, 1919; *Sissy*, 1932). By then Kreisler lived in the United States, and compositions of this kind may have expressed nostalgia for his native Austria. But his excellent cadenzas for violin concertos by Mozart (K. 216, 218, 219, 268), Beethoven, and Brahms show another side of his talent. Kreisler died in New York on 29 January 1962.

FINGERING

Joseph Hellmesberger, Sr., a violinist-philosopher with a sense of humor, supposedly distinguished between three kinds of fingerings: practical fingerings, artistic fingerings, and fingerings you use when the chips are down. A well-known French violinist remarked that Hellmesberger had omitted a fourth variety: fingerings taught at the conservatory. "Outside of the studio they become unplayable, and even the professor can't always bring them off!"

These remarks sum up well the problems with fingerings; actually, they apply to all instruments. Most violinists have gone through these stages: at first one forges ahead without thinking much about fingerings, avoiding the "uncomfortable" ones (those calling for the second, fourth, and sixth positions) and using only the "practical" ones, not yet knowing anything about others that may have artistic merit. But once the violinist is familiar with these and has practiced scales and arpeggios on one string (à la Ševčík and Flesch), a certain mastery of the fingerboard is acquired. From then on the violinist uses only the most complicated fingerings, playing in the first position only when absolutely necessary. During a performance, however, the ingenious fingering so cleverly worked out at home turns out, dismayingly, to be useless and unreliable. At that point, though it defies the rules, the player reverts to Hellmesberger's third category.

Complicated fingerings may also let the violinist down when sight reading in the orchestra, or when performing with only a few rehearsals—sure-fire fingerings are needed there. To survive in a professional orchestra one gradually returns to simple fingerings; the first position is newly appreciated!

The danger lies with violin teachers who have lost contact with the realities of public performance. They develop pedagogical systems and teach bowings and fingerings that they no longer have to test themselves on the concert stage. They come up with "conservatory" bowings and fingerings that only work in the studio, where even a weak player produces a large tone and never runs out of bow. So bowings are marked accordingly, but once onstage nothing seems to work. A large audience—their clothes, their bodies—absorbs half of that big tone, and the player resorts to "platform bowings" that are much shorter than those that sounded so beautiful at home.

One of the main fingering problems arises from the violin's being tuned in fifths which, coupled with the instrument's measurements, suggests diatonic fingering, whereas lute, guitar, and gamba call for chromatic fingering. As a result, violinists associate each note of the diatonic scale with a certain finger, including the raised or lowered form of that note. On the D string they will use the same third finger to play G, G-sharp, and G-flat. Even beginners find it easy to play E-flat, F, G, and A-flat on the D string with the first, second, third, and fourth fingers. But if these notes are written enharmonically as D-sharp, E-sharp, F-double-sharp, and G-sharp, a player may find it very difficult to sight read the passage and finger it properly. Though the fingers are in the same places, the violinist will play the first passage in the first position but the second one in the half position. He must be able to disassociate his playing from the "basic" fingering. During the first years of study it may be necessary to establish a quick, automatic association between basic tone and basic finger (e.g., G = third finger), but one must eventually get away from too rigid an association. A double stop such as E–B-flat already requires this, E being played with the second finger, so that one really plays in two positions. The two fingers are close to each other, which avoids a stretch. On the other hand, when playing E-flat–G-sharp, one will instinctively use the "basic" fingering 1–3, which results in a stretch larger than the major third that is likely to result in a tightening of the hand. One of the purposes of using sensible fingerings is to avoid these tensions.

A good example occurs in Kreutzer's Etude no. 7 (8, according to the new numbering; see first example opposite). Here, the fourth-finger marking goes back to Kreutzer himself, found in the second edition revised by the composer. (A digression: once during an exam at the conservatory I noticed that the student played the augmented sixth with the 2–3 fingering. Predictably, the A-sharp turned out to be too low. I asked the student to show me the music, to see which edition he was using. Actually, the teacher had crossed out the 4 and replaced it with a 3. Once more, progress had been stymied!) One might well sort out different editions of the Kreutzer etudes according to whether they called for a 4 or 3 in this place. A third group would consist of editions without any fingerings. Editors of violin music seem to be fond of printing fingerings in the most obvious places but remain silent when the player needs help the most.

The idea of putting fingers closely together—playing, in other words, in two positions at the same time, as in the example just cited—seems to have

been one of Paganini's basic principles. Fétis (*Revue musicale* of 1831) refers to it: "His fingerings in no way resemble those taught in conservatories. One finger often plays what rightfully belongs to another, and more often still, he uses the same finger for different notes." Nicely put—in the Kreutzer example the fourth finger plays the A-sharp that "rightfully" belongs to the third. In his *Grundlagen des violinistischen Fingersatzes. Paganinis Lehre* (Basics of violin fingering according to Paganini, Berlin 1920), Jarosy states that Paganini's fingerings may have been based on guitar playing and speaks of "natural" fingerings: "The four fingers will fall on the fingerboard easily . . . as soon as we stop requiring muscular stretches." On the A string in half position this would be B-flat–C–D-flat–D; in the first position B–C-sharp–D–E-flat. Starting from this premise, Jarosy investigated the fingerings in Ševčík's school of violin technique and suggested improvements:

This makes sense, but to apply such ideas too consistently becomes dangerous, as usual. The fingering in the next example will stop some violinists in their tracks because it implies that C is played in the "zero" position. Jarosy is right as far as logic is concerned, for such a fingering would be accepted without hesitation if moved up a half step: A–C-sharp–E–G. But scales and arpeggiated chords must work well more or less automatically, that is, based on practical and well-established considerations.

Jarosy recommends the following for an A major scale in the first movement of Tchaikovsky's Violin Concerto:

A person who plays scales that way—so different from standard fingering—may one day find it difficult to play *anything*—to make music on the violin. A well-known Russian violinist who taught in Germany during the 1920s supposedly used overly complex fingerings, which caused him such mental blocks that he had to cancel concert engagements. For the same A major scale, in his *Violin Fingering* (ex. 16), the practical musician Flesch recommends that because of the fast tempo, open strings should be used. Apparently he thought it obvious that the normal 1–2–3 fingering applies. Jarosy shows where an overly rigid application of basically good concepts can lead. The only good fingering is what will work on the concert platform, in chamber music, and in the orchestra. It is interesting to recall the advice Auer (1921) gave: use fingerings that will put the first finger *on* the beat. But even this kind of advice cannot be a rigidly applied, or a violinist would have to have three different fingerings for every scale, depending on whether it is played as eighth-note triplets, sixteenths, or sixteenth-note quintuplets.

Stretching and reaching (the fingering principles opposite to contracting) allow one to play in two or even three positions at the same time. Not all hands are physically capable of such extensions, which came into general use when playing the violin and composing for it became separate activities, that is, when composers were no longer guided in their writing for the violin by traditional finger patterns. Extending the fourth finger probably is as old as violin playing itself, and Vivaldi's original fingerings call for some remarkable extensions and reaches.

Nineteenth-century fingerings show that changing positions with a glissando was either an aesthetic expression or simply a way to go from one position to another. Listeners often did not know which of the two functions was intended. Modern violin playing has largely eliminated glissando in the second capacity; instead we establish the finger that serves as support in the new position without an audible change. Stretches and extensions can accomplish this, thereby avoiding a type of slide that no longer sounds pleasing to us. Concerning the following passage from the first movement of Beethoven's Violin Sonata op. 30, no. 3, Szigeti (1965) recommends avoiding Joachim's fingering (above the notes) in favor of the lower one.

Kulenkampff (1952) has pointed out the limits to extensions and stretches. "The degree of a stretch between two neighboring fingers is governed by the hand's anatomy. Stretches must not exceed what can be done with elasticity. One must not reach the very limit of what is possible as it would cause cramping and stiffening, whereas any stretch must be pliable."

Other ways to avoid undesirable slides when shifting are to accomplish the change of position outside of a legato phrase, or after a staccato note, or on a half-step progression. Sol Babitz, perhaps more than anyone else, explored the possibilities in his interesting study, *Principles of Extensions in Violin Fingering* (Philadelphia 1947). One passage he analyzed occurs in the first movement of the Beethoven Concerto (see next example). Flesch at one time saw fingering I as the only possibility, due to the inevitable shifting.

Not satisfied with this solution, he came up with two others, II and III, the latter printed in his book on violin fingering (his example 492). Babitz then supplied yet another solution (IV).

Babitz believed that all slides could be avoided by using extensions, so that "for the first time in the history of music absolute clarity [is possible], which is necessary for the playing of such transcendental music." We are still waiting for that great moment in the history of music—it is unlikely Babitz's fingering has ever been used successfully on the concert stage. Continually altering between contractions, reaches, and extensions, at a fast tempo and with fingers close to each other, the hand is likely to lose any feeling of security, of being anchored, and may stray far from D major.

In his highly instructive book on the Beethoven violin sonatas, Szigeti (1965), referring to the first movement of op. 30, no. 2, gives fingerings by Joachim and Kreisler, then provides one of his own, but cautions, "[It is] for my personal use . . . I hesitate to advocate [it] because of the contraction fingering at the crucial junction."

The chief objective of any fingering is good intonation, as Yampolski (1967) pointed out:

> The purity of the violinist's intonation depends to a certain extent on his choice of fingering. A bad fingering is often the reason for uncertain and inexact intonation, even in technically easy passages. This is the result of the awkward movements of the hand and fingers which are required by such fingerings.

He then compared two fingerings for a passage from the Beethoven Violin Concerto (see example below). He considered fingering A too risky for good intonation because no finger served as an anchor. In B, however, the first finger is well established on D''' and remains in place throughout the entire difficult measure. There are, to be sure, situations where no "good" fingering is possible, where one simply must weigh the advantages and disadvantages of two possible fingerings. As Strub put it, there are passages where the best one can do is to "use a bad fingering, but play well."

"Safety first" might be the main consideration. Just what fingering *is* safe depends on both the player's self-confidence on the concert platform and individual physical characteristics; for instance, having a very short fourth finger may mean that a player would not be able to carry off a fingering that would be good for others. Players must ultimately make their own decisions. Fingerings in printed editions or other sources can be no more than recommendations.

In some situations, a specific expressive effect may be impossible to achieve except with a fingering that differs from the usual, comfortable one. The following passage from a Beethoven sonata is so "easy" that most amateur players would sight read it using fingering A. Szigeti (1965) opted for the more difficult solution B, however, and gave his reasons:

> In the earthly folk-dance Finale of the Eighth Sonata [op. 30, no. 3] . . . playing it on two strings in the third and later in the fourth position will—I think—not only match the pianist's passage better, but bring out the appoggiatura dissonance latent in this folksy dance.

The introduction of continuous vibrato has supplanted an earlier principle of fingering, which was to keep fingers in place as much as possible. Twentieth-century pedagogy recommends otherwise, to facilitate vibrato. Even different concepts of tuning have affected fingering. Karl Courvoisier (*Die Violintechnik*, Cologne 1878) believed in pure intonation, but in practice advocated three different kinds: one when playing with piano, another with winds, and a third kind of intonation when playing with other strings. In the third case he urged that open strings be avoided as much as possible.

Fingerings tend to change as our ideas of taste and interpretation change, which means that new editions of music, with new fingerings, will become necessary from time to time. To appreciate how tastes have changed one need only look at the Beethoven fingerings advocated in 1889 by Eugène Sauzay in *Le violon harmonique* (see example below). Sauzay was no rank amateur but a pupil of Baillot, a violist in his quartet, and for many years a professor at the Paris Conservatoire.

One could cite many similar examples from that period. Flesch (*The Art of Violin Playing*, vol. 2) pointed out that Lalo, in his own edition of his *Symphonie espagnole*, carefully avoided the second and fourth positions. Lalo was a Habeneck pupil and a good quartet player, so it is doubtful that he used such primitive fingerings himself.

VIOLIN MUSIC SINCE 1900

A number of contrasting factors have affected developments in violin music since 1900. Traditions of the classic-romantic era continued to be observed; classicism was seen chiefly in formal aspects, while highly chromatic writing echoed nineteenth-century romanticism. The method developed and practiced by Arnold Schoenberg and members of his school—composing with twelve tones related only to each other—amounted to a drastic departure from traditional views of harmony. The concept of a row, or series, of tones, of "serial music," was then applied to other musical elements, especially rhythm, dynamics, and timbre. Other factors that substantially affected early twentieth-century developments came from folk music, especially from eastern Europe, which was based on rhythms and scales quite apart from the Western major-minor tradition. A renewed interest in older music manifested itself late in the century, evident in the cultivation of forms from the baroque and earlier periods. Finally, the advent of electronic music had a bearing on traditional instruments; their acoustically generated sounds were at times combined with those of electronic music.

For string players, the introduction of microtone music (using intervals smaller than the half-tone) had important consequences, for only string instruments can produce sounds such as quarter- or sixth-tones. As the father of quarter-tone music, Alois Hába achieved a modicum of fame, but microtone music itself eventually lost its significance because electronic music could produce any and all sounds synthetically.

Microtone music was an evolutionary development. Since most Western music had moved from diatonic to chromatic scales, it was thought that further developments must lead to even smaller intervals. In his investigations Busoni (1907) specifically referred to experimentation on the violin.

> The interval of a third-tone has been knocking on our door for some time, wanting to be admitted, but we continue to ignore it. I have experimented with it in a modest way, vocally and on the violin, trying to divide the whole tone into three equal distances, training fingers and ears to recognize them. Those who have made similar experiments will have found that third-tones are entirely autonomous intervals, with a character of their own, and certainly not to be confused with out-of-tune half steps.

Busoni later investigated a sixth-tone system and the dynamophone or telharmonium, which could produce electronically generated tones of any desired frequency of vibration; it was invented by the American Thaddeus Cahill.

Before long, traditional instruments were no longer widely used for explorations in microtone music. Only low-pitch string instruments can successfully play quarter-tones; on the violin, especially in high positions, fingers of normal thickness cannot produce them, and even for the lower positions a regular system of fingering cannot be established. In the traditional diatonic-chromatic musical environment, quarter-tones simply sound out-of-tune. That is how listeners usually experience the quarter-tones that occur in Hába's and Bartók's music; one does not have the impression of hearing music in a new tonal system, as can happen in purely electronic music.

Hába used quarter-tones in his second and third string quartets (1920, 1922), and sixth-tones in the fifth and tenth quartets (1923, 1953). He made the following comments in the preface to his second quartet:

> My interest in quarter-tone music goes back a long time. Ideas that could not be written down in the traditional system caused me to experiment again and again, both with instruments and notation. This quartet is the fruit of my having come to feel completely at home in a new language. My aim was to expand the conventional half-tone system with more subtle tone differences—not to endanger that system. I thought of the quarter-tone system not as a new language but as a further development of the old one. The traditional accidentals continue to be valid. The new ones are ♭ (raise the note by a quarter-tone) and ♩ (lower it by a quarter-tone).

An important tendency in violin music since 1900 has been the emphasis on linear, rather than chordal or harmonic texture, which went hand in hand with renewed interest in baroque music, both for concert performance and in the home. Reger's compositions reflect this particularly well. Polyphonic writing reappeared in the same forms and genres that had employed it in earlier times. Linear writing, of course, is idiomatic for melody instruments such as the violin. Nineteenth-century composers employed the violin chiefly as an ensemble instrument—*with* orchestra, *with* piano, in the string quartet. What little unaccompanied violin music was written was hardly ever heard in the concert hall. Beginning with Reger's op. 42, interest among composers in writing for unaccompanied violin and for two melody instruments was renewed. During the nineteenth century duets were rarely written except as teaching materials. It is indicative of the change that composers of Ravel's and Bartók's stature wrote duos for string instruments.

The following survey begins with these categories, for they also influenced the style and structure of violin sonatas with piano, of string quartets, and concertos for violin and orchestra.

WORKS FOR UNACCOMPANIED VIOLIN

| 1901 | Jongen, Sonata op. 22 |
| 1905 | Reger, Seven Sonatas op. 91 |

1907	Sauret, Suite in G minor, op. 68
1909/12	Reger, Seven Preludes and Fugues, Chaconne, op. 117
1911	Kreisler, Recitativo and Scherzo-Caprice, op. 6
1912	Karg-Elert, Sonata in E minor op. 88
	Karg-Elert, Partita no. 1 in D major, op. 89
1913	Jarnach, Sonata no. 1 in A minor, op. 8 (second version 1924)
1914	Reger, Six Preludes and Fugues, op. 131a
1919	Schnabel, Sonata or Five Pieces in the form of a suite
1921	Erdmann, Sonata op. 12
	Hopkins, Partita in G minor
1921/22	Courvoisier, Six Suites op. 31
1922	Hába, Fantasy in the quarter-tone system, op. 9a
	Hába, Music in the quarter-tone system, op. 9b
	Jarnach, Sonata no. 2 in D minor, op. 13
	Kahn, Sonata op. 2, no. 1
1923	Frenkel, Sonata in D op. 1
	Kadosa, Sonatina op. 2a
	Kempff, Sonata in C-sharp minor, op. 13
1923/24	Ysaÿe, Six Sonatas op. 27
1924	Hindemith, Two Sonatas op. 31
	Wellesz, Sonata op. 36
1924/25	Křenek, Sonata op. 33
1925	Ruyneman, Sonata
	Skalkottas, Sonata
1928	Ysaÿe, Ten Preludes "sur les intervalles"
1930	Koppel, Theme and Variations, op. 8
1931	Kadosa, Suite op. 16a
	Pijper, Sonata
1932	Brustad, Eventyr Suite
1933	Kletzki, Sonata in A minor, op. 26
1935	von Borck, Preludium in E, op. 11/2
1937	Jolivet, Incantation for violin (or flute) solo
1939	Knab, Twenty-four Variations on a folk song
1940	Badings, Sonata no. 1 for violin solo
	Honegger, Sonata
	Shostakovich, Three Pieces for violin solo
1941	Křička, Partita, op. 48b
	Mulder, Sonata "in modo classico"
1942	Bentzon, Suite op. 18
1943	Dresden, Sonata
1944	Bartók, Sonata
	Hovhaness, Chahagir for violin solo
1947	Prokofiev, Sonata in D major op. 115
1948	Arma, Sonata
	Křenek, Sonata
1949	David, Partita, op. 37, 1, *Es steht ein Lind in jenem Tal*

1950	Klebe, First Sonata op. 8
1951	Badings, Sonata no. 3
	Blacher, Sonata op. 40
	Hamilton, Variations op. 11
	Zimmermann, Sonata
1952	Ben-Haim, Sonata in G
	Müller-Zürich, Sonata op. 52
	Stam, Sonata and Partita
1953	Cage, *59½ Seconds for a String Player*
	Heiss, Twelve Inventions
	Nielsen, Prelude and Theme with Variations op. 48
1955	W. Bloch, Sonata
	Hába, Suite in the sixth-tone system, op. 85a (published 1981)
	Klebe, Sonata no. 2, op. 20
1957	Jelinek, Sonata op. 27
1958	Bacewicz, Sonata
	E. Bloch, Two Suites
1960	Logothetis, Agglomeration (with or without string orchestra)
	Shifrin, Concert Piece
1961	Antoniou, Sonata op. 13
	Halffter, Sonata op. 20
	Heider, Inventio I
1961/62	Baur, Sonata
1962	Finkbeiner, Sonata
1963	Bennett, Sonata no. 2
	Blacher, Perpetuum mobile
	Bussotti, Sensitivo no. 7 (from *Sette Fogli*)
	David, Sonata no. 2, op. 58/1
	Toch, Impromptu op. 90a
1965	Diamond, Sonata
	Grosskopf, Sonata no. 2
	Jolivet, *Suite rhapsodique*
1967	Lees, Invenzione
	Perle, Solo Partita (three movements for solo violin, two for solo viola)
1976	Khachaturian, Sonata-Monologue
1977	von Einem, Sonata op. 47
	Henze, Sonata (rev. ed. 1994)
	Steuermann, Dialogues

With his op. 42 Reger revived and gave new credibility to works for unaccompanied violin. He wrote about these works to a critic (4 July 1900):

You may think that I give no thought to what I am composing, but you are wrong. I am quite clear about my artistic goals. . . . When I point out to you that I have had all kinds of letters from violinists about my solo sonatas, what I quoted were not my own opinions but those of excellent performers, and not those of personal friends.

The enthusiastic reception of the four op. 42 sonatas inspired Reger to compose seven additional ones and two series of preludes and fugues. These presented real technical challenges, combining Bach-style polyphony with modern chromaticism. Reger's various dedications are expressions of his appreciation for the encouragement and inspiration he had received. The works are dedicated to, among others, Burmester, Busch, Eldering, Halir, Havemann, Heerman, Hess, Marteau, Moodie, Schnirlin, and Wendling— all among the leading violinists of the time.

Others soon took up Reger's lead in writing for unaccompanied violin. As time went on, these composers could be seen as representing three distinct orientations. First there were those who were primarily violinists and who, inspired by playing Bach, preserved elements of baroque style in their own etudes, caprices, sonatas, and concertos, at the same time introducing their own style characteristics. Since Bach's solo works show off the violin to such good advantage, it was natural for these composers to try their hands at that idiom. Outstanding among them was Émile Sauret who, as a teacher in Berlin, was close to developments in Germany. The Suite op. 68 is one of his best works. Ysaÿe's six solo sonatas also belong here, written after he had retired from performing in public. Their style is close to Reger's, and they are dedicated to his colleagues Szigeti, Thibaud, Enesco, Kreisler, Crickboom, and Quiroga. Szigeti (1947) said of them, "[They] probably are more important as a violinistic testament than as a creative effort that can stand critical evaluation in cold blood. What gives them significance is that they are a repository of the ingredients of the playing style of this incomparable interpreter."

Then there were the lesser composers, who guided by sincere enthusiasm for Bach's solo works tended to copy his style, resulting in a diluted neobaroque idiom. Sigfrid Karg-Elert, at one time a highly regarded composer, belongs to this group. His Partita consists of the typical baroque movements: Overture, Sarabande, Ritornello, Air, Alla Giga; the models are more in evidence than any individual, modern language.

Finally, there were the major composers who, in spite of Reger's examples, were slow to turn to unaccompanied violin writing. Thus Bartók's Sonata, perhaps the most significant work for solo violin after 1900, was not written until 1943–1944, commissioned by Menuhin. To be sure, Bach's influence can also be noticed in works by this third group of composers, but they possessed enough personality and individuality to create works of distinction. They may also have been reluctant to invite a comparison of their own creativity with Bach. At any rate, the medium offered rather limited possibilities for performance. They feared that a synthesis of Bach and a highly chromatic twentieth-century idiom might result in works that were unplayable or, at best, would be accessible only to a small number of world-class violinists (Flesch, *The Art of Violin Playing*, vol. 2). Then even virtuosos might not perform them, just as Paganini never played *Harold in Italy*, or Kreutzer "his" sonata!

Bartók's Sonata is a borderline case in that regard. When he sent the score to Menuhin, he accompanied it with a letter in which he wondered whether certain passages were unplayable, and he asked for suggestions. Menuhin studied the piece thoroughly. As Magidoff (1955) relates,

> The two met shortly before the first performance, on 26 November 1944, to discuss its final form. . . . Menuhin gave the sonata a magnificent first performance, but the critics, while applauding the violinist, reacted negatively to the composition.

Although twentieth-century composers must have recognized the problems inherent in the solo-sonata idiom, quite a few such works were written during and after the 1920s. This may in part be attributed to the trend toward polyphony, represented by Kurth (1917). From 1900 to 1927, no less than fifty-four sonatas, suites, and concert pieces for unaccompanied violin were published, fourteen of these between 1920 and 1922, and eleven in 1924 alone (Flesch, *The Art of Violin Playing*, vol. 2). The first after Reger (and independently of him) to write a sonata for unaccompanied violin was the Belgian Joseph Jongen (1873–1953) who, in his hometown of Liège, received much inspiration regarding technically demanding violin music. Probably at the suggestion of his duo partner Flesch, Artur Schnabel (1882–1951) began writing for solo violin immediately after World War I. Flesch (1957) recalled the 1919 Sonata thus:

> It is an interesting monstrosity, which takes nearly an hour to play, and offers a sample card of all the contradictions of the composer's personality. Its accumulation of minor seconds, augmented sevenths, and diminished tenths produced such an irritating effect on my nerves that in the middle of studying it I had a nervous breakdown, which manifested itself, above all, in acute insomnia and drove me away from my summer holiday. The first performance took place in my home before an invited audience. The effect was crushing.

An indication of the new interest in the medium is the fact that Stefan Frenkel (b. 1902 in Warsaw) published a solo sonata as his very first work. Interestingly enough, Křenek's solo sonata appeared almost simultaneously with his great operatic success, *Jonny spielt auf.*

Paul Hindemith (1895–1963) turned to writing for solo string instruments ca. 1923. His closeness to the Reger tradition is a matter of record: he made his own copy of Reger's G minor Chaconne, dated 6 September 1916. A group of Hindemith's works that began with sonatas for viola solo and cello solo includes the two sonatas for unaccompanied violin, op. 31, nos. 1 and 2. Hindemith's and Křenek's interest in solo composition is representative of their generation. These works do not represent pseudo-solo writing in which a heavy chordal texture simulates an effect of two or more instruments being heard. They are true one-voice compositions with only occasional hints at polyphony. Both major and minor composers of this persuasion turned away from the sound of late romanticism and impressionism to the "new classicism" championed by Busoni, with its clear, linear style. The two solo sonatas by Philipp Jarnach (1892–1982) are representative, steering clear of any imitation of baroque style.

Composers down to our own time have continued to create works for unaccompanied violin, a composer's most difficult task. This is remarkable, for such works are not standard recital fare. A violinist who performs Bach's six sonatas and partitas in two recitals can be reasonably sure of a good-sized audience everywhere, but to include a single contemporary solo sonata still amounts to a great risk, for which reason it is rarely done. Nor are many violinists likely to purchase such a piece—another disincentive for writing one. Nevertheless composers continue to write idiomatically for unaccompanied violin, rising to the challenges inherent in the medium.

Notation presents an additional challenge in avant garde compositions written since 1950. Improvisation often plays an important part in these, so traditional notation is inadequate. In *59½ Seconds for a String Player*, composer John Cage indicated that the piece may be played by itself, or in combination (simultaneously or successively) with other pieces yet to be composed. The illustration on p. 486 is a reproduction of the last page. Its notation is a kind of tablature, in principle similar to those used in the early seventeenth century. The figure 84 on top of the page is the metronome or speed indication; the horizontal distance of 2 cm represents the time interval indicated by the metronome marking. Below it are signs for vibrato, followed by others referring to bowing: W (wood, i.e., stick of the bow); H (hair). The next line defines the bow's point of contact with the string: B (bridge), N (normal), F (fingerboard), BN (nearer B than N), and so forth.

Bow pressure is indicated in the first space between lines. The upper line refers to lightest pressure, the lower one, strongest pressure. Lines 4, 6, 8, and 10 refer to the E, A, D, and G strings respectively. The space above each of these shows the upper limit (high), the space below, the lower limit. The distance of a half tone is 1 mm. "Sounds other than those indicated above (such as knocking on the violin's body)" are notated in the space between the lowest two lines. Further symbols are as follows:

- . = pizzicato
- ⁺. = vertical pizzicato, so that the string rebounds against the fingerboard
- ˟. = plucked with the fingernail
- ⋔ = simultaneous pizzicato-glissando

Cage further explains that additional lines indicate the length of very short tones produced with the bow. To avoid any misunderstanding, he wisely adds that other dots should be ignored, as they are mere blemishes in the photocopy.

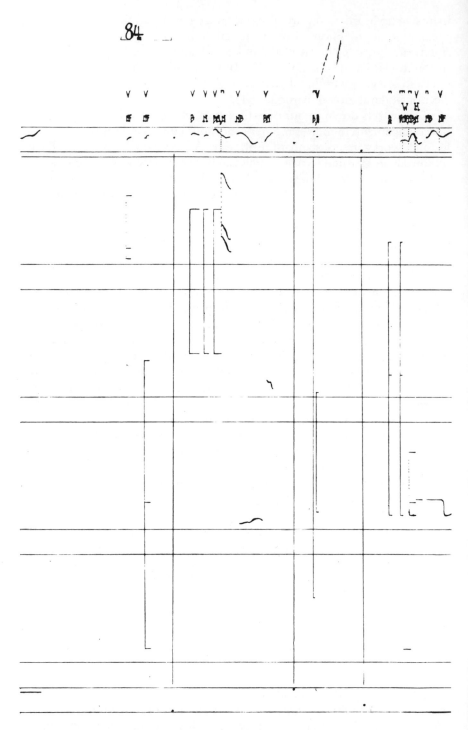

Page from Cage's *59½ Seconds for a String Player*

DUETS

While twentieth-century composers for solo violin represented the revival of an almost lost tradition, duets for strings (two violins, violin and viola, violin and cello) continued to be quite popular. As mentioned earlier, nineteenth-century duets were intended chiefly for instructional purposes and for amateur music making. In 1907, with Dancla's death, duets that required more advanced technique, sometimes entitled "duo brillant" or "concertant," disappeared, and in 1928 Flesch declared that duets for two violins, unaccompanied, were only of historical significance. He apparently did not consider those of contemporary composers, who had come to the duet from having explored the possibilities of a new style of writing for solo string instruments. He may not have been aware of new developments, or he looked at them only from the concertizing artist's point of view, for whom duets did not have much potential. A selection of duets written since 1900 shows their growing popularity. A few works for three or four violins have been included. [For editions of string music for duets, sonatas, concertos, and many other combinations, see Margaret K. Farish, *String Music in Print*, 2d ed. New York 1973, and 1984 supplement. *Ed.*]

1909	Toch, Duos for two violins, op. 17
1910/11	Draeseke, Suite for two violins, op. 86
1912	Karg-Elert, Ten Duets for two violins, op. 90
	Toch, Serenade for three violins, op. 20
1914	Kodály, Duo for violin and cello, op. 7
	Reger, Three Duos (Canons and Fugues) "in the old style," for two violins, op. 131b
1915	Ysaÿe, Sonata for two violins
1919	Fuchs, Fantasy Pieces for two violins, op. 105
1920	Honegger, Sonatina for two violins
1922	Ravel, Sonata for violin and cello
1925	Seiber, Sonata da camera for violin and cello
	Siegl, *Gartenmusik* for violin and cello, op. 19
1926	Harsányi, Duo for violin and cello
	Toch, Divertimento for violin and viola, op. 37/2
1927	Beck, Sonatina for flute and violin (or two violins)
	Hindemith, *Nine Pieces* in the first position for beginners, for two violins or two groups of violins, op. 44/1
	Křička, Sonatina for two violins, op. 48
ca. 1928	Eisler, Duo for violin and cello, op. 7
1928	Badings, Sonata for two violins
	Badings, Sonata for violin and viola
	Kósa, Duo for violin and double bass
	Szelényi, Duo for violin and cello
1930	Wildgans, Little Duo for two violins, op. 16a
	Zuckmayer, *Zusammenklänge, 7 Lehrstücke* for two violins

1931	Bartók, Forty-four Duos for two violins
	Brustad, Capricci for violin and viola
	Kadosa, Four Duets, op. 16b
	Kadosa, Five Short Rhythm Etudes, op. 16d
	Kadosa, Little Suite for two violins, op. 16e
1932	Copland, Elegies for violin and viola
	Doflein, ed. *Klang und Rhytmus*, Duets for two violins by Orff, Hindemith, Reutter, Bornefeld, Gebhard, Schröder, Doflein, Kelling, Katz, Irsen, and Maasz
	Doflein, ed. New Inventions and Fugues for two violins by Bornefeld, Doflein, Katz, Zuckmayer, Hindemith, van Leyden, Maler, Weismann, and Fortner
	Honegger, Sonatina for violin and cello
	Martinů, Easy Etudes for two violins
	Prokofiev, Sonata for two violins, op. 56
1933	Rózsa, Sonata for two violins, op. 15
1934	Beck, Duo for violin and viola
	Karel Hába, Duo for violin and cello, op. 19
1936	Gerster, Divertimento for violin and viola
1937	David, Duo Concertante for violin and cello, op. 19
	Hába, Duo for two violins (in the sixth-tone system)
1938	Jongen, Sonata-Duo for violin and cello, op. 109
	Shebalin, Sonata for violin and viola, op. 35
1939	Janáček, Duo for violin and viola, op. 19
	Skalkottas, Duos for violin and cello
1940	Milhaud, Sonatina for two violins
1941	Milhaud, Sonata for violin and viola
	Szelényi, Sonata for four violins
	Tcherepnin, Duo for violin and cello, op. 49
1942	Wildgans, Duo-Sonatina for violin and cello, op. 45
1943	Driessler, Duo for violin and cello, op. 1/1
1945	Badings, Little Duets for two violins, for beginners
	David, Sonata for two violins, op. 32/3
	Roos, Introduction, Adagio, and Allegro for two violins
1946	Ghedini, Three Canons for violin and cello
1947	Skalkottas, Four Duets for violin and cello
1948	Burkhard, Suite for two violins, op. 48
	Gaillard, Sonatina for violin and viola
	Hopkins, Prelude, Fugue, and Rondo for two violins
1949	Bacewicz, Quartet for four violins
	Egge, Duo Concertante for violin and viola, op. 23
1950	Holmboe, Duo Concertante for two violins
	Weiner, Duo for violin and viola
1951	Frid, Duos op. 37
	Raphael, *Dialoge*, twenty-five duets for two violins
1952	Szelényi, Duo for violin and cello

1953	Milhaud, Sonatina for violin and cello
	Seiber, Four Studies for two violins
1954	Skorzeny, Duo-studies for violin and viola
	Zbinden, Partita for violin and cello, op. 21
1957	Górecki, Sonata for two violins, op. 10
1958	Andriessen, Duo for two violins
	A. Kaufmann, Eight Duets in the first position, op. 76
1959	Bozza, Ricercare for violin and cello
	Raphael, *Kammermusik* for two violins, op. 47 (composed 1940)
1961	Beck, Duo for two violins
1963	Sommer, Sonata for two violins
1967	Gaburo, Ideas and Transformations no. 1 for two violins

Several of these compositions clearly reflect neobaroque tendencies: Reger's Three Duos "in the old style," also Siegl's *Gartenmusik*, a suite "in the old manner" consisting of Allemande, Gavotte, Musette, Sarabande, Menuet, and Gigue; Seiber's Sonata da camera, and many other duets. Others reveal a mixture of the old style with a new, personal idiom. Toch and Kodály found their way to chamber music with a small number of instruments without following such models.

In France, Honegger and Ravel turned to the string duo at approximately the same time, independently of each other. A high regard for Bach led Honegger to a modern linear style, while Ravel's tendency toward classic concepts led him away from the rich timbres of impressionism to a sparing use of expressive means. Honegger's Sonatina for two violins got off to a curious start. Its world premiere took place in a concert of the Société des Compositeurs in Paris. Funds were limited; the composer himself and his friend Milhaud were the performers. In their younger years, both had been fairly capable violinists but later had neglected the instrument. Reviewers praised the sonatina but had nothing good to say about the players who, perhaps reluctantly, ended their careers as violinists with the first performance of this attractive work.

Other twentieth-century duets were written for teaching purposes, Bartók's duos and Hindemith's *Nine Pieces* among them. Martinů and Badings too contributed valuable teaching materials that should be used more often. Bartók was a great master of "pedagogical music" (a term used disparagingly by Adorno) with a strong sense of mission and a comprehensive vision for education. He believed that a radical reform of music education would lead to a profound regeneration of society. His duos were originally intended for the series entitled *Spielmusik für Violine* (Pieces for [informal] music making, ca. 1932), edited by Erich Doflein, which included duets by important contemporary composers.

Many duets since have avoided technical difficulties and virtuoso effects—works written chiefly for a *Hausmusik* setting. Others explore to the maximum the possibilities of writing for two string instruments, creating a fullness of sound, a dense polyphonic texture that at times stretches the limits of duet writing.

Telemann's fine concertos for four unaccompanied violins may have been the models for the few contemporary works for three or four violins.

WORKS FOR VIOLIN AND PIANO

Among the various genres of violin music, the sonata for violin and piano has seen the fewest structural changes since 1900. Sonatas from Beethoven to Brahms and Franck were standard recital fare in the late nineteenth century; often they constituted the most substantial part of a program. This amounted to a strong tradition that affected developments during the first half of the twentieth century. Because the sonata maintained its central position, many new ones were added to the repertory. The following list represents little more than an overview. [For a detailed discussion of twentieth-century sonata repertory, see Abram Loft, *Violin and Keyboard*, vol. 2. *Ed.*]

1902	Jaques-Dalcroze, *Fantasia appassionata*
1902/03	Reger, Sonata no. 4 in C major, op. 72
1904	Szymanowsky, Sonata in D minor, op. 9
1905	Reger, Sonata no. 5 in F-sharp minor, op. 84
1906	Reger, Suite in F major "in the old style," op. 93
1908	Ives, Sonata no. 1
	Reger, Suite in A minor, op. 103a
1909	Jongen, Sonata no. 2, op. 34
	Reger, Two Little Sonatas in D minor and A major, op. 103b
	Sinding, Sonata in D minor "in the old style," op. 99
1910	Ives, Sonata no. 2
	Webern, *Four Pieces for Violin and Piano*, op. 7
1911	Ireland, Sonata no. 1
	Milhaud, Sonata no. 1
	Reger, Sonata no. 8 in E minor, op. 122
	Weiner, Sonata no. 1 in D major, op. 9
1912	Dohnányi, Sonata
1913	Martin, Sonata op. 1
1913/14	Kornauth, Sonata in E minor, op. 9
1914	Ives, Sonata no. 3
	Milhaud, Sonata for two violins and piano
1915	Ives, Sonata no. 4
	Reger, Sonata no. 9 in C minor, op. 139
	Sibelius, Sonatina in E major, op. 80
1916	Fauré, Sonata no. 2, op. 108
1916/17	Debussy, Sonata
1917	Ireland, Sonata no. 2
	Milhaud, Sonata no. 2
	Respighi, Sonata in B minor

1917/18	Elgar, Sonata in E minor, op. 82
1918	Hindemith, Sonata in E-flat, op. 11/1
	Hindemith, Sonata in D, op. 11/2
	Honegger, Sonata no. 1
	Pfitzner, Sonata in E minor, op. 27
	Weiner, Sonata no. 2 in F-sharp minor, op. 11
1919	Honegger, Sonata no. 2
	Křenek, Sonata in F-sharp minor, op. 3
	Pijper, Sonata no. 1
1920	E. Bloch, Sonata no. 1
1921	Bartók, Sonata no. 1
	Szymanowski, *Mythes* op. 30
1913/21	Janáček, Sonata
1921/22	Dale, Sonata op. 11
1922	Bartók, Sonata no. 2
	Pijper, Sonata no. 2
1922/23	Alfano, Sonata
1924	E. Bloch, Sonata no. 2
	Rathaus, Sonata no. 1, op. 14
1923/25	Kadosa, Sonata op. 5
1923/27	Ravel, Sonata
1924	Roussel, Sonata no. 2
1925	Delvincourt, Sonata
	Kadosa, Suite op. 6
	Roslavec, Sonata no. 3
1926	Harsányi, Sonata
	Haas, Two Church Sonatas for violin and organ, op. 62
1928	Bartók, Two Rhapsodies (also with orchestra)
	Beck, Sonatina no. 1
	Toch, Sonata op. 44
1929	Martinů, Sonata no. 1 in G minor
	Hennessy, Sonatina no. 2
	Rathaus, Suite op. 27 (also with chamber orchestra)
1930	Delius, Sonata no. 4
	Goossens, Sonata no. 2, op. 50
	Lajtha, Sonatina op. 13
1931	Kadosa, Partita op. 14
	Kaminski, Music for two violins and harpsichord
	Martinů, Sonata no. 2
1931/32	Martin, Sonata no. 2
1932	von Borck, Sonata op. 7
	Khachaturian, Sonata
	Stravinsky, Duo Concertant
1933	Badings, Sonata no. 1
1934	Françaix, Sonatina
	Stravinsky, "Pulcinella" Suite (*Suite italienne*)

1934/35	Britten, Suite op. 6
1935	Enesco, Sonata op. 26
	Hindemith, Sonata in E
1936	Lipatti, Sonatina
1937	Auric, Sonata
	Bridge, Sonata
	Martinů, Sonatina
	Pfitzner, Duo for violin and cello with piano, op. 43
	Rathaus, Sonata no. 2, op. 43
1938	Casella, Sonata a tre for piano, violin, and cello, op. 62
	Distler, Sonata for two violins and piano, op. 15a
1939	Badings, Sonata no. 2
	Creston, Suite op. 18
	Hindemith, Sonata in C
	Janáček, Sonata op. 21
	Lajtha, *Sonata a concerto*, op. 28
	Piston, Sonata
1940	Bantock, Sonata no. 3
1941	Kaminski, *Hauskonzert* for violin and piano
1942	Copland, Sonata
	Hessenberg, Sonata in F major, op. 25
	Hurnik, Duo
	Sessions, Duo for violin and piano
1942/44	Prokofiev, Sonata no. 2 in D major, op. 94
1943	Bentzon, Sonatas nos. 2 and 3, opp. 24 and 30
	Genzmer, Sonata no. 1
1943/44	Kuusisto, Sonata in B, op. 36
1944	Henkemans, Sonata
	Hovhaness, Arshalouis and Varak for violin and piano
	Martinů, Sonata no. 3
	Müller–Zürich, Sonata no. 2, op. 32
1944/45	Křenek, Sonata
1945	Cowell, Sonata
	Fortner, Sonata
	Milhaud, Sonatina
1938/46	Prokofiev, Sonata no. 1 in F minor, op. 80
1946	Beck, Sonatina no. 2
	Binet, Sonatina
	Fine, Sonata
	Henze, Sonata
1946/47	Dallapiccola, Two Studies
1947	Arnold, Sonata op. 15
	Blacher, Sonata op. 18
	Ferguson, Sonata no. 2, op. 10
	Ginastera, Pampeana no. 1

	Ginastera, Rhapsody for violin and piano
	Heiss, Sonata
1948	Cilèa, Suite
1948/50	Baur, Sonata in A
1949	Arma, Sonata
	von Einem, Sonata op. 11
	Müller-Zürich, Fantasy and Fugue for violin and organ, op. 45
	Schoenberg, Fantasy for violin with piano accompaniment, op. 47 (rev. 1978)
	Walton, Sonata
1950	Bentzon, Suite op. 67
	Cage, *Six Melodies*
	Fricker, Sonata op. 12
	Zimmermann, Sonata
1951	Diamond, Chaconne
	Genzmer, Sonata no. 2
	Lutoslawski, Recitative and Arioso
1952	Klebe, Sonatina op. 14
1953	Arnold, Sonata no. 2, op. 43
	Genzmer, Sonatina
	Járdányi, Concertino
1954	Bernstein, Serenade (also with orchestra)
	Genzmer, Sonata no. 3
	Klebe, Scene for four solo violins, tutti violins, and four-hand piano
	Lutoslawski, Ten Easy Pieces for violin and piano
	Powell, Divertimento for violin and harp
1955	Kirchner, Sonata Concertante
1959	Martinon, *Duo: Musique en forme de sonate*
	Penderecki, Three Miniatures
1961	Kurtág, Eight Duos for violin and cimbalom, op. 4
1963	Schnittke, Sonata no. 1
	Soukup, Sonata
	Yun, Gasa
1965	Amram, Sonata
1966	Gerhard, *Gemini*: Duo Concertante
1968	Adler, Sonata no. 2 (with piano or harpsichord)
	Anderberg, Duo
	Antoniou, Lyrics
	Schnittke, *Quasi una sonata* (Sonata no. 2)
	Shostakovich, Sonata op. 134
1969	Döhl, Pas de deux for violin and guitar
	Thärichen, *Klangstufen* op. 49
1970	Witzenmann, Concerto

Reger's op. 1 was a violin sonata. As an outstanding pianist and chamber music player, he was intimately acquainted with the genre and participated in the premieres of his seven long and two short sonatas, joined by some of the outstanding violinists of the day. His Suite "in the old style" helped establish the neobaroque concept. In these works Reger's distinct personal style prevails—fortunately, for other, less talented composers of his persuasion did little more than imbue their works for violin and piano with an archaic, historical flavor. Reger contributed another, rather odd piece to the repertory: he added a violin part to the six piano sonatinas of Clementi's op. 36.

The degree of a country's cultivation of violin playing and chamber music tends to have a strong effect on the composing of sonatas. In the Franco-Belgian region, violinists such as Ysaÿe and Thibaud inspired many works for violin and piano. Sonatas were written for them, or were inspired by their interpretations of other music.

Shortly before his death, Debussy began work on a cycle of six sonatas, but only three were completed. With the violinist Gaston Poulet, Debussy premiered his sonata on 5 May 1917; it was to be his last public appearance. Kulenkampff (1952) wrote about this sonata and its significance at an important moment in music history:

> In Debussy's *oeuvre* the violin occupies a subordinate place. Nevertheless this sonata, only thirteen minutes long, is of major significance, a milestone in the development of modern violin playing. Fleeting and phantomlike in character, it contains subtleties of virtuosity—possibilities disregarded by most modern composers. Its hallmark is *violinistic nuance*, avoiding pathos or romantic affectation. Instead, precision and concentration on what is absolutely essential determine the sonata's form. Indeed, for the realization of the subtle laws of this new tonal language, the violin is the predestined medium. To communicate these nuances with artistry—without heaviness or vagueness, clearly, yet in a vibrant, intense manner—requires a highly gifted violinist.

The middle movement of Ravel's Violin Sonata is entitled "Blues." According to Menuhin, an excited Ravel one day dropped in on Enesco, who was giving a lesson. The composer said that he was looking for a violinist with whom he could play the sonata that very evening for a publisher. Enesco's ability to sight read was as phenomenal as his memory. He agreed to do it, and after playing through the sonata once had it fully committed to memory! Other important contributions to the French repertory include Fauré's late sonata, those by Milhaud, Honegger, and Auric, and, more recently, by Claude Ballif (b. 1924).

Bartók's works for strings occupy a significant place in his *oeuvre*, inspired not only by the milieu of his youth, with its cultivation of chamber music, but also by the important Budapest school of violin playing. An early sonata of 1903 (not published until 1968) was followed by two sonatas (1921 and

1922) and two rhapsodies. Although he provided full orchestra accompaniment for the rhapsodies, Bartók did not view the versions for violin and piano as mere "reductions." His violin and piano works are among the most powerful twentieth-century contributions to the genre, yet they are seldom performed. Quite rhapsodic in character, they demonstrate the composer's superb knowledge of the violin's possibilities. Their ensemble writing may represent the highest phase of his development.

Hindemith, a violinist and violist, was among those who came to terms with Reger's ideas. While Hindemith's op. 11 greatly disturbed his contemporaries, we view it as clearly stemming from the Brahms-Reger heritage. He wrote the two later sonatas immediately after his book *Unterweisung im Tonsatz* (1937, 1939; Engl. trans. as *The Craft of Musical Composition*, 1941). A strong neobaroque flavor distinguishes the fast movements in particular.

Stravinsky's compositions for violin date from his time of close collaboration with the violinist Samuel Dushkin, from whom he obtained advice about the writing of his Violin Concerto. The Duo Concertant was followed by a series of arrangements, among them the "Pulcinella" Suite. All these arrangements were created with much care and in the spirit of the new (violin and piano) medium, so that they virtually amount to original compositions.

Composers of the Second Viennese School contributed rather little to the repertory for violin and piano, though both Schoenberg and Webern were good string players (cellists) in their youth. With *Four Pieces for Violin and Piano*, op. 7, Anton Webern (1883–1945) broke away from the excessive emotionalism of some early twentieth-century sonatas for violin and piano, but they were not published until 1922 and even then went largely unnoticed. Several decades ahead of their time, they represent Webern's striving for extreme conciseness and subdued expression, as did his slightly earlier *Six Pieces for Orchestra*, op. 6, the shortest of which lasts fifty seconds. Opus 7 consists of these four movements: Sehr langsam (very slow), nine measures long; Rasch (very quick), twenty-four measures; Sehr langsam, fourteen measures; and Bewegt (with motion), fifteen measures. During this period in his development, Webern combined extremely subtle timbres with tense harmonies, rich in intervals of a second.

The Fantasy for violin with piano accompaniment is Schoenberg's only contribution. The designation may seem anachronistic, for ever since Mozart's late sonatas the equality of the two parts had been well established, and composers wrote accordingly. But we know that Schoenberg actually completed the violin part before he added the piano part. It is doubtful, however, that the fantasy was intended for unaccompanied violin. The extant version reveals no traces of such a plan.

Avant garde composers have shown little interest in writing for violin and piano, as evidenced by the few works written since 1950. This is surprising, for violin and piano each played an important part in the exploration of new timbres. For the violin, this especially applies to the medium of the string quartet. Perhaps seemingly primitive essays like Cage's *Six Melodies* are harbingers of new developments.

WORKS FOR VIOLIN AND ORCHESTRA

During the nineteenth century, concerts by symphony orchestras were regular public events, and it soon became customary to include a concerto on the program. Most solo concertos of the late classic and romantic periods were written with this tradition in mind, a tradition that has changed very little since. Concertos for violin and orchestra remain therefore an important part of the repertory. The twentieth-century revival of interest in baroque music and its forms, including the concerto grosso, has provided new stimuli. [For a discussion of contemporary violin concertos, see part 4 of Roeder's *A History of the Concerto. Ed.*]

1901	Fitelberg, Concerto op. 13
1902	Jaques-Dalcroze, Concerto in C minor, op. 50
1902/03	Suk, Fantasy op. 24
1903	Glazunov, Concerto in A minor, op. 82
	Sibelius, Concerto in D minor, op. 47 (rev. 1905)
1907/08	Bartók, Concerto no. 1, op. posth. (premiered 1958)
	Reger, Concerto in A major, op. 101
1908	Enesco, *Symphonie concertante*
1910	Elgar, Concerto in B minor, op. 61
pre-1911	Stephan, *Musik für Geige und Orchester* in one movement
1914	Vaughan Williams, *The Lark Ascending*, a "romance"
1915/16	Delius, Double Concerto for violin, cello, and orchestra
1916	Delius, Violin Concerto
	Szymanowski, Concerto no. 1, op. 35
1916/17	Prokofiev, Concerto no. 1 in D major, op. 19
1918	Gretchaninov, Suite "in modo antico," op. 81
1921	Křenek, Concerto grosso no. 1 for six solo instruments and string orchestra, op. 10
	Respighi, *Concerto gregoriano*
1923	Pfitzner, Concerto in one movement in B minor, op. 34
1924	Karel, Symphony for violin and orchestra, op. 20
	Křenek, Concerto grosso no. 2 for violin, viola, cello, and orchestra, op. 25
	Křenek, Concertino for flute, violin, harpsichord, and string orchestra, op. 27
	Křenek, Violin Concerto no. 1, op. 29
	Ravel, *Tzigane*, Concert Rhapsody
1924/25	Berg, Chamber Concerto for piano, violin, and thirteen wind instruments
1925	Hindemith, *Kammermusik 4* for violin and chamber orchestra, op. 36/3

	Respighi, *Concerto all'antica*

Respighi, *Concerto all'antica*
Vaughan Williams, Concerto in D minor
Weill, Concerto for violin, wind orchestra, string bass, and
    percussion, op. 12

1927   K. Marx, Concerto for two violins and orchestra, op. 5
Milhaud, Concerto no. 1

1927/28   Janáček, Concerto (unfinished)

1928   Badings, Concerto no. 1 (unpublished)
Bartók, Two rhapsodies
Casella, Concerto in A minor, op. 48
Hauer, Concerto op. 54

1929   Rathaus, Suite for violin and chamber orchestra or piano, op.
    27

1930   Holst, Concerto for two violins
Jachino, *Sonata drammatica*

1931   Martinů, Concerto for string quartet and orchestra
Stravinsky, Concerto in D

1932   Gretchaninov, Concerto op. 132
Malipiero, Concerto
Szelényi, Triple Concerto for piano, violin, cello, and winds

1932/33   Szymanowski, Concerto no. 2, op. 61

1933   Absil, Concerto no. 1, op. 11
Casella, Concerto for trio (violin, cello, piano) and orchestra,
    op. 56

1934   Françaix, Suite for violin and orchestra

1935   Berg, Concerto
Milhaud, *Concertino de printemps* for violin and chamber
    orchestra
Prokofiev, Concerto no. 2 in G minor, op. 63
Sessions, Concerto

1935/36   Schoenberg, Concerto op. 36

1936   Egk, *Geigenmusik*

1936/37   Delannoy, *Sérénade concertante*

1937   Bax, Concerto in E major
Creston, Partita for flute, violin, and string orchestra, op. 12
Pfitzner, Duo for violin, cello, and small orchestra, op. 43
Wladimir Vogel, Concerto

1937/38   Bartók, Concerto no. 2

1938   Bloch, Concerto
Malipiero, Concerto a tre (violin, cello, piano)

1939   Barber, Concerto op. 14
Bresgen, *Jagdkonzert* for violin, ten woodwinds, and double bass
Britten, Concerto op. 15 (rev. 1958)
Hartmann, *Concerto funebre* for violin and strings (rev. 1959)
Hindemith, Concerto
Walton, Concerto (rev. 1945)

1939/40	Halffter, Concerto op. 11
	R. Kubelik, Concerto
	Skalkottas, Double Concerto for violin, viola, winds, and string bass
1940	Conrad Beck, Chamber Concerto
	Khachaturian, Concerto in D minor
1940/41	Kadosa, Concerto no. 2, op. 32 (rev. 1956)
1942	Jirák, Rhapsody, op. 44
	Pentland, Concerto
1943	Burkhard, Concerto no. 2, op. 69
	Holmboe, Chamber Concerto no. 6, op. 36
	Martinů, Concerto
1943/44	Gerhard, Concerto
1944	Gruenberg, Concerto op. 47
1945	Korngold, Concerto in D major, op. 35 (written 1937–1939)
1946	Amirov, Double Concerto for violin, piano, and orchestra
	Antheil, Concerto
	Fortner, Concerto for violin and large chamber orchestra
	Milhaud, Concerto no. 2
1947	Badings, Concerto no. 4
	Bialas, Concerto
	Ghedini, *Concerto detto "Il Belprato"* for violin and string orchestra
	Henze, Concerto no. 1
	Křenek, Double Concerto for violin, piano, and small orchestra
	Schuman, Concerto (rev. 1954, 1958)
1947/48	Shostakovich, Concerto no. 1 in A minor, op. 77 (rev. in 1955 as op. 99)
1948	Blacher, Concerto op. 29
	Alan Bush, Concerto op. 32
	Chávez, Concerto
	Kabalevsky, Concerto in C major, op. 48
1948/49	Harris, Concerto
1948/50	Henkemans, Concerto
1950	Hamilton, *Sinfonie concertante* for violin, viola, and orchestra, op. 8
1950/51	Martin, Concerto
	Zimmermann, Concerto in one movement
1952	Badings, Capriccio for violin and two soundtracks
	J. N. David, Concerto no. 1, op. 45
	Leighton, Concerto op. 12
1954	Fricker, *Rapsodia concertante*, op. 21
	Ghedini, *Concentus basiliensis* for violin and chamber orchestra
1955	Hlobil, Concerto op. 47
	Kalomiris, Concertino

	Klebe, Concerto for violin, cello, and orchestra
	Křenek, Concerto no. 2
	Martinů, *Suite concertante*
	A. Merikanto, Concerto no. 4
	Shostakovich, Concerto no. 1, op. 99
1956	Larsson, Concertino no. 8 for violin and string orchestra
1956/57	Nono, *Varianti* for violin, strings, and woodwinds
1957	Bartolozzi, Concerto for violin, string orchestra, and harpsichord
	J. N. David, Concerto no. 2, op. 50
1958	Lees, Concerto
	Milhaud, Concerto no. 3
1959	Archer, Concerto
	Baird, *Espressioni varianti*
	Genzmer, Concerto da camera
	Harrison, Concerto with percussion orchestra
	Malipiero, Concerto for violin and baritone voice
1960	Martinon, Concerto no. 2
1961	Khachaturian, Concerto-Rhapsody
	Sculthorpe, *Irlanda IV* for solo violin, strings, and percussion
1963	Ginastera, Concerto op. 30
	Malipiero, Concerto
1965	Amy, *Trajectoires*
	Bacewicz, Concerto no. 7
	Chávez, Concerto
1966	Blacher, Virtuoso Music for solo violin, ten winds, timpani, percussion, and harp
	Steffen, Concerto op. 32
1967	Grosskopf, Sonata Concertante no. 2
	R. Malipiero, Rhapsody
	Penderecki, Capriccio
	Shostakovich, Concerto no. 2, op. 129
1968	Antoniou, *Events I* for violin, piano, and orchestra, op. 36
	Martin, *Magnificat* for soprano, violin, and orchestra
	Penderecki, *Concerto per violino grande (o violoncello) ed orchestra*
1969	Maderna, Concerto
1970	K. Huber, Concerto
1971	Henze, Concerto no. 2 for violin, tape, and thirty-three instruments
1972	Jolivet, Concerto
	Wuorinen, Concerto for amplified violin and orchestra
1973	Maderna, Concerto
1975	Rochberg, Concerto
1976	Penderecki, Concerto
1979	Tippett, Triple Concerto (violin, viola, cello)
1985	Dutilleux, Concerto, *L'arbre des songes*

1986   Davies, Concerto
1993   Davies, Strathclyde Concerto no. 5 for violin, viola, and
                string orchestra (date of publication)

A less full-sounding version of Schumann's Cello Concerto, one for violin and orchestra, was discovered in Hamburg in 1986; it received its first modern performance the following year by Saschko Gawrilloff (b. 1929 in Leipzig of Bulgarian extraction).

Glazunov and Sibelius each wrote a major concerto at the beginning of the century. Their satisfying balance of virtuoso and symphonic elements has given them a secure place on concert programs, though they are less popular than the Beethoven and Brahms violin concertos. Reger's two romances opp. 40 and 50 are seldom heard, but they paved the way for his Violin Concerto, dedicated to Marteau, who premiered it. This is a gigantic work, requiring a soloist who commands an especially big tone. Even so, conductors will have to rein in the large orchestra to obtain the transparent sound envisioned by Reger. The Glazunov and Sibelius concertos are more rewarding for this reason, though the Reger is their equal in musical substance. Certain unwritten laws about the relative proportions of a concerto's solo and tutti parts must be observed if it is to be equally attractive to the violinist and the public. Reger showed less concern with these laws than his two colleagues did. In his youth, Sibelius performed the Mendelssohn Concerto often. Following the success of his own Violin Concerto he wrote several smaller works for violin and orchestra, but they were not as well received.

Josef Suk (1874–1935) was the second violinist in the celebrated Bohemian String Quartet and therefore well acquainted with the violin's possibilities. Kulenkampff called Suk's Fantasy an "outstanding concert piece," ranking it next to Dvořák's Violin Concerto.

The Violin Concerto no. 1 by Karol Szymanowski (1882–1937) is a significant addition to the repertory, though neglected by soloists. It owes its existence to a suggestion by the Polish violinist Pavel Kochanski. Highly personal, expressive language places it above the composer's later Concerto op. 61.

Various stylistic tendencies mark concertos written in the decade after World War I. Looking for new harmonic colors, Ottorino Respighi (1879–1936) turned to the ancient church modes, while in his *Concerto all'antica* he incorporated neobaroque formal features. Hans Pfitzner (1869–1949), the son of an orchestra violinist, dedicated his Violin Concerto to the Australian Alma Moodie, who was the soloist in its premiere [see also Schwarz 1983. *Ed.*]. It is a typical late romantic work, with an intense, virtuosic violin part.

The Concerto for violin and wind instruments by Kurt Weill (1900–1950) represents an interesting attempt to break away from standard instrumentation. Weill must have realized that such scoring limited the work's chances for performance. No doubt it is an attempt, characteristic for its time, to avoid the sound of the large, late romantic orchestra.

In his cycle of four violin concertos op. 36, Hindemith may have pursued similar objectives, though by different means. Neobaroque motoric energy and formal organization characterize the cycle; the solo violin is supported either by a group of solo instruments or by a chamber orchestra. Opus 36, no. 3 omits tutti violins altogether and is scored as follows:

> solo violin
> two piccolos
> E-flat clarinet
> B-flat clarinet
> B-flat bass clarinet
> two bassoons
> contrabassoon
> cornet a piston in B-flat
> trombone
> bass tuba
> four violas
> two cellos
> four double basses
> four drums (tambourines without jingles, notated in bass clef)

A cadenza twenty-two measures long, played by solo violin and drums, provides the transition from the fourth to the fifth movement.

Hindemith's cycle of chamber concertos was preceded by Berg's Chamber Concerto for violin, piano, and thirteen wind instruments, written in honor of Schoenberg's fiftieth birthday. An apparent extension of Schoenberg's type of chamber symphony, it contains the intense contrapuntal writing and basically lyrical mood so typical of Berg. In a letter to Schoenberg he explained and analyzed its construction.

Quite different in mood and concept is the quiet, introspective *Putovani dusicki* (Migration of the little soul) by Leoš Janáček (1854–1928), an unfinished violin concerto written at the same time as his opera *From the House of the Dead*. Some of the music occurs in both works. Its designation as a "violin concerto" may have affected its reception adversely; as an "elegy" or "symphonic poem" it might have succeeded better with the public.

Henk Badings (1907–1987) of Holland turned to the violin concerto in the 1920s. Along with Milhaud, Martinů, Vagn Holmboe (b. 1909) of Denmark, and Grazyna Bacewicz (1913–1969) of Poland, Badings was one of the few twentieth-century composers who provided a volume of soloistic works for the violin. They are all well written for the instrument and show good formal design.

During the nineteenth century, the concertante (or sinfonia concertante) for several instruments disappeared, but the revival of the baroque concerto grosso, which inspired Křenek's contribution after World War I, resulted in widespread activity. Alfredo Casella (1883–1947) incorporated neobaroque elements in his Violin Concerto, and baroque models (as well as Beethoven's Triple Concerto) are evident in the scoring of his Trio Concerto op. 56. Respighi's *Concerto a cinque*, in which the violin is one of several solo instruments, dates from the same year. Titles of this kind, however, do not necessarily imply a historicizing, backward look. Style characteristics of this kind were developed in an entirely personal way in the *Contrappunti* for string trio and orchestra by Ghedini (1892–1965) and in the Sinfonia Concertante by Martinů (1890–1959), the latter scored for violin, oboe, bassoon, cello, and orchestra. Nor is Pfitzner's Duo tied to baroque models.

The 1930s were a period of intensive concerto writing, producing distinguished works by Stravinsky, Schoenberg, Berg, Bartók, Hindemith, and Skalkottas. Though not a violinist, Stravinsky was always eager to include string instruments in his scores, and a penchant for virtuoso writing soon led him to the concerto. In his *L'histoire du soldat* he used a small complement of solo performers, partly out of necessity because of conditions in 1918, during the final months of the war. In this work the violin symbolizes the devil who, as an itinerant musician, tempts a returning soldier into parting with his fiddle. This is the devil of a Russian village tavern, whom Stravinsky imbues with a kind of stubborn nonchalance. *L'histoire* includes a small interpolated violin concerto. A number of other concerted compositions followed, the first of which, the *Concerto pour instruments à cordes*, was written soon after *L'histoire*. The Violin Concerto, as mentioned earlier, goes back to Stravinsky's friendship with the violinist Samuel Dushkin. At the time, the composer was fond of the driving rhythms of some baroque music. This is evident in the Piano Concerto of 1924 and in the Violin Concerto, whose movements are entitled Toccata, Aria I, Aria II, and Capriccio. Stravinsky gratefully acknowledged Dushkin's advice with a note in the score: "Violin part in collaboration with Samuel Dushkin." In his autobiography (1936) he recalls details from 1931:

> Before beginning the work I consulted Hindemith, who is a perfect violinist. I asked him whether the fact that I did not play the violin would make itself felt in my composition. Not only did he allay my doubts, but he went further and told me that it would be a very good thing, as it would make me avoid a routine technique, and would give rise to ideas which would not be suggested by the familiar movement of the fingers. . . . My faithful Dushkin, who was near Grenoble and not far from us, used to come to see me every day. He was assiduously studying his part so as to be ready in time, as the Berlin Rundfunk [radio] had secured the first audition of the *Concerto*, which was to be played under my direction on October 23.

Schoenberg's Violin Concerto, written after his 1933 emigration to the United States, was premiered in 1940 by Louis Krasner with the Philadelphia Orchestra. In this work Schoenberg amalgamates serial technique with the requirements of traditional concerto style. The composition, cyclical in form, has three movements: Poco Allegro/Vivace, Andante grazioso, and Finale-

Allegro. A virtuoso solo part with cadenzalike sections represents a conscious continuation of the best concerto traditions, but the musical material itself is typical Schoenberg. Its combination of seemingly heterogeneous elements makes it one of the most difficult works technically in the entire concerto repertory, for which reason it is rarely heard. Someone told Schoenberg that it required a soloist with six fingers, to which he replied, "I can wait."

Alban Berg's contribution, on the other hand, is one of the most frequently performed modern violin concertos. He dedicated it "To the memory of an angel," a reference to Manon Gropius, daughter of Alma Maria Mahler; Manon died at the age of eighteen. It is a magnificent, lyric poem, beautifully coherent, emphasizing the violin's lyrical powers of expression, which often are neglected in works with orchestra accompaniment. Listeners are not disturbed by its serial nature; the row on which it is based includes three overlapping triads, which helps those used to tonal, rather than serial music:

G–B-flat–D–F-sharp–A–C–E–G-sharp–B–C-sharp–D-sharp–E-sharp

The concerto is Berg's last completed work. It is a testimonial to the strength with which he established his own style, for he succeeded in combining with the tone row a folk song from Carinthia and the chorale "Es ist genug," largely using Bach's harmonization—all without any incongruity of style.

When speaking of Bartók's Violin Concerto, most people are referring to the one he wrote in 1937–1938. An early work of 1907–1908, lost for many years, was found in the possession of a private owner and finally published in 1958. Though a fine concerto, it is viewed rather as a station in Bartók's career, whereas the Second Concerto represents the "real" Bartók. In it we admire the composer's fortuitous combination of rhapsodic elements with concentrated motivic development. Like other twentieth-century composers, Bartók provided his own cadenza, to ensure its organic connection with the rest of the movement. In this work he employs quarter-tones that densely envelop the note D (see example below). The up-arrow signifies a quarter-tone above; the down-arrow a quarter-tone below. He also makes use of a vertical pizzicato, indicated by the ♭ sign; on release, the string sharply hits the fingerboard, adding special rhythm accents.

The writing of violin concertos continued with unabated vigor, as shown by those of Khachaturian (1940), Shostakovich (1947/48 and 1967), Blacher (1948 and 1966), Johann Nepomuk David (1952 and 1957, written for his son Lukas), and Penderecki (1967), to mention just a few. From 1949 to 1957 Lukas David (b. 1934 in Wels, Austria) was a pupil of Varga in Detmold, where he has taught since 1966. In 1955 Stuckenschmidt wrote, "Since the end of the war, Germany has produced no greater virtuoso than Lukas David."

Since ca. 1950, some composers have avoided the traditional designation "concerto" in favor of others, such as "virtuoso music" (Blacher) or "capriccio" (Penderecki). Other works for solo violin and orchestra (or smaller chamber groups) have been called, among other things, "dialoghi," "mutazioni," and "incontri." Nono's *Varianti*, written for and with Rudolf Kolisch, who premiered the piece, reflects the composer's interest in subtle nuances of color and expression, evidently influenced by electronic music.

VIOLIN PEDAGOGY SINCE 1900

Looking at the wealth of violin teaching materials available today, one wonders how teachers in less richly endowed times were able to train their students to become outstanding artists.   MAX GRÜNBERG,
FÜHRER DURCH DIE LITERATUR DER STREICHINSTRUMENTE, 1913

In arranging the many pedagogical works published since 1900 according to content, we note that they differ according to objectives and to the approaches chosen to reach those objectives. They can be assigned to three groups. First are study materials that follow traditional teaching methods. Their purpose is to produce competent professional violinists who can perform chamber and orchestra music and who, talent permitting, may also become accomplished soloists. Authors of such works were critical of earlier violin methods and saw a need for better ones. They were less inclined to add to the corpus of traditional etudes, believing there was little chance of replacing what was so firmly established.

The second group consists of works based on an analysis of the mechanisms of playing, with various specialized exercises provided. Ševčík did not invent these but developed them into a comprehensive teaching system. Emphasis is on short exercises, usually one to two measures long, each dealing with a narrowly defined task. The objective of this approach is to lead to a high level of virtuosity.

Finally there are materials intended for those, mostly amateurs, who want to develop their general musicianship, especially for the purpose of music making in the home, rather than aiming at the production of virtuosos, a goal inevitably reached by only a few. This very different approach was encouraged and nurtured, especially in German-speaking countries, by the *Jugendmusik* (music for young people) movement of the 1920s and 1930s.

Such classifications are arbitrary, to be sure, and amount to oversimplifications made to facilitate an overview. In practice, most pedagogues will choose their own approach, after evaluating and selecting teaching materials. The following remarks should be considered in that light.

Shortly after the turn of the century, Joachim and Moser published a comprehensive violin school in three volumes. Great things could be expected from the collaboration of a virtuoso violinist with a musician as experienced as Moser, the author of a history of violin playing. Joachim never taught beginners, but like most master teachers he was forever frustrated by insufficiently prepared students. In the preface, he warned that it was difficult to overcome such handicaps, and that only patient, energetic students, who were willing to spend time on their artistic preparation, would succeed, even if it meant postponing the day when they could earn a living with their playing. Moser authored the first and second parts; Joachim attended to the third, a discussion of masterworks for the violin. Both examined even seemingly insignificant details and included only material on which they agreed.

With its excess of dry exercises, somewhat like Ševčík's, and lesser concern for the pupil's musical development, their joint publication was not greatly successful. Part 3, however, based on Joachim's lifelong experience as a performer, consists of sixteen major works, carefully edited and provided with cadenzas.

In *Die Grundlagen der Technik des Violinspiels* (Foundations of violin technique), Amadeus von der Hoya came to terms with new musical trends. Aware of the high degree of chromaticism in works by Reger and his contemporaries, Hoya taught a system of chromatic fingerings, thereby addressing the most crucial and controversial issue in twentieth-century violin teaching: that students trained with outdated study material (etudes representing, at best, the state of composition at Spohr's time) will inevitably face difficulties when confronted with twentieth-century music. Unfortunately Hoya was methodical to a fault, far more so than Ševčík. I know of no other violin school that contains more than three hundred pages of purely abstract exercises, of which the page reproduced on p. 506 is an example.

All violin teaching must include four factors: the student, the violin, *music*, and the teacher. It is the teacher's task to have a strong personal interest in the first three, to observe a healthy balance between them, and to strive for a development that takes all three into consideration. In Hoya's two volumes we hardly find anything that could be regarded as music in the accepted sense, yet when children express an interest in playing an instrument, or when parents consider this desirable for the child's education, this normally stems from a love of music. Yet Hoya's method ignores music completely and uses music notation merely to fix on paper gymnastic exercises for the left and right hands. Others have imitated and possibly carried even farther the

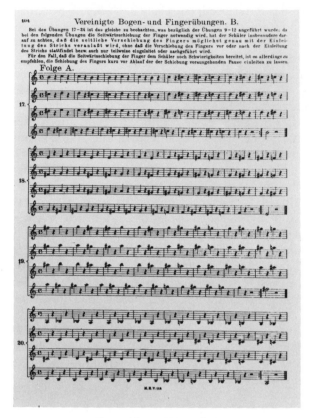

From Hoya 1904–1905

ideas of Ševčík and Hoya, among them Demetrius Dounis in *The Absolute Independence of the Fingers*:

In *Modern Violin Studies* (1944), Danish violinist Mogens Heimann, a Flesch pupil, takes up efficiently rational ways of practicing and suggests radical departures from tradition.

This collection of exercises aims at compensating for all generally applied studies; beside Flesch's *Basic Studies* and *Scale Systems* it should represent an effective help to every well-educated violinist, as it follows the sound principle of studying by small but regularly and often-repeated doses. The best possibility of rapid technical progress for the time being is the three-hour daily study of Ševčík's editions and various collections of etudes; but at the first place this plan of study cannot be put up with for more than a month; then one cannot be sure to deal equally thoroughly with all parts of technique; and lastly one cannot combine the normal study of repertory-pieces with such tiring and tedious work, which on the other hand is possible with the present collection, requiring only one to one and a half hours a day.

Heimann is not opposed to etudes in general, for he addresses only trained violinists who want to keep up their technique with a minimum of time. He claims that with a shifting study, one and a half pages in length, he "has reduced Ševčík's entire op. 8 to a five-minute exercise," but this implies that violinists will have gone through Ševčík's volume during their earlier course of study.

Several of the authors cited intended to prepare students to cope with the tonally different music of our time. More than accustoming the eye to reading accidentals, this requires a clear and quick recognition of the intervals involved. Violinists with a good technique but insufficient studies in music theory may still encounter difficulties with music that is more complex, freely tonal, or atonal. Intensive training in sight reading and dictation will help, along with constant analysis of intervals at an ever-faster tempo. Such analysis must be second nature and should include harmonic form, chord structure, and modulation. Music that is tonally free may also require unconventional fingering, including stretches and extensions.

Much remains to be done in adapting the teaching of violin technique to the requirements of twentieth-century music. The "Kreutzer etudes" for our time are yet to be written! In 1928 Flesch noted the lack of preparatory studies for atonal violin concertos. It is too bad that Czech composer Bohuslav Martinů did not provide them; his etudes for two violins, and for violin and piano, are valuable pedagogical studies, suggesting that he saw the need for a reevaluation of our entire repertory of etudes. Few violinists took up the ideas set forth in Hindemith's *Übungen für Geiger* or in Lilli Friedemann's *Studien für Violine*.

French music teaching has not ignored that students need to develop facility in reading handwritten music. *Solfèges manuscrits* may serve as preparation for works such as F. Gerlier's *30 études manuscrites*; its examples are photocopied, not engraved or printed. *Jugendmusik*, the youth movement in German-speaking countries, made simple pieces by Bach and other baroque composers available to amateur violinists, drawing much of its inspiration from folk music and from the relatively easy instrumental melodies and vocal music of the sixteenth and seventeenth centuries.

Violin tutors published during the 1920s and 1930s, some designed specifically for group or class lessons, were not intended to lead to advanced levels but rather to help those who wanted to acquire the basics needed for music making at home, in schools, and in other groups. Opinions about the merits of class lessons are divided. While some consider them the death knell for violinistic talent, others are convinced that a revitalization of violin playing could only be brought about by the discovery of real talent through group instruction. Instrument makers, of course, note that class lessons are the best way to promote the sale of instruments; though this might seem a crassly commercial point of view, it is true that a particular instrument's sales are a good indication of its future. In the United States, class lessons for all age groups, from young children to college students to adults, are widespread, and such instruction has stimulated vigorous musical activities in Japan and Russia as well.

The success of group instruction is determined by a teacher's personality and approach. Japan's Shinichi Suzuki (b. 1898) developed methods of group instruction especially for preschool-age children, and his results have attracted much attention. Suzuki clearly saw that traditional violin teaching methods were entirely unsuitable for four-year-olds, but he also realized that children learn their mother tongue, no matter how complicated, by imitating what they hear. Suzuki, by way of analogy, used recordings and had his young charges play back from memory what they were hearing. Note reading and playing from music were not taught until quite late. His *Suzuki Violin School* (Tokyo 1955) is based on this system. Each of the ten volumes is accompanied by a piano part and a recording.

The outstanding practitioner of violin teaching since 1900 was Carl Flesch, whose lifelong career as a pedagogue dealt with artistic interpretation. He was not a "born teacher"; only gradually did he come to realize that teaching was to be his profession. What he found sound and useful in teaching others he first tested on himself. Flesch (1957) reminisced about his first publication, brought out in 1911:

> About this time I made my debut as a writer on theory. For a number of years, I had employed for my own use a simplified method of "playing myself in" [warming up], exercises that had the purpose of lubricating, as it were, all the joints used in violin playing. One day, a pupil remarked that I had no right to keep this idea to myself. Thus, the *Urstudien* (Basic studies) came into being, and I prided myself not a little on enriching, as a Hungarian, the German language by that word. Though some considerable time has passed since the publication of the little treatise, the underlying idea does not seem to have become obsolete.

With these basic studies, Flesch appeared to continue along the paths of Ševčík and Hoya, but his true direction was indicated in the title of his second publication, *The Art of Violin Playing*, in which compendium Flesch takes up very subtle aspects of technique as well as other topics and problems: aesthetics, methodology, excessive practicing, and physiological and psychological problems such as stage fright. Beyond these, Flesch comments on

1970 Matsumoto Summer School, directed by Shinichi Suzuki

general musical matters: on contemporary musical life, on the violinist's profession, and on human problems that cannot be separated from violin teaching proper. Intensive research and an international perspective lent him by his own performance and life experiences in Vienna, Paris, Bucharest, Amsterdam, Berlin, and the United States enabled Flesch to convey a valid picture of violin playing since about 1880. His writings are a rich source of information, whether or not the reader agrees with all his views.

When the first volume of his *Art of Violin Playing* appeared, Flesch put in ten-hour days of playing, teaching, and writing, which regime required very rational working methods. For instance, he kept a card file of fingerings. Kulenkampff visited him one day, and, violins in hand, the two virtuosos exchanged experiences. As they discussed the fingering of a certain passage in the Brahms Concerto, Flesch suddenly stopped and said, "I must check whether this fingering is in my file." Based on decades of collecting material he was able, late in life, to write *Violin Fingering* (Milan 1960, London 1966), published posthumously. In this book's approximately two thousand examples, Flesch dealt with virtually all problems of fingering.

Flesch's achievements are distinguished by this unique combination: he never failed to submit the fruits of his fine speculative thinking to practical testing. His lofty concept of violin pedagogy raised it to the level required for professional training today. Naturally, his teaching methods were examined very critically. Mingotti (1949) called Flesch "the Sigmund Freud of the violin," offering the player a kind of safety net for all exposed climbs to high virtuosity. In his comprehensive book *Hemmung und Herrschaft auf dem Griffbrett* (Fingerboard problems and how to conquer them, 1931), Siegfried Eberhardt devoted an entire chapter to Flesch and the significance of his work. As a teacher, Flesch addressed himself mainly to professional students, but his influence went far beyond.

New approaches to teaching beginners required new teaching materials. Ferdinand Küchler (1867–1937) satisfied this need with his violin school, which went through many printings and revisions. Its progressive, well-planned arrangement moves at a sensible pace that does not overpower or discourage the student. Practicing material includes folk songs and melodies from well-known operas. Flesch praised Küchler's approach.

Erich Doflein's violin school is similarly organized. In an essay on contemporary issues in music teaching he referred to changes in the world of music during the 1920s and 1930s and their effect on music pedagogy. It was an age that favored adhering to original sources (the *Urtext* concept) rather than arrangements, with a new appreciation of the values and beauties of folk song. New teaching materials reflected this new attitude toward music, from Bach's time and before.

Continually improved teaching methods, along with teaching materials of comparable quality, have led to remarkably high standards of violin playing at national and international competitions. But great strides in technical prowess have not always been followed by rising standards of interpretation. Kreisler (quoted in Lochner 1950) voiced this concern in a 1932 newspaper article:

> The technical talent of the youth of today is almost unbelievable. I know five "wonder children" in New York alone who play anything, no matter how difficult, as if it were nothing. But they are all *technical* "wonder children," just as a child now can put a radio or an automobile together. This can never remain the object of music. People will get away from it again.

A list of selected teaching materials published since 1900 follows. [Some titles included in the German edition have been omitted; a few widely used American publications have been added. See also Schwarz 1983, which deals with DeLay, Galamian, Gingold, and Schneider in the valuable chapter "Great American Teachers." *Ed.*]

1901	Ševčík, *Preliminary Trill Studies*, op. 7, Leipzig
	Ševčík, *Preliminary Double-Stop Studies*, op. 9, Leipzig
1902/03	Sauret, *Vingt-quatre études caprices* op. 64, Berlin
1902/05	Joachim and Moser, *Violinschule* (3 vols.), Berlin (new ed. London and Hamburg 1956–1959)
1903	Ševčík, *School of Bowing Technique*, op. 2 (6 vols.), Leipzig

	Steinhausen, *Die Physiologie der Bogenführung* (The physiology of bowing), Leipzig (5th ed. 1928)
1904/05	Hoya, *Die Grundlagen der Technik des Violinspiels*, Leipzig
1904/08	Ševčík, *Violin School for Beginners*, opp. 6–9, Leipzig
1910	Marteau, *Bogenstudien* op. 14, Berlin
1911	Flesch, *Urstudien*, Berlin
	Küchler, *Praktische Violinschule* op. 2, Zurich (rev. ed. 1964)
1914	Stoeving, *The Elements of Violin Playing and a Key to Ševčík's Works*, London
1916	Capet, *La technique supérieure de l'archet*, Paris
1920	Moser, *Methodik des Violinspiels*, Leipzig
1921	Auer, *Violin Playing As I Teach It*, New York
	Dounis, *The Artist's Technique of Violin Playing* op. 1, New York
	F. Gerlier, *30 études manuscrites*, Paris
1922	Ševčík, *The School of Intonation* (14 vols.), New York
1923/28	Flesch, *Die Kunst des Violinspiels* (2 vols.), Berlin (Engl. trans. as *The Art of Violin Playing*, New York 1924, 1930; 2d rev. ed. 1939)
1924	Dounis, *The Absolute Independence of the Fingers*, op. 15, London
1925	Auer, *Violin Masterworks and Their Interpretation*, New York
1926	Auer and Saenger, *Graded Course of Violin Playing* (8 vols.), New York
	Flesch, *Das Skalensystem* (Scale studies), Berlin
	Hindemith, *Studies for Violinists*, Mainz and New York
1931	Flesch, *Das Klangproblem im Geigenspiel*, Leipzig (Engl. trans. as *Problems of Tone Production*, New York 1934)
1932	Martinů, *Rhythmische Etüden* (with piano), Mainz
1932–	Erich and Elma Doflein, *Das Geigen-Schulwerk*, Mainz (many editions; Engl. trans. Mainz and London 1957)
1937	Norden, *Harmony and Its Application in Violin Playing*, Boston
1944	Heimann, *Modern Violin Studies*, Copenhagen
1953	Gingold, ed., *Orchestral Excerpts* (3 vols.), New York
1960	Primrose, *Technique Is Memory: A Method for Violin and Viola Players Based on Finger Patterns*, London
1961	Havas, *A New Approach to Violin Playing*, London (5th ed. 1970; with videocassette 1991)
1962	Galamian, *Principles of Violin Playing and Teaching*, Englewood Cliffs, N.J.
1963	Hutton, *Improving the School String Section*, Boston
1964	Green, *Twelve Modern Etudes for the Advanced Violinist or Violist*, Philadelphia
	Szigeti, *A Violinist's Notebook*, London
1966	Flesch, *Violin Fingering: Its Theory and Practice*, London (1st publ. Milan 1960)

1967	Yampolsky, *The Principles of Violin Fingering*, London
	Ysaÿe, *Exercices et gammes* (Szigeti, ed.) Brussels
1969	Suzuki, *Nurtured by Love: Talent Education for Young Children*, New York
1971	Menuhin, *Six Lessons with Yehudi Menuhin*, London (rpt. 1974)
1972/73	Applebaum, *The Way They Play* (interviews), Neptune City, N.J.
1977	Zukofsky, *All-Interval Scale Book, Including a Chart of Harmonics*, New York
1982	Ben–Haim, *Three Studies for Violin Solo*, Tel Aviv
1985	Jacoby, *Violin Technique: A Practical Analysis for Performers*, London
1986	Igor Ozim, ed. *Pro Musica Nova: Studies for Playing Contemporary Music for Violin* (English and German text), Wiesbaden
1987	Rolland, *Young Strings in Action: A String Method for Class or Individual Instruction*, Farmingdale, N.Y.
1988	Ricci, *Left-Hand Violin Technique*, New York
1989	Rolland, *The Teaching of Action in String Playing* (with fourteen films on nine videocassettes), Urbana
1993	Kaufman, *Warming-Up Scales and Arpeggios for Violin*, New York
1996	Adler, *Meadowmount Etudes: Four Studies of Twentieth-Century Techniques for Solo Violin*, Bryn Mawr, Pa.

GREAT TWENTIETH-CENTURY VIOLINISTS: *VIRTUOSI*

It was easy to group violinists from the seventeeth and eighteenth centuries according to their significance. The Italians formed a fairly homogeneous group according to their origin, schooling, and interpretive style, whether they were active in Turin, Padua, London, Paris, Dresden, Stuttgart, or Vienna; it was therefore appropriate to discuss them in one chapter. The same was largely true for the nineteenth century, though some players defy such classification. Joachim, for instance, was a Jew born in Kitsee, which city—then in Hungary—counted many German immigrants among its inhabitants. He studied in Pest, Hungary, and then in Vienna before becoming Germany's leading violinist, active in Leipzig, Hanover, and Berlin. His style of playing was considered truly German, and his career so strongly affected German music that one is justified in including him among nineteenth-century German violinists. Flesch's situation, recalled in his memoirs, was similar.

I had in a short time become accepted in Germany and abroad as the leading German violinist. For the strange thing about my career has been that I, the German–Hungarian Jew, trained in the Franco–Belgian school, and therefore a decided opponent of the current German school, was all my life regarded as a violinist of purely German feeling.

Flesch's remarks apply until ca. 1910–1912. Up to that time, life was sufficiently stable, so that violinists, though traveling widely, could still take root in a new environment. With World War I, drastic changes occurred that also affected the field of music performance. The United States, the proverbial melting pot, became the destination of many who were eager to leave Europe, where the flames of nationalism were continually fanned by politicians. America's readiness to receive immigrants made it the world's foremost harbor for violinists such as Auer, Heifetz, Kreisler, Menuhin (of Russian-Jewish parents), and Milstein, to name just a few. In 1933, events in Nazi Germany caused another exodus of violin virtuosos and outstanding teachers; it continued through and even after the horrors of World War II and included composers, conductors, singers, and instrumentalists. Many acquired U.S. citizenship and traveled with U.S. passports. Although all these upheavals may not have entirely eradicated characteristics related to a violinist's ethnic background, it makes it difficult if not impossible to arrange a survey of violinists according to nationality.

Establishing categories according to schools of violin playing would be equally irrelevant. Such categorizing already led to questionable results during the nineteenth century. When we learn that the outstanding Polish violinist Ida Haendel studied at first with her father and then with Mihalowicz, Frenkel, Goldberg, Totenberg, Szigeti, Flesch, and Enesco, we realize that in the twentieth century the term "school" lost most of its earlier meaning. Even ordering players according to their dates of birth would cause confusion in regard to their artistic significance. Kubelik (b. 1880 in Prague), for instance, reached the height of his career ca. 1910, at a time when Kreisler, who was five years older, was just beginning to make a name for himself. On the other hand, Menuhin and Szeryng are almost the same age (b. 1916 and 1918), yet Menuhin's meteoric rise to fame began in 1926, whereas Szeryng did not receive widespread recognition until the 1940s. Therefore I judged that a neutral, impersonal alphabetic listing would be most useful for the readers of this book.

It was also difficult to decide whom to include in this list. The importance of earlier violinists (who may also have been composers and authors of teaching materials) was largely determined by the longevity of their works. The elapsed time gives us a clearer view of their significance, beyond trends and fashions of their day, and we can see more clearly their effect on the development of violin playing. We are helped in this by research and by the continued existence of their published editions. But as we come closer to our own time, decisions about rank, value, and importance are more difficult, for in many cases we deal with developments that are still in progress. Our opinions are largely affected by a player's participation in international concert life, and even by the degree to which the recording industry has championed certain soloists, both factors not entirely determined by artistic quality. More-over, the current state of violin playing is not reflected by soloists alone. Those who have distinguished careers as quartet players (even those playing second violin!) should not be overlooked; the same applies to outstanding teachers. Nor should orchestra players be forgotten. A concertmaster, sitting year after year at the same stand, may conscientiously carry out his or her duties, always prepared to play the solo in Strauss's *Ein Heldenleben* or in Mozart's "Haffner" Serenade. A concertmaster represents the orchestra and its standing, and is responsible for the quality of the string section as a whole. All this suggests a higher degree of importance than that of a soloist, who appears and quickly leaves again.

Given all these considerations, I trust that readers will understand why some names they consider important may be missing from the following overview. It is not intended to be a comprehensive account, which would have been impossible to compile. One should also remember that any selec-tive list is bound to be subjective to some extent.

[*Editor's note*: An attempt has been made, equally selective, to provide basic information about violinists who have come to the fore in recent years. Because of space limitations, these listings had to be very brief, and cannot be complete or definitive, for new virtuosos appear on the concert stage every year, if not every month. Thus Gil Shaham (often appearing with his sister, pianist Orli Shaham) has become a major performer, giving well over a hun-dred concerts a year (*The New York Times*, 11 March 1997). Among sources consulted, Boris Schwarz's outstanding compilation, *Great Masters of the Vio-lin* (New York 1983), was particularly helpful. Its section "The Twentieth Century" includes chapters on violin playing in America, subdivided accord-ing to the older, middle, and younger generations. Among the younger play-ers he includes Eugene Fodor, Erick Friedman, Caroll Glenn, Ani and Ida Kavafian, Jaime Laredo, Robert Mann, Michael Rabin, and Charles Treger. There also are chapters on Israeli and Asian violinists and a bibliography with biographies and memoirs of many violinists. A more recent listing of major violinists is included in Alain Pâris's *Dictionnaire des interprètes* (Paris 1995).]

Salvatore Accardo (b. 1941 in Turin)

Pupil of Luigi d'Ambrosio, Yvonne Astruc, and Milstein. Played the Paganini Caprices at the age of thirteen. Won numerous prizes including the Paganini competition (Genoa 1958). Many recordings, including two recordings of the Paganini Caprices and all his concertos. Also conducts.

Christian Altenburger (b. 1957 in Heidelberg)

Austrian. Studied with his father, who was chairman of the Vienna Phil-harmonic, then with Moravec in Vienna. Graduated at the age of sixteen. Further studies with DeLay at Juilliard. Many tours and recordings.

Pierre Amoyal (b. 1949 in Paris)

Took up the violin because there was no room for a piano at home. Premier prix at the Conservatoire at the age of twelve, then scholarship pupil of Roland Charmy. At seventeen, began five years of intensive study with Heifetz in Los Angeles, then made his first recording for Erato, followed by many others. Professor at the Paris Conservatoire 1977–1986.

Shmuel Ashkenasi (b. 1941 in Tel Aviv)

Several waves of immigration brought major performers and pedagogues to the young state of Israel. Huberman, Kestenberg, and others provided experience and funding, building up an intensive, high-quality musical life. Now Israel "exports" artists. Ashkenasi studied with Ilona Fehér, a Hubay pupil, then with Zimbalist at the Curtis Institute in Philadelphia. He is considered a Paganini specialist and is the founder of the Vermeer String Quartet, in residence at Northern Illinois University.

Gabriel Banat (b. in Transylvania)

Discovered by Bartók. Won the Hubay Prize at age seventeen. American sonata recitals with Enesco. Several works written for him, among them *Music Plus One* for violin solo and tape by Ilhan Mimaroglu (1970). Member of the New York Philharmonic. Published six volumes of *Masters of the Violin*, a facsimile edition of Mozart violin concerto autographs, and editions of baroque music (Mondonville, with E. Boroff).

Joshua Bell (b. 1967 in Indiana)

Gingold student. Carnegie Hall debut 1985. Many recordings, including Prokofiev concertos (1994).

Igor Besrodny (b. 1930 in Tiflis)

One of the many major Russian violinists who are as yet little known in the West. Attended the Central Music School for Children and Music Academy in Moscow, a Yampolsky pupil. A Strad was made available to him by the state; he used it on his tours. With Gidon Kremer and others he represents a new Russian style of playing, exemplified by his Bach interpretations, which eschew virtuosity *per se* in favor of a faithful rendering of each composition.

Kolja Blacher (b. 1963 in Berlin)

One of Germany's foremost young musicians. Concertmaster of Berlin Philharmonic since 1993.

Vadim Brodski (b. 1950 in Kiev)

Won first prize at the Wieniawski competition (Warsaw 1977). Member of Kiev Philharmonic; in Poland since 1981. Paganini competition (Genoa 1984) and Varga competition (Sion 1984). Toured the U.S. Many recordings, including Tchaikovsky's complete works for violin and orchestra and Paul McCartney's *Beatles Symphony* (1986).

Willy Burmester (b. 1869 in Hamburg, d. 1933)

At age twelve studied with Joachim in Berlin; at fifteen, graduated from the Berlin Academy. His report card stated, "Failing in all subjects except violin, for which he showed some talent." Yet Joachim's reputation as a teacher was substantially advanced by Burmester's later successful career. He amazed turn-of-the-century audiences with his phenomenal technique, demonstrated especially in his playing of Paganini. Arranged and performed many somewhat trivial arrangements, but never played the four sonatas Reger had dedicated to him. His star waned around the time of World War I. Like Kubelik he did not succeed in reestablishing himself as a concert artist, nor was he interested in teaching, so that he had little influence on the younger generation.

Adolf Busch (1891–1952)

Ever since Spohr (whose playing was contrasted with Paganini's), some violinists have been considered "typically German." These include Joachim, Flesch, Kulenkampff, and Adolf Busch. They shared one common characteristic: though they were all virtuosos, their concerts included very little music that merely displayed their virtuosity. Their chief intent was to interpret only the best violin music, with emphasis on Bach, Beethoven, and Brahms. Concentration on this repertory, and their strong devotion to chamber music, led to the neglect of music given to purely sensuous effects. This has been said of Adolf Busch in particular, who was considered one of the foremost interpreters of the "three Bs."

Busch's first teacher was his father, in whose dance band he soon played. He attended the Cologne conservatory, studying with Hess and Eldering, finishing the course of study there at eighteen. He became concertmaster of the Vienna *Konzertverein*; his success led to his appointment, at twenty-six, to the Berlin academy. Ever since his youth he was deeply committed to playing chamber music with his brothers Fritz (best known as a conductor) and Herrmann (a cellist). The Busch Quartet and the Busch-Serkin Duo established worldwide reputations. The Nazi regime led to an exodus of violinists, but Busch did not choose to take advantage of this to further his career in Nazi Germany. He left in 1933, settled in the U.S. in 1939, and founded the Marlboro School of Music in Vermont in 1950. His reputation was such that for several years he was entrusted with the teaching of the young Menuhin.

Alfredo Campoli (b. 1906 in Rome, d. 1991)

The son of a violin teacher and an outstanding singer, with whom he soon moved to England. Campoli won many prizes as a child prodigy, but his career was hindered by the depression that followed World War I. He made a living with a band he had founded, playing light music, but eventually made his way back to classical music. He was highly regarded as an interpreter of Tartini, Paganini, and Tchaikovsky; his recordings also included the Handel sonatas, the Mendelssohn Concerto, and works by Bach. He toured worldwide, making his U.S. debut in 1953.

Samuel Dushkin (b. 1891 in Poland, d. 1976)

Soon adopted by the American composer Blair Fairchild and taught by Auer and Kreisler. With this varied background Dushkin became an outstanding interpreter. As the result of their collaboration, we learn something about Stravinsky's view of virtuosos, included in his 1936 autobiography:

> Before knowing him I had been a little doubtful, in spite of the weight I attached to the recommendations of a man of such finished culture as my friend Strecker. I was afraid of Dushkin as a virtuoso. I knew that for virtuosi there were temptations and dangers that they were not all capable of overcoming. In order to succeed they are obliged to seek immediate triumphs and to lend themselves to the wishes of the public, the great majority of whom demand sensational effects from the player. This preoccupation naturally influences their taste, their choice of music, and their manner of treating the piece selected. How many admirable compositions, for instance, are set aside because they do not offer the player an opportunity of shining with facile brilliancy! Unfortunately, they often cannot help themselves, fearing the competition of their rivals and, to be frank, the loss of their bread and butter.
>
> Dushkin is certainly an exception in this respect among many of his fellow players, and I was very glad to find in him, besides his remarkable gifts as a born violinist, a musical culture, a delicate understanding, and—in the exercise of his profession—an abnegation that is very rare.

It may be that this "abnegation" or reticence prevented Dushkin from acquiring the position in international concert life to which his artistry had entitled him.

Mischa Elman (1891–1967)

Auer's reputation as a teacher, throughout Europe and then worldwide, was established by three violinists: Mischa Elman, Efrem Zimbalist, and Jascha Heifetz. When early in the century Elman first appeared on the concert stages of central Europe, Auer was almost sixty years old. His father, a village schoolteacher, gave him his first lessons; Mischa then went to conservatories in Odessa and St. Petersburg. He made his Berlin debut, playing the Tchaikovsky Concerto before he had started working with Auer, which indicates that that pedagogue provided only the finishing touches to Elman's studies. Flesch (1957) had words of high praise:

> His tone production, above all, overflowing as it is with a sensuous mellifluence, an Italian *bel canto* in oriental dress, impresses and at times stuns the listener. His intonation, which is clear as a bell, further enhances the charm of his tone.

This large and refined tone, carefully nurtured, was probably due in part to Auer's "Russian" way of holding the bow. Violinists with small hands that cannot execute large stretches may find consolation in knowing that for these reasons Elman was unable to play certain Paganini compositions, a problem he had in common with Sarasate. But the rest of his repertory was ample, including Handel and Mozart sonatas as well as the Beethoven and Tchaikovsky concertos. His strength was phenomenal; he continued to concertize even during the last years of his life, which ended in New York.

Georges Enesco (1881–1955)

The Romanian Enesco was one of the few twentieth-century musicians who were violinists, composers, and conductors. His early studies were with Hellmesberger in Vienna, then with Marsick in Paris. He also studied harmony and counterpoint. In time he acquired a worldwide reputation as a virtuoso, based especially on his interpretations of the repertory from Bach to Brahms. He also gained recognition as a composer (the opera *Oedipe*, Paris 1937; several symphonies, rhapsodies for orchestra, violin sonatas, and string quartets), as conductor of his own works in particular, and he was much in demand as a teacher.

Christian Ferras (1933–1982)

With the deaths of Jacques Thibaud (1943) and Ginette Neveu (1949), France lost their greatest violinists. In time, Ferras was able to fill this void. He was Enesco's private pupil and completed his studies at the Conservatoire in 1946, earning prizes in violin and chamber music. This double success of the barely thirteen-year-old boy was characteristic for Ferras. As a violinist he was the equal of colleagues who had concertized for decades, but he used his virtuosity for interpetations that were profoundly musical; among his favorites were the Brahms and Berg concertos. Ferras was appointed to the Conservatoire faculty in 1975. He died in Paris, only forty-nine years old.

Carl Flesch (1873–1944)

A doctor's son, born in a German-speaking region of Hungary. At the age of ten he went to Vienna to study with Maxintsack. In 1886 he was admitted to Grün's violin class at the conservatory. It was a stroke of luck that nearsightedness prevented his becoming a member of the court opera orchestra. Instead he went to Paris and became a student of Marsick. On leaving the Conservatoire he obtained a premier prix. Successful recitals in Vienna and Berlin led to teaching at the conservatory and other activities in Bucharest. After a short stay in Berlin he went to Amsterdam in 1903, teaching at the conservatory and becoming increasingly successful as a soloist. In 1908 he returned to Berlin, teaching at first privately, then, beginning in 1921, gave master classes at the academy. After five years in America he received a permanent professorship in Berlin in 1928 and also gave summer courses in Baden-Baden. By that time Flesch was one of the leading pedagogues. Many outstanding violinists benefited from his instruction or counsel, among them Gimpel, Goldberg, Haendel, Neveu, Odnoposoff, Rostal, Strub, and Szeryng. Several major publications resulted from his teaching experiences. For racial reasons he left Germany in 1934. Years of unrest, due to persecution and the war, took him to London, Amsterdam, Budapest, and Lucerne.

Flesch represented an unusual mixture of concertizing artist, scholar, and pedagogue. He saw his principal calling as teacher and writer, not having quite succeeded in taking his place among world-class virtuosos. As a performer he excelled as an interpreter of sonatas with Artur Schnabel. His memoirs are a good source of information about his life and work, though some of his very critical statements about his contemporaries must be taken with a grain of salt.

Zino Francescatti (1902–1991)

As a child in Marseille, he is said to have known the entire violin repertory, for his mother (who was also his first teacher) practiced the violin six hours a day. The family had come from Italy to Marseille, where the father taught cello. After studies at the Paris Conservatoire, Francescatti concertized in Europe and then went to America. From then on he seldom appeared on the Continent. His repertory included most of the great works for his instrument; he was highly regarded as a Paganini player. He retired in 1975 except for some teaching. The international violin competition in Aix was founded by him in 1987.

Erick Friedman (b. 1939 in New Jersey)

Pupil of Applebaum, Galamian, and Milstein. Studied with Heifetz 1956–1958. At Eastman School of Music since 1975.

Joseph Fuchs (1899–1997)

Continued in the tradition of Franz Kneisel, whose student he was. Concertmaster of the Cleveland Orchestra 1926–1940. Professor of violin at Juilliard from 1946 until his death.

André Gertler (b. 1907 in Hungary)

Pupil of Hubay in violin and Kodály in composition. Began performing at thirteen, often playing duos with Bartók. Founded the Gertler Quartet in 1931; the group played approximately one thousand concerts in twenty years. His repertory is unusual: works from the baroque and classic periods as well as twentieth-century compositions. He performs about thirty modern works, including nine dedicated to him. (He may also have given advice about their violin parts.) A Bartók specialist, Gertler also wrote cadenzas for the Beethoven Concerto and Mozart's K. 216 (published 1973 in Vienna).

Josef Gingold (b. 1909 in Russia, d. 1995)

Studied with Ysaÿe in Belgium. For seven years played under Toscanini in the NBC Symphony Orchestra, was concertmaster in Detroit, then thirteen years under Szell in Cleveland. Active as soloist and chamber music player. Joined the Indiana University School of Music faculty in 1960, also taught at the Manhattan School of Music 1980–1981. Two records, issued in celebration of his seventy-fifth birthday, demonstrate his talent.

Szymon Goldberg (1909–1993)

At the age of ten he became a Flesch student in Berlin; ten years later was appointed concertmaster of the Berlin Philharmonic. Dismissed by the Nazis in 1934. He was an outstanding leader, also a fine interpreter of classic concertos, and an occasional conductor. Performed recitals with Lily Kraus and Artur Balsam, trios with Hindemith and Feuermann. New York debut 1938. Became a U.S. citizen. Prisoner of war 1942–1945. Active participant in the Aspen Festivals, taught at Juilliard and Curtis. In 1990 became conductor of the New Japan Philharmonic Orchestra.

Arthur Grumiaux (1921–1986)

In relation to the Belgian generation of Ysaÿe, his place is similar to that of Besrodny and Kogan to the older Russian generation. Impeccable technique. First lessons with his grandfather, then, at the age of six, at the conservatory in Charleroi, and five years later at the Brussels conservatory. When eighteen, he studied with Enesco in Paris. Won many prizes, including the Prix Vieuxtemps. It is indicative of his clear, analytical mind that he passed all final exams in theory, including counterpoint and fugue. His career as a virtuoso was delayed by World War II, but not his development as a mature artist. Having twice recorded all Mozart concertos he was considered a Mozart specialist. Exemplary performances with pianist Clara Haskil.

Franco Gulli (b. 1926 in Trieste)

Played the Bach Chaconne when he was nine, pieces by Paganini at eleven. Later studied with Szigeti. Master classes in Siena and Lucerne since 1964; professor at Indiana University (Bloomington) since 1972. Appears in sonata performances with his wife, pianist Enrica Cavallo.

Jascha Heifetz (1899–1987)

Born in Vilnius, then Russian Poland, later Lithuania. His early training was substantial: first taught by his father, an orchestra violinist, then, aged five, by Malkin, three years later by Auer's assistant Nalbandian, finally by Auer himself. Without wanting to detract from Auer, it must be said that Malkin's role was decisive, for Heifetz performed the Mendelssohn Concerto at the age of seven. He once said that he had no idea what the Auer method was, even though he had studied with him. Much has been written about Heifetz and his phenomenal talent. He soon became one of the greatest violinists of the century, a reputation confirmed by his first New York recital in 1917.

Flesch (1957) wondered whether he really belongs among the truly great interpreters: "Without a question, he represents a culmination in the contemporary development of our art. . . . He got used to playing often with his hands alone and allowing his mind a Sleeping Beauty's rest." Few would agree with him. As Heifetz's recordings confirm, his mastery of technique led him to tempos that reach the limit of what the listener can hear clearly. His repertory included Bach and the classic composers, but he was best playing

Tchaikovsky, Vieuxtemps, Lalo, and other works of that age. Among composers who dedicated concertos to him were Korngold, Rózsa, Walton, and Gruenberg. He published numerous transcriptions. Heifetz last appeared in public in 1972, having taught extensively since 1959. Like many artists whose professional work requires supreme concentration, he had a hobby: under the pen name Jim Hoyl he composed popular tunes.

Jenö Hubay (1858–1937)

Son of Karl Huber, a violin teacher, conductor, and composer in Pest. Studied in Berlin (Joachim) and Paris, became Vieuxtemps's successor at the Brussels conservatory. After early successes as a soloist, he returned to Hungary in 1886 and devoted himself to quartet playing, teaching, and composing. Eldering was among his Brussels students; those in Budapest included Szigeti and Vécsey. He was largely responsible for the term "Budapest (or Hungarian) school." For a long time he directed the Budapest music academy.

A Hubay competition that all young Hungarian violinists hope to win has kept his name alive. His opera *The Cremona Violin Maker* (1894), with an important violin solo, and his once very popular "Hejre Kati" in the gypsy manner have largely disappeared from the repertory.

Bronislaw Huberman (b. 1882 near Warsaw, d. 1947)

Raised in an environment of poverty, a violin was chosen for him since a piano would have been too expensive. At age six he entered the Warsaw conservatory, then went to Berlin for further training. Joachim turned him over to an assistant; as a result, father and son Huberman soon left Berlin to seek better inspiration in Frankfurt (Hugo Heermann) and Paris (Marsick). Conventional lessons ended when he was twelve; after that he considered himself self-taught, saying that his real learning took place on the concert platform. When he was thirteen he played the Brahms Concerto in Vienna, in the presence of the composer, who was delighted. It seems the event made a lasting impression on Huberman, who throughout his career was particularly acclaimed for his Brahms interpretations. His rich repertory included virtually all masterworks, from Bach to Tchaikovsky and Lalo.

Beethoven's ethics must have greatly impressed Huberman, who passionately fought for the humanitarian concept of European unity in his writings and in speeches. He contributed heavily to provide for persecuted fellow Jews. In 1936 he founded the Palestine Orchestra that in 1948 became the Israeli Philharmonic Orchestra in Tel Aviv. In a charming, witty book *Aus der Werkstatt des Virtuosen* (From a virtuoso's workshop), Huberman told much about his career, problems of his development, and his thoughts about the violin and art in general.

Young-Uck Kim (b. 1948 in Seoul)

Aged seven, he won first prize in the Korean national competition. Studied with Galamian 1961–1966. In 1967, Bernstein presented him on television playing a Mozart concerto. Gave a New York recital in 1976. Formed trio with Yo-Yo Ma and pianist Emanuel Ax.

Franz Kneisel (b. 1865 in Bucharest, d. 1926)
Studied in his hometown and then in Vienna. Went to the United States, became concertmaster of the Boston Symphony Orchestra in 1885. Founded Kneisel Quartet in 1886, active until 1917. From 1905 on taught at Institute of Musical Art in New York. An important figure in the development of music, especially chamber music, in America.

Leonid Kogan (b. 1924 in Dnepropetrovsk, Ukraine, d. 1982)
Began violin lessons at age seven. Because of the boy's talent, the family moved to Moscow, where he was admitted to the Central Music School. Taught by Yampolsky, who prepared him for admission to the conservatory. At twenty-four he completed the course of study, then prepared for the Queen Elisabeth competition in Brussels, which he won three years later. He embarked upon a successful international career, but his was not a meteoric rise to fame; only after twenty years of hard work did he succeed in Brussels. Concertized extensively in Europe and, after 1954, in North America. In 1980 taught at Chigi Academy in Siena. His repertory was extensive, including much chamber music, in which field he concertized with Emil Gilels, his brother-in-law.

Louis Krasner (1903–1995)
Left his native Russia as a child, studied at New England Conservatory, from which he graduated in 1923. Further study in Europe with Capet, Flesch, and Ševčík. His great interest in contemporary music led to premieres of many major works, most importantly of Berg's Violin Concerto. Concertmaster of Minneapolis Symphony under Mitropoulos, 1944–1949. After 1974 taught at New England Conservatory.

Gidon Kremer (b. 1947 in Riga)
First lessons with father; a grandfather also was a professional violinist. Began eight years of study with Oistrakh at Moscow Conservatory in 1965. Participated in competitions in Brussels (1967), Genoa (1969), and Moscow (1970). New York debut 1977; left Russia 1980 to settle in the West. Published a volume of recollections (Munich 1993) and a collection of interviews, opinions, and such, edited by W. Lewinski (Munich 1982). Karajan called him "the greatest violinist of his generation."

Jan Kubelik (b. 1880 near Prague, d. 1940)
Studied with Ševčík in Prague 1892–1898. His sensational debut at the age of twenty helped to establish Ševčík among the top pedagogues. On his twenty-first birthday, Lord and Lady Palmer presented him with a 1687 Strad. Worldwide concert tours established his reputation, especially as a Paganini expert; he was considered one of the few legitimate heirs of that

wizard. This period of glory, however, lasted less than ten years. As Flesch (1957) recalled,

> The precision of his technical preparations was virtually unprecedented, but it was coupled with . . . a tendency to exaggeratedly long, slow, and mechanical studies resulting in an atrophy of elemental feeling [and] a disregard of purely musical thought in favor of a perfect but lifeless, soulless mechanization of the playing movements.

Kubelik composed a *Symphonie américaine* (1937) and several concertos and shorter pieces.

Sigiswald Kuijken (b. 1944 near Brussels)

Best known as a specialist in baroque violin and gamba playing. Premier prix, Brussels conservatory 1964. Performs on period instruments. In 1972 founded La Petite Bande, a baroque orchestra named after Lully's orchestra in Versailles, and the Kuijken Quartet in 1986. Has taught at Brussels conservatory since 1994. Many recordings, including Bach sonatas with Gustav Leonhardt.

Georg Kulenkampff (b. 1898 in Bremen, d. 1948)

With Adolf Busch, one of the few German violinists after 1900 to gain international recognition. Studied with Willy Hess. At eighteen became concertmaster of the Bremen Philharmonic but resigned after three years to devote himself entirely to a solo career. Taught at the Berlin academy and after 1944 at the Lucerne conservatory, as Flesch's successor. A well-rounded violinist, Kulenkampff excelled in the classic and romantic repertory.

Cho–Liang Lin (b. 1960 in Taiwan)

Began violin lessons aged five at the Sydney conservatory, where he gave his first public recital at seven. Robert Paler was his teacher in Sydney, Dorothy DeLay at Juilliard since 1975. Appeared at New York's Mostly Mozart Festival in 1979, the start of a brilliant career. Rostropovich invited him to play in Washington. Became U.S. citizen in 1988.

David Mannes (1866–1959)

Studied in New York, also in Brussels with Ysaÿe. In 1895 joined the New York Symphony, where he was concertmaster 1903–1912. His desire to make music lessons available to children from poor families in 1894 led to the founding of the Music School Settlement on New York's East Side. In 1916 he and his wife founded the Mannes Music School, which later became the Mannes College of Music. Published an autobiography, *Music Is My Faith*, in 1938.

Henri Marteau (b. 1874 in Reims, d. 1934)

The son of a French father and German mother, which during World War I caused him anxieties and difficulties. Studied with Léonard, then at the

Paris Conservatoire. Taught in Geneva and at the Berlin academy (1908–1915), where he succeeded Joachim. As a French army reserve officer he was arrested, then restricted to teaching at home. Other political problems followed, causing him to leave for Sweden, where he obtained citizenship. Older audiences considered him among the best Mozart and Bach interpreters, but he cultivated the modern repertory as well, giving the first performance of Reger's Violin Concerto, dedicated to him, in 1908. The war's interruption seriously affected Marteau's career.

Yehudi Menuhin (b. 1916 in New York)

To judge by some biographies of Lord Menuhin, his career consists of nothing but a series of crises. One wonders, then, where he found the time for the many achievements, on the concert platform and in the recording studio, that have established him as one of the greatest violinists of our age. His spectacular successes at the age of ten would hardly have justified that opinion. He then performed in San Francisco, New York, and Paris, playing Tchaikovsky and Lalo, followed by a Beethoven concert under Fritz Busch in Carnegie Hall in 1927.

Menuhin was the son of Russian immigrants, taught by Sigmund Anker and Louis Persinger. After the Paris recital he studied with Enesco, and in 1929 with Adolf Busch. In that year he performed, in one evening, three concertos with the Berlin Philharmonic under Bruno Walter: the Bach (in E major), the Beethoven, and the Brahms. The success was tremendous; few others would have had the stamina for such a tour de force, but it did not inhibit the boy's further development. The knowledge that some critics may just be waiting for him to follow this with a weak performance (using it to make a point about child prodigies) may have led to occasional tension, but this did not detract from his violinistic accomplishment.

For some time Menuhin was considered a Mozart specialist who also was fond of playing Bach, but who was always ready to oblige with a Paganini concerto. In recent years he has pursued additional interests as a writer, conductor, and organizer of the Bath Festival. In 1963, on a country estate near Stoke d'Abernon, southwest of London, he established his own music school for talented children. "It is not a breeding ground for prodigies . . . but a place where the musical mind can grow and expand according to its own God-given timetable, gently guided but never channeled." [Schwarz 1983 devotes a fine chapter to Menuhin. *Ed.*] Many works were commissioned by and dedicated to him, the composers including Bartók, Bloch, Frank Martin, Milhaud, and Takemitsu, to name a few. In 1993, Queen Elizabeth bestowed upon him the title Baron of Stoke d'Abernon. In 1996, having reached his eightieth birthday, he continued his career of conducting. Much has been written by and about Lord Menuhin.

Nathan Milstein (b. 1904 in Odessa, d. 1992)

Studied with Stoliarsky and Auer, the latter exerting a powerful influence on him. Milstein's performing career spanned nearly sixty years, which means that his playing was subject to evaluation by several generations. Reviewers of his later recordings praised his noble, singing tone, and the dancelike quality of his finales. Though considered a Mendelssohn and Tchaikovsky specialist, his repertory was catholic. He met Horowitz in Kiev in 1921; they became close friends and music partners. Milstein came to the U.S. in 1928 and made his debut with the Philadelphia Orchestra in 1929. Though he became a U.S. citizen, he returned to Europe after the war. His book, *From Russia to the West*, was published in 1990.

Shlomo Mintz (b. 1957 in Moscow)

Mintz grew up in Israel, where he studied with Ilona Fehér, then in New York with DeLay at Juilliard. Carnegie Hall debut 1973. International tours since 1976; at ease performing music from Bach to the present. Also a violist, a devoted chamber music player, and occasional conductor. Music advisor to the Israel Chamber Orchestra 1988; chief guest conductor, Maastricht 1994.

Ricardo Odnoposoff (b. 1914 in Buenos Aires)

Of Russian parentage, he played his first concert aged five. Flesch pupil. Successful in competitions in Vienna (1932) and with David Oistrakh in Brussels (1937). Concertmaster, Vienna Philharmonic, followed by teaching in New York (1944–1956), then at the academy in Vienna, and later in Stuttgart and Zurich. Extensive repertory, with special strength in nineteenth-century literature.

David Oistrakh (b. 1908 in Odessa, d. 1974)

Early training in his hometown; moved to Moscow aged twenty. His arrival at the top was not easy; after rigorous national competitions he won second prize in the Wieniawski competition (Warsaw 1935) and first prize in Brussels (1937). Though esteemed as an interpreter of classic sonatas and concertos, he championed those by many contemporary Russians—Prokofiev, Shostakovich, Khachaturian, Kabalevsky—and gave the premieres of some of these. In 1934 began teaching at the Moscow Conservatory, attracting many superior students. Some conducting, including accompanying his son, with whom he frequently performed the Bach Double Concerto. His partners in sonata recitals included Sviatoslav Richter.

Igor Oistrakh (b. 1931 in Odessa)

Won the Wieniawski competition (Warsaw 1953) and then embarked on a brilliant career—accomplishments that speak to the father's pedagogical skill, but also to the son's strongly independent personality. Growing up in the shadow of the great man, he became more than his imitator. Whether he performs with orchestra or with his wife, the excellent pianist Natalia Serzalova, one never thinks of him as an image of his father, though he plays with a similarly warm tone and energetic bow. He taught at the Moscow Conservatory until 1975.

Itzhak Perlman (b. 1945 in Tel Aviv)

Began violin study when he was five; gave his first concert four years later. Began studies with Galamian at Juilliard in 1958. Won the Leventritt competition in 1964, which furthered his rise to stardom. Worldwide concert tours followed, though polio has confined him to a wheelchair since childhood. As one of the top virtuosos of his generation he performs and records repertory from all periods with equal understanding, including some lighter music. Premiered concertos by Earl Kim (1979) and Robert Starer (1981), and interpreted those by Walton and Korngold.

Louis Persinger (1887–1966)

After early studies in the U.S. he attended the Leipzig conservatory and studied with Ysaÿe in Brussels. Philadelphia Orchestra debut under Stokowski 1912. Moved to San Francisco, where Menuhin was one of his pupils; upon hearing Persinger play, the three-year-old boy decided that this man ("I did not know his name") would be his teacher. In 1930, Persinger joined the Juilliard faculty, where his pupils included Stern and Ricci.

Váša Příhoda (1900–1960)

First taught by his father, director of a music school in Prague, then by Marák, a Ševčík student. As a child prodigy in Prague he performed the Beethoven and Brahms concertos. Dvořák, Tchaikovsky, and Lalo are said to be the composers who inspired him most, but he was famous for flawless Paganini interpretations. After teaching in Munich and Salzburg, he joined the Vienna academy faculty in 1950. Soon after the end of World War I he supported himself by playing in a Milan café, where Toscanini "discovered" him and gathered financial support for the concert tour that facilitated Příhoda's breakthrough to top virtuoso standing.

Michael Rabin (b. 1936 in New York, d. 1972)

The son of a New York Philharmonic violinist, he became a Galamian student when he was nine and made his Carnegie Hall debut, earning superlative reviews. Extensive tours followed, but his promising career was cut short by personal problems, allegedly involving depression and drugs. He had to retire from concertizing and died at the early age of thirty-five.

Ruggiero Ricci (b. 1918 in San Francisco)

After early studies with Persinger, he embarked on a most successful career, giving concerts in San Francisco (1928, accompanied by Persinger) and New York (1929). Despite various family crises and a change of teacher, Ricci eventually established himself as a brilliant virtuoso, retaining this reputation as an adult. He served in the U.S. Army, then made a brilliant comeback, concertizing and recording. Taught at Indiana University, then at Juilliard.

Max Rostal (b. 1905 in Bohemia, d. 1991)

Studied with Rosé, then with Flesch (1920–1924). Concertmaster in Oslo, Flesch's assistant in Berlin 1928–1930; continued to teach there 1930–1933. Went to England, where he began teaching at the Guildhall School in 1943, known as an outstanding teacher. Returned to Germany after the war, taught in Bern and in Cologne 1957–1982. Edited the Beethoven violin sonatas (1981) and wrote a book on their interpretation (1985).

Alexander Schneider (b. 1908 in Vilnius, d. 1993)

First lessons in his hometown, then in Frankfurt, and in Berlin with Flesch. Joined Budapest String Quartet in 1932 (his brother, Misha, was the cellist). The quartet then established itself in the U.S., with Schneider, who took up residence there in 1938. In 1944 left the Quartet and formed the Albeneri Trio, also a duo with Ralph Kirkpatrick, harpsichordist. Active in establishing the Casals Festival in Prades; played with Casals in other festivals as well. Rejoined the Budapest Quartet in 1955, but remained active in many other musical enterprises (New York; Marlboro, Vermont) as a performer, teacher, and organizer. *Sasha: A Musician's Life* (New York 1988) is a volume of his casual, frequently amusing reminiscences.

Wolfgang Schneiderhan (b. 1915 in Vienna)

Studied with Ševčík. Debut with orchestra 1926. Concertmaster Vienna Symphony 1933–1937; Vienna Philharmonic 1937–1949. First violin in his own string quartet. Turned increasingly to solo performance, excelling in concertos and sonatas from Mozart and Beethoven to Brahms. Resides in Lucerne, Switzerland; teaches there (Lucerne Festival Strings) as well as in Salzburg, Vienna, and Stockholm.

Jaap Schröder (b. 1925 in Amsterdam)

Violinist, conductor, and musicologist, specializing in performing eighteenth-century music on period instruments. Studied at Amsterdam conservatory and with Thibaud in Paris. Leader of several quartets and chamber orchestras. Has taught in Basel, at Salzburg Mozarteum, Yale University, Juilliard, and many other institutions. Leader, Smithsonian Chamber Players, Washington, D.C. Has recorded extensively, including the complete Mozart symphonies with the Academy of Ancient Music, London, also Schubert, Mendelssohn, and Schumann chamber music with the Atlantis Ensemble.

Oscar Shumsky (b. 1917 in Philadelphia)

Studied with Auer and Zimbalist. Aged eight, performed a Mozart concerto under Stokowski. Member of Toscanini's NBC Orchestra (1938), first violinist of Primrose Quartet. Concertmaster of several orchestras. Taught at Curtis, Juilliard, and Yale. Also performs on viola.

Albert Spalding (1888–1953)

Probably the outstanding American violinist of his generation. The child of a well-to-do family who spent their winters in Florence, where the boy studied and heard many violinists at the family residence. At fourteen he graduated from the Liceo Musicale in Bologna. Paris debut 1905; New York 1908. After wartime service in U.S. Army, pursued a successful concert career. Gave first U.S. performance of Dohnányi's Violin Concerto and premiere of the Barber Concerto (1941). His book *Rise to Follow* (1943) describes his earlier career.

Tossy Spivakowsky (b. 1907 in Odessa)

Studied in Berlin with Willy Hess; first recital at age ten, followed by touring. Concertmaster of Berlin Philharmonic under Furtwängler 1926–1933; of Cleveland Orchestra 1942–1945. Gave first U.S. performance of Bartók's Violin Concerto no. 2 (1943), its only performance heard by the composer. Many premieres of works by American composers. At Juilliard since 1974.

Isaac Stern (b. 1920 in Kremenets, Ukraine)

Came to the U.S. as a young child. Studied with Naoum Blinder and Persinger. Eleven years old, appeared with San Francisco Symphony. New York debut 1937. After further studies played there again in 1939 to an enthusiastic audience. During the war years performed for servicemen overseas, also gave recitals at home. Member and founder of various chamber music ensembles; formed trio with Emanuel Ax and Yo-Yo Ma (1987). Extensive touring and recording. Involved in various music causes such as the preservation of Carnegie Hall and support of study and performance opportunities in Israel and China (the film *From Mao to Mozart* is based on Stern's 1979 trip).

Josef Suk (b. 1929 in Prague)

Grandson of the Czech composer of the same name, also a great-grandson of Dvořák. Studied at Prague conservatory. Successful soloist and chamber music player (Suk Trio), appearing as both violinist and violist. Founded Suk Chamber Orchestra in Prague in 1974. Premiered Martinů's Violin Concerto no. 1 in 1973. Performed at Bath Festival 1991.

Henryk Szeryng (b. 1918 near Warsaw, d. 1988)

His parents nurtured his musical education; violin lessons began at age seven, including three years with Flesch. Highly successful concert career, begun when he was fifteen, was delayed by his broad musical interests, including counterpoint and composition. Studies in Paris led to a premier prix in 1937. Hartnack describes how his career really took flight during the war years, when he performed for allied troops from Poland, the U.S., and U.K. Settled in Mexico in 1946, touring and recording extensively. The night before his death he performed the Brahms Concerto.

Joseph Szigeti (b. 1892 in Budapest, d. 1973)

At age thirteen finished Hubay's advanced class. Soon came into contact with Bartók, who remained a friend throughout his life, including the last years in America; in 1929 they first performed Bartók's First Rhapsody, dedicated to Szigeti. His concert career began in Frankfurt, where he appeared as a special attraction in a circus, playing the Mendelssohn Concerto. Before long he had to begin shaving his legs, so that his billing as a child prodigy, in short pants, would still be credible. Berlin debut 1905. Declined Joachim's offer to take him on as a student. London debut 1907; Szigeti remained in that city until 1913, broadening his musical and general education. Taught in Geneva 1917–1924, becoming widely known as a virtuoso. Premiered Prokofiev's First Concerto in Russia. Philadelphia debut 1925. Premiered Bloch's Violin Concerto, dedicated to him, in Cleveland, 1938. Very successful tours, including Russia and America. Took up residence in U.S. in 1940. Continued friendship and joint appearances with Bartók, including a performance of Bartók's *Contrasts* with Benny Goodman. Widely admired, as a musician and person. Many great composers dedicated works to him. Among his books, *With Strings Attached* (1947) is deservedly popular.

Jacques Thibaud (b. 1880 in Bordeaux, d. 1953)

Early training in his hometown, where Ysaÿe was impressed by the thirteen-year-old boy's playing. Student of Marsick at Paris Conservatoire; won a premier prix in 1896, but forced to play in cafés to earn a living. Joined several orchestras and eventually established himself as a soloist. By 1903 he succeeded on an American tour. After service in the French army he returned, playing a New York recital in 1916; regularly visited America after that. In 1905 he became the violinist in the famed Cortot Piano Trio; Casals was the cellist. He was loved and admired by the public and by colleagues, including Ysaÿe, Kreisler, and David Oistrakh, who wrote his obituary. Thibaud was almost seventy-three years old when he died in a plane crash on his way to a concert tour of French Indochina. [See *Un violon parle: Souvenirs de Jacques Thibaut* (Paris 1953), and Christian Goubault's *Jacques Thibaud, violoniste français* (Paris 1988, with discography). *Ed.*]

Charles Treger (b. 1935 in Detroit)

Studied with Galamian and Szymon Goldberg. Founding member of Chamber Music Society of Lincoln Center, 1969. Formed duo with André Watts in 1978, and in 1984 became director of the Meadowmount School, Westport, N.Y.

Viktor Tretyakov (b. 1946 in Krasnoiarsk, Siberia)

First lessons from his mother, then at music school in Irkutsk, and in 1953 at Moscow. Won a first prize in Tchaikovsky competition (Moscow 1966). Leader of USSR State Chamber Orchestra in Moscow, 1983.

Tibor Varga (b. 1921 in Györ, Hungary)

Admitted to Hubay's class in Budapest (1931–1938) and studied with Flesch in Berlin. Began concertizing abroad at age fourteen, activities interrupted by the war. Performed and recorded works by Berg, Schoenberg, Bartók, and many other contemporary composers. Founded Varga Chamber Orchestra in Detmold, Germany, in 1954; directed it until 1988. In 1964 organized Festival Tibor Varga in Sion, Switzerland, including master classes and a violin competition. Directed chamber orchestra in Annecy, France, 1989–1993. His many students perform and teach in many countries.

Franz von Vécsey (b. 1893 in Budapest, d. 1935)

Studied with Hubay, amazed audiences in Berlin when he was ten. Being featured as a child prodigy caused problems. Bartók concertized with him in Portugal in 1906, complained to the boy's mother about the "forced labor" involved. "Nothing but practicing; he sees nothing of the country." Flesch commented about the seventeen-year-old in his memoirs:

> Purely as a violinist, to be sure, he made a spotless impression: his tone production was brilliant, his movements were correct, and his technical ability altogether was of a high order. But his playing did not seem to contain much: it was primitive and undistinguished musically. He seemed a pupil of unusual talent with all the necessary spiritual potentialities which, however, were destined to remain latent. . . . His last years were wrapped in mystery. He rarely appeared on the concert platform, and it was not known quite how he spent his time.

Nevertheless, Vécsey's playing during his best years impressed his contemporaries, including Sibelius, who dedicated his Violin Concerto to him.

Eugène Ysaÿe (b. 1858 in Liège, d. 1931)

Studied with his father, with Rodolphe Massart and Wieniawski, and for three more years with Vieuxtemps. Concertmaster of a Berlin orchestra (1880); some travels as soloist. Professor at Brussels conservatory 1886–1897, where he founded his own quartet. Conductor of the Concerts Ysaÿe beginning in 1894. First American tour; declined directorship of New York Philharmonic. "Maître de Chapelle de la Cour de Belgique" and violin tutor to Queen Elisabeth, the patron of the Brussels competition named after her, 1913. Conducted Cincinnati Symphony 1918–1922, also taught at local conservatory. A virtuoso with phenomenal technique combined with varied, colorful timbre. Championed contemporary music (premiered Franck's Violin Sonata and Debussy's String Quartet, which the composer dedicated to Ysaÿe's group); found the great classic concertos a serious challenge and repeatedly postponed performing them. Retired almost completely from concertizing after the war. A diabetic, he underwent the amputation of his right foot. Conducted his last concert in Brussels in 1930 and died there the following year.

Pinchas Zukerman (b. 1948 in Tel Aviv)

Early education in his hometown, with financial support from the Israel-America Foundation. Isaac Stern heard the boy in 1960, helped to arrange his studies with Galamian, from age fourteen to seventeen. Co-winner of 1967 Leventritt competition, the beginning of a spectacular concertizing and recording career that includes works from Vivaldi to Elgar, Bartók, and Claude Bolling's Suite for jazz piano (with string bass and percussion). He also performs on viola, plays chamber music with Stern, Perlman, and others, and conducts (St. Paul Chamber Orchestra, 1980–1987). Principal guest conductor of the Dallas Symphony 1993.

Paul Zukofsky (b. 1943 in New York)

Studied with Galamian; made his Carnegie Hall debut at age thirteen. Graduate degree from Juilliard 1964. Became an advocate of new violin repertory, first presented in a series of recitals 1968–1969. Remains a specialist in avant garde music, having recorded works by Penderecki, Babbitt, Cage, Feldman, and many others. Taught at New England Conservatory and at Tanglewood; at Juilliard 1984–1992. At University of Southern California since 1992, teaching violin, chamber music, and conducting. Artistic director, Museum of Modern Art, New York. Has written on aspects of contemporary violin technique.

GREAT TWENTIETH-CENTURY
VIOLINISTS: *VIRTUOSE*

If a separate section is devoted to *virtuose*, this does not imply a difference in importance or quality. Based on his own teaching, Ševčík was full of praise: "Young women do not drink or smoke to excess; they therefore tend to be in better physical condition. It is also evident that they are more patient than men." That women soloists are still a minority may be attributed to lingering social prejudices. The London Royal Academy of Music did not admit female students until 1872, and many orchestras did not appoint women players until very recently—in some cases, only because of a shortage of qualified men.

From older recordings we realize that two English Ševčík students, Marie Hall (d. 1956) and Kathleen Parlow (d. 1963), were outstanding performers. Older concertgoers still rave about the Australian Alma Moodie (d. 1943), a Flesch student, who was only forty-three at her death. She lived in Germany and was an advocate of contemporary music. Flesch (1957) considered her the oustanding female violinist of her time. Erica Morini (1904–1995), a naturalized American born in Vienna, also was a Ševčík student, known especially for her interpretations of Brahms and Tchaikovsky. Gioconda De Vito (1907–1994), born and trained in Italy, represented in her playing her country's best traditions. She has been called the "bel canto violinist."

Guila Bustabo (b. 1919 in Wisconsin) performed in Chicago at the age of four and six years later with the New York Philharmonic. Her virtuosity equals that of her greatest male colleagues; for a long time she was considered one of the best Paganini interpreters.

The promising career of Ginette Neveu (1919–1949) was tragically cut short when she (and her brother Jean) died in a plane crash, on the way to her fourth American tour. At her death, according to Schwarz (1983), Neveu was near to being "the most widely acclaimed woman violinist of her day." Only a week before the fatal accident she played a recital in Paris, where she had some of her training, receiving a premier prix at the Conservatoire at the age of eleven. Four years of study with Flesch followed. She won the Wieniawski competition (Warsaw 1935). A fine interpretation of the Brahms Concerto is preserved on one of her few recordings.

Ida Haendel (b. 1924 in Chelm, Poland) has been mentioned as a product of many teachers. To succeed with exposure to so many different, often conflicting schools requires a strong personality, which Haendel possesses. A British subject, she concertizes there, in the U.S., and in Israel, less on the Continent. Her autobiography was published in 1970.

The Hungarian Johanna Martzy (1924–1979), a Hubay pupil, won many prizes and for many years was considered an outstanding soloist, praised especially for a recording of the Dvořák Concerto. Wanda Wilkomirska (b. 1929) came from a prominent Polish family of musicians. She graduated with honors from the Lodz conservatory, then studied in Budapest. She is fond of performing Prokofiev and (unlike many of her colleagues) the Berg Concerto, as well as music by Penderecki, Szymanowski, and other Polish composers. After lessons from her father, Edith Peinemann (b. 1937 in Mainz) studied with Max Rostal. She cultivates the great classic and romantic works and excels in Beethoven and Brahms sonatas. In 1960 she formed a duo with Jörg Demus.

[To the following sketches additions have again been made, to call attention to at least a few *virtuose* who have reached prominence in recent years. The *Dictionnaire des interprètes* by Pâris (1995) is a valuable source of information about these and other violinists. *Ed.*]

Jenny Abel (b. 1942 near Husum, Germany)

Also studied piano, voice, and composition, and pursued a serious interest in painting. At fourteen began studies with Rostal in Cologne and consulted with Szeryng. Specializes in contemporary repertory and unusual recital programs, such as three unaccompanied sonatas by Henze, Bach, and Bartók. Also has performed works by female Polish composer Grazyna Bacewicz (1909–1969). Recordings include the Berg Concerto and Respighi's rarely performed *Concerto gregoriano*. In 1977 she received the prize of the German recording industry. Oskar Kokoschka featured her in a series of eight paintings entitled *Jenny Abel Plays Sonatas by Bartók and Bach* (1973).

Iona Brown (b. 1941 in Salisbury, England)

Studied with Odnoposoff and Szeryng. Member of London Philharmonic 1963–1966, as well as of the Academy of St. Martin in the Fields, serving as concertmaster and assistant conductor to Sir Neville Marriner (1974). Artistic director of Los Angeles Chamber Orchestra 1987–1992.

Pina Carmirelli (1914–1993)

Student of Abbado and Serato, directed violin class at Accademia S. Cecilia in Rome. Founded Quintetto Boccherini in 1949, also made a detailed study of that composer and prepared editions of his instrumental works and of music by Vivaldi. In 1970, with Rudolf Serkin, performed all Beethoven sonatas at Carnegie Hall.

Sarah Chang (b. 1980 in Philadelphia)

Prodigiously talented student of DeLay and Hyo Kang at Juilliard. Played Paganini's First Concerto with the New York Philharmonic at the age of eight. Recorded her first album when she was nine, playing on a quarter-size violin; subsequent releases feature the Tchaikovsky Concerto, Lalo's *Symphonie espagnole*, Vieuxtemps's Violin Concerto no. 5, and Vaughan Williams's *The Lark Ascending*.

Kyung-Wha Chung (b. 1948 in Korea)

Studied with Galamian at the age of twelve. Won 1967 Leventritt competition (sharing first prize with Zukerman). Her recorded repertory reaches from Bach to Berg, Bartók, and Stravinsky. Has recorded Debussy and Franck sonatas with Radu Lupu. Her six brothers and sisters are also fine instrumentalists. Plays violin in a piano trio with her brother Myung-Whun (piano) and sister Myung-Wha.

Christiane Edinger (b. 1945 in Potsdam)

Daughter of a pianist, with whom she recorded sonatas. Studied with Milstein, also with Joseph Fuchs at Juilliard. Berlin debut 1962. Performs much contemporary music: Maderna, Zimmermann, Blacher, and von Einem; one of the first to perform Penderecki Concerto. Recorded Bach's solo sonatas and partitas.

Miriam Fried (b. 1946 in Romania)

Studied in Tel Aviv, then in New York (Galamian) and Indiana (Gingold). Won first prizes in Paganini (Genoa 1968) and Queen Elisabeth (Brussels 1971) competitions. Teaches at Indiana University, concertizes extensively. Appearances with orchestras during 1994/95 seasons included Chicago, Cleveland, Boston, and Philadelphia. [See "Miriam Fried: A Profile" (videocassette, Indiana University 1985). *Ed.*]

Dylana Jenson (b. 1961 in California)

Studied with Compinski, then Gingold (1974) and Milstein. European debut Zurich 1974. Won second prize in Tchaikovsky competition (Moscow 1978), the youngest participant. Played Sibelius Concerto with Philadelphia Orchestra at Carnegie Hall 1980.

Midori (Goto Mi Dori; b. 1971 in Osaka)

After early lessons from her mother, she received a scholarship to go to Aspen, to study with Dorothy DeLay (1980). At Juilliard in 1982, she also studied with Zukerman and appeared at a Young People's Concert of the New York Philharmonic, followed by extensive touring. Carnegie Hall debut 1990. Many recordings, including Bach's Double Concerto with Zukerman. London Proms debut 1993.

Viktoria Mullova (b. 1959 in Moscow)

Pupil of Kogan and others at Moscow Central Music School and Conservatory. First public appearance at age twelve, playing works by Paganini and Wieniawski. Winner of competitions in Lublin (1975), Helsinki (1981), and Moscow (1982). Escaped from Russia 1983, seeking political asylum in the U.S., then embarked on an international concert career.

Anne-Sophie Mutter (b. 1963 in Germany)

Early studies with Erna Honigberger, then Aida Stucki, both Flesch students. Aged six, won first prize in German "Young People Make Music" contest. Played Tartini's "Devil's Trill" Sonata and Bach's Chaconne at a recital, Lucerne 1976. Performed in Salzburg (1977) as a soloist with Berlin Philharmonic under Karajan, who took a lively interest in her career. Recorded concertos by Mozart, Mendelssohn, Bruch, Brahms, and Beethoven, also under Karajan, 1978–1982. In 1985 Lutoslawski composed a partita for her. She formed string trio with Giuranna and Rostropovich. Appointed to London Royal Academy of Music 1986. Premiered Penderecki's Violin Concerto no. 2 in 1993.

Maud Powell (b. 1868 in Peru, Ill., d. 1920)

At the age of twelve was taken to study with Schradieck in Leipzig, where she performed the Bruch G minor Concerto in 1882. Further studies followed, at Paris Conservatoire and in Berlin with Joachim. Returned to U.S. in 1885; performed with New York Philharmonic, including Dvořák's new violin concerto, with the composer in the audience. Moved to England, where she was equally successful. Toured with Sousa's band in Europe, 1903, performing Bach and Mendelssohn concertos, also Saint-Saëns's *Introduction et rondo capriccioso* (Sousa arranged all the accompaniments for band), and a *Caprice on Dixie* for unaccompanied violin. Her piano trio toured England, South Africa, and America. She was an early champion of women composers and performers. See *Maud Powell, Pioneer American Violinist* by Karen Shaffer and Neva Greenwood (Ames, Iowa, 1988).

Nadja Salerno-Sonnenberg (b. 1961 in Rome)

Studied at Curtis Institute 1969; with DeLay at Juilliard 1975. Won Naumburg award 1981. Toured Europe with Juilliard orchestra; gave New York recital in 1982. Admired especially for her interpretations of twentieth-century works, including Prokofiev. A 1994 reviewer called her "a superb player with unlimited virtuosity and a tone that shimmers and glows," but was disappointed in her performance of an all–Bach program. Her book, *Nadja: On My Way* (New York 1989), is chiefly directed at young people.

STRING QUARTETS

Attitudes about string quartet players have changed. There was a time when violists were considered to be violinists past their prime, and playing "second fiddle" meant being "second-rate." Fees paid to professional quartets also indicated something about their standing. Managers were prepared to pay magnificent honoraria to virtuoso soloists appearing with an orchestra but were insulted if a famous quartet made similar demands, even though the fee had to be divided among four players. Nor was there general agreement among chamber music players about the proper apportioning of fees. Not long ago, a well-known flutist demanded half the total fee for recording a Mozart quartet for flute, violin, viola, and cello. (He did not receive it, for the string players refused to participate.)

During the early nineteenth century, most quartets (amateur or professional) played Haydn, Mozart, Boccherini, Romberg, and the Beethoven quartets up to op. 95. The late Beethoven quartets (from op. 127 on) were rarely tackled, nor were those by Schubert. Instead, works by Spohr, Mendelssohn, Onslow, and others augmented the repertory well into the nineteenth century.

Professional quartets appeared slowly: the Schuppanzigh Quartet, in Beethoven's time, was among the first. The Leipzig Quartet (including Campagnoli, second violin, and Dotzauer, cello) was among the better ones ca. 1800. In Paris, Baillot and other violinists improved the quality of quartet playing, as did Lipinski's quartet in Dresden.

Early quartets often consisted of first-chair players in the local orchestra. They mostly performed at home, but a few groups also toured. In 1782 the Berlin Quartet, which included the violinists E. Schick and W. H. Benda, performed in Hamburg, playing works by Haydn. A quartet formed by the Moralt brothers in Munich concertized successfully in France and England in 1810; their programs included Haydn and Mozart. The Müller brothers (1831–1855) were the first true touring quartet, founded by Karl Friedrich Müller (1797–1873) who, however, did retain a home base as concertmaster in Braunschweig. Beginning in 1847, the family quartet consisting of Wilma Neruda and her sister as violinists, and their brothers, acquired an international reputation.

Traveling had an important effect on quartet playing: one rehearsed more intensively and concentrated on a few programs that were performed frequently, which provided new insights into those works. On the other hand, Joachim maintained a quartet in London during the 1860s (with Ries, Strauss, and Piatti) that met during only a few months and then gave a recital every Monday. In Paris, Joachim played in public with members of the

Armingaud Quartet, in which Lalo played viola. Similarly, Sarasate appeared with Parent, van Waefelghem, and Delsart.

A new standard of quartet playing developed when Beethoven's late quartets began to be given public performances. Ferdinand Laub introduced them to Berlin audiences between 1855 and 1862; later he presented Beethoven cycles in Vienna. Performances by the Maurin-Chevillard Quartet impressed Wagner in Paris. Jean-Pierre Maurin, the first violinist, even founded a Société des Derniers Quatuors de Beethoven. Later nineteenth-century works made ever greater demands on players. Brahms's three quartets, for instance, were beyond most amateur players, but when Joachim scheduled seven rehearsals for the premiere of a Brahms quartet this was considered extraordinary.

Ensembles devoted primarily to public performances were forced to go on tour, for one series of concerts tended to be all the local public would support. Among the most successful groups were Joachim's Berlin Quartet (1869–1907) and the Florentine Quartet, which existed until 1880. Hugo Heerman's quartet in Frankfurt also had a distinguished career for several decades. Other ensembles of the time were the Singer (later Wendling) Quartet in Stuttgart and the Marsick Quartet in Paris. Around 1900 the Viardot Quartet was well known in Paris, as was the Hubay Quartet in Budapest.

Other groups owed their existence to violinists who had a special interest in certain repertory. The Bohemian String Quartet (founded in 1892) was devoted to masterworks by Dvořák and Smetana and interpreted these with attention to the most minute details. This group acquired a worldwide reputation for excellence, which led to a strong tradition of chamber music in Prague and other Czech cities, and to the founding of the Smetana and Novak Quartets, among others.

The history of the Rosé Quartet is an example of the high achievements of some of these groups. Arnold Rosé (1863–1946) became concertmaster of the Vienna Philharmonic at the age of seventeen. He presented his quartet to the public in 1883, after a year of rehearsing. The publication issued in honor of its fiftieth anniversary lists 455 concerts for Vienna alone, among them fifty-four premieres. The latter include five works by Brahms and Schoenberg's sextet *Verklärte Nacht* and his D minor and F-sharp minor quartets. Most works were performed from manuscript music. There were also fifty-two Vienna premieres of works by Dvořák, Reger, and Pfitzner. In 1938 Rosé emigrated to England, where he continued to play chamber music into his eighty-second year.

It was not uncommon then for the first violinist to be an autocratic, indeed, tyrannical leader. This was true of Rosé, who once, on the podium, hit one of his fellow players over the head with his bow for missing an entrance in a fugal passage. On tour, Rosé insisted on having his own green-room; for tuning, the second violinist was obliged to go there and say, "Herr Hofrat [an honorary title], may I ask you for your esteemed A?"

Belonging to a professional quartet—rehearsing, performing, and traveling together almost constantly—may be stressful even today, in a more

The Bohemian String Quartet (Karl Hoffmann, Josef Suk, Georg Herold, Hans Wihan), caricature in pencil by Hugo Böttinger, 1907

democratic environment. Alexander Schneider mused, "It is far easier to live with a woman than with three quartet colleagues, especially after the first three years." A second violinist may well be as good as the leader but must not show this by displaying a prima donna temperament. Truly great violinists tend to be modest. In London, Joachim would take turns playing second violin with Laub, and when playing quartets in Ysaÿe's home, Thibaud would play second violin, while Pierre Monteux, the conductor, played viola. Kreisler, Thibaud, and Ysaÿe often met in Paris to play quartets with Casals, purely for their own enjoyment—but no one wanted to play first violin, and everyone was eager to play viola!

Membership in a quartet tends to change, for the players' professional or personal reasons. Rosé's quartet had ten changes in fifty years, but there was always some continuity. Lucien Capet left Bordeaux for Paris in 1903. There he founded his second quartet, which functioned for seven years. He established a third one in 1910 with Hewitt and Henri and Marcel Casadesus. For a year they rehearsed three hours daily and gave their first concert after three hundred rehearsals. At the 1911 Beethoven festival in Bonn their playing of his works caused a sensation, but in 1914 the group's cellist died in the war. To be a replacement player is not easy: one has to fit in quickly with three others who may have performed together for years and want to continue offering their well-rehearsed repertory. It is most unusual, and fortuitous, for a quartet to have the same players for forty years, as did the Amadeus Quartet. When Schidlof, the violist, died, the quartet dissolved itself in 1987.

In addition to independently founded quartets there are some that form or formed part of an institution: the Leipzig Gewandhaus Quartet, the Vienna Konzerthaus Quartet, and the Zurich Tonhalle Quartet. Others are associated with an educational institution, often a very satisfactory arrangement. One of the outstanding ones is the Juilliard Quartet, founded in 1946. Robert Mann was its leader until his retirement in 1997. Other American schools have appointed groups as artists-in-residence, their on-campus teaching and playing obligations limited to specified periods, giving them time to tour. Among these are or were the LaSalle Quartet in Cincinnati, the Takacs Quartet in Boulder, and the Ying Quartet in Rochester, N.Y. Given the difficulties of establishing and maintaining a quartet, the number of outstanding groups is impressive. In addition to those listed below, some of the earlier quartets that must be mentioned are the Budapest, Busch, Calvet, Claremont, Drolc, Hollywood, Hungarian, Koeckert, Loewenguth, and Poltronieri Quartets, and the Quartetto Italiano. [See also Pâris 1995 for listings, including players' names. Ed.]

For string players, the choice of a fine instrument is a special concern. Old masters, of course, are most in demand, but musicians' earnings are modest. At times, wealthy patrons have given or loaned Strads or other precious instruments to an ensemble; other groups play on those by outstanding living luthiers. It has happened that after a recital enthusiastic concertgoers crowded the greenroom to admire the Strads that produced such delightful sounds, only to find that they had heard modern instruments; in retrospect, some disappointed listeners have been known to declare that the quartet didn't sound all that good after all.

To succeed on the international concert circuit quartet players, like soloists, have to be top performers. A superior technique is taken for granted, but the finer details of ensemble playing are nailed down in rehearsing and performing, often under greatly varying local conditions. After a magnificent performance of Debussy's Quartet by the Parennin Quartet the players were asked how often they had performed that work. After some thought, the answer came: "About six hundred times."

Rehearsing a composition may also involve analytical study of the music and investigation of the original sources. The Amadeus Quartet often studied works from the classic/romantic repertory using photographic reproductions of the autograph manuscript. Such concern with the *Urtext* is not snobbism but represents a desire to follow the composer's intentions as closely as possible. The cellist Siegfried Palm recalled that as a member of the Hamann Quartet he learned much from analyzing the music with the first violinist.

Many composers wrote and dedicated works to specific ensembles. This also applies to twentieth-century works for string quartet and orchestra (Conrad Beck, 1929; Virgilio Mortari, 1934; Alvin Etler, 1968).

In our time, compositions for string quartet have become increasingly complex and difficult, which has caused some ensembles to specialize in performing this kind of repertory. In the 1920s the Hungarian String Quartet began to cultivate Bartók's works, a tradition continued after World War II by the Végh Quartet, the Juilliard Quartet, and one or two other groups. Most quartets by Schoenberg, Berg, and Webern were first presented by Rudolf Kolisch (a violinist who bowed with his left hand) and his colleagues Kuhner, Lehner, and Benar Heifetz. The earlier music festivals in Donaueschingen, dedicated to contemporary music, prominently featured the Amar Quartet, in which Hindemith was the violist. Stravinsky's important *Three Pieces for String Quartet* (1914) and Concertino (1920) were premiered by the Flonzaley Quartet, organized by violinist Alfred Pochon. The Parrenin Quartet in Paris has given eighty premiere performances in twenty-five years, including *Livre pour quatuor* by Boulez. It was fascinating to watch the first violinist playing in triple time, without accents, while occasionally "conducting" with his violin in duple time, in which the others played. One realizes how many talents a modern quartet player must have. In the United States, the Kronos Quartet specializes in contemporary repertory.

Some recent works, such as Mauricio Kagel's Quartet (1974), require the players to produce all kinds of sounds not normally emanating from string quartets. The instruments are "prepared" with adhesive tape, coins, and pieces of cloth on the fingerboard. The first violinist wears a heavy glove on the left hand, and knitting needles are wedged between the cello strings, along with matches, paper clips, and other objects. Various kinds of *scordatura* are called for, and in some places the players are expected to sing. Needless to say that such activities are perceived as clowning by many listeners.

In recent years, many new quartets have been formed, often by young players out of the same music school, while other groups have been dissolved. The following list, as earlier ones, makes no claim to completeness (which would soon cause it to be out of date) but names some of the better known ensembles successfully concertizing today.

Alban Berg Quartet	Guarneri Quartet
Amati Quartet	Janáček Quartet
American String Quartet	Juilliard Quartet
Arditti Quartet	Kodály Quartet
Auryn Quartet	Kronos Quartet
Borodin Quartet	Lenox Quartet
Brahms Quartet	Lindsay Quartet
Brodsky Quartet	Manhattan Quartet
Carmina Quartet	Melos Quartet
Chilingirian Quartet	Mozarteum Quartet
Colorado Quartet	Muir Quartet
Eder Quartet	New Budapest Quartet
Emerson Quartet	New World Quartet
Fine Arts Quartet	Panocha Quartet
Franz Schubert Quartet	Parennin Quartet
Gabrieli Quartet	Philharmonia Quartet Berlin
Giovane Quartetto Italiano	Prague Quartet

Salomon Quartet	Takacs Quartet
Sequoia Quartet	Talich Quartet
Shanghai Quartet	Tatrai Quartet
Skampa Quartet	Tokyo Quartet
Smithsonian Quartet	Vermeer Quartet
Suk Quartet	Ysaÿe Quartet Paris

[*Editor's note*: The summer 1996 issue of *BBC Music Magazine* reviewed and advertised recent recordings by many quartets not listed here, an indication of the current interest in the medium. Among the quartets they included are the following:

Brindisi	Medici
Britten	Quatuor Mosaïques
Coull	Orpheus
Delmé	Petersen
Duke	Quartetto Puccini
Keller	St. Petersburg
Kontra	Sibelius Academy
Lyric	Vogler
Maggini	

Chamber Music America, in its 1996 directory, lists 121 professional string quartets currently performing in the United States!]

INTO THE TWENTY-FIRST CENTURY

On his first visit to Palestine in 1950, Menuhin was asked to listen to large numbers of budding violinists, presented by their proud parents. He recalled (as quoted in Magidoff 1955),

> At times it seemed as though all the violin prodigies in the world had crowded into my room and the hall leading to it. I had to listen to them all, of course, and they wore me out, I must admit, but I was also heartened, because no instrument is as sadly neglected as is the violin. It is an individual instrument expressing individual feelings.

Statistics for the 1950s and 1960s show that in Germany and Austria violin study significantly declined, and that more students of primary and secondary school age were enrolled in lessons for other instruments (piano, guitar, accordion) than the violin. This was attributed in part to a chronic shortage of string teachers. Making string instruments available to students on loan helped, but many music schools had one violin student for every four piano students. The ratio for recorder and guitar lessons to violin lessons was

10:1. One obvious reason for the disparity is the relatively long period of study needed to reach a certain level of proficiency on the violin.

Demonstrations and spectacular achievements by young role models at times have led to correspondingly spectacular results. In 1924, the seven-year-old Menuhin performed with the San Francisco Symphony; two weeks later the concert was repeated for an audience of six thousand schoolchildren. Within a very short time, all inexpensive and medium-priced violins in the city's music stores had been sold! No doubt the initial enthusiasm of some young players (and parents) faded when they realized there could be no progress without practicing. But if only a fraction stayed with the violin, the concert achieved a desirable result that could not have been reached without the child Menuhin as a role model—and without an enterprising concert manager.

Active promotion of string instruction, coupled with innovative teaching methods and materials, has attracted young violin players, especially in the United States. Effective methods of class instruction were developed there, and student orchestras—from grade schools to youth orchestras, college, conservatory, and university orchestras—provided training that for some led to membership in American symphony orchestras, which often have outstanding string sections.

In central and western Europe, a shrinking supply of young professional players has been attributed, from about 1900 on, to decreasing numbers of beginners. It is worth noting that at that time, music periodicals still regularly included inserts of sheet music, for violin and other instruments. Some of these magazines (*Le violon pour tous*, for instance) had a faithful clientele of subscribers for many decades, but such journals have largely disappeared. [In the U.S., *Etude* magazine suffered this fate in 1957. *Ed.*] The pieces they published may not always have been great music, but they reached enthusiastic players of all ages. Many a great violinist began like Enesco, who as a child tried to master Ivanovici's *Waves of the Danube Waltz* on his primitive half-size violin.

Records for the 1960s in Austria yield the following data: of a total of approximately one million schoolchildren (ages six to eighteen), only 140,000 played an instrument. Of these, 28 percent played the recorder, 19 percent piano and accordion, 14 percent guitar, 4 percent melodica, and 3.6 percent violin. For Germany, figures for conservatories (preparing students for professional careers) showed that not enough players would graduate to replace older musicians going into retirement. The situation was somewhat eased by an influx of refugees from Eastern Europe. Enrollment figures also showed that there were more conducting students than orchestra-bound violin players, and two and a half times as many musicology students in the universities than string students in conservatories and other music schools.

[*Editor's note*: Available statistics for the United States tell a somewhat different story. String programs in many public school systems have been curtailed or eliminated, largely due to budgetary strictures. As a result, many schools no longer have orchestras but continue to support bands. In October

1996, I spoke with Dr. Camille Smith of the University of Florida (Gaines-ville), who has made detailed studies of public school string programs. Her statistics cover every state and are broken down according to school districts and grade level: elementary, middle school, and high school. Results are fur-ther detailed according to socioeconomic level and the location and size of school districts. According to Dr. Smith, approximately 16 percent of U.S. schools offered string instruction in 1989; by 1994 that figure had dropped to ca. 14 percent. She judges the situation to be even more alarming in poor school districts, where such instruction is almost nonexistent. What is also disturbing is that in many states little if any string instruction is offered at the elementary level, generally thought to be the best age for beginning violin study.

More encouraging is the situation in American community music schools, in which young students are actively encouraged to study string instruments. In 1996, 473 individual string instrument lessons were taught at Philadelphia's Settlement Music School, along with 1193 keyboard and 304 wind lessons. String enrollment was gaining; the school has an "endangered instruments program"! Figures for the number of students enrolled at schools in other cities in the same year, though not necessarily representative of schools everywhere, also give cause for hope:

Cincinnati College-Conservatory of Music, preparatory division: piano, 283; strings, 128.
Community School of Music and Arts, Mountain View, Calif.: violin, 34; cello, 11; double bass, 2.
Merit Music Program, Chicago: piano, 216; strings, 387.
Michigan State University School of Music (community school): piano, 215; all strings, 225; violin, 173.
Suzuki-Orff School for Young Musicians, Chicago: piano, 30–35; violin, 65–75.

Certainly, the health of any local string program depends in part on the ini-tiative and enthusiasm of its director. I am indebted for the above statistics to Charles Farmer, director of the Community Music Center, Portland, Ore.]

In Europe, there were problems not only with the quantity but also with the quality of prospective violinists. The concertmaster of the Salzburg Mozarteum Orchestra recalled that in about twenty years he had auditioned four hundred violinists eager to join this state-supported orchestra. Among them, fifteen at most would have "materially added to the orchestra's qual-ity," thirty to forty might have been worth hiring with the hope "that they would improve in time," while the rest were "definitely unemployable." Of the actual auditions he said, "After listening to just a few bars of Mozart's *Eine kleine Nachtmusik* we knew enough."

My own impression, based on listening to many auditions, suggests that such applicants are not properly trained. They usually begin the audition by playing a concerto of their own choice, showing talent and some accomplishment, but when asked to sight read some orchestral excerpts it becomes clear that they do not know the standard orchestra repertory and that their ability to read music intelligently is woefully lacking. Fritz Weidlich, music director in Innsbruck, had his own auditioning routine. After candidates had played Beethoven, Brahms, or Tchaikovsky concertos with assurance and élan, he would ask them to play a passage from the second movement of Haydn's Piano Concerto in D major:

The results were often what one would expect from a second-year violin student. These young people evidently had been trained entirely (and unrealistically) for the career of a soloist. Subjects such as rhythm drill, orchestra playing, orchestra discipline, sight reading, and chamber music had been neglected if not ignored, though they are important skills for every professional musician. Their teachers at one time may have had dreams of becoming Paganinis themselves; disenchanted, they turned to teaching, hoping that their students would achieve what they had not. Every student was treated as a potential Menuhin, and the vicious circle would close: the student's dreams too are finally shattered, and only then does he or she consider auditioning for an orchestra position. If accepted, they feel that an unjust, cruel fate has kept them from the glorious career of a soloist, whom they now must accompany as an orchestra player. Thomas Beecham once said that all orchestra players are frustrated soloists; he may have spoken from experience.

[*Editor's note*: As for professional orchestras, the situation in the United States at the end of the twentieth century is in some ways different. Competition for vacancies in major symphony orchestras continues to be very keen; several hundred qualified applicants may apply for one opening. Law requires that such vacancies be advertised nationally, e.g., in the *Journal of the American Federation of Musicians*. Serious applicants are likely to be well trained, including experience gained by years of membership in public school, college, and conservatory orchestras.

In Germany, and in many other European countries, specialized music schools (rather than public schools) provide instrumental instruction at all levels, up to the professional training offered by the largely state–administered conservatories. Dr. Ulrich Wüster of the Association of German Music Schools (Verband deutscher Musikschulen) has supplied valuable general information and statistics for 1996–1997.

In 1960 there were fewer than a hundred music schools throughout Germany. There are now about a thousand, with more than a million students and ca. thirty-five thousand instructors. They offer general music training for children aged four to six and basic music instruction for the six-to-nine-year-olds. Nearly a quarter of a million children are enrolled in these two groups. Instruction includes ear training, singing, movement, dance, and elementary instrumental activity, especially on percussion instruments. At this age, some children already discover a preference for a certain instrument, at times even reveal a decided talent for it. In all, some forty-five thousand children study the violin. While group instrumental lessons are now being explored on an experimental basis, violin instruction is still chiefly given in individual lessons to some thirty-eight thousand children, at present. Virtually all standard instruments are taught; violin lessons hold the fourth place after piano, recorder, and guitar.

About 10 percent of the total enrollment in music schools consists of adults, from those in their twenties to senior citizens. All instructors are graduates of professional conservatories. Chamber music playing is stressed, and orchestras are formed at various levels of accomplishment including "mini orchestras" for small children. Very talented young players are chosen by audition for select orchestras at the regional, provincial, and state levels. There is a German Music School Orchestra, a string orchestra composed of players from all over Germany.

Many music schools also offer specialized instruction to young preprofessional players who plan to take conservatory entrance exams. In addition to intensive work on their major instrument, these players study a second instrument and participate in various activities, such as ensemble and orchestra playing and conducting.

The Association of German Music Schools cooperates with sister organizations in most European countries. A European Association of Music Schools was founded in 1973. Its twenty-one members are in close contact, exchanging information about their work. A book describing this work, including similarities and differences from country to country, was published in 1995 (text in English, French, and German) and is available from the Europäische Musikschul–Union (General Secretariat), St. Florinsgasse 1, FL–9490 Vaduz, Liechtenstein. The European String Teachers Association (ESTA) may be reached at its German address: Katzenberg 123, D–55126, Mainz.]

Today, a violinist has to come to terms with some new, entirely different problems. Beginning with Webern, Berg, and Bartók, composers have included in their writing a greater range of timbres than had been customary. Effects such as sul ponticello and col legno, used sparingly by earlier composers, are frequently called for, along with slow glissando, pizzicato-glissando, vertical pizzicato (with the string hitting the fingerboard), and audible re-tuning of a string. Rhythm (rather than melody and harmony) has been stressed by composers since Stravinsky, Cowell, and Orff. As a result, percussive effects such as knocking on or slapping the instrument are indicated, familiar for some time from string bass playing in popular music.

Composers have also attempted to have traditional string instruments imitate the sounds of musique concrète and electronic music. Some compositions require string players to produce more of these sounds than those of traditional writing. Composers at times have incurred protests from an orchestra's string section. In Munich this led to a full-fledged scandal when the orchestra of the Bavarian State Opera refused to play a work by Penderecki, for the good reason that their valuable instruments would suffer damage. Most critics sided with the composer, which shows that few people realize how delicate and fragile a good violin is. Composers also should know that they cannot expect a violinist to knock (with knuckles or bow) on seventeenth- or eighteenth-century varnish. Discussing the performance of such a work by Xenakis, H. H. Stuckenschmidt took the side of the string players, saying that the damage inflicted on their instruments was far more significant than the musical effect gained by such abuse. Music calling for such effects represents, of course, only a small facet of contemporary writing, but some musicians have asked whether it makes sense to use a precious instrument for such effects, the same instrument whose sound a Stradivarius or a Guarnerius took great pains to perfect. Many of the required sound effects could be created, as well or better, by percussion instruments built for these specific purposes.

The violin still holds a central place in our musical culture and its future is thus assured. Of music currently performed, in public or in private, at least 95 percent stems from roughly the last 350 years, the period from Monteverdi to Schoenberg, when traditional violin music flourished. There is, however, another danger. Concert pitch has risen steadily, especially in America. This high pitch is so hard on singers' voices that the time may come when the great works for soloists, chorus, and orchestra can no longer be performed. As for the violin family, the precious old instruments will deteriorate to the point of becoming useless, for they will no longer be able to support the enormous tension of strings tuned to this high level. Before long, all the magnificent instruments made by Amati, Stainer, Stradivarius, and Guarnerius del Gesù will have disappeared from our concert halls. Conferences to discuss the problem were held in Salzburg (1968), Toledo (1971), and Florence (1989); no solution was forthcoming.

Violin makers from many countries met in Cremona in 1988 to protest the "murderous race to an ever higher pitch." They urged the universal adoption of a pitch based on A = 432, as opposed to the A = 450 frequently encountered today. Instruments of the old masters were designed for a string pressure of 4 kg; now they are expected to withstand pressures up to 14 kg.

On 26 April 1988, the Paris newspaper *Le Figaro* ran a story about the Cremona meeting. Its title? "Pitié pour nos violons" (Have mercy on our violins).

BIBLIOGRAPHY

Editor's note: Given the encyclopedic nature of this book, which deals with many subjects related to the violin, this bibliography is necessarily selective. In particular, the literature on the subject of violin and bow making, only a small portion of which could be included here, is vast. A recent computer search on the subject of violin construction, excluding periodical articles, yielded 621 items; on violin varnish alone there were forty-eight.

For additional bibliography, especially older literature, the reader is referred to Edward Heron-Allen's *De fidiculis bibliographia* (London 1890–1894, rpt. 1961); for more recent literature to David D. Boyden's *The History of Violin Playing* (London 1965). Extensive bibliographies are also found in *The Violin Family* (New York 1989), derived from articles in *The New Grove Dictionary of Musical Instruments* (London 1984) and in *Musikinstrumente in Einzeldarstellungen, Band 1: Streichinstrumente* (Munich and Kassel 1981), based on articles in *MGG*. See also the bibliography in *The Cambridge Companion to the Violin* (Cambridge 1992), edited by Robin Stowell, especially valuable for works on the violin in traditional and non-Western music as well as in jazz, ethnic, and other popular music.

For this revised English-language edition, some entries from the earlier German editions have been omitted to make room for more recent titles, especially in English. Space limitations have prevented the inclusion of many valuable periodical articles. Among important American journals containing such articles are the following:

> *American Lutherie* (1973–; quarterly)
> *American Music Teacher* (1951–; bi-monthly)
> *American String Teacher* (1950–; quarterly)
> *Journal of the American Musical Instrument Society* (1975–; annual)
> *Journal of the American Viola Society* (1985–; irregular)
> *Journal of the Violin Society of America* (1973–; quarterly)
> *Strings* (1966–; bi-monthly)

Contents of these and other journals are indexed in *The Music Index* (1949–; monthly). *The Strad* (1890–; monthly), a British journal, provides excellent coverage of the United States and frequently carries in-depth interviews with rising stars.

Aarvig, Christian. 1884. *Den unge Ole Bull*. Copenhagen. Rpt. 1934.
Abbado, Michelangelo. 1937. "Quando è nato Antonio Stradivari." *Musica d'oggi*.
Abele, Hyacinth. 1864. *Die Violine, ihre Geschichte und ihr Bau*. Neuburg. Engl. trans. Boston 1920, 1977.

Abbott, R. B. 1936. "Response Measurements and Harmonic Analysis of Violin Tones." *Journal of the Acoustical Society of America* 7.

Adler, Eduard. 1895. *Die Behandlung und Erhaltung der Streichinstrumente.* Leipzig. Rev. ed. 1924.

Albrecht, Willi. 1940. "Vom Schafdarm zur Saite." *Zeitschrift für Instrumentenbau* 184.

Alexandru, Tiberiu. 1957. "Le violon comme instrument musical populaire." *Revista de folclor.* Bucarest.

Alton, Robert. 1978. *Violin and Cello Building and Repairing.* St. Clair Shores, Mich. 1st publ. London 1946; rev. ed. London 1964; rpt. 1986.

Anders, Gottfried Engelbert. 1831. *Biographical Sketch of Nicolo Paganini.* London.

————. 1832. "Beitrag zur Geschichte der Violine." *Cäcilia* 14, no. 56: 247ff.

Angeloni, Domenico. 1923. *Il liutaio, origine e costruzione del violino.* Milan.

Anonymous ("C. M."). N.d. *Theresa Milanollo et Maria Milanollo.* Nantes.

————. 1872. *Musical Recollections of the Last Half Century.* London.

————. 1788. "Anmerkungen über die Violine und den Violinspieler." *Musikalische Real-Zeitung* 2ff.

————. 1799. "Einige Tonkünstler älterer Zeiten." *Allgemeine Musikalische Zeitung*: 577ff.

————. 1804. "Über die heutige verworrene Strichbezeichnung." *Allgemeine Musikalische Zeitung*: 729.

————. 1886. *The Violin: How to Make It.* Boston.

————. 1937. *Antonio Stradivari: Notizie e documenti.* Cremona.

————. [1889]. *The Fiddler's Hand-Book.* London.

————. 1808. "Über die Violin." *Allgemeine Musikalische Zeitung* 50.

————. 1818. *Galérie des violons et luthiers célèbres.* Paris.

Anthony, James R. 1997. *French Baroque Music from Beaujoyeulx to Rameau.* Rev. and expanded ed. Portland, Ore. 1st publ. New York 1974.

Apian-Bennewitz, Paul Otto. 1892. *Die Geige.* Weimar. Facsim. rpt. Innsbruck 1976.

Arakélian, Sourène. 1958. *Le violon.* Tehran.

Armando, W. G. 1960. *Paganini.* Hamburg.

Arns, Ulrich. 1954. "Untersuchungen an Geigen." Diss., Karlsruhe.

————. 1957. "Eine neue Art objektiver Qualitätsbestimmung von Geigen." *Gravesaner Blätter.*

Atti, Gaetano. 1892. *Biografia di Bartolommeo Campagnoli da Cento, celebre violinista.* Bologna.

Auer, Leopold. 1921. *Violin Playing As I Teach It.* New York. 3d ed. 1960.

————. 1923. *My Long Life in Music.* New York.

————. 1925. *Violin Masterworks and Their Interpretation.* New York.

Auer, Leopold, and Gustav Saenger. 1926–1927. *Graded Course of Violin Playing*, 8 vols. New York.

Axelrod, Herbert. 1976. *Heifetz.* Neptune City, N.J. 2d rev. ed. 1981.

Azzolina, Umberto. 1964. *Liuteria italiana dell'ottocento e del novecento.* Milan.

————. 1967. *Liuteria veneziana del '700.* Milan.

Babitz, Sol. 1947. *Principles of Extension in Violin Fingering.* Philadelphia.

————. 1970. *Differences between Eighteenth-Century and Modern Violin Bowing.* Los Angeles.

Bachmann, Alberto. 1906. *Le violon*. Paris.

——. 1913. *Les grands violonistes du passé*. Paris.

——. 1914. *Gymnastique à l'usage des violonistes*. Paris

——. 1925. *An Encyclopedia of the Violin*. New York. Rpt. 1967.

Bachmann, Werner. 1969. *The Origins of Bowing and the Development of Bowed Instruments Up to the Thirteenth Century*. Oxford. 1st publ. in German, Leipzig 1964.

Baese, Geary L. 1985. *Classic Italian Violin Varnish*. Fort Collins, Colo.

Bagatella, Antonio. 1786. *Regole per la costruzione dei violini, viole, violoncelli e violoni*. Padua.

Baillot, Pierre. 1825. *Notice sur J.-B. Viotti*. Paris.

——. 1991. *The Art of the Violin*. Louise Goldberg, ed. and trans. Evanston, Ill. 1st publ. in French, Paris 1835.

Balfoort, Dirk J. N.d. *Antonius Stradivarius*. Amsterdam. Engl. trans. Stockholm 1940.

——. [1920]. *Het probleem van den vioolbouw*. The Hague.

——. 1931. *De Hollandsche Vioolmakers*. Amsterdam.

Balfour, Henry. 1900. *How to Tell the Nationality of Old Violins*. London. 2d enl. ed. 1901.

Barrett, Carolyn. 1995. *The Magic of Matsumoto: The Suzuki Method of Education*. Palm Springs.

Bast, C. 1920. *Die Lösung des physiologischen Problems der Technik der Streichinstrumente*. 2d ed. Neugilching.

Beck, Adolf. 1923. *Die proportionale Konstruktion der Geige*. Leipzig.

Becker, Wilhelm. 1948. "Der altitalienische Geigenlack." *Instrumentenbau-Zeitschrift* 1.

Beckmann, Gustav. 1918. *Das Violinspiel in Deutschland vor 1700*. Leipzig.

Bénédit, Pierre Gustave. 1854. *C. Sivori*. Marseille.

Berenzi, Angelo. 1906. *Di alcuni stromenti fabbricati da Gasparo da Salò*. Brescia.

——. 1890. *Di Giovanni Paolo Maggini celebre liutaio bresciano*. Brescia.

Berger, Achille. 1910. *Théorie scientifique du violon*. Paris.

Berr, Albert. 1949. *Geigengeschichten: Erinnerungen und Notizen*. Zurich. 2d ed. 1983.

——. 1961. *Geigen: Originale, Kopien, Fälschungen*. Frankfurt. 2d ed. 1975.

Bertolotti, A. 1891. *Gaetano Pugnani e altri musicisti di Torino al secolo XVIII*. Milan.

Bessaraboff, Nicholas. 1941. *Ancient European Musical Instruments*. Boston.

Besseler, Heinrich. 1949. *Zum Problem der Tenorgeige*. Heidelberg. Engl. trans. Lexington, Ky. 1978.

Bettoni, Pio. 1901. *Gasparo da Salò e l'invenzione del violino*. Salò.

Biancolli, Amy. 1998. *The Life of Fritz Kreisler*. Portland, Ore.

Billè, Isaia. 1928. *Storia degli strumenti ad arco e loro cultori*. Rome.

Blandin, Emile M. 1951. *Les luthiers en Normandie*. Le Havre.

Blaukopf, Kurt. 1955. *Grosse Virtuosen*. Teufen.

Bonaventura, Arnaldo. 1911. *Nicolò Paganini*. Rome.

——. 1906. *Storia del violino, dei violinisti e della musica per violino*. Milan. 2d ed. 1933.

Bonetti, Carlo, with Agostino Cavalcabò and Ugo Gualazzini. 1937. *Antonio Stradivari*. Cremona.

Bonn, J. Edwin. 1885. *Technical Notes on the Choice, Keeping, and Preparation of Violin Strings*. Brading, Isle of Wight.

Botti, F. 1962. *Paganini e Parma*. Parma.

Bouasse, Henri. 1926. *Acoustiques, cordes et membranes*. Paris. Rpt. 1987.

Boyden, David D. 1950. "The Violin and Its Technique in the Eighteenth Century." *The Musical Quarterly* 36: 9–38.

———. 1951. "Prelleur, Geminiani, and Just Intonation." *JAMS*, Fall issue.

———. 1959. "Geminiani and the First Violin Tutor." *Acta Musicologica* 31: 161–170.

———. 1960. "A Postscript to 'Geminiani.'" *Acta Musicologica* 32: 40–47.

———. 1961. "The Violin." In *Musical Instruments through the Ages*. Anthony Baines, ed. Harmondsworth.

———. 1958–1963. "Monteverdi's *Violini Piccoli* and *Viole da Braccio*." *Annales musicologiques* 6.

———. 1965. *The History of Violin Playing from Its Origins to 1761*. London. Rpt. 1975.

———. 1969. *Catalogue of the Hill Collection . . . in the Ashmolean Museum Oxford*. London.

———. 1980a. "Bow." In *The New Grove Dictionary of Music and Musicians* 3: 125–135.

———. 1980b. "The Violin Bow in the Eighteenth Century." *Early Music* 199–212.

Bracharz, Leopold. 1929. "Die Solovioline bei Beethoven." Diss., Vienna.

Brainard, Paul. 1959. "Die Violinsonaten G. Tartinis." Diss., Göttingen.

Brederode, W. 1938. *Carl Flesch, Een kleine biografische Studie*. Haarlem.

Bremt, Fr. van den. 1949. *Willem de Fesch*. Brussels.

Briqueville, Eugène de. [1894]. *Les pochettes des maîtres de danse*. Versailles.

Brijon, E. C. R. 1763. *Réflexions sur la musique et sur la vraie manière de l'exécuter sur le violon*. Paris. Facsim. rpt. Geneva 1971.

Brinser, Marlin. 1978. *Dictionary of Twentieth-Century Italian Violin Makers*. Irvington, N.J.

Broadhouse, John. [1892]. *How to Make a Violin*. London. Rpt. 1910; rev. ed. 1939.

Brook, Donald. 1948. *Violinists of Today*. London. 2d ed. 1953.

Brown, Clive. 1984. *Louis Spohr: A Critical Biography*. Cambridge.

Bull, Sara C. 1883. *Ole Bull*. London.

Burmester, Willy. 1975. *Fifty Years as a Concert Violinist*. Linthicum Heights, Md. 1st publ. in German, Berlin 1926.

Burney, Charles. 1773. *The Present State of Music in France and Italy*. London. Rpt. New York 1969.

Busch, Fritz. 1953. *Pages from a Musician's Life*. London. Rpt. St. Clair Shores, Mich. 1973; 1st publ. in German as *Aus dem Leben eines Musikers*, Zurich 1949.

Busoni, Ferruccio. 1907. *Entwurf einer neuen Ästhetik der Tonkunst*. Trieste. Engl. trans. New York 1911.

Buttorini, Mattia. 1901. *Gasparo da Salò, inventore del violino moderno*. Salò.

Cabos, Francine. 1948. *Le violon et la lutherie*. Paris.

Campbell, Margaret. 1980. *The Great Violinists*. New York.

Capet, Lucien. 1916. *La technique supérieure de l'archet*. Paris. Rpt. 1952.

Capri, Antonio. 1945. *Giuseppe Tartini*. Milan.

Careri, Enrico. 1993. *Francesco Geminiani, 1687–1762*. Oxford.

Chabert, H. 1900. *Le violon, sa pédagogie, son travail, dangers d'un mauvais enseignement*. Paris.

Chenantais, Jules Edward. [1905]. *Le violoniste et le violon*. Nantes.

Christ-Iselin, Wilhelm. 1920. *Zur Frage des Cremoneser Geigenlackes*. Leipzig.

Christen, Ernest. 1946. *Ysaÿe*. Geneva.

Clarke, A. Mason. 1895. *A Biographical Dictionary of Fiddlers*. London.

Clarke, Mary Gray. 1967. "The Violin Sonatas of F. M. Veracini." Diss., University of North Carolina.

Clerjot, Maurice. 1907. *Essai de philosophie instrumentale: L'art du violon*. Paris.

Codignola, Arturo. 1935. *Paganini intimo*. Genoa.

Common, Alfred F. [1909]. *How to Repair Violins and Other Musical Instruments*. London. Rpt. 1969.

Courcy, Geraldine I. C. de. 1957. *Paganini, the Genoese*. Norman, Okla. Rpt. New York 1977.

Courvoisier, Karl. 1878. *Die Violintechnik*. Cologne. Engl. trans. 1880.

Coutagne, Henry. 1893. *Gaspard Duiffoproucart et les luthiers lyonnais du XVIe siècle*. Paris.

Coventry, W. B. 1902. *Notes on the Construction of the Violin*. London.

Cozio di Salabue. *See* Salabue

Cremer, Lothar. 1984. *The Physics of the Violin*. Cambridge, Mass. 1st publ. in German 1981.

Crosby, Alpheus B. 1877. *The Art of Holding the Violin and Bow as Exemplified by Ole Bull*. New York.

Curry, Pat Bryan. 1968. "The François Tourte Violin Bow." Diss., Brigham Young University.

Cutter, Benjamin. 1903. *How to Study Kreutzer*. Boston.

Czach, Rudolf. 1927. "Fr. W. Rust." Diss., Berlin.

Dancla, Jean-Baptiste-Charles. 1893. *Notes et souvenirs*. Paris. 2d ed. 1898; Engl. trans. Linthicum Heights, Md., 1981.

Dasseno, T., and Ugo Ravasio, eds. 1990. *Gasparo da Salò e la liuteria bresciana tra Rinascimento e Barocco*. Brescia. Exhibition catalog.

Denis, Valentin. 1944. *De Muziekinstrumenten in de Nederlanden en in Italie*. Antwerp.

Desfossez, Achille. 1856. *Henri Wieniawski*. The Hague.

Devoney, Frank. 1893. *The Acoustics of Violin Making*. Edinburgh.

Diehl, Nicolaus Louis. 1864. *Die Geigenmacher der alten italienischen Schule*. Hamburg. 5th ed. 1877.

Diestel, Hans. 1912. *Violintechnik und Geigenbau*. Leipzig. 2d ed. 1919.

Dieu. 1875. *Essai sur les notes défectueuses des instruments à archet*. Paris.

Dissmore, George A. 1895. *The Violin Gallery*. London.

Doerr, Ray. 1985. *Violin Maker's Handbook*. Battle Creek, Mich.

Donington, Robert. 1977. *String Playing in Baroque Music*. New York.

Dorian, Jean-Pierre. [1947]. *Un violon parle: Souvenirs de Jacques Thibaut*. Paris. 2d ed. 1953.

Doring, Ernest N. 1945. *How Many Strads?* Chicago.

———. 1949. *The Guadagnini Family of Violin Makers*. Chicago.

Doring, Ernest N., and Harvey S. Whistler. 1961. *Jean-Baptiste Vuillaume of Paris*. Chicago.

Dounias, Minos. 1935. *Die Violinkonzerte Giuseppe Tartinis*. Wolfenbüttel. Rpt. 1966.

Dräger, Hans-Heinz. 1948. *Prinzip einer Systematik der Musikinstrumente*. Kasel.

———. 1937. *Die Entwicklung des Streichbogens und seine Anwendung in Europa*. Kassel. Diss., Berlin.

Drögemeyer, Hermann August. 1891. *Die Geige*. Bremen. 3d ed. Berlin 1903.

Dubal, David. 1991. *Conversations with Menuhin*. London.

Dubourg, George. 1836. *The Violin*. London. 5th ed. 1878.

Eberhardt, Goby. 1926. *Erinnerungen an bedeutende Männer unserer Epoche*. Lübeck.

Eberhardt, Siegfried. 1910. *Der beseelte Violinton*. Dresden. Engl. trans. New York 1911.

———. 1922. *Die Lehre von der organischen Geigenhaltung*. Berlin.

———. 1926. *Der Körper in Form und Hemmung*. Munich.

———. 1938. *Wiederaufstieg oder Untergang der Kunst des Geigens*. Copenhagen.

Eckhardt, Julius. 1888. *Ferdinand David und die Familie Mendelssohn*. Leipzig.

Edler, Hans. 1970. *Geigen-f-Modelle nach den Originalen alter Meister*. Siegburg. 2d ed. 1976.

Emery, Frederic B. 1912. *The Violinist's Dictionary*. London. 3d ed. Chicago 1928.

———. 1928. *The Violin Concerto through a Period of Nearly Three Hundred Years*. Chicago. Rpt. 1969.

Engel, Carl. 1883. *Researches into the Early History of the Violin Family*. London. Rpt. Amsterdam 1965.

Engl, Rafael. 1897. *Österreichs Cremona*. Schönbach.

Escudier, Léon. 1868. *Mes souvenirs: Les virtuoses*. Paris.

Farga, Franz. 1940. *Geigen und Geiger*. Zurich. 7th ed. 1983; Engl. trans. London 1950, 1969.

Farish, Margaret K. 1965. *String Music in Print*. New York. 2d ed. 1973; supplement 1984.

Farrell, William James. 1921. *The True-Tone Violin*. London.

Ferris, George T. [1884]. *Sketches of Great Pianists and Great Violinists*. London.

Fétis, François Joseph. 1851. *Notice biographique sur Nicolo Paganini*. Paris.

———. 1856. *Antoine Stradivari*. Paris. Engl. trans. London 1864; rpt. 1964.

Fleming, James M. 1883. *Old Violins and Their Makers*. London.

———. 1892. *The Fiddle Fancier's Guide*. London.

Flesch, Carl. 1924, 1930. *The Art of Violin Playing*, 2 vols. New York. 2d rev. ed. 1939; 1st publ. Berlin 1923, 1928.

———. 1934. *Problems of Tone Production*. New York. 1st publ. Leipzig 1931.

———. 1957. *The Memoirs of Carl Flesch*. London. Rpt. New York 1979.

———. 1966. *Violin Fingering: Its Theory and Practice*. London. 1st publ. Milan 1960.

Folegatti, Ercole. 1873–1874. *Storia del violino e dell'archetto*, 2 vols. Bologna.

———1874. *Il violino, esposto geometricamente*. Bologna.

Forster. 1864. *The History of the Violin*. London.

Frank-Reiner. 1923. *Das Problem der Tonveredlung bei Streichinstrumenten*. Mainz.

Friedmann, Martin. 1971. "Francesco Geminiani's *The Art of Playing on the Violin* in Perspective." Diss., University of Washington.

Freeman, T. C. 1901. *Old and New Violins*. New York.

Fry, George. 1904. *The Varnishes of the Italian Violin-Makers*. London.

Fuchs, Albert. 1960. *Taxe der Streichinstrumente*, 6th ed. Frankfurt. 13th ed. 1991.

Fuhr, Karl. 1926. *Die akustischen Rätsel der Geige*. Leipzig. Rpt. Frankfurt 1958.

Gai, Vinicio. 1969. *Gli strumenti musicali della corte medicea*. Licosa.

Galamian, Ivan. 1962. *Principles of Violin Playing and Teaching*. Englewood Cliffs, N.J. 2d ed. 1985.

Galamian, Ivan, and Frederick Neumann. 1963, 1966. *Contemporary Violin Technique*, 2 vols. New York.

Galpin, Francis W. 1937. *A Textbook of European Musical Instruments*. London. 4th ed. 1956.

Gates, Willis C. 1950. "The Literature for Unaccompanied Solo Violin." Diss., North Carolina University.

Geiringer, Karl. 1978. *Instruments in the History of Western Music*. 3d ed. New York. Earlier editions published as *Musical Instruments*, 1943, 1945.

Gelrud, Paul Geoffrey. 1941. "A Critical Study of the French Violin School (1782–1882)." Diss., Cornell University.

Geminiani, Francesco. 1751. *The Art of Playing on the Violin*. London. Facsim. rpt., with introduction by David D. Boyden, 1952.

Gemünder, Georg. 1881. *Georg Gemünder's Progress in Violin Making*. Astoria, N.Y. 1st publ. in German 1880.

Gerhartz, Karl. 1924. "Die Violinschule in ihrer musikgeschichtlichen Entwicklung bis Leopold Mozart." Diss., Bonn.

Gerle, Robert. 1983. *The Art of Practicing the Violin*. London.

Giazotto, Remo. 1956. *Giovanni Battista Viotti*. Milan.

Gill, Dominic. 1984. *The Book of the Violin*. New York.

Giltay, J. W. N.d. *Bow Instruments: Their Form and Construction*. London.

Ginzburg, Lev. 1980. *Ysaÿe*. Neptune City, N.J.

———. 1981. *Giuseppe Tartini: His Life and Times*. Neptune City, N.J. 1st publ. Moscow 1969.

———. 1984. *Vieuxtemps: His Life and Times*. Neptune City, N.J.

Göthel, Folker. 1935. "Das Violinspiel L. Spohrs." Diss., Berlin.

Goffrie, Charles. [1876]. *The Violin: A Condensed History*. Philadelphia.

Gontershausen, Welcker von. N.d. *Neueröffnetes Magazin musikalischer Tonwerkzeuge*. Frankfurt.

Grabkowski, Edmund. 1986. *Henryk Wieniawski*. Warsaw. In English.

Greilsamer, Lucien. 1910. *L'hygiène du violon*. Paris.

———. 1924. *L'anatomie et la physiologie du violon*. Paris.

Gretschel, H. 1869. *Lehrbuch der Geigen- und Bogenmacherkunst*. Weimar.

Greulich, Martin. 1934. "Beiträge zur Geschichte des Streichinstrumentenspiels im 16. Jahrhundert." Diss., Berlin.

Grillet, Laurent. 1901–1905. *Les ancêtres du violon et du violoncelle: Les luthiers et les fabricants d'archets*. Paris. Rpt. New York 1969.

Grossmann, Max. 1907. *Kritische Übersicht über Neuerungen und Streitfragen im Geigenbau im Jahre 1906*. Berlin.

———. 1927. *Das Geheimnis der alten italienischen Geigenbauer*. Lübben-Steinkirchen.

Grube, Max-Ludwig. 1961. *Probleme des Violinspiels*. Berlin.

Grünberg, Max. 1913. *Führer durch die Literatur der Streichinstrumente*. Leipzig.

———. 1925. *Meister der Violine*. Stuttgart.

Guéroult, A. 1842. "P. Baillot." *Gazette musicale* 25 September.

Haas, de. 1909. *On the Motion of the Bridge of the Violin*. Amsterdam.

Hadden, Cuthbert J. 1914. *Modern Musicians*. London.

Haendel, Ida. 1970. *Woman with Violin: An Autobiography*. London.

Haesler, Oskar Erich. 1968. *Beseelter Geigenklang*. Hofheim.

Hajdecki, Alexander. 1892. *Die italienische Lira da Bracchio*. Mostar. Rpt. Amsterdam 1965.

Hamma, Fridolin. 1931. *Meisterwerke italienischer Geigenbaukunst*. Stuttgart.

———. 1948. *Meister deutscher Geigenbaukunst*. Stuttgart. Engl. trans. London 1961.

———. 1959. *Wie kam es zu einem Geigenprozess in der Schweiz*. Stuttgart.

———. 1961. *Die D'Egville-Del Gesù*. Stuttgart.

Hamma, Walter. 1964. *Meister italienischer Geigenbaukunst*, 2d enl. ed. Stuttgart. 8th ed. 1993.

———. 1986. *Violin Makers of the German School from the Seventeenth to the Nineteenth Century*, 2 vols. Tutzing. In English, French, and German.

Hardy, Joseph. 1910. *Rodolphe Kreutzer*. Paris.

Hart, George. 1875. *The Violin: Its Famous Makers and Their Imitators*. London. 4th ed. 1909; rpt. New York 1978.

———. 1881. *The Violin and Its Music*. London. Rpt. Boston 1973.

Hartnack, Joachim W. 1967. *Grosse Geiger unserer Zeit*. Munich. 4th ed. Zurich 1983.

Harvey, Brian W. 1995. *The Violin and Its Makers in the British Isles: An Illustrated History and Directory*. Oxford.

Hasselt, Ernestine-André van. [1899]. *L'anatomie des instruments de musique*. Brussels.

Haubensack, Otto. 1930. *Ursprung und Geschichte der Geige*. Marburg.

Hauck, Werner. 1962. *Kleiner Katechismus für den Geiger*. Kassel.

———. 1966. *Die physikalische Einheit des Violinspiels*. Kassel.

———. 1975. *Vibrato on the Violin*. London. 1st publ. in German 1971.

Haugen, Einar Ingwald. 1993. *Ole Bull: Norway's Romantic Musician*. Madison, Wis.

Havas, Kato. 1968. *The Violin and I*. London.

Haweis, Hugh Reginald. 1898. *Old Violins*. London. 3d ed. 1910.

Hayes, Gerald R. 1930. *Musical Instruments and Their Music 1500–1750*, 2 vols. London. Rpt. New York 1969.

Heartz, Daniel. 1995. *Haydn, Mozart and the Viennese School*. New York.

Heller, Karl. 1997. *Vivaldi*. Portland, Ore. 1st publ. in German, Leipzig 1991.

Helmholtz, Hermann von. 1862. *Die Lehre von den Tonempfindungen*. Braunschweig. Engl. trans. London 1875; rev. ed. New York 1948.

Henley, William. 1959–1960. *Universal Dictionary of Violin and Bow Makers*, vols. 1–5. Brighton. Vol. 6, 1965; vol. 7, 1969; rpt. in a single vol. 1973.

———. 1961. *Antonio Stradivari*. Brighton.

Heron-Allen, Edward. 1882–1883. *Opuscula fidicularum*. Vol. 1, *The Ancestry of the Violin*; vol. 2, *Hodges Against Chanot*. London.

———. 1884. *Violin Making, As It Was and Is*. London. 2d ed. 1885; facsim. rpts. London 1973, 1984.

————. 1890–1894. *De fidiculis bibliographia*, 2 vols. London. Rpt. 1961.

Hill, Alfred Ebsworth. 1931. *The Violin-Makers of the Guarneri Family*. London. Rpt. 1980.

Hill, John Walter. 1972. "The Life and Works of Francesco Maria Veracini." Diss., Harvard University. Ann Arbor, Mich. 1974, 1979.

Hill, William Ebsworth. 1893. *Violins and Their Makers*. London.

Hill, William Ebsworth, and Sons. 1891. *The Tuscan and the Salabue Stradivari (Le Messie)*. London. Rpt. 1976

————. 1892. *Giovanni Paolo Maggini, His Life and Work, Compiled and Edited from Material Collected and Contributed by W. E. Hill and His Sons William Arthur & Alfred Hill by Margaret L. Huggins*. London. 2d ed. 1976.

Hill, W. Henry, Arthur F. Hill, and Alfred E. Hill. 1902. *Antonio Stradivari: His Life and Work*. London. Rpts. New York 1963; London 1980.

Hjorth, Arne. 1963. *Danish Violins and Their Makers*. Copenhagen.

Hoe, William. [1884]. *A Dictionary of the Fiddle and Other Stringed Instruments Played with the Bow*. London.

Homberg, Herfried. 1968. *Louis Spohr. Bilder und Dokumente seiner Zeit*. Kassel.

Honeyman, William C. 1893. *The Violin: How to Choose One*. Edinburgh.

————. 1899. *Scottish Violin Makers Past and Present*. Edinburgh. Rpt. 1981.

Honold, Eugen. 1922. *Von der Geige*. Stuttgart.

Hosiasson, S. 1939. *La maîtrise du violon par l'entrainement psycho-dynamique*. Paris.

Huberman, Bronislaw. 1912. *Aus der Werkstatt des Virtuosen*. Leipzig and Vienna.

Huet, Félix. 1880. *Etude sur les différentes écoles de violon*. Châlons-sur-Marne.

Huggins, Margaret. 1892. *Gio. Paolo Maggini: His Life and Work*. London.

Iviglia, Giovanni. 1957. *Cremona, wie es nicht sein soll*. Bellinzona.

Jacquot, Albert. 1882. *La musique en Lorraine*. 2d ed. Paris.

————. 1896. *Les Médards, luthiers lorrains*. Paris.

————. 1912. *La Lutherie Lorraine et Française*. Paris. Rpt. New York 1969.

Jahn, Arthur. 1913. *Die Grundlagen der natürlichen Bogenführung auf der Violine*. Leipzig.

Jalovec, Karel. 1964. *Italian Violin Makers*. 2d ed. London.

————. 1967. *German and Austrian Violin Makers*. London.

Jambe-de-Fer, Philibert. 1556. *Épitome musical*. Lyon. Facs. rpt. and Engl. trans. in *Annales musicologiques* 6 (1958–1963).

James, E. 1845. *Camillo Sivori: A Sketch of His Life, Talent, Travels and Successes*. London.

James, William. N.d. *Introduction in Fiddle-Making*. London.

Jones, Sterling Scott. 1995. *The Lira da Braccio*. Bloomington, Ind.

Jung, Hans. 1956. "Johann Georg Pisendel." Diss., Jena.

Kapp, Julius. 1913. *Paganini*. Leipzig. 15th rev. ed. Tutzing 1969.

Kaul, Paul. 1927. *La querelle des anciens et des modernes: Lutherie italienne ou lutherie française*. Nantes.

Kayser, Hans. 1947. *Die Form der Geige*. Zurich.

Kehr, Günther. 1942. "Untersuchungen zur Violintechnik um die Wende des 18. Jahrhunderts." Diss., Cologne.

Kendall, Alan. 1982. *Paganini: A Biography*. London.

Kern, Walter. 1924. *Das Violinspiel*. Vienna.

Kidd, Ronald Ray. 1968. "The Sonata for Keyboard with Violin Accompaniment in England." Diss., Yale University.

Kish, Anne L. 1964. "The Life and Works of J. B. Senaillé." Diss., Bryn Mawr College.

Kleverkaus, Friedrich. 1929. *Die Konstruktion des Geigenkörpers aus der Teillänge der Saite*. Leipzig.

Klingler, Karl. 1921. *Über die Grundlagen des Violinspiels*. Leipzig.

Koch, Franz Joseph. [ca. 1921?]. *Homogene Streichinstrumente*. Dresden.

Köhler, Louis. 1858. *Die Gebrüder Müller und das Streichquartett*. Leipzig.

König, Adolf. 1958. *Die Schweizer Geige*. Bern.

Kollmann/Schneider-Böhner. 1966. *Untersuchungen über die Erwärmung und Trocknung des Holzes mit Infrarotstrahlen*. Opladen.

Kolneder, Walter. 1970. *Antonio Vivaldi*. Berkeley, Calif. 1st publ. in German 1965.

———. 1979. *Performance Practices in Vivaldi*. Winterthur. 1st publ. in German 1955.

Kosnick, Heinrich. 1927. *Lebenssteigerung. Ein neuer Weg zur Heilung und zur Lösung technischer Probleme des Instrumentalspiels und des Gesanges*. Munich.

Kreisler, Fritz. 1915. *Four Weeks in the Trenches: The War Story of a Violinist*. Boston.

Kufferath, Maurice. 1882. *Henri Vieuxtemps: Sa vie et son oeuvre*. Brussels.

Kulenkampff, Georg. 1952. *Geigerische Betrachtungen*. Regensburg.

Kurth, Ernst. 1917. *Grundlagen des linearen Kontrapunkts. Bachs melodische Polyphonie*. Bern. Rpts. 1948, 1956.

Lahee, Henry C. 1899. *Famous Violinists of Today and Yesterday*. Boston. Rev. ed. 1925.

Lanfranco, Giovanni Maria. 1533. *Scintille di musica*. Brescia. Rpt. Bologna 1969.

Laurencie, Lionel de la. 1922–1924. *L'école française de violon de Lully à Viotti*, 3 vols. Paris. Rpt. Geneva 1971.

Layer, Adolf. 1959. *Matthias Klotz von Mittenwald*. Feldafing.

Le Blanc, Hubert. 1740. *Défense de la basse de viole*. Amsterdam. Facsim. rpt. Geneva 1975.

Leipp, Emile. 1946. *Essai sur la lutherie: Le vernis de Crémone*. Paris.

———. 1952. *La sonorité du violon, de l'alto, du violoncelle*. Paris.

———. 1969. *The Violin: History, Aesthetics, Manufacture, and Acoustics*. Toronto. 2d ed. 1989; 1st publ. as *Le violon*, Paris 1965.

Lentner, F. 1898. *Des Geigenmachers Jakob Stainer's Lebenslauf im Lichte archivalischer Forschung*. Leipzig.

Leonhardt, Konrad. 1969. *Geigenbau und Klangfarbe*. Frankfurt. 2d ed. 1981.

Leoni di Pienza, Raimondo. 1793. *Elogio di Pietro Nardini*. Florence.

Linge, Ola. 1953. *Ole Bull*. Oslo.

Lipizer, Rodolfo. 1967. *L'arte e la technica del vibrato sul violino e viola*. Florence.

Livi, G. 1896. *I liutai bresciani*. Milan.

Lochner, Louis P. 1950. *Fritz Kreisler*. New York. Rev. ed. Neptune City, N.J., 1981.

Loft, Abram. 1973. *Violin and Keyboard*, 2 vols. New York. Rpt. Portland, Ore., 1991.

———. 1992. *Ensemble! A Rehearsal Guide to Thirty Great Works of Chamber Music*. Portland, Ore.

Lombardini, Paolo. 1875. *Cenni sulla celebre scuola cremonese degli strumenti ad arco*. Cremona.

Lowendall, Louis. 1900. *Fachmännische Erläuterungen über den von mir erfundenen Resonator-Stimmbalken für Streichinstrumente*. Berlin.

Lozzi, Carlo. [1891]. *I liutai bresciani e l'invenzione del violino*. Milan.

Lütgendorff, Willibald Leo. 1922. *Die Geigen-und Lautenmacher vom Mittelalter bis zur Gegenwart*, 2 vols. Frankfurt on the Main. Rpt. Tutzing 1975.

McArtor, Marion E. 1951. "Francesco Geminiani, Composer and Theorist." Diss., University of Michigan.

Magidoff, Robert. 1955. *Yehudi Menuhin: The Man and the Musician*. New York. 2d ed. London 1973.

Mahillon, Victor Charles. 1874. *Eléments d'acoustique musicale et instrumentale*. Brussels.

Mailand, Eugène. 1859. *Découverte des anciens vernis italiens employés pour les instruments à cordes et à archet*. Paris.

Maillot, Charles. 1952. *La fabrication des cordes harmoniques*. Paris.

Malibran, Alexander. 1860. *Louis Spohr: Sa vie et ses oeuvres, par son élève*. Frankfurt.

Mannes, David. 1938. *Music Is My Faith*. New York. Rpt. 1978.

Marcan, Peter. 1983. *Music for Solo Violin Unaccompanied: A Performer's Guide*. High Wycombe.

Maroncelli, Piero. 1819. *Vita di Arcangelo Corelli*. Milan.

Martens, Frederick H. 1919. *Violin Mastery: Talks with Master Violinists and Teachers*. New York.

Marx, Klaus. 1979. *The Evolution of the Violoncello and Its Playing Technique*. Lexington, Ky. 1st publ. in German, Regensburg 1963.

Massart, Lambert-Joseph. [1850?]. *L'art de travailler les études de Kreutzer*. Paris. Engl. trans. Detroit 1940, 1983.

Matzke, Hermann. 1931. *Grundzüge einer musikalischen Technologie*. Breslau.

———. 1949. *Unser technisches Wissen von der Musik*. Vienna.

Maugin, J. C. 1834. *Manuel du luthier*. Paris. 2d ed. 1869; rev. and enl. ed. 1977.

McVeigh, Simon. 1989. *The Violinist in London's Concert Life, 1750–1784: Felice Giardini and His Contemporaries*. New York.

Meinel, Hermann. 1937. *Über die Beziehung zwischen Holzdicke, Schwingungsform, Körperamplitude und Klang eines Geigenkörpers*. Berlin.

Melkus, Eduard. 1960. "Eine vollständige 3. Violinsonate Schumanns." *Neue Zeitschrift für Musik* 446.

———. 1962. "Zur Frage des Bach-Bogens." *Neue Zeitschrift für Musik* 502–507.

Menuhin, Yehudi. 1981. *Violin*. London. 1st publ. 1971.

———. 1986. *The Compleat Violinist*. New York.

———. 1996. *Unfinished Journey*. London. 1st publ. 1976.

Menuhin, Yehudi, and William Primrose. 1976. *Violin and Viola*. London.

Metzner, Curt. N.d. *Kunst und Wissenschaft im Geigenbau*. Frankfurt.

Meyer/Buchmann. 1931. *Die Klangspektren der Musikinstrumente*. Berlin.

Meyer, Fritz. 1919. *Berühmte Geigen und ihre Schicksale*. Cologne.

Migge, Otto. 1894. *Das Geheimnis der berühmten italienischen Geigenbauer, ergründet und erklärt*. Frankfurt.

Millant, Roger. 1972. *J. B. Vuillaume: Sa vie et son oeuvre*. London.

Millant, Roger, and Max Millant. 1952. *Manuel pratique de lutherie*. Paris. 2d ed. 1979.

Mingotti, Anton. 1949. *Das Bewegungsgesetz im Streichinstrumentenspiel*. Lindau. Rpt. 1973.

Möckel, Max. 1925–1927. *Das Konstruktionsgeheimnis der alten italienischen Meister: Der Goldene Schnitt im Geigenbau*, 2 vols. Berlin.

———. 1935. *Die Kunst der Messung im Geigenbau*. Berlin.

Möckel, Otto. 1930. *Die Kunst des Geigenbaues*. Berlin. 6th ed. 1984.

Möller, Max, and Max Möller (father and son). 1938. *Italiaansche Vioolbouw van Gasparo da Salò tot Pressenda*. Amsterdam.

Möller, Max. 1955. *The Violin Makers of the Low Countries*. Amsterdam.

Mordret, Léon. 1885. *La lutherie artistique*. Paris.

———. 1898. *Les violons de Crémone*. Rouen.

Morris, W. Meredith. 1904. *British Violin Makers*. London. 2d ed. 1920; rpt. 1981.

Moser, Andreas. 1901. *Joseph Joachim: A Biography*. London. 1st publ. in German, Berlin 1898; rev. ed. 1908.

———. 1920. "Zu Joh. Seb. Bachs Sonaten und Partiten für Violine allein." *Bach-Jahrbuch*.

———. 1923. *Geschichte des Violinspiels*, 2 vols. Berlin. 2d ed. Tutzing 1966–1967.

Moser, Andreas, and Joseph Joachim. 1902–1905. *Violinschule*, 3 vols. Berlin. New ed. London and Hamburg 1956–1959.

Mozart, Leopold. 1756. *Versuch einer gründlichen Violinschule*. Augsburg. Engl. trans. London 1948, 1985.

Mucchi, Antonio Maria. 1940–1943. *Gasparo da Salò: La vita e l'opera 1540–1609*. Milan.

Müry, Albert. 1941. "Die Instrumentalwerke Gaetano Pugnanis." Diss., Basel.

Nabering, Dirk. 1968. *David und Igor Oistrach*. Berlin.

Nelson, Sheila M. 1972. *The Violin and Viola*. New York.

Nelson, Suzanne. 1994. "Twentieth-Century Violin Technique: The Contributions of Six Major Pedagogues." Diss., University of South Carolina.

Neurath, Herbert. 1926. "Das Violinkonzert in der Wiener klassischen Schule." Diss., Vienna.

Niederheitmann, Friedrich. 1876. *Die Meister der Geigenbaukunst in Italien und Tyrol*. Vienna.

———. 1877. *Cremona. Eine Charakteristik der italienischen Geigenbauer und ihrer Instrumente*. Leipzig. 8th ed. Frankfurt 1956.

Nissel-Nemenoff, Elfriede. 1930. *Die Violintechnik Franz Bendas und seiner Schule*. Kassel.

Norden, Hugo. 1937. *Harmony and Its Application in Violin Playing*. Boston.

Nunamaker, Norman Kirt. 1968. "The Virtuoso Violin Concerto before Paganini: The Concertos of Lolli, Giornovichi, and Woldemar (1750–1815)." Diss., Indiana University.

Orestad, Ivar. 1943. *The Riddle from Cremona*. Oslo.

Ottani, Giancarlo. 1945. *Stradivari*. Milan.

Otto, Jacob Augustus. 1817. *Über den Bau und die Erhaltung der Geige und aller Bogeninstrumente*. Halle. Engl. trans. London 1833; 5th ed. 1875.

Paganelli, Sergio. 1967. *Gli strumenti musicali nell'arte*. Milan.

Panum, Hortense. 1940. *Stringed Instruments of the Middle Ages*. London. Rpt. 1971.

Pâris, Alain, ed. 1995. *Dictionnaire des interprètes*. Paris.

Pasquali/Principe. 1951. *Il violino*. 3d ed. Milan.

Pearce, Joseph, Jr. 1866. *Violins and Violin Makers*. London.

Peluzzi, Euro. 1941. *Antonio Stradivari ha parlato*. Milan.

Peterson, John. 1911. *Ein Deklamationsfehler beim Lagenwechsel auf den Streich-instrumenten in vergleichender Darstellung mit dem Gesang*. Berlin.

Petherick, Horace. 1900. *A. Stradivari*. London. 2d ed. 1913.

———.1906. *Joseph Guarnerius: His Work and His Master*. London.

Petrobelli, Pierluigi. 1968. *Giuseppe Tartini: Le fonte biografiche*. Vienna.

———. 1992. *Tartini: Le sue idee e il suo tempo*. Lucca.

Pfäfflin, Clara. 1936. *Pietro Nardini*. Wolfenbüttel.

Pfau, S. 1931. "Die Violinmusik in Italien 1600–1650." Diss., Berlin.

Phipson, Thomas Lamb. 1877. *Biographical Sketches and Anecdotes of Celebrated Violinists*. London.

———. 1886. *Guido Papini and the Italian School of Violinists*. London.

———. 1896. *Famous Violinists and Fine Violins*. London.

Piancastelli, Carlo. 1913. *In onore di Arcangelo Corelli*. Fusignano.

Piccolellis, Giovanni de. 1885. *Liutai antichi e moderni*. Florence. Rpt. Bologna 1969.

———. 1886. *Genealogia degli Amati e dei Guarneri*. Florence.

Pierrard, Louis. 1902. *Le violon*. Gand.

Pierre, Constant. 1893. *Les facteurs d'instruments de musique, les luthiers*. Paris. Rpt. Geneva 1971.

Pierrotet, Adèle. 1896. *Camillo Sivori*. Milan.

Pincherle, Marc. 1922. *Les violinistes, compositeurs et virtuoses*. Paris. Rpt. 1984.

———. 1927. *Feuillets d'histoire du violon*. Paris.

———. 1948. *Les instruments du quatuor*. Paris.

———. 1952. *Jean-Marie Leclair l'aîné*. Paris.

———. 1956. *Corelli: His Life, His Work*. New York. 1st publ. in French, Paris 1933.

———. 1957. *Vivaldi: Genius of the Baroque*. New York. 1st publ. in French, Paris 1955.

———. 1963. *The World of the Virtuoso*. New York. 1st publ. in French, Paris 1961.

———. 1966. *Le violon*. Paris. Rev. ed. 1974.

Plowright, Dennis G. 1994. *Dictionary of British Violin and Bow Makers*. Exmouth.

Poidras, Henri. 1924–1932. *Dictionnaire des luthiers anciens et modernes*, 2 vols. Rouen.

Polnauer, Frederick, and Morton Marks. 1964. *Senso-Motor Study and Its Application to Violin Playing*. Urbana, Ill.

Porter, Thomas. [1879]. *How to Choose a Violin*. London.

Pougin, Arthur. 1924. *Le violon, les violonistes et la musique du violon du XVIe au XVIIIe siècle*. Paris.

Poznanski, Misha. 1962. "Violin Harmonics and Their Usage in Performance." Diss., Columbia University.

Praetorius, Michael. 1980. *The Syntagma Musicum of Michael Praetorius*. Vol.

2, *De organographia*. Engl. trans. by Harold Blumenfeld. New York. 1st publ. 1619.

Preston, Robert Elwyn. 1959. "The Forty-eight Sonatas for Violin and Figured Bass of Jean-Marie Leclair, l'aîné." Diss., Michigan University.

Profeta, Rosario. 1942. *Storia e letteratura degli strumenti musicali*. Florence.

Pulver, Jeffrey. 1923. *A Dictionary of Old English Music and Musical Instruments*. London.

———. 1936. *Paganini: The Romantic Virtuoso*. London.

Quantz, Johann Joachim. 1752. *Versuch einer Anweisung die Flöte traversière zu spielen*. Berlin. Rpt. Kassel 1992; Engl. trans. New York 1966, 1985.

Racster, Olga. 1905. *Chats on Violins*. London.

Radoux, J.-Théodore. [1891]. *Vieuxtemps: Sa vie et ses oeuvres*. Liège. Engl. trans. Linthicum Heights, Md. 1983.

Ravizza, Victor. 1967. "Das instrumentale Ensemble von 1400–1550 in Italien." Diss., Bern.

Reade, Charles, 1872. *Cremona Fiddles*. Birdsfield. Rpt. London 1981.

———. 1873. *Cremona Violins*. Gloucester.

Reiter, Johann. 1935. *250 Jahre Mittenwalder Geigenbau 1685–1935*. Mittenwald.

Retford, William C. 1964. *Bows and Bow Makers*. London. 3rd ed. 1984.

Reuchsel, Maurice. 1907. *Un violoniste en voyage: Notes d'Italie*. Paris.

Reuter, Florizel von. 1926. *Führer durch die Solo-Violinmusik*. Berlin.

Rho-Guerrieri, Vittorio Emmanuele. 1892. *Gasparo da Salò*. Rome.

Richelme, Antoine Marius. 1868. *Études et observations sur la lutherie ancienne et moderne*. Marseille.

Riechers, August. [1893]. *Die Geige und ihr Bau*. Göttingen. Rev. ed. Wiesbaden [1955].

Riley, Maurice Winton. 1954. "The Teaching of Bowed Instruments from 1511 to 1756." Diss., Univeristy of Michigan.

———. 1980. *History of the Viola*, vol. 1. Ypsilanti, Mich. Vol. 2, Ann Arbor, Mich., 1991.

Rinaldi, Gioffredo Benedetto. 1873. *Classica fabbricazione di violini in Piemonte*. Turin.

Ritter, Hermann. 1889. *Professor Ritters dreifüssiger Normalsteg für Geigeninstrumente*. Würzburg.

Ritz, J. 1883. *Untersuchungen über die Zusammensetzung der Klänge der Streichinstrumente*. Munich.

Robinson, John Stuart. 1982. *The Guarneri Mold and the Modern Violin Maker*. Oklahoma City.

Roda, Joseph. 1959. *Bows for Musical Instruments of the Violin Family*. Chicago.

Roeder, Michael. 1994. *A History of the Concerto*. Portland, Ore.

Rödig, Hans. 1962. *Geigenbau in neuer Sicht*. Frankfurt on the Main. 2d ed. 1976.

Roeseler, Albrecht. 1987. *Grosse Geiger unseres Jahrhunderts*. Munich. 2d ed. 1996.

Ronze-Neveu, Marie Jeanne. 1957. *Ginette Neveu*. London. 1st publ. in French, Paris 1952.

Rösing, Helmut. 1967. "Probleme und neue Wege zur Analyse von Instrumenten- und Orchesterklängen." Diss., Vienna.

Rostal, Max. 1985. *Beethoven, the Sonatas for Piano and Violin: Thoughts on Their Interpretation*. London.

Rousseau, Jean. 1687. *Traité de la viole*. Paris. Facsim. rpts. Amsterdam 1965; Geneva 1975.

Roussel, André. 1956. *Traité de lutherie*. Paris. 4th ed. Frankfurt 1974.

———. 1963. *Nouveau traité de lutherie*. Paris.

Rühlmann, Julius. 1882. *Die Geschichte der Bogeninstrumente*. Braunschweig. Rpt. 1974.

Ruf, S. 1872. *Der Geigenmacher Jakob Stainer von Absam in Tirol*. Innsbruck.

Sacchi, Federico. 1898. *Il Conte Cozio di Salabue*. London. Engl. trans. 1900; rpt. 1983.

Sachs, Curt. 1913. *Real-Lexikon der Musikinstrumente*. Berlin. Rpts. 1964, 1979.

———. 1920. *Handbuch der Musikinstrumentenkunde*. Leipzig. Rpt. 1979.

———. 1940. *The History of Musical Instruments*. New York.

Saint-George, Henry. 1896. *The Bow: Its History, Manufacture and Use*. London. Rpt. New York 1969.

Salabue, Count Cozio di. 1950. *Carteggio*. Mod. ed. by G. Iriglia.

———. 1987. *Observations on the Construction of Stringed Instruments*. Oxford. 1st publ. 1804.

Sandys, William, and Simon Forster. 1864. *The History of the Violin*. London. Rpt. St. Clair Shores, Mich., 1976.

Santoro, Elia, ed. 1993. *L'epistolario di Cozio di Salabue (1773–1845)*. Cremona. In English and Italian.

Schebeck, Edmund. 1874. *Der Geigenbau in Italien und sein deutscher Ursprung*. Prague.

Schenk, Erich. 1955. *The Italian Trio Sonata*. Cologne.

Schering, Arnold. 1904a. "Verschwundene Traditionen des Bachzeitalters." *Neue Zeitschrift für Musik*, September.

———. 1904b. "Verschwundene Traditionen des Bachzeitalters" (expanded version). *Bach-Jahrbuch*, October.

———. 1905. *Geschichte des Instrumentalkonzerts*. Leipzig. 2d ed. 1927; rpt. 1972.

Schlesinger, Kathleen. 1910. *The Instruments of the Modern Orchestra*. Vol. 2, *The Precursors of the Violin Family*. London. Rpt. 1969.

Schmidt, W. 1908. *Das Schleifen, Beizen und Polieren des Holzes, Elfenbeins usw*. 8th ed. Leipzig.

Schmolzi, Herbert. 1948. "Die Behandlung der Violine in den Werken Johann Sebastian Bachs." Diss., Cologne.

Schneider, Albin. 1902. *Akustik und Harmonie . . . Abhandlung des mathematischen Problems für Geigenbau und Streichinstrumente*. Dresden.

Schneider, Alexander. 1988. *Sasha: A Musician's Life*. New York.

Schröder, Fritz. 1922. "Bernhard Molique und seine Instrumentalkompositionen." Diss., Munich.

Schroeter, Kurt. 1924. *Flesch-Eberhardt: naturwidrige oder natürliche Violintechnik?* Leipzig.

Schubert, Franz Ludwig. 1865. *Die Violine*. Leipzig. 5th ed. 1922.

Schuler, Johannes. 1861. *Jakob Stainer*. Innsbruck.

Schulmann, Otto von. 1961. *Echt oder falsch?* Siegburg. 2d ed. 1976.

Schulze, Carl. 1901. *Stradivaris Geheimnis: Ein ausführliches Lehrbuch des Geigenbaus*. Berlin.

Schwarz, Boris. 1983. *Great Masters of the Violin: From Corelli and Vivaldi to Stern, Zukerman, and Perlman*. 2d ed. 1987, with bibliography.

————. 1987. *French Instrumental Music between the Revolutions (1789–1830)*. New York. Diss., Columbia Univ., 1950.

Schwarz, Vera, ed. 1975. *Violinspiel und Violinmusik in Geschichte und Gegenwart*. Vienna.

Schweitzer, Albert. 1962. *J. S. Bach*, 2 vols. New York. 1st publ. in French, Paris 1905; various rpts.

Seagrave, Barbara Anne Garvey. 1958. "The French Style of Violin Bowing." Diss., Stanford University.

Seiffert, Alfred. 1922. *Eine Theorie der Geige auf mechanischer Grundlage*. Leipzig.

Senn, Walter. 1951. *Jakob Stainer*. Innsbruck. Rev. ed. Frankfurt 1984.

Shackford, Charles Reeves. 1954. "Intonation in Ensemble String Performance." Diss., Harvard University.

Sibire, Abbé Antoine. 1806. *La chélonomie, ou Le parfait luthier*. Paris.

Silverman, William Alexander. 1957. *The Violin Hunter: The Story of the Life of Luigi Tarisio*. New York.

Simoutre, Nicolas Eugène. 1883. *Aux amateurs du violon*. Basel.

————. 1886. *Un progrès en lutherie*. Basel.

————. 1889. *Supplément aux amateurs du violon et au progrès en lutherie*. Basel.

Smith, H. P. 1877. *The Construction of the Violin*. 3d ed. Syracuse, N.Y.

Smith, Mortimer Brewster. 1947. *The Life of Ole Bull*. Princeton, N.J. Rpt. 1973.

Spalding, Albert. 1943. *Rise to Follow*. New York.

Spitta, Philipp. 1951. *J. S. Bach*, 3 vols. in 2. New York. 1st publ. in German, Leipzig 1873, 1880.

Spohr, Louis. 1833. *Violin School*. London. 1st publ. in German, Vienna 1832.

————. 1865. *Louis Spohr's Autobiography*. London. Rpt. New York 1969; 1st publ. in German, Kassel 1860–1861; also published as *The Musical Journeys of Louis Spohr*, Henry Pleasants, trans., Norman, Okla., 1961, rpt. 1990.

Stainer, Cecil. 1896. *A Dictionary of Violin Makers*. London. Rpt. Boston 1973.

Starcke, Hermann. 1884. *Die Geige, ihre Entstehung, Verfertigung und Bedeutung*. Dresden.

Stern, Isaac. 1993. *Isaac Stern: A Life. A Biography in Music*. New York. Videodisc.

Stillings, Frank Stuart. 1956. "Arcangelo Corelli." Diss., Michigan University.

Stoeving, Paul. 1904. *The Story of the Violin*. London.

————. 1928. *The Violin: Its Famous Makers and Players*. Boston.

Stolba, K. Maria. 1965. "A History of the Violin Etude to About 1800." Diss., Iowa University. Rpt. 1979.

Stoll, Barrett. 1978. "Joseph Joachim: Violinist, Pedagogue, and Composer." Diss., University of Iowa.

Stowell, Robin. 1984. "Violin Bowing in Transition." *Early Music* 12: 317–327.

————. 1985. *Violin Technique and Performance Practice in the Late Eighteenth and Early Nineteenth Centuries*. Cambridge.

————, ed. 1992. *The Cambridge Companion to the Violin*. Cambridge.

Straeten, Edmund van der. 1933. *The History of the Violin*, 2 vols. London. Rpt. New York 1968.

Stravinsky, Igor. 1936. *An Autobiography*. New York. Rpt. 1962.

Strocchi, Giuseppe. 1913. *Liuteria: Storia ed arte*. Lugo. 3d ed. 1937.

————. 1937. *Le origini del violino*. Lugo.

Suzuki, Shinichi. 1969. *Nurtured by Love*. New York.

Swalin, Benjamin. 1941. *The Violin Concerto: A Study in German Romanticism*. Chapel Hill, N.C. Rpt. New York 1973.

Szigeti, Joseph. 1947. *With Strings Attached*. New York. Rpt. 1967.

————. 1964. *A Violinist's Notebook*. London.

————. 1965. *The Ten Beethoven Sonatas for Piano and Violin*. Urbana, Ill.

————. 1969. *Szigeti on the Violin*. London. 2d ed. 1979.

Tartini, Giuseppe. [1752–1756?]. *Regole per arrivare a saper ben suonar il violino*. [Bologna].

————. 1961. *Treatise on Ornaments in Music*. Erwin Jacobi, ed. Celle and New York. Trans. of *Traité des agréments de la musique*, Paris 1771.

Themelis, Dimitris. 1967. "Étude ou Caprice. Die Entstehungsgeschichte der Violinetüde." Diss., Munich.

Thomastik, Franz. 1932. *Die Stahlseite als Kulturfaktor*. Vienna.

Tolbecque, Auguste. 1890. *Quelques considérations sur la lutherie*. Paris.

————. 1898. *Notice historique sur les instruments à cordes et à archet*. Paris.

————. 1903. *L'art du luthier*. Niort. Facsim. rpts. New York 1969, Marseille 1978.

Toskey, Burnett R. 1983. *Concertos for Violin and Viola: A Comprehensive Encyclopedia*. Seattle.

Tottmann, Albert. 1874. *Führer durch den Violin-Unterricht*. Leipzig. 2d ed. 1886; 4th ed. 1935 as *Führer durch die Violin-Literatur* by Tottmann and Wilhelm Altmann.

Trendelenburg, Wilhelm. 1925. *Die natürlichen Grundlagen der Kunst des Streichinstrumentenspiels*. Berlin. Rpt. Kassel 1974.

Tua, Teresina. 1907. *Joseph Joachim: Ricordi e note*. Rome.

Twinn, Sidney. 1963. *The Study of Harmonics as an Aid to Technical Mastery of the Violin*. London.

————. 1905. *Storia del violino*. Milan.

Valdrighi, Luigi Francesco. 1878. *Ricerche sulla liuteria e violineria modenese*. Modena.

————. 1884–1894. *Nomocheliurgografia antica e moderna*. Modena. Rpt. Bologna 1967.

Vannes, René. 1951–1959. *Dictionnaire universel des luthiers*, 2 vols. Brussels. 5th ed. 1981; supplement 1985.

Vercheval, Henri. 1923. *Dictionnaire du violoniste*. Paris.

Vidal, Antoine. 1876–1878. *Les instruments à archet*, 3 vols. Paris. Rpt. London 1961.

————. 1889. *La lutherie et les luthiers*. Paris. Rpt. New York 1969.

Walls, P. 1984. "Violin Fingering in the Eighteenth Century." *Early Music* 12: 300–315.

Wasielewski, Wilhelm Joseph von. 1869. *Die Violine und ihre Meister*. Leipzig. 8th ed. 1927; rpts. Wiesbaden 1968, Schaan 1981.

————. 1874. *Die Violine im 17. Jahrhundert und die Anfänge der Instrumental-*

komposition. Bonn. 2d ed., with vol. of music examples, Berlin 1905; rpt. Bologna 1969; Engl. trans. Lexington, Ky., 1978.

―――. 1878. *Geschichte der Instrumentalmusik im 16. Jahrhundert*. Berlin.

Wechsberg, Joseph. 1972. *The Glory of the Violin*. New York.

Weissmann, Adolf. 1918. *Der Virtuose*. Berlin.

Wettengel, Gustav Adolf. 1828. *Lehrbuch der Geigen- und Bogenmacherkunst*. Ilmenau. 2d ed. Weimar 1869.

White, E. Chappell. 1957. "Giovanni Battista Viotti and his Violin Concertos." Diss., Princeton University.

Williams, Michael. 1972. "The Violin Concertos of Rodolphe Kreutzer." Diss., Indiana University.

Winckel, Fritz. 1952. *Klangwelt unter der Lupe*. Berlin.

Winternitz, Emanuel. 1966. *Musical Instruments of the Western World*. London.

―――. 1967a. *Musical Instruments and Their Symbolism in Western Art*. New Haven, Conn. Rpt. 1979.

―――. 1967b. *Gaudenzio Ferrari: His School and the Early History of the Violin*. New York.

Wirsta, Aristide. 1955. "Écoles de violon au 18e siècle d'après les ouvrages didactiques," 3 vols. Diss., Paris.

―――. 1971. *L'enseignement du violon au 19e siècle*. Paris.

Wit, Paul de. 1902. *Geigenzettel alter Meister vom 16. bis zur Mitte des 19. Jahrhunderts*. Leipzig. 2d ed. 1910; facsim. rpt. Frankfurt 1976.

Witting, Carl. 1900. *Geschichte des Violinspiels*. Cologne.

Wolff, William. 1894. *Fiddle Frauds and How to Detect Them*. London.

Würtz, Roland. 1969. "Ignaz Fränzl." Diss., Mainz.

Wunderlich, Friedrich. 1933. *Der Geigenbogen: Ratschläge für alle Geiger*. Leipzig.

Yampolsky [Iampolskii], I. M. 1967. *The Principles of Violin Fingering*. London. Rpt. 1984; 1st publ. in Russian 1933.

Young, T. Campbell. 1939. *The Making of Musical Instruments*. Oxford.

Ysaÿe, Antoine, and B. Ratcliffe. 1947. *Ysaÿe: His Life, Work, and Influence*. London. 2d ed. Brussels 1974.

Ysaÿe, Eugène. 1968. *Henri Vieuxtemps, mon maitre*. Brussels.

Zanier, Ferruccio. 1931. *Il violino*. Milan.

―――. 1937. *Come costruisco un violino*. Genoa.

Zschinsky-Troxler, Elsa Margherita von. 1939. *Gaetano Pugnani*. Berlin.